Drafting and Negotiating
Commercial Leases

Drafting and Negotiating Commercial Leases

Third edition

MURRAY J ROSS   Solicitor

Foreword by John Stuart Colyer   QC

Butterworths
London and Edinburgh
1989

United Kingdom	Butterworth & Co (Publishers) Ltd, 88 Kingsway, LONDON WC2B 6AB and 4 Hill Street, EDINBURGH EH2 3JZ
Australia	Butterworths Pty Ltd, SYDNEY, MELBOURNE, BRISBANE, ADELAIDE, PERTH, CANBERRA and HOBART
Canada	Butterworths Canada Ltd, TORONTO and VANCOUVER
Ireland	Butterworth (Ireland) Ltd, DUBLIN
Malaysia	Malayan Law Journal Sdn Bhd, KUALA LUMPUR
New Zealand	Butterworths of New Zealand Ltd, WELLINGTON and AUCKLAND
Puerto Rico	Equity de Puerto Rico, Inc, HATO REY
Singapore	Malayan Law Journal Pte Ltd, SINGAPORE
USA	Butterworth Legal Publishers, AUSTIN, Texas; BOSTON, Massachusetts; CLEARWATER, Florida (D & S Publishers); ORFORD, New Hampshire (Equity Publishing); ST PAUL, Minnesota; and SEATTLE, Washington

A CIP Catalogue record for this book is available from the British Library.

First edition 1980
  Reprinted 1982
Second edition 1984
  Reprinted 1985 (twice)

ISBN 0 406 35909 1

Typeset by Phoenix Photosetting, Chatham
Printed and bound in Great Britain by
Biddles Ltd, Guildford and King's Lynn

Foreword

It seems only yesterday that I was writing a Foreword to the First Edition of this then slimmer volume. But nine years have gone by, and since the legal public knows a good thing when it sees one, now – by popular demand – we have the *Third Edition*. It preserves all the qualities of its predecessors except brevity, and makes some new departures which I am sure most readers will appreciate. So no justification is needed for this edition – it comes because readers wanted it.

Nevertheless, before diving into the text or precedents, I think that readers (and especially *new* users of the book) would be assisted by the reflections upon this work of a practitioner in this field who comes from that part of the profession which so often sees the deals that went wrong, and has to litigate about the resulting débris of broken (or misunderstood) promises. Perhaps this viewpoint gives one a jaundiced view: but even if it does have that effect, the viewer is in a good position to spot recurring problems and to assess the value of any volume which sets out to be an aid to avoiding those problems.

So 'justifying' this time the fact that I dare to express views on the book, I proceed to offer you those reflections.

As I said in 1980: 'The granting of a lease of commercial premises is today a matter which calls for the exercise of considerable professional skill and "know-how" on the part of the intended landlord's solicitor and for close co-operation between that solicitor and the surveyors or other property advisers of his client. The taking up of the lease of commercial premises is an even more hazardous operation, calling for still more experience, skill and collaboration on the part of those who are involved professionally in advising the intended tenant. Unfortunately, although there are many precedents of leases available, there has until now been no volume available to the solicitors acting for the intended tenant or landlord of commercial premises which is of a size small enough to ensure that it will be read and which communicates to its reader the know-how and experience of an author who is thoroughly versed in the current practical problems of commercial leasing, and especially the practical problems of the incoming commercial tenant'.

Later I continued: 'Now to some of those who read this book some of [the author's] observations may seem to be statements of the obvious. I would say two things to those readers. First, it always is the case that when set out in print much professional know-how does seem obvious – and that is not surprising since what is such distilled experience other than particularised or specialised common-sense? Many matters, however, that appear obvious after one has read a clear exposition of them must have been rather less obvious before publication to the advisers of the numerous litigants who have kept the courts so busy in the last decade with litigation on "obvious" points. No, the "obvious" usually only becomes obvious when it is set out clearly in black and white, whether it be in a judgment by a court or in a book by an author. Secondly, I would commend the clear and easily understandable style of writing of the author. I think that that clarity of style also makes some things seem to be simpler and more obvious than they really were before you had read his text'.

Now in this edition the text has expanded in the light both of the use made of the first two editions by practitioners and of the developments which have occurred in the law, such as VAT invading the realms of property transactions. The 'mix' of text and precedent, commentary and footnote has changed, but usefully so. Still the book avoids being a legal 'tome', and I hope it will continue to avoid that development, for its utility was initially and still is that 'there is enough law in the book to make the practical observations useful and intelligible, enough precedents to meet most needs, and enough useful commentary and alternative clauses, and explanations of those precedents, to enable the reader who uses them to understand what he is doing and to use them intelligently.'[1] The main difference is that the developed fuller explanations which are now given us, assist us rather better than before.

So, so far, so good. An enthusiastic reader of the First Edition greets the Third Edition with renewed or increased pleasure in so far as it is an update. But what about the new departures? The major one is the Rosscastle Letting Conditions, appropriately named by combination of the two authors' surnames. Do we really need such a document?

So far attempts to standardise leases have foundered. Leases Acts have been tried and found to be wanting (or unwanted) and become a dead letter. Why? I believe that it is because the precedents which they offered were too jejune to be of use in the often complex commercial transactions which form the contexts in which much modern conveyancing had to be carried out. So no set of letting conditions will be of general use unless it contains a great number of clauses. *Brevity* in such a document is not a virtue; for the short 'omnibus' precedent is bound to omit a provision which is needed. So it comes as no surprise to me to find that the Rosscastle Letting Conditions are formidable in their length – *they have to be*. I think that they represent a useful collection of clauses which with a few necessary deletions and sometimes a few additions would enable almost all transactions to be framed by reference to them.

That it can be done does not mean that it will be done, and the real question is whether conveyancers will try to use them, or will continue each with his pet formulary (usually a draft lease – 'letting conditions' introduce a flexibility of purpose which is useful in itself). *I urge readers to use them*, even if they engraft upon them their own pet additions (for which, who knows, there may be room in the Fourth Edition, even if only in a footnote!). I commend the authors for the courage, skill and draftsmanship they have shown in presenting us with their Letting Conditions, and I hope they have struck the first blow in the battle which will lead to a single set of Conditions emerging as the standard basis for leasing, the basic form to which only a few special provisions need to be added. We have seen in the last few months how in respect of sales the profession can accept that there is no virtue in a choice of different National and Law Society Conditions of Sale: now let us hope that the documentation for the necessarily more complex and subjective transaction of leasing can at least progress towards some degree of uniformity, whilst not forgetting that the very nature of the transaction involves a continuing relationship between landlord and tenant the regulation of which calls for many stipulations unnecessary where a conveyance (even of an existing leasehold interest) is being effected. It is not true to say 'Anybody can convey: nobody can lease'; but it is true that the latter transaction is more likely to go wrong and requires more attention than the former. Happily, Messrs Ross and Castle provide us with first-rate equipment for the more complex of the two transactions, equipment which if you use it properly you will find invaluable.[2] So even if it seems 'new' or innovative in the production of and space devoted to the Letting Conditions, I feel sure that the extra space is well spent and 'Rosscastle' merits both close attention and *use*.

John Stuart Colyer   QC
Temple
London

October 1989

---

1   May I be forgiven for adding by way of a footnote that the separate point I then made in the original foreword that one must use the precedents appropriately still applies. As I said in 1980: 'That is what really matters – to use precedents intelligently; for again and again legal problems are created, not by bad drafting in that as a work of draftsmanship the lease or other document may be impeccable, but by the use of the document unintelligently, and without it being appreciated that it does not precisely fit the circumstances of the case or the intentions of the client. The precedent which is perfect for one occasion can be disastrous in even a slightly different situation, and I think that this book does a very good job indeed of ensuring that its readers do understand those documents which are presented to them within the book. It is much better that a few precedents be well explained than that a much larger book be produced containing many different documents, the choice of which must largely be left to the reader, who may not be sufficiently assisted by the footnotes or commentary to make that choice'.
2   Gentle reader, read *again* footnote 1, for it applies with double truth and validity to the use of Letting Conditions!

Preface

The third edition of this book has the same objective as the first and second – to provide ready guidance for those engaged in drafting and negotiating leases of business premises. Each edition seems to be significantly longer than its predecessor and there are four main reasons for this. The first is the simple fact that there is so much more law to be considered. For example, rent review is now an overwhelming subject, and yet when I was writing the first edition in 1979 most of the reported cases dealt with the procedure of review, and in particular whether time was of the essence. Courts then were asked only occasionally to look at the substance of the clause, and to consider the terms of the hypothetical letting. It would be a fascinating exercise – alas, I have found it hard enough to create the time to produce this third edition without embarking upon further *divertissements* – to establish how many of the cases cited in Chapter 6 have been decided during the last five years. Secondly, I have (perhaps unwittingly at first) extended the scope of the work beyond the grant of a new lease. Now it should assist on many of the estates management points that arise during the term and also guide the solicitor who is reviewing an existing lease prior to reporting to a client contemplating acquiring the reversion or taking an assignment of the lease.

The third reason is my growing interest in the language in which legal documents are written and the way in which they are presented. I am convinced that even complex documents can be drafted in what has come to be called plain English or is perhaps better described as good normal English. I have expanded my comments on drafting in Chapter 1 (paras 1.1–1.5).

Finally I have collaborated in Appendix 1 with my good friend Richard Castle in a venture aimed at reducing the length of commercial leases, or more accurately, the length of time that has to be spent on them. Our submission is simple. Everybody's standard lease deals in broadly the same way with basically identical topics and takes over fifty pages to do so. If we could all (or even some of us) agree on one standard, then so much time would be saved in drafting and negotiating, while it should still be possible to introduce variations required in view of the letting in question.

It is interesting to review some of the developments since the second edition appeared in 1984. Cases still come before the courts fairly regularly where conveyancers have been unable to describe the property with adequate certainty (para 3.7) and, although there are obviously practical difficulties involved and not every client would readily pay for it, one has to ask how many of these defective descriptions would have been avoided if the draftsman had inspected the property. The unfortunate position of a person persuaded to enter into a lease as the tenant's guarantor is becoming better known (paras 5.5–5.11) but the continuing liability to the landlord of the original lessee has attracted even more recent attention (paras 5.5 and 5.14–5.15). This aspect of the law of landlord and tenant is an anachronism and it is to be hoped that reform is indeed on the way (para 5.16).

Rent review clauses continue to take up a great deal of judicial time although there seem to have been fewer reported cases in the last year or so. So far as the procedure of review is concerned, this may be because the courts do seem to have reiterated (paras 6.10 and 6.12) the principle of *United Scientific* (para 6.6), after at times seeming to move away from it (paras 6.9 and 6.11). The current trend against drafting clauses that have to be instigated by formal notices (para 6.5) has also helped – if no notice is needed, there can clearly be no dispute as to *when* it should be served. It is to be hoped that the purposive approach to construction is here to stay (para 6.17:2) while the views of the appellant courts are still awaited on whether the approach of severely limiting rights of appeal, apparently welcomed in other types of arbitration, applies to a rent review arbitration (para 6.46).

It is probably true to say that there have not been any fundamental changes in the courts' attitude to repairing covenants although the Court of Appeal has reminded us that before repair there has to be disrepair (para 8.3). In fact this will rarely be an issue – in most instances, the presence of disrepair is blindingly obvious.

The steady flow of cases under Part II of the Landlord and Tenant Act 1954 has continued. The Act has withstood several initiatives for reform and the Law Commission are reviewing it again (para 14.2). There are few who would not reform the detailed operation of the Act, particularly in relation to the service of notices and the commencement of proceedings, where a failure to take the appropriate action within the time prescribed can have such critical consequences for a party (and all too often for his advisers and their insurers). Others go further and advocate abolishing the Act altogether, arguing that similar legislation is rarely seen elsewhere in the world, with business life not apparently suffering as a result, and that the Act was introduced to deal with a specific short term problem – the post war shortage of business premises. HM Government, however, when last commenting on the Act, were against *any* changes (para 14.2).

Some developments are too recent for a considered view. Early signs are that the Landlord and Tenant Act 1988 is instilling a greater sense of urgency in landlords and their advisers in dealing with applications from tenants for consents under their leases but exactly how its remedies will operate remains to be seen (para 7.6). The decision of the European Court of Justice that prompted the introduction of VAT into commercial property has not been welcomed nor has the somewhat retrospective way in which it has been implemented (paras 2.23–2.25). Only time will tell what effect VAT will have on the real and the hypothetical (para 6.29) letting markets.

I acknowledge the assistance that I have received from so many people, to coin a phrase, too numerous to mention in preparing this edition. I thank them all most sincerely. I repeat my thanks to those who helped with previous editions.

Richard Castle and I have participated over the last few years in a residential course on drafting (para 1.2, footnote 1) and it was our work together on this that prompted the discussions on drafting commercial leases that eventually led to the Rosscastle Letting Conditions (Appendix 1). We would like to think that our work has not merely been some type of academic exercise but that it will assist (the parties as well as the lawyers) in the leasing of business premises. I thank Richard for all the time that he has so readily given to the venture.

Thanks too are due to Cynthia Digby who assisted on Chapter 6 and was largely responsible for Chapter 7. She has admirably expanded on the (by comparison) rather superficial treatment of the tenant's covenants that appeared in previous editions, and has not shirked from dealing with a number of difficult topics. Her practical experience in the property department of a well known City firm is much in evidence. Cynthia was a member of the team that produced 22 Encyclopaedia of Forms and Precedents (5th edn) to give the volume its formal title and the following pages consciously or unconsciously owe much to that highly fruitful (and, with hindsight, enjoyable) collaboration.

This edition is dedicated to the memory of Iain Buist and my father. Iain was an intellectual without whose industry, wisdom and good cheer Volume 22 of the Encyclopaedia would never have appeared. His fellow contributors will always regard the volume as Iain's memorial. By his death, at the tragically early age of 37, we lost a greatly respected colleague, an outstanding lawyer and a dear friend. Gordon Ross had intended to be a surveyor and began his working life in an estate agent and surveyors office but after wartime service as a pilot in the Royal Air Force, he forsook property for sport as a journalist, editor, author and public relations consultant. He greatly encouraged me in my writing and was proud to add my first and second editions to the nine books that he had written and the numerous other publications and periodicals that he wrote or edited or to which he contributed. My sports writing was confined to the school magazine (with the occasional contribution to a publication edited by Father) and I think he felt that my writing on property matters somehow completed the circle.

I have done my very best to state the law as it stands on 31 August 1989.

Murray J Ross
20 Essex Street
London
WC2R 3AL

September 1989

Contents

Contents

Table of statutes

References in this Table to Statutes are to Halsbury's Statutes of England (Fourth Edition) showing the volume and page at which the annotated text of the Act may be found.

References in right-hand column are to paragraph and page numbers. Numbers printed in *italic* type refer to pages of the Appendix. Page numbers printed in **_bold italic_** type indicate where the section of an Act is set out in part or in full.

Table of cases

References are to paragraph and page numbers. Numbers printed in italic type refer to pages of the Appendices.

A

B

C

E

G

I

J

K

M

O

P

Q

R

S

U

X

Y

Z

Author's note on terminology

The Landlord and Tenant Acts 1927 and 1954 are referred to throughout as 'the 1927 Act' and 'the 1954 Act'.

I have generally avoided words such as 'potential' or 'prospective', and used 'landlord' and 'tenant' to include, where the context so requires, the time when the terms of a *possible* letting are being discussed and negotiated.

The landlord, the tenant, and the client are regarded throughout as individuals, although the parties to most commercial leases are corporations. It seemed awkward, however, to have to refer to 'advising it' or 'it should bear in mind', and thus preferable to regard every such party as the individual responsible for the corporation's property affairs.

Finally, I hope that my female colleagues in the profession will forgive me for not stating 'he or she' whenever referring to the parties and their advisers. Such an approach would hardly have improved the style, but I can assure them that no discrimination is intended. In this, as in so many other contexts, the principle of s 6 of the Interpretation Act 1978 applies, the 'words importing the masculine gender include the feminine'.

Chapter 1

Drafting and negotiating leases

A DRAFTING

1.1 *Duty to draft well.* A lease of commercial premises will be read by many people between the preparation of the first draft and completion. The parties to the transaction themselves will review the document and, as corporate bodies rather than private individuals are usually involved, the lease may have to be studied by more than one person within the organisation. It will also be considered by the parties' solicitors, and no doubt by their property, insurance, and other advisers, including the agents who negotiated the commercial terms of the letting. After completion, the lease will become a reference document and will be consulted on estate management matters as they arise during the term, when it will not always be the case that a lawyer is on hand to explain any mysteries that the document may contain. Many people, therefore will have cause to curse the original draftsman if his work does not readily lend itself to these types of scrutiny. Any solicitor acting for a landlord should feel that there is a duty imposed upon him to produce a draft lease that is (to adopt terminology favoured by parliamentary draftsmen) as readable 'as is reasonably practicable'. So before he begins drafting, the landlord's solicitor should give careful thought to the task ahead of him.

1.2 *The aim of a document.* Drafting[1] is a subject that is very much taken for granted, and it must be assumed that lawyers are automatically able to draft, because it plays little or no part in university or professional syllabuses, and there are few works on the subject.[2] Drafting is a difficult topic about which to write – it is all too easy to find oneself, for example, stating the obvious, appearing to claim novelty for a practice that has been in use for many years, or dogmatically insisting that one's own preferred way is the only means of achieving a particular end. Two points, however, are fundamental. It must be the case that any document has failed in its purpose if it cannot be understood by its audience or readership. Thus a 'man of property' should be able to read and understand – and find his way about – a lease. Secondly, the object of a legal document is to set out clearly, unambiguously, and as simply as possible, the terms of the bargain struck between the parties. With these points in mind, it is possible to evolve a series of general guidelines.[3]

1 My interest in drafting has been further stimulated by my involvement in the annual courses run since 1984 on the principles of legal drafting by the Centre for Commercial Law Studies, Queen Mary College, London E1 4NS (assisted by the Law Society's Commerce and Industry Group) and I readily acknowledge that what follows owes much to my colleagues on those courses, particularly Professors John Adams and Roy Goode, Richard Castle and Carolyn Walton.
2 Two fairly slim paperbacks are recommended for the practitioner who is anxious to improve and modernise his drafting, although neither is published in the UK: E L Piesse: *The Elements*

1

of Drafting (7th edn, 1985, Editor: J. K. Aitkin), The Law Book Company Ltd (Australia), R. C. Wydick: *Plain English for Lawyers* (2nd edn, 1985) Carolina Academic Press (USA). For a wider treatment of the subject, see David Mellinkoff: *The Language of the Law* (1963) Little, Brown and Company (Boston USA) and *Legal Writing: Sense and Nonsense* (1982) West Publishing Co (St Paul, Minnesota, USA); Reed Dickerson; *The Fundamentals of Legal Drafting* (2nd edn, incorporating *Legislative Drafting*, 1986) Little, Brown and Company, and *Materials on Legal Drafting* (1981) West Publishing Co; and Stanley Robinson: *Drafting: Its Application to Conveyancing and Commercial Documents* (1980) Butterworths.

3   See paras 1.3–1.5 below.

1.3   *Drafting: what to do.* It is suggested that leases can and should be drafted in normal English, rather than in the pompous, wordy, artificial style that conveyancers have often used. The modern draftsman should depart from normal English only where there is a good reason, and should be aware that the reasons put forward (for example, the need to be unambiguous and comprehensive) will frequently be suspect. Although it may take some effort, the draftsman ought in most instances to be able to produce a clause in normal English that will be every bit as certain and comprehensive as its 'legal English' predecessor.[1] Our landlord-clients, their tenants and both parties' successors will have cause to thank us for that effort, because it will produce leases that they will be able to read more quickly and understand more easily. Good drafting involves two sets of guidelines – those to be followed[2] and those to be avoided.[3] The good draftsman will decide what he is going to say before he begins drafting. He will use plain modern words[4] in short, simply constructed sentences.[5] He will state who does what,[6] and will adopt the active rather than the passive voice, and whenever possible, the affirmative rather than the negative.[7] He will gather sentences into clauses of manageable length and avoid long clauses by dividing them into several sub-clauses, or by introducing paragraphing.[8] To avoid repetition and to create certainty he will use defined terms,[9] and put into schedules material that otherwise would 'clutter' the document. He will present the document in a 'user friendly' way – for example, the provisions that deal with a particular topic will appear together, and the various topics will be set out in a logical order. The document will be complete.[10] The clauses and sub-clauses will be well spaced, there will be a margin on all four sides of the page and each line will be of a sensible length. Every clause will have a heading and all but the simplest documents will have a list of contents. The number of each clause will appear in full[11] and the numbering system will facilitate paragraphing.[12] Punctuation will be used as an aid to reading but not as an aid to construction.[13] Any cross-referencing will be correct,[14] and there will be no pages or plans missing and no plans uncoloured.

1   The draftsman, however, has to be a good lawyer and to submit his modern clause to close scrutiny, however superficially attractive it may appear – for an example of the dangers when neither was the case, see [1984] Conv 325 at 328.

2   See this paragraph.

3   See para 1.4 below.

4   The draftsman should adopt a style and a vocabulary that will be familiar to the readership of the document. In a commercial agreement it should be very similar to what his clients would themselves use in an important 'considered' document, such as a report or proposal to management. A good test for commercial conveyancers is – if the property manager was writing a report on this matter to his managing director, would he use that language? If the answer is no, then it should not appear in a draft.

5   Wydick (see footnote 2 to para 1.2 above) . . . suggests (p 34) that most sentences should contain only one thought and that the average sentence length should be kept below 25 words. A document that adopts this approach will be easier to read and less likely to contain

the type of ambiguities that can be hidden away in a long, complicated sentence. But short sentences are not ambiguity-proof: see para 1.5 below.

6   Legal language often describes an action or process without specifying who does what ('agent deletion'). Such sentences can be harder to understand and create and artificiality common in legal writing. Whenever practical, the subject of the verb should be specified. For example replace: 'Where it has been determined that an interim payment has . . .' by 'Where the Architect has determined that an interim payment has . . .'.

7   Sentences written in the affirmative are easier to understand than those expressed in the negative. This means that: 'You should only use negatives if you have to' and not 'Do not use negatives unless you have to'. Double negatives ('do not . . . unless', 'shall not . . . without') are even more difficult. Usually this can be avoided by the use of 'only . . . if'.

8   Some long clauses can simply be *divided* into two or more clauses or sub-clauses. In others, the introduction of *paragraphing* or tabulation will often help considerably – many long clauses consist of some introductory (or concluding) words following (or preceding) a list. This can be broken up by setting out each item in the list on a new line and giving it a number. Indeed, in certain instances paragraphing/tabulation can remove an uncertainty (see para 1.5:1 below). 'Paragraphing' is not used here in the strict dictionary sense, but to refer to a passage which commences on a new line and ends without running on to the next passage.

9   A defined term produces clarity, brevity and consistency but substantive points should be included in the body of the document and not in the definition. A development from the use of definitions is a particulars clause – here the principal variable terms are set out in a tabulated or block form at the beginning of the lease. This has two advantages – all the 'blanks' that have to be completed are contained in this initial clause and the information required to answer a great number of the estate management queries that will arise during the term of the lease will be readily available.

10 The agreement must always be *complete* – for example if a document has been incorporated by reference (for example printed terms or a previous lease that is being renewed), the original or a copy of that document must always be retained. Indeed it is preferable to bind the original document into the subsequent one.

11 In order to avoid having to refer back in the document to see that sub-clause 6(a) is in fact a part of clause 3. That time would have been saved if the sub-clause had been numbered 3.6:1.

12 The decimal system of numbering provides unlimited potential for paragraphing, but there is an alternative view. In the drafting manual of the Law Reform Commission, State of Victoria (the most recent overview of the subject) the conventional 2(3)(b)(i) is used and the authors say sub-paras should be divided only in very exceptional circumstances. Some find 2(3)(b)(i)(C) easier to follow than 2.3:2.1:3. Because there is unlimited potential in the decimal method there may perhaps be a temptation to go into too many sub-divisions. Critics of decimal numbering find constant repetition of the numbers irksome and (depending upon layout) the decimal system can make the columns absurdly narrow and (more importantly) difficult to read. They believe that there is an argument for adopting the same layout for private documents as the parliamentary draftsman does for acts. It is suggested that decimal numbering does have a distinct advantage in overcoming the problem mentioned in footnote 11 above, but where this is not a factor, the method numbering is a matter of personal preference.

13 See *R v Casement* [1917] 1 KB 98, CCA and *Re Steel, Public Trustee v Christian Aid Society* [1979] Ch 218, [1978] 2 All ER 1026. In particular, a comma should be used between items in a list, to mark the end of a condition and the beginning of the substantive part of a clause, and commas should be used in pairs to enclose subordinate phrases and so make the main provisions of the clause easier to identify, for example: 'If, on an application made pursuant to the preceding clause, the Board refuse to give a direction under this sub-section, the parent body may, by notice in writing given to the Board within thirty days after the refusal, appeal to the Special Commissioners who, if satisfied that the requirement in question ought not to have effect, may determine accordingly.' The draftsman should not, however, rely on punctuation to remove an ambiguity, but should draft the provision in another way. If in doubt first draft the provision without punctuation, and only insert punctuation when satisfied that the clause is unambiguous without it.

14 A specific check should be made of every document to ensure that the cross-references are correct, especially if amendments have been made since the previous draft. Sometimes the risk can be limited by the drafting ('in accordance with its obligations in this Lease' rather than 'in accordance with clause 7.2') but generally a specific reference will be more helpful for the parties. When a clause is deleted at the last moment of negotiations it may be preferable for the document to read: '7. Clause Deleted' to save re-numbering and consequential amendments. Excessive cross-referencing should be avoided.

1.4 *Drafting: what not to do.* The good draftsman will avoid all aspects of legalese – for example 'hereby' and 'thereby';[1] 'hereof' and 'hereto';[2] 'such' and 'the same';[3] 'said' and 'aforesaid';[4] the exaggerated use of 'any', 'each', 'every', and 'all';[5] unnecessary expressions;[6] superfluous pairs;[7] circumlocutions;[8] Latin terms;[9] and unnatural uses of the future tense.[10] He will avoid technical language, 'buzz words' or jargon relating to the subject matter of the document.[11] He will *never* change his language unless he wishes to change his meaning but will *always* change his language when he does wish to change his meaning.[12]

1 The use of compounds of 'there' and 'here' are prime examples of legalese – their insertion adds nothing. In normal life we do not 'hereby give you a book' or 'hereby invite you to lunch' and there seem no grounds for parting from this normality in drafting.

2 These words should not be used, because the point they seek to make is self evident – in the absence of any indication to the contrary 'clause 7' or 'Schedule 2' would be taken to refer to the document in question without 'hereof' and 'hereto'. If, however, the document, or the transaction of which it formed part was complicated (or if the point really worried him) the draftsman could put the matter beyond doubt by adding the following clause: 'References in this Agreement to any clause, sub-clause or schedule without further designation are to that clause, sub-clause or schedule of this Agreement.' Many would think that goes overboard. The following provision from the Education (School Governing Bodies) Regulations 1981 certainly does: 'In these Regulations any reference to a Regulation is a reference to a Regulation of these Regulations, any reference in a Regulation to a paragraph is a reference to a paragraph of that Regulation and any reference in a paragraph to a sub-paragraph is a reference to a sub-paragraph of that paragraph.'

3 Only a lawyer would state: 'to sell such products', or 'to sell the same'. The layman refers to 'the product', 'that product', 'those products' or 'them' and the draftsman should follow his example.

4 The point that these words, when used as demonstrative adjectives, seek to make is generally self evident – a second reference to a person or item will, in the absence of an indication to the contrary, be taken to refer to the same person or item that was mentioned previously ('my said wife . . .' is a favourite of the author) and in a case of genuine confusion 'said and aforesaid' may well not help (see *Campbell v Bouskell* (1859) 27 Beav 325). Where the point does need to be dealt with, adopting a defined term is a better solution '"Wife" means . . .'. In some instances, for example, 'that' may assist.

5 Lawyers have a tendency to use these words too frequently. In many instances the word 'a' can be substituted for 'any': 'any person may enter the park', may be written; 'a person may enter the park'. Similarly with 'each' and 'every'. On many occasions the word 'all' can be deleted altogether (in for example 'all persons may go into the park') without loss of effect. Generally these words should not be used except where the sense overwhelmingly requires it.

6 Such as 'In consideration of . . .' or 'Subject to the terms of this Agreement . . .'.

7 For example 'agreed and declared', 'execute and perform', 'settle and compromise', 'well and sufficiently' etc.

8 For example replace: 'in the event that' by 'if'; 'in any case where' by 'where', and 'shall be at liberty to' or 'shall be entitled to' or 'shall have the right to' or 'power is reserved to' by 'may'.

9 Latin terms do not very often crop up today in Board Rooms, business parks or High Streets, and so should not appear in legal documents. 'If that phrase had not been in Latin, nobody would have called it a principle': Lord Shaw of Dunfermline in *Ballard v North British Rly Co* 1923 SC (HL) 43 at 46.

10 Lawyers favour one unique misuse of 'shall'. In normal English (which happens to be grammatically correct) we say 'If the Solicitor loses his dictaphone he will have to use another one'. Lawyers wrongly insert 'shall': 'If the Solicitor shall lose his dictaphone . . .'. To put it in a more likely context, lawyers tend to write: 'If the Tenant shall go into liquidation . . .'. In fact we should follow normal English and say: 'If the Tenant goes into liquidation . . .'. Conveyancers often avoid another potential problem with 'shall' by imposing obligations on parties in the forms of covenants: 'The Landlord covenants with the Tenant as follows:'. When they do not, however, they sometimes use 'shall': 'The Tenant shall pay the interim service charge . . .'. There are two difficulties with such use – (a) 'shall' can be used as an obligation, or simply as an indication of the future, or misused when only a discretion is intended, and (b) one should never use the same term for different meanings and one should always use the same term for the same meaning. Draftsmen who recognise these points frequently use 'shall' for the obligation, 'may' for the discretion and 'will' to indicate

the plain future tense. But this is not entirely satisfactory. Textbooks on grammar tend to suggest that 'shall' should be used in the first person and 'will' in the second and third so that 'he shall go' is grammatically incorrect. Moreover it is suggested that to use 'shall' as the obligation is to use it in a way in which it has not been used in normal English for many centuries. When acknowledging or imposing a commitment or obligation in normal English, we use 'must'. 'I must go to the office early in the morning', 'You must pick me up at half-past seven' state commitments or obligations. Substitute 'shall' for 'must' and you produce something which is far short of an obligation or commitment. If we agree with the simple policy statement that legal documents should be written in normal English and not in some special language used only by lawyers then we should use 'must' when an obligation is intended. The prudent draftsman and student of linguistics would be well advised never to use 'shall'.

11 The danger is that not everybody 'in the industry' would regard them as having exactly the same meaning and that the Judge, if the agreement ever has to be litigated, will not understand them.

12 A person or thing should always be called by the same name and a circumstance, condition or result should always be described in the same words, while the same word should never be used for different circumstances or conditions or results. Having referred to 'a sum of money', it should not afterwards be called 'the amount'. Having spoken of the object of a gift as 'the legatee', he should not later be called 'the beneficiary'. If 'on the cessation of his employment' has been written, 'on the termination of his employment' should not afterwards be used if the same thing is meant because, for example, the latter expression might be interpreted as being restricted to termination by the act of the employer or the employee.

1.5 *Avoiding ambiguity.* The good draftsman will realise that the lessons of the previous two paragraphs will minimise, but not eliminate altogether, the risk of his work containing ambiguities.[1] He should, however, be aware of a few key areas in which even a short sentence drafted in the most simple of English can contain uncertainties. For example:

1.5:1 *The 'wandering' word or phrase.* The uncertainty here is to which part of a sentence does a word or phrase refer. For example: 'tenants who are in arrears frequently cannot be re-housed'. Does the 'frequently' refer to the payment of the rent by the tenants and set out a rule or policy statement – ie the rule is that 'tenants who are frequently in arrears cannot be re-housed' – or to the re-housing – ie sadly it is a fact that 'frequently tenants who are in arrears cannot be re-housed' however much we should like to. Another example arises where an adjective or adverb precedes a list of nouns or verbs. For example: 'No dangerous shoulder-pads, buckles or rings may be worn'. Does 'dangerous' apply to all three terms, so that a buckle or ring that is not dangerous *could* be worn, or only to shoulder-pads, so that *no* rings or buckles could be worn, whether dangerous or not.[2] A more complicated variation occurs where a number of statements are made followed by some words of qualification, often referred to as a modifier, and the question is whether the modifer applies only to the last, or to all the preceding statements.[3] For example, the tenant may have covenanted:

'not to make any structural alteration or addition to the Premises or use or permit any part of the Premises to be adapted or used so that the gross covered floor area of the Premises available for use or letting is decreased'.

It is not clear from this if there is an absolute covenant against structural alterations or additions, or if the prohibition applies only where the floor area is increased – ie does the modifier ('so that . . .') apply to alterations etc *and* use or only use. Assuming that *both* are intended, a re-draft resolving the ambiguity would read:

'Not to:
(a) make any structural alteration or addition to the Premises, or
(b) use or permit any part of the Premises to be adapted or used
so that the gross covered floor area of the Premises available for use or letting is decreased'.

If the modifier was intended to apply only to (b), then the words 'so that . . . decreased' would have been included in (b).

1.5:2 *The fundamental word.* Courts are frequently asked to construe a common everyday word, perhaps even when it appears in a short sentence drafted in plain English.[4] The draftsman should be alive to situations where the interpretation of such a word could be fundamental and discuss this with his client. There are essentially three approaches. The client may prefer to leave the term as it is on the basis that the uncertainty could work in his favour. The other extreme is to define precisely what the term means when used in that context.[5] The danger is that the definition may in practice prove not to be comprehensive and, for example, an activity that would, by any commonsense interpretation of the term be included, will be excluded because of the special meaning given to the term when used in that document. The midway position is to assist in the interpretation without actually 'closing the class'.[6]

1.5:3 *When does the term begin?* It can be vital to know the exact date upon which a term begins – not only will this indicate when it will end, but it will also control the validity of a notice that has to be served for example 'within six days of the commencement of the term' or 'at any time before the expiry of the second year of the term'. The question that frequently arises is whether the date expressed in the document is included in the term. The general rule is that a term expressed to commence *from* a certain date commences on the first moment of the *next* day unless the document contains a clear indication that the parties had a different intention.[7] It is suggested that good drafting demands clarity on this point and that it will usually be preferable to rebut the presumption and to indicate that the commencement date in included. So rather than 'from' the lease should state 'from and including' or 'beginning on' or, where a period is involved, 'after 31 March 1988 and before 1 September 1988' is preferable to 'within the period from 1 April 1988 to 30 August 1988.'

1.5:4 *Which is 'the fifth year of the term'?*   Expressions such as 'the fifth year of the term' should be avoided. Leases are often granted (ie dated) during a year subsequent to the year in which the term is expressed to commence. For example, a draft lease submitted in December may indicate that the term will commence on the 25 December of that year. Completion might take place on the 1 February of the following year. There could be more extreme cases – for example where the last unit on an estate is let several years after the first, but for estate management reasons the landlord insisted upon standard commencement and expiry dates.[8] Disputes can therefore arise as to which is the 'fifth year'. Should time be computed from the commencement of the term, or the date of the grant (ie the date of the lease)? There are two lines of contrasting cases. In the *Earl Cadogan v Guinness*[9] and *Roberts v Church Comrs for England*[10] the date of the lease was taken as the commencement date for the purposes of calculating the length of the term whereas in *Bird v Baker*[11] and

Page v Mallow Investments Ltd[12] time was held to run from the date on which the term was expressed to begin for calculating when a break clause ('at the end of seven years') or an option ('within eighteen months of the commencement of the term') could be exercised. Where a period is referred to in a lease, the latter would probably prevail,[13] but there is no excuse for introducing any element of uncertainty especially where it is so easy to put the matter beyond doubt – for example by stating the review dates themselves or by specifically referring to the date from which the periods should be computed.[14]

1 Long, complicated sentences are likely to hide ambiguities.
2 A further example is statements like 'wilfully defacing damaging or destroying the premises'. Does 'wilfully' apply to defacing, and so any type of damage or destruction falls within the provision, or does 'wilfully' apply to all three verbs?
3 The term 'squinting modifier' is sometimes used to describe a modifier the application of which is uncertain.
4 The danger inherent in simple everyday words is illustrated by the statutory provisions that indicate when the two major landlord and tenant Acts apply. The Rent Act 1977, s 1 stated that 'a tenancy under which a dwelling-house (which may be a house or part of a house) is let as a separate dwelling is a protected tenancy for the purposes of the Act' (and the Housing Act 1988, s 1(1) adopts similar wording). The Landlord and Tenant Act 1954, s 23 states that 'this Part of this Act applies to any tenancy where the property comprised in the tenancy is or includes premises which are occupied by the tenant and are so occupied for the purposes of a business carried on by him or for those and other purposes.' (See Appendix 3 below.) The sections could hardly have been drafted using more simple language . . . and yet, probably no two sections have been more frequently litigated – see 27 Halsbury's Statutes (4th edn) pages 410–413 and 139–141, and as to the latter, para 14.3 below.
5 For example, 'For the purposes of this Agreement "Business" means . . .'.
6 For example, 'For the purposes of this Agreement, the term "Business" includes [excludes] . . .'. See for example Landlord and Tenant Act 1954, s 23(2) and (3) (see Appendix 3 below). Here the natural meaning of the term is enlarged, restricted or clarified.
7 *Ladyman v Wirral Estates Ltd* [1968] 2 All ER 197 – note the discussion of factors that the court will consider are indications that the parties *did* intend to rebut the presumption that the term should commence on the first moment of the next day, and intended the term to begin on the day itself.
8 The tenant also needs to note that this approach can serve to shorten the term of the lease and the first review period: as to the latter see para 6.4:2 below.
9 [1936] Ch 515, [1936] 2 All ER 29.
10 [1972] 1 QB 278, [1971] 3 All ER 703, CA. See also *Brikom Investments Ltd v Seaford* [1981] 2 All ER 783, [1981] 1 WLR 863, CA.
11 (1858) 1 E & E 12.
12 (1974) 29 P & CR 168.
13 *Bradshaw v Pawley* [1979] 3 All ER 273 [1980] 1 WLR 10; *Beaumont Property Trust v Tai* (1983) 265 Estates Gazette 872; *Keen v Holland* [1984] 1 All ER 75, [1984] 1 WLR 251, CA.
14 See Appendix 1, Form 3, clause 1.7 below.

B TAKING INSTRUCTIONS

1.6 *Basic agreement rarely complete*. The function of the solicitors involved in the grant of a lease is to embody the agreement made by their clients.[1] Such an agreement is usually complete in the case of the sale of freehold land, but will rarely be complete on the granting of a lease because the parties never (or at least 'hardly ever'[2]) deal with the details of the lease. For example, the parties and the premises may have been identified, and the initial rent, review period and length of the term agreed. One or two well-known phrases may well have been used such as 'tenant's full repairing and insuring lease' or 'tenant to pay a percentage of the cost of the services'. It will fall to the landlord's solicitor to ensure that his client has adequately considered *all* the key issues and given specific instructions on them. These include, for example, the precise extent of the premises to be let,[3] any rights that the tenant would require over the landlord's adjoining land to enable the tenant to use the premises,[4] the rights that the landlord might require over the demised premises to enable him and his other tenants to occupy[5] (and perhaps be free to develop[6]) adjoining premises, the detailed arrangements for repair and maintenance of the demised premises[7] and, when relevant, the building of which they form part.[8] Much time will be wasted, which will not be in his client's interests, if the landlord's solicitor does not deal properly with these matters in his initial draft and, as such, taking instructions should not be regarded purely as a passive exercise.[9] The tenant's solicitor clearly has a duty to explain the effect of clauses that he inserts in the draft lease.[10]

1   It is to be hoped 'subject to lease'. See para 1.8 below.
2   W. S. Gilbert: 'HMS Pinafore', Act I.
3   See Chapter 3 below.
4   See paras 4.2–4.9 below.
5   See paras 4.10–4.17 below.
6   See para 4.15 below.
7   See Chapter 7 below.
8   See Chapter 11 below.
9   The preparation of check lists (see Appendix 2 below) or model forms of lease for various types of premises will assist by reminding the draftsman of the issues upon which instructions are needed.
10   As to the duty of the tenant's solicitor to explain, see para 1.18 below but it is suggested that a similar duty is imposed on the landlord's solicitor, especially where the landlord is not in the business of property and in the case of clauses the implications of which are not obvious. For example, a landlord should be alerted to the fact that a narrow user covenant may not be in the landlord's interest when it comes to reviewing the rent (see para 7.10:3 below). Where the landlord is proposing to let off part of his business premises, his solicitor should always raise the question of excluding the security of tenure provisions of Part II of the 1954 Act (see para 14.5 below).

1.7   *The emphasis of the lease.* The landlord's solicitor will rarely be assisting his client by producing a draft, so weighted in favour of the landlord, that no properly advised tenant would accept. The risks of so doing are two-fold. In an extreme case the tenant might decide there and then that he wants no more of the matter and look for alternative premises. More likely, the legal negotiations will get off on a 'contentious' footing, and be more protracted than they need. If a fairer draft had been submitted, the lease might have been completed more quickly and the landlord would have begun to receive rent at an earlier date. Sometimes one feels that if only the landlord had fully understood the intricacies of the draft lease at the time that it was submitted, he would have preferred to adopt a more reasonable stance from the beginning. By the time the issues are fully explained to him, however, he feels obliged to support the line adopted by his solicitor. It follows that the landlord should be sent a copy of the draft lease (together with the appropriate explanations[1]) before it is submitted to the tenant's solicitor.[2]

1   See footnote 10 to para 1.6 above.
2   Alternatively a copy of the draft lease could be sent to the landlord at the same time that it is sent to the tenant's solicitor, who should be told that the draft has not been reviewed by the landlord and is sent subject to any changes that he may wish to make.

C 'SUBJECT TO LEASE'

1.8 *Subject to contract today*. Practitioners brought up to believe that one of the greatest sins that they could commit was to create 'a Section 40 memorandum' will find it difficult to accept that the section and therefore its memoranda are no more. The Law of Property Act 1925, s 40 provided that contracts for the sale or disposition of any interest in land,[1] in order to be enforceable, had to be in writing *or evidenced in writing* and signed by or on behalf of the party against whom the contract was being enforced.[2] Generally a solicitor retained to act for a client who proposes to purchase land[3] has no authority to bind his client unless authority has been expressly conferred upon the solicitor or is necessarily implicit in the terms of his retainer.[4] The danger was that when he did have that authority, a solicitor's letter confirming an agreement to buy and sell land, or grant a lease, could constitute the memorandum or note of an oral contract and thus provide the written evidence and the signature required by s 40 to produce an enforceable agreement. Hence the obsession with marking communications 'subject to contract' to guard against that risk by clearly indicating that no unconditional agreement existed. Section 40 has, however, been repeated[5] by the Law of Property (Miscellaneous Provisions) Act 1989 that provides that contracts for the sale or other disposition of an interest in land:[1]

(a) must be in writing,[6]

(b) must incorporate all the terms of the agreement in one document (or in each where there is an exchange of documents),[6]

(c) may incorporate the terms by reference to another document,[7]

(d) must be signed by or on behalf of all the parties (or on different parts where there is an exchange of documents).[8]

1 Which by virtue of the Law of Property Act 1925, s 205(1) includes a lease.
2 Unless there had been part performance: Law of Property Act 1925, s 40(2).
3 It is suggested that the position is the same where the client is taking a lease.
4 See for example 44 Halsbury's Laws of England (4th edn) para 108; *Griffiths v Young* [1970] Ch 675, [1970] 3 All ER 601, CA.
5 With effect from 27 September 1989.
6 Law of Property (Miscellaneous Provisions) Act 1989, s 2(1) Act 1986. The section does not apply to short leases (not exceeding three years at the best rent with no premium; Law of Property Act 1925, s 54(2)), a contract made in the course of a public auction or a contract regulated by the Financial Services Act 1986.
7 Ibid, s 2(2).
8 Ibid, s 2(3).

1.9 *Consequences of the new Act*. The consequences of the Law of Property (Miscellaneous Provisions) Act 1989 are considerable – for example:

(a) the law has been simplified – the agreement for the sale etc of land now has to be in writing and the concept of an oral agreement being evidenced in writing (by a 'Section 40 memorandum') has been abolished,[1]

(b) accordingly correspondence concerning a proposed sale or lease need not be marked 'subject to contract',

(c) contracts can still be created in correspondence but only where the correspondence complies with the rules of the new Act set out in para 1.8 above,

(d) a contract therefore could come into existence as a result of correspondence between the parties' solicitors[2] but only where both solicitors were authorised to enter into that agreement,[3]

(e) a solicitor worried that he might be thought to have the authority of his client could protect both himself and his client by indicating at the beginning of the matter that he does not have that authority.

1   As has the concept of part performance that can be longer cure a breach of the formal requirements: the Law of Property Act 1925, s 40(2) has also been repeated.
2   As to what would have to be in that correspondence, see para 1.10 below.
3   See para 1.8 footnote 4 above.

1.10   *How comprehensive an agreement is needed?* In order to constitute a binding contract, there must be a concluded bargain which settles everything that is necessary to be settled and leaves nothing to be settled by agreement between the parties.[1] The issues involved in the sale of freehold land are few and can easily be agreed. It could be argued, that no agreement in correspondence relating to a lease could be complete unless it dealt with *all* the terms of the lease, because without this, there would still be matters 'to be settled by agreement between the parties'. That would not be so, however, if the court was satisfied that the intention of the parties really was to enter into a binding commitment, because an agreement for lease does not specify the covenants and provisos that are to be included in the lease, there is an implied term that the lease will contain the usual and proper covenants and provision.[2] What these are in each case is a question of fact to be determined in default of agreement by the court.

1   *May and Butcher Ltd v R* [1934] 2 KB 17n. (Decided in 1929.) This very strict approach of the House of Lords appears to be in conflict with later decisions, for example *Hillas & Co Ltd v Arcos Ltd* [1932] All ER Rep 494. Note Lord Tomlin at 499: 'The problem for a court of construction must always be to balance matters so that, without a violation of essential principles, the dealings of men may as far as possible be treated as effective and that the law may not incur the reproach of being the destroyer of bargains.' See also for example *Smith v Morgan* [1971] 2 All ER 1500, [1971] 1 WLR 803; *Brown v Gould* [1972] Ch 53, [1971] 2 All ER 1505; *Thomas Bates & Son Ltd v Wyndham's (Lingerie) Ltd* [1981] 1 All ER 1077, [1981] 1 WLR 505, contra *King's Motors (Oxford) Ltd v Lax* [1969] 3 All ER 665, [1970] 1 WLR 426; *Courtney and Fairbairn Ltd v Tolaini Bros (Hotels) Ltd* [1975] 1 All ER 716, [1975] 1 WLR 297. See also *Beer v Bowden* [1981] 1 All ER 1070, [1981] 1 WLR 522, CA; *Sudbrook Trading Estate Ltd v Eggleton* [1983] 1 AC 444, [1982] 3 All ER 1, HL; *Trustees of National Deposit Friendly Society v Beatties of London Ltd* [1985] 2 EGLR 59, 275 Estates Gazette 54.
2   See para 2.20 below and Hill & Redman *Law of Landlord and Tenant* (18th edn) para A698.

1.11   *When formal agreements are contemplated.* A party seeking to prove a binding obligation can still be in difficulties even where there is an agreed form of lease, because he will then be confronted with the decision of Harman J in *Hollington Bros Ltd v Rhodes*[1] which was followed by Plowman J in *Leveson v Parfum Marcel Rochas (England) Ltd.*[2] In *Hollington*, the defendants were tenants of a block of offices under a long lease. In 1945 they negotiated through agents for the grant of an underlease for a term of seven years of certain rooms in the block next to the plaintiffs. Negotiations were completed in August 1945 and the plaintiffs executed the counterpart of the underlease and returned it to the defendants. The defendants executed the underlease but it was never granted to the plaintiffs, although their agents informed the plaintiffs that the lease was being executed. The plaintiffs were let into possession in September 1945 and they paid the rent quarterly to the defendants' agents. The agreement for the underlease was never registered as a land charge. In September 1947 the defendants assigned the headlease to D 'subject to and with the benefit of such tenancies as may affect the premises'. D immediately gave the plaintiffs notice to quit on the footing that they were in possession only as annual tenants. The plaintiffs were obliged to negotiate with D who were prepared to grant them an underlease for the residue of the term of the alleged underlease but only on payment of a premium and an increased rent. Harman J held that no contract to grant an underlease was ever made between the plaintiffs and the defendants, their conduct constituting only ordinary business negotiations. He said:

'It is commonplace that in many, indeed, in most cases where a lease is to be granted everything remains in negotiation until the lease and its counterpart are finally exchanged between the parties[3] and it seems to me impossible to spell out of the course of business which I have described, and which appears from correspondence, anything more than the ordinary course of negotiations . . . In my judgment such a contract cannot be spelled out of this state of things. There was, I think, no intention on either side to be bound by the course which negotiations took until the lease was exchanged with the counterpart, and this was never done.'

Plowman J went further[4] and considered that there was a presumption that where parties were negotiating the terms of a proposed lease, the approval of the draft lease did not conclude a contract, which was concluded only upon the exchange of the lease and counterpart. This is a further reason for preferring 'Subject to Lease' to 'Subject to Contract', where no contract is envisaged, in that the former strengthens the presumption that the parties do not intend to be bound until the lease and counterpart are exchanged.

1   [1951] 2 All ER 578n, [1951] 2 TLR 691.
2   (1966) 200 Estates Gazette 407.
3   See para 1.12 below.
4   See note 2 above.

1.12   *Sealing the lease may bind.* It is suggested that it is an over simplification to say that everything remains in negotiation until the lease and counterpart are finally *exchanged*. A party that has *executed* the lease or counterpart could well find itself bound, even where there had been no exchange, providing the other party executes its part within a reasonable time. As Lord Denning MR said in *Vincent v Premo Enterprises (Voucher Sales) Ltd*:[1]

'A deed is very different from a contract. On a contract for the sale of land, the contract is not binding on the parties until they have exchanged their parts. But with a deed it is different. A deed is binding on the maker of it, even though the parts have not been exchanged as long as it has been signed, sealed and delivered. "Delivery" in this connection does not mean "handed over" to the other side. It means delivered in the old legal sense, namely, an act done so as to evince an intention to be bound. Even though the deed remains in the possession of the maker, or his solicitor, he is bound by it if he has done some act evincing an intention to be bound as by saying: I deliver this my act and deed. He may, however, make the "delivery" conditional: in which case the deed is called an "escrow" which becomes binding when the condition is fulfilled.'

When a party seals the lease or counterpart there will always be an implied term that (by adapting the principles of *Glessing v Green*[2] to the grant of a lease) this is conditional upon the other party executing its document and the tenant paying such sums as are due by way of rent and other payments 'within a time that is reasonable in all the circumstances'.[3] This concept was illustrated in *Beesly v Hallwood Estates Ltd*[4] where an engrossed counterpart of a proposed lease, to be granted in pursuance of the tenant's exercise of an option, was sent to the tenant's solicitors. The landlord executed the lease intending to deliver it conditionally only (so the Court found) upon the tenant executing the counterpart. The counterpart was executed by the tenant, but before the lease and counterpart was exchanged, the landlord declined to proceed, on the ground that the option had not been validly exercised. The Court of Appeal held that the lease, having been executed by the landlord as an escrow, could not be recalled by the landlord pending performance of the condition on which it was delivered (ie the sealing of the counterpart by the tenant) and thus the tenant was entitled to a new lease, even though the lease and counterpart had not been exchanged, nor the renewal registered as a C(iv) land charge.[5]

1 [1969] 2 All ER 941 at 944. See also the cases mentioned in note 1 to para 15.5 below and P. H. Kenny: 'Dating an Escrow' [1982] Conv 409. As to the validating of a deed that lacks a seal, see *TCB Ltd v Gray* [1986] Ch 621, [1986] 1 All ER 587.
2 [1975] 2 All ER 696, [1975] 1 WLR 863.
3 *Kingston v Ambrian Investment Co Ltd* [1975] 1 All ER 120 at 125.
4 [1961] Ch 105, [1961] 1 All ER 90.
5 The 'no exchange of lease and counterpart' cases and the escrow cases are, however, reconcilable. In *Hollington* and *Leveson* (see para 1.11 above), agreements for leases were not binding because they were equitable interests not protected by registration and the dispute was with the third party purchaser of the reversion. In the escrow cases, performance of the condition allowed the deed (escrow) to take effect, thus creating a legal estate against the landlord and (although not necessarily arising) against a third party, irrespective of notice, just as the annual tenancy in *Hollington* bound the purchasers although the unregistered agreement did not.

D THE ROLE OF THE TENANT'S SOLICITOR

1.13 *Immediate action.* In due course, therefore, the draft lease (and a copy for his use), will arrive on the desk of the tenant's solicitor. There is a great temptation at this stage to say 'Oh no, that's three days work, just to go through it', and put the file firmly at the bottom of the pile. It is quite true that the solicitor will have to set aside several hours in which to review the draft, and it may well be that, because of other commitments, he is unable to do so at once. There is, however, much that he can and should do immediately that will take up very little time and that may avoid delays later. For example:

(a) He can put in hand and without a detailed study of the lease, many of the non-drafting steps referred to in Chapter 2, below. He can always reserve the right to raise further enquiries after his review of the lease, but at least time will have begun to run on these matters so that the appropriate replies and information should be to hand by the time the wording of the lease is nearing agreement, thus avoiding further delays at this stage.

(b) It will not take very long to check that the lease is complete (no pages missing and no passages illegible), that the plans have been included and are properly coloured, and that the basic elements (rent, term, etc) correspond with his instructions. Not only is it annoying to find when one settles down to review the draft in detail that it is not in order, but once again valuable time may be lost if the need to remedy these matters is only discovered at a later stage. If the basic terms of the lease do not correspond with the instructions that the tenant's solicitor has received, then he should take up this point with his client at once.

(c) A solicitor's relationship with his client depends of course very much upon the individuals involved, but there may be instances where it would be appropriate to pass on to his client a copy of the unread draft at this stage. Alternatively, or in addition, it may be beneficial to provide the tenant's surveyor with a copy of the draft. There can be no general rule – the tenant's solicitor will need to decide in the light of the circumstances of the case and the individuals involved.

(d) He should acknowledge receipt of the draft lease. At least then the landlord's solicitor will be reassured by the news that his draft has not gone astray in the post and many a matter has got off on the wrong foot because the landlord's solicitor had to send a reminder where no acknowledgment had been received.

1.14 *Detailed review.* In due course, what some would call 'the evil day' can be postponed no longer, and the tenant's solicitor will settle down to study the draft lease in depth. A lease is not a novel and should not be read as such. It is sensible initially to glance quickly through the document to get some idea of its structure, and where the various components are located. Then the tenant's solicitor should look individually at each of these components, dealing thoroughly with each one, and noting the amendments that he feels necessary, before moving on to the next point. The checklist in Appendix 2, below, and the subsequent chapters of this book, should assist this systematic review. It is important to consider not only the language set out in the draft but also the matters that have been *omitted* altogether. Many of the amendments proposed by the tenant's solicitor will involve introducing a totally new clause into the lease, rather than amending some existing provision. The tenant's solicitor should always remember that there are really only four good reasons for amending a draft document:

(a) to make it more accurately reflect the intentions of the parties;
(b) to deal with a point omitted altogether from the draft that should be included in order to avoid future disputes between the parties;
(c) to remove a possible ambiguity;
(d) in respect of a matter of detail not previously 'agreed' between the parties, to make the document more favourable to the tenant.

A solicitor needs to take care not to amend for the sake of amending. The tenant's solicitor should resist redrafting the document to put it into a style and form that he finds more acceptable unless and to the extent that this is required to achieve one or more of these objectives. There is also a need to be realistic when the draft under review is an underlease[1] because the immediate landlord will be restricted, and will clearly not enter into an obligation with his tenant that he may be unable to meet in view of the terms of the headlease. The prospective sub-tenant must either accept the position or, where the issue is so fundamental that the underletting can only proceed if it is resolved, inform the landlord accordingly, and suggest that he approach the superior landlord with a view to seeking an amendment to the headlease.

1 See Chapter 13, below.

1.15 *The next step.* When the tenant's solicitor has reviewed the draft lease and decided the changes that he feels should be made, he can either take them up at once with the landlord's solicitor, or report on them to his client and seek instructions. The course he adopts will be influenced by his relationship with his client, and the nature of the proposed changes. Where the draft lease contains an inconsistency with his instructions, then clearly the solicitor should first consult his client, because, if there remains a misunderstanding between the parties over a fundamental term of the letting, there must be a risk that the matter would not proceed, and as such any detailed legal work would be premature. In many cases, however, the draft lease will comply with the instructions received by the tenant's solicitor and all his proposed changes will be of a 'legal' nature. In such instances, and especially where either the tenant's solicitor knows his client's policies on these matters, or the client tends 'to leave all such matters to my solicitor', it seems sensible to avoid further delay by writing direct to the landlord's solicitor.[1]

1   It would be worth making the point that the reply is subject to any points that the tenant himself may have.

1.16   *Explain concerns.* When the tenant's solicitor responds on the draft lease, it is important for him to indicate why he has proposed the changes. Armed with these explanations, the landlord's solicitor may be able to find compromises by which both parties' aims can be accomplished. There are essentially two forms in which the tenant's solicitor can respond. Where only a few amendments have been made to the draft, it is normal to return the draft amended in longhand (usually in red ink). This document then becomes known as the 'travelling draft'. Where, however, the draft needs (in the view of the tenant's solicitor) substantial amending, it may be more sensible to write, explaining the general nature of the changes required, on the basis that any detailed drafting is premature until the principles have been agreed or compromised. In many such cases, the drafting causes few problems between the solicitors once the parties have agreed upon the principles.

1.17   *Relationship with client.* A solicitor's relationship with his client will depend upon the individuals – in some instances it might be helpful for the solicitor to send to his client copies of all correspondence with the other party's solicitor that deals with substantive matters including, where necessary, a copy of the amended draft. This will not only help to keep the client informed on the progress of the matter, but will also give him the option of taking up the outstanding matters with the other party (or his agent) direct. Whether or not copies of correspondence are sent, the tenant's solicitor will need to report to his client on the terms of the lease. The exact form of that report and its timing will depend upon the tenant's requirements and the relationship between the solicitor and his client – sometimes a report is sent as soon as the draft lease is received but in other cases, where the client's requirements are well known to his solicitor, this might be deferred until the amendments had been proposed and accepted or rejected by the landlord.

1.18   *Duty to explain to client.* Copy letters and reports are not, however, sufficient in themselves. It is the duty of the tenant's solicitor to *explain* to the tenant the effect of all the terms of the lease, and in particular any unusual or onerous terms. In *Sykes v Midland Bank Executor and Trustee Co Ltd*[1] a firm of architects and surveyors entered into a lease that prohibited any user other than their own business unless 'the permission in writing of the lessor and the superior lessors has first been obtained, such permission *by the lessor* not to be unreasonably withheld'. The tenant's solicitor was held to be negligent for failing to advise his clients that the *superior lessor's* consent could be arbitrarily withheld.[2] Thus the tenant's solicitor will need to go through the draft lease with his client pointing out the effect of the various provisions. It will, of course, be in the solicitor's interests either to do this in writing, or, where the lease was reviewed with the client at a meeting, to write confirming that the meeting took place, and specifically referring to any particularly onerous clauses.

1   [1971] 1 QB 113, [1970] 2 All ER 471, CA but note *Aslan v Clintons* (1984) 134 NLJ 584 July 13. See also *GP & P Ltd v Bulcraig and Davis* [1986] 2 EGLR 148, 280 Estates Gazette 356; *County Personnel (Employment Agency) Ltd v Alan R Pulver & Co* [1987] 1 All ER 289, [1987] 1 WLR 916. As to calculation of damages for solicitor's negligence see also *Hayes v Dodd* [1988] BTLC 380, CA and *Walker v Griffen Couch & Archer* [1988] EGCS 64.
2   Only nominal damages of £2 were awarded because the Court of Appeal found that even if the clauses had been fully explained, the plaintiffs would nevertheless have proceeded.

E   SUBSEQUENT NEGOTIATIONS

1.19   *The tenant's position is known.* Thus the landlord's solicitor receives from the tenant's solicitors either an amended draft or a letter indicating those changes that the tenant is proposing. There are some transactions – although probably not many – when all the amendments are acceptable and/or utterly unacceptable. In other words, there are no issues for subsequent negotiation. In these cases, the landlord's solicitor writes to the tenant's solicitor, indicating what amendments (if any) are accepted, and pointing out that the remaining amendments are not agreed, that they will not in any circumstances be agreed, and that if the tenant finds this unacceptable, he should proceed elsewhere. A landlord's solicitor needs to have obtained very specific instructions in order to write in this way, even if the suggestion to withdraw from the matter is left to be inferred, because his client will not thank him if the proposed tenant decides not to proceed, where, in fact, the landlord would have been prepared to compromise on some of the issues. Normally, however, the position is less clear-cut – the landlord's solicitor amends (usually in green) the travelling draft and returns it to the tenant's solicitor, or responds to the tenant's solicitor's letter, where no amended draft has been sent.[1] The next step, whenever practical, should be a *meeting* between the solicitors, with a senior representative of both parties present. It needs to be someone with authority, not because any binding commitments are going to be made, but to lessen the chance of compromises worked out at the meeting, that appear acceptable to everyone there, subsequently being rejected by the senior management of one of the parties. Clearly a meeting will save time, because exchanges between the parties, that may take several weeks when reduced to writing and sent in the post, can often be accomplished at a single meeting. There is, however, a further advantage. A meeting gives each solicitor the opportunity of explaining, more fully than is usually possible in correspondence, his reason for inserting a clause, or making an amendment.

In a surprising number of instances when these reasons are known, both parties' positions can be accommodated. Solicitors are human and do sometimes tend to over-react. A landlord's solicitor will draft a clause wider than his client really requires, while the tenant's solicitor will strike out a provision altogether when in fact his client could accept a 'watered-down' version. Matters such as these can be explored much more easily face to face than in correspondence.

1   See para 1.16 above. In fact in these circumstances it would often be preferable to proceed straight to the meeting without there being any written response from the landlord at this stage.

1.20   *'Be prepared'*. The way in which the negotiations will be conducted will depend upon the circumstances of the individual case. The vital lesson to those involved is simply – *be prepared*. One should clearly establish before the meeting, or set out in correspondence where a meeting is not practical, not why the amendment would be in the client's interest, but rather why the amendment would be *reasonable in all the circumstances*. The two may be virtually synonymous, and the distinction will generally only involve a slight change of emphasis, but this is important when seeking to persuade the other side to concede. As part of this preparation, one should consider possible counter-arguments that may be raised and be ready to deal with them. It may even be helpful to 'rehearse' the matter in the office with a colleague taking the other side's position. There is a need also to consider any law that relates to the issues in dispute. It can be disconcerting to the unwary if the other solicitor says, with a sweeping gesture, 'But that's covered by Section 19 anyway'. It does strengthen your position to know what the section says, and to be able explain why, for example, the provision that you are seeking would not be implied by s 19(3) of the 1927 Act.[1]

1   See para 7.16:2 below.

1.21   *Strength of the parties*. It is rare in any negotiations for the strength of the parties to be evenly balanced, and the relative positions of the landlord and tenant will be relevant during negotiations. If the premises in question are much in demand, the landlord may feel himself able to adopt a 'take it or leave it' approach. Where on the other hand the premises have been on the market for a while, the landlord is likely to be more amenable to proposed amendments to the lease, especially where the tenant is a significant undertaking and can thus provide a 'good covenant'. A solicitor about to be involved in detailed negotiations should, therefore, always establish the background to the proposed letting.

1.22   *Lease terms affect rent*. In some circumstances, the tenant may wish to reopen the 'commercial negotiations' if his solicitor is unable to persuade the landlord to concede on a point of substance especially the amount of the rent. This may arise particularly where the draft appears at variance with the terms previously agreed, or where some burdensome obligation to be imposed on the tenant is disclosed, for the first time, when the draft lease is submitted and thus after the rent has been 'agreed' between the parties. For example, the proposed rent might have been agreed, subject to lease, on the basis of a 'tenant's internal repairing lease' but the draft lease provides for the tenant to be responsible for the structure of part of the building, including perhaps the roof and foundations, or the tenant understood that this would mean that the landlord would be responsible for the exterior, but the draft is silent on the point. If the landlord will not accept amendments making the tenant liable only for interior decorative repair and imposing a positive obligation on the landlord for the exterior and structure, the tenant will need to enquire of his surveyor whether or not it would be appropriate for this to be reflected in a reduced rent. If the tenant's surveyor does feel that the market rent of the premises let on the terms now envisaged would be less than the rent previously agreed, he should seek to reopen negotiations. The reverse could also be true. If the tenant is pressing for a particular amendment which, in the view of the landlord or his surveyor, would lessen the value of the reversion, the landlord could offer to accept the amendment only in return for an increase in the rent.

F   TERMS FOR THE FUTURE

1.23   *Never lower standards for short lease.* There is one final general point that should be remembered by parties and solicitors concerned with proposed leases for relatively short terms. An atmosphere can be created that 'It does not matter too much because it's only for a year or two'. This is often emphasised when one party is most anxious for a quick completion, especially where the tenant is acquiring the premises for what he sees a short-term need. In these circumstances, the landlord's solicitor may be tempted not to give the drafting of the lease quite the same attention that he would were the term longer, and the tenant who is desperate to obtain possession may be prompted to suggest to his solicitor 'not to be too fussy over the small print' provided the basic elements of the lease are acceptable. This philosophy should be resisted. It is a fallacy to suggest that there is a direct relationship between the length of the term and the potential for disputes. Over and above this, however, the parties may be defining the terms of a relationship for many more years than they intended, in the event of the tenancy being renewed under the 1954 Act.[1] Section 35 provides that the terms of the new tenancy shall (in the absence of agreement between the landlord and the tenant) be determined by the court 'and in determining those terms the court shall have regard to the terms of the current tenancy and to all relevant circumstances'. A party's property demands change, as its business and the economic climate fluctuate, and many a tenant has found himself renewing a lease of premises which, at the time of the original negotiations, he did not think that he would require beyond the initial term. Conversely many premises are assigned or underlet because it turns out that the tenant requires them for a shorter term than he anticipated, and such leases may, in due course, be renewed by the assignees or underlessees. On any renewal under the 1954 Act, the parties (or their successors in title) may have many years to regret any careless drafting, or concessions made, on the grounds of speed or expediency, during the preparation and negotiation of the original lease. It is true that variation to the terms can be ordered by the court,[2] but the case law clearly establishes a presumption in favour of the original terms. The prudent party, and his advisers, should aim to get the terms right from the beginning and thus avoid the risk of costly and possibly unsuccessful litigation in the future.

1   See Chapter 14 below.
2   See paras 14.56 and 14.60 below.

Chapter 2

Non-drafting steps

A PROCEDURAL MATTERS

2.1 *Non-drafting steps.* The drafting and negotiation of the terms of the lease are only part of the work that will be undertaken by the parties' solicitors, and it seems appropriate to consider the non-drafting steps before looking in depth at the lease itself.

2.2 *Landlord's costs.* Leases are often negotiated on the basis that the tenant will pay the landlord's legal fees.[1] This, however, will only assist the landlord if the lease is completed. If it is not, the landlord will be responsible for his own legal fees. So, when the lease has been negotiated on the footing that the tenant will pay the landlord's costs, the landlord's solicitor should write at once and ask the tenant's solicitors to undertake that they will be responsible for the landlord's legal charges and disbursements *whether or not the matter proceeds.* It is a brave tenant who will not agree, because without his agreement the landlord is unlikely to proceed, unless the parties are operating in a strong tenant's market. Nevertheless, even where the tenant does agree, his solicitor should make it quite clear that the tenant will not be responsible for such costs if the landlord withdraws from the matter for reasons unrelated to the negotiations with the tenant. This at least means that, while the prospective tenant is at risk to pay the landlord's legal fees if he decides not to proceed, he would not be liable for the fees if it was the landlord who unilaterally withdrew from the matter. Indeed, it would seem not unreasonable to ask the landlord's solicitor to confirm that the landlord would be responsible for the tenant's legal fees if the landlord were to withdraw in such circumstances.

1 See para 7.32 below.

2.3 *Superior landlord's licence.* Whenever instructed to prepare a draft underlease,[1] a solicitor should refer to the headlease to establish what licences will be needed. The superior landlord's consent will almost certainly be required for the underletting,[2] but it may be that, in addition, consent will be needed for a change of user, having regard to the business that the tenant proposes to carry on at the premises.[3] The sub-lessor's solicitor should enquire of his client or his surveyor what steps (if any) have been taken in relation to obtaining such consents. It may well be helpful to telephone the superior landlord or his solicitors (if known) to find out what documentation in the form of references and accounts will be needed and to whom they should be sent. The sub-lessor's solicitor needs to keep the questions of the superior landlord's licence very much in mind throughout the matter to avoid a possible delay when the form of the lease has been agreed between the sub-lessor and the tenant, but still no licence is to hand.

1   See Chapter 13.
2   As to alienation generally, see paras 7.1–7.7 below.
3   See paras 7.8–7.18. A licence for alterations may also be required: see paras 7.19–7.26.

B   USE

2.4   *Tenant's responsibility*. Devlin J said in *Edler v Auerbach*:[1]

> 'It is the business of the tenant, if he does not protect himself by an express warranty,[2] to satisfy himself that the premises are fit for the purposes for which he wants to use them, whether such fitness depends on the state of their structure or the state of the law or any other relevant circumstances.'

This statement was approved by the Court of Appeal in *Hill v Harris*.[3] I turn later to the question of structure[4] but examine first the 'state of the law or any other relevant circumstances'.

1   [1950] 1 KB 359, [1949] 2 All ER 692.
2   And in practice, no landlord will give one.
3   [1965] 2 QB 601, [1965] 2 All ER 358. See para 2.8, n 4, below.
4   See para 2.16 below.

2.5   *Planning*. The tenant's solicitor has to be satisfied that the use for which his client requires the premises will be permitted under Town and Country Planning legislation. A tenant should not take a lease unless he is satisfied that there is already in existence an express planning permission for the use that he requires (effective for the period of the proposed lease and not expressed to be personal to another party), or that there is an established use certificate for the appropriate use, or that the landlord has provided sufficient evidence that the use required by the tenant has been carried on continuously since at least December 1963. The aim of an established use certificate is to enable the owner of premises to record the fact that the current use of the premises, although originally unauthorised, is safe from enforcement proceedings because that use began before the end of 1963.[1] If the owner of premises obtains a certificate that a particular use of the premises is established, the certificate is a complete answer to any enforcement proceedings brought in respect of that use. There is, however, no obligation to obtain such a certificate, and a party can still resist enforcement proceedings if he can prove that the user began before the end of 1963. Thus, in the absence of an express permission or established use certificate, the tenant needs to be satisfied that his proposed user has been carried on continuously since at least December 1963.

1   The Town and Country Planning Act ('T&CPA') 1968 abolished the four-year time limit on the service of an enforcement notice in respect of development constituting an unauthorised change of use (with one exception, that is not relevant to commercial leases – see T&CPA 1971, s 87(3)(c)). Thus planning authorities can now claim *at any time* that the use of land is unauthorised. These provisions are now re-enacted in T&CPA 1971, ss 94 and 95.

2.6   *Consequences of lack of permission for proposed use*. There are two contrasting cases on the status of a lease where the user to which the tenant is putting the premises is not permitted. In *Best v Glenville*[1] the landlord let a room for the purpose of a bridge club; both the landlord and tenant knew that would involve a material change of use for which planning permission was required, and it was understood by both parties that the tenant would apply for such permission. The tenant went into possession and the club was opened, but when an application for planning permission was made by the tenant it was refused. The landlord sued for arrears of rent and the tenant contended that the purpose for which the premises were let was unlawful and therefore the contract of letting was illegal and unenforceable. The Court of Appeal held that the tenancy was not illegal because the parties had contemplated that planning permission should be obtained and that its refusal did not affect the legality of the agreement. In *Turner and Bell v Searles (Stanford-le-Hope) Ltd*,[2] however, the tenant had applied for a new tenancy under Part II of the 1954 Act. The tenant intended to continue a use which was in contravention of an enforcement notice although for various reasons the planning authority was reluctant to 'enforce' the notice. The Court of Appeal upheld the county court judge in refusing to grant a new lease. Bridge LJ said:

> 'This is a case where the Court would be bound to refuse the relief claimed on the simple ground that if the Court were to order a new tenancy in the circumstances indicated it would be ordering parties to enter into an illegal contract which the Court could not enforce because the illegal purpose of the tenant was clearly known to both parties.'

The distinction is the position at the commencement of the two tenancies. In *Best*, the parties recognised the problem, were proposing to put in hand the remedy, and (presumably) believed that they would be able to obtain the necessary planning permission. In *Turner and Bell*, the parties were aware of the problem, but there was obviously no way in which it could be rectified. Nevertheless it appears from the report of *Best* that some of the arrears of rent ordered to be paid by the tenant to the landlord covered the period *after* the planning application had been refused and the appeal rejected. So by this time the situation was the same as that envisaged in *Turner and Bell*. The court, however, was clearly not prepared to hold that an agreement that had begun as a legal one could subsequently become illegal.[3]

1   [1960] 3 All ER 478, [1960] 1 WLR 1198. As to the implications on a rent review of a use for which there is no planning permission, see *6th Centre Ltd v Guildville Ltd* [1989] 1 EGLR 260.
2   (1977) 33 P & CR 208.
3   As a general rule, a covenant to do anything illegal or immoral, or prejudicial to public interest is void. If legal and illegal divisible, only illegal part will be void but if whole purpose is illegal all covenants will be void; see *Upfill v Wright* [1911] 1 KB 506 (no rent could be recovered where property was to the knowledge of landlord let for immoral purpose).

2.7   *Misrepresentation as to planning.* The landlord's solicitor should always confirm, or advise his client to check, that there is a planning permission covering the use for which he is offering the premises that will apply for the full term of the lease. In *Laurence v Lexcourt Holdings Ltd*,[1] the plaintiff offered premises to the defendant as offices. The premises had the appearance of offices, but in fact there was planning permission only for part of them. The defendant went into possession without making the usual searches and enquiries. When the omission was discovered and a planning application made, permission was ganted for a limited period of time. Mr Brian Dillon QC,[2] sitting as a deputy judge, held that the defendants were entitled to have the agreement rescinded on the ground of misrepresentation. In his view, the plaintiff's description of the premises as offices amounted to a representation, not merely as to the physical state of the premises, but also as to the availability of planning permission for them to be used for the full term of the proposed lease for this purpose.

1   [1978] 2 All ER 810, [1978] 1 WLR 1128. Note also *Collins v Howell-Jones* (1980) 259 Estates Gazette 331, CA and comments of Eveleigh LJ re estate agents' particulars relating to user in *Bovis Group Pension Fund Ltd v GC Flooring & Furnishing Ltd* (1984) 269 Estates Gazette 1252 at 1253, CA.
2   As he then was.

2.8   *Restrictions affecting the freeholder headlease.* The matter does not end with planning, however, as there may be restrictions that would bind the tenant, even if he had no knowledge of them, affecting either the freehold, or where an underlease is being contemplated, the headlease. The tenant will be bound by restrictive covenants affecting the freehold that have been registered as land charges, or, if not registrable, of which he has notice under the equitable rules.[1] Further, a lease of registered land takes effect subject both to any entries appearing on the register of the landlord's title, and also to any overriding interest.[2] Finally, the tenant is bound by the covenants in the headlease which extend to the sub-tenant's user. In *Hill v Harris*[3] a sub-tenant was prevented by a restriction in the headlease from carrying on the business which he had contemplated when he took the underlease, and Russell LJ concluded his judgment with the following words, that should be taken to heart by every solicitor acting for a sub-tenant:[4]

> 'I am not surprised that the sub-lessee is disappointed, and grievously disappointed, by the fact that he cannot, in the face of opposition by the freeholders, use these premises for the business of a retail tobacconist; but his claim to compensation for that disappointment against the defendant, the sub-lessor, must for the reasons I have given, fail.[5] This is not to say that he must necessarily be permanently disappointed, because, although the matter is not for decision before us, I find it at the moment not easy to see what conceivable defence the solicitors then acting for him would have to a claim for equivalent damages for negligence, in that they did not take the ordinary conveyancing precaution, before allowing their client to take a sub-lease, of finding out by inspection of the headlease what were the covenants, restrictive of user or otherwise, contained in the headlease.'

1   See *Dartstone Ltd v Cleveland Petroleum Co Ltd* [1969] 3 All ER 668, [1969] 1 WLR 1807.
2   See para 2.21, footnote 2 below.
3   [1965] 2 QB 601, [1965] 2 All ER 358, CA.
4   At pp 618, 363.
5   In *Hill v Harris* the sub-tenant had sued the sub-lessor for damages for breach of warranty that the premises could lawfully be used for the business in question, but the Court of Appeal held that, on the facts of the case, the discussions and letters did not amount to an *express* warranty, and that there is no *implied* contract or condition, when property is let, that it is fit for the purposes for which it is let.

C   TITLE

2.9   *Limited rights to require title to be deduced.* In the absence of a provision in the contract to the contrary,[1] if the proposed landlord is the freeholder, the tenant cannot require him to deduce title but must assume it is such as to enable him to grant the lease.[2] Where an underlease is being granted, the proposed sub-tenant will be able to call upon the landlord to produce his lease or underlease, and any assignment of it during the preceding fifteen years, but will not be entitled to call for the reversionary title, be it the freehold (if the proposed lease is an underlease) or another lease (if the proposed lease is a sub-underlease). Establishing ownership is only one reason for deducing title – the other is to permit investigations to be made as to the matters to which the land is subject. In practice, people who claim they own land generally do[3] and the inability of the tenant to satisfy himself as to any restrictions that affect the land is in many ways more serious, especially as s 44(5) of the Law of Property Act 1925[4] does not give the tenant the protection that, at first sight, it appears to afford. It seems to provide that where an intending tenant is not entitled to call for the title to the freehold (or to a leasehold reversion) he will not be deemed to be affected with notice of any matter or thing of which, if he had contracted that such title should be furnished, he might have had notice. This does not, however, extend to matters (for example restrictive covenants affecting the freehold registered under the Land Charges Act) of which a purchaser (and thus a tenant) is deemed by statute[5] to have *actual notice*.[6] It is also inapplicable in the case of a lease of registered land because the lease, being a disposition of registered land, takes effect subject to any enumbrance and other entries appearing on the register of the landlord's title and to any overriding interests affecting the estate created.[7] This is so, even though in the absence of any special agreement with the landlord, the tenant may not have been entitled to inspect the register of the landlord's title.

1 See Law of Property Act 1925, s 44(11).
2 The Law of Property Act 1925, ss 44(2)–(4) provides:
   '(2) Under a contract to grant or assign a term of years, whether derived or to be derived out of freehold or leasehold land, the intended or lessee or assign shall not be entitled to call for the title to the freehold.
   (3) Under a contract to sell and assign a term of years derived out of a leasehold interest in land, the intended assign not have the right to call for the title to the leasehold reversion.
   (4) On a contract to grant a lease for a term of years to be derived out of a leasehold interest, with a leasehold reversion, the intended lessee shall not have the right to call for the title to that reversion.'
3 But not always – see *Industrial Properties (Barton Hill) Ltd v Associated Electrical Industries Ltd* [1977] QB 580, [1977] 2 All ER 293, CA.
4 The Law of Property Act 1925, s 44(5) provides:
   '(5) Where by reason of any of the three last preceding subsections, an intending lessee or assign is not entitled to call for the title to the freehold or to a leasehold reversion, as the case may be, he shall not, where the contract is made after the commencement of this Act, be deemed to be affected with notice of any matter or thing of which, if he had contracted that such title should be furnished, he might have had notice.'
5 Law of Property Act 1925, s 198.
6 See para 2.8 above.
7 Land Registration Act 1925, ss 2(1)(a), (b), 23, 50(2), 42, 112. See para 2.21, footnote 2 below.

2.10 *Must press for title.* In view of the points made in paragraphs 2.8 and 2.9, above, the tenant's solicitor should press to have title deduced. In the case of registered land, he should ask for office copies of the landlord's freehold title and an authority to inspect the register. In the case of unregistered land, as well as receiving an abstract of the landlord's title, he would theoretically need to know the names of the previous freeholders to enable him to search at the Land Charges Registry for restrictive covenants affecting the land. If the tenant's solicitor is unable to satisfy himself that his client's user will be permitted, he should require an express warranty from the landlord to the effect that the proposed user will indeed be permitted, and that provided he complies with the terms of the lease, he will not be in breach of any restrictions affecting the premises.[1] At least then the tenant will have a claim against the landlord if that is not so.[2]

1   The reverse is usually the case – see for example Rosscastle Letting Conditions (Appendix 1, Form No 1 below) Conditions 10.2 and 10.3 and 22 Encyclopaedia of Forms and Precedents (5th edn) Form 22 clauses 9.2 and 9.4.
2   Without an express warranty, the sub-tenant will have no such claim – see *Hill v Harris* [1965] 2 QB 601, [1965] 2 All ER 358. Doubts as to whether or not the proposed user is, or will be, permitted are most likely to arise in shop lettings, or other leases where the permitted user is narrow.

D   SEARCHES AND ENQUIRIES

2.11   *Status of parties*. It is assumed that, before instructing his solicitor, the landlord will have satisfied himself as to the tenant's creditworthiness and desirability as a tenant, and that he will not therefore wish his solicitor to make any enquiries about the tenant other than when required in relation to a superior landlord's consent.[1] The tenant's solicitor should, however, consider making a company search against the landlord unless the landlord is a very well-known corporation. His client is, after all, contemplating embarking upon what may be a long relationship and deserves to know in advance all that can reasonably be found out about his potential partner. Where the search reveals the landlord to be a company of no great substance, the question of a guarantee should be considered.[2]

1   See para 2.3 above.
2   See para 5.3 below.

2.12   *Local search*. A local search should also be made so that the tenant may be provided with as much information as is possible before deciding whether or not to proceed. This may or may not provide the answer to the question of the permitted user under planning legislation referred to in para 2.5 above, and, if it does not, further enquiries must be pursued. A failing of the local search system, that is likely to be more relevant in a residential matter is that, with a few exceptions (for example a proposed road scheme within a few hundred yards of the property), the local authority merely provides information about the premises that are the subject of the search, and says nothing about the surrounding area. Thus a solicitor acting for a potential residential buyer and possibly, in certain circumstances, a potential commercial tenant, should, whenever the point may be relevant, ask his client to confirm that he has not decided to proceed with these premises wholly or partly because of some nearby open space, or other area, which, if developed, would have an adverse effect on the property. If a prospective tenant of an office building were to reply to this question by saying that he was particularly impressed by the premises in question because of the open and unspoiled landscape around them, his solicitor should arrange for an inspection to be made of the register of planning permissions at the local planning authority. For all his unsuspecting client may know, permission to develop that surrounding land may recently have been given, and thus the landscape will be dramatically changed in the long term, not to mention the short-term problems involved when there is a major construction work taking place on adjoining land.[1]

1   The situation is rather more serious if the tenant will require adjoining land to be available for
    use in conjunction with his development, for example as car parking. The squash club must
    have considered itself fortunate to have some success in *Lyme Valley Squash Club Ltd v Newcastle
    under Lyme Borough Council* [1985] 2 All ER 405 for reasons discussed in (1985) 274 Estates
    Gazette 1259. It is unlikely that a search under the Commons Registration Act 1965 of the
    registers of common land and town or village greens would even be relevant to a commercial
    letting (unless a large open space was included or perhaps on a first letting of a development on
    a green field site) but a Map Index search at HM Land Registry may be relevant when the
    lease will be registered (see para 15.11 below) and occasionally as a means (to a limited extent)
    of revealing items to which the freehold may be subject.

2.13   *Mining search.* If a solicitor's knowledge of an area tells him that coal
mining may have taken place under or near the demised premises, or mining
rights are reserved to the landlord or a third party in the draft lease,[1] the
tenant's solicitor should make a mining search. For a modest fee, British Coal
will provide detailed information about mining in any area in the United
Kingdom.[2] This information could be vital for a prospective tenant. The
premises may be built over disused underground workings, and thus be liable
to subsidence, or their presence may restrict or prevent (or increase the cost of)
a development on the land that the tenant may wish to make.

1   If minerals are not excepted, the tenant is entitled to working existing mines and quarries
    (*Clavering v Clavering* (1726) 2 P Wms 388), but may not open new as this would be voluntary
    waste (*Viner v Vaughan* (1840) 2 Beav 466). But see the Coal Industry Nationalisation Act, 1946,
    ss 1(1)(a), 5, and 36. As to the construction of phrases 'mines and minerals' and 'mineral
    substances' see *Earl of Lonsdale v A-G* [1982] 3 All ER 579, [1982] 1 WLR 887.
2   The Law Society and British Coal have recently produced a standardised search form and a
    directory of areas where searches are needed: see [1989] Gazette 27 September 4 & 23. The
    search fee is £14.65 plus £2.20 VAT. Forms and the directory are available from Oyez.

2.14   *Enquiries before contract.* The standard form of preliminary enquiries[1]
should be submitted having deleted those items which are relevant only to a
residential purchase. It is also appropriate to amend the form to 'proposed
tenant's solicitor' and 'proposed landlord's solicitor' instead of referring to
purchaser and vendor.

1   See also 22 Encyclopaedia of Forms and Precedents (5th edn) Forms 226, 227 and 231.

2.15   *Copy documents.* The tenant's solicitor should ensure that he has seen a
copy of every document referred to in the draft lease. For example, an
underlease invariably contains a covenant by the tenant to comply with the
terms of the headlease. The sub-tenant will only know if he will be able to
comply with the terms if he has seen them. The tenant also invariably
covenants not to do anything by which the insurance of the premises is
vitiated, or the premium increased. He can only know what acts would vitiate
the policy or increase the premium if he has seen the policy.

E   SURVEY AND INSPECTION

2.16   *Survey.* It may be desirable to leave the survey until the terms of the lease
have been agreed, especially where the repairing covenants and other relevant

provisions[1] are the subject of negotiation between the parties. A tenant proposing to take any premises on a full repairing lease should have them surveyed before proceeding and the survey should extend to the landlord's fixtures especially when these include valuable plant and equipment. A copy of the survey report should be supplied to the tenant's solicitor – if it reveals major problems, amendments to the draft may well be needed (if the matter is to proceed) but even when it does not the survey report will contain information about the property and the tenant's solicitor should welcome all such information that is available. It is easy to believe that no such survey is required where the repairing obligation is limited to the interior decorative facings. Such covenants, however, are generally found in leases of suites of offices or units in shopping centres where the tenant also agrees to reimburse the costs incurred by the landlord in performing various specified services one of which will almost certainly be the maintenance of the structure of the building.[2] Thus a tenant holding such a lease of a suite of offices in a building that required major structural repairs could find himself paying a share of the cost of such work.[3] Accordingly, a tenant proposing to take such a lease would do well to satisfy himself as to the general condition of the building before proceeding.[4] A cesser of rent provision[5] that operated only where the damage was due to an insured risk, and the lack of a provision permitting the tenant to terminate the lease after the premises had been unfit for a considerable period, would be further arguments in favour of a survey, in that, with such terms, the tenant could find himself liable to pay rent when the premises had become unfit for use due to some structural defect.

1 For example, cesser of rent (see para 10.23 below) and termination if premises not restored within a reasonable period (see para 10.24 below).
2 See for example Appendix 1 Form No 6 below and 22 Encyclopaedia of Forms and Precedents (5th edn) Forms 29, 30 and 31.
3 See para 11.18:3 below.
4 But note the practical problems mentioned in para 11.18:3 below – a tenant taking a small unit in a major shopping development can hardly have the entire Centre surveyed.
5 See para 10.23 below.

2.17 *Solicitor's site inspection.* In the ideal world, a solicitor would always inspect any premises with which he was concerned, and if it is reasonably practical, and especially where there are complex rights to be granted and excepted, the solicitor should make every effort to do so.

2.18 *Photographs in lieu of inspection.* A very useful substitute for an inspection is photographs of the property. The tenant's solicitor should ensure that he is supplied with the letting agent's particulars, so that he can check that they are reflected in the draft lease, other than any that have been varied by agreement. The particulars may contain a photograph, but where they do not it is worth establishing a system with property clients by which they supply their solicitor with photographs of all properties on which he is instructed. Somebody on behalf of the client will always have inspected the property and, bearing in mind that modern cameras require (or are claimed to require) less and less skill on the part of the photographer, it should be easy enought for him to take some photographs. How many will depend upon the nature of the property. In the case of a lock-up shop (with no rear access) one or two would be sufficient, but the photographer should ensure that he covers aspects that may have significance during the legal negotiations – for examples, boundaries and any rights that will be required by the tenant in order to use the premises. Not only will such a set of photographs give the tenant's solicitor a much better idea of the property with which he is dealing, but they may well prompt suggestions that might not have occurred to him in those cases where an inspection would not be practical, for example that an inappropriate description of the structure of the building has been used[1] or that a tenant's full repairing lease may not be practical.[2]

1 See Chapter 3 below.
2 See para 8.9 below.

F AGREEMENT FOR LEASE AND ITS REGISTRATION AND STAMPING

2.19 *Agreement.* In the case of most commercial leases, there is little need for an agreement for lease to precede completion, because the lease and counterpart can generally be exchanged, and the various payments due on the grant of the lease made, as soon as the wording of the lease has been agreed. Sometimes, however, there may be special circumstances where an agreement is necessary – perhaps the building is not yet completed. Alternatively, the freeholder's consent to an underletting may not yet be to hand, or there may be some other contingency upon which the grant of the lease has to be subject. There is a great temptation at this stage of an agreement to be entered into (either by a formal document or exchange of letters) by which the landlord agrees to grant and the tenant agrees to accept 'a lease in the form that has been agreed between the parties' solicitors'.[1] This should be avoided where the draft has been much amended because there could be great difficulties if it was found, when the engrossment was prepared, that there remained disputes as to wording that had either been overlooked, or where there had been some misunderstanding. The only sure way of proceeding is to annex an agreed form of lease to the agreement. This can simply be the travelling draft, although both solicitors should be given the opportunity of examining it 'one last time' to ensure that it does correctly set out what they have agreed. It may well be that by this time the travelling draft has been so much amended as to be almost unrecognisable. In these circumstances, a fair copy should be prepared and agreed by the parties.

1 For further comments and precedents of agreements for lease see 22 Encyclopaedia of Forms & Precedents (5th edn) paras 27–29 and Forms 1–10.

2.20 *Agreement before form of lease agreed.* There are always those dynamic men of commerce who want to sign a contract at once. In the landlord and tenant context, this is generally linked or prompted by a tenant who requires immediate possession, and a landlord equally keen to begin collecting rent but unwilling to give that possession until there is a binding contract or until the lease has been granted.[1] The only satisfactory solution – which demands co-operation between the parties and their advisers – is to set-to and quickly draft and agree a form of lease.[2] Where this is not possible, two alternatives are worth considering. In both cases, there is set out in the agreement for lease the basic 'commercial terms' and as many other terms of the letting as possible.[3] Then the agreement should provide either:

(a) that the remainder of the lease will be in a form that is for example 'fair and reasonable between the Landlord and the Tenant' or 'of the type currently used in lettings of this nature' or 'as shall reasonably be required by the Landlord' to be determined in default of agreement by a third party specified in the agreement, perhaps a well-respected local conveyancer, acting as an expert and not an arbitrator.[4] Unless the third party has already agreed to act, there should be a provision for the appointment of an alternative, should the nominee decline, or

(b) that the lease should contain 'the usual covenants and provisions'. There are two instances where the concept of the 'usual covenants' operates – if an agreement for lease does not specify the covenants and provisos which are to be inserted in the lease there will be an implied term in the agreement that the lease will contain the usual and proper covenants and provisions.[5] The other application is where the agreement expressly provides that the lease shall contain 'the usual covenants'. What these are is a matter for the Court. As Maugham J said in *Flexman v Corbett*:[6]

> 'The question whether particular covenants are usual covenants is a question of fact, and . . . the decision of the Court on that point must depend upon the admissible evidence given before the Court in relation to that question. I think that it is proper to take the evidence of conveyancers and others familiar with the practice in reference to leases and that it is also permissible to examine books of precedents. It is permissible to obtain evidence with regard to the practice in the particular district in which the premises in question are situated'.

The judgment of Foster J in *Chester v Buckingham Travel Ltd*[7] provides a more recent example of the Court deciding what covenants were 'usual' in a lease of business premises.

The two alternatives are basically the same, the only difference being the identity of the party who decides the terms of the lease, should there be a dispute – in the former it is a third-party expert and in the latter, the Court. It must be stressed, however, that they are both very much less satisfactory than agreeing all the terms of the lease prior to making the commitments.[2] Either option, assuming both parties agree, can provide the means of producing a binding agreement in a short time but there is no guarantee that the parties will be satisfied with the final form of the lease – both may have ample time to 'repent at leisure'.

1 As to the position of an intending tenant who has access to the premises prior to completion, see 22 Encyclopaedia of Forms and Precedents (5th edn) paras 121–125.

2 It is suggested that the Rosscastle Letting Conditions (see Appendix 1 below, Form No 1) will greatly facilitate this task, especially if both parties are familiar with them.

3 If the Rosscastle Letting Conditions (see footnote 2 above) are not used, it should be possible to deal with the question of rent review by means of incorporation – for example 'such rent to be reviewed on (insert review dates) in accordance with the latest Model Form of Rent Review Clause prepared by the Joint Committee of the Law Society and the Royal Institution of Chartered Surveyors, the reviewed rent to be ascertained in default of agreement by an independent valuer'. See 22 Encyclopaedia of Forms and Precedents (5th edn) Form 117.

4 As to the distinction between expert and arbitrator see para 6.45 below. For a precedent, see 22 Encyclopaedia of Forms and Precedents (5th edn) Form 5. See *Sweet and Maxwell Ltd v Universal News Services Ltd* [1964] 2 QB 699, [1964] 3 All ER 30, CA.

5 See para 1.15 above, *Church v Brown* (1808) 15 Ves 258; *Propert v Parker* (1832) 3 My & K 280; *Blakesley v Whieldon* (1841) 1 Hare 176.

6 [1930] 1 Ch 672. See also *Hodgkinson v Crow* (1875) LR 19 Eq 591; *Hampshire v Wickens* (1878) 7 Ch D 555; *Hart v Hart* (1881) 18 Ch D 670; *Charalambous v Ktori* [1972] 3 All ER 701, [1972] 1 WLR 951.
7 [1981] 1 All ER 386, [1981] 1 WLR 96.

2.21 *Registration and stamping of agreement.* The tenant's solicitor needs to bear in mind that, if the landlord's title is unregistered, an agreement for lease should be protected by registration as a Class C (iv) Land Charge (estate contract)[1] or if the title is registered at HM Land Registry by the entry of a notice, caution or restriction on the landlord's title.[2] If the appropriate registration is not made, and the landlord disposes of his interest after the date of the agreement but before completion, the purchaser would not be bound by the agreement to grant the lease. The original landlord would remain liable to the tenant for breach of contract, but money is not always an adequate compensation for a loss, and there could be situations in which the landlord, notwithstanding the fact that he had received the proceeds of sale, was unable to meet the tenant's claim.[3] It should also be remembered by the tenant's solicitor that an agreement for lease is liable to stamp duty as if it were the lease itself.[4]

1 Land Charges Act 1972, s 2. Non-registration makes the agreement void against a purchaser of the legal estate for money or money's worth (ibid ss 4, 5(7)(8), 6(4)(5)(6), 7(2), Sch 1 para 4) even if the purchaser had actual knowledge: Law of Property Act 1925, s 199, *Hollington Bros Ltd v Rhodes* [1951] 2 All ER 578n, TLR 691; *Midland Bank Trust Co Ltd v Green* [1981] AC 513, [1981] 1 All ER 153, HL.
2 Land Registration Act 1925, ss 48–62. A purchaser of registered land takes the legal estate subject to the entries on the register, and to overriding interests, but otherwise free from all other interests whatsoever: ibid ss 3(xv), 5, 9, 20, 23, 59(6) and 74, *Williams and Glyn's Bank Ltd v Boland* [1981] AC 487, [1980] 2 All ER 408, HL. Overriding interests are defined in ibid s 70(1) – essentially they are the type of rights that a purchaser of unregistered land would discover by inspection and enquiries and not from an examination of the title deeds. Note particularly that 'the rights of every person in actual occupation of the land, or in receipt of the rents and profits thereof' is an overriding interest except 'where enquiry is made of such person and the rights are not disclosed' (ibid s 70(1)(g)).
3 For an example of the dangers of non-registration, see *R J Stratton Ltd v Wallis Tomlin & Co Ltd* [1986] 1 EGLR 104, 277 Estates Gazette 409, CA although the judgments leave registration issues to be inferred. The agreement was for the grant of a new lease and the proposed tenant was in occupation of the premises under the original lease. Thus had the landlord's title been registered, the tenant would have had an overriding interest (Land Registration Act, s 70(1)(g): see footnote 2 above) at least in the absence of non-disclose by the tenant in response to any enquiry by the purchaser. (This point is referred to somewhat obliquely by May LJ at 106F.) As the original landlord was in receivership, the tenant no doubt recovered little if anything under the contract. See also *Ashburn Anstalt v Arnold* [1989] Ch 1, [1988] 2 All ER 147, CA.
4 Stamp Act 1891, s 75. The exemption of an agreement for lease for a term exceeding 35 years has been removed in relation to any agreement entered into on or after 20 March 1984: Finance Act 1984, ss 111(1)(5), 128(b), Sch 23, Pt X. For stamp duty generally, see para 15.10 below.

G TAXATION

2.22 *Brief over-view.* There is no place in a work of this nature for a detailed discussion of the fiscal implication of the grant of a lease. Suffice to say that the landlord's solicitor should ensure where appropriate that his client receives, or has received, adequate specialist advice.[1] *Income tax* is chargeable under Schedule A[2] on the annual profits or gains arising as follows:

(a) rents under leases of land in the United Kingdom;
(b) rent charges and any other annual payments reserved in respect of or charged on or issuing out of such land;
(c) other receipts arising to a person from, or by virtue of, his ownership of an estate or interest in or right over such land or incorporeal hereditament in the United Kingdom.[3]

Capital gains tax is chargeable in respect of chargeable capital gains computed in accordance with the Capital Gains Tax Act 1979 and accruing to a person on disposal of assets. Section 106 and Sch 3 of the Act relate to leases. A company is chargeable to *corporation tax* on all its profits wherever arising.[4] The amount of its income is, for the purposes of corporation tax, to be computed in accordance with income tax principles,[5] and the amount to be included in respect of chargeable capital gains is to be computed in accordance with the principles applying to capital gains tax.[6]

1 See Spencer, *Property Tax Planning Manual* (Butterworths) (2nd edn, 1989).
2 Income and Corporation Taxes Act 1988, ss 1, 15.
3 Ibid s 15.
4 Ibid s 8.
5 Ibid s 9.
6 Ibid s 345(2).

2.23   *VAT – background.* Value Added Tax ('VAT') is charged on the supply of goods and services in the United Kingdom when a taxable supply[1] is made by a taxable person[2] in the course or in furtherance of any business[3] carried on by him.[4] A taxable person[2] is required to charge VAT on taxable supplies[1] made by him[5] (output tax) and to pay this to Customs and Excise but before doing so he can deduct the VAT paid by him on goods and services supplied to him (input tax) and account for only the balance.[6] If the input tax paid by a taxable person exceeds the output tax collected by him, he is entitled to a refund from Customs and Excise.[7] The supply of any goods and services will, for VAT purposes, fall within one of three categories – taxable at standard rate,[8] taxable but zero rated[9] or exempt.[10] VAT is generally charged at the standard rate of 15%[8] but Schedule 5 to the Value Added Tax Act 1983 ('VATA')[9] sets out seventeen categories of goods and services that are zero rated.[11] Thus the taxable person is not required to charge any VAT on them, but as they are taxable supplies, the principle of deducting input tax that is attributable to them still applies.[9] So a taxable person who supplies mainly zero rated goods will collect little output tax. If the output tax that he does collect is less than the input tax that he pays, he is entitled to a refund of the difference.[7] Schedule 6 to VATA,[10] however, provides that other goods and services are exempt.[12] These are outside the VAT system altogether and a business that supplies exempt goods and services has nothing to deduct from the input tax charged to it that is attributable to those exempt supplies. It has to absorb the VAT that it has paid, in the same way as the end (ie non-business) user.

1 Value Added Tax Act 1983 ('VATA'), s 3.
2 VATA, s 2(2), Sch 1.
3 VATA, s 47.
4 VATA, s 2(1).
5 Tax on any supply of goods and services is a liability of the person making the supply and becomes due at the time of the supply: VATA s 2(3).

6 VATA, ss 14, 15.
7 VATA, s 14(5).
8 VATA, s 9.
9 VATA, s 16.
10 VATA, s 17.
11 Including, for example, food, sewerage and water, books, newspapers, fuel and power etc.
12 Including, for example, insurance, financial services, education, burial and cremation etc.

2.24 *VAT and property – the old law.* Until 1989, VAT did not often concern property lawyers, because most property supplies were either zero rated or exempt. The freehold sale (or the grant of a lease for more than 21 years) of a new building by the person who has constructed it,[1] the freehold sale (or the grant of a lease of more than 21 years) of a listed building by a person who has substantially reconstructed it[2] and the supply of construction services in connection with the erection of a new building (or an approved alteration to a listed building) were *zero rated*.[3] Any other freehold sale or any grant, assignment or surrender of a lease or tenancy of land or buildings was *exempt*.[4] All other supplies of goods and services made in connection with property transactions were standard rated.

1 VATA, Sch 5 Group 8 Item No 1 as originally enacted.
2 VATA, Sch 5 Group 8A Item No 1 as originally enacted.
3 VATA, Sch 5 Groups 8 and 8A Item No 2 as originally enacted.
4 VATA, Sch 6 Group 1 as originally enacted. This was subject to certain exceptions set out in Group 1.

2.25 *VAT and property – the new law.* The Finance Act 1989[1] has so changed the position that VAT has become a constant factor in commercial conveyancing.[2] Now the only *zero rated*[3] supplies are:
(a) the sale of the freehold or the grant[4] of a lease for a term certain exceeding 21 years by a person constructing a building designed as a dwelling[5] or a number of dwellings or intended for use solely for relevant residential[6] or relevant charitable purposes[7]
(b) work in the course of the construction of a building designed as a dwelling or number of dwellings or intended for use solely for relevant residential or relevant charitable purposes or any civil engineering work necessary for the development of a permanent park for residential caravans[8]
(c) the sale of the freehold or the grant of a lease for a term certain exceeding 21 years by a person substantially reconstructing a protected building[9]
(d) work in the course of an approved alteration of a protected building[9]
(e) the supply of materials and builders' hardware by a supplier of construction work of the type mentioned above.[10]
The following are *standard rated*:[11]
(a) the sale of a partly completed building which is neither designed as a dwelling or number of dwellings nor intended for use solely for a relevant residential purpose or a relevant charitable purpose[12]
(b) the sale of a new building which is neither designed as a dwelling or number of dwellings nor intended for use solely for a relevant residential purpose or a relevant charitable purpose after the grant[12]
(c) a partly completed civil engineering work[12]
(d) a new civil engineering work[12]
(e) the surrender of any interest in or right over land or of any licence to occupy land[13]

(f)   the provision of work to existing buildings (other than in the course of an approved alteration of a protected building)[14]

(g)   the grant of any interest, right or licence consisting of a right to take game or fish[15]

(h)   the provision in an hotel, inn, boarding house or similar establishment of sleeping accommodation or of accommodation in rooms which are provided in conjunction with sleeping accommodation or for the purpose of a supply of catering[16]

(i)   the provision of a holiday accommodation in a house, flat, caravan, houseboat or tent[17]

(j)   the provision of seasonal pitches for caravans, and the grant of facilities at caravan parks to persons for whom such pitches are provided[18]

(k)   the provision of pitches for tents or of camping facilities[19]

(l)   the grant of facilities for parking a vehicle[20]

(m)   the grant of any right to fell and remove standing timber[21]

(n)   the grant of facilities for housing, or storage of, an aircraft or for mooring, or storage of, a ship, boat or other vessel[22]

(o)   the grant of any right to occupy a box, seat or other accommodation at a sports ground, theatre, concert hall or other place of entertainment[23]

(p)   the grant of facilities for playing any sport or participating in any physical recreation.[24]

The grant of any other interest in or right over land or any licence to occupy land continues to be *exempt*[25] but subject to one major qualification. Owners or landlords can elect on a property-by-property basis to waive the exemption and to charge VAT at the standard rate on the otherwise exempt rents and proceeds of sale.[26]

1   Section 18, and Sch 3.

2   VAT is a European Community tax and these changes were forced on the UK by a decision of the European Court of Justice. The VAT system envisaged by European Community law does not provide for any supplies of goods or services to be zero rated. As a transitional measure, member states where zero rating was in force on 31 December 1975 were allowed to retain their zero rating provisions until the advent of the Single European Market on 31 December 1992 provided the zero rates in question are applied 'for clearly defined social reasons and for the benefit of the final consumer . . .'. The Commission took the view that certain of the UK's zero rating provisions did not comply with the condition and took proceedings in the Court of Justice to compel the UK to abolish them. The court *upheld* the Commission's view in the case of the construction and sale of commercial and industrial buildings; non-domestic supplies of water and sewerage services; news services other than those supplied to final consumers; non-domestic supplies of fuel and power; and protective boots and helmets supplied to employers for use by their employees. The court *rejected* the Commission's arguments on the construction and sale of new *domestic* buildings and the supply of animal feedstuffs, seeds and live animals for human consumption.

3   VATA, Sch 5 Group 8 and Group 8A (as amended by the Finance Act 1989, s 18, Sch 3).

4   Grant includes assignment: VATA, Sch 5 Group 8 (as amended by the Finance Act 1989, s 18, Sch 3) Note (1).

5   As to 'dwelling', see ibid, Note (2).

6   As to 'relevant residential purpose', see ibid, Note (3).

7   As to 'relevant charitable purpose', see ibid, Note (4).

8   See VATA, Sch 5 Group 8 (as amended by the Finance Act 1989, s 18, Sch 3) Item No 2, Note (10).

9   See VATA, Sch 5 Group 8A (as amended by the Finance Act 1989, s 18, Sch 3).

10   See VATA, Sch 5 Group 8 Item No 3.

11   ie in most instances by virtue of being the exclusions from the exempt supplies set out in VATA, Sch 6 Group 1 (as amended by Finance Act 1989, s 18, Sch 3).

12   Ibid, Item No 1.

13   Finance Act 1989, s 18, Sch 3 has amended the opening words to VATA, Sch 6 Group 1 Item No 1 by deleting the words 'assignment or surrender'. Many surrenders show no financial consideration and are effected as part of a broader transaction, for example surrender followed by the grant of a new lease of the property. VAT will still be payable – the surrender will be deemed to be for an amount equal to the market value of the surrendered lease: VATA, s 10(3).

14   ie because such work is not zero rated under VATA, Sch 5 (as amended): see above.
15   VATA, Sch 6 Group 1 (as amended by Finance Act 1989, s 18, Sch 3) Item No 1(b).
16   Ibid, Item No 1 (c).
17   Ibid, Item No 1 (d).
18   Ibid, Item No 1 (e).
19   Ibid, Item No 1 (f).
20   Ibid, Item No 1 (g).
21   Ibid, Item No 1 (h).
22   Ibid, Item No 1 (i).
23   Ibid, Item No 1 (j).
24   Ibid, Item No 1 (k).
25   Ibid, Item No 1 opening words.
26   See para 2.26 below.

2.26   *VAT and property – election to waive the exemption.* Apart from the specified exceptions,[1] the grant of any interest in or right over land, or any licence to occupy land, remains an exempt supply.[2] Schedule 6A to VATA,[3] however, gives a person the right to elect that a particular grant will *not* be exempt, enabling him to charge VAT on rent or proceeds of sale, except[4] where:

(a)   the building (or a part of it) is intended for use as a dwelling, or number of dwellings[5] or solely for a relevant residential purpose

(b)   the building (or part of it) is intended for use solely for a relevant charitable purpose, other than as an office[6]

(c)   the grant is made to a registered housing association and the association has given to the grantor a certificate stating that the land is to be used for the construction of a building or buildings intended for use as a dwelling or number of dwellings or solely for a relevant residential purpose; or[7]

(d)   the grant is made to an individual and the land is to be used for the construction, otherwise than in the course of furtherance of a business carried on by him, of a building intended for use by him as a dwelling.[8]

The election must be made on a property-by-property basis[9] and once made cannot be varied for future supplies in relation to that property by the person who has made the election.[10] The aim of the concept of waiving the exemption is to overcome the hardship that would apply if the grant of a lease or sale of a freehold was always an exempt supply. A person who had paid VAT and incurred input tax on, for example, the construction or purchase of a new commercial building and who then let it would be unable to collect any output tax if the rent (which was his only supply) was always exempt. Thus he would have nothing to set off against the input tax paid on the cost of construction or the purchase price and would pay this in full. The fact that he can waive this exemption gives him the opportunity to collect output tax against which his input tax can be credited.[11]

1   ie those specified in VATA, Sch 6 Group 1 Item No 1 (a)–(k) (as amended by the Finance Act 1989, s 18, Sch 3).
2   Ibid, Item No 1.
3   Paragraph 2(1): inserted by the Finance Act 1989, s 18, Sch 3.
4   These (and the supplies that are not exempt: see footnote 1 above) are the only exceptions. So the election to waive the exemption applies to all other properties, including (for example) new and old buildings, agricultural land (see VATA, Sch 6A Paragraph 2(4).
5   VATA, Sch 6A Paragraph 2(2)(a).
6   Ibid, Paragraph 2(2)(b).
7   Ibid, Paragraph 2(3)(a), 3(9).
8   Ibid, Paragraph 2(3)(b).

9   Ibid, Paragraph 2(1). As to when an election is made in relation to part of a building see ibid, Paragraph 3(3).
10   Ibid, Paragraph 3(b). The timing of the election is vital if all the input tax is to be allowable: ibid, Paragraphs 2(4), (5), (6), (7), 3(1). As to when an election is made in relation to an existing lease, see ibid, Paragraph 4. There are transitional provisions (VAT reduced by 50% up to 31 July 1990) for buildings completed before 1 August 1989 and for charities (VAT introduced in four stages up to 31 July 1993): ibid, Paragraph 4(5).
11   See para 2.23 above.

2.27   *VAT and property development.* The Treasury and Customs and Excise had several false starts before they decided how VAT should be applied to development land.[1] The Finance Act 1989 finally contained no special provisions as to development land; it is to be treated in the same way as any other land or property – the sale will be exempt[2] unless the vendor has waived his exemption, in which case VAT will be payable at the standard rate.[3] The commencement of development of land will not have any consequences for VAT purposes. If, however, work has commenced on a commercial development at the time of the sale, VAT will be charged at the standard rate.[4] On completion of a non-residential building, one of four events will follow:

2.27:1   *The freehold will be sold.* The purchase price, including the value attributed to the land, will be subject to VAT at standard rate, and, provided the vendor/developer has given an undertaking to dispose of the freehold on completion of the development, he will have been able to reclaim all the input tax paid on the construction costs.[5]

2.27:2   *A lease or leases will be granted.* If the landlord/developer has not waived his exemption[6] the rents payable will be exempt and the landlord/developer will be unable to recover the input tax incurred in the development.[7] If, as would usually be the case, the landlord/developer waives his exemption,[6] the tenants will pay VAT on the rent and the landlord/developer will be able to deduct the input tax that he has incurred from the output tax collected by him on the rent, and account to Customs and Excise with the balance.[7]

2.27:3   *The developer who is not a fully taxable person goes into possession.* Here the developer will be deemed to have made a supply of the property to itself at market value on which VAT would be chargeable.[8]

2.27:4   *The developer who is a fully taxable person may go into possession.* There are two alternatives here. If the developer undertook the construction work itself, using its own employees rather than an outside contractor, the developer will be treated as making a supply to itself and VAT will be payable on the sum that it would have had to pay to a contractor.[9] Where, however, an outside contractor has been used, the self supply provisions as finally enacted do not apply and the developer follows the normal practice of deducting from the output tax that he collects on his taxable supplies input tax paid in relation to the construction of the building.[10]

1   The UK government published a consultation paper in June 1988 following the decision of

the European Court (see para 2.25 footnote 2 above) and then draft legislation early in 1989. The proposals in the Finance Bill were slightly different and these were amended during the passage of the Bill. Many of the provisions as to VAT came into force on 1 April 1989 (ie long before the Finance Act 1989 was passed) and practitioners are warned to check that any articles and publications to which they may refer that appeared before August 1989 are dealing with the law as it is rather than the law as it might have been.

2 See para 2.25 above.

3 See para 2.26 above.

4 See para 2.25 above and VATA, Sch 6 Group 1 Item No 1(a)(i) and (iii) as amended by Finance Act 1989, s 18, Sch 3.

5 See ibid, Item No 1(a)(ii) and (iv).

6 See para 2.26 above.

7 See para 2.23 above.

8 See VATA, Sch 6A paras 5 and 6 (inserted by Finance Act 1989, s 18, Sch 3).

9 VATA 1983, Sch 6A para 5 (inserted by Finance Act 1989, s 18, Sch 3) and Value Added Tax (Self Supply of Construction Services) Order 1989.

10 Providing it remains a fully taxable person for ten years: see ibid.

2.28 *VAT now payable – who suffers?* A purchaser or tenant who is himself a taxable person supplying standard or zero rated supplies will have no fundamental concern if the purchase price or rent of his property attracts VAT.[1] It will no doubt increase his input tax but as he can deduct this from his output tax and claim a refund if inputs exceed outputs his only potential problem could be one of cashflow, having to fund the inputs before he has received outputs to set off against them or (where inputs exceed outputs) before he receives the refund at the end of the prescribed accounting period.[1] The purchasers or tenants who will suffer will be those who supply exempt services, for example banks, building societies, insurance companies and private schools. They will have nothing to set against the additional 15% payable on their rent and purchase price and will simply have to absorb this or pass it on as higher charges or fees.[2]

1 See para 2.23 above. The only qualification to this statement is that he will have to pay stamp duty on the VAT as well as the purchase price on VAT: note VATA, s 10(2); *Independent Television Authority v IRC* [1961] AC 427, [1960] 2 All ER 481, HL; *Coventry City Council v IRC* [1979] Ch 142, (1989) 10 PLB 28.

2 See VATA, Sch 6 (as amended by the Finance Act 1989, s 18, Sch 3). According to *The Times* (27 June 1989) Barclays Bank plc estimates that its head office development in Lombard Street will cost an additional £40 million in irrecoverable VAT. It is these types of tenant who will be seeking covenants from landlord not to waive the exemption: see para 2.29:4 below.

2.29 *VAT – practical issues.* The property lawyer will now need to consider the VAT implications in a number of situations – for example:

2.29:1 *Property development.* VAT will now have to be added to the list of factors that will need considering during the planning stage of any proposed commercial development by all the parties and their advisers.[1]

2.29:2 *Waiving exemption.* When a sale or lease of commercial premises is being contemplated that would otherwise produce exempt proceeds of sale or rents, the advisers to the potential vendor or landlord need to consider if their client should elect to waive the exemption so as to be able to charge VAT and collect output tax on the proceeds of sale or rent.[2]

2.29:3 *Registered for VAT.* Where a party has not made taxable supplies before, he will need to be registered. A purchaser or tenant who wishes to set off the input tax paid by him against the output tax charged to him must also be registered.[3]

2.29:4 *Purchaser's and tenant's concerns.* A purchaser's or tenant's solicitor should whenever it could be appropriate enquire of the vendor's or landlord's solicitor if the exemption has been waived.[4] A vendor who has not done so should be required in the contract to warrant that the exemption has not been waived and to covenant that it will not be waived after exchange of contracts. A tenant who supplies mainly goods and services that are exempt[5] should seek to introduce a covenant into the lease, preventing the landlord from waiving the exemption at any time during the term of the lease.

2.29:5 *VAT invoice.* Whenever a person pays VAT, he should obtain a VAT invoice otherwise his claim to set the input tax incurred on that supply against his output tax is at the discretion of Customs and Excise.[6]

2.29:6 *Exclusive of VAT.* Every contract for the sale of commercial property must provide that the purchase price is exclusive of VAT. When drafting a new lease, the landlord's solicitor must ensure that the rent is expressed to be exclusive of VAT, so that the landlord will be able to add VAT onto the rent payable under the lease. It would appear that in a pre-April 1989 lease the landlord will be able to add VAT onto the rent unless the lease states otherwise and specifically refers to VAT or VATA, s 42.[7] In a lease completed after April 1989 the rent will apparently be inclusive of VAT unless the lease states otherwise.[8] Thus the effect of an election to waive the exemption in the case of a VAT inclusive rent would be that 15/115 of the rent then payable under the lease would be regarded as VAT[9] and that the landlord would not be able to add VAT of 15% onto the rent.

2.29:7 *Rent review.* Both parties are likely to consider if additional assumptions and disregards should be included to deal with any implications that VAT may have on the hypothetical letting of the premises required for the purposes of the rent review.[10]

1 See para 2.27 above.
2 See para 2.26 above.
3 VATA, ss 14, 15, Sch 1.
4 See para 2.26 above.
5 See para 2.23 footnotes 10 and 12 above.
6 VATA, s 14 and the Value Added Tax (General) Regulations 1985, regs 12 and 62.

7 Although the point could certainly have been better dealt with, this seems to be the effect of the addition made to VATA, s 42 set out in VATA, Sch 6A paragraph 7 that was added by Finance Act 1989, Sch 3.

8 VATA, s 10(2).

9 Because VAT is inclusive – thus the rent payable is rent (100) and VAT (15).

10 See para 6.29 below.

Chapter 3

The parcels

A THE NEED FOR CERTAINTY

3.1 *Leases can pose special problems.* The parcels must define, with absolute certainty, the property that is to be included in the lease. Those involved in the negotiations need to satisfy themselves that the description in the document, including any plan that may be annexed, is such that there could never be a dispute as to the extent of the premises demised. Any ambiguity must be resolved before the final wording is agreed. All too often this is not done, and the parties become 'the victims of sloppy conveyancing'.[1] Many of the cases referred to in this chapter concerned freehold land, but the principles apply equally to leases. Indeed it may be said that they are, if anything, more relevant to leases. The problems have generally arisen as a result of inadequate descriptions of parts of buildings.[2] A sale of the freehold of part of a building is relatively unusual – leases of part are commonplace. Nor are the consequences of poor drafting limited to disputes between the parties. A landlord could experience difficulties in selling his fully-let development to an institutional purchaser where the leases inadequately define the premises let.

1 Per Cumming-Bruce LJ in *Scarfe v Adams* [1981] 1 All ER 843 at 845, CA.
2 For example *Kingston v Phillips* [1976] CA Transcript 279 and *Scarfe v Adams* above.

3.2 *Basic principles.* The drafting of the parcels should be straightforward in the case of a detached building standing in its own ground. Commercial men talk in areas, while lawyers all too often do not, and thus dimensions and areas ought to be referred to whenever possible.[1] The question of ownership of boundary walls and fences must also be dealt with. The landlord's solicitor should refer to his client's title deeds for the description of the property, but should bring this up to date, where appropriate. Names of roads, counties, and districts can change over the years and what used to be an unnamed track or estate road may well, in time, acquire a name.

1 See para 6.18, footnote 6 below.

3.3 *Registered land.* If the lease in question will have to be registered at HM Land Registry[1] the parcels should refer to the title number, and where, as is so often the case, part only of the land in the title is being let, the lease must contain a plan signed by the parties enabling the land to be identified on the filed plan.[2]

1 See para 15.11 below.
2 Land Registration Act 1925, ss 18(1)(e), 21(1)(d); the Land Registration Rules 1925, r 113(1).
  A plan may be dispensed with if the area leased is clearly defined from words in the deed on the general map kept at the Land Registry, but in practise a plan should generally be provided. See too M M Barrett 'Surveys and Plans in the Sale of Land' [1981] Conv 257.

B AIRSPACE AND SUB-SOIL

3.4 *Above and below.* A lease includes everything directly beneath the surface of the land demised and the space directly above it unless a contrary intention appears from the lease.[1] Thus in *Kelsen v Imperial Tobacco Co of Great Britain and Ireland Ltd*[2] a one-storey building had been let, and a sign was erected that extended some eight inches into the air space above the demised premises. It was held that this was a trespass, entitling the tenant to an injunction for the removal of the sign. It is no answer to say that the damage is trivial and that the plaintiff's ordinary business is not interfered with.[3]

1 See *Cooke v Yates* (1827) 4 Bing 90; *Newcomen v Coulson* (1877) 5 Ch D 133, CA; *Laybourn v Gridley* [1892] 2 Ch 53; *Mithcell v Mosley* [1914] 1 Ch 438; *Woollerton and Wilson Ltd v Richard Costain Ltd* [1970] 1 All ER 483, [1970] 1 WLR 411 and *Grigsby v Melville* [1973] 3 All ER 455, [1974] 1 WLR 80, CA. Airspace will be excluded where the upper limit of the demised premises is specifically defined in the lease (see for example 22 Encyclopaedia of Forms and Precedents (5th edn) Form 22, clause 3.5) or where the roof is excluded from the demised premises and the upper limit thereby defined. The exclusion of the roof may have been dealt with expressly (see for example Appendix 1 below, Form No 6) or impliedly (see para 3.11 below especially footnote 10).
2 [1957] 2 QB 334, [1957] 2 All ER 343.
3 *Anchor Brewhouse Developments Ltd v Berkley House Docklands Developments Ltd* [1987] 2 EGLR 173, 284 Estates Gazette 625 (tower cranes oversailing plaintiff's properties). In *Baron Bernstein of Leigh v Skyviews and General Ltd* [1978] QB 479, [1977] 2 All ER 902 the defendant flying over the plaintiff's country residence to take aerial photographs was held not to be trespassing in the plaintiff's airspace. 'The difficulties posed by overflying aircraft or balloons, bullets or missiles seem to me to be wholly separate from the problem which arises where there is invasion of air space by a structure placed or standing upon the land of a neighbour . . . In my judgment, if somebody erects on his own land a structure, part of which invades the airspace above the land of another, the invasion is a trespass.': *Anchor Brewhouse* per Scott J at 175, 176. Note *Davies v Yadegar* [1989] EGCS 68, CA.

3.5 *Should the upper limit be defined?* It follows, therefore, that unless the upper limit of the demised premises is defined, the tenant will not need any further grant from the landlord to extend the building upwards.[1] What he *will* need is consent from the landlord to carry out the alterations, but the landlord may be required not unreasonably to refuse that consent.[2] The landlord would have been in a stronger position if the upper extent of the demised premises had been limited, because he could then have refused to lease the additional airspace required by the tenant for the alterations, or been prepared to do so only in return for an additional rent. This sometimes prompts landlords and their advisers to seek to exclude from the letting the airspace over the demised premises. This is often not as straightforward as it first appears. For example, a lease of a plot of land with a factory on part of it may state that the term 'demised premises' 'includes no airspace above the height of the building'. There are two potential problems with this:
(a) if the lease is a full repairing one, the tenant will need to be granted the right to enter the airspace above the building for the purposes of inspecting and repairing the roof,[3] and
(b) such expressions can be ambiguous in relation to the airspace over the unbuilt parts of the demised premises.[4]
The drafting complications often persuade landlords that the powers that they have in the lease to control alterations are a sufficient safeguard.

1 See para 3.4 above.
2 See paras 7.19–7.26 below.

3   Unless he is prepared to rely on the fact that such a right should be implied see Hill & Redman's *Law of Landlord and Tenant* (18th edn) para A672 and footnote 1 to para 4.7 below.

4   Any ambiguity could be avoided by stating 'includes no airspace over any part of the demised premises above the height of the Building'. Thus the top of the building forms a 'lid' over all of the site.

3.6   *Unusual shaped buildings.* The parties do need to consider the question of airspace and the space below ground level when dealing with unusual buildings. For example the term 'dwelling house' has been held[1] to include all parts of the dwelling house, including the footings and eaves, even where these were outside the area coloured on the plan annexed to the conveyance as indicating the property conveyed. The column of air between the footings and the eaves was not, however, included. The parcels were drafted in a slightly unusual way by modern standards, but the point could still arise in relation to 'shop', 'factory', or 'building'. Similar problems can arise when there is a 'projection' such as a fire escape.

1   *Truckell v Stock* [1957] 1 All ER, [1957] 1 WLR 161, CA.

C   THE PLAN

3.7   *Words used to refer to the plan.* Where the demised premises are clearly defined there is no need for a plan, and indeed a purchaser (and presumably a tenant) cannot insist upon a plan where the description is otherwise suifficient.[1] If, however, a plan is to be used, the draftsman has a decision to make – should the plan or the verbal description prevail in the event of conflict? Where a large-scale plan is available, on which the extent of the demised premises may be shown with precision, then the plan should be made to prevail and words such as 'more particularly delineated' or 'more particularly described' used when referring to the plan.[2] Where only a small-scale plan is to hand, the premises should be described in detail in the lease and the plan should be included 'for the purpose of identification only'. Here the description will prevail over the plan.[3] There seems to exist confusion over these words. As Romer LJ said in *Webb v Nightingale*:[4]

> 'Now it seems to me that the words "for the purposes of indentification only" are virtually meaningless in the context in which they are found in this particular document and I have the greatest doubt as to whether the draftsman had the smallest idea of what he meant by putting them in.'

These words should only properly be used when a plan is annexed to indicate the *location* of the premises, and *not* to establish the *precise* boundaries and area of the land in question. A problem that has come before the courts several times is, where the parcels do *not* contain an adequate description, can a plan expressed to be 'for the purposes of identification only' be used to establish the boundaries of the land? In *Wigginton & Milner Ltd v Winster Engineering Ltd,*[5] the Court of Appeal held that, although a plan annexed to a conveyance and so described could not *contradict* anything which was explicit in the description of the parcels, it could be used to elucidate the identity of the property which the conveyance was intended to convey, where it was not made explicit in the description of the parcels. In *Spall v Owen,*[6] Peter Gibson J said that he did not understand the decision in *Wigginton* as meaning that the court should *ignore* any other available means to determine what land had passed. As such, he considered extrinsic evidence in resolving a dispute as to the ownership of a strip of land between neighbouring properties on an estate development.[7]

1   *Re Sharman and Meade's Contract* [1936] Ch 755, [1936] 2 All ER 1547. The Council of the Law Society has recommended (Digest (1954) Col 1, p 44 Opinion No 157, dated 7 October 1949) as good conveyancing practice that the parties should sign any annexed plans. As to unincorporated plans, see J T Ferrand ('Conveyancer's Notebook') [1983] Conv 333.
2   *Lyle v Richards* (1866) LR 1 HL 222; *Eastwood v Ashton* [1915] AC 900, HL; *Wallington v Townsend* [1939] Ch 588, [1939] 2 All ER 225. But see para 3.8 below.
3   *Horne v Struben* [1902] AC 454, PC.
4   [1957] CA Transcript 84. See also *Willson v Greene* [1971] 1 All ER 1098, [1971] 1 WLR 635 and *Nelson v Poole* (1969) 20 P & CR 909; *Smout v Farquharson* (1972) 226 Estates Gazette, CA.
5   [1978] 3 All ER 436, [1978] 1 WLR 1462. Applied also in *Scott v Martin* [1987] 2 All ER 813, [1987] 1 WLR 841, CA and *Hatfield v Moss* [1988] 2 EGLR 58, 40 EG 112 (see H W Wilkinson: 'The extent of the propoerty conveyed: using the plan' (1989) 139 NLJ 235) but note *A J Dunning & Sons (Shopfitters) Ltd v Sykes & Son (Poole) Ltd* [1987] Ch 287, [1987] 1 All ER 700, CA, discussed [1987] Conv 214.
6   (1981) 44 P & CR 36.
7   Extrinsic evidence (a planning permission) was considered in *Scott v Martin* [1987] 2 All ER 813, [1987] 1 WLR 841, CA.

3.8   *Plan not to limit or enlarge.* In the light of *Wigginton*,[1] the most satisfactory course, where a plan that defines the premises is not available, is to ensure that a sufficient and accurate description in words of the demised premises is set out in the deed, and then stipulate that the plan 'shall not limit or enlarge' this description. Even this, however, should often be regarded very much as a last resort – except where the premises can adequately be described in words alone, the solution is to obtain a professionally prepared plan that properly defines the land.

1   [1978] 3 All ER 436, [1978] 1 WLR 1462, CA.

3.9   *Conveyancers criticised.* Conveyancers have been criticised all too often in recent years for using inadequate plans when conveying complex properties.[1] The words of Cumming-Bruce LJ in *Scarfe v Adams*[2] should be in the forefront of the mind of every conveyancer:

> 'Though the general description of the property, and reliance on a small scale Ordnance map, may once have been sufficient for the purpose of conveying to a single purchaser a whole great property, together with its surrounding land, such a description and such a plan is likely to be wholly inappropriate to achieve, without uncertainty and resulting confusion, the conveyance of the small divided parts of big buildings or to define the boundaries between the small gardens and courtyards of the adjoining plots into which the Vendor has divided the land around the house.'
>
> 'The facts of the present case are really very simple, but I hope that this judgment will be understood by every conveyancing solicitor in the land as giving them warning, loud and clear, that a conveyancing technique which may have been effective in the old days to convey large property from one vendor to one purchaser will lead to nothing but trouble, disputes and expensive litigation if applied to the sale to separate purchasers of a single house and its curtilage[3] divided into separate parts. For such purposes it is absolutely essential that each parcel conveyed shall be described in the conveyance or transfer deed with such particularity and precision that there is no room for doubt about the boundaries of each, and for such purposes if the plan is intended to control the description, an Ordnance map of a scale of 1:2500 is worse than useless. The plan or other drawing bound up with the deed must be on such a large scale that it clearly shows with precision where each boundary runs. In my view the parties to this appeal are the victims of sloppy

conveyancing for which the professional advisers of vendor and purchasers appear to bear the responsibility. We are not concerned in this appeal with determining or apportioning that responsibility. This Court has to try to reduce to order the confusion created by conveyancers.'

The most satisfactory way of avoiding such disputes will generally be to obtain or have prepared a plan of an appropriate scale. The plan, however, is a means to an end and not an end in itself. The conveyancer's objective is for the transfer, conveyance or lease (including the plan, where one is included) to define the property with particularity and precision and it may well be that boundaries can be dealt with in writing in the deed. This would be of assistance when an appropriate plan is not available. Certainly the boundary that was considered by the Court in *Scarfe v Adams*[2] could easily have been defined in words.

1   *Kingston v Phillips* [1976] CA Transcript 279; *Scarfe v Adams* [1981] 1 All ER 843, CA; *Mayer v Hurr* (1983) 49 P & CR 56, CA.
2   [1981] 1 All ER 843 at 845, CA.
3   For an indication of the meaning of 'curtilage', see *Dyer v Dorset County Council* [1989] QB 346, CA.

3.10   *No points of identification of the site.* There can be instances when a plan is of little assistance in actually defining the land involved, for example where there are no points of indentification on the ground. This could arise where unfenced plots are being leased for building purposes, and where the landlord has 'drawn lines on a plan'. It could prove very difficult for surveyors in the future to 'plot' all the points involved on the land, and disputes could arise. Therefore either as many measurements as possible should be included on the plan, and confirmation obtained from a surveyor that this would provide him with sufficient information to define the area in question, or (better still) the plots should be 'pegged out' or some form of simple fencing erected, with the agreement on the site of the parties. The land would then be leased with reference to the pegs or fencing, and there would be a stipulation to the effect that the plan would neither limit nor enlarge that description.[1]

1   See *Willson v Greene* [1971] 1 All ER 1098, [1971] 1 WLR 635, and J T Farrand ('Conveyancer's Notebook') [1983] Conv 338.

D   LEASE OF PART OF A BUILDING

3.11   *Must define in detail.* Where the premises to be let form part of a building, it is essential to define specifically their extent in relation to the exterior walls, and the walls and floors that divide the premises from the other parts of the building.[1] If the parcels are inadequately defined, disputes as to the extent of the premises might arise, for example where the tenant covenants to repair 'the demised premises'. The point could also be relevant in less obvious instances – in *Sturge v Hackett*[2] a distinguished soldier succeeded in burning down a country mansion of which he was tenant of part in an attempt to smoke out a sparrow's nest by lighting a rag soaked in paraffin. The vital question for insurance purposes was whether or not the fire started on premises demised to the defendant. The need for precision on the part of the draftsman is all the more important because of the very limited authorities. Such as there are provide as follows:

3.11:1   Vertical

(a)   *External*

In the absence of provision in the lease to the contrary, a demise of part of a building divided, horizontally or vertically includes the external walls of the part so demised[3] including an external fixture, whether ornamental or not, that may be affixed to such external walls.[4]

(b)   *Interior*

In *Phelps v City of London Corpn*[5] Peterson J was required to construe an exception in a lease by which the landlord reserved to himself a passage and a basement under the same. During the course of his judgment he said:[6]

> 'As Joyce J said in *Hope Brothers v Cowan*[5] "the demise of a room must necessarily include, unless it be excepted, some part of the wall which bounds it". The walls are, in fact, part of the room. In the case of an external wall the demise of a room includes the whole of the wall *while in the case of a partition wall it seems to be clear that some part of the wall is included in the demise.*'

The colouring of the plan annexed to the lease in question meant that the learned Judge did not have to come to any general view as to the extent of that 'some part'.

3.11:2   Horizontal

In *Sturge v Hackett*[2] the Court of Appeal held that the defendant's flat extended *at least* to the underside of the floor joists to which his ceiling was attached. The Court found it unnecessary to decide whether it extended half way through the thickness of the floor joists or to the top side of them. Thus this question remains unanswered. In *Phelps*, Peterson J stated he did[8] 'not see any difference in law between the horizontal division between an upper and a lower room and the vertical division between two adjoining rooms'. It would seem to follow from this therefore that his Lordship believed that 'some part' of the floors and ceilings would be included but again the case did not require him to be more precise. In *Graystone Property Investments Ltd v Margulies*,[9] Griffiths LJ referred to a submission by Counsel that 'the general rule is that the upper boundary of a flat is the lower boundary of the flat immediately above' and said that 'it may, I think, be rather too strong to state this proposition as a normal rule, but I have no doubt that it is the general expectation of anyone who takes the lease of a flat that he acquires the space between the floor of his flat and the underneath of the floor of the flat above'. There seem no principles of general application as to whether the roof is included in the demised premises – this is simply a matter of construction of the individual lease.[10]

1   See too comments on a modern commercial building in paras 3.13–3.17 below.
2   [1962] 3 All ER 166, [1962] 1 WLR 1257, CA.
3   *Carlisle Cafe Co v Muse Bros & Co* (1897) 67 LJ Ch 53; *Hope Bros Ltd v Cowan* [1913] 2 Ch 312 and *Goldfoot v Welch* [1914] 1 Ch 213.
4   *Sturge v Hackett* [1962] 3 All ER 166, [1962] 1 WLR 1257, CA; *Boswell v Crucible Steel Co* [1925] 1 KB 119, CA; *Holiday Fellowship Ltd v Hereford* [1959] 1 All ER 433, [1959] 1 WLR 211, CA and as to a skylight, see *Taylor v Webb* [1936] 2 All ER 763; revd on other grounds [1937] 2 KB 283, [1937] 1 All ER 590, CA.
5   [1916] 2 Ch 255.
6   At 263. The emphasising is the author's.
7   See note 2 above.
8   At 264.
9   (1983) 269 Estates Gazette 538. For valuable comments on the case, see [1984] Conv 171.
10   *Cockburn v Smith* [1924] 2 KB 119, CA; *Douglas-Scott v Scorgie* [1984] 1 All ER 1086, [1984] 1

WLR 716, CA; *Straudley Investments Ltd v Barpress Ltd* [1987] 1 EGLR 69, 282 Estates Gazette 1124, CA. *Hatfield v Moss* [1988] 2 EGLR 58, [1988] 40 EG 112, CA. The related problem of whether the roof is within the exterior or structure of the building of which the demised premises form part (ie for the purposes of the Housing Act 1961, s 32(1)(a) or service charges) has frequently been considered: *Campden Hill Towers Ltd v Gardner* [1977] QB 823, [1977] 1 All ER 739, CA; *Douglas-Scott v Scorgie* [1984] 1 All ER 1086, [1984] 1 WLR 716, CA; *Rapid Results College Ltd v Angell* [1986] 1 EGLR 53, 277 Estates Gazette 856; *Tennant Radiant Heat Ltd v Warrington Development Corpn* [1988] 1 EGLR 41, [1988] 11 EG 71, CA.

3.12 *Authorities often refer to different buildings.* The authorities, therefore, provide a very incomplete picture. Equally unhelpful is the fact that the structure of most contemporary commercial buildings is very different from that of the buildings considered by the courts. The walls and floors of modern buildings are made up of a series of layers, and which of these layers is included in the demised premises must either be set out in words, or dealt with on a plan or section. It is very dangerous for solicitors to rely upon one set of general words which they hope will apply to the division of all buildings. These 'standard words' may prove totally unsuitable for that particular building, having regard to the methods of construction used, and thus leave unresolved the very uncertainty that they were seeking to cure. This is a matter in which surveyors and engineers must be involved and each building looked at individually. The experts must advise on the nature of the building and where it is appropriate to make divisions, and assist in the drafting of the definition of the demised premises. It is the horizontal division that is so often overlooked, and the drafting of this part of the lease will have failed unless the parties can easily ascertain from a study of the lease the precise point at which the premises cease to be within the demise, for example 'along the underside of the beams' or 'along the topmost side of the joists'.

3.13 *Typical modern building.* These principles are well illustrated by looking at a typical modern multi-storey office building. The basement consists of reinforced concrete floors and the walls covered by a waterproofing membrane. Unless the contrary is shown, a demise of the basement would presumably include both sides of the wall, and the waterproofing membrane, even though the outside of the wall is below ground level. It may be that the expense involved in repairing the membrane could be considerable and the tenant should resist its inclusion in the premises demised to him. A tenant of a basement needs to take great care over the horizontal divisions, as an oversight here could mean that the foundations of the building were included in the demise. It would be a somewhat unwelcome surprise for a tenant, who had taken a lease of some basement premises for storage, to find that he was responsible for the foundations of the whole building.

3.14 *Horizontal boundary.* The building consists of a framework of structural steel columns and beams, with reinforced concrete laid onto the beams to form the floors. This is topped by a sand/cement screed, on which there are applied finishes, for example tiles, terrazzo, plastic sheeting, wood block, carpet, etc. This will illustrate why it is vital to define the horizontal boundary – the floor of this (and virtually any other modern) building consists of various layers and in the absence of an express provision, there are no principles of law as to where the division will be. A practical problem that might arise could be the failure of the sand/cement screed and the responsibilities of the parties regarding its repair. If this topping fails, the structure of the building will not be at risk, but the finish applied to the screed, such as the tiles, may loosen or break up due to lack of support.[1] The law would provide little assistance as to whether or not the screed was within the demised premises, where the definition was limited to 'all that part of the third floor shown edged on the plan annexed hereto'. The ceilings will often be suspended from the underside of the floor above and there is a need to deal precisely with the boundary here.[2]

1 Even where the definition of premises was such that it was clear that the screed was not within the demise (and thus the tenant's repairing covenant), it does not automatically follow that the landlord will be obliged to repair it. He will only have to undertake such repairs if he has covenanted so to do.
2 See note 9 to para 3.11 above.

3.15 *Flank walls.* Each flank wall of the building is in fact a number of individual walls built on the edge of each concrete floor up to the underside of the floor above. It is not, therefore, one wall built from the foundations to the roof, as would be the case in a conventional brick-built building, and nor are these 'individual' walls load-bearing. (Sometimes a brick cladding is used which may extend from the ground to the roof, but this is not load-bearing, and would merely be fixed to the building at various points.) A large part of the individual walls are likely to be taken up with windows – the remainders may be reinforced concrete panels or brickwork, often with a cavity for heating and air-conditioning installations. The walls, therefore, are also made up of vertical layers and a clear definition is needed of the boundary of the demised premises.

3.16 *Columns.* In the building, there are columns a few feet inside the walls forming the vertical part of the steel framework of the building. Columns are sometimes located as part of the walls, or may be on the outside of the wall. The columns will rarely be restricted to in or near the walls (other than in a very narrow building) and there will generally be lines of columns running through each floor. In these columns, the structural steel is protected by reinforced concrete, before the applied finish of plaster or panelling. Again, the law would be of very little assistance in defining the boundary of the demised premises in relation to such columns and in the absence of any wording to the contrary it would probably be held that *all* the column (including that part representing the steel framework of the building) was included in the demise, thus imposing a considerable burden on the tenant if a full repairing covenant is given.

3.17 *Roof.* The tenant of the top floor of the building has to pay particular regard to the horizontal division to ensure that he is not also responsible for the roof, which is likely to be a metal deck or reinforced concrete slab,[1] although there may just be an advantage in some circumstances for there to be no top limitation of the demised premises.[2]

1 But see *Cockburn v Smith* [1924] 2 KB 119 and the cases referred to in para 3.11, footnote 10 above.
2 See para 3.5 above.

E FIXTURES

3.18 *Types and tenant's ability to remove.* Modern commercial buildings frequently contain valuable plant and equipment, the ownership of which could be significant, for example in relation to the repairing covenant,[1] on a rent review or renewal under the 1954 Act,[2] as to whether or not the tenant will be entitled to remove the items on the expiry of the term and install them in his new premises,[3] and in relation to the tenant's tax affairs.[4] For the avoidance of doubt, the demised premises should be expressed to include landlord's fixtures.[5] This will cover three categories of fixtures – those attached to the premises (by the landlord or a previous tenant)[6] on the date of the lease, any items brought into the premises by the landlord during the term of the lease, and items installed by the tenant that, by operation of law, have become landlord's fixtures. Prima facie however whatever is annexed to the property becomes part of it and vests in the landlord,[7] and the tenant will be guilty of waste if he removes it. Thus a tenant can fix items to premises during the term and have no right to remove them on its expiry or prior determination. A tenant can, however, remove trade fixtures,[8] and the mode of annexation is important – an item will not be a fixture if it can easily be removed without injuring the building or, providing it can be removed without serious injury, if annexed for a temporary purpose and not as a permanent improvement to the building.[9] All rights of removal are subject to the terms of the lease and thus the landlord can vary the general law, with a view to making part of the premises items that the tenant would normally be permitted to remove.[10]

1   That will generally apply to the landlord's fixtures, including those installed by the tenant that by operation of law have become landlord's fixtures.

2   Because items installed by the tenant that become landlord's fixtures will be 'improvements' for the purposes of s 34 of the 1954 Act and any rent review clause based on it: *New Zealand Government Property Corpn v HM & S Ltd* [1982] QB 1145.

3   He will not if they have become landlord's fixtures.

4   See para 3.20 below.

5   For a full discussion of fixtures, see 27 Halsbury's Laws (4th edn) para 142 and *Hill & Redman's Law of Landlord and Tenant* (18th edn) para 2416, Legal Notes (1987) 281 Estates Gazette 1332.

6   But not those installed by the *same* tenant during a *previous* tenancy: see *New Zealand Property Corpn v HM & S Ltd* [1982] QB 1145, [1982] 1 All ER 624 in which the Court of Appeal established that when a lease expires or is surrendered and is followed immediately by another to the same tenant remaining in possession, the tenant does not lose his right to remove tenant's fixtures but is entitled to remove them at the end of the new tenancy.

7   *Bain v Brand* (1876) 1 App Cas 762, HL; *Wake v Hall* (1880) 7 QBD 295, CA; *Boswell v Crucible Steel Co* [1925] 1 KB 119, CA.

8   *Poole's Case* (1703) 1 Salk 368; *Climie v Wood* (1869) LR 4 Exch 328; *Smith v City Petroleum Co Ltd* [1940] 1 All ER 260.

9   *Hellawell v Eastwood* (1851) 6 Exch 295; *Holland v Hodgson* (1872) LR 7 CP 328; *Bain v Brand* (1876) 1 App Cas 762; *Leigh v Taylor* [1902] AC 157; *Re Hulse, Beattie v Hulse* [1905] 1 Ch 406; *Billing v Pill* [1954] 1 QB 70, [1953] 2 All ER 1061.

10   Although where a tenant's right to remove tenant's fixtures is excluded, clear language to that effect is needed: *Lambourn v McLellan* [1903] 2 Ch 268, CA.

3.19 *Inventory of fixtures.* The tenant must insist upon a comprehensive inventory of the landlord's fixtures and the survey[1] that the prudent tenant has made prior to proceeding should extend to fixtures. In particular he must be satisfied that any major items such as the air conditioning or central heating system are in good working order. The landlord should be required to remedy any defects prior to completion. If for whatever reason there will be defective fixtures at the time of the grant, then this must be dealt with in the lease otherwise there would be a danger that the tenant would have to remedy such defects under his repairing covenant.[2] If necessary an agreed schedule indicating the wants of repair should be prepared and the tenant's covenant to repair and maintain fixtures should be so expressed as not to require standards greater than this.[2] Alternatively an allowance could be made to the tenant to put the fixtures into repair, but the tenant should be wary of this approach because, if the sum proved insufficient, the tenant would have to make up the shortfall in order to comply with his repairing covenant.

1 See para 2.16 above.
2 For a typical covenant see Rosscastle Letting Conditions (Appendix 1 below) Conditions 3.4:1 and 3.4:2. Note that by virtue of Condition 2.1:5, fixtures are included within the defined team 'Property' and so Condition 3.4:1 encompasses the fixtures as well.

3.20 *Capital allowances.* A further consequence of the change of ownership that comes about when a tenant installs an item in premises that then becomes a landlord' fixtures[1] was seen in *Stokes (Inspector of Taxes) v Costain Property Investments Ltd.*[2] The tenant company installed lifts and central heating equipment in buildings at which it was undertaking development work. When the development was completed, it was entitled to a lease of the buildings. It was common ground that on installation, the items became landlord's fixtures. The tenant claimed that they belonged to it for the purposes of s 41(1)(b) of the Finance Act 1971, and that accordingly the expenditure incurred on the items qualified for capital allowances, but the Revenue, Harman J and the Court of Appeal disagreed – they took the view that a thing could not 'belong' to a person who, although having a right to possession of it, had no right of disposition by sale, gift or destruction. In the particular case, one cannot be certain that any drafting could have assisted[3] but where the items in question were less significant the landlord might be prepared to agree for the lease to provide that the items would not become landlord's fixtures. The Court of Appeal suggested that the legislation should be reviewed because its purpose was to encourage investment in machinery and plant, whereas in *Stokes* nobody would receive the tax allowance: the freeholder did not incur the expenditure and the tenant would not receive it because the items in issue did not belong to the tenant. The point has, perhaps, become less significant with the restructuring of capital allowances.[4]

1 See para 3.18 above.
2 [1984] 1 All ER 849, [1984] 1 WLR 763. It is understood that an appeal to the House of Lords is pending. See also Larry Chrisfield 'Capital Allowances on Plant and Machinery' [1984] Gazette 11 April 1037.
3 But see (1983) 4 PLB 14 (written, although this does not seem to be material, after the decision at first instance and before the appeal).
4 See Finance Act 1984.

Chapter 4

Rights, exceptions and reservations

A GENERAL WORDS

4.1 *Deal expressly with required rights.* By virtue of ss 62 and 205(1)(ii) of the Law of Property Act 1925, a lease is deemed to include, in the absence of any contrary intention, 'all . . . waters, watercourses, liberties, privileges, easements, rights, and advantages whatsoever appertaining . . . to the land' at the time of the lease. As such, there is no need in a lease to insert general words in relation to the grant of rights such as 'all ways and other easements used therewith'. The draftsman may be tempted to rely wholly on these statutory provisions, and not to specify the rights granted, on the basis that statute provides that all rights enjoyed in relation to the property at the time of the grant will be automatically included.[1] It would be an unwise tenant's solicitor, however, who allowed the matter to proceed on this footing and he should insist that the rights that will be required are granted specifically. Section 62 operates with effect from the *date of the demise* and thus, if there was a subsequent dispute as to whether or not a right was included, it would be necessary to produce evidence that such a right was used by the occupier of the land at the time of the grant.[2] This may well not be easy. The second advantage of specifying the rights that are included is that it has been held[3] that s 62 does not apply to services (such as the supply of hot water) because these are not property rights but a question of contract between the landlord and the tenant. Finally, expressly dealing with the rights serves as a reminder to make proper provision for the upkeep and maintenance of the item over which, or through which, the right will be exercised.[4]

1   Especially where the lease relates to an existing building, the landlord might be well advised to express the contrary intention, and state that the only rights granted to the tenant are those set out in the lease and that the tenant shall not be entitled to any rights that would be included by virtue of s 62. This could prevent the inadvertent inclusion of a right that the landlord had no intention of granting and so also avoid uncertainties on a rent review (see para 6.18:1 below) or renewal under the 1954 Act (see para 14.43 below).
2   Note *Graham v Philcox* [1984] QB 747, [1984] 2 All ER 643, CA.
3   See *Regis Property Co Ltd v Redman* [1956] 2 QB 612, [1956] 2 All ER 335, CA. Nor can implications be made under s 62 to supply omissions in the description of the parcels – see *Altmann v Boatman* (1963) 186 Estates Gazette 109, CA.
4   See Chapter 11 below.

B RIGHTS OF WAY

4.2 *When needed.* In many leases, the tenant will need a right of way in order to gain access to the demised premises.[1] He will not need such a right where the demised premises directly abut a public highway. It is easy to think that the

48

only public highways are those adopted by the highway authority and 'maintained at the public expense'. This is not so – a highway may be created under the provisions of a statute (for example the Highways Act 1980), but can also come into existence by dedication, express or implied. Thus if a landowner dedicates a right of passage across land for use by the *public at large*, and the public accepts and uses the way *as of right*, a public highway is created. Where the tenant will require to use an unadopted public highway in order to gain access to the premises his solicitor should always try to obtain confirmation (a) that there was an intention to dedicate (this will be relevant when no formal document can be produced), (b) that the right is exercised by or granted to the public *at large*[2] (c) that the grantor had sufficient title to grant the right and (d) that adequate arrangements are in force regarding the maintenance of the road. Where a right of way has been enjoyed by the public as of right and without interruption for twenty years, the way is deemed to have been a dedicated highway, unless there is sufficient evidence to the contrary.'[3]

1   See for example, Appendix 1, Form No 4 below, clause 1.3:1.
2   See *Poole v Huskinson* (1843) 11 M & W 827.
3   See Highways Act 1980 ss 31 and 32, *Merstham Manor Ltd v Coulsdon and Purley UDC* [1937] 2 KB 77, [1936] 2 All ER 422; *Fairey v Southampton County Council* [1956] 2 QB 439, [1956] 2 All ER 843, CA.

4.3   *Is the right of way sufficient?*   The tenant's solicitor should ensure that his client will be granted a *sufficient*[1] right of way, as the tenant will need a right of way over the whole distance from the highway to the demised premises. This could be particularly relevant in a lease of a factory or warehouse on an industrial estate where the tenant is granted rights of way over the estate roads. The tenant's solicitor needs to confirm that the estate roads lead directly to a public highway. If they do not, and there is a further stretch of 'private road' between the industrial estate and the public highway, then the tenant will require rights over this.

1   And (where appropriate) the right will extend to vehicles as well. Subsequent changes to the land over which the right of way is exercised may prompt further questions of whether or not it is sufficient. An interference with a private right of way is actionable only if it is substantial, and it would not be substantial if it did not interfere with reasonable use of the right of way: *Celsteel Ltd v Alton House Holdings Ltd* [1985] 2 All ER 562, [1985] 1 WLR 204.

4.4   *Loading and parking.*   There is an implied right for vehicles to stop on a right of way for the purposes of loading and unloading, but there is no implied right to park[1] – an express provision would be required. Thus the tenant's solicitor needs to seek instructions from his client, and if it is felt that rights would be needed to park on a road over which the tenant will have a right of way, this point must be specifically negotiated with the landlord. Megarry J was required in *VT Engineering Ltd v Richard Barland & Co Ltd*[2] to consider a number of aspects relating to the extent of a right of way over the estate roads of an industrial estate where the plaintiffs, who made steel beams up to 30 ft long, had been granted a right of way to their factory. He held that:
(a)   a right of way includes a right to load and unload, but not a right to place cranes and hoists on the road, and not a right to park vehicles which are not being loaded or unloaded.
(b)   although it may be that a grantor cannot fence up to the edge of a winding right of way, but should leave a tolerance of a foot or two for wide loads,

there is no lateral swing space (ie space for swinging loads being hoisted by crane) over an undefined area of a neighbour's land, and

(c) if an unlimited grant of a right of way is given over land which at the time of the grant is open to the skies, it cannot be roofed-in so as to interfere with the plaintiff's use. In this case the defendant was about to put a building on stilts over the right of way with merely a 9 ft to 11 ft clearance, something which would have severely prejudiced the plaintiffs.

1   *Bulstrode v Lambert* [1953] 2 All ER 728, [1953] 1 WLR 1064; *McIlraith v Grady* [1968] 1 QB 468, [1967] 3 All ER 625, CA; but note *Papworth v Linthaven Ltd* [1988] EGCS 54.
2   (1968) 19 P & CR 890.

4.5 *Shared rights of way.* In many instances, the right of way will be enjoyed with others and the tenant should always make enquiries to those with whom he will be sharing this right. The nature and the amount of the use to which the right of way is put will be directly linked with the cost of the upkeep of the right of way, which will no doubt in part be the tenant's expense.[1] To return to the example of the light industrial building on a small estate, the tenant may assume that the only other users of the estate roads are the other occupiers of the similar buildings on the estate. In fact the local farmer may have rights of access to his fields beyond the estate, and if this was found to be so, enquiries should be made to ensure that the farmer is alone responsible for removing mud from the roads. Alternatively, one party who has rights may have a significantly heavier user than the others, and should be responsible for a greater share of the cost of upkeep and maintenance of the right of way.[2]

1   See Chapter 11 and Appendix 1 below, Form No 4 clauses 1.3:1, 4.1, 4.2, 5.1 and 5.2.
2   See Chapter 11 below.

C OTHER RIGHTS

4.6 *Conducting media.* Unless the mains supply of gas, electricity, sewage, etc passes under a public highway[1] adjacent to the demised premises, or directly over, under or through the demised premises, rights will be needed through conducting media on the adjoining land in order to connect up with and use these services.[2] There is a tendency of landlords' solicitors not specifically to grant such rights, presumably on the basis that they are granted under s 62, but for the reasons set out above, the tenant should insist upon a specific grant.[3]

1   It is important to ensure that the demised premises abut the highway and that there is not a small strip of land between the highway and the boundary of the premises under which an easement would be required for services. Where a tenant is granted a right to receive a supply of gas he is entitled to enter the landlord's property and lay a new gas main: *Coopind (UK) Ltd v Walton Commercial Group Ltd* [1989] 1 EGLR 241 but note *Trailfinders Ltd v Razuki* [1988] 2 EGLR 46.
2   Where the demised premises consist of a part of a building, further services may be required through conducting media in other parts of the building, for example television, telecommunications, data processing etc.
3   See for example Appendix 1, below, Form No 4 clauses 1.2 and 1.3:2 and Form No 6 clauses 1.4 (see footnote 2 above) and 1.5:3.

4.7 *Access to adjoining land.* Every lease contains a tenant's repairing covenant and very often the tenant will only be able to comply with his covenant if he has the right to go onto adjoining property. The obvious example is flank walls which represent the boundary of the demised premises. By definition the outside of these can only be repaired from neighbouring land.[1] Where these are party walls, the tenant has a right to enter his neighbour's land under s 38 of the Law of Property Act 1925, but this is a complex section. In any event there will be cases where part of the demised premises that is not a party wall could only be repaired from the neighbour's premises. When the neighbouring land is in the ownership of the landlord, the tenant should always insist upon an express right in the lease.[2]

1 It is possible that such a right could be held to be an easement of necessity (see *Wong v Beaumont Property Trust Ltd* [1965] 1 QB 173, [1964] 2 All ER 119 and *Nickerson v Barraclough* [1981] Ch 426, [1981] 2 All ER 369)] but, to avoid any doubt, an express right should always be sought. The same point arises where the right to airspace is excluded but the tenant is responsible for the repair of the roof.
2 See Appendix 1 below, Form No 5, clause 1.5:3.

4.8 *Support and protection.* Where the demised premises form part of a larger building, the tenant should always insist upon specific rights of support and protection which strengthen the landlord's covenant for quiet enjoyment.[1]

1 See Appendix 1 below, Form No 6, clause 1.5:4.

4.9 *Toilets.* The tenant's solicitor should insist upon a specific right to use defined toilets when none are included in the demised premises.[1] Statutory obligations are imposed on the landlord to provide and maintain in efficient working order and good repair sufficient and suitable sanitary conveniences.[2] As the number of conveniences required depends upon the number of persons employed in the building,[3] there may be cases where the landlord will need to obtain a covenant from the tenant limiting the numbers working at the demised premises.

1 See Appendix 1 below, Form No 6, clause 1.5:2.
2 Factories Act 1961, ss 7(1), 122. Offices Shops and Railway Premises Act 1963, ss 9(1), 42(6), 43(4).
3 Sanitary Accommodation Regulations 1938.

D   EXCEPTIONS AND RESERVATIONS

4.10 *Terminology.* There is a subtle, but not irrelevant,[1] distinction between and exception and a reservation, although most of those matters that are regarded today as exceptions and reservations are, in fact, neither. An exception is a subtraction from the demise that was *in existence at the time of the lease* – for example, the rights of a third party to use conducting media or to take minerals under the land. A reservation is a right or profit issuing out of the demised premises which previously had no separate existence and that *comes into being by virtue of the lease.* Only the rent and payments in the nature of rent issue out of the demised premises[2] and so a right for the landlord over the demised premises created by the lease is neither an exception, because it was not in existence before lease, nor a reservation as it does not issue out of the demised premises. Technically, such a right is a regrant. Nevertheless, the term 'exceptions and reservations' is used here to cover all rights to which the demised premises are subject. Where the tenant has been granted rights, the landlord will impliedly be entitled to reciprocal rights[3] but the prudent landlord will, in the interests of certainty, require the exceptions and reservations to be expressly set out. The doctrine not to derogate from a grant applies to exceptions and reservations.[4]

1 The only distinction would seem to be in whose favour they are construed – see para 4.11 below and footnotes 2 and 3 thereto.
2 *Doe d Douglas v Lock* (1835) 2 Al & El 705.
3 *Re Webb's Lease, Sandom v Webb* [1951] Ch 808, [1951] 2 All ER 131, CA.
4 *Johnston & Sons Ltd v Holland* [1988] 1 EGLR 264, CA.

4.11 *Construction and categories.* The landlord and his advisers should give careful consideration to the exceptions and reservations to be included in the lease. An exception[1] (but not necessarily a reservation or regrant)[2] will in cases of doubt be construed in favour of the tenant, so that if the landlord wishes to retain a part of or a right over the demised premises, he must expressly so provide in the lease, unless the right in question amounts to an easement of necessity.[3] Exceptions and reservations can essentially be divided into two groups – rights enabling the landlord and his other tenants to use and be free to develop neighbouring land,[4] and those rights that the landlord will need to supervise the tenant and to ensure that he is complying with the terms of the lease.[5]

1 Sheppard's Touchstone (7th edn) 100; *Earl of Cardigan v Armitage* (1823) 2 B & C 197; *Bullen v Denning* (1826) 5 B & C 842; *Savill Bros Ltd v Bethell*]1902] 2 Ch 523, CA.
2 *Re Webb's Lease, Sandom v Webb* [1951] Ch 808, [1951] 2 All ER 131, but see *St Edmundsbury and Ipswich Diocesan Board of Finance v Clark (No 2)* [1975] 1 All ER 772, [1975] 1 WLR 468, CA.
3 *Liddiard v Waldron* [1934] 1 KB 435, CA.
4 See paras 4.12–4.17 below.
5 See for example Rosscastle Letting Conditions (Appendix 1 below, Form No 1) Condition 3.6.

4.12 *Conducting media.* Where the landlord requires the use of conducting media[1] in the demised premises, he will need a re-grant to this effect in the exceptions and reservations. This should be expressed to apply to any that come into existence during the term, and not just those that are there at the time of the grant.[2] The landlord should also reserve an express right to enter the demised premises to introduce new conducting media[3] because no such right will be implied even where the lease grants the landlord the right to use new media once installed.[4]

1 For discussion of in, on, under or over, see *Trailfinders Ltd v Razuki* [1988] 2 EGLR 46, [1988] 30 EG 59.
2 See for example Appendix 1 below, Form No 6, clause 1.6:1.
3 See ibid clause 1.6:2. He could hardly object if the tenant requires him to agree to make good: See Rosscastle Letting Conditions (Appendix 1 below, Form No 1) Condition 4.2.
4 *Taylor v British Legal Life Assurance Co* [1925] 1 Ch 395; revsd 94 LJ Ch 284, CA; *Trailfinders Ltd v Razuki* [1988] 2 EGLR 46, [1988] 30 EG 59.

4.13 *Repairs and scaffolding.* Where the landlord will be retaining adjoining premises he will wish to reserve a right of access to the demised premises if this may be required to inspect and repair the retained premises.[1] Where the landlord will be retaining premises above the demised premises, his solicitor will need to consider the principles illustrated in *Owen v Gadd*.[2] Soon after the lease of a shop was granted, scaffolding poles were erected in front of the windows and door of the ship so that necessary repairs could be carried out by the landlord to the upper part of the building which he occupied. The Court of

Appeal held that as the premises were let as a shop, the erection of the scaffolding constituted an interference that was sufficiently physical and direct to be a breach of the covenant for quiet enjoyment. In fact, only nominal damages were awarded but the principle had been established and the landlord's solicitor should ensure that a right is specifically reserved.[3]

1   See Appendix 1 below, Form No 6, clause 1.6:3. Note also clause 1.6:5.
2   [1956] 2 QB 99, [1956] 2 All ER 28. Note also *Queensway Marketing Ltd v Associated Restaurants Ltd* (1984) 271 Estates Gazette 1106.
3   See Appendix 1 below, Form No 6, clause 1.6:4.

4.14   *Tenant's amendments.* The tenant's solicitor will always wish to mitigate the severity of the exceptions and reservations. In relation to any rights of access, he should propose amendments so that these can only be exercised (except in cases of emergency, where relevant) on reasonable notice and at reasonable times during working hours and by prior appointment. So far as the last point is concerned, the landlord could quite properly insist upon adding: 'except where the Tenant unreasonably refuses or delays in making an appointment'. This must be dealt with differently in an underlease, because if the headlease does not oblige the superior landlord to give reasonable notice or other similar provision, there can be no such provision in the underlease that purports to apply to the superior landlord. That does not, however, prevent the *sub-lessor* from accepting such provisions *in relation to himself*. If there is an exception or reservation permitting the landlord and others to enter the demised premises to carry out work the tenant should always insist upon a covenant to make good.[1] Whenever there is an exception and reservation in relation to mining rights the tenant's solicitor should make a mining search.[2]

1   See Rosscastle Letting Conditions (Appendix 1 below, Form No 1) Condition 4.2.
2   See para 2.13 above.

4.15   *Rights of light and air.* On a lease of one of two adjoining premises by the owner of both, the tenant will be entitled to the access of light and air to the demised premises over the adjoining property, if that right had been enjoyed through a definite aperture such as a window or through a definite channel over the adjoining property.[1] A right to light or air will not, however, be implied against the landlord if it would be inconsistent with the intention to be implied from the circumstances existing at the date of the lease and known to the tenant – for example when the tenant knew that the adjoining land was intended to be used for building although the circumstances must clearly be established.[2] In practice, whenever the landlord is retaining adjoining land he should always expressly reserve to himself the right to develop it, notwithstanding the fact that light to the demised premises may be affected.[3] The tenant should seek to qualify the landlord's freedom to develop around the demised premises in such a way that all light to the demised premises is cut out by adding a proviso preventing this where the demised premises or the tenant's use and occupation of them would be materially affected.

1   But if the land has been let for a particular purpose, the tenant's rights are wider, and the landlord is bound to abstain from doing any act on the adjoining retained property which would prevent the use of the demised premises as intended as this would be derogating from his grant – see *Aldin v Latimer Clar, Muirhead & Co* [1894] 2 Ch 437. The entitlement is to such access of light as will leave the premises adequately lit for all ordinary purposes for which they may reasonably be expected to be used: *Carr–Saunders v Dick McNeill Associates Ltd* [1986] 2 EGLR 181, 279 Estates Gazette 1359, discussed in Legal Notes (1986) 279 Estates Gazette

1239. Note also *Lyme Valley Squash Club Ltd v Newcastle under Lyme Borough Council* [1985] 2 All ER 405 discussed and criticised in Legal notes (1986) 274 Estates Gazette 1259.
2   *Birmingham, Dudley and District Banking Co v Ross* (1888) 38 Ch D 295; *Broomfield v Williams* [1897] 1 Ch 602; *Long v Gowlett* [1923] 2 Ch 177.
3   See for example Appendix 1 below, Form No 6, clause 1.6:6.

E   THE RULE AGAINST PERPETUITIES

4.16   *Future grants.* Where a lease of part of a building or development is involved, the landlord will invariably reserve to himself the right to use any conducting media which may in the future be constructed in the demised premises for the benefit of his adjoining property,[1] and the right to construct and maintain them.[2] A magnanimous landlord may grant the tenant the right to use pipes that may be constructed on the landlord's adjoining premises. Where this arises, the draftsman will need to consider the rule against perpetuities. The old rule was that a grant of a future interest in any property was void if it could vest after the perpetuity period had expired. The period comprised a life or lives in being when the grant took effect plus twenty-one years and, in the absence of any reference to lives in being, the period was twenty-one years from the effective date. In *Dunn v Blackdown Properties Ltd*[3] Cross J had to consider the validity of a right to use sewers then passing or thereafter to pass under a certain road. At the time of the grant there were no such sewers and he held that the grant was void.[4] The severity of the old law was mitigated by the Perpetuities and Accumulations Act 1964 that made two important changes:

(a)   a period of years not exceeding eighty could be expressly specified[5] as the perpetuity period[6] and if this is done, the concept of a life or lives in being is excluded, and

(b)   where a grant would fail under the old Rule because it *could* vest outside the perpetuity period, it was now possible to *wait and see* – if the grant vests within the period, it will be valid.[7]

1   See Appendix 1 below, Form No 6, clause 1.6:1.
2   See ibid clause 1.6:2.
3   [1961] Ch 433, [1961] 2 All ER 62.
4   And was not saved by the Law of Property Act 1925, s 162(1)(d)(iv).
5   See *Re Green's Will Trusts* [1985] 3 All ER 455.
6   The Perpetuities and Accumulations Act 1964, s 1(1).
7   The Perpetuities and Accumulations Act 1964, s 3.

4.17   *Drafting.* Thus a draftsman dealing with the grant of a future easement should specify a perpetuity period. Where freehold land is involved, he is likely to choose eighty years, and the grant will only be void if it does not vest within that period. The principle applies equally to a grant[1] contained in a lease, although it is suggested that there is no need in a lease for less than twenty-one years to deal with the subject of perpetuities, because by virtue of s 3(4)(b) of the Perpetuities and Accumulations Act 1964 there is always a period of twenty-one years which is available as the perpetuity period.[2] It is tempting in a lease for a term exceeding twenty-one years, to specify the term of the lease as the perpetuity period but there could be a problem with this approach. Section 1(1) of the Act demands the specification of 'such number of years not exceeding eighty' and it seems at least arguable that this must be a determinate period, and not one liable to be cut short by forfeiture, surrender etc or extended by virtue of the provisions of Part II of the 1954 Act. In the light of this, it would seem prudent to specify a finite term.[3] That being so, many leases for terms of longer than twenty-one years state that the period of eighty years shall be the perpetuity period.[4] This may look somewhat bizarre in a lease, for example, of twenty-five years and the landlord's solicitor may prefer to specify a period amounting to the term of the lease plus perhaps five years as the perpetuity period, on the grounds that the risk of the term being extended under the 1954 Act by more than five years *and* a future right vesting after this period is outweighed by the advantage of producing a provision that appears sensible.

1   Used here to include a regrant (ie exception and reservation – see para 4.10 above).
2   Except perhaps in the case of say a twenty-year lease – if the term of the lease was extended by the 1954 Act, any future interest that vested more than 21 years after the grant would be void. (See below in this para).
3   See *Re Green's Will Trusts* [1985] 3 All ER 455.
4   See Rosscastle Letting Conditions (Appendix 1 below, Form No 1, Condition 10.9).

Chapter 5

Before the covenants

A THE PREMISES: DATE AND PARTIES

5.1 *Defined.* 'The premises', as properly defined,[1] comprise the date of the lease, the names and descriptions of the parties, the subject matter of the lease, and (where appropriate) the consideration and recitals. This chapter deals with those parts of the premises not dealt with already,[2] together with the habendum and reddendum.

1 Shep. Touchstone, p 74.
2 Parcels (Chapter 3) and rights, exceptions and reservations (Chapter 4).

5.2 *The date.* A deed takes effect from the date upon which the last party unconditionally[1] delivers it.[2] The date of a deed is not an essential part of it, so that an undated deed, or one with an impossible date (for example 30 February), is not invalid, but takes effect from unconditional delivery. It is an offence to insert the wrong date in a deed with intent to defraud or deceive,[3] and in any event the presumption that a document was executed on the date which it bears may be rebutted by contrary evidence.[4]

1 A deed has not, however, been delivered when sent 'in escrow' or 'as an escrow' – see paras 1.11 above and 15.2 below.
2 *Browne v Burton* (1847) 17 LJQB 49. Where agreements are intended to be exchanged, see *Eccles v Bryant and Pollock* [1948] Ch 93, [1947] 2 All ER 865, CA.
3 Forgery Act 1913, s 1; *R v Wells* [1939] 2 All ER 169, CCA.
4 *Browne v Burton* (1847) 17 LJQB 49.

5.3 *The landlord.* The landlord's solicitor should always check his client's title to ensure that the name of the correct party is inserted in the lease.[1] This is particularly necessary in those cases where the tenant will not be entitled to see the landlord's title[2] and thus be unable to check this point. It would be catastrophic – if unlikely – to discover later that some third party was the owner of the reversion. On the other hand, what is always possible is that the client may have overlooked the fact that the property in question is held in the name of a 'related party' – for example an associated or subsidiary company, rather than the parent.[3] The identity of the landlord can be relevant to the tenant in another way. The terms of a proposed letting could have been negotiated with a significant property company but when the lease is submitted, the landlord is shown as an unknown company. The landlord is probably a company within the property company's group, and the tenant's solicitor should make a search at the Companies Registry to confirm this. The search may show, however, that the landlord is a company of no great substance. It must always have a least one asset, being the premises to be demised by the lease, but these may be mortgaged. In these circumstanes, the tenant would be perfectly reasonable in asking the parent company to guarantee the performance of its subsidiary landlord, especially where the landlord gives significant covenants, perhaps in relation to repairs and maintenance or services. In the final analysis, the only circumstances in which the tenant could suffer in the event of the landlord's performance not being guaranteed would be if the tenant's claim exceeded the difference between the value of the landlord's interest in the demised premises and the amount for which they were mortgaged. This may be unlikely but the more practical argument that the tenant should advance is why should the tenant be forced to sue the insignificant subsidiary for damages, forcing it into liquidation if necessary, rather than have a simple action against the company who it believed, at the time of the negotiations, would be his landlord?[4]

1   He should also consider the capacity of the landlord to grant the lease. An owner absolutely entitled to the fee simple in land who is an individual and under no personal incapacity may grant leases for such periods and on such terms and conditions as he pleases. Persons who are entitled only to a limited or defeasible or partial interest in property or who are under a disability, or trustees or corporations etc can grant leases for the extent permitted by law: see 22 Encyclopaedia of Forms and Precedents (5th edn) paras 2 (The Crown), 3 (Persons suffering from a mental disorder), 4 (Infants), 5 (Universities and colleges), 6 (Settled land), 7 (Trustees for sale), 8 (Executors and administrators), 9 (Charities), 10 (Local and public authorities), 11 (Building etc societies, trade unions), 12 (Corporations and companies), 13 (Mortgagors and mortgagees), 14 (Receivers), 15 (Liquidators) and 16 (Trustee in bankruptcy). As to mortgagees, receivers, liquidators, administrators, administrative receivers and trustees-in-bankruptcy, see also paras 15.4–15.7 below.
2   See para 2.9 above.
3   Some of the problems that may result are illustrated by *Industrial Properties (Barton Hill) Ltd v Associated Electrical Industries Ltd* [1977] QB 580, [1977] 2 All ER 293, CA.
4   Damages will not be an adequate remedy because what the tenant wants is undisturbed occupation of the premises with the landlord's covenants being performed thereby enabling the tenant to get on with his business.

5.4   *The tenant.* The landlord's solicitor needs to ensure that the lease is granted to the party to whom the landlord has agreed to grant the lease.[1] For example, the landlord may have agreed the commercial terms of the tenancy with a company known as Judge and Jury (Manchester) Ltd. The landlord would have investigated the creditworthiness of this company and decided, as a result, to grant a lease to it. In due course, the draft lease is returned by the proposed tenant's solicitor and the landlord's solicitor notices that the name of the tenant has been amended to Judge and Jury Ltd. The landlord's solicitor should never assume that this is merely a correction, and that it was as a result of some unimportant misunderstanding or error, earlier in the matter. There must always be the possibility that the tenant has in fact decided that it wants to take the lease in the name of a subsidiary or associated company. In many instances, this would be of no concern to the landlord, because any group of companies must be free to hold its property as it thinks fit, providing that in do soing it does not prejudice its landlord. The obvious situation in which this might arise would be if Judge and Jury Ltd were a wholly-owned subsidiary of Judge and Jury (Manchester) Ltd but with a share capital of £100 and no assets. If the matter were allowed to proceed on this footing, the landlord may have obtained a totally worthless covenant, and the tenant, by winding up his subsidiary, would have found a way to opt out of the letting at any time. In these circumstances, the landlord would clearly require a guarantor.[2]

1 The tenant's solicitor for his part needs to consider the capacity of the tenant to accept the lease. An individual who is under no personal incapacity which disables him from contracting for or from holding land is able to accept a lease on such terms as he pleases. The rights of other persons to accept leases are limited by law: see 22 Encyclopaedia of Forms and Precedents (5th edn) paras 18 (Persons suffering from a mental disorder), 19 (Infants), 20 (Co-owners, trustees and personal representatives), 21 (Unincorporated associations), 22 (Charities), 23 (Corporations and companies), 24 (Building etc societies and trade unions) and 25 (Local authorities).
2 See paras 5.6–5.13 below. In a lease containing tenant's covenants to repair, not to assign or underlet etc, it is of great importance to the landlord to know the identity of the tenant. Accordingly a person named as tenant cannot be agent for an undisclosed principal, nor can two tenants contract for themselves and a third person as undisclosed principal also – see *Hanstown Properties Ltd v Green* (1977) 246 Estates Gazette 917, CA.

B   GUARANTORS AND QUASI GUARANTORS

5.5 *Guarantor, original tenant and distinctions.*[1] Where the landlord has any doubts about the ability of the tenant to pay the rent and perform the covenants and conditions of the lease, he is likely to require a third party to be joined in the lease to guarantee the tenant's obligations.[2] After an assignment, the original tenant[3] will become a quasi-guarantor for the assignee and any subsequent assignee because, by privity of contract, the original tenant remains liable to the landlord for any breach of the tenant's obligations contained in the lease throughout the term granted by the lease and notwithstanding the assignment.[4] There are, however, important distinctions between the liability of a guarantor and that of an original tenant:

5.5:1 *Discharge by variation of terms.* A guarantor will be discharged by any variation in the terms of the agreement between the creditor (the landlord) and the debtor (the tenant) that could prejudice the guarantor.[5] An original tenant will not, however, be so discharged because, by assigning its interest, the original tenant has put the assignee into its own position and consequently empowered the assignee (and any subsequent assignees) to act in any way that the original tenant could himself have done.[6]

5.5:2 *Breaches by the tenant.* Whether a guarantor's obligations extend to breaches by the tenant occurring during a statutory continuation of the lease is a question of fact in each case.[7] It would appear probable, however, that an original tenant would always continue to be liable during such a statutory continuation.[8]

5.5:3 *More than one guarantor.* Where there is more than one guarantor, the release of one may operate to release the other(s). An original tenant, however, is not released by the landlord releaseing the current assignee's guarantor.[9]

1 For a detailed discussion of this topic see K Reynolds and S Fogel (1984) LS Gaz 2214; S Murdoch *Tenants, assignees and sureties* (1984) 272 Estates Gazette 732, 857.
2 See eg Rosscastle Letting Conditions (Appendix 1, Form 1 below) condition 5. Guarantors (normally in the form of the directors) are most common in the case of private companies with limited assets but are seen also where the parent or holding company guarantees a subsidiary or where a United Kingdom party guarantees a tenant incorporated outside the jurisdiction. Nor should a guarantor, assuming that one can be found, be overlooked in the case of a letting to an individual.

3   If the original tenant has a guarantor, the latter will be guaranteeing not only the original tenant's 'actual' performance but also the continuing obligation: see *Selous Street Properties Ltd v Oronel Fabrics Ltd* (1984) 270 Estates Gazette 643; *Thames Manufacturing Co Ltd v Perrotts (Nichol & Peyton) Ltd* (1984) 271 Estates Gazette 284 and para 5.10:1 note 2 below.

4   See 27 Halsbury's Laws (4th edn) para 389 and Paragraph 115 post, paras 5.14–5.16 below. By privity of contract, the original landlord is bound by its covenants after it has parted with the reversion, but this is likely to be of less practical significance, but see 22 Encyclopaedia of Forms and Precedents (5th edn) Form 243.

5   *Holme v Brunskill* (1877) 3 QBD 495, CA. A variation that does not prejudice the guarantor may not release it: see para 5.7:2 below.

6   *Baynton v Morgan* (1888) 22 QBD 74, CA; *Centrovincial Estates plc v Bulk Storage Ltd* (1983) 268 Estates Gazette 59; *Allied London Investments Ltd v Hambro Life Assurance Ltd* (1983) 269 Estates Gazette 41; *Selous Street Properties Ltd v Oronel Fabrics Ltd* (1984) 270 Estates Gazette 643.

7   Ie under the Landlord and Tenant Act 1954 s 24 (23 Halsbury's Statutes (4th edn) LANDLORD AND TENANT). See *Junction Estates Ltd v Cope* (1974) 27 P & CR 482; *A Plesser & Co Ltd v Davis* (1983) 267 Estates Gazette 1039.

8   There is no direct authority on the point but this would seem to be the case because: (1) the courts have tended to treat the Landlord and Tenant Act 1954 as effecting a continuation of the current lease subject only to a modification of the ways in which it can be terminated (see *HL Bolton (Engineering) Co Ltd v TJ Graham & Sons Ltd* [1957] 1 QB 159, [1956] 3 All ER 624, CA; *Scholl Manufacturing Co Ltd v Clifton (Slim-Line) Ltd* [1967] Ch 41, [1966] 3 All ER 16, CA; (2) it is clear that the original tenant's guarantor can be liable for breaches occurring during a statutory continuation, provided that the terms of its guarantee expressly say so; given that a guarantor's liability cannot normally exceed that of the principal debtor, this again tends to suggest that the original tenant would be held responsible for breaches committed by a subsequent assignee during a statutory continuation; (3) of the reasoning in *GMS Syndicate Ltd v Gary Elliott Ltd* [1982] Ch 1, [1981] 1 All ER 619.

9   *Allied London Investments Ltd v Hambro Life Assurance Ltd* (1985) 50 P & CR 207, CA.

C   GUARANTORS

5.6   *The wisdom of seeking a guarantor.* A significant number of businesses fail every year. Throughout the 1970s, there were on average nearly 4,500 company liquidations a year. This had risen to almost 15,000 in 1985.[1] Accordingly, a landlord contemplating leasing commercial premises should consider requiring a third party to guarantee the tenant's obligations under the lease if he has any reservations about the tenant.[2] Small private companies of limited means are not the only tenants for which a guarantor should be required – subsidiaries should not be neglected. Times have changed since 1959 when Danckwerts J, on being asked to hold that a landlord was unreasonably refusing to grant licence to assign where the proposed assignee owed its parent company a large sum of money, said:[3]

> 'The other criticism is that . . . the holding company . . . could at any time demand . . . payment of that sum and wreck the proposed assignee . . . Lawfully, a demand could be made to the proposed assignee for payment of the whole of this large sum at any moment, but . . . as a practical matter it seems to me quite out of the question that any such demand would be likely to be made. The holding company . . . can have no interest except to keep its subsidiary company going as a part of its trading amalgamation and *it seems unthinkable, as a practical matter, that the proposed assignee is going to be brought to an end suddenly by reason of a demand for this debt.*'

Today, the financial pressures on a parent company could be such that it feels that it has no option but to put a subsidiary into liquidation, irrespective of the consequences in terms of goodwill or reputation.[4] A guarantor within the jurisdiction would also be desirable where the tenant is an overseas company. The need to consider guarantors similarly applies to lettings to individuals – there were nearly 7,000 bankruptcies in 1987.[5]

1   Department of Trade and Industry Statistics Division. The current trend is down: 14,898 in 1985, 14,405 in 1986 and 11,182 in 1987.

2   Although it is suggested that this and other devices (see for example 22 Encyclopaedia of Forms and Precedents (5th edn) Form 248) are no substitute for carefully selecting tenants and rejecting altogether those of doubtful status. As to whether a guarantor can be required when a lease is renewed under Part II of the 1954 Act see para 14.61 below.

3   *Re Greater London Properties Ltd's Lease* [1959] 1 All ER 728 at 732. The emphasising is the author's.

4   There have, however, been cases in which the basic principle of *Salomon v A Saloman & Co Ltd* [1897] AC 22, HL, one effect of which is not to make a company liable for its subsidiaries' debts, seems to have been weakened. It was held in *Smith, Stone & Knight Ltd v Birmingham Corpn* [1939] 4 All ER 116 and *DHN Food Distributors Ltd v London Borough of Tower Hamlets* [1976] 3 All ER 462, [1976] 1 WLR 852, CA that a parent company was entitled to receive compensation payable in respect of a subsidiary's land. In *Amalgamated Investment & Property Co Ltd v Texas Commerce International Bank Ltd* [1982] QB 84, [1981] 3 All ER 577, CA a parent was in effect held (admittedly very much on the unusual facts of the case) liable for the debts of its subsidiary.

5   Department of Trade and Industry Statistics Division: Bankruptcy 5448, Receiving Orders 1628, Other 433.

5.7   *Landlord's concerns.* The guarantor's covenant will probably be construed against the landlord[1] whose solicitor should consider the following points:

5.7:1   *Giving time.* If a creditor 'gives time' to the debtor in a binding manner, this will serve to release the guarantor.[2] The guarantee should, therefore, be expressed to apply notwithstanding any time or indulgence granted by the landlord to the tenant, or neglect or forbearance on the part of the landlord in enforcing the payment of rent and the other covenants in the lease.[3]

5.7:2   *Variations.* Any variation of the terms of the contract between the creditor and the debtor will discharge the guarantor,[4] unless the guarantor consents,[5] although it has been suggested[6] that an immaterial variation (and one that was not prejudicial to the guarantor) might not release it. No properly advised guarantor should accept a provision by which the guarantee would be expressed to continue 'notwithstanding that the terms of the Lease may have been varied by agreement between the Landlord and the Tenant', but on the other hand it seems unfair on the landlord for the guarantor to escape his liability merely because a minor change has been agreed between the landlord and the tenant. A provision that the guarantee shall continue to apply notwithstanding an immaterial variation not prejudicial to the guarantor seems a fair compromise.[7]

5.7:3   *Acceptance of lease of residue of term.* A disclaimer of a lease by the original tenant's trustee in bankruptcy or liquidator releases the guarantor as from the date of the disclaimer[8] and as such the guarantor's covenant should require the guarantor, in the event of such disclaimer, to accept a lease of the premises for the residue of the term which would have remained had there been no disclaimer.[9]

5.7:4   *Statutory continuation.* In the absence of wording to the contrary, a guarantee does not extend to a period after the expiry of the term of the lease where the tenant remains in occupation under a statutory continuation of the tenancy.[10] If the term is not defined elsewhere in the lease in a way that covers such a continuation, the point should be dealt with specifically in the guarantor's covenant.[11]

5.7:5   *Replacement guarantor.* A corporate guarantor may go into liquidation or have a receiver appointed, and an individual guarantor may become bankrupt or die.[12] Therefore, the lease may either provide that a right of re-entry arises on any of these eventualities occurring,[13] or impose on the tenant the requirement of finding a replacement guarantor, reasonably acceptable to the landlord, within a specified time.[14] The former would not preclude the latter because the tenant, in claiming relief against forfeiture,[15] would be able to argue that another acceptable guarantor was available, if that was indeed so. In the case of the latter, the landlord would be able to seek forfeiture for breach of covenant if no acceptable guarantor was produced, although at least this alternative does give the tenant time in which to find a replacement. Again the tenant would be able to seek relief,[15] perhaps claiming that the landlord had been unreasonable in rejecting a candidate put forward by the tenant.

5.7:6   *Take reasonable steps against the tenant.* The landlord ought to take reasonable steps against the tenant if he fails to observe or perform the provisions of the lease, and a landlord who acts in a desultory way vis-a-vis the tenant, and then seeks to recover from the guarantors could be in difficulties. This is in view of the decision in *Standard Chartered Bank Ltd v Walker*[16] in which the Court of Appeal held that a mortgagee or receiver exercising a power of sale owed a duty to both the mortgagor *and any guarantor of the loan in question* to obtain the best reasonable price. If the courts are prepared to extend this principle, any creditor (such as a landlord) could be held to owe a duty to the guarantor to take reasonable care and exercise reasonable skill in enforcing against the principal debtor (ie the tenant) the liability in respect of which the guarantee is given.[17]

1   *Bacon v Chesney* (1816) 1 Stark 192; *Stamford Spalding and Boston Banking Co v Ball* (1862) 4 De GF & J 310; *Blest v Brown* (1862) 8 Giff 450; affd 4 De GF & J 367; *Eastern Counties Building Society v Russell* [1947] 1 All ER 500; *Associated Dairies Ltd v Pierce* (1982) 265 Estates Gazette 127, CA; *Pinemain Ltd v Welbeck International Ltd* (1984) 272 Estates Gazette 1166. *Capital and City Holdings Ltd v Dean Warburg Ltd* [1989] 1 EGLR 90, [1989] 25 EG 97, CA.

2   See *Swire v Redman* (1876) 1 QBD 536; *Holme v Brunskill* (1877) 3 QBD 495, CA; *Selous Street Properties Ltd v Oronel Fabrics Ltd* (1984) 270 Estates Gazette 643; and 20 Halsbury's Laws (4th edn) paras 258, 259. See 22 Encyclopaedia of Forms and Precedents (5th edn) Form 79.

3   It has been suggested that a landlord who refuses to accept rent so as not to waive a breach of covenant by the tenant (see para 12.5 below) would not be protected by such wording. This is unresolved but to avoid any doubt the point should be expressly dealt with: see for example Rosscastle Letting Conditions (Appendix 1, Form No 1 below) Condition 5.2:2. It would appear that any provision in a guarantor's covenant that purported to exonerate the landlord from the consequences of its own negligence would have to satisfy the reasonableness test of the Unfair Contract Terms Act 1977: see para 11.16 below.

4   *Holme v Brunskill* (1877) 3 QBD 495, CA: see 20 Halsbury's Laws (4th edn) para 259.

5   See 20 Halsbury's Laws (4th edn) para 258.

6   See the dissenting judgment of Brett LJ in *Holme v Brunskill* (1877) 3 QBD 495 at 508, CA.

7   In the light of *Holme v Brunskill* (1877) 3 QBD 495, CA the point of the surrender of part of the premises should be dealt with expressly: see for example Rosscastle Letting Conditions (Appendix 1, Form No 1 below) Condition 5.2:4. An alternative approach might be to require the landlord to give notice to the guarantor of a proposed variation and to provide that the variation will be binding on the guarantor unless he objects within a certain period.

8   *Stacey v Hill* [1901] 1 KB 660, CA; *Re Katherine et Cie Ltd* [1932] 1 Ch 70 at 73; 20 Halsbury's Laws (4th edn) para 287.

9   See for example Rosscastle Letting Conditions (Appendix 1, Form No 1 below) Condition 5.1:3.2. Leases often include a provision that the guarantee will continue to apply

'notwithstanding the fact that the Tenant may have ceased to exist'. If the principal debtor/tenant has ceased to exist, it cannot have any liability to the creditor/landlord. As a guarantor's liability is co-extensive with that of the principal debtor, it would appear that the guarantor would also have no liability where the tenant ceases to exist, and as such the provision is meaningless. The landlord is protected (1) where the tenant is an individual by the general law to the effect that on the death or bankruptcy of the tenant, the leasehold interest vests in his personal representatives or trustee in bankruptcy respectively ie the tenant as defined in the lease does not cease to exist and (2) where the tenant is an individual or a corporation by the express provision in the guarantor's covenant requiring the guarantor to take a lease of the premises on any disclaimer following the bankruptcy or liquidation of the tenant.

10 Ie under the Landlord and Tenant Act 1954, s 24 (23 Halsbury's Statutes (4th edn) LANDLORD AND TENANT). See *Junction Estates Ltd v Cope* (1974) 27 P & CR 482 followed in *A Plesser & Co Ltd v Davis* (1983) 267 Estates Gazette 1039.

11 See for example 22 Encyclopaedia of Forms and Precedents (5th edn) eg Form 22 clause 3.6. For an alternative approach, see Rosscastle Letting Conditions (Appendix 1, Form 1 below) Condition 10.8.

12 In the absence of a provision to the contrary, the death of the guarantor does not terminate a continuing guarantee (*Lloyd's v Harper* (1880) 16 Ch D 290, CA) and therefore the guarantor's personal representatives would be liable under the guarantee but only to the extent of the assets in their hands (*Wentworth v Cock* (1839) 10 Ad & El 42; *Ahmed Angullia Bin Hadjee Mohamed Salleh Angullia v Estate and Trust Agencies (1927) Ltd* [1938] AC 624, [1938] 3 All ER 106, PC). The guarantor may also become a patient within the meaning of the Mental Health Act 1983. As to the death of the guarantor see 20 Halsbury's Laws (4th edn) para 301.

13 Where the lease gives the landlord the right to re-enter on the bankruptcy of the guarantor, this is a 'breach of condition' within the Law of Property Act 1925 s 146(1) (37 Halsbury's Statutes (4th edn) REAL PROPERTY) and as such the landlord must serve notice under ibid s 146 before exercising its right of re-entry. It is nevertheless an irremediable breach: see *Halliard Property Co Ltd v Jack Segal Ltd* [1978] 1 All ER 1219, [1978] 1 WLR 377.

14 See Rosscastle Letting Conditions (Appendix 1, Form 1 below) Condition 3.21. No express reference is needed in this case in the proviso for re-entry.

15 See para 12.2 below.

16 [1982] 3 All ER 938, [1982] 1 WLR 1410, CA, overruling *Barclays Bank Ltd v Thienel and Thienel* (1978) 122 Sol Jo 472 and *Latchford v Beirne* [1981] 3 All ER 705.

17 The Landlord's solicitor could expressly provide that the guarantee would continue to apply 'notwithstanding any failure by the Landlord to take reasonable care or exercise reasonable skill in the enforcement of the terms hereof against the Tenant'. This is hardly an 'attractive' provision which may in any event have to be read subject to the reasonableness test of the Unfair Contract Terms Act 1977 – see para 11.16 below.

5.8 *Drafting matters.* There are two matters that relate to guarantors who may come into being during the course of the lease that should be considered:

5.8:1 *Directors and others.* Leases often provide that, where there is an underletting or assignment to a private limited company, its directors may be required to enter into direct covenants of guarantee with the landlord.[1] This limitation seems unnecessarily restrictive on the tenant who would wish to be free to provide some other reasonably suitable guarantor(s). It would, for example, often be inappropriate for the directors of a subsidiary company to be called on to guarantee the company's obligations, although it seems unlikely that any landlord's refusal to grant consent could be reasonable where the parent company was willing to provide a guarantee, even if the lease specified only directors.[2]

5.8:2 *Form of guarantee.* Such a clause also leaves unresolved the exact form of the covenant of guarantee that these 'new' guarantors can be required to enter into.[3] To avoid such uncertainty, the lease, where the guarantor is being made a party, should specify that the covenant from the guarantor of an assignee or undertenant will be in the form of the guarantor's covenant in the lease.[2] Where there is no such covenant in the lease, a model form should be set out,[4] and the covenant should require the 'new' guarantor to enter into a deed in that form.

1 Where there is no express provision for an assignee to be guaranteed, whether or not guarantors can be required by the landlord is a question of reasonableness where the Landlord and Tenant Act 1927 s 19(1) (23 Halsbury's Statutes (4th edn) LANDLORD AND TENANT) applies. The landlord was held to have been unreasonable in *Re Greater London Properties Ltd's Lease, Taylor Bros (Grocers) Ltd v Covent Garden Properties Co Ltd* [1959] 1 All ER 728, [1959] 1 WLR 503.
2 See for example Rosscastle Letting Conditions (Appendix 1, Form 1 below) Condition 3.7:5.
3 Eg is the guarantee to apply for the residue of the term of the lease, notwithstanding a subsequent assignment or only while the lease is vested in the assignee in question, and can the guarantors be compelled to agree to a provision requiring them to accept a lease on the bankruptcy or liquidation of the assignee?
4 See for example 22 Encyclopaedia of Forms and Precedents (5th edn) Form 244.

5.9 *The guarantor's liability.* A guarantor who has accepted a standard guarantor's covenant[1] is in a most undesirable position[2] because his guarantee:

(a) cannot be revoked or withdrawn;
(b) will apply throughout the term of the lease, not merely in respect of the original tenant with whom the guarantor presumably has some connection, and so the guarantor[3] may be agreeing to guarantee the performance of future, and as yet unknown, parties;
(c) will apply not only to the rent as reserved, but where the lease provides for the rent to be reviewed, to the reviewed rent,[4] but the guarantor will be unable to play any part in the operating of the rent review provision;[5] and
(d) will impose no obligation on the landlord to keep him informed as breaches occur and so the guarantor has no opportunity of exercising control over the tenant – thus a minor breach may have deteriorated into something altogether more serious before the guarantor becomes aware of the problem, and even then there will be no action that he (as opposed to the landlord) will be able to take against the guarantor.[6]

1 See for example Rosscastle Letting Conditions (Appendix 1, Form 1 below) Condition 5.
2 See eg *Torminster Properties Ltd v Green* [1983] 2 All ER 457, [1983] 1 WLR 676, CA; *Associated Dairies Ltd v Pierce* (1982) 265 Estates Gazette 127, CA.
3 Ie unless released by the landlord: see 22 Encyclopaedia of Forms and Precedents (5th edn) Form 238.
4 Ie unless the lease provides otherwise.
5 See para 5.10:5 below.
6 Ie unless the guarantor and the tenant have entered into a separate deed.

5.10 *Advising the guarantor.* The final form of any lease of business premises depends on the relative bargaining positions of the parties. Where the landlord is able to insist upon a standard covenant, the guarantor must carefully weigh up its potential exposure under the proposed covenant against the need of the tenant (with whom he is presumably connected) for the premises.[1] The guarantor should argue for the following amendments:

5.10:1 *Limitation in time.* The guarantee should be expressed to apply only while the lease is vested in the tenant.[2] Should this be rejected by the landlord, the guarantor should seek a provision permitting the substitution of a new guarantor of equal status.[3]

5.10:2 *Copies of notices.* The lease should contain a covenant by the landlord to provide the guarantor with a copy of all notices served by the landlord on the tenant. The drafting should be wide enough to cover any 'informal notices', for example, any communications from the landlord drawing the tenant's attention to a breach of covenant.

5.10:3 *Late payment of rent.* The lease should contain an obligation on the landlord to inform the guarantor if the tenant is persistently late in paying rent.

5.10:4 *Enforcement of covenants.* The lease should contain a covenant by the landlord to enforce the landlord's covenants against the tenant and perhaps to have regard to any representations made by the guarantor.[4]

5.10:5 *Participation in rent review.* The lease should contain the facility for the guarantor to participate in the rent review. Detailed provisions would need to be included which provide for the guarantor to be alerted when the process of review commences, and give the guarantor the right to be involved in the negotiations with the landlord's surveyor and, when appropriate, the determination of the rent by a third party. It is unlikely that landlords would accept the involvement of guarantors in the rent review process, unless the property market dramatically changes, but to give the guarantor at least some protection by allowing him to conduct the rent review negotiations, it has been suggested[5] that the tenant should appoint the guarantor as his attorney for the operation of the rent review clause. This raises two problems:
(a) it would probably be necessary to link this with an undertaking by the tenant to take no part himself in the review; and
(b) where the guarantee was expressed to apply throughout the term of the lease, there would have to be a provision dealing with assignments, because the original tenant could hardly purport to appoint an attorney on behalf of its assigns.[6]

5.10:6 *Assignments to the guarantor.* The lease should contain a provision for the tenant to be compelled to assign the lease to the guarantor in the event of default.[7] This gives the guarantor the facility to limit his liability, especially where there is a demand for the premises, permitting the guarantor to complete the assignment himself and then (subject to the landlord's consent as to the proposed assignee) dispose of the lease. A guarantor cannot apply for relief against forfeiture,[8] at least unless the tenant has agreed to execute a mortgage of the lease in favour of the guarantor.[9] A provision requiring assignment to the guarantor will overcome this problem, the assignment giving the guarantor the status he needs to seek such relief, and thus thwarting the landlord's efforts to regain possession, while vesting what could be a valuable asset in the guarantor.

5.10:7 *Indemnity.* Having paid sums to the landlord pursuant to his guarantee, the guarantor will normally have an implied right of indemnity against the tenant, even where no express provisions are made. As with most implied terms, there could be technical difficulties[10] and the guarantor would be well advised to enter a separate deed with the tenant setting out his rights should the guarantee ever be enforced, and dealing in detail with matters such as costs and interest. Such a deed could also grant the guarantor certain rights where the tenant is in breach, for example, to enter the premises after notice and carry out repairs that the tenant has refused to do, the cost of which is to be reimbursed by the tenant.[11] The guarantor should seek a covenant from the landlord to co-operate with the guarantor when the guarantor enforces his rights against the tenant. Where there is to be a guarantor, the tenant should avoid a proviso for re-entry that is expressed to be exercisable on the bankruptcy, liquidation or death of a guarantor.[12] As the guarantee will apply throughout the term to breaches by future assignees, the guarantor might contemplate a provision requiring the guarantor's consent for an assignment, such consent not to be unreasonably refused.

1   It is submitted that the guarantor should be represented separately from the tenant.
2   The original tenant will remain liable to the landlord for breaches after it has parted with the lease: see paras 5.14–5.16 below. Thus the only absolute release for the initial guarantor would be to provide that the guarantee applies only to breaches actually committed by the named initial tenant.
3   See Encyclopaedia of Forms and Precedents (5th edn) Forms 238, 239.
4   A similar obligation may be implied (see para 5.7:6) but the tenant should seek to put the matter beyond doubt by proposing an express covenant.
5   See (1980) LS Gaz 787.
6   See Clarke and Adams *Rent Reviews and Variable Rents* (2nd edn, 1984) p 172.
7   See Encyclopaedia of Forms and Precedents (5th edn) Form 234.
8   See the Common Law Procedure Act 1852, s 210 (23 Halsbury's Statutes (4th edn) LANDLORD AND TENANT); the Law of Property Act 1925, s 146(2), (4), (5) (37 Halsbury's Statutes (4th edn) REAL PROPERTY).
9   *Egerton v Jones* [1939] 2 KB 702, [1939] 3 All ER 889, CA; *Re Good's Lease, Good v Wood* [1954] 1 All ER 275, [1954] 1 WLR 309.
10   It seems unlikely that any problem would arise in a landlord/tenant/guarantor situation, but for examples of difficulties that have arisen in relation to the implied right of indemnity in guarantees generally see Putnam *Suretyship* (1981) Ch 6. On paying the debt, a guarantor is entitled to be subrogated to those rights which the creditor has against the debtor but as to distress see *Selous Street Properties Ltd v Oronel Fabrics Ltd* (1984) 270 Estates Gazette 643 where the question was left open.
11   The drafting could be based on Encyclopaedia of Forms and Precedents (5th edn) Form 235.
12   See para 5.7:5 above.

5.11 *Advice to a purchaser of the reversion.* When acquiring the reversion to a lease that contains a guarantor's covenant, the purchaser would still be wise to obtain an express assignment of the benefit of the covenant.[1] There were indications that this was essential if the guarantor was still to be bound[2] but in *P & A Swift Investments v Combined English Stores Group plc*[3] the House of Lords held that a claim to enforce a guarantor's covenant, can, where there is no express assignment, be based upon the common law rule that the assignee has the legal estate and the covenant 'touched and concerned'[4] the land. Thus the guarantor's covenant will generally run with the reversion and will not have to be expressly assigned.

1   And thereby avoid any arguments as to whether the covenant in question falls within the criteria set out in footnote 4 below. See 22 Encyclopaedia of Forms and Precedents (5th edn) Forms 255 and 261.
2   *Pinemain v Welbeck International Ltd* (1984) 272 Estates Gazette 1166; *Re Distributors and Warehousing Ltd* [1986] 1 EGLR 90, 278 Estates Gazette 1363.
3   [1988] 2 All ER 885, [1988] 3 WLR 313. *Kumar v Dunning* [1989] QB 193, [1987] 2 All ER 801, CA was approved. In *Coronation Street Industrial Properties Ltd v Ingall Industries plc* [1989] 1 All ER 979, [1989] 1 WLR 304 the House of Lords held that a covenant by a guarantor to accept a lease replacing the leased disclaimed on behalf of an insolvent tenant (see Rosscastle Letting

Conditions, Appendix 1, Form No 1 below, Condition 5.1:3) touched and concerned the demised premises so that the benefit of the covenant ran with the reversion and did not have to be expressly assigned.

4   The House of Lords held that a covenant touched and concerned land (a) where it benefited only the reversioner for the time being; (b) the covenant affected the nature, quality, mode or user or value of the reversioner's land; (c) the covenant was not expressed as personal; and (d) a covenant to pay money would still touch and concern land so long as the three foregoing conditions were satisfied and the covenant was connected with something to be done on, to or in relation to the land.

5.12   *Insure against tenant default.* The landlord ought to consider other ways in which he might obtain protection against the tenant's failings, apart from requiring a third party to join in the lease as guarantor. The insurance market provides policies known as Tenant Default Indemnities that seek to compensate a landlord of business premises upon the insolvency of the tenant.[1] The tenant applies for the policy that is issued in favour of the landlord. The policies cover some or all of the types of loss that the landlord may suffer such as loss of rent until a new lease is granted, certain legal expenses and the cost of dilapidatons. The details of the policies vary according to market conditions. These policies have certain disadvantages when compared with a conventional guarantor – for example:

(a)   like all policies of insurance, the duration is short – generally one or two years, although apparently in exceptional cases a policy can be for as long as five years. Thus the landlord will not always be able to ensure at the time of the letting that the tenant's liability is guaranteed throughout the term. True, it will generally prove possible to renew the policy but on terms to be agreed at that time. If by then the financial standing of the tenant has decreased, the insurers would no doubt insist upon an increased premium, or in extreme cases, even decline to renew the policy;[2]

(b)   the 'indemnity' is subject to the financial limit set out in the policy, which will have been based upon the annual rent and other sums for which the tenant is responsible. Thus, where the insolvent tenant is, for example, in breach of the repairing covenant, the sum recovered from the insurers may not extend to the cost of remedying the dilapidations. Further, the landlord could be in difficulties if the rent was reviewed during the duration of the policy;[2]

(c)   the question arises of who is ultimately to be responsible for the payment of the premium, that will generally be between 1% and 3% of the total annual rental and other charges payable by the tenant to the landlord. If the landlord does so, in effect out of the rent, he has to recognise that this 'protection' means that he is not receiving the full market rent, while a tenant called upon to pay (either directly or via a service charge) will, on the face of it, be paying 'over the odds' for the property;

(d)   payment will generally only be made when the tenant is bankrupt or in liquidation, or a receiver has been appointed. Thus if no other creditor of the tenant has taken such action, the landlord would himself have to put the tenant into bankruptcy or liquidation. This would not be the case where the tenant's obligations were guaranteed in the usual way.[3]

1   The author is indebted to Willis Wrightson South Ltd for information provided on these policies but the comments are entirely his. See also (1983) 4 PLB 37.
2   Nevertheless, one does have to concede in relation to points (a) and (b) that the mere fact that the original tenant's obligations under a lease are guaranteed by a third party does not mean that the landlord has thereby eliminated all risk. Times, and guarantor's financial states, change and when many years after the commencement of the letting the landlord seeks to

enforce the guarantor's covenant, he may find that the guarantor has ceased to exist, or is unable to meet the claim. At least this type of insurance provides virtually 'absolute' protection, be it only in the short term.

3 But this could be the case anyway: see para 5.7:6 above.

5.13 *Bank guarantee.* An attractive thought, so far as the landlord is concerned, is that the tenant's bank might guarantee their customer's liabilities under the lease. The author understands, however, that a clearing bank would never enter into a lease as a conventional guarantor, and generally will give no other form of guarantee for a customer's liabilities as a tenant. In some cases however a bank may be prepared to provide a guarantee by means of a separate deed but this would only be in respect of the liabilities of the customer while he or she remained a tenant in possession of the property. The bank would require that in the event of any assignment by its customer its guarantee would automatically cease. Further, banks will only provide a guarantee covering a relatively short period and subject to an overall maximum figure. Thus a clearing bank can sometimes offer assistance but there will be shortcomings not present in a conventional guarantee ... although the credit worthiness of the guarantor could not be bettered!

D ORIGINAL TENANT AS GUARANTOR

5.14 *Original tenant as quasi-guarantor.* By privity of contract, the original tenant[1] remains liable to the landlord[2] for any breach of the tenant's obligations[3] contained in the lease,[4] notwithstanding the fact that the tenant may have assigned the lease.[5] The original tenant will no doubt have obtained an express or implied[6] covenant of indemnity in respect of a breach committed at any time[7] after it has assigned the lease[8] but this will be of no assistance to it if the assignee is insolvent.[9] Therefore the original tenant will have many of the concerns of a guarantor.[10] Similarly, the original landlord remains liable to the tenant after he has parted with the reversion.[11]

1 *Baynton v Morgan* (1888) 22 QBD 74, CA; *Thames Manufacturing Co Ltd v Perrotts (Nichol & Peyton) Ltd* (1984) 271 Estates Gazette 284. See for example *Weaver v Mogford* [1988] 2 EGLR 48, [1988] 31 EG 49, CA. It follows that the original tenant's guarantor (where there was one) will also be liable: see *Selous Street Properties Ltd v Oronel Fabrics Ltd* (1984) 270 Estates Gazette 643.

2 Ie the landlord for the time being: see the Law of Property Act 1925 s 141 (37 Halsbury's Statutes (4th edn) REAL PROPERTY); *Re King, Robinson v Gray* [1963] Ch 459, [1963] 1 All ER 781, CA; *Arlesford Trading Co Ltd v Servansingh* [1971] 3 All ER 113, [1971] 1 WLR 1080, CA.

3 The liability remains even if the original tenant has not covenanted on behalf of itself and its successors in title: see the Law of Property Act 1925, s 79.

4 The liability remains notwithstanding the death of the original tenant: see para 5.7 note 12 above. Furthermore, where an assignee goes bankrupt and his trustee in bankruptcy disclaims the lease, the original tenant will remain liable for rent accruing after the disclaimer: *Warnford Investments Ltd v Duckworth* [1979] Ch 127, [1978] 2 All ER 517. If the lease is extended, the original tenant's liability will continue: see *Baker v Merckel* [1960] 1 QB 657, [1960] 1 All ER 668, CA. It will not apply where the lease is renewed. As to the court's powers to require guarantors on a lease being renewed under the 1954 Act, see para 14.61 below.

5 The liability remains notwithstanding any variation of the terms of the lease: see para 5.5:1 above. As to the date from which interest is payable under the Supreme Court Act 1981 on sum payable by original tenant following an assignee's default, see *Allied London Investments Ltd v Hambro Life Assurance Ltd* [1985] 1 EGLR 45, 274 Estates Gazette 48, CA.

6 Ie implied by the Law of Property Act 1925, s 77 and the Land Registration Act 1925, s 24 (37 Halsbury's Statutes (4th edn) REAL PROPERTY).

7 The indemnity should apply to breaches occurring at any time during the remainder of the term which will include breaches by the immediate assignee or any subsequent assignee. The original assignee will, in effect, be giving to the original tenant a guarantee (in the form of an indemnity) against breaches by subsequent assignees and as such the original assigneee may be tempted to try and limit its liability to breaches occurring while it is the tenant. By privity of estate, an assignee will be liable to the landlord only for breaches of covenant that occur while it holds the lease (*Valliant v Dodemede* (1742) 2 Atk 546) but landlords seek to obtain direct covenants from each assignee to observe the provisions of the lease during the remainder of the term (see Form 22 clause 5.9:4 post). As Asquith J pointed out in *J Lyons & Co Ltd v Knowles* as reported in [1942] 2 All ER 393 at 396, after an assignment there are always two persons liable to be sued for rent, the original tenant who is liable by privity of contract and the assignee who is liable by privity of estate, but by taking the precaution of obtaining direct covenants from assignees (and undertenants) the number of such persons can be increased almost indefinitely.

8 On an assignment there will usually be an indemnity in respect of future breaches given by the assignee to the assignor: see note 7 above. The original tenant could be in difficulties where the immediate assignee has ceased to exist and the default is by a subsequent assignee. There is an implied indemnity on the part of each successive assignee to indemnify the original tenant at least in the case of the current assignee: *Moule v Garrett* (1872) LR 7 Exch 101; *Duncan, Fox & Co v North and South Wales Bank* (1880) 6 App Cas 1, HL. The original tenant may not be able, however, to recover from an intermediate assignee unless there has been an express assignment to the original tenant of the benefit of the intermediate assignee's guarantee.

9 See eg *Selous Street Properties Ltd v Oronel Fabrics Ltd* (1984) 270 Estates Gazette 643; *Thames Manufacturing Co Ltd v Perrotts (Nichol & Peyton) Ltd* (1984) 271 Estates Gazette 284. See also *Weaver v Mogford* [1988] 2 EGLR 48, [1988] 31 EG 49, CA; *Becton Dickinson UK Ltd v Zwebner* [1989] QB 208, [1989] 1 EGLR 71.

10 See para 5.9 above.

11 This is likely to be of less practical significance but note 22 Encyclopaedia of Forms and Precedents (5th edn) Form 243.

5.15 *Tenant's proposals.* There are a number of proposals that the tenant should consider advancing:

5.15:1 *Absolute release.* As the principle stems from contract, it follows that it applies unless the parties agree otherwise. There is nothing to prevent the lease from providing that the liability of the tenant to observe and perform the covenants and conditions shall cease on any assignment. Tenants would argue that this is entirely fair and reasonable because, as the consent of the landlord will be required before the assignment can be made, the landlord has the opportunity to evaluate the assignee, and if the assignee subsequently defaults, the landlord bears as much responsibility as the assignor. Even if there might possibly be some justification for the tenant remaining liable for breaches by its immediate assignee, it is difficult, however, to see why it should also be liable for the acts and omissions of a subsequent assignee of whom the tenant has no knowledge, but who once again has been approved by the landlord.

5.15:2 *Qualified release.* Here the lease provides for the original tenant to be released on an assignment but only when the assignee is of comparable or better financial standing. The lease can provide either for release with the landlord's consent, such consent not to be unreasonably refused, for example, where the assignee's financial standing is comparable with or better than that of the tenant or for a specific provision which sets out certain criteria which, if met by the assignee, will cause the tenant to be released.[1]

5.15:3 *Insurance.* If the tenant cannot obtain an absolute or qualified release, he should consider insuring against liability following an assignment.[2]

5.15:4 *Covenant by the landlord to enforce covenants against assignees.* An original tenant is entitled to feel aggrieved if his liability arises only as a result of poor estate management by the landlord, for example, by allowing considerable arrears of rent to accrue or permitting minor wants of repair to become serious, before taking any action against the tenant. In fact, a duty may be imposed on the landlord to take reasonable care and exercise reasonable skill in enforcing the covenant against the current tenant,[3] but to avoid any uncertainty the original tenant should consider proposing that the landlord should give in the lease an express covenant to this effect.

5.15:5 *Avoiding the situation.* The problem can arise only where the lease has been assigned and it is suggested that in most cases where an original tenant does incur such liability, there have been further assignments. A short term must lessen the likelihood of numerous assignments,[4] while the insertion of a break clause would be an added protection enabling the tenant to determine the lease rather than assign it. Where none of these is included in a lease, a tenant wishing to dispose of the premises should perhaps consider underletting rather than assigning, because then it would at least retain control[5] over the occupier of the premises and itself be able to exercise all the landlord's remedies against the occupier in the event of default by him.[6] Where an underlease would not be acceptable, the original tenant should consider inserting in the assignment rights of entry and provisions that would enable the original tenant to require compliance with the terms of the lease and/or making use of the opportunity contained in the Law of Property Act 1925[7] to require that the premises are charged with the payment of all sums that may be payble under an indemnity covenant. The original tenant would then acquire the remedies of a mortgagee.[8]

1 See 22 Encyclopaedia of Forms and Precedents (5th edn) Form 239.
2 See (1986) 277 Estates Gazette 944.
3 See *Tucker v Linger* (1882) 21 Ch D 18 at 24; affd (1883) 8 App Cas 508, HL.
4 Yet the tenant will in consequence expose itself to a risk which may be of greater concern ie the tenant's application for a new tenancy on the expiry of the short lease being successfully resisted by the landlord under the Landlord and Tenant Act 1954, s 30(1) (23 Halsbury's Statutes (4th edn) LANDLORD AND TENANT). The tenant should consider seeking an option to renew. See 22 Encyclopaedia of Forms and Precedents (5th edn) Form 83.
5 The lack of control which the original tenant can exercise over the current assignee is one of the very real concerns of the concept of such continuing liability, because it will only be when the original tenant makes a payment to the landlord that it will have any rights to enforce either by virtue of the indemnities (see Paragraph 115 notes 7, 8 ante) or by subrogation (see *Duncan, Fox & Co v North and South Wales Bank* (1880) 6 App Cas 1, HL; *Selous Street Properties Ltd v Oronel Fabrics Ltd* (1984) 270 Estates Gazette 643 where the question of whether or not the original tenant is subrogated to the landlord's right of distress was left open).
6 This view was advanced by Harman J in *Centrovincial Estates plc v Bulk Storage Ltd* (1983) 268 Estates Gazette 59 at 60.
7 Ie the Law of Property Act 1925, s 77(7) (37 Halsbury's Statutes (4th edn) REAL PROPERTY).
8 Ie sale, possession, foreclosure and the appointment of a receiver.

5.16 *The Law Commission's views.* The Law Commission has recommended that the responsibilities of both the landlord and the tenant under the lease should generally end as soon as they dispose of the property.[1] So, when a tenant assigns, he would be released from any further liability under the lease except (as would nearly always be the case where a business letting is involved) where the lease contains a covenant against assignment, when the landlord could:

(a) at his discretion, if the covenant is absolute,[2] or

(b) if it is reasonable to do so, if the covenant is qualified[2]

require the tenant to guarantee the performance of the covenants by his immediate successor.[3] When a tenant's obligations cease, his guarantor would similarly be released. Landlords, it is suggested, should be treated similarly, and should be able to obtain release from their covenants on an assignment of the reversion, where this would be reasonable.[4]

1   Landlord and Tenant Law – Privity of Contract and Estate [1988] Law Comm No 174. A draft bill is annexed. The report was prepared in the light of the responses to the Law Commission's working paper (Landlord and Tenant – privity of contract and estate [1986] LCWP No 95). The general reaction to the working paper convinced the Law Commission that reform of the continuing liability law was needed. They discovered some alarming cases – an original tenant who transferred an office lease a year after it was granted had to pay £48,000 rent arrears run up by a later tenant; after tenants had improved their offices, the rent was revised and they failed to pay it – the original tenant had to pay £110,000 arrears, partly based on improvements he knew nothing about and had had no benefit from; in another case a tenant had paid £300,000 and a further company paid a total of £500,000 over recent years. For further discussion, see 'Continuing Liability of Original Tenants' (1989) 139 NLJ 51.
2   As to absolute and qualified, see paras 7.4 & 7.5 below.
3   Ie but not beyond that.
4   Contracting out would be prohibited. The Bill does not provide an immediate release for all those tenants who have already assigned if it is enacted. On the first assignment after the Act came into force, however, the assignor would have the possibility of release referred to in the Bill and his predecessors in title would be automatically released.

E   RECITALS

5.17   *Rarely required.* A recital in a deed will estop the parties to that deed, and the parties claiming through them, from showing that a statement contained in a recital is incorrect. In addition, s 45(6) of the Law of Property Act 1925 provides that recitals, statements and descriptions of facts in documents 20 years old must be taken as sufficient evidence as truth of the facts, unless and except in so far as they may be proved to be inaccurate. Recitals do not control the operative part of the document.[1] There are two types of recitals – narrative, that relate past history and introductory, that indicate the purpose of the deed. Recitals are not generally included in a lease but where the lease is entered into pursuant to an agreement, this fact should be recited.[2] If the lease was to be the subject of litigation, this recital would alert the parties to the fact there had been an agreement prior to the exchange of the lease and counterpart. This could be relevant because the contract may contain terms that had not merged, and that could still therefore be enforced. The general rule is that the terms of the contract will be merged in the lease, and so usually the rights of the parties will depend solely upon the lease, and neither of them will be able to rely upon a term of the contract. The rule, however, only applies to so much of a contract as was intended to be executed by the lease, and to the extent that the contract contains other matters, it will remain in force.[3] There should always be inserted in any agreement for a lease containing terms that the parties do not wish to merge in the lease, a declaration to that effect. Furthermore, it may become relevant at a future date to know *why* the lease was entered into, and recitals as to the intended purpose of the deed may turn out to be of assistance in construing that document at a later date.[4]

1   *Re Moon, ex p Dawes* (1886) 17 QBD 275, CA.
2   There are various choices of format open to the draftsman who has to include recitals in a document that makes considerable use of defined terms. The conflict that he has to resolve is

that terms should not be defined in the recitals and yet one cannot refer to a defined term in a document *before* the definition has appeared. One approach is not to use the defined terms in the recitals and to refer, for example, to 'certain premises that are defined below'. This is somewhat clumsy, especially when several defined terms are used in the recitals. An alternative is to use the defined terms in the same way as in the operative part of the document but to state after the first use of a defined term in the recitals '(all terms with initial capital letters are defined in clause 1)'. This at least alerts the reader to the fact that these terms have a special meaning, and directs him where to find that meaning, but again is not entirely satisfactory because it requires the reader to read the document out of order. Neither approach, in addition, deals with the question of where to insert recitals when the 'Particulars style' of draft is used. The most satisfactory course would seem to be to insert the recitals in the operative part of the document *after* the defined terms, in a clause perhaps headed 'Background'.

3 See *Leggott v Barrett* (1880) 15 Ch D 306, CA; *Greswolde-Williams v Barneby* (1900) 49 WR 203; *Millbourn v Lyons* [1914] 2 Ch 231, CA. See also *Hill v Harris* [1965] 2 QB 601, [1965] 2 All ER 358, CA. As to applicability of the doctrine to registered land, see *Knight Sugar Co v Alberta Rly and Irrigation Co* [1938] 1 All ER 266, PC; *Palmer v Johnson* (1884) 13 QBD 351, CA; *Clarke v Ramuz* [1981] 2 QB 456, CA; *Lawrence v Cassel* [1930] 2 KB 83, CA (building agreement contained in simple contract held not to be merged in the conveyance).

4 An example of general application is the 1927 Act, s 19(1)(b) which will turn upon whether the lease was made 'in consideration wholly or partially of the erection [etc] of buildings'. For another example (not ordinarily likely to be relevant to commercial lettings) see Leasehold Reform Act 1967, s 4(1) proviso.

F THE HABENDUM

5.18 *Function.* The habendum specifies the commencement and duration of the term granted by the lease, and should be quite straightforward for the draftsman. The term may be expressed to commence on any past, present or future date.[1] The tenant's solicitor will need to ensure that the term will in fact be of the duration that was agreed, and not shortened by the use of a retrospective 'commencement date'.[2]

1 For the reasons explained in para 1.5:3 above 'from and including', 'commencing on' or 'beginning on' is preferable to 'from' when referring to the commencement date.

2 For example the parties may have agreed a ten year term. The draft lease submitted in early January may state that the term begins on 25 December. If negotiations take a while, and the lease is not agreed until March, the term will have been reduced by nearly three months if the commencement date remains unchanged. A similar problem occurs in relation to the review dates: see para 6.

5.19 *When rent commences.* Although the term will commence only when the lease is executed,[1] it will often be 'limited' by reference to an earlier date eg a lease made on 1 February may well express the term to be seven years from[2] the previous 25 December.[3] If the term is so defined care must be taken specifically to indicate from which date the rent is to be paid, because presumably in the example given the tenant will only envisage paying rent from 1 February. Unless the draftsman deals with the point, the tenant may find himself paying rent as from the date used to define the length of the term, ie 25 December in the above example.[4] It is suggested that the rent be either expressly reserved 'from and including' a specified date, or that the traditional formula for part payment until the next quarter day be adopted so as to read: 'the first payment being a proportionate sum in respect of the period beginning [date desired that rent commences – perhaps "today" or "on" the Rent Commencement Date] and ending on the day before the next quarter day'[5]

1 *Earl of Cadogan v Guinness* [1936] Ch 515, [1936] 2 All ER 29; *Roberts v Church Comrs for England* [1972] 1 QB 278, [1971] 3 All ER 703. See para 1.7 above.

2   As to 'from', see para 5.20 above and notes 1 and 2 thereto.

3   Where this has occurred, expressions such as 'every fifth year' should not be used in the lease – see note 74 to P1, appendix 1 below.

4   As he did in *Bradshaw v Pawley* [1979] 3 All ER 273, [1980] 1 WLR 10. See also *Beaumont Property Trust v Tai* (1983) 265 Estates Gazette 872 and *East v Pantiles (Plant Hire) Ltd* (1982) 263 Estates Gazette 61. The point is particularly relevant where the lease is being granted as the result of the renewal of a former lease under the provisions of Part II of the 1954 Act, and the term has been expressed to commence from the contractual term date of the old lease, despite any continuation thereof which may have occurred under the 1954 Act, s 64.

5   This wording would have avoided the problem seen in *Bradshaw v Pawley* [1979] 3 All ER 273, [1980] 1 WLR 10.

5.20   *Stamp duty implications.* In deciding the length of the term that he requires, the tenant should not lose sight of the stamp duty implications.[1] The rate of duty depends upon the length of the term,[2] increasing not evenly, but in the form of 'steps' at seven, thirty-five, and one hundred years. A tenant's only period of absolute security of tenure is the term of the lease, as the landlord may, in certain circumstances,[3] be able to oppose the renewal of the lease under Part II of the 1954 Act. Thus a tenant would be unwise to seek a term not exceeding seven years, when a longer one had been offered, purely to save a relatively small amount of stamp duty, although this could be a factor where the tenant is taking premises to meet what he is certain will be a short-term need. Where a long lease is being contemplated, however, the thirty-five and (should it ever be relevant) one hundred year 'landmarks' should not be overlooked by the tenant's advisers. There would need to be, for example, a very good reason for taking a lease a term of thirty-six years!

1   And his other reasons for acquiring the premises. Where the proposed lease is of short duration, the tenant needs to consider (and be advised by his surveyor on) the market for such premises on very short lettings, ie if the tenant no longer required the premises when his lease had say less than two years to run, would there be potential and suitable assignees or underlessees (or might the landlord be prepared to accept a surrender) or would the tenant probably have to retain the premises for the full term and remain liable for rent.

2   For stamp duty, see paras 15.16–15.18.

3   See para 5.21.

4   The 1954 Act, s 30(1).

5.21   *Option may save stamp duty.* No duty is payable on an option to grant a further lease, although of course duty will be payable on the second lease, in the normal way, if the option is exercised. Thus a tenant, uncertain as to how long he will require premises, might seek a lease for a term of five years, with an option for a further lease, also of five years at the 'open market rent' on the date upon which the second lease commences, the option providing for this to be agreed, or fixed by a third party. Thus, assuming the annual rent to be £100,000, he will pay £1,000 stamp duty on the grant of the first lease, and, providing the rates of duty remain the same, another £1,000 if he exercises the option. If he no longer requires the premises after five years, however, he will have 'saved' the extra £1,000 duty that he would have paid had he originally taken a lease of ten years and will have the added advantage of not having to find a purchaser for the residue of the lease. The danger is that if the tenant *does* require the premises for ten years, he might pay *more* stamp duty by adopting this method, because the rates of duty or the rent[1] could have been increased by the time the second lease is granted.

1   If the rent under the new lease is to be the market rent at the time that the new lease is granted, and this exceeds £100,000, the tenant would have lost out by this option rate, because no extra duty would have been payable on a ten-year lease where there was a rent review after five years.

G   THE REDDENDUM

5.22   *Function.* The reddendum fixes the amount of rent and specifies the dates upon which it is to be paid. The amount of rent must be certain, but the actual figures for the whole of the term need not be stated in the lease, provided the rent throughout the term can be ascertained with certainty.[1] The reddundum should cause the draftsman no great problems – he needs to provide clearly and unambiguously the amount of rent, or the means to determine the rent for any period in respect of which the sum is not specified in the lease.[2] Then he should set out the date from which the rent will become payable,[3] the dates upon which the rent is to be paid, the date of the first payment, and the amount of the first payment (or the period which it is to cover) in the event of the initial payment being other than a complete instalment provided for in the lease.[4] Finally the draftsman should provide, if it is so agreed, that the rent should be payable in advance, in the absence of an express provision it will be paid in arrears. Rent falls due on the morning of the day upon which it is payable (including Sundays[5]), but will not be in arrears until midnight[6] except that rent due on a Bank Holiday is not payable until the following day.[7] A reference to 'the usual quarter days'[8] is all that is required when the rent is to be paid on these days – there is no need to set out the dates in full.

1   *Parker v Harris* (1692) 1 Salk 262; *Selby v Greaves* (1868) LR 3 CP 594; *Lloyds Bank Ltd v Marcan* [1973] 3 All ER 754, [1973] 1 WLR 1387, CA; *Re Knight, ex p Voisey* (1882) 21 Ch D 442, CA.
2   For rent reviews see Chapter 6 below.
3   Although this may be set out in the Particulars.
4   See para 5.19 above.
5   *Child v Edwards* [1909] 2 KB 753.
6   *Dibble v Bowater* (1853) 2 E & B 564; *Re Aspinall, Aspinall v Aspinall* [1961] Ch 526, [1961] 2 All ER 751.
7   Banking and Financial Dealings Act 1971, s 1.
8   The usual quarter days are the four feast days – Lady Day (25 March), Midsummer Day (24 June), Michaelmas Day (29 September) and Christmas Day. The old quarter days still occasionally referred to were 12 days later in each case. The Scottish quarter days are Candlemas (2 February), Whitsunday (15 May), Lammas (1 August) and Martinmas (11 November).

Chapter 6

Rent review

A INTRODUCTION

6.1 *The purpose of the clause.*

'A rent review clause is designed to deal with a particular commercial problem, namely that of the tenant who wants security of tenure for a lengthy term, and the landlord who, in times of inflation or a rapidly changing property market, does not want to commit himself to a fixed rent for the whole of that term.'[1]

A rent review clause attempts to resolve this problem by providing for the rent initially reserved by the lease to be reviewed at some time or times during its subsistence. The clause may provide for the rent to be reviewed, for example, by reference to the price of a particular commodity, or to a particular index of prices.[2] It will usually provide, however, for the rent to be reviewed by reference to the property market, normally to market rents, and the most common type of rent review clause provides for the rent to be reviewed by reference to the market rent of the particular property which is the subject of the lease.

1 *MFI Properties Ltd v BICC Group Pension Trust Ltd* [1986] 1 All ER 974 per Hoffmann J at 975. In addition, of course, one must not forget the landlord (particularly the institutional landlord) who is also eager to secure a tenant for a long term in order to guarantee a return on his investment for a minimum period.

2 This chapter deals primarily with the form of rent review clause most commonly found. For alternative methods of review, however, see Section J below.

6.2 *The drafting of the clause.* Although, generally, a particular property has a market value, it does not, without more, have a market rent. What does have a market rent is *a leasehold interest in that property*, the duration, terms and conditions of which are defined.[1] The most common type of rent review clause therefore requires the parties to assume that certain property (usually the property which is the subject of the existing lease) is being let in the open market on a particular date (usually referred to as the review date), on a lease for a specified duration and containing specified terms and conditions (usually bearing some relationship to the duration, and terms and conditions, of the existing lease), and to agree upon the yearly rent which a hypothetical tenant in the market would pay for that lease. If they cannot agree, a third party will determine that rent for them. The lease then usually provides for the rent reserved by the existing lease to be increased to that figure. The draftsman of such a rent review clause will be well advised to work closely with his client's surveyor, and must deal with:

6.2:1 *The implementation of the clause.*[2] The clause must indicate when[3] and how the review is to be implemented. Some rent review clauses provide for a formalistic approach, involving the service of notices and counter-notices by the parties.[4] The draftsman must address his mind to the question of delay – if the implementation of the review is delayed, is it nonetheless to take place? If one or other of the parties delays in a step which is to be taken in implementing the review, should he lose his rights?[5]

6.2:2 *The assumption of a hypothetical letting.*[6] The draftsman must ensure that the parties are required to assume a hypothetical letting[6] and must apply sufficient information about the premises which are to be the subject of the hypothetical letting[7] and the duration[8] and terms of the hypothetical letting,[9] to enable the valuation to take place.

6.2:3 *Other assumptions and disregards.* It must be remembered that on the review date, in reality, the premises will already be let to the tenant and may have been so for some years, and that no new letting is in fact taking place. As a result, it is not sufficient simply to require the parties to assume that certain premises are being let on a particular date for a specified period on certain terms. To enable the hypothetical letting to operate as the parties intend and to prevent injustice to one or other of the parties, it is necessary for them to be required to make other assumptions about the hypothetical letting and the premises which are to be the subject of that letting which will, or may, not in fact be correct on the review date, and also to disregard certain matters which may in fact exist on the review date.[10]

6.2:4 *The valuation.*[11] Having provided for the implementation of the review, having required the parties to assume a hypothetical letting, and having inserted such other assumptions and disregards as are necessary, the draftsman must go on to specify what the parties are to ascertain, and how. Usually they will be asked to ascertain the yearly rent which a hypothetical tenant in the open market would pay under the hypothetical letting, and the way in which the valuation is to be conducted will be left to them, but some clauses adopt other valuation terms,[12] and prescribe the method of valuation to be adopted.[13]

6.2:5 *Third party.* A rent review clause will usually specify what is to happen if the parties are unable to agree on the revised rent, and the most common form of rent review clause will provide for the revised rent to be determined by a third party in the absence of agreement. The draftsman must direct his mind to the capacity of that third party – should he act as an expert or an arbitrator?[14]

6.2:6 *Procedural matters.* The clause must deal with such procedural matters as what is to happen if the revised rent is not determined by the review date, and whether or not the agreement or determination of the revised rent is to be documented.[15]

6.2:7 *Ancillary matters.* Generally, it is in the interests of both landlord and tenant that the rent review clause should be properly and comprehensively drafted, and that it addresses all necessary matters. There are, however, certain ancillary matters about which the landlord is particularly concerned,[16] such as the question of what is to happen if counter-inflation legislation is in force on the review date, or even (if the lease is for a relatively long term) whether or not the rent review clause itself should be reviewed, and others to which the tenant should give consideration,[17] such as whether or not the rent review clause should provide for upwards and downwards review, rather than the traditional upwards-only review.

1 Rent review clauses have come before the courts where this fundamental concept had been overlooked and where the clause provided no guidance as to the duration, terms and conditions of the hypothetical letting – see for example *Sterling Land Office Developments Ltd v Lloyds Bank plc* (1984) 271 Estates Gazette 894 and *Ipswich Town Football Club Co Ltd v Ipswich Borough Council* [1988] 2 EGLR 146, [1988] 32 EG 49. In both cases the reviewed rent was to be the 'market rental' at the review date. As Harman J said: 'Any person practising nowadays in the field of landlord and tenant will at once think of a number of questions as to the meaning of these artless phrases; for example: in what state are the premises assumed to stand – as they in fact are at the date of review, in proper repair, or in some other, and what, state? For what term are the premises assumed to be available – for 21 years or some other term? On what conditions are the premises offered for letting . . . on the "usual" covenants, on the covenants in the Underlease, or on some other, and, if so, what, covenants? The lease offers no express answer to any of these questions' Harman J held on the facts in *Sterling* that the duration and covenants of the hypothetical letting should be as in the actual lease and that, there being no reference to improvements made by the tenant nor to the state of repair, the premises should be valued as they stood.
2 See section B below.
3 See para 6.5 below.
4 See paras 6.13–6.14 below.
5 See paras 6.6–6.16 below.
6 See para 6.17 below.
7 See para 6.18:1 below.
8 See para 6.18:2 below.
9 See para 6.18:3 below.
10 These then are the 'assumptions' and 'disregards' – see sections D, E and F below.
11 See section G below.
12 See para 6.41 below.
13 See para 6.39 below.
14 See section H below.
15 See paras 6.52–55 and 6.58 below.
16 See paras 6.56–57 below.
17 See para 6.59 below.

B IMPLEMENTATION

6.3 *Introduction.* The draftsman should put himself in the position of the parties as they approach the first review. He must ensure that his drafting will leave no uncertainties on the questions that may arise then – for example:
(a) What are the review dates?[1]
(b) How is the review mechanism to be instigated?[2]
(c) If the review date has been allowed to pass with the landlord taking no action to instigate the review, has he lost the right to that review?[3]
(d) Where the clause sets out a formal procedure of notices and counter notices (and perhaps other steps as well[4]) will a failure to comply strictly with the timetable cause the landlord to lose his right to review, or the tenant to lose the right to contest the landlord's proposed rent?[5]

1 See para 6.4 below.
2 See para 6.5 below.
3 See para 6.6–6.16 below.
4 For example, the appointment of the third party: see section H below.
5 See paras 6.13–6.14 below.

6.4 *What are the review dates?* The draftsman's instructions will usually include details of the review dates, and it should be a simple task for him to refer to these instructions and specify the review dates in the lease.[1] It is advisable to avoid expressions like '25th March in every fifth year' because, for example, if the term is expressed to commence on 25 December 1987, but the lease is actually granted on 1 February 1988, it will be unclear which is the first review date – will it be 25 March 1992 or 25 March 1993?[2] The answer is probably the former, but there is no excuse for leaving any uncertainty – the review dates should be expressed to be '25th March in the years . . .'[3] or '25th March in the year . . . and every fifth anniversary of that date'[4] There is one drafting point, and three commercial points which should be considered:

6.4:1 *What is to happen on the review dates?* It is easy for the draftsman to forget that the mere specification of particular dates, or definition of particular dates as 'review dates' or similar, in the rent review clause will not have any magical effect. He has to make it clear in the rent review clause what will happen on those dates. Usually it is intended that, in respect of each review, a date will be specified which is to be both the date on which the premises will be valued for rent review purposes and the date from, or commencing on, which the revised rent will be payable. It is, of course, perfectly possible for different dates to be specified for these two purposes, and this may be required by the parties. The draftsman should, however, ensure that this does not occur inadvertently. There have been a number of cases[5] in which, because of the drafting of the rent review clause, it was either assumed or argued that the valuation date for the purpose of a rent review should not be a fixed date, but the date on which the revised rent was actually ascertained. This may be required by the parties in particular circumstances, but generally, as it could mean that delay would cause the revised rent to be ascertained on the basis of rent current perhaps years after the commencement of the period in respect of which it is payable,[6] it is inadvisable.[7]

6.4:2 *Short initial review period.* The tenant's solicitor ought to ensure that he does not inadvertently allow a retrospective term commencement date to shorten the first review period – for example, a draft lease submitted in July may indicate that the term commences on 24 June and that the review dates are to be anniversaries of that date. If the lease is not completed until early September, but no amendment is made to the term commencement date or review dates, the rent will be first reviewed after a little over four years and nine months rather than the agreed five years.[8]

6.4:3 *Term-end review date.* A business tenancy within the protection of the 1954 Act[9] continues, by virtue of the provisions of that Act[10] beyond the expiry of the term granted by the lease (the 'contractual term'). Under the 1954 Act, the tenancy continues on the same terms and at the same rent, except that the landlord is entitled to apply to the court for the determination of an interim rent to be paid in respect of this period of statutory continuation.[11] Landlords generally do not consider this to be wholly satisfactory. A landlord's entitlement to an interim rent depends upon the service of a statutory notice and the making of an application to the court, and if the landlord should delay, or forget to take the necessary procedural steps, he may not be entitled to an interim rent in respect of part, or indeed the whole, of the period of statutory continuation.[12] In addition and in any event, an interim rent is very seldom actually paid until long after the expiry of the contractual term.[13] Landlords do not consider this to be fair, nor do they consider it fair that the somewhat unusual guidelines which are laid down for the determination of an interim rent[14] result, in their view, in a rent which is 'unrealistic'. These concerns have prompted landlords to attempt to provide in the lease for a rent review to take place at, or near, the expiry of the contractual term. The purpose of this is to ensure that, not only will there be no need for any application to be made for an interim rent, but also that a 'realistic' rent, more quickly agreed or determined without reference to the court, will be payable during the statutory continuation period. Tenants raise three main objections to such a rent review:

(a) Landlords intend it to result in what they consider to be a 'realistic' rent. Usually, they consider this to be a rent similar to that which would have been payable under the new lease,[15] had it been granted on the expiry of the contractual term, with the result that the rent review clause will provide for the review to be conducted on the basis of a hypothetical letting for a fixed term of a particular length. Tenants argue that, if the landlord is obtaining such a 'realistic' rent, it will shift the balance in negotiations on the new lease in favour of the landlord, who will have no incentive to reach agreement on the rent and terms, with the result that the tenant's bargaining position will be adversely affected. They also argue that, if the landlord is receiving such a 'realistic' rent, there will be less to discourage him (when not opposing[16] the grant of a new lease) from attempting to delay ascertainment of the new lease rent, when delay might result in an increase of the new lease rent because it will defer the valuation date and allow in expected helpful comparables,[17] or (when opposing the grant of a new lease) from attempting to defer the hearing until he has established his ground or grounds of opposition[16] under the Act. The tenant's most persuasive argument against such a rent review is, however, that the tenant will be paying rent for something he does not have. At the time of the rent review, all that the tenant will have is the right to a new tenancy which the landlord may, or may not, be opposing. If the rent review is to result in a truly 'realistic' rent, it should *not* be conducted on the basis of a hypothetical letting for a fixed term, but on the basis of a hypothetical letting reflecting the true position. It is questionable to what extent the landlord would consider a revised rent assessed on such a basis to be any more 'realistic' than an interim rent![18]

(b) Tenants also object to the practical disadvantages inherent in the existence of a review date at the end of the contractual term, particularly at a time of rapidly increasing rents. They argue that the landlord could implement the review, bring an interim rent application for hearing some time later, and then bring the main proceedings to hearing some time after that, with the result that the tenant may have the expense and inconvenience of three separate valuations and negotiations, and three separate increases in rent, within a period far shorter than a normal review period.

(c) The third objection raised by tenants is that one of the purposes of an interim rent is to 'cushion' the tenant against a substantial increase in rent on renewal. This view of interim rents has recently been endorsed by the courts.[19]

If it is not intended that any such review should be provided for in the lease, the parties should ensure that it is not incorporated in error. For example if, in the lease, the 'term' is defined as including any continuation of the tenancy created by the lease, and the review dates are expressed to be '24th June 1990 and every fifth anniversary thereof during the term', it is arguable that the rent can be reviewed every five years for so long as that tenancy subsists, both before the expiry of the contractual term and afterwards when the term is being continued by the 1954 Act. In most cases, however, the term will have been defined as including any statutory extension 'where the context so admits', and a tenant might with some justification suggest that the context did not so admit in relation to the review dates, because statute provides an alternative means of determining a rent to be payable in respect of the period of any statutory continuation. If it is intended that the lease should provide for such a review, both the landlord and the tenant should bear in mind that this could have valuation implications, both on the grant of the lease and, if rent reviews are to be conducted on the basis of a hypothetical letting on the same terms as those contained in the lease, on rent review. The way in which it should be incorporated depends very much on the format of rent review clause adopted. It is suggested that the point should be specifically dealt with either by setting out the review dates[20] or by making it plain that the anniversaries extend beyond the expiry of the contractual term.[21]

6.4:4   *Long review period.* Although the market will usually prescribe the frequency of review, it is of course possible for the parties to agree upon any frequency, greater or less than that which is normally found. The parties should, however, bear in mind that, both on the grant of the lease and on rent review, it might be difficult for the valuer to assess the effect which an abnormally long or short review period will have on the rent. In the same way as a lease containing no provision for review will generally command a higher rent,[22] it would seem inevitable that a tenant in the open market will generally pay more for a lease with a longer than normal period before the first review, both on the grant of a lease, and (if, as is normal, the rent review clause incorporates the terms of the actual lease in the hypothetical lease) on rent review.[23] In the case of a lease providing for reviews at twenty-one yearly intervals, for example, it might be common ground at one of the review dates that a new lease granted on that review date would provide for a review of the rent every five years and, accordingly, there would be no comparable transactions to assist in determining the revised rent.[24] It would seem that the valuer would not have the power to direct that a further review should take place after five years, nor to order a revised rent which increased every five years throughout the review period.[25] Indeed, this would be altering the bargain between the parties and might produce a substantially different result, to the benefit of one of the parties and to the detriment of the other. Unless there are special circumstances, therefore, it is advisable for the parties to avoid any such departure from the norm if possible.[26]

1   But this is not always the case – see *Prudential Assurance Co Ltd v Gray* [1987] 2 EGLR 134, 283 Estates Gazette 648; *Parkside Knightsbridge Ltd v German Food Centre Ltd* [1988] 8/2 2 RRLR 131; *Ladbroke Group plc v Bristol City Council* [1988] 1 EGLR 126, [1988] 23 EG 125, CA; *Finger Lickin Chicken Ltd v Ganton House Investments Ltd* [1989] EGCS 99.
2   See para 1.5:4 above.
3   But see para 6.18:3(d) below. If the hypothetical letting on rent review is to be on the same terms as those contained in the actual lease, but for a term longer than the residue of the contractual term of the actual lease, the insertion of specific dates as review dates could have the result of increasing the revised rent on later review dates because the hypothetical lease rent will be constant during the latter part of the hypothetical term, unless it is made clear in

the rent review clause that the hypothetical letting is to include reviews at the relevant intervals throughout the whole term.

4 But see para 6.4:3 below. This could result in the incorporation of reviews during any period of statutory continuation. It should be made clear whether or not this is intended.

5 See *Accuba Ltd v Allied Shoe Repairs Ltd* [1975] 3 All ER 782; *London and Manchester Assurance Co Ltd v GA Dunn & Co* (1982) 265 Estates Gazette 39, CA; *Touche Ross and Co v Secretary of State for the Environment* (1982) 265 Estates Gazette 982, CA; *Prudential Assurance Ltd v Gray* (above); *Webber v Halifax Building Society* [1985] 1 EGLR 58 but note *Glofield Properties Ltd v Morley (No 2)* [1989] 32 EG 49, CA.

6 A query arises as to the effect of such delay on the term commencement date, and the length of the term, of the hypothetical lease.

7 See *Glofield v Morley* (above) in which the court acknowledged that if the landlord's contention (that the valuation date was the date of the determination of the revised rent) was accepted it might produce results not intended by the parties, as the longer the landlord waited, the higher the rent in a period of inflation. On the other hand, it also said that if the intention of the parties is clearly and unequivocally expressed, the court is bound by it, however capricious it may be, unless it is plainly controlled by other parts of the lease. The court held that although the tenant's construction would produce a far more sensible and realistic commercial result, the decision of the Court of Appeal in *London and Manchester* (above) had to be followed and the proper date of valuation was the date when the arbitrator made his award.

8 The landlord's agent may have made it clear during initial negotiations that the first review date would remain the same however long the delay before the lease was granted. This may have been for estate management reasons – it may be important to a landlord that the rent reviews on all premises within a development coincide. On the other hand, some landlords impose such a requirement, with other similar requirements, to give the tenant an incentive to complete the lease quickly (and, of course, to give themselves an advantage during negotiations on the draft lease). If the tenant's agent has accepted the principle, it will be difficult for his solicitor to alter the position unless, perhaps, a delay in completing the lease has been caused exclusively by the landlord. Even if the principle has not been accepted, the tenant's solicitor will usually be unable simply to require that the review dates are calculated from the date of the grant of the lease, as most landlords require the review dates to fall on quarter days. Some negotiation will therefore usually be required. In the example given in the text, if the September quarter day were taken, the initial review period would exceed five years, which the landlord may find unacceptable.

9 See Chapter 14 below.

10 See paras 14.6 and 14.14 below and the 1954 Act (ss 24 and 64).

11 As to interim rents generally, see ibid s 24A and para 14.15 below.

12 An interim rent is payable only from the later of the date specified in the landlord's notice under s 25 or in the tenant's request under s 26 of the Act, and the date of the landlord's application for an interim rent (see para 14.15 below and ibid s 24A(2)). Accordingly, if the landlord delays in serving a notice under s 25 of the Act (with the result that he has to specify in it a date later than the contractual term date, or with the result that the tenant serves a s 26 notice specifying a date later than the contractual term date) or delays in making an application for an interim rent, the interim rent will not be payable in respect of the commencement of the period of statutory continuation. Even where the matter is agreed between the parties without resort to the court, a well-advised tenant will not agree to make any payment in lieu of interim rent for any part of the period of statutory continuation in respect of which the landlord would not be entitled to interim rent through the court, unless in doing so he obtains some compensating benefit.

13 The hearing of the application for an interim rent is usually adjourned for hearing with the main proceedings, with the result that, even if the landlord serves his notice, and makes his application for an interim rent in time, the interim rent will seldom actually be paid until long after the expiry of the contractual term. Even where the matter is agreed between the parties without resort to court proceedings, a tenant will seldom make any additional payment in respect of rent for the period of statutory continuation until the new lease is granted.

14 As to the calculation of interim rent, see para 14.15 below and ibid s 24A(3). In fact, in practice, this disadvantage does not always exist. Where the matter is agreed between the parties without resort to court proceedings, the tenant will frequently agree that the rent agreed in respect of the new lease will be back-dated to the date on which the landlord's entitlement to interim rent commenced. A well-advised tenant, however, will require the valuation date to be similarly back-dated, and perhaps some other benefit, as a quid pro quo.

15   Provided that the statutory procedures are followed, a tenant under a lease protected by the Act is entitled to be granted a new tenancy on the determination of his lease. As to this entitlement, and the calculation of rent under the new lease, see paras 14.1 and 14.50 below.

16   Provided that the statutory procedures are followed, a landlord has the right to resist the tenant's application for a new tenancy on certain grounds. As to this right, and these grounds, see ibid s 30(1) and para 14.29 below.

17   As to the valuation date and comparables, note paras 6.4:1 above and 6.41, 6.42, 14.50 and 14.51 below. See also *Lovely and Orchard Services Ltd v Daejan Investments (Grove Hall) Ltd* (1977) 246 Estates Gazette 651.

18   Although, of course, a rent review, even on a realistic basis, would avoid the landlord's other concerns mentioned above. From the tenant's point of view, the objection mentioned in paragraph (a) would be met, but those mentioned in paragraphs (b) and (c) below would not.

19   See *Charles Follett Ltd v Cabtell Investment Co Ltd* [1987] 2 EGLR 88, CA; *Conway v Arthur* [1988] 2 EGLR 113, [1988] 40 EG 120, CA.

20   Ie in a lease for twenty years commencing in 1990: '24th June in the years 1995, 2000, 2005 and 2010'. Assuming that the term of the lease commenced on 24 June 1990 (ie so that 24 June 1990 was included in the term – see para 1.5:3 above) this would mean that the last review date was after the expiry of the contractual term. There seems in principle no objection to this. If the lease is not continued by virtue of s 24 (see para 14.14 below) then the tenancy would have terminated before that last review date and no review would arise. The draftsman with this format must decide if he thinks that a continuation under s 24 of more than five years is likely and thus if he need insert 2015! See note 3 above for the potential danger of inserting specific dates as review dates.

21   Using the same example as in footnote 20 above: '24th June 1990 and every fifth anniversary thereof for so long as this tenancy shall subsist including any extension or continuation whether by statute or common law'. At least here no decision has to be made as to the year 2015!

22   See para 6.18.3(d) below.

23   Although the validity of such an uplift was put in doubt by Tudor Evans J in *Lear v Blizzard* [1983] 3 All ER 662. The case concerned an option for a new lease for a term of 21 years at a rent to be agreed between the parties or, in default of agreement, to be determined by an arbitrator. One of the questions which arose was what uplift, if any, should be made to the rent to take into account this long term without review. The judge held that the introduction of an uplift on that which would otherwise be the open market rent would, in effect, be contrary to the judgment in *National Westminster Bank Ltd v BSC Footwear Ltd* (1980) 257 Estates Gazette 277 (in which the Court of Appeal held that there was no power for an arbitrator determining the open market rent for a lease being granted pursuant to an option to insert a rent review clause), and that no such uplift should therefore be permitted. It must be said, however, that the Court of Appeal in *National Westminster* did not seem to preclude the possibility of an uplift, Templeman LJ indicating that 'the hypothesis which the arbitrator has to make is that this lease, with a 21 year term at a fixed rent, is on offer and he must decide the market price for a rent as between landlord and tenant if that lease came on the market'. This is a question for the valuer to decide and if, on the evidence before him, he believes that the rent for a 21 year term at a fixed rent would be higher than that for a lease for a 21 year term with five-yearly reviews, there would appear to be nothing to preclude him from fixing a higher rent. Recent cases concerning the effect on the revised rent of a hypothetical lease making no provision for review (see para 6.18.3(d) below) support this view.

24   As to comparables, see paras 6.41 and 6.42 below.

25   See *National Westminster Bank Ltd v BSC Footwear Ltd* (1980) 257 Estates Gazette 277, CA; *Bracknell Development Corpn v Greenlees Lennards Ltd* (1981) 260 Estates Gazette 500; *Clarke v Findon Developments Ltd* (1983) 270 Estates Gazette 426.

26   Indeed, even if the lease provides for reviews at a frequency normal at the time of its grant, this may well change at some point if the lease is granted for a long term, causing difficulty on rent review. In such circumstances, the parties might like to consider the possibility of providing for a 'review' of the frequency of review at each review date, although this could, of course, cause further valuation problems (see para 6.57 below).

6.5   *How is the review mechanism to be instigated?* Broadly rent review clauses fall into two categories – the formalistic that provides for the service of notices and counter-notices – and sometimes for the taking of certain other steps[1] – and the informal that merely provides for the rent to be agreed or, in the absence of agreement,[2] determined by a third party, without specifying a detailed timetable of various steps that are required to begin and to continue the process of review.[3] The latter informal approach is more often seen today[4] and would seem to have three advantages:

(a) it is fairer than a formalistic clause that is drafted[5] so that a tenant (or sometimes either party) will lose all his rights[6] at that review if he delays in taking a certain step;[7]

(b) the absence of dates by which steps have to be taken avoids the much litigated question of whether the parties intended their rights[6] to be lost by delay – in other words, was time to be of the essence?[7]

(c) the lack of any requirements for notices and counter notices avoids that other frequently litigated point of whether a particular document was drafted and served in such a way to constitute a valid notice for the purpose of the clause.[8]

1   For example, the appointment of the third party who will determine the rent in the absence of agreement.

2   Such wording does not imply that there must have been an attempt to agree: *Re Essoldo (Bingo) Ltd's Underlease, Essoldo Ltd v Elcresta Ltd* (1971) 23 P&CR 1; *Laing Investment Co Ltd v GA Dunn & Co* (1981) 262 Estates Gazette 879; *Wrenbridge Ltd v Harries (Southern Properties) Ltd* (1981) 260 Estates Gazette 1195.

3   Apart, of course, from giving preferably either party the right at (more or less) any time to apply for a third party to be nominated to determine the rent in the absence of agreement. There are those draftsmen who, while basically preferring an informal approach, like to provide for the review process to be triggered by a notice. They need to take great care in so doing – clumsy drafting could have lost the advantages set out in this paragraph in a way that could only benefit the tenant (ie only the landlord could fall foul of the problems referred to in this paragraph) while if the lease contains a break clause the mere insertion of the need to serve a trigger notice could make time of the essence; see paras 6.11 and 6.12 below and *Edwin Woodhouse Trustee Co Ltd v Sheffield Brick Co plc* (1983) 270 Estates Gazette 548.

4   This approach is adopted, for example, in 22 Encyclopaedia of Forms and Precedents (5th edn) Forms 22 (Second Schedule), 117 (prepared by the Joint Committee of the Law Society and the Royal Institution of Chartered Surveyors), and 118 (recommended by the Incorporated Society of Valuers and Auctioneers), the Rosscastle Letting Conditions (see Appendix 1, Form 1 below) condition 7. The Joint Committee of the Law Society and the RICS state in their Background Notes (ibid p 505): 'In the light of the *Burnley* and *Cheapside* decisions, the Joint Committee have continued to avoid, so far as possible, strict time-limits and notices, in order to give effect to the contract between the parties (ie a letting for a term of years with rent reviews at specified intervals) and remove the risk of that contract being frustrated by human error. There is, however, provision, as an alternative, for a time limit after which a review can no longer be initiated.'

5   Admittedly not every formalistic clause is drafted so that a failure to comply with the timetable means that rights are lost but (a) all too many such clauses leave uncertain this point (a fact that prompted many of the cases referred to in paras 6.6–6.16 below) and (b) if a timetable does not have to be followed (ie time is *not* to be of the essence) why bother to specify one?

6   The term 'the parties rights on a review' is used to mean the landlord's right to review the rent and the tenant's right to have some involvement in the negotiation of that rent and, more particularly, the right to have it determined by a third party.

7   See paras 6.6–6.14 below.

8   See paras 6.13:1 and 6.13:5 below.

6.6   *Time of the essence: the presumption.* The possibility of the informal approach[1] did not often occur to draftsmen of early rent review clauses who, in many ways understandably, allowed themselves to be influenced by the 1954 Act.[2] Thus the landlord was frequently required to serve a notice 'not more than twelve months nor less than six months before the review date' while the tenant had to serve a counter-notice within a certain time. Many of the early reported cases on rent reviews related to a situation in which a party had failed to comply strictly with these requirements – did this mean that a defaulting landlord was debarred from benefiting from that review, and had to wait until the next review date (if there was one) before increasing the rent, or that a defaulting tenant could no longer dispute the revised rent proposed by the landlord, and had lost the right to have it determined by a third party? The general rule was established by the House of Lords in *United Scientific Holdings Ltd v Burnley Borough Council* and *Cheapside Land Developments Co Ltd v Messels Service Co.*[3] It is easy to over simplify this decision and regard it as authority for the statement that time is not of the essence on a rent review. In fact, the decision was summarised by Lord Diplock as follows:[4]

> 'So upon the question of principle which these two appeals were brought to settle, I would hold that in the absence of any contra-indications in the express words of the lease, or in the interrelation of the rent review clause itself and other clauses, or in the surrounding circumstances, the presumption is that the timetable specified in a rent review clause for completion of the various steps for determining the rent payable in respect of the period following the review date is not of the essence of the contract.'

It follows, therefore, that time *will* be of the essence if the lease expressly so provides and, as Lord Diplock said[5] 'the best way of eliminating all uncertainty in future rent review clauses is to state expressly whether or not stipulations as to the time by which any step provided for by the clause is to be taken shall be treated as being of the essence.' In fact, the current trend is not to have any stipulations as to time as such, but rather to indicate that the steps can be taken *at any time*.[1]

1 See para 6.5 above and the precedents referred to in footnote 4 to that para.
2 See Chapter 14 below.
3 [1978] AC 904, [1977] 2 All ER 62.
4 At 930 and 72.
5 At 936 and 77.

6.7 *Time of the essence: the presumption rebutted.* Time will be of the essence in relation to the steps of a rent review clause, if the parties expressly make it so,[1] or if there are contra-indications in either the lease,[2] in the interrelation of the rent review clause and other clauses,[3] or in the surrounding circumstances.[4] Since *United Scientific*,[5] courts have frequently been invited to hold that the presumption that time is not of the essence should be rebutted[6] – and sometimes they have held that it should be – but recent indications are that the presumption is a strong one that will not easily be rebutted.[7]

1 See para 6.8 below. As to when the tenant can serve notice making time of the essence when the clause indicates that it is not, see *Factory Holdings Group Ltd v Leboff International Ltd* [1987] 1 EGLR 135, 282 Estates Gazette 1005; Legal Notes (1987) 282 Estates Gazette 873.
2 See paras 6.9 and 6.10.
3 See paras 6.11 and 6.12.
4 The meaning of this concept was not explored in the speeches in *United Scientific* (see footnote 3 to para 6.6 above) and there have been no reported cases. For discussion of the point, see D N Clarke and J E Adams: *Rent Reviews and Variable Rents* (Oyez Longman) 2nd edn, p 123.
5 See footnote 3 to para 6.6 above.
6 See the cases cited in paras 6.9–6.12 below.
7 See *Phipps-Faire Ltd v Malbern Construction Ltd* [1987] 1 EGLR 129, 282 Estates Gazette 460 (paras 6.9 and 6.10 below) and *Metrolands Investments Ltd v J H Dewhurst Ltd* [1986] 3 All ER 659, CA.

6.8 *Time of the essence: by express agreement.* As has already been suggested[1] the parties to a lease should be reluctant to make time of the essence in relation to any steps of the review procedure and should adopt clauses of the informal type discussed above.[2] If, however, they chose to depart from this, the draftsman should ensure that the clause clearly indicates that time shall be of the essence in relation to those parts of the clause that are required by his client.[3] This task has not always proved as easy as it appears. There is a line of cases dealing with a similar clause in which the expression 'time of the essence' appears and yet the court held that the landlord was able to review the rent after the dates in question.[4] In *Wrenbridge Ltd v Harries (Southern Properties) Ltd*[5] the reviewed rent was to be:

(a) agreed by 29 September 1979 'in respect of which time is to be deemed the essence of the contract',

(b) if not so agreed fixed by an arbitrator 'appointed for that purpose by the parties hereto', or

(c) failing agreement as to such appointment '. . . by 25 December 1979 time in this respect deemed to be of the essence of the contract then by an arbitrator to be appointed by the President of the RICS . . .'

The landlord did nothing until 4 February 1980 when he wrote proposing a new rent and in default of agreement suggesting the President be asked to appoint an arbitrator. The tenant took the position that as time was of the essence in relation to the review the landlord was not entitled to the new rent. Lloyd J stated that it was difficult to see what the draftsman had meant by making time of the essence in relation to dates by which agreement had to be reached rather than a date by which a specific action had to be taken, as was the case in the *United Scientific*.[6] He decided that the clause provided three alternative ways for the rent to be reviewed and thus the landlord was entitled to his late review. A similar situation arose in *C Bradley & Sons Ltd v Telefusion*[7] in which Walton J was required to construe a two stage clause (agreement/ arbitration) and decide if the words '(time to be of the essence of this provision)' inserted in the middle of the clause referred to the whole clause, the first part only or (as the judge held) the second part only. Thus in this case, as no arbitrator had been appointed, the landlord lost his right to review. Again the lesson in clear – the draftsman must be totally unambiguous on the crucial issue of whether or not time is of the essence in relation to the timetable on review.

1   See para 6.5 above and note para 6.14 below.
2   See paragraph 6.5 above and the precedents referred to in note 4 to that paragraph.
3   See for example *Weller v Akehurst* [1981] 3 All ER 411.
4   *Amherst v James Walker Goldsmith & Silversmith Ltd* (1980) 254 Estates Gazette 123, CA; *Wrenbridge Ltd v Harries (Southern Properties) Ltd* (1981) 260 Estate Gazette 1195; *Laing Investment Co Ltd v GA Dunn & Co* (1981) 262 Estates Gazette 879. See also *Million Pigs Ltd v Parry* (1983) 268 Estates Gazette 809.
5   (1981) 260 Estates Gazette 1195.
6   See para 6.6 above.
7   (1981) 259 Estates Gazette 337.

6.9   *Time of the essence: presumption rebutted by contra-indications in the wording of the lease: early cases.* There have been a number of cases in which it has been argued that the parties intended to rebut the presumption, and to make time of the essence, without stating this in so many words. For example, in *Drebbond Ltd v Horsham District Council*,[1] Megarry V-C held that the words 'but not otherwise' made time of the essence in relation to a provision that the revised rent should be referred to an arbitrator '. . . if the Landlord shall so require by notice in writing given to the Tenant within three months thereafter but not otherwise.'

Then in recent years there have been a series of decisions that are not always easy to reconcile. The lease in *Lewis v Barnett*[2] provided that:

'. . . if the Landlord and Tenant shall not have agreed the open market rent at least six months before the rent review date and the Landlord shall neglect to make the application referred to in paragraph 3 hereof [ie to the President of the Royal Institution of Chartered Surveyors to appoint a surveyor to determine the rent] then (unless the parties hereto shall in writing agree otherwise) any notice already given by the Landlord to the Tenant under the provisions of paragraph 2 hereof shall be void and of no effect.'

The Court of Appeal held that time *was* of the essence. And yet in *Touche Ross & Co v Secretary of State for the Environment*[3] the lease provided that if within two months of the landlord's notice the revised rent had not been agreed the question 'shall as soon as practicable and in any event not later than three months after the service of the said notice be referred' to a third party. Perhaps somewhat surprisingly in the light of *Drebbond*,[1] the Court of Appeal decided that time *was not* of the essence, Dillon LJ observing:[4]

'Obviously it is undesirable that questions of whether time is of the essence on a rent review clause should depend upon minute differences of language. Since there is no magical formula it is possible that small differences of language will lead in some cases to opposite conclusions. I do not need to express any view either way on whether the *Drebbond*[1] case was rightly decided on the terms of the lease which the court had to consider in that case.'

1 (1978) 246 Estates Gazette 1013. Harman and Scott JJ took the same view of the effect of 'but not otherwise' in *Norwich Union Life Insurance Society v Tony Waller Ltd* (1984) 270 Estates Gazette 42 and *Norwich Union Life Insurance Society v Sketchley plc* [1986] 2 EGLR 126, 280 Estates Gazette 773.
2 (1981) 264 Estates Gazette 1079, CA. Note para 6.10 below and *Power Securities (Manchester) Ltd v Prudential Assurance Co Ltd* [1987] 1 EGLR 121, 281 Estates Gazette 1327.
3 (1982) 265 Estates Gazette 982. This approach was followed on similar wording by Goulding J in *Thorn EMI Pension Trust Ltd v Quinton Hazell plc* (1983) 269 Estates Gazette 414.
4 At 984.

6.10 *Time of the essence: presumption rebutted by contra-indications in the wording of the lease: later cases.* Shortly after *Touche Ross*,[1] the Court of Appeal had to consider a complex clause in *Henry Smith's Charity Trustees v AWADA Trading and Promotion Services Ltd*.[2] It provided for the landlord to serve a notice stating his proposed rent. The tenant had a month in which to serve a counter-notice indicating his proposed rent and in the absence of a counter-notice within the month, the landlord's rent was to prevail. Paragraph 7 of the rent review schedule read:

'If on the expiration of two months from the date of sevice of such counter-notice the Landlords and the Tenant shall not have agreed in writing an amount to be treated as the market rent and the Landlords shall not have applied for the appointment of a Surveyor in accordance with paragraph 6 of this Schedule [ie to determine the open market rent as an expert] the amount stated in such counter notice shall be deemed to be the market rent.'

There was no express reference to time being of the essence. No rent was agreed, and the landlords failed to apply for the appointment of an expert within the two month period. The Court of Appeal cited *Lewis v Barnett*[3] with approval and held that time *was* of the essence and thus the rent referred to in the tenant's counter-notice should be the revised rent. Then in *Mecca Leisure Ltd v Renown Investments (Holdings) Ltd*,[4] the lease provided that the reviewed rent was to be the sum specified in the landlord's notice, unless the tenant served a counter-notice within a specific period, in the absence of which he would be deemed to have agreed the rent specified in the landlord's notice. The Court of Appeal held that the deeming provision did *not* rebut the presumption, and so time *was not* of the essence in relation to the tenant's counter-notice. The lease in *Greenhaven Securities Ltd v Compton*[5] provided that the reviewed rent should be the current rent if the parties had not within fifteen months agreed on an arbitrator or made an application for the appointment of an arbitrator. No application was made and Goulding J held that this clause *did rebut* the presumption and so time *was* of the essence. Mr B A Hayter QC, sitting as a deputy judge, had the unenviable task in *Taylor Woodrow Property Co Ltd v Lonrho Textiles Ltd*[6] of reconciling *Henry Smith*[2] and *Mecca*[4] . . . or acknowledging that they were irreconcilable. The lease before him provided that if the tenant failed to serve a counter-notice within the period it would be deemed to have agreed to the landlord's rent. The learned deputy judge decided, albeit with some hesitation, that the reconciliation between *Henry Smith*[2] and *Mecca*[6] could be found in the difference between the deeming provisions – in the former, they applied to both parties, whereas in the latter it applied only to the tenant. As the clause in the present case was materially identical to that in *Mecca*,[4] he followed *Mecca*,[4] and held that the presumption was *not rebutted*, so time *was not* of the essence and the tenant's counter-notice served out of time was valid. Then in *Phipps-Faire Ltd v Malbern Construction Ltd*,[7] Warner J rejected the tenant's 'attractive' arguments that the lease in question contained contra-indications. He said that 'the authorities[8] seem to me to show that the presumption that time is not of the essence of a provision in a rent review clause is strong and that it will not be rebutted by any contra-indication in the express terms of the lease unless it is a compelling one.' Thus time was not of the essence.[9] The lesson from these complicated cases is simple. If it is the intention of the parties that time should be of the essence, then the lease should state this and make it clear to which step or steps of the review process it is intended to apply. If, on the other hand, it is the parties' intention that time is not to be of the essence, then either the clause should be drafted in such a way that no periods are referred to, or a statement should be included that time is not of the essence.[10]

1   (1982) 265 Estates Gazette 982.
2   (1983) 269 Estates Gazette 729.
3   (1981) 264 Estates Gazette 1079.
4   (1984) 271 Estates Gazette 989.
5   [1985] 2 EGLR 117, 275 Estates Gazette 628.
6   [1985] 2 EGLR 120, 275 Estates Gazette 632. Note also *Power Securities (Manchester) Ltd v Prudential Assurance Co Ltd* [1987] 1 EGLR 121, 281 Estates Gazette 1327 and *Panavia Air Cargo Ltd v Southend-on-Sea Borough Council* [1988] 1 EGLR 124, [1988] 22 EG 82, CA in which time was held *not* to be of the essence.
7   [1987] 1 EGLR 129, 282 Estates Gazette 460. See also *Power Securities* and *Panavia*: footnote 6 above.
8   Ie the cases referred to in this paragraph.
9   This general approach seems to be in line with that adopted in the case of the effect of a break clause by the Court of Appeal in *Metrolands Investments Ltd v J H Dewhurst Ltd* [1986] 3 All ER 659 – see para 6.12 below. It is to be hoped that the time of essence pendulum has stopped swinging, and that the approach adopted in *Phipps-Faire*, *Power Securities* and *Panavia*, and in *Metrolands* (see above) will be applied constantly in the future.
10   See para 6.5 above.

6.11   *Presumption rebutted by the interrelation of the rent review and other clauses: break clause: early cases.* In *United Scientific*,[1] Lord Fraiser said:[2]

'For these reasons, I am of the opinion that the equitable rule against treating time as of the essence of a contract is applicable to rent review clauses unless there is some special reason for excluding its application to a particular clause. The rule would of course be excluded if the review clause expressly stated that time was to be of the essence. It would also be excluded if the context clearly indicated that that was the intention of the parties – as for instance where the tenant had a right to break the lease by notice given by a specified date which was later than the last date for serving the landlord's trigger notice. The tenant's notice to terminate the contract would be one where the time limit was mandatory, and the necessary implication is that the time limit for giving the landlord's notice of review must also be mandatory. An example of such interlocked provisions is to be found in *Richard v Karevita*[3] where the decision that time was of the essence of the landlord's notice could be supported on this ground, although not, as I think, on the ground on which it was actually rested. The case of *Samuel Properties (Developments) Ltd v Hayek*[4] is not in this class because, although there was a tenant's break clause, the time allowed to the tenant for giving notice was automatically extended until one month after the notification of the reviewed rent to the lessee.'[5]

The presence of a break clause has sometimes been held to rebut the presumption and to make time of the essence as to the landlord's implementation of the rent review.[6] But the rent review machinery and the break clause have to be interrelated for this to arise. In *Edwin Woodhouse Trustee Co Ltd v Sheffield Brick Co plc*[7] Judge Finlay, sitting as a deputy judge of the High Court, decided that there was no such interrelationship where the rent review clause was of the type discussed above – it required no 'trigger' notice and the rent was to be agreed *at any time* and referred to the third party *at any time* after a certain date. Thus the presence of a break clause in the lease was held not to make time of the essence so far as implementing the review clause was concerned.

1 See para 6.6 above.
2 At 962 and 98.
3 (1971) 221 Estates Gazette 25.
4 [1972] 3 All ER 473, [1972] 1 WLR 1296, CA.
5 The reason for this is because time will be of the essence under the general law as to options in relation to the break clause. So if the parties genuinely did intend the rent review and the break clause to be linked, so that the tenant could terminate the lease if the reviewed rent was not to his satisfaction, the landlord could defeat this object by delaying the review. Thus, the argument runs, time must be of the essence in relation to the rent review. As the courts have recognised, however, break clauses are sometimes inserted into leases quite coincidentally of the rent review clause and there is no valid reason why this should serve to rebut the presumption that time is not of the essence (see for example *Edwin Woodhouse* and *Metrolands*, footnote 7 and para 6.12 below).
6 *Al Saloom v Shirley James Travel Services Ltd* (1981) 259 Estates Gazette 420, CA; *Rahman v Kenshire* (1980) 259 Estates Gazette 1074; *Coventry City Council v J Hepworth & Son Ltd* (1982) 265 Estates Gazette 609, CA; *Legal & General Assurance (Pension Management) Ltd v Cheshire County Council* (1983) 269 Estates Gazette 40, CA; *William Hill (Southern) Ltd v Govier and Govier* (1983) 269 Estates Gazette 1168.
7 (1983) 270 Estates Gazette 548.

6.12 *Presumption rebutted by the interrelation of the rent review and other clauses: break clause: recent case.* The question of whether or not a break clause made time of the essence came before the Court of Appeal in *Metrolands Investments Ltd v J H Dewhurst Ltd*.[1] Slade LJ (who delivered the judgment of the court) pointed out that since the ultimate object of the court in construing a rent review clause was to ascertain the parties' intention from the words used, and since the rent review could only result in an increase in rent and was thus only for the landlord's benefit, it followed that the test to be applied was whether, from the words used, the proper intention to be imputed to the parties was that the landlord should lose his right to a rent review if the stipulated timetable was not strictly adhered to. Having regard to the facts that (a) the landlord was likely to suffer greater detriment if he lost the right to a rent review than the tenant would suffer if the assessment of the new rent was delayed, (b) what was required by the rent review clause was the actual obtaining of the arbitrator's decision,[2] which was an event substantially outside the landlord's control since the arbitrator might be dilatory or the tenant's submissions might delay the proceedings, and (c) the tenant had it in his own power to obviate any hardship arising from the landlord's delay by himself initiating the rent review, the Court of Appeal decided that the interrelation between the rent review and break clauses was not sufficient to rebut the presumption that time was not of the essence in the rent review clause, and accordingly the intention properly to be attributed to the parties was that time was not of the essence. The judgment indicates that *William Hill (Southern) Ltd v Govier and Govier*[3] may have been wrongly decided but also seems to suggest that judicial approach may have been swinging too much in favour of finding time to be of the essence.

1   [1986] 3 All ER 659. Surprisingly, *Edwin Woodhouse* (see para 6.11 above) does not appear to have been cited.
2   The provision in the lease that the landlord had not complied with in time was to seek the determination of the revised rent by an arbitrator.
3   (1983) 269 Estates Gazette 1168.

6.13   *A common counter-notice clause and its problems.* Many landlords today seem content with the informal type of clause discussed above by which the revised rent is to be agreed, and in the absence of agreement referred to a third party.[1] They feel that this ability to refer is a sufficient sanction to impose upon a tenant who is delaying. There are some landlords, however, who believe that a sense of urgency needs to be introduced from the beginning into the review process. They want a tenant who delays to be penalised by having to accept the rent specified by the landlord. There are a number of variations of these clauses but a common one[2] provides that there are three alternative ways in which the revised rent is to be determined – specified in a notice served by the landlord, or agreed between the parties within say two months of that notice, or determined by a third party at the election of the tenant 'such election to be made by counter-notice in writing served by the Tenant upon the Landlord not later than the expiration of two months from the Landlord's notice'. All provisions as to time are expressed to be of the essence. The dangers to the tenant will be obvious – the second and third methods of determining the rent will be lost two months after the service of the landlord's notice. Thus a tenant who has neither agreed the rent nor served a counter-notice by then will have to pay the rent specified in the landlord's notice.[3] Not surprisingly, these or similar clauses have frequently been before the courts, and a number of questions have been posed:

6.13:1   *Has the landlord effectively implemented the clause?* This is a vital question because if the landlord's attempt was ineffective – because, for example, his initial notice was defective – the review mechanism would not have been triggered and thus any subsequent failings by the tenant would be immaterial.

The proper approach would seem to be whether a tenant reading the document would think that it was a trigger notice. 'It is simply necessary that the letter, fairly read, should bring to the mind of the reader that it was intended to set in motion the rent review procedures . . .'.[4]

6.13:2 *Must the rent specified in the landlord's notice be reasonable?* In *Davstone (Holdings) Ltd v Al-Rifai,*[5] Goulding J rejected a submission by a tenant who had failed to respond in time that, as the notice indicated the landlord's wish to increase the rent to the full yearly market rental, it should be implied that the landlord could not validly propose a rental wholly outside the full yearly market rental as such term was defined in the lease. Goulding J was not prepared to read anything into the lease along these lines, but he did leave open the question of whether or not a false and fraudulent expression of opinion as to the rent in the landlord's notice, that was not the genuine opinion of the writer, could invalidate the notice.

6.13:3 *Is time of the essence in relation to the landlord's implementation of the clause?* Here the normal rules will apply – the presumption is against time being of the essence but this can be rebutted if the parties expressly so provide or if the court decides that it was their intention to do so.[6]

6.13:4 *Is time of the essence in relation to the service of the tenant's counter-notice?* Again the normal principles will apply,[6] although if the type of clause outlined above is intended,[7] the lease will indicate that time is of the essence in relation to the landlord's counter-notice.

6.13:5 *Has the tenant served a valid counter-notice?* Time will generally be of the essence in relation to the service of the tenant's counter-notice, and so the prudent tenant should serve on the landlord within the relevant period a document that is unequivocally a formal counter-notice.[8] Many tenants have failed to do this and there has been a series of cases in which tenants have invited the court to hold that a letter objecting to the rent specified in the landlord's notice sent within the period should be construed as a counter-notice indicating an election by the tenant to have the rent determined by the third party.[9] In all these cases, the argument failed and the rent in the landlord's notice prevailed.[9] Then in *Nunes v Davies Laing & Dick Ltd*[10] the tenant's agent wrote to the landlord's solicitors, in a letter that was headed in the matter of the lease and the rent review: 'I am instructed by the tenants to give you hereby formal notice that the open market rental is £12,000 per annum and call on you under the terms of the above lease to agree this. Please confirm that this is accepted as due notice.' There was no mention to the clause of the lease and no express exercise of the right of election to go to the third party. Sir Nicolas Browne-Wilkinson V-C held that this letter *did* constitute a valid counter-notice, reiterating that the test to be applied was that the document would be held to be a counter-notice if it was in terms that were sufficiently clear to bring home to the ordinary landlord that the tenant was purporting to exercise his right to have the rent determined by the third party. The clause that Vinelott J had to consider in *British Rail Pension Trustee Co Ltd v Cardshops Ltd*[11] was a complex one, and the counter-notice that the tenant had to serve was not an election to have the rent determined by a third party. The judge felt that the proper test was would a reasonably sensible businessman, in the light of all the surrounding circumstances, have been left in no real doubt that the tenant wished to bring the review machinery into operation, or could he have been reasonably mistaken as to what was meant? Applying that test, Vinelott J held that a letter marked 'Subject to Contract' *was* a valid counter-notice.[12]

6.13:6 *Does a tenant who has failed to serve a counter-notice in time have any rights to apply for an extension?* The answer depends upon the nature of the counter-notice, and in particular if it is an election for a determination by a third party, and upon the status of that third party. If the counter-notice is not an election, but the lease merely provides that, unless the tenant serves a counter-notice in time, he will be deemed to accept the rent in the landlord's notice, then the tenant will have no redress if he fails to serve the counter-notice.[13] If the third party is an expert, then a failure to serve a counter-notice electing for his determination will similarly be fatal. If, however, the counter-notice is an election for determination by an arbitrator the tenant may apply to the court for an extension of time in which to serve his counter-notice under s 27 of the Arbitration Act 1950.[14] This states that where an agreement to refer future disputes to arbitration provides that the rights shall be lost unless notice to appoint an arbitrator is given within a fixed time, the High Court 'if it is of opinion that in the circumstances of the case under hardship would otherwise be caused, and notwithstanding that the time so fixed has expired, may, on such terms, if any, as the justice may require . . . extend the time for such period as it thinks proper.' Vinelott J extensively reviewed the relevant authorities in *Chartered Trust plc v Maylands Green Estate Co Ltd*.[15] He adopted the principles set out by Brandon J in *The Jocelyne*:[16]

> '. . . In deciding whether to extend time or not, the court should look at all the relevant circumstances of the particular case . . . In particular the following matters should be considered: (a) the length of the delay; (b) the amount at stake; (c) whether the delay was due to the fault of the claimant or to circumstances outside his control; (d) if it was due to the fault of the claimant the degree of that fault; (e) whether the claimant was misled by the other party; (f) whether the other party has been prejudiced by the delay, and if so, the degree of such prejudice.'

Vinelott J felt that the extent, if any, to which an applicant under s 27 may have a remedy against his professional advisers in relation to the failure to serve a counter-notice, and the time that elapsed before the application was made, were relevant factors. In the case before him, he granted leave but on the basis that interest would be paid on the shortfall of rent, as there was no provision to this effect in the lease.

6.13:7 *Where the clause requires further steps from either party after the service of the tenant's counter-notice, is time of the essence?* Here again the normal principles will apply – the presumption will be against time being of the essence but this can be rebutted if the parties expressly so provide, or if the court decided that it was their intention to do so.[6]

6.13:8 *What constitutes 'application' when the landlord has to apply for the nomination of an arbitrator or expert?* One variation of the counter-notice clause requires the landlord to apply for the appointment of an arbitrator or expert within a certain period of the tenant's counter-notice, if the rent has not been agreed in the meantime. The clause considered by the court in *Staines Warehousing Co Ltd v Montague Executor and Trustee Co Ltd*[17] did not call for counter-notices, but the question that it posed would be equally relevant to this variation of the counter-notice clause. The clause here called for the landlord to have applied by a certain date to the President of the Royal Institution of Chartered Surveyors to nominate an expert surveyor to determine the rent. It was common ground that time was of the essence. Before the relevant date, the landlord's agents wrote to the President indicating that 'no rent has yet been agreed in this case, negotiations are continuing between ourselves and the tenants, and we are, therefore, writing in accordance with the terms of the second schedule to the lease to make an in time only application for the appointment by the President of an expert surveyor to determine a revised rent.' Notice of this was not given to the tenant nor was the fee paid or the Institution's application form completed and a copy of the lease sent, until after the relevant date but the Court of Appeal agreed with Knox J that the letter constituted a genuine application.

6.13:9 *If the landlord fails to take some further step in respect of which time is of the essence, can he simply activate the whole review process again?* In *Norwich Union Life Assurance Society v Sketchley plc*[18] the landlord served a valid notice triggering the clause. There was no agreement as to the revised rent, but the landlord did not give the tenant notice of his intention to refer the determination of the revised rent to a third party, as he was required to do, within the relevant time limit, time being of the essence. Time had not been of the essence as to the implementation of the clause, and the landlord argued that he could simply start the same review again by serving another trigger notice. Scott J disagreed – he gave a literal construction to the lease that provided that the 'Landlord shall be entitled by notice in writing given to the Tenant at any one time . . . to call for a review of the initial market rent . . .'. Thus he held that this gave the landlord the opportunity to call for a review once and only once. His decision was very much one of construction rather than principle, and so presumably a second review might be possible under a differently worded clause and indeed Harman J had come to a differing view on the same clause.[19]

1   See para 6.5 above and the precedents referred to in note 4 to that paragraph.
2   See 22 Encyclopaedia of Forms and Precedents (5th edn) Form 127. This is sometimes known as a 'specification – agreement – determination clause'.
3   As to an 'agreement' that is expressed to be 'subject to contract' or 'without prejudice', see *Henderson Group plc v Superabbey Ltd* [1988] 2 EGLR 155, [1988] 39 EG 82. Older leases sometimes include more complex variations of counter-notice clauses that can be fairer for the tenant, in the sense that the landlord is subjected to the same regime – some, for example, require the landlord to take a further step within a specified time after the receipt of the tenant's counter-notice. Thus the landlord may have to refer the determination of the rent to the third party by a certain date after the service of the tenant's counter-notice if the rent has not been agreed in the meantime (see for example *Henry Smith's Charity Trustees v AWADA Trading and Promotion Services Ltd* (1983) 269 Estates Gazette 729, CA). It is difficult, however, to see what attracts landlords to these alternatives because a failure by the landlord to take action at some stage during a review where time is of the essence could cause him to lose that chance to review the rent which happened, for example, in *Henry Smith*. In fairness, most of these clauses that are still being litigated are in leases granted either before *United Scientific* (see para 6.6 above) or before the lessons of it had been digested. Landlords today seem generally to favour either clauses of the type advanced in para 6.5 above and in footnote 4 to that paragraph or the simple counter-notice clause of the type referred to in this paragraph that in fact bites only on the tenant, although a landlord should consider very carefully if such a clause is wise in the wider context of landlord and tenant relations.

4 *Norwich Union Life Insurance Society v Sketchley plc* [1986] 2 EGLR 126, 280 Estates Gazette 773 per Scott J applying the test of the Court of Appeal in *Amalgamated Estates Ltd v Joystretch Manufacturing Ltd* (1980) 257 Estates Gazette 489. (Note also *Darlington Borough Council v Waring & Gillow (Holdings) Ltd* [1988] 2 EGLR 159, [1988] 45 EG 102.) In *Shirlcar Properties Ltd v Heinitz* (1983) 268 Estates Gazette 362 the Court of Appeal held that a letter from the landlord's agents, sent more than two months before the notice had to be served and expressed to be subject to contract, stating that 'the rent required as from the review date is £6,000 per annum exclusive and we look forward to receiving your agreement' was not a notice and thus the clause had not been 'triggered'. Harman J seemed to have applied a rather stricter and more specific standard in *Norwich Union Life Insurance Society v Tony Waller Ltd* (1984) 270 Estates Gazette 42 (and in particular to have suggested that a letter marked 'without prejudice' could never constitute a trigger notice) but the more general approach of whether the person reading it would regard it as a notice was preferred by Scott J in *Sketchley*, by Sir Nicolas Browne-Wilkinson V-C in *Nunes v Davies Laing & Dick Ltd* [1986] 1 EGLR 106, 277 Estates Gazette 416, by Hutchison J in *Glofield Properties Ltd v Morley* [1988] 1 EGLR 113, [1988] 02 EG 62 and by Vinelott J in *British Rail Pension Trustee Co Ltd v Cardshops Ltd* [1987] 1 EGLR 127, 282 Estates Gazette 331 who held that a letter marked 'Subject to contract' did constitute a valid counter-notice (but note *Darlington Borough Council v Waring & Gillow (Holdings) Ltd* [1988] 2 EGLR 159, [1988] 45 EG 102). See para 6.13:5 and note Legal Notes [1988] 05 EG 69. See also *Durham City Estates Ltd v Felicetti* [1989] EGCS 23, CA. As to the dangers when the reversion is sold at a time when notices should be served, see *Cordon Bleu Freezer Food Centres Ltd v Marbleace Ltd* [1987] 2 EGLR 143, 284 Estates Gazette 786.

5 (1976) 32 P & CR 18. This view was confirmed by Templeman LJ in *Amalgamated Estates Ltd v Joystretch Manufacturing Ltd* (1980) 257 Estates Gazette 489: 'If a landlord puts forward a preposterous figure for rent, the tenant can always serve a counter-notice. It would be ludicrous if the court were obliged to decide whether the landlord's figure was a bona fide and genuine pre-estimate in order to decide whether the landlord's request for an increased rent was valid or wholly void. The court does not exist to punish a landlord for being greedy, especially as the definition of 'greed' varies from Shylock to Portia and from landlord to tenant.'

6 See paras 6.5–6.12 above and *Maraday Ltd v Sturt Properties Ltd* [1988] 2 EGLR 163, [1988] 46 EG 99.

7 See 22 Encyclopaedia of Forms and Precedents (5th edn) Form 127.

8 See 22 Encyclopaedia of Forms and Precedents (5th edn) Form 129.

9 *Bellinger v South London Stationers Ltd* (1979) 252 Estates Gazette 699 ('. . . we would hardly add that we do not accept the revised figure.'); *Oldschool v Johns* (1980) 256 Estates Gazette 381 ('Our client . . . contends that the open market rental value . . . is at this time less than the present rental value'. The tenant's argument failed that the landlord was estopped from relying upon the rent contained in the notice by writing *after* the period had expired 'in the event of non-agreement between the respective valuers, then the issue will have to go to arbitration'); *Amalgamated Estates Ltd v Joystretch Manufacturing Ltd* (1980) 257 Estates Gazette 489 ('We cannot agree with your rent increase'); *Edlingham Ltd v MFI Furniture Centres Ltd* (1981) 259 Estates Gazette 421 ('Will you please accept this letter as counter-notice to the effect that we consider that the rent of £50,000 is excessive and will appreciate it if you will kindly forward to us comparables on which you have based this figure'); *Horserace Totalisator Board v Reliance Mutual Insurance Society* (1982) 266 Estates Gazette 218 ('I am writing to inform you that the Board does not accept your proposed increase of £6,500'); *Sheridan v Blaircourt Investments Ltd* (1984) 270 Estates Gazette 1290 ('In view of the obvious disagreement between us, I suggest that it would be appropriate to make application to the Royal Institution of Chartered Surveyors for an independent valuer'. The letter was also marked 'subject to contract'); *Glofield Properties Ltd v E B Tobacco Ltd* [1985] 1 EGLR 56, 273 Estates Gazette 74 ('but please note at this stage that the proposed rent . . . is not accepted by the tenant as representing the present open market rental value of the premises.' The tenant's argument that the landlord was estopped from relying upon the rent contained in the notice, in the light of subsequent negotiation's between the parties, was rejected). See also para 6.13 and footnote 1 above.

10 [1986] 1 EGLR 106, 277 Estates Gazette 416. Note too *Glofield Properties Ltd v Morley* [1988] 1 EGLR 113, [1988] 02 EG 62 in which Hutchison J held that a letter from the tenant's agents that included the words 'Please accept this letter as formal objection and counter-notice' *did* constitute a valid counter-notice. He expressed doubt as to whether there was any conflict between the decisions in *Edlingham* (see footnote 9 above) and *Nunes* but, if there was, would follow the latter.

11 [1987] 1 EGLR 127, 282 Estates Gazette 331.

12 See footnote 4 above.

13 For an example of a deemed acceptance of the landlord's rent clause, see *Mecca Leisure Ltd v Renown Investments (Holdings) Ltd* (1984) 271 Estates Gazette 989, CA.

14 For a time it was believed that no application could be made in relation to these clauses following *Tote Bookmakers Ltd v Development and Property Holding Co Ltd* [1985] Ch 261, [1985] 2 All ER 555 but the Court of Appeal overruled this decision in *Pittalis v Sherefettin* [1986] QB 868, [1986] 2 All ER 227.

15 (1984) 270 Estates Gazette 845. See also *S I Pension Trustees Ltd v William Hudson Ltd* (1977) 242 Estates Gazette 689; *Sioux Inc v China Salvage Co* [1980] 3 All ER 154, [1980] 1 WLR 996; *Amalgamated Estated Ltd v Joystretch Manufacturing Ltd* (1980) 257 Estates Gazette 489; *Edlingham Ltd v MFI Furniture Centres Ltd* (1981) 259 Estates Gazette 421; *Pittalis v Sherefettin* [1986] QB 868, [1986] 2 All ER 227, CA.

16 *Moscow V/O Exportkhleb v Helmville Ltd, The Jocelyne* [1977] 2 Lloyd's Rep 121 approved by the majority of the members of the Court of Appeal in *Libra Shipping and Trading Corpn Ltd v Northern Sales Ltd, The Aspen Trader* [1981] 1 Lloyd's Rep 273, CA.

17 [1987] 2 EGLR 130, 283 Estates Gazette 458, CA.

18 [1986] 2 EGLR 126, 280 Estates Gazette 773.

19 *Norwich Union Life Insurance Society v Tony Waller Ltd* (1984) 270 Estates Gazette 42.

6.14 *Counter-notice clauses: general advice.* The tenant's advisers should strongly resist any clause by which an administrative failure could cause the tenant to lose his right to participate in the review process.[1] The punishment of having to pay[2] a rent which could exceed (and indeed that may even bear no relationship to) the market rent[3] does not fit the crime of failing to serve a counter-notice. Landlords really cannot suggest as a point in favour of the clause that it is no more burdensome than the provisions for renewing a lease under Part II of the 1954 Act.[4] On a renewal, it is arguable that there needs to be a strict timetable imposed on the tenant, so that the landlord knows in good time whether or not he will have to re-let the premises. Moreover any tenant's failings under the 1954 Act mean that he will lose the right to a *new* lease – when the tenant does not comply with the procedural requirements of this type of review clause, he could be saddled with an inequitable rent in an *existing* lease. A lease renewal is not comparable to a rent review because under the latter the landlord knows that the letting will continue, that he will receive the revised rent backdated to the review date (even if that revised rent is only determined later),[5] and that in many instances he will receive interest on the shortfall between the revised rent and the prevailing rent.[6] As such, there seems no valid reason for landlords to impose these types of clause upon unwilling tenants.

1 If for no other reason than that any administrative failure may be that of those same advisers rather than the tenant himself.

2 Subject to any limited rights of 'appeal': see para 6.13:6 above.

3 As to how near to the market rent the rent prescribed in the landlord's notice has to be, see para 6.13:2 above.

4 See paras 14.8 and 14.9 below.

5 See paras 6.52–6.54 below.

6 See para 6.55 below. He may even receive an interim rent: see para 6.56 below.

6.15 *Landlord's delay when time not of the essence: generally does not preclude review.* *United Scientific*[1] was a decision welcomed by landlords but tenants' advisers derived some comfort from the suggestion of Lord Salmon that if 'the lessors had been guilty of unreasonable delay which caused prejudice or hardship to the lessees they would have forfeited their rights to be paid the market rent from April 8th 1975 to April 8th 1982 . . .'[2] ie notwithstanding the fact that time was *not* of the essence. Lord Salmon's dicta was followed and even extended in *Telegraph Properties (Securities) Ltd v Courtaulds*[3] where a landlord sought to invoke a rent review clause in 1978 where the review date was 1973. Foster J held that such a delay was unreasonable and it was unfair for the landlord to invoke the clause. He said that in his 'judgment the plaintiff has been guilty of such a delay as to make it unreasonable for it to call on the defendant for a rent review and to do so would be *of necessity* unfair for the defendant.' In other words there was no need to prove the 'prejudice or hardship' referred to by Lord Salmon. Then followed a gradual wind of change. In *H West & Son Ltd v Brech*[4] Cantley J said:

> 'I am not satisfied that unreasonable delay of itself precludes a landlord from relying on a review clause. It is otherwise if such delay causes prejudice or hardship to the tenant, or if such delay is so inordinate as to leave reasonably to the inference that the right to review has been abandoned or that there is a tacit agreement not to enforce it.'

His Lordship held that an eighteen month delay did not preclude the landlord from obtaining his review and this approach was apparently adopted by Dillon J in *Printing House Properties Ltd v J Winston & Co Ltd*.[5] Nevertheless there was still the suggestion that 'if prejudice or hardship was caused to the tenant', the landlord would be prevented from operating the review. Two cases in the Court of Appeal, while differing on certain matters, established that this is not the case.[6] In *London and Manchester*,[6] Oliver LJ said that 'where the contract itself . . . envisages that the landlord may exercise his right at any time early or late in the period he cannot be said to be guilty of unreasonable delay if he simply does what the contract entitles him to do', while in *Amherst*[6] he reiterated that he knew 'of no ground for saying that mere delay, however lengthy, destroys the contractual right'. *Telegraph Properties*,[7] in so far as the decision rested on simple delay, was held in *Amherst*[6] to have been wrongly decided.

1 See paras 6.6–6.12 above.
2 [1977] 2 All ER at 89, 93.
3 (1981) 257 Estates Gazette 1153. In *Amherst v James Walker (Goldsmith and Silversmith) Ltd* [1983] Ch 305, [1983] 2 All ER 1067 the Court of Appeal held that this case in so far as it rests on simple delay or alternatively abandonment was wrongly decided.
4 (1982) 261 Estates Gazette 156.
5 (1982) 263 Estates Gazette 725.
6 *London and Manchester Assurance Co Ltd v GA Dunn & Co* (1982) 265 Estates Gazette 39, 131 and *Amherst v James Walker (Goldsmith and Silversmith) Ltd* [1983] Ch 305, [1983] 2 All ER 1067. Note too decision of Goulding J in *Million Pigs Ltd v Parry* (1983) 268 Estates Gazette 809.
7 See footnote 3 above.

6.16 *Landlord's delay where time not of the essence: estoppel.* Both cases, however, indicate that a review could be lost through estoppel.[1] As Lawton LJ said in *Amherst*:[2]

> 'They (the tenants) could only be relieved of this obligation (to pay a revised rent) in a way known to the law. One way was by agreement with the landlord.[3] There was no such agreement in this case. Another way of their getting relieved of their liability to pay a higher rent would have arisen if they could have shown that the landlord's conduct had been such that he was estopped from relying on the rent assessment notice which he did serve. He would only have been estopped if the tenants could have proved that by his words or conduct he had represented that he did not intend to ask for the payment of a higher rent and in reliance on that representation they had altered their position to their prejudice. In my judgment nothing short of estoppel would have relieved the tenants from their liability to pay a higher rent . . .

if a landlord by his words or conduct leads his tenant reasonably to infer that he did not intend to claim a higher rent he makes a representation to that effect so that the foundation of an estoppel is laid; but the landlord will not be estopped unless the tenant has acted on the representation to his prejudice. A landlord who over a long period makes no attempt to set a rent review procedure in motion may be adjudged to have represented that he did not intend to exercise his rights; but whether he did would be a matter of inference from the circumstances in which the delay had occurred not from the mere fact of delay'.

Where the two cases differ is whether or not the concept of abandonment[4] has a place in rent reviews. Slade LJ believed in *London and Manchester*[5] that it did – Oliver and Lawton LJJ felt in *Amherst*[5] that it did not. In summary therefore, the landlord will not lose his review simply by delaying[6] (where time is not of the essence) but could be estopped from reviewing the rent, although it is questionable how often in practice the somewhat strict criteria for estoppel set out by Lawton LJ (and in particular the fact that the tenant must have acted on the representation to his prejudice[7]) will be met.

1   The doctrine of equitable estoppel was successfully applied in *James v Heim Gallery (London) Ltd* (1979) 252 Estates Gazette 1017 at first instance but Court of Appeal reversed the decision (1980) 256 Estates Gazette 819 holding that the tenant had not established promissory estoppel. See also *Essoldo Ltd v Elcresta Ltd* (1971) 23 P & CR 1; *CH Bailey Ltd v Memorial Enterprises Ltd* [1974] 1 All ER 1003, [1974] 1 WLR 728; and *Accuba Ltd v Allied Shoe Repairs Ltd* [1975] 3 All ER 782, [1975] 1 WLR 1559.
2   See footnote 6 to para 6.15 above at 1077.
3   But any agreement not to review has to be a formal one – an informal agreement that no increase was necessary did not stop the landlords from subsequently operating review in *Esso Petroleum Co Ltd v Anthony Gibbs Financial Services Ltd* (1983) 267 Estates Gazette 351, CA.
4   For a definition of abandonment see *The Hannah Blumenthal* [1983] 1 All ER 34 per Lord Brandon at 47.
5   See footnote 6 to para 6.15 above.
6   Although there was an obiter suggestion by Sir Douglas Frank QC (sitting as a deputy High Court judge) in *Chrysalis Properties Ltd v Secretary of State for Social Services* (1983) 133 NLJ 473 that, as a matter of principle, only one rent review notice should be current at any one time and so the period for serving a trigger notice expires when the time comes for the next one to be served. These remarks were before *London and Manchester* in the Court of Appeal had been fully reported (although it had by then been heard) and before *Amherst* had been heard.
7   But note the remarks of Lord Denning MR in *WJ Alan & Co Ltd v El Nasr Export and Import Co* [1972] 2 QB 189, [1972] 2 All ER 127, CA that there is no need now for the representee to act to his prejudice. This view was adopted by Graham J in *Ogilvy v Hope-Davies* [1976] 1 All ER 683 but doubted by Balcombe J in *Fontana NV v Mautner* (1979) 254 Estates Gazette 199.

C   THE HYPOTHETICAL LETTING: ASSUMPTIONS AND DISREGARDS

6.17   *Introduction.* The most common type of rent review clause provides for the revised rent to be that which the parties agree or, in the absence of agreement, that which an expert or arbitrator determines to be the rent obtainable on a hypothetical letting of the premises demised by the lease on the review date – in other words, it directs the parties or a third party to establish the *actual* rent to be paid after the review under the *existing* lease by reference to the rent payable on a *hypothetical* letting of the premises.[1] The draftsman of such a rent review clause must not only require the parties to assume a hypothetical letting, but must also define in the lease with great precision the premises which are to be the subject of that hypothetical letting, the duration and terms of that hypothetical letting, and any other matters which are to be assumed or disregarded in relation to that hypothetical letting, so that it is clear what falls to be valued.[1] The parties and their advisers would do well to consider some general points as they approach this aspect of the rent review clause:

6.17:1   *'False' assumptions and disregards.* It is by means of assumptions[2] and disregards[3] that the form of rent review clause under discussion not only requires the parties to imagine that there is a hypothetical letting, but also describes that which the parties must imagine to be the circumstances of that hypothetical letting. All assumptions and disregards are 'false', to the extent they require the parties to imagine something on rent review which is not the case in reality. The assumption of a hypothetical letting itself is 'false' in one sense, but is inserted in order to enable the parties to assess the rental value of the premises.[4] Other assumptions and disregards generally found in a rent review clause are also 'false' in that sense as they remove the hypothetical lettings from reality, but do so only in order to support the basic hypothesis of a letting, and/or render the hypothetical letting like the actual letting.[5] It is not to these, but to assumptions and disregards which remove the circumstances of the hypothetical letting from those of the actual letting, which this paragraph relates. It is, of course, possible for the parties to insert *any* assumptions and disregards in the rent review clause. So, for example, the rent review clause may specify that the premises which are to be the subject of the hypothetical letting are to be totally different premises from those comprised in the lease. Even if it specifies that they are to be the premises comprised in the lease, it may require the rent review valuation to be conducted on the basis that they are in a totally different state and condition to that in which they actually are on the review date. Similarly, the rent review clause may require the terms of the hypothetical letting to be totally different from those in the actual lease, or it may require the parties to assume, on rent review, that the premises have the benefit of rights, licences and permissions which they do not, in fact, have on the review date, or vice versa. As a general rule, however, in the absence of special circumstances, it is inadvisable for the hypothetical letting to differ from the actual letting any more than is necessary. In *Norwich Union Life Insurance Society v Trustee Savings Bank Central Board*,[6] Hoffmann J said: 'There is, I think, a presumption that the hypothesis upon which the rent should be fixed upon review should bear as close a resemblance to reality as possible.' This statement was made in relation to the construction of existing clauses, but it is good advice to parties negotiating new clauses. So, for example, the parties should generally avoid assumptions and disregards that will require the rent to be determined on the basis of a hypothetical tenancy of premises other than those comprised in the lease, or a hypothetical tenancy the terms of which are significantly different from those of the actual letting. There are two reasons why, as a general rule, the circumstances of the hypothetical letting should bear as close a resemblance to the circumstances of the actual letting as possible:

6.17:1.1   *Fairness.* It is suggested that, generally, a tenant should pay rent on the basis of what he actually has. Landlords often seek to 'improve' the terms of the hypothetical lease. A tenant in the real open market would probably refuse to accept a lease containing onerous provisions without a discount in the rent. Conversely, a lease that was generous to the tenant might command a higher rent. A similar result will flow on rent review. The tenant's advisers, in particular, must therefore be wary that the landlord does not use assumptions and disregards to produce a generous hypothetical lease when the actual lease is onerous, in order to achieve a higher rent on rent review. For example, the actual lease might restrict the tenant as to the use to which he can put the premises,[7] might contain an absolute prohibition on underletting,[8] and might impose other onerous restrictions. If the hypothetical lease was assumed to permit a wide range of uses,[7] to permit underletting of whole or part,[8] and to contain no such onerous restrictions, the tenant might find himself paying a far higher rent on rent review than that which a lease similar to his actual lease would command on the open market.[9]

6.17:1.2 *Drafting difficulties.* Assumptions and disregards which remove the circumstances of the hypothetical letting from those of the actual letting may not always operate unjustly. Indeed, some of the most commonly found assumptions and disregards have this effect, and yet are inserted to achieve justice between the parties.[10] Nonetheless, assumptions and disregards which have the effect of rendering the circumstances of the hypothetical letting different from the actual letting, even those clearly intended to achieve justice between the parties, should not be inserted without caution and should be avoided if possible if they involve, or may involve, too extreme a departure from reality. This is because rent review clauses attempting to achieve this have often been found inadequate in that they do not provide *all* the information that is needed to determine the rent. For example, in *Trust House Forte Albany Hotels Ltd v Daejan Investments Ltd*[11] a lease of a hotel provided that it was to be assumed that part of the premises in fact used as part of a hotel were 'actually let for or available for shopping and retail purposes'. The question arose on review as to whether it should be assumed that the premises had planning permission for this hypothetical use, and that they had been physically adapted for such use. Fox J held that the valuation should be conducted on the basis that there were no obstacles to such use (ie that it was permitted under the lease and for Town and Country Planning purposes) but that it did not have to be assumed that the premises had been adapted for that use. It will never be easy for the draftsman to anticipate all the valuation issues that may arise when assumptions and disregards are included in the rent review clause which render the circumstances of the hypothetical letting significantly different from those of the actual letting and, accordingly, these assumptions and disregards should be avoided whenever possible.[12]

6.17:2 *Construction of rent review clauses.* The aim of the draftsman is to ensure that his documents are drafted in such a way that no dispute can ever arise as to their meaning.[13] In order to achieve this, it is essential that the draftsman of rent review clauses should give some consideration to cases on their construction. On a simple level, he needs to know how, in the past, the courts have interpreted particular words and phrases, in order that he should use them to the correct effect. More generally, however, he needs to be aware of the principles which the courts follow when construing rent review clauses, and should bear these in mind when drafting. In particular, the draftsman must bear in mind that the courts will be unable to accept evidence of the negotiations leading up to the transaction, and will be attempting to derive the presumed intention of the parties from the words used, in the rent review clause and elsewhere, and, to some extent, from the circumstances surrounding the transaction, including its commercial purpose. How, and the extent to which, the commercial purpose of the rent review clause should be taken into account in its construction has been the subject of considerable debate in recent years, with certain decisions of the courts appearing to reflect a more 'literal', and others a more 'purposive' approach to construction. It is perhaps decisions concerning the construction of assumptions as to the terms of the hypothetical letting which have caused the most controversy. Much concern was expressed[14] following several cases in each of which the court felt obliged to hold that a rent review clause required it to be assumed that the hypothetical lease on rent review contained no rent review provisions whilst, of course, there were rent review provisions in the actual lease.[15] Thus, because the terms of the hypothetical letting were less onerous than those of the actual letting, a higher revised rent resulted than would have been determined if the hypothetical letting had been on the same terms as the actual letting. Commentators[14] – and men and women of property generally – found it difficult to believe that the court's construction of these rent review clauses reflected the intentions of the parties to the relevant leases. The Vice-Chancellor proposed certain guidelines[16] encouraging a more 'purposive' approach to the construction of rent review clauses which arguably required a hypothetical letting without review that the Court of Appeal (in a different case[17]) endorsed, whilst making it clear that they were not rules of construction to be applied rigidly in every case (and, indeed, they were not applied in that case) and that they did not entitle the court to construe and apply, not the clause which the parties had entered into, but the different clause which they might have entered into if their lawyers had thought rather more deeply about how the intricate scheme they were setting up would work in practice. A few months later, a differently constituted Court of Appeal[18] took the opportunity to lay down guidelines for the construction of rent review clauses in *Basingstoke and Deane Borough Council v Host Group Ltd*. The main issue was whether the terms and conditions of the hypothetical lease (which were not defined) should be the same as those in the actual lease or such as the valuer would regard as reasonable for the lease of a bare site for development (which is what the premises were assumed to be on rent review). Nicholls LJ (giving the judgment of the court) said:[19]

> 'The question raised on this appeal is one of construction of a rent review clause in a lease. In answering that question it is axiomatic that what the court is seeking to identify and declare is the intention of the parties to the lease expressed in that clause. Thus, like all points of construction, the meaning of this rent review clause depends upon the particular language used interpreted having regard to the context provided by the whole document and the matrix of the material surrounding circumstances. While recognising, therefore, that the particular language used will always be of paramount importance, it is proper and only sensible, when construing a rent review clause, to have in mind what normally is the commercial purpose of such a clause.[20]
>
> The means by which rent review clauses afford landlords relief in respect of increases in property values or falls in the value of money is by providing, normally, for the valuer, in default of agreement, to assess the up-to-date rent for the demised premises at successive review dates. In making that assessment the valuer will be achieving the intended purpose of keeping the rent in line with current property values having regard to the current value of money if, but only if, he assesses the up-to-date rent on the same terms (other than as to quantum of rent) as the terms

still subsisting between the parties under the actual, existing lease. If he departs from those terms, and assesses the up-to-date rent on the footing of terms materially less onerous to the tenant than those in the actual, existing lease, the rental at which he arrives will reflect, in addition to the rental increases attributable to a rise in property values or a fall in the value of money, an additional element, namely the increased rental attributable to the fact that he is calculating the rent of a lease on terms more favourable to the tenant than the terms in the actual existing lease. Conversely, if he assesses the up-to-date rent on the basis of terms materially more onerous to the tenant than those in the actual existing lease, the rental figure at which the valuer arrives will not fully reflect the rise in property values or the fall in the value of money since the lease was granted or the rent was last fixed.

Of course rent review clauses may, and often do, require a valuer to make his valuation on a basis which departs in one or more respects from the subsisting terms of the actual existing lease. But if and in so far as a rent review clause does not so require, either expressly or by necessary implication, it seems to us that in general, and subject to a special context indicating otherwise in a particular case, the parties are to be taken as having intended that the notional letting postulated by their rent review clause is to be a letting on the same terms (other than as to quantum of rent) as those still subsisting between the parties in the actual existing lease. The parties are to be taken as having so intended, because that would accord with, and give effect to, the general intention underlying the incorporation by them of a rent review clause into their lease.'

There can be few involved with commercial property who would disagree with this approach but only time (or a decision of the House of Lords) will tell if it represents a settled view.[21] Nonetheless, the lessons to be learned from the cases are clear. It cannot be guaranteed that the court, in any particular case, will adopt this, less 'literal', approach to construction and even one which does may sometimes (albeit reluctantly) be unable to construe a rent review clause in such a way as to produce the effect intended by the parties, because the words used either clearly result in a different construction,[22] or create some doubt as to the commercial purpose of the clause.[23] The draftsman cannot rely on the courts to rescue sloppy drafting, but must ensure that his wording unambiguously produces the required result.[24]

6.17:3 *Surveyors.* The drafting and negotiating of the rent review clause is a matter for close co-operation between each party and his surveyor and solicitor. The first reason for this is information. The solicitor must be given all the information he needs about the premises (particularly if he is unable to inspect them himself), the arrangements between the parties and his client's proposals to enable him to ensure that the rent review clause is appropriate to the circumstances and produces a just result between the parties. The second reason is skill. The solicitor working alone will often be unable to identify all the valuation difficulties which might arise from the nature of the premises or the parties' arrangements. If, for example, the premises are unusual,[25] a surveyor may well suggest that the clause ought to give more help to the valuer,[26] or that a significant departure from the normal form of clause might, for once, be advisable.[27] Ideally, the solicitor should involve his client and surveyor at each stage of the drafting and negotiation of the rent review clause. Failing that, there should be a discussion between them at the outset to identify difficulties and concerns and then, when the clause has been agreed between the solicitors (subject to final instructions), each solicitor should submit it to his client and his client's surveyor for approval, with a request to both for confirmation that no relevant alteration in arrangements has arisen since the initial discussion, and to the surveyor for confirmation that, were he to be appointed as arbitrator or expert on the first review, he would encounter no difficulties in operating the clause. It is suspected that the close co-operation advocated above seldom exists during the drafting and negotiation of a rent review clause. This is partly the fault of the solicitor, who fails to appreciate, or request, the input which can be given by his client and his surveyor. It is also the fault of the client and surveyor, however, who fail to appreciate that a standard form of rent review clause may not be appropriate in every case. Often, the landlord's solicitor receives instructions to despatch a draft lease immediately on the basis of brief heads of terms because the tenant's rent free period will start to run on receipt of the draft lease. Often the tenant's solicitor will be advised 'not to make a meal of' the draft lease because the tenant would like to complete the lease and start his fitting out works the following week. Such haste, without a willingness to devote the time available to discussion, may be an example of false economy. It is suggested that a 'brainstorming' session while the lease was being negotiated might well have avoided many of the difficulties seen in the cases referred to in this chapter, and thus not only much time-consuming and costly litigation, but also loss to one or other of the parties when the rent review clause was construed to have an effect which they did not suspect at the time of the grant of the lease.

1 See para 6.2 above.
2 See section D. For a typical set of assumptions, see Rosscastle Letting Conditions (Appendix 1, Form 1 below) Condition 7.2:2.
3 See sections E and F below. For a typical set of disregards, see Rosscastle Letting Conditions (Appendix 1, Form 1 below) Condition 7.2:3.
4 For the way in which the assumption of a hypothetical letting enables the parties to assess the rental value of the premises, see para 6.2 above.
5 Such as an assumption of vacant possession (see para 6.19 below), or an assumption of a willing landlord and willing tenant (see para 6.22 below).
6 [1986] 1 EGLR 136, 278 Estates Gazette 162. See also *Sterling Land Office Developments Ltd v Lloyds Bank plc* (1984) 271 Estates Gazette 894; *Scottish and Newcastle Breweries plc v Sir Richard Sutton's Settled Estates* [1985] 2 EGLR 130, 276 Estates Gazette 77; *General Accident Fire and Life Assurance plc v Electronic Data Processing Co plc* [1987] 1 EGLR 112, 281 Estates Gazette 65; *Basingstoke and Deane Borough Council v Host Group Ltd* [1988] 1 All ER 824, [1988] 1 WLR 348, CA; *Ravenseft Properties Ltd v Park* [1988] 2 EGLR 164, [1988] 50 EG 52.
7 As to user provisions generally, see paras 7.8–7.18 below.
8 As to alienation provisions generally, see paras 7.1–7.7 below.
9 As to the possible effect of lease terms on rent, see para 6.18:3 below.
10 Such as an assumption that the tenant has complied with his covenants (see para 6.25:1 below), or a disregard of improvements carried out by the tenant (see paras 6.34–6.40 below) or of goodwill built up by the tenant (see para 6.33 below).
11 (1980) 256 Estates Gazette 915. See also *Bovis Group Pension Fund Ltd v G C Flooring & Furnishing Ltd* (1984) 269 Estates Gazette 1252, CA; *Exclusive Properties Ltd v Cribgate Ltd* [1986] 2 EGLR 123, 280 Estates Gazette 529; *Basingstoke and Deane Borough Council v Host Group Ltd* [1988] 1 All ER 824, [1988] 1 WLR 348, CA; *Wallace v McMullen* [1988] 2 EGLR 143, [1988] 28 EG 81; *Trusthouse Forte Albany Hotels Ltd v Daejan Investments Ltd (No 2)* [1989] 30 EG 87, CA; *Rushmoor Borough Council v Goucher and Richmond* [1985] 2 EGLR 140, 276 Estates Gazette 304; provides an example of the problems that can arise from what appears to have been a superfluous assumption.
12 Sometimes 'false' assumptions and disregards can be avoided by giving a little more thought to the drafting of the lease. For example, in a case where the tenant wants to use the premises for a use peculiar to himself, the lease is often drafted in such a way as to permit only that user whilst the rent review clause contains an assumption that the hypothetical lease permits another use. In such a situation, this false assumption can be avoided, and a more safe and just result achieved, by redrafting the user clause to permit other uses with the consent of the landlord, such consent not to be unreasonably withheld – see para 7.16 below. In a case where the value of the premises depends on the existence of a licence which may be lost by the default of the tenant, a more just and safe result can be achieved by placing the tenant under

an obligation not to jeopardise the licence, and by inserting in the rent review clause the usual assumption that the tenant has complied with his covenants, than by inserting an assumption in the rent review clause that such a licence is available on the review date. Sometimes, the arrangements between the parties can be adjusted. For example, in a case where the tenant wants to use the premises in such a way that a valuable planning permission will be lost, the parties may consider the possibility of the tenant paying once-and-for-all compensation to the landlord, rather than inserting in the lease a rent review assumption to the effect that the premises have the benefit of such planning permission. Another possibility which the parties might consider, before introducing unusual assumptions or disregards into the rent review clause in an attempt to deal with unusual commercial factors, is that of providing for the revised rent to be a specific percentage of the open market rent for the premises (which may be more or less than 100% depending on the circumstances) – see 22 Encyclopaedia of Forms and Precedents (5th edn) Form 121 – or of adopting some other form of rent review clause – see section J below. Naturally, there will be circumstances in which there is no alternative to inserting unusual, false assumptions and disregards in the rent review clause (see, for example, *Jefferies v O'Neill* (1983) 269 Estates Gazette 131 – discussed at para 6.18:2 below). In such circumstances it is essential that the parties, together with their solicitors and surveyors, spend sufficient time on consideration and discussion to ensure that the false scenario is complete and achieves justice and their business objectives.

13   'Mr Piesse considered that a document should be expressed with sufficient clarity to make it unnecessary to have recourse to the rules of interpretation or decisions of the courts on points of language' – see Piesse: *The Elements of Drafting* (The Law Book Company Ltd, Australia: 7th edn, 1987, Editor: J K Aitken) Introduction. See also Reed Dickerson: *The Fundamentals of Legal Drafting* (Little Brown and Company, 1986) para 3.9.

14   See para 6.18:3(d) below and for example John Stuart Colyer QC and Peter Banks: 'Paying for the notional or for the real' (1986 Blundell Memorial Lecture), Legal Notes (1987) 282 Estates Gazette 719, (1987) 7 PLB 73.

15   See *Pugh v Smiths Industries Ltd* (1982) 264 Estates Gazette 823; *Lister Locks Ltd v TEI Pension Trust Ltd* (1981) 264 Estates Gazette 827; *Safeway Food Stores Ltd v Banderway Ltd* (1983) 267 Estates Gazette 850; *National Westminster Bank plc v Arthur Young McClelland Moores & Co* [1985] 1 EGLR 61, 273 Estates Gazette 402; *Securicor Ltd v Postal Properties Ltd* [1985] 1 EGLR 102, 274 Estates Gazette 730; *General Accident Fire and Life Assurance plc v Electronic Data Processing Co plc* [1987] 1 EGLR 112, 281 Estates Gazette 65; *Equity and Law Life Assurance Society plc v Bodfield Ltd* [1987] 1 EGLR 124, 281 Estates Gazette 1448, CA.

16   *British Gas Corpn v Universities Superannuation Scheme Ltd* [1986] 1 All ER 978, [1986] 1 WLR 398. See also *Datastream International Ltd v Oakeep Ltd* [1986] 1 All ER 966, [1986] 1 WLR 404; *MFI Properties Ltd v BICC Group Pension Trust Ltd* [1986] 1 All ER 974; *Electricity Supply Nominees v F M Insurance Co Ltd* [1986] 1 EGLR 143, 278 Estates Gazette 523; *Amax International Ltd v Custodian Holdings Ltd* [1986] 2 EGLR 111, 279 Estates Gazette 762; *British Home Stores plc v Ranbrook Properties Ltd* [1988] 1 EGLR 121, [1988] 16 EG 80.

17   *Equity and Law Life Assurance Society v Bodfield* [1987] 1 EGLR 124, 281 Estates Gazette 1448 (19 March 1987: Fox, Dillon & Russell LJJ).

18   [1988] 1 All ER 824 (3 November 1987: Slade, Glidewell & Nicholls LJJ).

19   At 828.

20   Nicholls LJ referred here to the judgments of Sir Nicholas Brown-Wilkinson V-C in *British Gas* (see footnote 16 above) and Dillon LJ in *Equity and Law* (see footnote 17 above).

21   The decisions for example in *Equity and Law* (see footnote 17 above) and in *Stroud v Weir Associates Ltd* [1987] 1 EGLR 190, 281 Estates Gazette 1198 suggest that the *Basingstoke* approach may not be shared by all the members of the Court of Appeal.

22   See *Pugh v Smiths Industries Ltd* above.

23   See *Equity and Law Life Assurance Society v Bodfield* above.

24   It has been suggested that if, despite all efforts, he is concerned that he might not have achieved this, he might consider introducing a clause which clearly explains what the parties are intending to achieve, and why, thus bringing in 'by the back door' evidence of negotiations.

25   See para 6.18:1(d) below.

26   For example, an assumption as to access would have assisted in *Jefferies v O'Neill* (1983) 269 Estates Gazette 131 – see para 6.18:1(b) below.

27   For example, 22 Encyclopaedia of Forms & Precedents (5th edn) Form 122 would have assisted in the lease considered in *F R Evans (Leeds) Ltd v English Electric Co Ltd* (1977) 36 P & CR 185.

D   ASSUMPTIONS

6.18   *The subject and terms of the hypothetical letting.* The first, and fundamental, assumption which the most common type of rent review clause requires the parties to make, is that there is to be a hypothetical letting.[1] This is not necessarily implied from the existence of a rent review clause with the result that, if it is intended, the rent review clause should specifically require the assumption of a letting.[2] As previously explained,[1] it should then define, with great precision, the premises which are to be the subject, and the duration and other terms and conditions of, that hypothetical letting.

6.18:1   *The premises.* As previously mentioned,[1] it will generally be intended that the premises that are to be the subject of the hypothetical letting will be those which are the subject of the existing lease on the review date.[3] This will not always be the case, however,[4] and the rent review clause should make this clear if it is intended. Even if the premises which are to be valued are those comprised in the lease, there are a number of factors which require consideration:

(a) *Defective definition.* If the premises which are to be the subject of the hypothetical letting are to be described by the specification of a defined term, such as 'the demised premises' the definition should be carefully checked by both parties.[5] Does it, for example, include tenant's fixtures?[6]

(b) *Rights.* Disputes could also arise on the review as to the rights enjoyed with the letting by virtue of s 62 of the Law of Property Act 1925.[7] This is a further reason for defining with precision what rights are enjoyed with the premises (and even specifically excluding the operation of s 62) together with such rights as are excepted and reserved. The particular premises which are the subject of the hypothetical letting should be considered separately, as they will be on review. For example, if the tenant occupies two adjoining units, in only one of which there are cloakroom facilities, under separate leases, the draftsman might insert an assumption in the rent review clause of the lease of the premises without cloakroom facilities that the tenant has the right to use the facilities in the adjoining unit. If the tenant occupies adjoining premises through which he gains access to the demised premises, the draftsman should specifically provide that an alternative access be assumed, in order to defeat the argument that the demised premises are incapable of being let to anyone else.[8]

(c) *Ancillary rights.* Disputes could occur in relation to ancillary rights similar to those that have occurred in relation to s 32 of the 1954 Act.[9] These rights may perhaps have been dealt with by means of a licence or side-letter from the landlord. It is suggested that there should be a specific provision in any document that grants additional rights indicating whether or not these matters ought to be regarded as part of the premises for the purposes of the rent review.[10] An example would be the right to use certain car parking spaces. The presence or lack of parking would affect the open market rent of an office in a town centre, and uncertainties could arise if there was no specific direction as to whether or not car parking enjoyed by the tenant by virtue of a document other than the lease should be regarded for the purposes of arriving at the revised rent.

(d) *Unusual buildings.* Difficulties may arise on any rent review where there is likely to be a lack of evidence of comparable transactions.[11] This can arise where the premises are unusual, because of their scarcity – such as hypermarkets, supermarkets or department stores – or simply because they are significantly larger than buildings of that type in the area in question.[12] The parties should explore the possibility of agreeing the method of valuation to be adopted and then setting this out in the lease. For example, in the case of a particularly large industrial building, it might be helpful to specify that the revised rent per square foot should bear a specified relationship to the market rent per square foot of a normal-sized unit on the same site, let on a hypothetical tenancy similar to those applying to the demised premises.[13] Similarly the rent of department stores, supermarkets and hypermarkets could be related to the market rent per square foot of a shop of a more normal (and specified) size on the same site.[14]

6.18:2 *Duration*: There must also be defined the duration of the term of the hypothetical letting.[15] There are essentially five alternatives: the review period itself, the full term of the actual lease, the residue of the term of the actual lease unexpired at the relevant review date, a compromise between the full term and the residue[16] (so that the term of the hypothetical letting is expressed to be the residue of the term unexpired or, for example, ten years whichever is the longer), or a completely independent term that is not linked to the term of the actual letting.[17] It is always dangerous for solicitors to play at being valuers. The preferred term for the hypothetical letting can vary from property to property and from time to time. Indeed what may have seemed ideal for one party at the commencement of the letting may prove otherwise if the market has changed by the review dates. As such, it is important for the solicitor acting for each party to seek the advice of his client's surveyor on this point specifically in each case.

6.18:3 *Other terms of the lease*. It is essential that the rent review clause should clearly define the terms of the hypothetical letting.[18] Generally, in the absence of unusual circumstances, it is advisable for the hypothetical letting to bear as close a resemblance to the actual letting as possible.[19] As a result rent review clauses usually specify that the hypothetical letting is to be 'subject to the provisions of this Lease'.[20] Unfortunately, a failure on the part of many draftsmen fully to appreciate the importance and implications of these few words has given rise to a certain amount of litigation on this aspect of rent review clauses.[21] The terms of a lease can, of course, have a considerable effect on the rent obtainable on its grant and, in the same way, the terms of the hypothetical lease may affect the rent determined on rent review. In the open market, a lease containing provisions which are unusually onerous[22] or restrictive,[23] or which contains deficiencies which are to the disadvantage of the tenant,[24] will often command a lower rent, for two reasons. First of all, the restrictions may reduce the number of tenants who are able to take the lease,[25] and secondly, those tenants who are able to take the lease may not be willing to do so at all, or may not be willing to do so without a discount in rent by way of compensation, because of these provisions or deficiencies. On the other hand, a lease which is unusually generous, or which gives the tenant greater freedom of action than is usual, or which contains deficiencies which are to the advantage of the tenant,[26] might command a higher rent, because a greater number of tenants will be able to take the lease, and because they will be more eager to obtain that lease than others which are not so advantageous. If the terms of the actual lease are incorporated in the hypothetical lease, both parties must bear in mind that those terms may affect the revised rent.[27] Accordingly, when drafting and negotiating the lease, each party must consider its terms not only from his own point of view, but also from the point of view of the other party. For example, a landlord who grants a lease to a tenant who is poorly advised or in a weak bargaining position, and who therefore accepts a lease containing provisions which are to his disadvantage, should bear in mind that, on rent review, that tenant or his assignee may argue strenuously for a discount in the revised rent as a result of that provision. Furthermore, because on rent review the parties are hypothetical,[28] the landlord must consider the terms from the point of view of a hypothetical tenant, and the tenant from the point of view of a hypothetical landlord. If, for example, the actual tenant is not concerned about a particular provision because of his own peculiar circumstances, but the majority of tenants would be, the landlord should bear in mind that this provision might operate to decrease the revised rent on rent review despite the fact that the actual tenant is not adversely affected by it. There are a few particular points which the parties should bear in mind:

(a) *Unilateral waiver of restrictions.* Restrictions contained in the lease generally fall within one of three basic categories: absolute, qualified or fully qualified. An absolute restriction takes the form, for example, of a covenant by the tenant 'not to apply for planning permission'. The general rule[29] is that, although it is open to the tenant to apply for consent to do the prohibited act, and to the landlord to waive the relevant prohibition, the tenant is completely at the mercy of the landlord, who may decide whether or not to consider the tenant application, and whether or not to waive the restriction, at his absolute discretion. A qualified prohibition takes the form, for example, of a covenant by the tenant 'not to apply for planning permission without consent'. The general rule[30] is that this has the same effect as an absolute covenant, in that the landlord may decide whether or not to consider the tenant's application, and whether or not to grant consent, at his absolute discretion. A fully qualified covenant takes the form of a covenant on the part of the tenant 'not to apply for planning permission without consent, such consent not to be unreasonably withheld'. In such a case, the landlord's ability to withhold consent is limited to circumstances in which it is reasonable for him to do so. The difference in effect on rent review between absolute and fully qualified prohibitions, particularly those relating to alienation,[31] change of use,[32] and alterations,[33] can be substantial, although this is of course a question of valuation and will depend on all the circumstances. Landlords should bear in mind that, if they include an absolute prohibition in the lease which is incorporated into the hypothetical lease, the possibility that the landlord will waive the restriction must be ignored,[34] even though the landlord may in fact have waived the restriction on many occasions in the past, and even though it might be entirely in his interests to do so in many circumstances. It seems that a qualified prohibition should have the same effect, although this is not beyond doubt.[35] Futhermore, it seems that neither of the parties may purport unilaterally to waive or vary the provisions of the lease in order to obtain a benefit on rent review.[36]

(b) *References to the actual tenant.* Sometimes leases are granted which make reference to the actual tenant, either directly or indirectly. So, for example, they might permit only the actual original tenant to allow group companies to occupy the premises,[37] or they might define the permitted user of the premises by reference to the actual original tenant or his business.[38] This is obviously inadvisable in the case of a lease containing a rent review clause which incorporates the terms of the actual lease in the hypothetical lease, and the failure to appreciate this has led to capricious results on rent review in the past.[38] In most cases, it is possible for the problem to be avoided if thought is given to the drafting of the lease. So, for example, a lease which permits use for the purposes of the tenant's business, which refers to the actual original tenant by name, may also permit other uses with the consent of the landlord, such consent not to be unreasonably withheld. If it cannot be avoided, consideration should be given as to whether or not the relevant provision should be considered to apply to the hypothetical tenant on rent review, and appropriate directions should be included in the rent review clause.

(c) *Unusual provisions.* Sometimes the parties enter into particular arrangements which are reflected in unusual provisions in the lease. For example, the tenant may receive a rent free period in return for entering into an obligation to carry out works in the future, the landlord or tenant may be given an option to break the lease on, before or after a particular date, or the parties may agree that the revised rent will actually be a percentage of the open market rent.[39] Whenever there are unusual provisions, a certain amount of thought should be given as to the way in which they should be treated on rent review. The parties should decide whether they should be included in the hypothetical lease or disregarded, or if they should be assumed to be included in the hypothetical lease with amendment.[40]

(d) *Rent and rent review.* Clearly, the rent initially reserved by the lease should not be included in the hypothetical lease, as the whole point of the exercise is to determine the rent payable under that lease.[41] Until a series of recent, much-publicised (and much-criticised) decisions of the courts,[42] however, draftsmen did not realise that, in excluding the amount of the reserved rent from the hypothetical lease, they might inadvertently use wording which operated so as also to exclude other provisions relating to the rent (and in particular the rent review provisions) from that lease. Although it is, of course, a question of valuation, it is inevitable that generally, in times of inflation and rising rents, a tenant who is offered a lease for a relatively long term which does not contain provision for the review of the rent initially reserved will pay more for that lease than he would for a lease which provides for the rent to be reviewed at, say, five yearly intervals.[43] Accordingly, in those cases referred to above in which it was held that the wording of the rent review clause did operate so as to exclude from the hypothetical lease not only the amount of rent initially reserved by, but also the rent review provisions contained in, the actual lease,[44] the revised rent determined was higher than it would otherwise have been.[45] Despite recent indications that the courts may be adopting a less literal approach to the construction of this aspect of rent review clauses,[46] the tenant and his advisers should ensure that the rent review clause makes it clear that the hypothetical lease is to include the rent review provisions contained in the actual lease.[47]

(e) *Other deeds and documents.* The question arises as to whether the provisions of deeds and documents other than the lease should be taken into account on rent review. Prior to the review date, the landlord and tenant may have varied the terms of the lease, or entered into some other document, such as a licence granting consent to alterations or change of use, or a document granting rights to the tenant, such as rights to use car parking spaces. Although it is generally accepted that if, as is usual, the hypothetical lease incorporates the terms of the actual lease, it will take the form of the actual lease as varied from time to time,[48] this may not be the case[49] and, if this is intended by the parties, it is advisable for them to make it clear in the rent review clause or elsewhere in the lease that references to the lease are references to the lease as varied from time to time, with the result that all variations will be taken into account in the valuation unless the document specifies to the contrary. If a document entered into between the parties to a lease does not constitute a variation of the lease it seems that, generally,[50] its provisions will not be taken into account and, accordingly, if the parties intend the provisions of any licence or other such document to be taken into account,[51] this should be made clear in the document.[52]

1   See para 6.2 and *Ravenseft Properties Ltd v Park* [1988] 2 EGLR 164, [1988] 50 EG 52.
2   See, for example, the arguments put forward on behalf of the tenant in *SI Pension Trustees Ltd v Ministerio de Marina de la Republica Peruana* [1988] 1 EGLR 119, [1988] 13 EG 48.
3   So, for example, if part of the premises has been surrendered, it will normally be the remaining premises which are the subject of the valuation.
4   See para 6.18:1(d) below.
5   See *Ipswich Town Football Club Co Ltd v Ipswich Borough Council* [1988] 2 EGLR 146, [1988] 32 EG 49 and *New Zealand Government Property Corpn v H M & S Ltd* [1982] QB 1145, [1982] 1 All ER 624, CA.
6   See *New Zealand Government Property Corpn v H M & S Ltd above*. At first sight, there seems much to commend setting out in the lease the dimensions or area of the demised premises but methods of measurement might change during the term of the lease: see *National Westminster Bank plc v Arthur Young McClelland Moores & Co* [1985] 1 EGLR 61, 273 Estates Gazette 402 and John Stuart Colyer QC and Peter Banks 'Paying for the notional or for the real' (Blundell Memorial Lectures 1986). It might be preferable to provide that 'The then current edition of the Royal Institution of Chartered Surveyors and the Incorporated Society of Valuers & Auctioneers "Code of Measuring Practice" shall apply to any calculations of areas required under this clause'. The first edition of the Code was published in 1979 and the second in 1987. The Code has no mandatory status but its purpose is to provide accurate definitions relating to the measurement of buildings and sites to enable practitioners to adopt a common language of measurement practice. Figures should not be taken from letting particulars or the plans of the property as neither may be accurate. If the area of the demised premises is to be altered with the consent of the landlord, it might be as well to set out in the licence how the alteration is to be regarded for rent review purposes and thereby remove the uncertainty present in *A Hudson Pty Ltd v Legal and General Life of Australia Ltd* [1986] 2 EGLR 130, 280 Estates Gazette 1434, PC.
7   See para 4.1 above.
8   In fact this might be implied anyway: see *Jefferies v O'Neill* (1984) 269 Estates Gazette 131.
9   For example *G Orlik (Meat Products) Ltd v Hastings and Thanet Building Society* (1974) 234 Estates Gazette 281, CA. See paras 14.43 and 14.60 below.
10 As to consents granted by the landlords and others generally, see paras 6.18:3(e) and 6.27.
11 See para 6.42 below.
12 As was the case, for example, in *F R Evans (Leeds) Ltd v English Electric Co Ltd* (1977) 36 P & CR 185, 245 Estates Gazette 657. Note also *Leigh v Certibilt Investments Ltd* [1988] 1 EGLR 116, [1988] 04 EG 127 and *Lansdown Estates Group Ltd v TNT Roadfreight (UK) Ltd* [1989] 38 EG 120.
13 See 22 Encyclopaedia of Forms and Precedents (5th edn) Form 122. It is vital that the premises that will be the subject of the hypothetical letting are fully defined – in *Standard Life Assurance Co v Oxoid Ltd* [1987] 2 EGLR 140, 283 Estates Gazette 1219, CA the size of the hypothetical premises was not specified. The greatest care is needed in describing what is to be valued on the review whenever there is to be any departure (or possible departure) from the premises as demised: See *Ipswich Town Football Club Co Ltd v Ipswich Borough Council above*. If the demised premises are not to be the premises for the hypothetical lease, it may be

necessary to amend the terms of the lease as well (*Basingstoke and Deane Borough Council v Host Group Ltd* [1988] 1 All ER 824, [1988] 1 WLR 348, CA).

14 Nevertheless, the parties need to be certain that the 'appropriate' rent of the unusual premises will throughout the term bear the same relationship to the rent of more normal premises. The linking of the rent of the demised premises to some other hypothetical premises is akin to linking the rent to an index with all the inherent dangers (see para 6.64 below), and in particular the possibility that over the years the rental value of the premises will not move in the same way as the index, or in this case as the rent of normal sized premises.

15 In the absence of express provision, it seems that it will generally be implied that the term of the hypothetical lease is to be equivalent to the residue of the term of the actual lease on the review date – see *Basingstoke and Deane Borough Council v Host Group Ltd* [1988] 1 All ER 824, [1988] 1 WLR 348, CA and *Norwich Union Life Insurance Society v Trustee Savings Banks Central Board* [1986] 1 EGLR 136; *Ritz Hotel (London) Ltd v Ritz Casino Ltd* [1988] EGCS 142. Historically, tenants have sought, and landlords have avoided, short hypothetical terms, in the belief that a shorter term will result in a lower rent because a tenant in the open market would pay less if he did not have a relatively long period of security of tenure. As a result many landlords automatically require the term of the hypothetical letting to be the length of the actual term, while many tenants automatically require it to be the residue of the actual term, without consideration of the particular circumstances. This is inadvisable. Whilst in many cases it may be true that a longer term will result in a higher rent, and vice versa, this is not inevitable. Even a tenant for a short term will bear in mind the possibility of renewal under the 1954 Act, and it has now been established that the court may take this into account on rent review (see para 6.28 below). It should also be borne in mind that, although many institutional landlords refuse to grant leases for a short term because they need a relatively long period of guaranteed income, there may be a demand for such leases from tenants who are reluctant to undertake onerous obligations for a long period, particularly in the light of recent publicity about original tenant liability. All the circumstances of the letting need to be taken into account. Consideration should be given, for example, to the terms of the lease and the nature of the premises. A tenant taking on a full-repairing lease of an elderly building, or a lease of a unit on a large estate (which will quite clearly need costly works to be carried out in the relatively near future) which contains wide service charge provisions, may well prefer a shorter term. For examples on the term of the hypothetical lease being specified, see 22 Encyclopaedia of Forms and Precedents (5th edn) Forms 22 (Second Schedule, para 1.3:7) 117 (Clause 3(A)(i)(a)) and 118 (Clause 1.3), Rosscastle Letting Conditions (Appendix 1, Form No 1 below) Condition 7.2:2.7.

16 The Joint Committee of the Law Society and the RICS that produced the Model Forms of rent review clause (see 22 Encyclopaedia of Forms and Precedents (5th edn) Form 117) 'were of the view that the unexpired term subject to a minimum term (suggested to be ten years or a figure closest thereto which represents a multiple of the "review period") was the most appropriate compromise' (see Background Notes to Model Forms, para 6, ibid p 505). The clause recommended by ISVA (ibid Form 118) provides for 'a term of 10 years or a term equal to the residue then unexpired . . .' and a footnote states 'This valuation holds the balance firmly between the interests of landlord and tenant on the occasion of the last rent review. Note that, where the reviews are at intervals other than 5 years, the figure "10" should be adjusted to the figure nearest to 10 which is divisible by the interval between reviews eg 9 for 3 year reviews, 14 for 7 year reviews.' (ibid p 512).

17 It is interesting to surmise what prompted the most unusual hypothetical term of five and a half years found in the *Secretary of State for the Environment v Pivot Properties Ltd* (1980) 256 Estates Gazette 1176 – see para 6.28 below.

18 See para 6.2.

19 See para 6.17:1.

20 For various forms of words, see Encyclopaedia of Forms & Precedents (5th edn) Forms 22 (Second Schedule para 1.3:6), 117 (para 3(A)(i)(b)) and 118 (para 1.3), Rosscastle Letting Conditions (see Appendix 1, Form No 1 below) Condition 7.2:2.7. Many leases follow the wording of the 1954 Act, s 34(1) (see paras 14.50–14.55 and Appendix 3 below) and provide for the revised rent to be determined 'having regard to the terms of this lease'. It was accepted in *Plinth Property Investments Ltd v Mott, Hay and Anderson* (1978) 249 Estates Gazette 1167, CA that where the words 'having regard to' relate to the terms of the hypothetical letting rather than to evidential matters, they do prescribe the basis of valuation. Nonetheless, the words should generally be avoided to avoid dispute, as should any confusion between assumptions relating to the terms of the hypothetical lease and the terms of comparables (see *99 Bishopsgate Ltd v Prudential Assurance Co Ltd* (1984) 270 Estates Gazette 950; on appeal (1985) 273 Estates Gazette 984, CA; *SI Pension Trustees Ltd v Ministerio de Marina de la Republica Peruana* [1988] 1 EGLR 119, [1988] 13 EG 48).

21   Much of the litigation has related to user and alienation, but of course all the terms of the lease are relevant.

22   Such as, for example, a lease which places onerous repairing obligations on the tenant. As to repair generally, see Chapter 8. In *Norwich Union Life Insurance Society v British Railways Board* [1987] 2 EGLR 137, 283 Estates Gazette 846, Hoffmann J upheld the decision of an arbitrator who had reduced the market rent by 27.5% on the basis that a covenant 'to keep the demised premises in good and substantial repair and condition and when necessary to rebuild, reconstruct or replace the same' placed upon the tenant a more onerous obligation than the usual covenant to keep the premises in good and substantial repair. (The term of the lease, however, was 150 years with 21 year reviews and, as the arbitrator pointed out: 'it is not inconceivable that [rebuilding] might indeed become necessary at some point in this time span no matter what the standard of construction of the original building might have been'.) The reverse could presumably be true – a less onerous covenant could cause the rent to be uplifted.

23   Such as, for example, a lease which describes the permitted use by reference to the tenant's business – see para 6.18.3(b) below and, as to user generally, see paras 7.8–7.18 below – or contains an absolute prohibition against assignment or alterations – see para 6.18:3(a) below and, as to assignment and alterations generally, see paras 7.1–7.7 and 7.19–7.26 below.

24   Such as, for example, a lease of a suite of offices which makes no proper provision for the upkeep of the common parts of the building or for the provision of services essential to the tenant's enjoyment of the premises.

25   This will be the case of the provisions have the effect of limiting the user of the premises (see paras 7.8–7.18 below).

26   Such as, for example, a lease of a suite of offices which places obligations on the landlord in respect of the repair and maintenance of the building but which contains defective service charge provisions which do not enable him to recover the entire cost.

27   For a more detailed discussion of the way in which this consideration should be balanced with other considerations when drafting those provisions of the lease relating to user, alterations and alienation, see paras 7.8–7.18, 7.19–7.26 and 7.1–7.7 below.

28   See para 6.22 below.

29   As to the effect of statute on absolute restrictions against alienation, change of use and alterations, see paras 7.3 (alienation), 7.16:1 (user) and 7.24:1 (alterations) below.

30   As to the effect of statute on qualified restrictions against alienation, change of use and alterations, see paras 7.4–7.6 (alienation), 7.16:2 (user) and 7.24:2 (alterations) below. It has been suggested (see, for example, the dictum of Megaw LJ in *Bocardo SA v S and M Hotels Ltd* [1979] 3 All ER 737 at 741, CA with regard to a covenant not to assign without consent) that the words 'such consent not to be unreasonably withheld', or words to similar effect, should be implied in any qualified covenant as a matter of course, but see *Price v Bouch* [1986] 2 EGLR 179, 279 Estates Gazette 1226 (no general rule of law that such words should be implied); *Guardian Assurance Co Ltd v Gants Hill Holdings Ltd* (1983) 267 Estates Gazette 678 (no such words implied in covenant against change of use without consent); *Pearl Assurance plc v Shaw* [1985] 1 EGLR 92 (no such words implied in covenant against applying for planning permission without consent); but see also *Cryer v Scott Bros (Sunbury) Ltd* (1986) 55 P & CR 183, CA, in which it was held that there was no rule of law either way, and whether or not such words should be implied depends on the circumstances of the particular case. In the special circumstances of that case, the words were implied in a covenant concerning the approval of works.

31   See paras 7.3–7.6 below.

32   See paras 7.16:1 and 7.16:2 below.

33   See paras 7.24:1 and 7.24:2 below.

34   See *Plinth Properties Ltd v Mott, Hay and Anderson* (above). This related to a lease containing an absolute prohibition against user otherwise than 'as offices in connection with the lessee's business of consulting engineers', but there seems to be no reason why the principle should not apply in the case of any absolute restriction. For a criticism of the reasoning of the case, see Bernstein and Reynold's *Handbook of Rent Review*, para 5.5.

35   Valuers may consider that the addition of the words 'without consent', or the equivalent, is an indication that the landlord may more readily consider a change of use – see the comments of Peter Gibson J in *Forte & Co Ltd v General Accident Life Assurance Ltd* [1986] 2 EGLR 115: 'The decision in the *Plinth* case in my view turned on the particular wording of the particular lease which permitted only one form of user. It does not follow that the decision applies to a case where the lease expressly contemplates that other forms of user might be authorised. Of course it would be open to the arbitrator to say that the possibility of the superior lessors acting arbitrarily, as they are entitled to do, when asked for their authority has the effect in valuation terms that the rental value has to be assessed on the footing that the specified forms of user are the only permitted forms of user. But equally, in my judgment, if he were to say that the hypothetical lessee would pay more for a lease which expressly contemplated the possibility of change of use, I do not see that he could be faulted.'

36 See *C & A Pensions Trustees Ltd v British Vita Investments Ltd* (1984) 272 Estates Gazette 63 and, for the corresponding position on lease renewal, see *Charles Clements (London) Ltd v Rank City Wall Ltd* (1978) 246 Estates Gazette739; *Aldwych Club Ltd v Copthall Property Co Ltd* (1962) 185 Estates Gazette 219 and para 14.52. See also D W Williams 'Improvements and User at Rent Reviews' (1984) Estates Gazette 1673. It is suggested by D N Clarke and J E Adams (*Rent Reviews and Variable Rents*, 2nd edn, p 209) that the landlord might insert, in the lease, a provision which would allow him to waive restrictions at his discretion, and which would enable him to relax the restrictions in the lease immediately prior to a review date so as to avoid a lower rent. It is true that this would allow the landlord to wait and see whether or not the tenant is sufficiently well advised at rent review to argue for a lower rent on the basis of a restrictive clause. In the majority of cases, however, it is suggested that it will simply result in a deferring of the evil moment when the landlord has to decide whether his priority is control or income. It would normally be imprudent for a tenant to accept such a provision. Indeed, perhaps the greatest argument against this suggestion, is that a tenant in so weak a position as to accept such a provision would probably also accept an assumption, in the rent review clause, rendering the terms of the hypothetical lease wider than that in the actual lease would normally be preferable from the landlord's point of view.

37 See paras 7.1–7.7 below and *James v British Crafts Centre*. Note also *Ritz Hotel (London) Ltd v Ritz Casino Ltd* [1988] EGCS 142.

38 See paras 7.8–7.18 below.

39 For example, in *Guys 'n' Dolls Ltd v Sade Bros Catering Ltd* (1983) 269 Estates Gazette 129, CA the lease provided that the revised rent was to be £7,500 above the fair rack market rental value. The question for the court was whether account should be taken of the obligation to pay this extra rent in determining the rental value. Note also *Lister Locks Ltd v TEI Pension Trust Ltd* (1981) 264 Estates Gazette 827.

40 So, for example, if the actual lease contains a break clause exercisable by the tenant on a specified date, the parties might decide to incorporate the clause in the hypothetical lease in the case of reviews which take place before that date only. Alternatively, they might decide to incorporate the clause in the case of all reviews, and include an assumption as to the date on which it is exercisable.

41 Although the point is probably self-evident, and it is no doubt for this reason that it is not expressly dealt with in the form of rent review clause recommended by the ISVA (22 Encyclopaedia of Forms and Precedents (5th edn) Form 118 para 1.3. As the form contains no provision for the disregard of the rent the dangers mentioned later in this paragraph are avoided.

42 See *Pugh v Smiths Industries Ltd* (1982) 264 Estates Gazette 823; *Lister Locks Ltd v TEI Pension Trust Ltd* (1981) 264 Estates Gazette 827; *Safeway Food Stores Ltd v Banderway Ltd* (1983) 267 Estates Gazette 850; *National Westminster Bank plc v Arthur Young McClelland Moores & Co* [1985] 1 EGLR 61, 273 Estates Gazette 402; *Securicor Ltd v Postal Properties Ltd* [1985] 1 EGLR 102, 274 Estates Gazette 730; *Datastream International Ltd v Oakeep Ltd* [1986] 1 All ER 966, [1986] 1 WLR 404n; *MFI Properties Ltd v BICC Group Pension Trust Ltd* [1986] 1 All ER 974; *British Gas Corpn v Universities Superannuation Scheme Ltd* [1986] 1 All ER 978, [1986] 1 WLR 398; *Electricity Supply Nominees v F M Insurance Co Ltd* [1986] 1 EGLR 143, 278 Estates Gazette 523; *Amax International Ltd v Custodian Holdings Ltd* [1986] 2 EGLR 111, 279 Estates Gazette 762; *General Accident Fire and Life Assurance plc v Electronic Data Processing Co plc* [1987] 1 EGLR 112, 281 Estates Gazette 65; *Equity and Law Life Assurance Society plc v Bodfield Ltd* [1987] 1 EGLR 124, 281 Estates Gazette 1448, CA; *British Home Stores plc v Ranbrook Properties Ltd* [1988] 1 EGLR 121, [1988] 16 EG 80.

43 See note 45 below, but see also *Lear v Blizzard* [1983] 3 All ER 662 discussed at para 6.3:4 above.

44 The landlord's argument was successful in all but *Datastream*, *MFI Properties*, *British Gas*, *Amax* and *Electricity Supplies*, and *British Home Stores* and the decisions in the other cases have been considerably criticised – see for example John Stuart Colyer QC and Peter Banks: 'Paying for the notional or for the real' (Blundell Memorial Lecture 1986), Legal Notes (1987) 282 Estates Gazette 719, (1987) 7 PLB 73. Common sense suggests that none of the parties to the leases that were before the courts in all these cases consciously and genuinely intended that the reviewed rents should be determined on this artificial basis, and as such it is unfortunate that the courts, subject to the few exceptions, felt that the principles of construction compelled them to construe the clauses in this way. Nor was it easy to follow the Court of Appeal's views in *Equity and Law* of the 'commercial' guidelines proposed by Sir Nicolas Browne-Wilkinson V-C in *British Gas*. A bold statement from the Court of Appeal to the effect that the parties should, in the absence of very clear words to the contrary, be

presumed to have intended that the hypothetical letting should be on the same terms as the actual letting (other than quantum of rent) that might have been expected in *Equity and Law* was not forthcoming until *Basingstoke and Deane Borough Council v Host Group Ltd* [1988] 1 All ER 824, [1988] 1 WLR 348: see para 6.17:2 above. In the light of *Basingstoke*, it seems unlikely that the landlord's argument would succeed today in the way in which it did in those cases referred to in footnote 26 above that were determined in the landlord's favour . . . although note the rather stricter approach adopted by the Court of Appeal in for example *Stroud v Weir Associates Ltd* [1987] 1 EGLR 190, 281 Estates Gazette 1198, CA and in *Equity and Law*.

45 The uplift in rent has, in some of the cases mentioned, been considerable. In *Pugh* it was 22.5% (£30,000/36,750) and in *National Westminster* 20.5%.

46 See para 6.17:2 above.

47 See 22 Encyclopaedia of Forms and Precedents (5th edn) Forms 22 (Second Schedule para 1.3:6) and 117 (para 3(A)(i)(b)), Rosscastle Letting Conditions, (see Appendix 1, Form No 1 below) Condition 7.2:2.6. Some leases provide for the rent to be revised on specified dates, often referred to as the 'Review Dates'. If the terms of the actual lease are incorporated in the hypothetical lease and the term of the hypothetical letting is longer than the residue of the term of the actual lease, this could cause similar problems to those mentioned above. See para 6.4 and in particular note 20 above and para 6.18:3(d) below. In such circumstances, therefore, the rent review clause should include an assumption that the hypothetical lease contains provision for the review of the rent at similar intervals to the reviews provided for under the actual lease.

48 See, for example, Bernstein and Reynold's *Handbook of Rent Review*, para 5.12: 'The user covenant in the lease must of course be considered in conjunction with any licences entered into to vary the permitted use.'

49 See *SI Pension Trustees Ltd v Ministerio de Marina de la Republica Peruana* [1988] 1 EGLR 119, in which the rent review clause provided for the valuation to be carried out 'having regard to rental values . . . for similar property . . . subject to the provisions similar to those contained in this lease', and in which Mervyn Davies J said that this referred 'to the provisions of the lease, not to the provisions of the lease as they may be varied from time to time' and *Pleasurama Properties Ltd v Leisure Investments (West End) Ltd* [1986] 1 EGLR 145, CA in which the rent review clause provided for the hypothetical lease to be 'subject to covenants on the part of the tenant and conditions herein contained . . .' and in which Lloyd J said 'I will assume – though I certainly do not accept – that the deed of licence is to be regarded as a variation of the lease. I prefer the view that the licence is what it purports to be, namely, a licence granted pursuant to the lease . . . Even so, it does not follow that the covenant contained in the licence is to be read into . . . the lease . . . The question we have to ask ourselves is whether, on a fair reading of the deed of licence, the parties intended the covenant [to reinstate] to be brought within the lease. I am quite clear that they did not.'

50 See *Pleasurama Properties Ltd v Leisure Investments (West End) Ltd*, discussed in note 49 above. Nonetheless, there may be factors which, arguably, cause them to be taken into account. Many licences for change of use or alterations specify that the lease is to be varied to incorporate the tenant's covenants, to ensure that a tenant in breach of covenants contained in a licence will be liable to forfeiture (see, for example, 22 Encyclopaedia of Forms and Precedents (5th edn) Form 144). Some leases provide that references to the lease are to be interpreted as including references to all supplemental deeds and documents, and it could be argued that a document such as a licence for alterations or change of use is supplemental to a lease. Furthermore, assumptions included in the rent review clause may have the effect of incorporating the provisions of licences. Both the model form of rent review clause prepared by the Law Society and RICS and that prepared by the ISVA (see 22 Encyclopaedia of Forms and Precedents (5th edn) Forms 117 and 118) include general provisions of this nature. The Law Society/RICS clause contains an assumption that the premises 'may be used for any of the purposes permitted by this lease as varied or extended by any licence granted pursuant thereto'. This, of course, only relates to user, and may not apply to licences which cannot be considered to have been granted 'pursuant to' the lease. It should be noted that it does not deal with problems which may arise from licences referring to the actual tenant by name (see note 52 below). One concern which tenants will have when presented with such an assumption is that, if a particular use is permitted by the landlord but not, for example, by planning legislation, could it be argued, as a result of this assumption, that the premises may lawfully be used for that purpose (see para 6.27, note 11 below)? The ISVA model form contains an assumption that 'the benefit of any planning or other consent current at the relevant Review Date is available also for such willing tenant'. Assuming that this assumption will be construed as applying to consents from the landlord as well as consents in the nature of statutory consents, it should be noted that it does not specify that the tenant must have the benefit of the relevant consent. The fact that a subtenant (or, indeed the landlord) has the right, for example, to use the premises for a particular purpose may have a substantially different effect on valuation than the fact that the tenant has that right! A further concern is that neither form of assumption makes it clear that covenants given by the tenant in the relevant licence as a result of the consent granted (such as, for example, a covenant to obtain, and not to jeopardise, a justices' licence in a licence granting consent for change of use to a public house, or a covenant to keep the premises open in a licence granting consent to change of use to a shop) should be considered to be incorporated in the hypothetical lease.

51 Should licences which entitle the tenant to carry out alterations, change the use of the premises, apply for planning permission or otherwise be taken into account? Usually there is no need. If a lease contains a fully qualified prohibition against change of use, the valuer is entitled to value the premises on the basis of the use commanding the highest rent to which consent could not be unreasonably withheld. Similarly, if the lease contains a fully qualified prohibition against alterations, the valuer will take into account the fact that the hypothetical tenant will be able to carry out alterations to which consent could not be reasonably withheld. There are circumstances where hardship could occur if licences are not taken into account, however. If the lease contains a qualified prohibition against change of use the landlord is entitled to withhold consent at his discretion and, accordingly, the valuer is probably not entitled to take into account the possibility of consent being granted. If the landlord has, in fact, granted permission for a change of use, it would seem unfair for this to be disregarded. This problem can, however, be avoided by the landlord by drafting any such consent as a variation. As to user generally, see paras 7.18–7.18 below.

52 This has been discussed elsewhere in connection with rights such as rights to use car parking spaces (see para 6.18:1(c)) where it was said that any such licence should clearly specify whether or not its existence should be taken into account on rent review. In addition, of course, if its existence is to be taken into account and it refers to the actual tenant by name, it should usually specify that it is to be assumed on rent review that the name of the hypothetical tenant is substituted for that of the actual tenant. Care should be taken in the drafting of any document which is to be taken into account on rent review: for example, many licences granted pursuant to a lease contain time limits within which they are to be implemented, failing which they are to become void.

6.19 *Vacant possession: purpose and potential concerns.* It has already been suggested that the hypothetical letting required to be assumed by the rent review clause should bear as close a resemblance to reality as possible.[1] The very fact that in reality the premises are already let to the tenant, and usually have been for some years, and that no new letting is in fact taking place, requires the assumption of certain matters which may not, in fact, be the case on the review date. For example, a rent review clause commonly provides that it should be assumed that the premises are being let with vacant possession.[2] It has been held that this means that the tenant should be deemed to have moved out of, or never to have occupied, the premises.[3] The main purpose of such an assumption is self-evident. It directs the valuation of a new leasehold interest in the premises similar to, and in substitution for, the interest which the tenant actually has, rather than the valuation of a new intermediate leasehold interest in the premises, subject to the existing lease. However, such an assumption may have other significant consequences. For example:

6.19:1 *Property already sublet.* In the case of property subject to one or more sublettings on the review date, any such subletting would be ignored in arriving at the revised rent where vacant possession had to be assumed. This could work in either party's favour, depending on the circumstances – a landlord might have wished that a profitable subletting could have been taken into account, but might be pleased, in the case of a shop with accommodation above, if an existing residential subletting of the latter subject to the Rent Acts would be disregarded, because such a subletting might serve to depress the rental value of the demised premises, particularly if that accommodation had potential for office user.[4]

6.19:2 *Incoming tenant unlikely to occupy whole.* In the case of premises of such a nature that an incoming tenant would be unlikely to occupy them all himself, it could mean that a deduction would be made from the revised rent when market forces prevailing at the review date were such that, on a new letting at that time, an incoming tenant would obtain a reduction in rent, or rent-free period or other benefit, to compensate him for the fact that he will need to find subtenants.[5]

6.19:3 *Fixtures and fittings/equipped for immediate use.* It seems to have been assumed by the courts and commentators[6] that, because such an assumption means that the tenant should be deemed to have moved out of or never to have occupied the premises,[7] the tenant should be deemed to have removed all those tenant's fixtures and fittings which he would be entitled to remove on the determination of the existing lease.[8] The effect of this on rent review will, of course, depend on the quantity and nature of tenant's fixtures and fittings at the premises. However, it could again mean that a deduction would be made from the revised rent when market forces prevailing at the review date were such that, on a new letting at that time, an incoming tenant would obtain a reduction in rent, rent free period or other benefit to compensate him for the fact that he will need to fit out the premises. The landlord frequently seeks to overcome this risk by providing that it must be assumed that the premises that are to be the subject of the hypothetical letting are fit and available for immediate occupation and use, or words to similar effect.[9]

1 See para 6.17 above.
2 See, for example, 22 Encyclopaedia of Forms and Precedents (5th edn) Forms 22 (Second Schedule, para 1.3:4), 117 (para 3(A)(i)(a)) and 118 (para 1.3), Rosscastle Letting Conditions (Appendix 1, Form No 1 below) Condition 7.2:2.4. If there is no express assumption to this effect, the question of whether one should be implied is a matter of construction having regard to the circumstances of the original letting, for example, was it the party's intention that the tenant would sublet, and was there a subletting in existence at the time of the lease: *Avon County Council v Alliance Property Co Ltd* (1981) 258 Estates Gazette 1181; *Oscroft v Benabow* [1967] 2 All ER 548, [1967] 1 WLR 1087, CA; *Scottish and Newcastle Breweries plc v Sir Richard Sutton's Settled Estates* [1985] 2 EGLR 130, 276 Estates Gazette 77, (see Legal Notes (1985) 276 Estates Gazette 311); *Forte & Co Ltd v General Accident Life Assurance Ltd* [1986] 2 EGLR 115, 279 Estates Gazette 1227.
3 *F R Evans (Leeds) Ltd v English Electric Co Ltd* (1977) 245 Estates Gazette 657 per Donaldson J.
4 See para 6.19 below. Note *Royal Exchange Assurance v Bryant Samuel Properties (Coventry) Ltd* [1985] 1 EGLR 84, 273 Estates Gazette 1332.
5 The review clause in *99 Bishopsgate Ltd v Prudential Assurance Co Ltd* [1985] 1 EGLR 72, 273 Estates Gazette 984 provided that the revised rent was to be '. . . a fair yearly rent for the demised premises as at [the review date] having regard to rental values current at such day for property let without a premium with vacant possession and to the provisions of this Lease (other than the rent hereby reserved) . . .' – ie the vacant possession assumption was expressed to apply to the comparables and not, as such, to the demised premises. For an example of this type of clause, see the two previous forms of the Draft Model Forms of rent review clause prepared by the Law Society and the RICS: (1979) Gazette 6 June 564, (1980) Gazette 26 March 82. The latter was set out in full in the 2nd edition of *Drafting and Negotiating Commercial Leases*. In fact, it seems that generally this has the same effect (see para 6.18:3, note 3 above). In that case, the arbitrator found that an incoming tenant on the review date would obtain an initial rent free period of sixteen months, and the Court of Appeal upheld the arbitrators alternative award in which an allowance for that sixteen month period was made, discounted, not over the review period, but for the likely term (as found by the arbitrator) of underlettings of the type envisaged.
6 See Bernstein and Reynold's *Handbook of Rent Review*, para 4.48.
7 See note 3 above.
8 See *New Zealand Government Property Corpn v H M & S Ltd* [1982] 2 QB 1145, [1982] 1 All ER 624, CA; *Young v Dalgety plc* [1987] 1 EGLR 116, 281 Estates Gazette 427, CA. For the right of the

tenant to remove fixtures and fittings, see Halsbury's Laws of England Vol 27 (Landlord and Tenant) para 142 et seq.

9 See para 6.20:2 below, 22 Encyclopaedia of Forms and Precedents (5th edn) Forms 22 (Second Schedule para 1.3:5), 117 (clause 3(A)(i)(c) and 118 (clause 1.3(A) and Rosscastle Letting Conditions (Appendix 1, Form No 1 below) Condition 7.2:2.5.

6.20 *Vacant possession: drafting.* So far as the problem referred to in para 6.19:1 above is concerned, the solution is self-evident. The rent review clause should specify whether vacant possession of the whole should be assumed, or whether the hypothetical letting is to be subject to particular subleases, or all subleases, in existence at the review date.[1] If at the date of the grant of the lease there are existing subleases, it is likely to be fair that these should be taken into account on rent review. On the other hand, it may be that the parties will require the existence of subleases granted during the subsistence of the lease to be disregarded on rent review, certainly if the landlord is to have limited control over their grant. The solution to the problems referred to in para 6.19:2 and 6.19:3 above is less simple. Any attempt to draft a provision that aims to ensure that the vacant possession assumption would not bring about a reduction in the revised rent for the reasons set out in those paragraphs needs to recognise that, generally, rent-free periods (or reductions in rent in lieu of rent-free periods or other benefits) are granted essentially for three distinct reasons:

6.20:1 *Subletting.* Frequently the length of a rent-free period, or the value of a reduction in rent or other benefit, granted at the commencement of a new letting reflects a genuine attempt by the parties to compensate the tenant who does not propose to occupy the whole or some of the premises himself for the time, and sometimes also for the expense, involved in finding subtenants at the commencement of the term. To the extent that the parties take this disadvantage to the tenant into account in the bargain which they strike at the commencement of the letting, the tenant cannot reasonably expect it to be taken into account once more on rent review. It has to be stressed that the precise solution to this problem depends on the extent to which, and manner in which, this disadvantage is taken into account at the commencement of the letting, and on what the position is at the commencement of the letting. The following three suggested solutions[2] may be appropriate, with or without adaptation, in particular circumstances:

(a) If there are subleases, or agreements for sublease, in existence at the commencement of the term, or if the parties have entered into arrangements by virtue of which the landlord will be closely involved in the granting of subleases after the commencement of the term, it may be possible to resolve the problem by providing for existing subleases to be taken into account on rent review, as mentioned above.

(b) Another possible solution is to include in the rent review clause an assumption that the premises are being let with vacant possession, and also an assumption that a rent-free period or other benefit is being given at the commencement of the hypothetical letting, to compensate the tenant for those matters mentioned above in respect of which the tenant actually receives once and for all compensation on the grant of the lease. The clause should then provide that the revised rent will be the yearly rent which would be payable by the hypothetical tenant on the determination of that rent-free period, or taking into account the fact that the tenant has received that other benefit. The parties should consider whether the length of the rent-free period, or value of the other benefit assumed should be the same as that actually given on the grant of the lease, or that which is normally given in the market prevailing on the review date, by way of compensation for the relevant matters.

(c) A further possible solution is for the rent review clause to include an assumption that, on the review date, there are potential subtenants in existence, who are ready, willing and able to take subleases on completion of the hypothetical lease, or that the premises are fully sublet.[1] The draftsman will have to include in the rent review clause sufficient information about the subleases to enable the valuation to take place.[3]

6.20:2 *Fitting out and fit for immediate occupation.* Again, the length of a rent-free period, or the value of a reduction in rent or other benefit, granted at the commencement of a new letting frequently reflects a genuine attempt by the parties to compensate the tenant for the time, and sometimes also for the expense, involved in fitting out the premises. Again, to the extent that this disadvantage to the tenant has been taken into account at the commencement of the letting, the tenant cannot reasonably expect it to be taken into account once more on rent review and again, the precise solution to the problem will depend on the extent to which, and the manner in which, it was so taken into account. There are a number of ways in which landlords attempt to deal with this problem. The most popular is to include, in the rent review clause, an assumption that the premises are 'fit and available for immediate occupation',[4] or 'fully fitted out and equipped so as to be ready for immediate occupation and use',[5] on the review date, or words to similar effect.[6] Tenants raise two main objections to such assumptions, resulting from the fact that they may achieve far more than the avoidance of a rent-free period on review:

(a) Statute, or disrepair, or damage by an insured or uninsured risk, may have rendered the premises legally or physically 'unfit', or 'unready', for occupation and use on the review date. Such unfitness, or unreadiness, may have resulted from, or may not have been remedied by the review date as a result of, the tenant's default, but it may alternatively have resulted from, or not been remedied as a result of, the landlord's default, or the default of neither party. Whether or not such matters should be taken into account on rent review is discussed elsewhere,[7] but the tenant's advisors should bear in mind that the former wording given above will almost undoubtedly prevent their being taken into account, and it is certainly arguable that the latter may have the same effect in certain circumstances.

(b) Both forms of wording given above require it to be assumed that fitting out works have been done, with the result that the premises should, presumably, be valued with the benefit of those hypothetical fitting out works. Two obvious questions arise. First, to what standard should the hypothetical fitting out works be assumed to have been done? and secondly, what fitting out works should be assumed to have been done? These could be areas of potential dispute. In addition consider, for example, premises which are hypothetically available on rent review for a number of different uses, some of which, while requiring more time-consuming and costly fitting out works than others, may command a higher rent.[8] Should the landlord be able to obtain a rent on rent review which a hypothetical tenant wanting to use the premises for the higher rental-producing use would pay if such time-consuming and costly fitting out works had been done by the landlord prior to the grant of the lease, notwithstanding the fact that at the commencement of the term the tenant, who did not intend to use the premises for any such use, received once and for all compensation only for far less time-consuming and costly works?

An alternative way in which landlords seek to avoid any reduction in the revised rent resulting from the deemed removal of tenant's fixtures and fittings is actually to direct in the rent review clause that no reduction in the revised rent should be made to take account of any rent-free period or other rental concession which, on a new letting with vacant possession, an incoming tenant might be granted to compensate him for the time it will take him to carry out his fitting out works.[9] Landlords adopting such an alternative should be aware that it does not achieve the collateral advantages mentioned above. In addition, they may prefer the rent review clause to contain an assumption that such a rent-free period or other concession is being offered to the hypothetical tenant, together with a direction that the revised rent is to be the yearly rent payable by that tenant on the expiry of that rent-free period, or after the making of that other concession. Tenants generally accept that this method of dealing with the problem achieves a fair result, although they might consider it more fair (particularly if the premises are available for a wide variety of uses) if the length of the rent-free period or value of the concession were actually the same as that given to the original tenant on the grant of the lease or, at least, that which would be given to a tenant using the premises for the original tenant's use.

6.20:3 *Inducements.* There are cases, however, when market conditions are such that an incoming tenant would be able to obtain a rent-free period very much longer than, or some other benefit far in excess of, that which would be required to compensate him for the need to fit out the premises or find subtenants, as an inducement to enter into the lease.[10] It is suggested that, where this state of affairs subsists at the time of the review date in relation to premises of the type in question, it ought *not* to be disregarded in determining the revised rent, and any drafting that sought to provide otherwise would be an attempt to remove from comparables,[11] where such inducements were present, a vital element of those comparables. This would be 'tinkering' with the evidence and would be likely to cause legal and valuation difficulties, quite apart from being unfair on the tenant.[12] And yet, some landlords would argue that the provision of 'one-off' inducements on the grant of leases of a type of premises in a certain area is no reason for 'depressing' the rent of comparable premises, let sometime previously, that fall to be reviewed while inducements are being offered.[13] Finally, when the parties have introduced such provisions as they consider to be fair to deal with the matters set out in paras 6.20:1 and 6.20:2, they should ensure that the arrangements are not upset, and that ambiguities are not created, by provisions of the hypothetical lease. If (as will normally be the case) the hypothetical lease incorporates the terms of the actual lease[14] and, for example, the actual lease provides for a rent-free period, it will normally be advisable for the rent review clause to specify that those provisions are to be excluded.[15]

1   See 22 Encyclopaedia of Forms & Precedents (5th edn) Form 123.

2   Another solution can be seen in *Leigh v Certibilt Investments Ltd* [1988] 1 EGLR 116, [1988] 04 EG 127 in which the rent review clause provided for the rent to be 50% of the aggregate rent which would be achieved on hypothetical lettings of individual parts of the premises. The 50% discount was designed, in the opinion of the judge, to compensate the tenant for potential voids, for the expense of management, including the cost of reletting units from time to time, and a profit rental.

3   See 22 Encyclopaedia of Forms and Precedents (5th edn) Form 123. In *Leigh v Certibilt Investments Ltd* (see note 2 above), counsel conceded that, in the absence of any appropriate assumption in the rent review clause, the valuer had a free hand to assume whatever term, duration and provisions would be appropriate in an underlease of the appropriate part.

4   See ibid Form 117.

5   See ibid Form 118.

6   See ibid Form 22 (Second Schedule para 1.3:5), Rosscastle Letting Conditions (see Appendix 1, Form No 1 below) Condition 7.2:2.5.

7   See para 6.25:2, note 5 below.

8   As to valuation when the premises are available for a variety of uses, see para 7.11:3 below.

9   See ibid Form 117.

10   Such inducements are not uncommon because landlords, when operating in a tenants' market, frequently prefer quite generous 'one-off' incentives at the commencement of the term (such as rent-free or concessional rent periods, a payment to the tenant for fitting out or otherwise (limited) responsibility for the tenants' existing lease etc) to a reduction in the rent that they were seeking for the premises. Previously rents were generally negotiated to represent the value of the premises and to become payable either immediately or after a fairly short period for fitting out – the inducement was simply a reduction in the 'asking rent'.

11   See para 6.41 below.

12   Thus it is suggested that if the rent review is taking place in a market in which all new lettings are accompanied by 'inducements' (see above), the rents reserved by these leases should be discounted in order to allow for the inducements when assessing the value of the premises that are being reviewed. There is no authority, however, as to the way in which such inducements should be reflected and in particular the period over which any discount should be made (see note 4 to para 6.19 above). For example, in a depressed market the comparables might suggest that an incoming tenant would obtain a rent-free period of a year and then pay £10,000 per annum up to the first review in five years. A tenant on a rent review might suggest that the rent for the next five year Review Period should be £8,000 per annum (ie $4 \times £10,000$ – being the total rent paid during the review period – $\div$ 5). In support of this view, the tenant might argue that a rent-free period should be regarded as a reverse premium. If a premium had been charged, so the argument goes, this would have had to be written off over the review period unless the lease provided that once the open market rent had been determined, there should be a deduction to allow for the premium. Nevertheless, an alternative would be that the rent should be discounted over the full term rather than the review period. Thus if the term of the hypothetical letting in the above example was 20 years, the rent should be £9,500 ($19 \times £10,000 \div 20$). But is this the correct approach when the rent will be reviewed again every five years? (These calculations have been included for illustrative purposes – it is recognised that in practice life is rarely this simple!)

13   The logic of such an argument is difficult to follow. Nonetheless, for suggested assumptions for landlords who do endorse it, see 22 Encyclopaedia of Forms and Precedents (5th edn) Form 124.

14   See para 6.18:3 above.

15   See para 6.18.3(c) above and, for examples of the way in which this might be done, ibid Form 22 (Second Schedule paras 1.3:6 and 1.3:7) and Rosscastle Letting (see Appendix 1, Form No 1 below) Conditions 7.2:2.6 and 7.2:2.7.

6.21   *Let by one lease.* Another assumption which is inserted in appropriate circumstances to ensure that the hypothetical letting reflects the actual letting as nearly as possible, is an assumption that the premises are let on one lease.¹ This means that the revised rent will be determined on the basis of a single letting of the whole of the premises, rather than on the basis of a number of separate lettings of parts of the premises. In a lease of an industrial estate, for example, such an assumption would prevent the revised rent from being determined by aggregating the rents that might be obtained on separate lettings of each unit on the estate.[2] The assumption does not, however, prevent the third party from having regard to the possibility of the tenant subletting parts of the premises. The hypothetical letting will usually be made on the same terms as the actual lease, including the alienation convenants[3] and if these permit subletting of part, the third party should take this into account in determining the revised rent.[4]

1   See for example 22 Encyclopaedia of Forms and Precedents (5th edn) Form 22 (Second Schedule para 1.3:4), Rosscastle Letting Conditions (Appendix 1, Form No 1 below) Condition 7.2:2.4. It is often said that, when the rent review clause requires the assumption of a letting of the premises rather than the ascertainment of the rental value, this is not necessary – *sed quaere*: it seems that this must depend on the precise wording of the rent review clause, and that the expression should be included for the avoidance of doubt. Another form of assumption commonly employed is that the premises are 'let as a whole' (see, for example, the 1985 edition of the Law Society/RICS Model form of rent review clause (22 Encyclopaedia of Forms and Precedents (5th edn) Form 117). It is arguable that this, if taken in isolation, would be consistent with the grant of two or more hypothetical leases, each demising part of the premises and between them demising the whole of the premises. In *Avon County Council v Alliance Property Co Ltd* (1981) 258 Estates Gazette 1181 the words 'the whole of the demised premises' were taken as an indication that existing subleases should be disregarded.

2   See *F R Evans (Leeds) Ltd v English Electric Co Ltd* (1977) 245 Estates Gazette 657 and, for a lease in which the rent review clause was held to have this effect, *Leigh v Certibilt Investments Ltd* [1988] 1 EGLR 116.

3   See para 6.18:3 above.

4   It has been suggested that the assumption 'let as a whole' (see note 1 above) is a direction to the valuer to disregard the possibility of sub-letting part, but it is extremely difficult to understand how this can be the case. The tenant's ability to sublet or otherwise deal with the premises once the hypothetical lease has been granted depends upon the terms of the hypothetical lease as to alienation (see para 6.18:3 above). If these terms permit sublettings of part by the tenant, there is no reason why this should be over-ridden by an assumption that the premises are let as a whole (or on a single lease) to the tenant. If the draftsman wishes the valuer to disregard the possibility of subletting part, an express provision to this effect should be included. Where subletting of individual floors of a large office block is permitted, the market value of the whole building can often only be determined by aggregating the rental values of each floor (especially where the premises are such that the whole building is unlikely to be occupied by a single tenant): see *99 Bishopsgate Ltd v Prudential Assurance Co Ltd* [1985] 1 EGLR 72, 273 Estates Gazette 984, CA; *Leigh v Certibilt Investments Ltd* [1988] 1 EGLR 116, [1988] 04 EG 127.

6.22   *Willing landlord and willing tenant.* Section 34(1) of the 1954 Act dealing with the renewal of leases refers to a willing lessor and it is normal for rent review provisions to direct that a willing landlord and a willing tenant be assumed.[1] Again the purpose of such an assumption is to facilitate the operation of the hypothetical letting. These terms were considered by Donaldson J in *F R Evans (Leeds) Ltd v English Electric Co Ltd.*[2] The lease here concerned sixty acres of land together with buildings amounting to nearly a million square feet of floor space. The rent review provision provided that the reviewed rent should be the 'full yearly market rental' at the time of the review which was defined as 'the rent at which the demised premises are worth to be let with vacant possession on the open market as a whole between a willing lessor and a willing lessee for the remainder of the said term outstanding . . .'. Donaldson J held that it had to be assumed that there was a willing landlord and a willing tenant and any particular circumstances affecting the landlord and tenant in question which would not affect the hypothetical landlord and tenant should be ignored. Negotiations would be conducted fairly with all the appropriate bargaining advantages and disadvantages. The hypothetical willing landlord was neither one who was forced to let the premises nor one who could afford to wait until the market improved and the hypothetical willing tenant was one who was actively seeking premises like those that were the subject of the lease but who was not under any pressure to do so. It was implicit in the clause that there was in fact a rent upon which a willing landlord and a willing tenant would have agreed and it was to be assumed that there was at least one willing tenant in the market. Section 34 of the 1954 Act[3] makes no reference to a willing tenant but it is considered[4] that the court would infer that there was at least one willing tenant from the fact that the tenant was making an application for a new tenancy of those premises under the Act. Nevertheless, until *Dennis & Robinson Ltd v Kiossos Establishment*,[5] it was felt that the answer need not be the same in the case of a rent review where the rent review clause made no express reference to a willing tenant. In times of recession, there are tenants who have either moved out of premises because they have no further need for them, or who would do so if only they were able to dispose of their lease. If such a tenant had offered to surrender the lease back to the landlord for no consideration, and the landlord had refused, and if he had made extensive efforts to dispose of the property by means of an assignment or sublease without success (and perhaps even offered a reverse premium for so doing), he may be able to satisfy the arbitrator or expert that, assuming the lease in question had not existed and the landlord was seeking to let the premises, he would not at that time have found a party who was prepared to take a lease similar to that being offered hypothetically on the rent review. In such a case, where there was a lack of any express provision that a willing lessee is to be assumed, a tenant might well think that he has strong grounds for submitting that one should not be assumed, because such an assumption was contrary to reality, and not justified by the express terms of the lease. This was the argument advanced by the tenant in *Kiossos*.[5] Mr Michael Wheeler QC, sitting as a deputy Judge of the Chancery Division agreed – he came to the conclusion that to say that it must be assumed that there will be a letting is to incorporate into the hypothetical exercise a situation which the language of the rent review clause did not warrant and which was completely unreal.[6] The Court of Appeal,[5] however, allowed the landlord's appeal and held that the following assumptions had to be made: (1) there will be a letting of the property, (2) there is a market in which that letting is agreed, (3) the landlord is willing to let the premises, (4) equally, the supposed tenant is willing to take the premises. The court decided that although there was no express reference to a willing lessor and a willing lessee, such an implication was necessary to achieve an open market letting and the fact that the above assumptions are artificial is irrelevant. And yet, the landlord may have achieved only a pyrrhic victory[7] because Fox LJ seemed to be suggesting that when there is little or no demand for the premises, it might be of little consequence that a willing tenant had to be assumed. He said:[8]

'But the dispute which had arisen has, I think, some unreality about it. The assumptions are only a part of the process of computation of the full yearly market rent. It is assumed that there is a willing lessee. But the willing lessee is not going to pay more than the market requires him to pay. It is essentially a matter for the valuer to inquire into and determine the strength of the market. He is, for example, entitled, if such is his expert opinion on the facts, to say that, having regard to the state of the market and the condition of the property, a tenant, though a willing tenant, could not be expected to take the stipulated lease save at a low or nominal rent and that the full yearly market rent must be determined accordingly. Further, any determination below £30,000 will leave the existing rent unaltered anyway.'[9]

Dillon LJ, after confirming that a willing tenant had to be assumed said[10] that:

'the strength of the market and the rental value of the premises in the market are matters for the valuer's discretion based on his own knowledge and experience of the letting value of such premises.' In fact, as Fox LJ indicated, in the case of an upwards-only review, the best that the tenant could achieve would be to maintain the rent at the level being paid at the review date, even if the third party accepted that the open market rent had, in fact, dropped below that during the review period.

1 See for example 22 Encyclopaedia of Forms and Precedents (5th edn) Forms 22 (Second Schedule, para 1.3:4), 117 (para 3(A)(i)(a) and 118 (para 1.3), Rosscastle Letting Conditions (see Appendix 1, Form No 1 below) Condition 7.2:2.4.
2 (1977) 245 Estates Gazette 657.
3 See Chapter 14 below.
4 R Bernstein QC and K Reynolds: *Handbook of Rent Review* (Sweet & Maxwell) 1981 at para 6.23.
5 [1987] 1 EGLR 133, 282 Estates Gazette 857, CA. See Legal Notes (1987) 282 Estates Gazette 1547.
6 [1986] 2 EGLR 120, 280 Estates Gazette 200.
7 Pyrrhus exclaimed after his defeat of the Romans at Heraclea on the Siris (280 AD) that 'Another such victory and we are lost'.
8 At 134.
9 It was an upwards-only clause (see para 6.59:1 below) so the current rent of £30,000 would continue to be payable even if the open market rent on the review date was found to be less.
10 At 135.

6.23 *Premium.* The valuer should be directed to assume that no premium is payable by either party[1] on the commencement of the hypothetical letting.[2] The drafting should make it clear that the assumption extends to both parties especially if the lease is granted at a time when landlords are paying tenants premiums as inducements to take premises.[3] If the premium or any other 'inducements' are referred to in the lease there should generally be a direction in the rent review clause to the effect that they should be disregarded on reviews.[4]

1 The question of a reverse premium must always be considered when examining comparable transactions – ie a landlord rather than granting a rent-free period (that would be obvious on the face of the lease) may instead have paid for the tenant's fitting out, etc (and these costs may or may not have been reflected in the initial rent).
2 See for example 22 Encyclopaedia of Forms and Precedents (5th edn) Forms 22 (Second Schedule, para 1.3:4), 117 (Clause 3(A)(i)(a)), Rosscastle Letting Conditions (Appendix 1, Form No 1 below) Condition 7.2:2.4.
3 See para 6.20:3 above.
4 See paras 6.18:3(c) and 6.20 above.

6.24 *Rental value not diminished.* Although the hypothetical letting required to be assumed by the rent review clause should bear as close a resemblance to reality as possible,[1] the very fact that, in reality, the premises are already let to the tenant, and usually have been for some years, and that no new letting is in fact taking place, requires the assumption of certain matters which may not, in fact, be the case on the review date.[2] Those assumptions so far discussed[3] have been those generally necessary to support, and facilitate the correct operation of, the hypothesis of a letting. The purpose of other assumptions, however, is to ensure that the landlord does not suffer a diminution in rent on review as a result of the acts or omissions of the tenant or those deriving title under the tenant during the period of the tenant's interest in the premises prior to the review date. One such assumption commonly found, is an assumption that no work has been carried out to the premises by the tenant or those deriving title under him which has diminished the rental value.[4] There is an argument, however, to the effect that such an assumption may not be as effective as would first appear, which is as follows: works carried out by the tenant during the subsistence of the lease could be said to fall within four basic categories: decoration, repair, works required by statute and voluntary works. Statutory works can themselves be divided (very broadly speaking) into two main categories: those which any tenant would have to carry out before he could use and occupy the premises, and those which are necessary because of the particular way in which the tenant uses, or has adapted, the premises. Suppose the tenant has repaired the premises, or carried out works required by statute which fall within the first category mentioned above, in a shoddy way, or has decorated the premises in appalling taste. Will the assumption result in these works being disregarded? Arguably, only in the (presumably extremely unlikely) event that the works were so badly effected that the premises would have commanded a higher rent if they had been left undecorated, or unrepaired, or if the statutory works had not been effected at all, as only then would the works have produced a net diminution in the rental value. With regard to statutory works falling within the second category and voluntary works, it is quite possible that these will reduce the rental value of the premises, and that the assumption will be effective to prevent their reducing the revised rent. However, the effect on rent of such works may well be disregarded in any event, by virtue of other provisions in the rent review clause.[5] Whether or not this argument is correct, the landlord should bear it in mind, and ensure that the tenant's covenants are drafted in such a way as to give the landlord control over the manner in which works of repair and decoration, and statutory works, are effected. It has become popular in recent years, for tenants to attempt to exclude from this assumption works carried out by them pursuant to statute,[6] on the grounds that if they involve themselves in the cost and inconvenience of carrying out works, not because they want to carry them out, but because statute requires them to, and those works diminish the rental value of the premises, they should not then be further penalised by having to pay a revised rent on the assumption that the works have not been carried out. They take the view that such an exclusion is also for the benefit of the landlord, because without it the assumption might result in the conclusion that the premises are lawfully unusable, because the relevant statutory works have not been carried out. Again, there is an argument that this view is invalid. If one can say that statutory works will generally fall within one of the two categories mentioned above, it seems that statutory works falling within the first category will only be caught by the assumption in the extremely unlikely event that they were carried out so badly that the premises were worth more before they were carried out than after whilst, as statutory works falling within the second category mentioned above will result from the tenant's particular use or adaptation of the premises, again it would seem to be fair for these to be disregarded on rent review if they diminish the rental value of the premises. The above discussion relates to an assumption which requires the disregard of works which reduce the rental value of the premises and, naturally, will not necessarily apply to assumptions adopting different wording. Landlords occasionally attempt to provide, not for the disregard of the works which reduce the rental value of the premises, but for the disregard only of the diminishing effect on rent of such works. Whilst, in certain circumstances, this may produce a fair result, it could also produce great injustice to the tenant, and is generally strongly resisted by the tenants, on the basis that, in most circumstances, it will result in the landlord 'having his cake and eating it'.

1   See para 6.17:1 above.
2   See paras 6.1:2(c) and 6.19 above.
3   See paras 6.19–6.23 above.
4   See for example 22 Encyclopaedia of Forms and Precedents (5th edn) Form 22 (Second Schedule, paragraph 1.3:1) and 117 (paragraph 3(A)(iii)), Rosscastle Letting Conditions (Appendix 1, Form No 1 below) Condition 7.2:2.1.
5   See paras 6.34–6.40 below.
6   See ibid Form 22 (Second Schedule para 1.3:1).

6.25   *Covenants complied with.* The draftsman must consider each party's covenants in turn:

6.25:1   *Tenant's covenants.* Another assumption designed to ensure that the landlord does not suffer on rent review as a result of the acts and omissions of the tenant is an assumption that the tenant has complied with his covenants.[1] It seems reasonable that a tenant who is in breach of, for example, his covenant to repair, or to comply with statutes, should not be entitled to take advantage of his own wrong by obtaining a reduction in rent.[2] The effect of such an assumption is that the premises will be valued as if the tenant's covenants had been complied with.[3] Although some tenants argue that, in such circumstances, the rent should reflect the actual situation, because the landlord has separate remedies for breach of covenant, few landlords would be prepared to delete such an assumption.[4]

6.25:2   *Landlord's covenants.* It has become more popular in recent years for landlords to insert in rent review clauses assumptions and disregards which have the effect of requiring the premises to be valued disregarding certain legal or physical factors reducing their rental value which have arisen since the grant of the lease, even if such factors exist otherwise than as a result of the tenant's acts or omissions (or the acts or omissions of those deriving title under the tenant) – ie even if they exist on the review date as a result of the landlord's acts or omissions, or as a result of the default of neither party. One such assumption[5] is an assumption that the landlord has complied with his covenants.[6] If, for example, the landlord is under an obligation to carry out certain repairs or provide particular services to the premises, or perhaps to the building or estate of which the premises form part, and he fails to, should it be assumed that he has done so? It would initially appear unfair that he should because, in such circumstances, this would involve the tenant in paying rent for something better than that which he actually had.[7] Although there are arguments both for and against the insertion of such an assumption in the rent review clause,[8] it seems that, on balance, commentators consider that the arguments against have greater force.[9] Certainly, most tenants attempt to resist the insertion of this assumption, arguing that the premises should only be assumed to be in a better state and condition than they are to the extent that their existing condition is attributable to the tenant's own breach of covenant. If the landlord accepts that the revised rent will take into account factors reducing the rent which exist as a result of his own breach, he may consider the possibility of including provisions in the rent review clause which enable the parties to agree, or the third party to determine, a variable rent in such circumstances: one rent to apply so long as the rent-reducing factor subsists, and another following its removal.[10]

1   See, for example, 22 Encyclopaedia of Forms and Precedents (5th edn) Forms 22 (Second Schedule para 1.3:3), 117 (para 3(A)(ii)) and 118 (para 1.3(B)), Rosscastle Letting Conditions (Appendix 1, Form No 1 below) Condition 7.2:2.3. If the lease is not elsewhere defined as meaning the lease as varied from time to time the parties may want this referred to here (see para 6.18:3(e) above). It is interesting to speculate on the effect of this assumption if the lease has been varied to include, for example, tenant's covenants contained in licences for alterations, if such alterations are to be disregarded. Presumably the disregard would take priority. For a discussion of some of the effects of such an assumption, see D W Williams: 'Disrepair on rent reviews – some problems exposed' (1986) 278 Estates Gazette 380.

2   Although the tenant cannot reasonably expect the revised rent to be reduced because of damage which he should repair by virtue of his repairing obligations, there are situations in which the tenant might feel that such an assumption operates unjustly. It should be remembered, for example, that the tenant's repairing obligation will apply, in the absence of contrary provision, to the repair of damage caused by an inherent defect or other uninsured risk, to the extent that the remedying of that damage does not go beyond repair (see Chapter 8). This is, of course, a wider point, but the fact that the revised rent will not reflect any such damage is a further point to bear in mind when the tenant is considering the repairing obligations he is prepared to undertake.

3   It seems, however, that the assumption will only operate for the benefit of the innocent party, ie the landlord – see *Hamish Cathie Travel England Ltd v Insight International Tours Ltd* [1986] 1 EGLR 244, in which the tenant attempted to argue that certain improvements carried out without the landlord's consent should be disregarded on rent review, notwithstanding the fact that the rent review clause provided for a disregard only of improvements carried out with consent. He argued that, because the landlord's consent was required to the relevant improvements, and the rent review clause contained an assumption that the tenant had complied with his covenants, it should be assumed, for the purposes of the rent review, either that he had not carried out the improvements at all, or that he had obtained consent for them. This argument was rejected by the judge on the basis, mentioned above, that the assumption was only designed to benefit the innocent party.

4   It should be mentioned that, even if he were to do so, this would probably not alter the position: it seems that in the absence of contrary provision, the tenant would not be entitled to take advantage of his own wrong in any event – see *Family Management v Grey* (1979) 253 Estates Gazette 369, CA; *Harmsworth Pension Funds Trustees Ltd v Charringtons Industrial Holdings Ltd* [1985] 1 EGLR 97 (distinguishing *Fawke v Viscount Chelsea* [1980] QB 441, [1979] 3 All ER 568, CA, and the comments of Millet J in *Leigh v Certibilt Investments Ltd* [1988] 1 EGLR 116, [1988] 04 EG 127: 'It is well established that the lessee cannot rely, in diminution of the rent, upon his own breach of covenant.'

5   See paras 6.19:3 and 6.20:2 above.

6   See, for example, 22 Encyclopaedia of Forms and Precedents (5th edn) Forms 22 (Second Schedule para 1.3:3) and 117 (para 3(a)(ii)), each of which provides for this as an option. It is difficult to imagine a situation in which the landlord's failure to comply with his covenants will have the effect of reducing the rental value and the assumption will, accordingly, generally apply to the landlord's benefit. And yet, it has been held that an assumption that the tenant's covenants have been complied with will only apply to benefit the innocent party (see note 3 above).

7   Although, of course, if the tenant is under an obligation to reimburse the landlord for the cost of compliance by way of service charge, it can perhaps be argued that to some extent he cannot be said to be paying rent for the relevant repairs or services.

8   See ibid (5th edn) Form 117, Background Note 8 and note 5 above for a discussion of these arguments. It seems that, in the absence of an express assumption, none will be implied – see *Fawke v Viscount Chelsea*, above, and *Clarke v Findon Developments Ltd* (1983) 270 Estates Gazette 426.

9   See, for example, Bernstein and Reynold's *Handbook of Rent Review*, para 4.56.

10   The court does have power to order a variable rent on an application for an interim rent under s 24A of the 1954 Act (see para 14.54 below and *Fawke v Viscount Chelsea*, above) but it is clear that, in the absence of express provision, the valuer will have no power to order such a rent on rent review – see *National Westminster Bank Ltd v BSC Footwear Ltd* (1981) 257 Estates Gazette 277, CA; *Bracknell Development Corpn v Greenlees Lennards Ltd* (1981) 260 Estates Gazette 500; *Clarke v Findon Developments Ltd*, above; *Compton Group Ltd v Estates Gazette Ltd* (1977) 244 Estates Gazette 799, CA.

6.26 *Premises restored*. Another assumption of the nature discussed in para 6.25:2 above which is frequently required by landlords is an assumption that, if the premises have been damaged or destroyed at the review date, they have been fully restored.[1] At first sight, this does not appear unreasonable from the tenant's point of view, because if the tenant is in breach of his repairing obligations he cannot reasonably expect the revised rent to be reduced to reflect those wants of repair, and if the damage has been caused by an insured risk the cesser of rent proviso[2] will protect him from having to pay the revised rent (or a fair proportion of it) until the premises are again fit for use. Nevertheless, there are situations in which such an assumption could create hardship for the tenant:

6.26:1 *Damage which the tenant is under an obligation to repair*. It has been mentioned,[3] in connection with an assumption that the tenant has complied with his covenants, that although the tenant cannot reasonably expect the revised rent to be reduced because of damage which he should repair by virtue of his repairing obligations, he might well suffer hardship as a result. This is because his repairing obligation[4] will apply, in the absence of contrary provision, to the repair of damage caused by an inherent defect or other uninsured risk,[5] to the extent that the remedying of that damage does not go beyond repair. This is, of course, a wider point, but the fact that the revised rent will not reflect any such damage is a further matter to be borne in mind when the tenant is considering the repairing obligations he is prepared to undertake.

6.26:2 *Damage by an insured risk*. As pointed out above, if damage or destruction existing at the review date has been caused by an insured risk, the cesser of rent provisions will apply. This, however, may not always provide as complete protection as the tenant believes. First of all, it should be remembered that cesser of rent provisions usually only appear if the premises are so damaged or destroyed as to be unfit for occupation and use.[6] An insured risk may have damaged the premises in such a way as to reduce their rental value substantially, without rendering them unfit for occupation and use. Secondly, the cesser of rent provisions may be limited in time,[7] with the result that the premises remain unfit on the expiry of the period of rent suspension. This is a general point in relation to cesser clauses and it is assumed that the tenant will have effected his own insurance or consciously made the decision to carry the risk himself. In effecting that insurance, or making that decision, however, he should bear in mind the effect of an assumption such as that under discussion on the level of the revised rent.

6.26:3 *Damage which the tenant is not liable to repair, and which has not been caused by an insured risk*. Damage may exist on the review date otherwise than as a result of the acts or omissions of the tenant or as a result of an insured risk. It may exist as a result of the landlord's breach of covenant, such as breach of his covenant to repair, or damage may exist which neither party is under an obligation to make good, such as damage or destruction caused by an inherent defect, or other uninsured risk, which goes beyond repair.[8]

6.26:4 *Consequences*. As a result most tenants attempt to resist the insertion of this assumption, arguing that the premises should only be assumed to be in a better state and condition than they are to the extent that their existing condition is attributable to the tenant's own breach of covenant, and that this will be the case in any event by virtue of the usual assumption that the tenant has complied with his covenants. Landlords should be reluctant to allow the deletion of the assumption altogether. Most landlords will want such an assumption in relation to damage or destruction which the tenant is under an obligation to repair and in relation to damage or destruction by an insured risk, and most tenants will be prepared to accept such a qualified assumption. Furthermore, if the landlord accepts that the revised rent will take into account damage which exists as a result of his own breach, or extraneous factors, he may consider the possibility of including provisions in the rent review clause which enable the parties to agree, or the third party to determine, a variable rent in such circumstances.[9]

1 See for example 22 Encyclopaedia of Forms and Precedents (5th edn) Forms 22 (Second Schedule, para 1.3:2), 117 (para 3(A)(iii) and 118 (para 1.3(D)), Rosscastle Letting Conditions (Appendix 1, Form No 1 below) Condition 7.2:2.2. Where there is an upwards-only clause (see para 6.60:1 below) a rent not less than the current would continue to be payable even where the state of the premises *could* be taken into account. The issue would be what increase (if any) should there be? It has been pointed out (D N Clarke and J E Adams: *Rent Review and Variable Rents* (Oyez Longman) 2nd edn at p 221) that a possible consequence of the restoration of any destroyed premises assumption if the provision was literally construed, might be that if any part of the demised premises had been destroyed with the landlord's consent, subsequent reviews would be undertaken on the footing that this building was there. For example, a single letting of several factory or warehouse buildings may include some outbuildings that have outlived their useful purpose and that the tenant may wish to demolish. On a more day to day level, most alterations carried out by the tenant will involve the damage or destruction of part of the premises, albeit often only a small part. If the assumption is limited, as suggested below, to damage or destruction existing as a result of the tenant's breach of covenant or caused by an insured risk, this problem does not arise. If it is not so limited, it should be expressed not to apply to damage or destruction permitted by the landlord.
2 See paras 10.13, 10.15 and 10.23 below.
3 See para 6.25:1 note 2 above.
4 As to repair generally, see Chapter 8.
5 See paras 8.15–8.20 below.
6 See para 10.23 below.
7 See para 10.23 below.
8 For a discussion of the arguments raised when considering assumptions and disregards which have the effect of requiring the premises to be valued disregarding certain legal or physical factors reducing their rental value which have arisen since the grant of the lease, even if such factors exist otherwise than as a result of the tenant's acts or omissions (or the acts or omissions of those deriving title under the tenant), see para 6.25:2 note 5 above.
9 See para 6.25:2 (and in particular note 10) above.

6.27 *Statutory restrictions.* It is becoming popular for landlords to insert assumptions in the rent review clause which relate to statutory consents. The way in which statute may affect the tenant's ability to use the premises is discussed elsewhere.[1] In the absence of directions to the contrary, the premises will be valued as they are on the review date, with the result that existing statutory restrictions, and existing statutory consents of which the premises have the benefit, will be taken in to account. It seems that the valuer will not be entitled to value the premises on the basis that they will be used in breach of statutory restrictions,[2] whether or not the lease contains (as it normally will) a covenant on the part of the tenant not to breach such restrictions,[3] but that he will be entitled to take into account the possibility that a statutory consent will be granted, to the extent that the hypothetical tenant would take into account that possibility.[4] Landlords have two concerns:

6.27:1 *Personal permissions etc.* What will happen if the planning permission or other statutory consent relating to the premises is personal to the actual tenant? If the lease permits a user limited by reference to the name of the actual tenant, the courts have held in certain circumstances that the name of the hypothetical tenant should be substituted.[5] Generally,[6] this seems fair, because it places the hypothetical tenant in the same position as the actual tenant – he can use the premises himself, but his ability to dispose of the lease is limited because no one else can. At first sight it seems fair that this should apply to personal planning permissions and other statutory consents as well. The ISVA model form contains an assumption that 'the benefit of any planning or other consent current at the relevant Review Date is available also for such willing tenant'.[7] Tenants should, however, look closely at any such assumption. Sometimes a statutory consent will have been granted to the tenant as a result of his personal efforts. It is clearly accepted in other areas that the efforts of the tenant should not be taken into account to benefit the landlord.[8] In such cases, the tenant might consider it unfair if the consent were taken into account. Some statutory consents are only granted to people with particular qualifications, or will not be granted to people falling into a particular category. It seems that the hypothetical tenant should only be assumed to have such a consent if it is so qualified or is not so disqualified. The landlord should also consider whether or not such an assumption is desirable, as it may not be to his benefit in all circumstances. If the personal statutory consent relates to an unusual user peculiar to the actual tenant, it might be better from the landlord's point of view if the personal consent were disregarded, and if a different planning permission were asumed to exist.[9] So far as the ISVA model form wording is concerned, it should be noted that it does not specify that the actual tenant must have the benefit of the relevant consent. Furthermore, it may not be limited to statutory consents, but may apply to consents granted by the landlord,[10] or adjoining owners, or indeed anyone else.[11]

6.27:2 *Permission lost.* There is a possibility that a consent in existence on the date of the grant of the lease will have been lost prior to the review date, and, as a result, landlords sometimes attempt to insert assumptions to the effect that the premises and/or the hypothetical tenant have the benefit of all statutory consents necessary to enable the premises to be used by the hypothetical tenant for the permitted user. Tenants object to such an assumption for a number of reasons. The fact that all hypothetical tenants might not be able to obtain the relevant statutory consents has already been mentioned. In addition, of course, a consent may have been lost prior to the review date otherwise than as a result of the acts or omissions of the tenant, or indeed after the date of the grant of the lease statute might have introduced the need for a new consent which the actual tenant was unable to obtain.[12] Finally such an assumption does not deal with the question of the duration of the consent which should be assumed to be in existence, or the conditions (if any) subject to which it should be assumed to have been granted. Tenants will, accordingly, usually resist the insertion of any such assumption,[13] on the basis that

125

if the lease contains an obligation on the part of the tenant to use best endeavours to obtain and renew, and not to jeopardise, the relevant consents[14] and an obligation to comply with legislation,[15] and the rent review clause contains an assumption that the tenant has complied with his covenants in the lease[16] (as it usually will) it would seem that any consent lost as a result of the tenant's default should be assumed to be in existence in any event.

1   As to user generally see paras 7.8–7.18 below.
2   See *Compton Group Ltd v Estates Gazette Ltd* (1977) P & CR 148, CA.
3   See para 7.28 below.
4   ie 'hope value' – see *Railstore Ltd v Playdale Ltd* [1988] 2 EGLR 153, [1988] 35 EG 87.
5   See para 7.17 below.
6   Although draftsmen should avoid user clauses which refer to the actual tenant by name, as unexpected and arbitrary results can occur on rent review, depending on the precise wording.
7   See 22 Encyclopaedia of Forms and Precedents (5th edn) Form 118.
8   See paras 6.30–6.40 below.
9   Although, as a general rule, it is advisable for the hypothetical situation on rent review to bear as close a resemblance to reality as possible (see para 6.17:1 above) there may well be circumstances in which it is fair for planning permission to be assumed to be in existence when it is not. Suppose, for example, that premises have the benefit of planning permission for a wide and profitable use, but that the tenant would like to change the use to one which is more narrow and/or less profitable. The landlord may be prepared to agree to the change of use, provided that he receives due compensation from the tenant for the lower rent which he will receive both during the subsistence of the lease and after the tenant quits the premises. Although it is often advisable in such circumstances for the landlord to receive a one-off payment by way of compensation (see para 6.17:1 note 12 above) this may not always be possible, and the parties might decide to include an assumption in the rent review clause that the premises have planning permission for the originally permitted wide and profitable use. Naturally, when including such an assumption, a great deal of consideration should be given to ensuring that such other assumptions are inserted as are necessary to complete the hypothetical scenario (see para 6.17:1 above).
10   See para 6.18:3(e) above.
11   If, for example, the tenant, as a result of a special relationship, or arrangement, with an adjoining owner receives consent to cross, or park on, his land should such consent be taken into account?
12   For a discussion of the arguments raised when considering assumptions and disregards which have the effect of requiring the premises to be valued disregarding certain legal or physical factors reducing their rental value which have arisen since the grant of the lease, even if such factors exist otherwise than as a result of the acts or omissions of the tenant or those deriving title under the tenant, see para 6.25:2 note 5 above.
13   The parties should be aware that such an effect may be achieved to some extent without so specific an assumption. In *Bovis Group Pension Fund Ltd v GC Flooring & Furnishing Ltd* (1983) 266 Estates Gazette 1005; affd (1984) 269 Estates Gazette 1252, CA the revised rent was to be assessed on the basis that the premises were 'let for office purposes' and the Court of Appeal held that planning permission for office use should be assumed, although in *Daejan Investments Ltd v Cornwall Coast Country Club* [1985] 1 EGLR 77, 273 Estates Gazette 1122, no assumption was made that the hypothetical tenant would have a certificate from the gaming board permitting the premises to be used as a gaming club. See also *Ritz Hotel (London) Ltd v Ritz Casino Ltd* [1988] EGCS 142; *Trust House Forte Albany Hotels v Daejan Investments Ltd*, discussed at para 6.17:3 above and consider the possible effect of the assumption contained in the Law Society/RICS model form of rent review clause (see 22 Encyclopaedia of Forms and Precedents (5th edn) Form 117) to the effect that the premises 'may be used for any of the purposes permitted by this lease as varied or extended by any licence granted pursuant thereto'. If a particular use is permitted by the landlord but not, for example, by planning legislation, could it be argued, as a result of this assumption, that the premises may lawfully be used for that purpose?
14   See for example 22 Encyclopaedia of Forms and Precedents (5th edn) Form 22 clause 5.12, Rosscastle Letting Conditions (Appendix 1, Form No 1 below) Condition 3.13.
15   See para 7.28.
16   See para 6.25:1.

6.28 *Renewal under the 1954 Act: the problem.* The draftsman should consider the question of whether any assumptions are needed in relation to the renewal of the hypothetical tenancy under the terms of the 1954 Act[1] in the light of the *Secretary of State for the Environment v Pivot Properties Ltd.*[2] This case concerned two large office blocks in Croydon and the question posed by the arbitrator for determination by the court was: 'Whether upon the true construction of the underlease . . . the rack rental market value of the premises (which is to be assessed on the assumption that they are to be let as a whole for a term of five and half years[3]) is also to be assessed upon the assumption that no account is to be taken of any possibility of the tenancy being continued or renewed under the provisions of Part II of the Landlord and Tenant Act 1954'. Phillips J and the Court of Appeal decided that although the parties and the term were hypothetical, the amount at which the demised premises could reasonably be expected to be let in the open market had to be determined according to the facts as they were in the real world, and here the possibility of renewal under the 1954 Act would affect the rent at which the premises could be let in the open market. As such the answer to the arbitrator's question was that account *was* to be taken of the possibility of renewal under the 1954 Act. The situation, therefore, is that in determining a revised rent the valuer needs to consider the likelihood of the hypothetical tenancy being renewed under the 1954 Act. In *Pivot*[2] the situation must have been relatively straightforward for the valuer, because it was clear from the premises which were the subject of the hypothetical letting in that case that an application by the tenant for a new lease would probably succeed. The premises were new, and also extremely large, with the result that, whoever the landlord was, he would be unlikely to oppose the grant of a new lease to the tenant under s 30(1)(f)[4] or (g).[5] As will usually be the case, s 30(1)(e)[6] did not apply. The situation will not always be so straightforward, however, because very often, in making an assessment as to whether or not a tenancy is likely to be renewed under the 1954 Act, the *identity* of the landlord is relevant. For example, if the landlord were a property company, then it would be unlikely that an opposition under s 30(1)(g)[5] would be raised, but 30(1)(f)[4] would always pose a risk, even in the case of premises which were not near the end of their useful life. On the other hand, if the landlord occupied adjoining premises himself, s 30(1)(g)[5] could be relevant. On rent review, the identity of the landlord is generally unknown: he is usually simply a hypothetical willing landlord[7] and, accordingly, it will often be difficult for the valuer to be able to assess the likelihood of the tenant succeeding in an application for a new lease.[8] Nevertheless the fact remains that, in the absence of any specific assumption or disregard in the lease to the contrary, the valuer on a rent review needs to consider the possibility of a renewal under the 1954 Act, and is entitled to take into account this factor in arriving at the revised rent. Needless to say a rent will be higher when there is a likelihood of renewal, and indeed the range in *Pivot*[2] was enormous – before the reference to the court, the arbitrator had determined that if the answer to his question was in the negative the rent should be £2,950,000, and if in the affirmative £2,100,000. Thus a landlord may seek to include in the rent review provision an assumption that *the premises would be renewed under the 1954 Act* after the expiry of the hypothetical letting. The tenant should resist and if he feels himself unlikely to achieve the opposite position of an assumption that the valuer should assume that the hypothetical letting will *not* be renewed,[9] then at least propose that the provision be struck out altogether, so that the question is left to the general law, however difficult that may be for the valuer.

1 See Chapter 14 below.
2 (1980) 256 Estates Gazette 1176.
3 It will be noted that the term of the hypothetical letting was a most unusual one referring as it did to so short a period when in fact the leases were for forty two years.
4 See para 14.33 below.
5 See para 14.35 below.
6 See para 14.29 below.
7 See para 6.22 above.
8 From another point of view, the difficulty for the valuer highlighted in para 6.28 is not perhaps as unusual as may initially appear, in that a tenant on the grant of a lease, attempting to assess the likelihood of renewal at the end of the term, is not in very much better a position than the hypothetical tenant on rent review. Although he is aware of the identity of the original landlord, he will usually be unable to assess the likelihood of that landlord assigning the reversion prior to the end of the term, and will almost certainly have no control over any such assignment. From another point of view, however, there is no doubt that if, on rent review, the actual landlord is of such a nature as to be likely to oppose renewal the tenant will feel it unjust if the valuer assesses the rent on the basis that the tenancy is likely to be renewed because all other factors indicate that that will be the case. Similarly, a landlord who, at the review date, has no intention of assigning the reversion prior to the end of the term or of opposing the grant of a new lease, and who is not of such a nature as to be likely to be able to oppose even if he wanted to, will consider it unfair if the valuer on rent review is unable to allow the likelihood of renewal to affect his valuation because all other factors tend to the opposite conclusion. There seems to be no reason why the parties should not include in the rent review clause a direction that the valuer should take into account the possibility of renewal at the end of the hypothetical lease only if, and to the extent, that that possibility exists on the review date in respect of the actual lease.
9 For an example of an assumption which (apparently inadvertently) had this effect, see *Toyota (GB) Ltd v Legal and General (Pensions Management) Ltd* [1988] EGCS 148.

6.29 *VAT.*[1] One aim of the rent review clause is to create certainty, and to address the issues that might have a bearing on the rent of the hypothetical letting. If the implications of VAT are having an affect on the rent real lettings in certain markets, it seems to follow that they should be dealt with in the rent review clause, so that guidance is given to the valuer as to what assumptions should be made in arriving at the rent of the hypothetical letting. A further objective of any clause is that it should be in the interest of the party on whose behalf it is advanced and, it is here that the current difficulty arises. Only considerable experience after the implementation of the VAT legislation of letting all types of commercial property in all areas will indicate what effect it is having in the real markets. Thus, only time will tell how this topic should be dealt with in rent review clauses, and it may well be that a different approach is needed for different types of commercial premises and for different locations. As is so often the case individual advice will be needed, and the solicitor should work very closely with his client's surveyor and accountant. These few comments are offered as a starting point for the deliberations on any specific letting:

6.29:1 *VAT sensitive areas.* Early indications are that VAT is only likely to have any real effect on rents in what are beginning to be called 'VAT sensitive areas'. These are areas where a significant proportion of the occupiers are VAT adverse organisations – ie those who supply mainly exempt goods and services.[2] It may well be that VAT need not be dealt with in rent review clauses of lettings outside for example the City of London and other VAT sensitive areas.

6.29:2 *Onerous leases.* Landlord's solicitors must constantly balance the desire to benefit the landlord by inserting extra assumptions and disregards with the fact that their insertion may provide the tenant with an argument that the rent should be discounted on review to reflect the fact that the terms of the hypothetical letting are more onerous than the norm.

6.29:3 *Protection from tenants who cannot recover.* Landlords currently[3] seem to be fearing that, especially where it can offer a good covenant as will often be the case in financial services, a VAT adverse organisation may be able to negotiate a reduced rent on a new open market letting so as to mitigate the severity of the full impact of VAT. Thus landlords' advisors are providing that the incoming tenant on the hypothetical letting will be assumed to be able to recover any VAT that may be chargeable on the rent so that the hypothetical tenant would be assumed not to be seeking any such reduction. It has been suggested[4] that this could have an adverse effect so far as the landlord is concerned because it is said to limit the market and that it is preferable to assume that the landlord has covenanted on behalf of himself and his successors not to elect to charge VAT on the rent. And yet would any tenant accept this and if he did would he not have a strong argument for a discount?[5]

1 As to VAT generally, see paras 2.23–2.29 above.
2 And who will suffer from having to pay VAT: see para 2.28 above.
3 During 1989.
4 Steven Fogal and Graham Plumbe: 'VAT and rent review clauses' [1989] 16 EG 76, Patrick C Soares: 'VAT and rent review' (1989) 10 PLB 14.
5 See para 6.29:2 above.

E DISREGARDS

6.30 *Basic principle.* The basic principle of s 34 of the 1954 Act[1] and the disregarding provisions of rent review clauses is a recognition that it is unfair for the landlord to derive benefit in the form of increased rent from certain matters that may enhance the rental value of the demised premises, but that arise purely from the efforts or presence in the premises of the tenant or his predecessors. The tenant, however, must ensure that the landlord does not require there to be disregarded any matters so that the reviewed rent is thereby increased. A frequent example concerns user[2] – landlords seek all the estates management advantages of a narrow user covenant and none of the rent review disadvantages by providing that any restriction as to user contained in the lease shall be disregarded. Such provisions should be resisted by the tenant. If he is to be subjected to the problems of narrow user covenants, he deserves to benefit from such advantages to him that they may bring on the rent review. Sometimes too the valuer will be directed to disregard restrictions contained in a planning permission or other statutory restriction[3] that applies to the demised premises and the tenant will need the advice of his surveyor as to the reasonableness or otherwise of such provisions.[4]

1 See paras 14.50–14.54 below.
2 See paras 6.17:1, 6.18:3(a) above and 7.10:3 below.
3 See para 6.27 above.
4 Two examples would be a local user restriction (ie demised premises could only be occupied by

a tenant already located in the area) or a personal planning consent (ie permission to use large country house as a conference centre limited to the tenant).

6.31 *Background.* There was little to assist the draftsmen of the early rent review clauses as they wrestled with the assumptions, but s 34 of the 1954 Act[1] did provide guidance in relation to the matters to be disregarded. Many adopted it in full, providing that there shall be disregarded 'any matter which would be disregarded if the rent of the demised premises was being determined by the court under s 34 of the Landlord and Tenant Act 1954'. There were those, however, who sought to deal with the point by providing 'that there shall be disregarded the matters referred to in s 34, of the Landlord and Tenant Act 1954'. The problem with this latter form (and its numerous slight variations) was that it might have achieved a result that was quite the opposite of that intended by the draftsman. This was because it could be argued that such a clause should be construed as a direction on the review to disregard the direction to disregard contained in the Act and accordingly to *regard* the matters in question in arriving at the revised rent. In fact s 34 whether in its original or amended form is somewhat restrictive[2] especially so far as the tenant is concerned and the approach of incorporating it into the rent review clause is not to be recommended today.[3] Instead the rent review clause should set out the specific matters that are to be disregarded.

1 See paras 14.50–14.54 below.
2 For example, neither form of the section refers to subtenants or their predecessors in title, with the result that there is no specific direction to disregard the occupation and goodwill of such people, nor any improvements carried out by them (although this might be achieved by other means, see for example *Young v Dalgety plc* [1987] 1 EGLR 116, 281 Estates Gazette 427, CA); neither form of the section specifically requires improvements carried out at the tenant's cost by another person to be disregarded (although this might be implied, see *Scottish and Newcastle Breweries plc v Sir Richard Sutton's Settled Estates* [1985] 2 EGLR 130, 276 Estates Gazette 77); the section in its original form has been held only to apply to improvements carried out by the tenant in his capacity as tenant under the subsisting lease or by a predecessor in title of him to the same tenancy, with the result that works carried out prior to the grant of that lease will not be disregarded (see *Brett* below); the section in its amended form relates only to improvements carried out by someone who was actually the tenant at the time the works were carried out (and it has been held that this does not include a licensee prior to the grant of the lease – see *Euston Centre Properties Ltd v H & J Wilson Ltd* (1982) 262 Estates Gazette 1079) and will only relate to improvements carried out under a previous tenancy if certain conditions are satisfied.
3 If the parties do want to incorporate the disregards set out in s 34 of the Landlord and Tenant Act 1954 in the rent review clause, they should make it absolutely clear whether they are referring to s 34 in its original, or amended, form (see *Euston Centre Properties Ltd v H & J Wilson Ltd* (1981) 262 Estates Gazette 1079 in which it was assumed that the reference was to the section as amended and *Brett v Brett Essex Golf Club Ltd* [1985] 1 EGLR 154, CA in which it was held that the reference was to the statute in its amended form, both leases having been granted after 1969). They should also remember that, in defining those improvements which are to be disregarded, the section in its amended form refers to 'the application for the new tenancy', the 'holding', and tenancies of the description specified in s 23(1) of the Act, with the result that it cannot be incorporated into a rent review clause without amendment (particularly if the provisions of ss 24–38 of the Act have been excluded in relation to the tenancy granted by the lease!).

6.32 *Occupation.* The fact that the tenant or his subtenant or their predecessors in title have been in occupation of the property should be disregarded.[1] This acknowledges the fact that a tenant in possession may pay slightly in excess of the market rent in order to avoid the disruption to his business that leaving one property and acquiring another may involve. This is something quite separate from goodwill and may apply even where there is no goodwill – for example because the tenant has only recently acquired the premises in question or they are premises such as a warehouse to which no goodwill attaches. Nevertheless the tenant's advisers need to note that this provision applies only to the occupation of the premises themselves. Thus it could be argued that 'marriage value' as a result of the tenant being in occupation of *neighbouring* premises should be regarded on a rent review unless there was a specific direction to disregard. There certainly would be cases in practice where a tenant in occupation of adjoining premises might well pay more than the open market rent in order to secure the premises in question. Furthermore there are companies who occupy numerous premises in certain areas. Perhaps they may be prepared to pay a slightly higher rent there, not because of their local presence, but for the convenience of not having to go further afield to satisfy their expanding property needs. The alternative argument is that as the landlord and the tenant are hypothetical figures,[2] marriage value is irrelevant. From a practical point of view there is much to support this view, but it might be worthwhile to put the matter beyond doubt by providing in cases where the tenant occupies adjoining premises for the disregarding provision to be extended to deal with the occupation of other properties in the locality.

1 See para 14.50 below. See for example 22 Encyclopaedia of Forms and Precedents (5th edn) Forms 22 (Second Schedule para 1.4:1), 117 (clause 3(B)(i)) and 118 (clause 1.3(E)), Rosscastle Letting Conditions (Appendix 1, Form No 1 below) Condition 7.2:3.1.
2 *F R Evans (Leeds) Ltd v English Electric Co Ltd* (1977) 245 Estates Gazette 657 – see para 6.25 above.

6.33 *Goodwill.* The valuer should be directed to disregard any goodwill[1] attached to the premises by reason of the carrying on there of the business tenant whether by him or by a predecessor of his in that business.[2] The direction to disregard goodwill should be drafted in such a way that it extends back beyond the commencement of the term of the lease so if 'A butcher's business has been carried on at these premises for 75 years' all the goodwill relating to it will be disregarded. Moreover if at some stage the business was conducted by the landlord then goodwill relating to that period will also be disregarded because he is a predecessor in that business.

1 'Goodwill' was described by Lord Eldon in *Cruttwell v Lye* (1810) 17 Ves 335 at 346 as 'nothing more than probability that the old customers will resort to the old place' and by Lord MacNaghten in *IRC v Muller & Co's Margarine Ltd* [1901] AC 217 at 223, HL as 'the benefit and advantage of the good name, reputation and connection of a business. It is the attractive force which brings in custom. It is the one thing that distinguishes an old established business from a new business at its first start. The goodwill of a business must emanate from a particular centre or source. I for my part think that if there is one attribute common to all cases of goodwill it is the attribute of locality.' See also *Trego v Hunt* [1896] AC 7, HL; *Whiteman Smith Motor Co Ltd v Chaplin* [1934] 2 KB 35; and *Rialto Cinemas Ltd v Wolfe* [1955] 2 All ER 530, [1955] 1 WLR 693.
2 See for example 22 Encyclopaedia of Forms and Precedents (5th edn) Forms 22 (Second Schedule para 14:2), 117 (clause 3(B)(ii)) and 118 (clause 1.3(F)), Rosscastle Letting Conditions (Appendix 1, Form No 1 below) Conditions 7.2:3.2.

F DISREGARDING IMPROVEMENTS

6.34 *Introduction.* If a property is improved, the rental value may increase and it is obviously unfair for the tenant to pay on a review additional rent that reflects an increase in rental value attributable to improvements made by him.[1] Rent review provisions[2] seek to guard against this injustice. A number of questions repeatedly arise in relation to these clauses:

(a) what is an improvement?[3]
(b) what improvements will be disregarded?[4] In practice, much can turn on *when* the improvement was undertaken,[5] the status of the person who undertook it[6] and the *obligations* that this person owed to his landlord[7]
(c) how is the improvement to be disregarded in order to determine the rent that the tenant will be required to pay?[8]

1   For examples of that unfairness, see *Ponsford v HMS Aerosols Ltd* [1979] AC 63, [1978] 2 All ER 837, HL approving the then unreported decision of *Cuff v J and F Stone Property Co Ltd* [1979] AC 87, [1978] 2 All ER 833. See for example 22 Encyclopaedia of Forms and Precedents (5th edn) Forms 22 (Second Schedule para 1.4:3), 117 (clause 3(B)(iii)) and Rosscastle Letting Conditions (Appendix 1, Form No 1 below) Condition 7.1:3.3.
2   Whether contractual provisions in a lease (ie a rent review clause in the conventional use of the term) or those imposed by statute upon the renewal of a lease (see the 1954 Act, s 34, paras 14.50–14.54 below) or in an option to renew a lease (see for example *Lear v Blizzard* [1983] 3 All ER 662).
3   See para 6.35 below.
4   See para 6.36 below.
5   See para 6.36:1 below.
6   See para 6.36:2 below.
7   See paras 6.36:3–6.36:5 below.
8   See paras 6.37 and 6.38 below.

6.35   *What is an improvement?* The term is used but not defined in either the 1927 Act nor the 1954 Act. Cases under s 19 of the former indicate that an alteration to the premises that from a tenant's point of view improves the premises may be an improvement[1] and it has been suggested that this principle can be applied for rent review purposes.[2] In order to be an improvement, the alteration must go beyond repair.[3]

1   See in particular *Balls Bro Ltd v Sinclair* [1931] 2 Ch 325 but note *National Electric Theatres Ltd v Hudgell* [1939] Ch 553, [1939] 1 All ER 567.
2   See for example Ronald Bernstein QC and Kirk Reynolds: *Handbook of Rent Review* (Sweet and Maxwell) paras 6–14.
3   *Morcom v Campbell-Johnson* [1956] 1 QB 106, [1955] 3 All ER 264, CA; *Mullaney v Maybourne Grange (Croydon) Management Co Ltd* [1986] 1 EGLR 70, 277 Estates Gazette 1350; *Post Office v Aquarius Properties Ltd* [1987] 1 All ER 1055, CA.

6.36   *What improvements will be disregarded?* Generally some limitations are included and the answer to the question turns on the construction of the individual clause. There are a number of areas that need careful consideration:

6.36:1   *Time.* A rent review clause will generally provide that in order to be disregarded the improvement must have been undertaken during the current tenancy.[1] When appropriate, however, the tenant's advisers should extend this to cover any work done by the tenant *before* the commencement of the tenancy.[2] This could be relevant, for example, where a prospective tenant has entered into an agreement to carry out work to premises on condition that, when undertaken to the landlord's satisfaction, he will be granted a lease, or where a tenant is so confident that the lease will be granted, that he begins fitting out before completion. It will be particularly relevant where a tenant is taking a new lease on the expiry of a previous one. The 1954 Act imposes a condition that the improvement must have been completed within 21 years of the application to renew,[3] but it is suggested that any such limitation is inappropriate in a rent review clause, unless there have been a number of previous lease renewals.

6.36:2 *The status of the person who carried out the improvement.* Section 34 (as amended) refers to 'a person who at the time [the improvement] was carried out was the tenant'. Because of this wording, the suggestions put forward in para 6.36:1 above would not have assisted in the unusual circumstances that arose in *Euston Centre Properties Ltd v H & J Wilson Ltd.*[4] The prospective tenant had entered into an arrangement with the landlord by which he was entitled *but not obliged* to undertake certain defined works to a property. If and when those works were completed, he was to be granted a lease.[5] It was held that because he was not a tenant at the time the works were carried out, the works did not fall within the disregarding provisions of s 34.[6] This case serves as a warning that the wording of the disregard should be checked extremely carefully.[7] Whilst such a result would probably not have occurred if the lease had included the form of disregard now more commonly adopted, there is no excuse for failing to place the matter beyond doubt by making it clear, in appropriate circumstances, that improvements carried out by the tenant prior to the grant of the lease, whether or not he was the tenant at the time, should be included in the disregard. There are three other points which should be borne in mind:

(a) Improvements may be carried out, either before or after the grant of the lease, by someone other than the tenant, at the tenant's cost. Whilst the courts may well consider such works to fall within a disregard of improvements 'carried out by the tenant'[8] there is nothing to be lost by making express provision.

(b) Some forms of disregard refer only to improvements 'carried out at the cost of the tenant' or 'carried out by the tenant at his own cost'. This is apparently because landlords are concerned to ensure that works for which they have paid should not be disregarded, although it is difficult to imagine circumstances in which a landlord would pay for the cost of the tenant's improvements to the premises without having an opportunity to make appropriate arrangements for the treatment of such works on rent review. However, it is suggested that a better way of dealing with the matter is to refer to improvements carried out 'otherwise than at the landlord's cost', as there may be circumstances in which, strictly speaking, the tenant does not himself pay the whole or part of the cost of improvements.

(c) It should be remembered that it will usually also be appropriate for improvements carried out by subtenants or their predecessors in title to be disregarded.[9]

6.36:3 *Obligation to the landlord.* Section 34 excludes from the direction to disregard improvements any work carried out in pursuance of an obligation to the landlord and a similar provision is often set out in the rent review clause.[10] At first sight, there seems nothing unreasonable in this from the tenant's point of view because clearly he should not be entitled to benefit from work that he is obliged to do, and no doubt this provision was inserted to cover work undertaken by a tenant pursuant to his covenant to repair. The obligation does not, however, have to be contained in the lease.[11] There has been a tendency in recent years for landlords to impose in licences permitting alterations a covenant by the tenant to carry out the work in question, and concern was expressed as to whether such a covenant would be construed as an obligation to the landlord, as the expression is used within s 34. If it was, then any such improvements would not be disregarded on a rent review or renewal under the 1954 Act. Clearly every case will depend upon the terms of the covenant in question, but in the light of *Ridley v Taylor*[12] and *Godbold v Martin The Newsagents Ltd*[13] the courts seem anxious to construe such covenants as meaning that, if the tenant decides to go ahead with the work, he must do so in a certain way rather than as obligations to carry out the work.[14]

6.36:4   *Obligation to the landlord: fitting-out.* Leases, or more usually agreements for lease, frequently provided for the tenant to undertake certain fitting-out works.[15] These may be extensive or may simply be the installation of a shop front. To the extent that these fitting-out works constitute tenant's fixtures and fittings, it seems that they will be deemed to have been removed for the purposes of the rent review if the clause contains an express or implied assumption of vacant possession.[16] If there is no such assumption,[17] and to the extent that the works do not constitute tenant's fixtures and fittings, fitting-out work will not normally be disregarded because it will have been done pursuant to an obligation to the landlord.[18] Where this is likely to be a factor, a specific direction will be required to disregard fitting-out works.

6.36:5   *Obligation to the landlord: to observe statutes etc.* Leases invariably contain a covenant by the tenant to observe statutory obligations.[19] Thus, if legislation was introduced that required certain categories of shops to install sprinkler systems it would fall to the tenant of the shop, by virtue of such a covenant, to undertake such work. It may well concern a tenant whose lease had rent review provisions closely modelled on s 34 that this work would *not* constitute a 'disregarded improvement' because *it was carried out pursuant to an obligation to the landlord* albeit an indirect one. In *Forte & Co Ltd v General Accident Life Assurance Ltd*[20] Peter Gibson J held that substantial work to the Cafe Royal in Regent Street carried out by the tenant pursuant to the Fire Precautions Act 1971 in order to obtain a fire certificate had been done in pursuance of an obligation to the landlord[21] and thus was not to be disregarded on review. The tenant's solicitor should always seek to amend the clause to provide that all work done pursuant to the statutory obligations covenant is to be disregarded.[22] Landlords sometimes resist by suggesting that one way of disregarding work for valuation purposes is to assume that the work had not been done and then to value the unimproved building.[23] If the work had not been undertaken, the legislation would probably provide that the premises could not be used. In these circumstances, the landlord's argument continues, the rent would be depressed because an incoming tenant would have to incur expenditure on the work before he could occupy the premises.

6.36:6   *Obligation to the landlord: to obtain consent.* Rent review clauses often provide that only improvements for which the landlord has given his consent will be disregarded.[24] The lease that was considered in *Hamish Cathie Travel England Ltd v Insight International Tours Ltd*[25] contained such wording but the tenant argued that the landlord had unreasonably withheld consent and that the direction to disregard should be read as covering, not only improvements for which the landlord had given consent, but also those to which he had unreasonably withheld his consent. Mr Francis Ferris QC, sitting as deputy judge of the Chancery Division held that the landlord has not unreasonably withheld consent, a finding that apparently disposed of this aspect of the case. Nevertheless, he reviewed the most recent authority as to when a court should imply into an instrument terms which are not there[26] and held that he could make no implication to the effect that the clause should be construed as including improvements for which the landlord had unreasonably withheld consent. The effect of this decision would seem to be that even if a landlord unreasonably refuses to give consent, the improvements in question will not be disregarded because the provision that the landlord's consent is required will be construed literally.[27]

1   Even in the absence of specific provision to this effect, this will usually be the case, unless the disregard specifically provides to the contrary. This will either be because works carried out before the grant of the lease are not considered to be 'improvements', but part of the premises provided by the landlord (see *Scottish and Newcastle Breweries plc v Sir Richard Sutton's Settled Estates* [1985] 2 EGLR 130, 276 Estates Gazette 77; *Brett v Brett Essex Golf Club Ltd* (1984) 273 Estates Gazette 507; *Panther Shop Investments Ltd v Keith Pople Ltd* [1987] 1 EGLR 131, 282 Estates Gazette 594; *Hambros Bank Executor and Trustee Co Ltd v Superdrug Stores Ltd* [1985] 1 EGLR 99, 274 Estates Gazette 590 (where the point was apparently not addressed to the court), or because works carried out before the grant of the lease are not considered to have been carried out by the 'tenant' within the meaning of the disregard (see para 6.36:2 below).

2   For example by amending the clause to read '. . . during the term or during any period of occupation prior to the term . . .' See 22 Encyclopaedia of Forms and Precedents (5th edn) Forms 22 (Second Schedule para 1.4:3.1), 117 (clause 3(B)(iii)), Rosscastle Letting Conditions (Appendix 1, Form No 1 below) Condition 7.1:3.3. Despite the decisions in *Scottish and Newcastle*, *Brett* and *Panther* (see note 1 above) it seems that it is possible for the word 'improvements' to include works carried out before the grant of the lease which are not, strictly speaking, improvements by making it clear that that is what is intended in the rent review clause (see *Euston Centre Properties Ltd v H & J Wilson Ltd* (1981) 262 Estates Gazette 1079 and s 34 of the Landlord and Tenant Act 1954 (as amended)). See also para 6.36:2 below.

3   1954 Act, s 34(2)(a). See para 6.31 above and Appendix 2 below.

4   (1982) 262 Estates Gazette 1079. See also *Henry Smith's Charity Trustees v Hemmings* (1982) 265 Estates Gazette 383, CA; *Hambros Bank Executor and Trustee Co Ltd v Superdrug Stores Ltd* [1985] 1 EGLR 99, 274 Estates Gazette 590; *Panther Shop Investments Ltd v Keith Pople Ltd* [1987] 1 EGLR 131, 282 Estates Gazette 594.

5   This arrangement may perhaps have been put forward in an attempt to take the work out of the 'deemed premium' provisions of the Income and Corporation Taxes Act 1988, s 34(2), (3). See para 7.18 below.

6   The tenant sought to argue that, as there was an agreement for lease, he was at the time an equitable tenant by virtue of the principle of *Walsh v Lonsdale* (1882) 21 Ch D 9, CA. The operation of this case, however, depended upon the person going into possession being entitled to a decree of specific performance, and it was held that the argument failed because until the work has been done no such order would have been made, *Walsh v Lonsdale* might, however, assist where, at the time the improvements were carried out, an agreement for lease had been entered into and the tenant was entitled to specific performance. See *Scottish and Newcastle Breweries plc v Sir Richard Sutton's Settled Estates* [1985] 2 EGLR 130, 276 Estates Gazette 77.

7   The question of whether or not 'improvements' carried out before the grant of a lease were carried out by the tenant for the purposes of a disregard has been considered in a number of recent cases. In *Brett*, improvements carried out during a previous tenancy were not considered to have been carried out by the tenant for the purposes of a disregard in the form of s 34(2)(c) of the Landlord and Tenant Act 1954 in its original form, despite the fact that the person who carried out the work was defined as 'the tenant' in the lease, because such improvements had to have been carried out by the tenant in his capacity as tenant under the subsisting lease. In *Scottish and Newcastle*, improvements carried out prior to the grant of the lease whilst an agreement for lease was subsisting were considered to have been carried out by the tenant for the purpose of a disregard of 'any effect on rent of any improvement . . .

carried out by the tenant' because the improvements were carried out by the person defined in the lease as the tenant and the improvements were referable to the grant of the lease in subsistence and not a previous lease. In *Hambros Bank* improvements carried out prior to the grant of the lease were held to have been carried out by the tenant for the purposes of a disregard of 'any effect on rent of any improvement carried out by the tenant . . .' because the person who carried out the improvements was defined as the tenant in the subsisting lease and the matrix of facts indicated that the parties intended the improvements to fall within the disregard.

8   See *Scottish and Newcastle* (above).
9   For example by amending the clause to read '. . . by the tenant its subtenants or their respective predecessors in title . . .'. See examples referred to in footnote 2 above.
10   1954 Act, s 34(2).
11   'Section 34(2) . . . in its tortuous language applies to any improvement, but only if it was carried out otherwise than in pursuance of an obligation to the tenant's immediate landlord. My impression is that the draftsman had in mind primarily, an obligation imposed by the lease. But of course the provision can also apply to an obligation imposed by some other contractual document.' Per Judge Blackett-Ord in *Godbold v Martin The Newsagents Ltd* (1983) 268 Estates Gazette 1202.
12   [1965] 2 All ER 51, [1965] 1 WLR 611, CA.
13   (1983) 268 Estates Gazette 1202.
14   In *Godbold* the licences were not in identical form but the first contained a covenant by the tenant 'to carry out the said works of alteration in a proper and workmanlike manner' while in the second and third licences the tenant covenanted 'at its own expense to complete the said Works in conformity with the said drawings . . . and in a good and substantial and workmanlike manner with new good and sound materials' within a specified period. The judge concluded that: 'Looking at the licences it is clear that they were all granted at the request of the tenant and the language of the clauses in each case is the language of permission. Those clauses do not say that it has been agreed that the tenant shall carry out; he is simply granted permission. In my judgment the following clauses [ie the covenants set out above to carry out the work] are in each case subsidiary to that. Although the wording is different in each case the effect is that the improvements authorised are not to be taken into account in fixing the rent under the present review'.
15   See for example 22 Encyclopaedia of Forms and Precedents (5th edn) Form 22 Third Schedule para 1.
16   See para 6.13:3 above.
17   Or the effect of it is mitigated in the way envisaged in para 6.13:3 above.
18   Whether the fitting out work should be regarded or disregarded is, of course, a commercial matter to be negotiated and agreed between the parties. The important point for the tenant and his advisers to note is that unless this is specifically dealt with such work will not be excluded under the normal disregarding provision where the tenant covenants to do it.
19   See for example 22 Encyclopaedia of Forms and Precedents (5th edn) Form 22 Clause 5.7, Rosscastle Letting Conditions (Appendix 1, Form No 1 below) Condition 3.11.
20   [1986] 2 EGLR 115, 279 Estates Gazette 1227.
21   The tenant had covenanted 'to do and to execute . . . all such works as under or by virtue of any Act or Acts of Parliament for the time being in force are or shall be properly directed or necessary to be done or executed upon or in respect of the demised premises or any part thereof whether by the owner landlord lessee tenant or occupier . . .'
22   This can be done, for example, either specifically '. . . carried out otherwise that in pursuance of an obligation (except an obligation contained in clause 5.7:1) to the Landlord . . .' (22 Encyclopaedia of Forms and Precedents (5th edn) Form 22 Second Schedule para 1.4:3) or generally 'carried out . . . otherwise than in pursuance of an obligation to the Landlord . . . except obligations requiring compliance with statutes or directions of local authorities or other bodies exercising powers under statute or Royal Charter . . .' (ibid Form 117, Model Forms of Clause prepared by the Joint Committee of the Law Society/RICS). See also Rosscastle Letting Conditions (Appendix 1, Form No 1 below) Condition 7.2:3.3.
23   See para 6.37:3 below.
24   See for example 'any improvement to the demised premises carried out with consent where required . . .' (22 Encyclopaedia of Forms and Precedents (5th edn) form 117: Model Clause prepared by the Law Society/RICS, 'any alteration or improvement to the Demised Premises made . . . by the Tenant . . . with any necessary prior consent of the Landlord . . .' ibid Form 118: Clauses recommended by ISVA).
25   [1986] 1 EGLR 244.
26   *Liverpool City Council v Irwin* [1977] AC 239, HL. See especially Lord Wilberforce at 253–4, Lord Cross at 258 and Lord Edmund Davies at 266.

27   And yet one questions if this is the last word on the topic because in certain circumstances this
could cause real hardship for a tenant. Perhaps the answer is that the tenant needs to seek a
declaration that consent is being unreasonably withheld before turning to the question of rent
review.

6.37   *How is the improvement to be disregarded?*   Lawyers must not play at being
valuers but may well be called upon to advise their client's valuer and as such
it is important that they understand something of the methods of valuation
and the approach adopted by the courts. They would be well advised to read
the judgments of Forbes J in *Grea Real Property Investments Ltd v Williams*[1] and
Estates Projects Ltd v Greenwich London Borough[2] from which a number of points
emerge:

6.37:1   *No one method.* Valuers are not required to adopt any one particular
method of valuation in order to disregard improvements. As Forbes J said in
GREA:[3] 'The only principle of law which I think it necessary to enunciate is
thus the simple one that any method of valuation must properly reflect the
intention of the parties as expressed in the lease'.

6.37:2   *Intention.* The intention of the parties in this aspect of the lease is
essentially to ensure that the landlord does not have during the term any rental
benefit from improvements carried out by the tenant at its own cost and that as
such the rental equivalent of these improvements should be eliminated from
the rent agreed or determined on the rent reviews.

6.37:3   *Use unimproved comparables where possible.* 'It is a fundamental aspect of
valuation that it proceeds by analogy. The valuer isolates those characteristics
of the object to be valued which, in his view, affect the value and then seeks
another object of known or ascertainable value possessing some or all of these
characteristics with which he may compare the object that he is valuing.
Where no directly comparable object exists the valuer must make allowances
of one kind or another, interpolating or extrapolating from his given data. The
less closely analogous the object chosen for comparison is, the greater the
allowances which have to be made and the greater the opportunity for error.'[4]
As such 'where there are premises properly comparable with the subject
premises in an unimproved state, it seems to me, as I said in the GREA case
that it is sensible to use such comparables to arrive directly at a rent for the
premises which disregards the effect on rent of improvements; it does not seem
to me that it is necessary to start off by finding what is the improved rent and
then deducting something to arrive at the unimproved rent if you have
unimpeachable comparables which you can use to arrive at the unimproved
rent direct.'[5]

6.37:4   *If not, whatever reflects the intention.* There will be many cases where it
will not be possible to find unimpeachable comparables in an unimproved
state. Here it will be necessary to use some other method of valuation[6] but again
there is no right or wrong – an award should only be set aside on the ground
that the wrong method of valuation has been adopted if the judge is satisfied
that it does not, as a result, reflect the intention of the parties.

1   (1979) 250 Estates Gazette 651.

2 (1979) 251 Estates Gazette 851. For a discussion of these cases, see Christopher Priday and Dr T Hoyes 'Improvements and redevelopments by lessees' (Blundell Memorial Lecture 1980) Gazette 1 October 958 and 3 December 1208.

3 At 654.

4 Per Forbes J in *GREA* at 653.

5 Per Forbes J in *Greenwich* at 853. And yet, it would presumably be possible in a certain case for this method not to reflect the intention of the parties. Factors similar to those discussed under the vacant possession assumption (see paras 6.19 and 6.20 above) could sometimes arise. For example, it would be unfair to the landlord, if the tenant could argue that in respect of each review period he is entitled to an adjustment in the rent to reflect the market reality that part of his hypothetical term would be lost to him during the fitting-out of the premises – something which in reality the landlord may have already provided for by agreeing a one-off rent-free period at the commencement of the term or in the rent for the initial period. The landlord might consider adding a provision to the effect that in making such disregard 'no allowance shall be made for loss of the use of the Premises whilst such improvement [fitting-out and finishing] [and the installation of trade fixtures] are being carried out it being the intention of the parties that due allowance for such loss of use has already been made [by the initial rent-free period of occupation permitted under this lease] [and/or] [in the assessment of the initial rent].'

6 See for example those discussed in para 6.38 below.

6.38 *The facts of the case. GREA*[1] was a case in which no unimpeachable comparables in an unimproved state were available in view of the extent of the tenants' improvements. The developers had run out of funds before the building was completed and the tenants of the third floor carried out at their own cost all the work required to make the floor fit for use, in recognition of which they paid only a peppercorn rent for the first six months of their tenancy. The lease provided for a rent review after seven and fourteen years and in arriving at the 'fair rack rental market value' the parties (or in default of agreement the arbitrator) were directed to disregard: 'Any effect on the rental value of any improvement carried out by the Tenants or their predecessors in title otherwise than in pursuance of an obligation contained in this lease and in particular but without prejudice to the generality of the foregoing any such effect of any work of fitting out and finishing the demised premises to acceptable office standards carried out by the Tenants at the commencement of the term hereby negotiated.' At the first rent review, there was a dispute between the valuers instructed by the parties as to the correct approach to adopt. Two alternatives were canvassed:

(a) Establish by the normal use of comparables the rental value of the premises as improved on the review date ('the Actual Rental Value'). Then calculate what the cost of carrying out the improvements would have been on the review date. Determine the annual equivalent of this cost (by dividing the cost by the number of years of the lease) and deduct this from the Actual Rental Value, the balance representing the reviewed rent.[2]

(b) The rent for the remainder of the initial seven years had been discounted to reflect the condition of the premises, over and above the initial rent-free period of six months. By the normal use of comparables, the percentage could be determined by which this rent was less than the market rent at the commencement of the term, assuming that the improvements had been carried out. Thus the rent payable on the review should be the Actual Rental Value discounted by the same percentage.[3]

1 (1979) 250 Estates Gazette 651.

2 This method, however, assumes that inflation has proceeded at the same rate for rental values and the cost of carrying out the improvements. Further, it may be presumed that the tenant, having made at the commencement of the term the calculations which produced the annual equivalent of the capital cost of the works, thought it justifiable to incur that cost because he would reap the benefit over the full period of the lease plus any statutory extension. It does not follow that a tenant, faced with such expenditure at the first review date, would regard it as viable to pay the capital cost of a benefit which would only accrue to him over a shorter period. At the second review date it is even less likely that incurring such expenditure would be considered worthwhile.

3   But as Forbes J pointed out (*GREA* at 655): 'this assumes that the proportion which the value of the tenants' work bears to the whole will remain constant whatever happens. It may be, however, that inflation has had, or would have in the future, different effects on site values, major construction works and works of improvement such as the tenants' here; these are the three components which make up the total value of the building. It may be also that, even if inflation has had different effects, the comparative magnitude of the three components figures mean that wide variation between the rate of inflation for one component on the one hand and the other two on the other would not seriously affect the validity of the final calculations.' He referred to this method again in *Estates Projects Ltd v Greenwich London Borough* (1979) 251 Estates Gazette 851 at 855: 'As I indicated in the *GREA* case this method has considerable attraction but I had at that stage some doubt about the validity of assuming that the proportion was always constant. [The landlord's] counsel said that the doubt that I had in that case is unnecessary because once the improvements are completed, they become part of the reality so that there is no necessity to divide the value of the premises into its component parts. I find that an attractive argument but again, as in the *GREA* case, I have no valuation evidence upon that point and although such a method may have been adumbrated by the landlord before the arbitrator it was certainly not pursued in any depth. Now, I put it in that way because, as I sought to say in the *GREA* case, that method of valuation in cases such as this seems to me to have a great many attractions. I am not sure that the assumption that the proportion always remains constant is necessarily valid in every circumstance and before being satisfied about that one will, it seems to me, require some valuation evidence on that point. It may be that my doubts about it are fanciful and that valuers could indicate that one need not bother one's head about that sort of thing. It may be, on the other hand, that evidence would show that, in fact, there are differences. I do not know, and as I have indicated, this court, not being a valuer, cannot supply its own view about these matters for proper expert valuation evidence'.

6.39   *GREA*[1]*: the lessons.* Forbes J made certain observations as to the intention of the parties in the case but declined to indicate whether any of the various methods of valuation would reflect these intentions. He left that for the arbitrator and hoped that what he had said would 'enable the parties to address their minds to the question of what further evidence their valuers should adduce and the arbitrator to decide how far their valuations coincide with the intention of the parties as I have sought to express it'. It follows, of course, that there would be nothing to stop the parties to a lease, especially one where major and specific tenant's improvements were contemplated immediately the lease was granted, themselves assisting the arbitrator by setting out in the lease what their intention was as to the method of valuation to be used in disregarding these improvements.[2] In practice, however, parties seem to prefer to retain flexibility and finally to settle on their method of valuation only when the rent review is upon them and the comparables and other surrounding circumstances are known.

1   (1979) 250 Estates Gazette 651.
2   For example by providing in the lease 'that in making such disregard the following method of valuation shall be used . . .'

6.40   *Drafting – how to direct that improvements are to be disregarded.* There are at least four ways in which the valuer can be directed to deal with improvements:
   (a) *Disregard the effect on rent* – ie . . . 'there being disregarded any effect on rent of an improvement . . .',[1]

(b) *Disregard the improvement* – ie '. . . there being disregarded any improvement . . .',[2]

(c) *Disregard the increase in rent* – ie '. . . disregarding any increase in the rental value of the demised premises attributable to the existence at the relevant review date of any improvement to the demised premises . . .',[3] or

(d) *Make a fair allowance* – ie '. . . making a fair allowance to the Tenant in respect of any alteration or improvement to the Demised Premises made . . . by the Tenant . . .'.[4]

Draftsmen should not play at being valuers but must work very closely with their client's surveyor on this aspect of the draft lease. In practice, there will probably be few instances where valuation would be different depending upon whether alternative (a), (b) or (c) was used.[5] Perhaps when the improvement itself must be disregarded (alternative (b)), the valuer has to determine the rent of the premises on the basis that the improvement had not been carried out,[6] whereas other methods of valuation, if considered more appropriate, could be adopted where the direction is to disregard the effect on, or increase in, the rent attributable to the improvement.[7] The requirement to make a fair allowance is novel and does not appear to have been widely adopted in practice. It may well permit a more flexible approach to be used and would seem to presume that the premises are to be valued with the improvement, and then a fair allowance, arrived at 'in a commonsense way', is to be subtracted from that rental valuation.[8]

1 This adopts the wording of the Landlord and Tenant Act 1954, s 34(1)(c).
2 Ibid s 34(1)(b) states that there should be disregarded any goodwill – ie the words 'any effect on' included in s 34(1)(a) (occupation) and s 34(1)(c) are omitted. As such the draftsman of the Act presumably saw a distinction between disregarding a factor and disregarding the effect of that factor on the rent.
3 The form followed by the Model Clause prepared by the Law Society/RICS (see 22 Encyclopaedia of Forms and Precedents (5th edn) Form 117). The Background Notes give no indication as to why this format had been chosen.
4 The form adopted by the ISVA Model Clause (ibid Form 118). A footnote states 'This method avoids the difficulties which arise in respect of the "disregard" of the effect on rent of tenant's improvements, eg the problems of "fitting out time" or of works paid for partly by the landlord and partly by the tenant. Improvements can now be treated in a commonsense way'.
5 Indeed Ronald Bernstein QC and Kirk Reynolds the distinguished authors of the *Handbook of Rent Review* (Sweet & Maxwell) had not (as of 1988) met a case where on the facts the distinction of wording between (a) and (b) would have pointed to a difference in results.
6 And yet this method of valuation requires the availability of unimpeachable comparables in an unimproved state (see para 6.37:4 above). If none is available, the valuer would have to adopt some other method whatever the wording.
7 As to other valuation methods, see para 6.38 above.
8 But as has been pointed out (see Philip Freedman and Steven Fogel: 'ISVA Recommended Rent Review Clauses – some first impressions' (1984) 272 Estates Gazette 498 and 618 14 November 3169) 'fair' is capable of several interpretations and this could cause uncertainty – for example fair to the actual tenant (ie taking account of his financial and other circumstances), fair to both the actual tenant and the actual landlord, fair to a hypothetical tenant (ie without regard to the actual tenant's personal circumstances), or fair to a hypothetical landlord and hypothetical tenant. Note the problems that have arisen with 'fair' and 'reasonable' rents – see para 6.41 below.

G VALUATION TERM

6.41 *The expression defined.* The draftsman must define the rent that is to be determined on the review[1] and there are at least five such definitions in current use:

6.41:1 *Open market rent.* Such clauses are generally based upon s 34 of the 1954 Act[2] and provide that the revised rent is to be that at which the demised premises might reasonably[3] be expected to be let in the open[4] market on the terms that are defined in the lease, that is to say on a new hypothetical letting.[5] The valuer, therefore, is required to be objective. The similarity to s 34 can be an advantage because a rent review and a lease renewal of similar premises are, strictly speaking, only comparable transactions for the purposes of valuation where the rent has been determined on the same basis.[6] This would be so in the case of a renewal under the 1954 Act and a review where the rent review clause was based upon s 34. It need not be so where the rent had been reviewed in accordance with a clause that differed markedly from s 34. Thus a rent review clause similar to s 34 increases the likelihood of there being directly comparable transactions, and itself may be a transaction that would be comparable for other reviews or renewals.[7] In addition valuers are familiar with the term[8] and there is a certain amount of case law on open market valuations[9] that should provide some guidance. Draftsmen would be well advised to adopt his wording.

6.41:2 *Rack rent.* This means the rent which represents the full annual value of the holding[10] but it is suggested that when such an approach is required, an open market rent clause is clearer, while there could be problems with this expression if rents were frozen under counter inflation legislation.[11]

6.41:3 *Best rent.* Here the revised rent is to be the best rent at which the premises might be let.[12] Often 'the best rent' and 'the open market rent' would be the same,[13] but there will be instances where a direction to determine the best rent may increase the revised rent and tenants should therefore resist this term. This could occur, for example, where there had been a recent letting of similar premises to a large corporate tenant, that had made the decision to take premises in that particular locality, and was (if necessary) prepared to pay a little in excess of the market rent in order to do so. Where upon a review, the comparable transactions produce a range of rents, 'the best rent' would be at the top of the range, whereas, in determining the open market rent, the valuer may well be entitled to take the average or mean rent of the comparables. In the words of the valuers, the expression 'best rent' 'lets in the special purchaser's bid'.[14] The open market price (and therefore presumably rent) on the other hand, is the best sum obtainable in the market place,[15] such expression meaning, not the highest possible sum, but the best sum using acceptable valuation criteria.[16]

6.41:4 *Fair or reasonable rent.* In the interests of certainty, such expressions should be avoided. Frequently they might well be construed in the same way as open market rent, although a rent that is to be 'in all the circumstances reasonable' or 'which is reasonable for the Tenant to pay' would seem to require the application of a subjective test, rather than the objective test required to determine the open market rent – for example circumstances affecting the parties could be taken into account.[17] If it is the parties' intention that other than open market valuation matters should be considered, the lease should expressly deal with the point.

6.41:5   *Having regard to open market rental values.* In the initial versions of the model clause,[18] the Joint Committee of the Law Society and the Royal Institution of Chartered Surveyors provided that the revised rent, in default of agreement, was to be such that the arbitrator or valuer 'shall decide . . . should be the yearly rent at the relevant review date for the demised premises' let on the hypothetical term and subject to the assumptions and disregarded matters 'and having regard to[19] open market rental values current at the relevant review date'. The background notes did not indicate why the Committee had departed from the format of s 34, but it is understood[20] that the basic concept of the clause was to base the review on market forces and that the wording was prompted by the desire of the Joint Committee to make it clear that the reviewed rent should be determined by reference, not to the 'real' open market rent of the premises (the rent for which the landlord would be able to let the premises on the open market), but to the 'hypothetical' market rent (the rent for which the premises would be let on the hypothetical tenancy, and subject to the various assumptions and disregarded matters specified in the rent review clause). The importance of this distinction was illustrated in the *F R Evans case*[21] where the 'real' open market rent would have been low in view of the finding that the tenant was the only party who required the unusual premises in question. The 'hypothetical' market rent was rather higher,[22] although in most instances, it is probable that the rent will be the same as if determined under a clause that adopts the s 34 approach. It has been suggested that the 'having regard to' wording may introduce an element of subjectivity into the determination of the rent,[23] that is not present when the s 34 wording is used, and it is interesting to note that in the latest version of the clause the Joint Committee has reverted to the s 34 approach.[24]

1   Where the reviewed rent is not defined, see *Beer v Bowden* [1981] 1 All ER 1070, [1981] 1 WLR 522; *Thomas Bates & Son Ltd v Wyndhams (Lingerie) Ltd* [1981] 1 All ER 1077, [1981] 1 WLR 505, CA; *King v King* (1980) 255 Estates Gazette 1205. As to attitude of House of Lords on drafting omissions, see *Sudbrook Trading Estate Ltd v Eggleton* [1983] 1 AC 444, [1982] 3 All ER 1, HL. Sometimes, the parties will require an unconventional approach for determining the rent – the lease considered in *Leigh v Certibilt Investments Ltd* [1988] 1 EGLR 116, [1988] 04 EG 127 provided that the reviewed rent was to be one half of 'the estimated aggregate rack rental value of the premises' but very careful consideration by the parties, their solicitors and their surveyor is required before moving away from a conventional approach for reasons similar to those set out in para 6.17:1 above. For example, in *Leigh* it would probably have been preferable for the rent to be half of the aggregate of the rents actually received from the sublet units plus the market rent of parts not sublet (see para 6.65 below).

2   See paras 14.50–14.54 below.

3   There is no authority as to the correct intepretation of 'reasonably' and here there is perhaps an uncertainty as to whether the arguments similar to those advanced in the cases cited in note 17 below could be applied.

4   In fact 'open' probably only states the obvious because in determining a market rent the valuer, in the absence of any direction to the contrary, would assume that the property was being offered generally and not only to a 'closed or circumscribed market to which only certain bidders are admitted': see *Sterling Land Office Developments Ltd v Lloyds Bank plc* (1984) 271 Estates Gazette 894 per Harman J.

5   See for example 22 Encyclopaedia of Forms and Precedents (5th edn) Forms 22 (Second Schedule para 2.3), Rosscastle Letting Conditions (Appendix 1, Form No 1 below) Condition 7.3:3.

6   The better evidence, of course, is new comparable lettings in the open market, because a rent determined or agreed on a rent review or lease renewal is based upon the opinions of the parties' valuers etc.

7   Although for the reason set out in footnote 6 above, valuers are likely to prefer evidence of new lettings, freely negotiated in the open market, rather than rents determined on reviews or lease renewals.

8 See the definition of 'open market value' adopted by the Assets Valuation Standards Committee of the Royal Institution of Chartered Surveyors in Guidance Note 22 (although not directly relevant to rent reviews) helpfully set out in Ronald Bernstein QC and Kirk Reynolds *Handbook of Rent Review* (Sweet and Maxwell) paras 4–22.

9 Although it has to be admitted that most of the cases concern the expression as used in revenue statutes (see for example Inheritance Tax Act 1984, s 160 and Capital Gains Tax 1979, s 150). The price which a property is expected to fetch in the open market (and thus presumably the open market rent) is found by reference to the expectations of properly qualified persons who have fully informed themselves of all relevant information about the property, its capabilities, the demand for it and the likely purchasers (tenants): *IRC v Clay; IRC v Buchanan* [1914] 3 KB 466, CA; *Glass v IRC* 1915 SC 449; *Lynall v IRC* [1972] AC 680, [1971] 3 All ER 914, HL. See too *F R Evans (Leeds) Ltd v English Electric Co Ltd* (1977) 245 Estates Gazette 657.

10 See *Compton Group Ltd v Estates Gazette Ltd* (1977) 244 Estates Gazette 799, CA. As to 'current market rack rental value' see *Royal Exchange Assurance v Bryant Samuel Properties (Coventry) Ltd* [1985] 1 EGLR 84, 273 Estates Gazette 1332.

11 In *Compton* (see above) Pennycuick VC indicated that the expression can mean either the rent which represents the full annual value of the holding or the maximum rent permitted by law. See also *Newman v Dorrington Developments Ltd* [1975] 3 All ER 928, [1975] 1 WLR 1642.

12 Sometimes the expression 'highest rent' is seen.

13 A view perhaps confirmed by the comments of Peter Gibson J in *Daejan Investments Ltd v Cornwall Coast Country Club* [1985] 1 EGLR 77 that 'highest' in the expression 'the highest rent at which . . . the premises might reasonably be expected to be let in the open market . . .' added only emphasis because without the words 'the rent at which the premises might reasonably be expected to be let in the open market' would be the highest rent obtainable.

14 See *IRC v Buchanan* [1914] 3 KB 466, CA; *IRC v Crossman* [1937] AC 26, [1936] 1 All ER 762, HL; and *Re Lynall, Lynall v IRC* (1971) 47 TC 375.

15 *Earl of Ellesmere v IRC* [1918] 2 KB 735 at 740.

16 *Re Hayes's Will Trusts, Pattinson v Hayes* [1971] 2 All ER 341, [1971] 1 WLR 758. For examples of how a special purchaser's bid can be relevant even when the revised rent is to be determined on an open market basis, see Robert Lyons (1983) 265 Estates Gazette 451 and John Marples and Robert Lyons 'Rent Reviews in shopping developments' (1984) 271 Estates Gazette 515 and 602 (Abridged Blundell Memorial Lecture 1984).

17 *John Kay Ltd v Kay* [1952] 2 QB 258, [1952] 1 All ER 813, CA; but see *Ponsford v HMS Aerosols Ltd* [1979] AC 63, [1978] 2 All ER 837, HL; *Cuff v J and F Stone Property Co Ltd* [1979] AC 87, [1978] 2 All ER 833; *Thomas Bates & Son Ltd v Wyndham's (Lingerie) Ltd* [1981] 1 All ER 1077, [1981] 1 WLR 505, CA; *Lear v Blizzard* [1983] 3 All ER 662. In *99 Bishopsgate Ltd v Prudential Assurance Co Ltd* (1985) 273 Estates Gazette 984, CA the lease in question referred to 'a fair yearly rent'. Oliver LJ said 'that "fair", of course, means not "fair" between these particular parties, circumstances being what they are, but what a hypothetical tenant would fairly be expected to pay if taking the premises from a hypothetical landlord.'

18 See [1979] Gazette 6 June 564, [1980] Gazette 26 March 82.

19 The term 'have regard to' is not unfamiliar, appearing as it does in s 34 and s 24A of the 1954 Act (interim rents – see para 14.15 below). It has not been without its critics – in *English Exporters (London) Ltd v Eldonwall Ltd* [1973] Ch 415, [1973] 1 All ER 726 Megarry J said 'that the term "have regard to" is almost of necessity bound to create difficulties. How much regard is to be had, and what weight is to be attached to the regard when it has been had?' He agreed with the sentiments expressed by Stamp J in *Regis Property Co Ltd v Lewis and Peat Ltd* [1970] Ch 695, [1970] 3 All ER 227 as to the difficulties of construing 'shall have regard to the rent payable under the terms of the (existing) tenancy' in s 24A(3) of the 1954 Act. Stamp J did not feel that the rent under the existing tenancy assisted him. Thus, having regard to it, he took no account of it. The words, therefore, seem to mean that the item in question must be considered but can then be disregarded.

20 The publishers are much indebted to Messrs J R S Grimwood-Taylor MA LLB, Solicitor, and J P Wainwright MA FRICS, the then Chairmen of the Joint Committee for their assistance on this point.

21 (1977) 36 P & CR 185, 245 Estates Gazette 657.

22 Some valuers also suggest that 'having regard to open market rental values' enables them to disregard an apparently comparable transaction but where the rent appears out-of-line with the norm, and where special circumstances may well have been prevailing. They feel that they would have had to consider that transaction if required to determine the rent 'at which the premises might reasonably be expected to be let in the open market' – ie because these special circumstances may prevail again. There is also perhaps a possible danger that 'having regard to open market rental values' could be interpreted as 'having regard *only*

143

to . . .' thereby limiting the comparable transactions to which the valuer may refer to (new) open market lettings only and not to lease renewals or rent reviews.

23 See the arguments addressed to the court (but rejected) on the review clause in *99 Bishopsgate Ltd v Prudential Assurance Co Ltd* [1985] 1 EGLR 72, 273 Estates Gazette 984 which contained the words 'the amount which shall in [the arbitrator's] opinion represent a fair yearly rent for the demised premises having regard to rental values current . . .'

24 See 22 Encyclopaedia of Forms and Precedents (5th edn) Form 117.

6.42 *Comparables.* As has already been pointed out,[1] valuation proceeds by analogy, the valuer seeking an object of known or ascertainable value that is comparable with the object that he is valuing. In the case of a rent review, the valuer requires evidence[2] of lettings[3] of comparable premises on leases of comparable terms. Many of the issues that arise on a lease renewal are relevant to a rent review[4] but a question that arises only in the latter[5] is whether post review date comparables can be considered – ie lettings made *after* the review date.[6] The preferred view would seem to be that a subsequent comparable can be admitted, provided that, between the review date and the date of the comparable, no event has occurred that has altered the conditions that were prevailing at the review date.[7]

1 See para 6.37:3 above.
2 As to hearsay evidence, see para 14.51 footnote 1 below.
3 As to evidence of rent reviews and lease renewals, see para 6.41:1 footnotes 6 and 7 above.
4 See para 14.51 below.
5 It does not arise on lease renewals because the rent is being determined for a letting that will commence on the coming to the end of the current tenancy and therefore *after* the determination by the court (see 1954 Act, s 64 and paras 14.14, 14.49 and 14.50 below). Thus the court has to determine the rent on the basis of rents prevailing at the date of the hearing, although it can have regard to matters that could reasonably be expected to happen between then and the commencement of the new tenancy: *Lovely and Orchard Services Ltd v Daejan Investments (Grove Hall) Ltd* (1977) 246 Estates Gazette 651. A rent review arbitration, however, is likely to take place months or even years after the review date and during this period new comparables may have come into being.
6 *Bwllfa and Merthyr Dare Steam Colleries (1891) Ltd v Pontypridd Waterworks Co* [1903] AC 426, [1900–3] All ER Rep 600, HL; *Re Bradberry, National Provincial Bank Ltd v Bradberry* [1943] Ch 35, [1942] 2 All ER 629; *Ponsford v HM Aerosols Ltd* (1976) (Whitford J) (unreported but summary in *Handbook of Rent Review*); *Industrial Properties (Barton Hill) Ltd v AEI* (1976) (Judge Fay QC, Official Referee) (ibid); *Melwood Units Pty Ltd v Main Roads Comrs* [1979] AC 426, [1979] 1 All ER 161, PC; *Australian Mutual Provident Society v Overseas Telecommunications Commission (Australia)* [1972] 2 NSWLR 806; *Duvan Estates Ltd v Rosette Sunshine Savouries Ltd* (1981) 261 Estates Gazette 364; *Gaze v Holden* (1982) 266 Estates Gazette 998; *Segama NV v Penny Le Roy Ltd* (1983) 269 Estates Gazette 322.
7 See in particular *Australian Mutual, Melwood* and *Segama* (see footnote 6 above).

6.43 *Lack of comparables.* Where it is recognised that there may be a lack of evidence of comparable transactions, the parties and their advisers need when the lease is being negotiated to consider the problems that could arise on the rent reviews, and whether it would be helpful to address these issues in the lease.[1] Comparables can be unavailable where, for example, the premises are unusual, because of their scarcity – such as hypermarkets, supermarkets or department stores – or simply because they are significantly larger than buildings of that type in the area in question.[2]

1 See *Trust House Forte Albany Hotels Ltd v Daejan Investments Ltd* (1980) 256 Estates Gazette 915; *Bovis Group Pension Fund Ltd v GC Flooring & Furnishing Ltd* (1984) 269 Estates Gazette 1252, CA; *John Lewis & Co Ltd v Goodwin (V/O) and Westminster City Council* (1979) 252 Estates Gazette 499. In *National Car Parks Ltd v Colebrook Estates Ltd* (1982) 266 Estates Gazette 810 Foster J held that where no true comparables are available, the revised rent can be fixed by reference to the general increase in rent levels. For further discussion, see Blundell Memorial Lectures 1979 (Mr John C Hill TD, FRICS) [1979] Gazette 5 September 841, (1979) 251 Estates Gazette 147.

2 See para 6.18 above.

H THE THIRD PARTY: ARBITRATOR OR EXPERT?

6.44 *Introduction.* The rent review clause contemplates two stages. Initially it is hoped that the revised rent will be agreed between the landlord and tenant, but there must be a provision for it to be determined by a third party in the absence of agreement.[1] The third party will be either an independent valuer acting as an expert[2] or an arbitrator, and the draftsman must ensure that the lease leaves no doubt as to the status of the third party.[3] The lease must also provide who should appoint the arbitrator or expert if this cannot be agreed.[4] It could be important from the tenant's point of view that he can activate a rent review. Normally he will be quite happy to continue paying the existing rent if the landlord overlooks a review date,[5] but there may be circumstances where the tenant would require the revised rent to be determined, for example where he was proposing to dispose of the lease. It is true that where the landlord can instigate the review, the tenant could serve a notice making time of the essence, but this step raises a number of problems and the far more satisfactory solution is to provide in the rent review clause itself for either party to be able to implement the review.[6] In practice, this concern ought to be met if *either party* (and not just the landlord) can apply to the President to appoint the arbitrator or expert, because this means that the tenant is in a position to precipitate the determination of the rent by the third party.[7]

1 Where the lease provides that the revised rent 'shall be agreed between the parties hereto . . . and in the event of the parties failing to reach such agreement determined . . .' there is no implied term that there must have been an attempt to agree: *Re Essoldo (Bingo) Ltd's Underlease, Essoldo Ltd v Elcresta Ltd* (1972) 23 P & CR 1; *Laing Investment Co Ltd v G A Dunn & Co* (1982) 262 Estates Gazette 879; *Wrenbridge Ltd v Harries (Southern Properties) Ltd* (1981) 260 Estates Gazette 1195. See para 6.50:1 below.
2 The words 'acting as an expert and not as an arbitrator' should be inserted in this case to make clear the status of the third party, and to exclude the application of the Arbitration Acts 1950 and 1979.
3 Where the clause is not clear as to that status, see *Langham House Developments Ltd v Brompton Securities Ltd* (1980) 256 Estates Gazette 719; and *Safeway Food Stores Ltd v Banderway Ltd* (1983) 267 Estates Gazette 850; *Palacath v Flanagan* [1985] 2 All ER 161; *North Eastern Co-operative Society Ltd v Newcastle upon Tyne City Council* [1987] 1 EGLR 142, 282 Estates Gazette 1409.
4 See para 6.50 below. The correct procedure where a person believes that an appointment is void is to apply to the court for a declaration and not to commence proceedings against the appointer: *United Co-operative Ltd v Sun Alliance and London Assurance Co Ltd* [1987] 1 EGLR 126, 282 Estates Gazette 91.
5 See paras 6.53–6.56 below. If the tenant's only concern is having to pay a large shortfall between the current and the revised rent back-dated to the review date his surveyor could no doubt advise the tenant as to the likely rent and he could annually accrue a sum for the 'arrears' on this basis.
6 As to making time of the essence, see *United Scientific Holdings Ltd v Burnley Borough Council* [1978] AC 904, [1977] 2 All ER 62, HL; *Factory Holdings Group Ltd v Leboff International Ltd* [1987] 1 EGLR 135, 282 Estates Gazette 1005; *Panavia Air Cargo Ltd v Southend-on-Sea Borough Council* [1988] 1 EGLR 124, [1988] 22 EG 82, CA.
7 See for example Rosscastle Letting Conditions (Appendix 1, Form No 1 below) Condition 7.3:5.

6.45 *Distinctions between independent valuer and arbitrator.* In essence, two quite different processes are involved. An independent valuer acting as an expert is required to exercise his own skill and judgment and make a valuation, having sought out the relevant facts for himself,[1] while an arbitrator has to perform a judicial function and resolve a dispute upon evidence and arguments submitted to him.[2] Other distinctions are:

(a) the procedure for arbitration is set out in the Arbitration Acts[3] whereas an independent valuer is subject to no statutory control;

(b) an arbitrator is immune from actions for negligence, but an independent valuer is not;[4]

(c) a party dissatisfied with a valuation may appeal to the court where the valuer has set out the reasons upon which the valuation is based, and these demonstrate that the valuation has been made on a fundamentally erroneous basis.[5] There may be no such appeal when no reasons are given.[6] There are statutory rights of appeal against an arbitrator's award;[7]

(d) an arbitrator's fee can be taxed by the court[8] but there is no control over the fees of a valuer;

(e) an arbitration award may be enforced as a judgment of the court[9] whereas there is no means of enforcement of an independent valuation;[10]

(f) an arbitrator can order that one party shall pay the other's costs[11] but an independent valuer has no power (unless conferred by the lease[12]) to award costs.

1 An expert may accept information and submissions from the parties, although there is no authority for saying that he must have regard to them, even where the lease requires him to afford the parties an opportunity to make representations. As to the meaning of 'have regard to' see footnote 19 to para 6.41 above.

2 Thus the arbitrator's award (unlike the expert's determination) must be within the range of figures submitted to him by the parties. As to when an arbitrator is entitled to act on his own knowledge, see *Mediterranean and Eastern Export Co Ltd v Fortress Fabrics (Manchester) Ltd* [1948] 2 All ER 186 and *Fisher V P G Welfair Ltd* (1982) 263 Estates Gazette 589 at 657, [1981] 2 Llolyd's Rep 514, CA; *Top Shop Estates Ltd v Danino* [1985] 1 EGLR 9, 273 Estates Gazette 197; *Zermalt Holdings SA v Nu-Life Upholstery Repairs Ltd* [1985] 2 EGLR 14, 275 Estates Gazette 1134. For comments on a variation of the normal arbitration (sometimes known as a flip-flop or pendulum arbitration), by which the arbitrator must confirm the figure put forward by one or other of the parties, see *Henry Smith's Charity Trustees v A WADA Trading and Promotion Services Ltd* (1983) 269 Estates Gazette 729 at 731, CA, per Sir John Donaldson MR, Ronald Bernstein QC et al: 'Raising the efficiency and lowering the cost of rental review' (Blundell Memorial Lecture 1983), and Tony R Langridge: (1987) 284 Estates Gazette 882. For a precedent (that refers to an expert but that could readily be adapted for an arbitrator), see 22 Encyclopaedia of Forms and Precedents (5th edn) Form 130.

3 For example, s 12 of the 1950 Act refers to the conduct of proceedings requiring the arbitrator to hold a hearing (although this can be dispensed with in favour of written submissions by agreement between the parties) and dealing with such matters as the production of documents, the calling of witnesses and the power of the arbitrator to compel them to attend, giving evidence on oath and by affidavit, security for costs, and discovery of documents.

4 *Arenson v Arenson* [1972] 2 All ER 939, [1972] 1 WLR 1196; *Sutcliffe v Thackrah* [1974] AC 727, [1974] 1 All ER 859, HL; *Palacath Ltd v Flanagan* [1985] 2 All ER 161. But note the view that the Supply of Services (Exclusion of Implied Terms) Order 1985 could apply to arbitration, in which event obligations would be imposed upon the arbitrator to act with reasonable care and skill, and to do so within a reasonable time – see Professor J E Adams: 'New Basis of Liability for Negligence' (1984) 270 Estates Gazette 26. For examples of actions for negligence (that failed) by disgruntled landlords against an expert, see *Belvedere Motors Ltd v King* (1981) 260 Estates Gazette 813; *Wallshire Ltd v Aarons* [1989] 1 EGLR 147. Indeed, if the parties are bound by a wrong valuation given honestly and in good faith (see sub para (c) and footnote 5 below), then the injured party's *only* remedy may be an action for negligence against the expert.

5 *Johnston v Chestergate Hat Manufacturing Co Ltd* [1915] 2 Ch 338; *Dean v Prince* [1954] Ch 409, [1954] 1 All ER 749, CA; *Frank H Wright (Construction) Ltd v Frodoor Ltd* [1967] 1 All ER 433,

[1967] 1 WLR 506; *M Jones v R R Jones* [1971] 2 All ER 676, [1971] 1 WLR 840; *Arenson v Arenson* [1973] Ch 346, [1973] 2 All ER 235; *Sutcliffe v Thackrah* [1974] AC 727, [1974] 1 All ER 859; *Campbell v Edwards* [1976] 1 All ER 785, [1976] 1 WLR 403, CA; *Baber v Kenwood Manufacturing Co Ltd* [1978] 1 Lloyd's Rep 175, CA; *Burgess v Purchase & Sons (Farm) Ltd* [1983] Ch 216, [1983] 2 All ER 4; *Heyes v Derby* (1984) 272 Estates Gazette 935; *Apus Properties Ltd v D H Farrow Ltd* [1989] NPC 38.

6   And yet, one questions if it can be said that a valuation without reasons by an expert is by definition non-appealable, or whether there should be a substantive distinction between speaking and non-speaking determinations. The prospects of a successful appeal against the latter must be slender, but it may be that the courts would be prepared to consider a case where the expert must have mistaken what he was meant to be doing, and come to a valuation that no reasonable surveyor could possibly have arrived at, for example where evidence is called that shows that the valuation is significantly outside the range of what was possible. Where the expert sets out the factors upon which he has relied upon making his valuation, the position is clearer because, if one of these was materially in error, then an application could be made to the court (see footnote 5 above). Nevertheless this safeguard would generally be of little practical assistance, because experts tend to make their valuations without setting out reasons, and an expert cannot be required to give a reasoned determination, unless this is stipulated as being a condition attaching to his appointment. As such the parties might never know that the valuation was based, for example, upon an incorrect construction of the rent review clause. Where a dispute as to the construction of the clause can be anticipated before the review, however, it would be possible for either party to apply to the court for a declaration as to the proper construction of the clause.

7   See para 6.46 below.
8   Arbitration Act 1950, s 19.
9   Arbitration Act 1950, s 26.
10 The point is of little practical effect on a rent review because the amount fixed by valuation is rent and can be recovered in the usual ways.
11 Arbitration Act 1950, s 18.
12 See para 6.49:2 below.

6.46   *Appeal from the award of an arbitrator.* Section 1 of the 1979 Act[1] provides that there is an appeal from the award of an arbitrator only on a point of law, and, unless the parties agree, only with leave of the court.[2] Section 1(4) states that leave may not be granted unless the point 'could substantially affect the rights of one or more of the parties'.[3] The appeal is heard by a single judge and there is appeal to the Court of Appeal only with leave.[4] There were two early cases[5] (neither of which concerned rent reviews) in which the House of Lords laid down guidelines as to how a judge should approach the exercise of the discretion to give leave to appeal. In *The Nema*[5] the House of Lords held that in a case that is 'one off', either because the facts are singular to the case and not likely to occur again, or because it involves the construction of a clause singular to that particular case, the judge should not give leave to appeal if he thinks that the arbitrator was right, or probably right, or may have been right. Leave should only be given if the judge forms the provisional view that the arbitrator was wrong on a point of law which substantially affect the rights of one or other of the parties.[3] In a case that is not 'one off', but gives rise to a question of construction of a standard form with facts which may occur repeatedly, or at least from time to time, the judge should give leave if he thinks that the arbitrator may have gone wrong on the construction of the standard form, and if the decision will add significantly to the clarity of the law. The categorising of contracts as 'one-offs' or 'others' is more appropriate to shipping and insurance where many major contracts incorporate standard terms. Such an approach, does not readily lend itself to rent reviews, and difficulty was experienced in determining the extent to which those guidelines were applicable to appeals from arbitrator's awards under rent review clauses.[6] As Sir Nicholas Browne-Wilkinson V-C said in *Lucas Industries plc v Welsh Development Agency*:[7]

'This approach is difficult, if not impossible, to apply to arbitrations on rent review clauses. First, although there are precedents of such clauses in the books, they are frequently modified in practice: they in no way correspond to the standard printed terms of contract commonly incorporated into commercial contracts. Second, although the exact words used in rent review clauses vary from lease to lease, there are questions of law which apply generally to rent review clauses of a particular type, eg the question in this case whether in the absence of express provision the hypothetical lease is to be treated as having the same terms as the actual lease between the parties. Third (and to my mind the most important), save in the case of the last review, the proper legal effect of a rent review clause will be material on future reviews between the same parties under the same lease. Thus in the present case exactly the same point will arise between these parties (or their successors in title) on the reviews which will have to take place in the 10th, 15th and 20th years of the term. There are strong dicta which suggest that the decision by the arbitrator on this point of law will constitute an issue estoppel which will prevent a different arbitrator taking a different view of the point of law on future reviews; see per Diplock LJ in *Fidelitas Shipping Co Ltd v V/O Exportchleb* [1966] 1 QB 630 at 643, CA. In all the commercial decisions I have seen, the point of law in question has always been "one off" as between the parties to the arbitration and did not regulate their future contractual relationships. For these reasons,[8] I do not think that the House of Lords guidelines are capable of direct application to arbitrations on rent review clauses.'

Sir Nicholas felt that in cases where the same point of law will regulate future rent reviews, a lower standard than a strong prima facie case is appropriate – if the judge was left in real doubt whether the arbitrator was right in law, leave should be granted, especially where the point in question may be relevant to other rent review clauses.[9]

1   As amended by the Supreme Court Act 1981, s 148.
2   Formerly under the Arbitration Act 1950, s 21 either party could ask the arbitrator to state his award or any question of law in the form of a special case for the decision of the High Court and, if the arbitrator refused, the party could ask the court for a direction to that effect. Section 21 was repealed by the 1979 Act, the aim of which was to introduce greater finality into arbitrators' awards – it was felt that arbitrations were being lost to England in the shipping field because of the lack of finality (and privacy) brought about by the case stated procedure. For a brief background, and an indication of how the question of *The Nema* guidelines and rent reviews could have been resolved without 'the need for a great deal of judicial effort' see *Aden Refinery Co Ltd v Ugland Management Co Ltd* [1986] 3 All ER 737 per Sir John Donaldson MR at 739, CA.
3   See *Duvan Estates Ltd v Rossette Sunshine Savories Ltd* (1981) 261 Estates Gazette 364.
4   Arbitration Act 1979, s 1(6A), (7). As to the application of s 1(6A) see *Aden Refinery Co Ltd v Ugland Management Co Ltd* [1986] 3 All ER 737. As to the application of s 1(7) see *National Westminster Bank plc v Arthur Young McClelland Moores & Co* [1985] 2 EGLR 13, 275 Estates Gazette 717, CA.
5   *Pioneer Shipping Ltd v BTP Tioxide Ltd, The Nema* [1982] AC 724, [1981] 2 All ER 1030, HL; *Antaios Cia Naviera SA v Salen Rederierna AB, The Antaios* [1985] AC 191, [1984] 3 All ER 229, HL.
6   See for example *Segama NV v Penny Le Roy Ltd* (1983) 269 Estates Gazette 322. In *Norwich Union Life Insurance Society v Trustee Savings Banks Central Board* [1986] 1 EGLR 136, 278 Estates Gazette 162, Hoffmann J had pointed out that there was nothing in *The Nema* to indicate that the guidelines did not apply to rent reviews, but indicated that he did not 'think that the distinctions between "prima facie case", "arguable case" and various other grades of persuasion which might exist really have very much meaning. One thinks either that the arbitrator was right or that he was wrong . . .'
7   [1986] 1 EGLR at 148C, 278 Estates Gazette 878.
8   The Vice Chancellor added at the end of his judgment that the landlord had granted other leases in the same form and commented: 'I would have granted leave to appeal in the absence of this factor: but it provides an additional reason for so doing'.
9   The test proposed in *Lucas Industries* (see footnote 7 above) has been applied by Warner J in *Warrington and Runcorn Development Corpn v Greggs plc* [1987] 1 EGLR 9, 281 Estates Gazette

1075, Harman J in *Triumph Securities Ltd v Reid Furniture Co Ltd* [1987] 2 EGLR 139, 283 Estates Gazette 1071, Knox J in *Railstone Ltd v Playdate Ltd* [1988] 2 EGLR 153, [1988] 35 EG 87; by Peter Gibson J in *Manders Property (Estates) Ltd v Magnet House Properties Ltd* [1989] EGCS 54 and by Sir Nicolas Browne-Wilkinson V-C again in *Ipswich Borough Council v Fisons plc* [1989] 2 All ER 737; but has not been approved by the Court of Appeal. As to extension of time in which to seek relief under the Arbitration Acts, see *Learmouth Property Investment Co Ltd v Amos Hinton & Sons plc* [1985] 1 EGLR 13, 274 Estates Gazette 725.

6.47 *Preliminary point of law.* Section 2 of the 1979 Act permits an application to the court to determine a preliminary point of law but only where this approach 'might produce substantial savings in costs to the parties'. Again it would seem likely that leave will only be rarely given – as Lord Scarman said in *Tilling v Whiteman:*[1] 'Preliminary points of law are too often treacherous short cuts. The price can be, as here, delay, anxiety and expense.' In *Chapman v Charlwood Alliance Properties Ltd*[2] an application for determination of a preliminary point of law was refused because in the view of Hodgson J it amounted to a mixture of findings of law and fact and 'the point of construction ought not to be decided before the arbitrator has made his findings as to fact'. There was also unlikely to be a saving of costs because the valuers' submissions had already been prepared. As with s 1, an appeal to the Court of Appeal from the judge's decision may only be made with leave and this leave will only rarely be given.[3]

1   [1980] AC 1, [1979] 1 All ER 737, HL.
2   (1981) 260 Estates Gazette 1041.
3   *Babanaft International Co SA v Avant Petroleum Inc* [1982] 3 All ER 244, [1982] 1 WLR 871, CA; *Antaios Cia Naviera SA v Salen Rederierna AB, The Antaios* [1985] AC 191, [1984] 3 All ER 229, HL.

6.48 *Misconduct.* Although the case stated procedure of s 21 of the 1950 Act has been abolished,[1] ss 22–24 remain in force. These sections deal with the power of the High Court to remit matters to the reconsideration of the arbitrator, the removal of an arbitrator, the setting aside of the award where the arbitrator has misconducted himself,[2] and the power of the court to give relief where the arbitrator is not impartial or the dispute involves a question of fraud. 'Misconduct' includes what is misconduct by any general meaning of the word (such as being bribed or corrupted) but also mere 'technical' misconduct.[3] In view of the limited rights of appeal conferred by the 1979 Act,[4] it may well be that unsuccessful parties' advisers will seek to get the matter before the court on the basis that there has been technical misconduct by the arbitrator.[5]

1   See footnote 1 to para 6.46 above.
2   *London Export Corpn Ltd v Jubilee Coffee Roasting Co Ltd* [1958] 1 All ER 494, [1958] 1 WLR 271.
3   'The jurisdiction of the court under s 23 rests on what is, most unfortunately, called "misconduct". That gives the impression that some impropriety or breach of professional conduct or lack of integrity or incompetence is involved. In 99 cases out of a hundred an application under s 23 involves nothing of the kind. It involves usually a procedural lapse of a kind that any arbitrator or magistrate or judge may be guilty of. I should emphasise further at the outset, that [the Landlord's counsel], for the landlords in this application, disclaims any criticism whatever of the professional integrity, impartiality or competence of the arbitrator in this case' per Bingham J in *Zermalt Holdings SA v Nu-Life Upholstery Repairs Ltd* [1985] 2 EGLR 14, 275 Estates Gazette 1134.
4   See para 6.46 above.
5   For example the recent cases where it was alleged that the arbitrator had wrongly acted on his own knowledge (see footnote 2 to para 6.45 above) were brought under s 23. See also *Shield Properties and Investments Ltd v Anglo-Overseas Transport Co Ltd* [1985] 1 EGLR 7, 273 Estates Gazette 69 (admission of without prejudice discussion and hearsay evidence and failure by arbitrator to disclose to one party a letter sent to him by the other), and *Control Securities plc v*

Spencer [1989] 1 EGLR 136, [1989] 07 EG 82 (failure to disclose to landlord's surveyor a letter from the tenant and not discussed with the parties whether an oral hearing required).

6.49   *Expert: drafting*. The draftsman should consider:

6.49:1   *Representations*. Requiring the expert to afford to the parties an opportunity to make representations, and comments upon the other party's representations.[1]

6.49:2   *Costs*. Clauses often provide merely that the fees and expenses of the valuer (including the cost of his appointment) are to be borne equally by the parties, and there is a view that it is inappropriate for an expert to make decisions as to costs, perhaps because only an arbitrator has the opportunity to follow the practice of the court and invite submissions as to costs following his decision. A conflicting opinion is that if, during the negotiations, one party offers to agree to the rent that is subsequently determined by the expert, it is unfair on him to have to pay half the costs of an expert required solely because of the other party's unreasonable refusal to accept that rent. If there is a wish to give the expert that power, he needs some direction as to how to exercise it – for example by providing that he shall have regard to any offers made by either party and the manner in which the parties conducted the negotiations[2] or by requiring the parties to make to each other their final offers (perhaps on the basis that they are 'Without Prejudice save as to costs') and for any direction as to costs to be based upon these offers when the determination has been made.

1   Where the lease is silent on the point, most experts offer (and many encourage) the parties to make representations and cross representations together with the submission of an agreed statement of facts. But at times the reverse could also be the case – the parties might prefer the revised rent to be determined by an expert without either party instructing surveyors where the landlord's initial offer set out in a (trigger) notice is rejected by the tenant. It is probably the case that the determination of a narrow question of fact by an expert originally envisaged a quick and cheap method of resolving the issue by leaving it entirely to the expert without the parties instructing their own valuers. This is one of the attractions of this method and if valuers are to be retained, and representations made and exchanged, the parties may as well opt for arbitration with the additional safeguards that this provides (see para 6.51 below).
2   It would be advisable to indicate specifically whether any without prejudice correspondence or offers should be considered by the expert on the question of costs.

6.50   *Arbitrator or expert: drafting*. There are several drafting points worthy of consideration regardless of whether an expert or arbitrator is involved:

6.50:1   *Absence/default of agreement*. It is preferable to provide for the rent to be determined by the arbitrator or expert in the absence of agreement rather than in default of agreement and great care must be taken over the drafting if it is intended that an application to the President can only be made after a certain period.[1]

6.50:2   *Deputy appointer*. It is desirable specifically to provide for the appointment to be made by the deputy of the appropriate President or his nominee in the event of the President's unavailability.[2] This may avoid delay in the appointment being made, where the President is likely to be unavailable for some time, and in addition it removes the possibility of challenge should an appointment be made other than by the President personally where this is not specifically permitted in the lease.

6.50:3 *Replacement.* Provision should be made for the President to appoint another arbitrator if the original dies or declines to act, which is more straightforward than relying upon the provisions of the Act,[3] or, where appropriate, to appoint another expert.[4]

6.50:4 *Experience.* Consideration should be given as to whether the clause should specify that the arbitrator or expert must have experience of lettings of the type in question in the locality in which the premises are situated. Unless the letting is a particularly unusual one, it is suggested that this provision should be avoided on the grounds that it could cause uncertainty, for example, as to the meaning of locality and experience.[5]

1 See *Staines Warehousing Co Ltd v Montague Executor and Trustee Co Ltd* [1987] 2 EGLR 130, 283 Estates Gazette 458, CA; *United Co-operative Ltd v Sun Alliance and London Assurance Co Ltd* [1987] 1 EGLR 126, 282 Estates Gazette 91. See also para 6.44 footnote 1 above.
2 See for example Rosscastle Letting Conditions (Appendix 1, Form No 1 below) Condition 7.3:5.
3 Arbitration Act 1950, s 10.
4 See for example 22 Encyclopaedia of Forms and Precedents (5th edn) Form 117 (clause prepared by Law Society/RICS), Rosscastle Letting Conditions, Condition 7.3:6.
5 Indeed there could be occasional cases where a local man would not be appropriate. For example, if the demised premises were the only hypermarket in the locality, a valuer with experience of other hypermarkets but with little or no experience in the locality, might be preferred.

6.51 *Arbitrator or expert: the choice.*[1] Arbitration has a number of advantages over determination by an expert. The parties can be more confident that their case and the perceived weaknesses in their opponent's case will be fully presented to the third party, and that he is not influenced by matters to which he should not have regard. If an arbitrator makes significant errors of law or procedure there will generally be a right of appeal to the court.[2] If there is a very clear cut point of law of fundamental significance to the proceedings, then it may be possible to obtain a preliminary ruling on this from the court.[3] The disadvantages are that arbitrations are more expensive, especially if there is to be a hearing, because not only may the fees of a surveyor/arbitrator be more than a surveyor/expert, but the parties themselves will probably incur more professional fees in presenting their cases to the arbitrator. It is said that determination by an expert is quicker – and this will certainly sometimes be so – but where the revised rent will be back-dated to the review date, with interest payable on the shortfall, this may not be a prime consideration. As a general rule, arbitration will clearly be a safer choice. It is suggested that a landlord and his advisers could at least consider determination by an expert where all the following factors are present:
(a) the property is an entirely conventional one with no unusual history;
(b) the drafting of the rent review clause follows a straightforward and well known format, with no unusual assumptions or disregards;
(c) there are numerous comparables in the locality apart from those in the same development as the demised premises. The qualification is

important, because problems best suited to resolution by arbitration could arise if, for example, the only light industrial units in the area were those in the development in which the premises were located;

(d) the rent is modest.

1 See J E Adams: 'Expert or Arbitrator' (1981) 258 Estates Gazette 627. Ronald Bernstein QC, Peter Purton and David Marsh suggested in their 1983 Blundell Memorial Lecture entitled 'Raising the efficiency, and lowering the cost, of rent review' that determination by an arbitrator should be required unless it was intended that the rent be decided by an independent expert without either party instructing surveyors where the landlord's initial rental offer contained in a trigger notice (see para 6.49:1 footnote 1 above) is not accepted by the tenant.
2 See paras 6.46 & 6.48 above.
3 See para 6.47 above.

I   PROCEDURAL MATTERS

6.52   *Introduction.* When the draftsman has dealt with the implementation of the clause,[1] clearly set out the assumptions,[2] the disregarded matters[3] and the valuation term[4] and defined the status of the third party,[5] he needs to consider a number of procedural points, and to do so on the basis that the revised rent will generally be determined after – and perhaps long after – the review date. For example:

(a) what rent will be paid from the review date until the determination of the reviewed rent?[6]
(b) how will the shortfall be paid for that period?[7]
(c) can the landlord's 'cash-flow' be protected during the period – he may eventually get the reviewed rent back-dated to the review date, but ideally he would have preferred to receive it on each rent day, and the landlord would certainly not want there to be any advantage for a tenant in delaying the determination of the rent?[8]
(d) what rights would the landlord require if counter-inflation legislation was prevailing at the time of the rent review?[9]
(e) where the term is a long one, would there be merit in providing for the rent review provisions themselves to be reviewed at some stage so that they could be brought into line with the type of clause then in use?[10]
(f) what steps must be taken to record the reviewed rent once it has been agreed or determined?[11]

The tenant's advisers would do well to consider two commercial matters.[12]

1 See section B above.
2 See section C above.
3 See sections D and E above.
4 See section F above.
5 See section G above.
6 See para 6.53 below.
7 See para 6.54 below.
8 See paras 6.55–6.56 below.
9 See para 6.57 below.
10 See para 6.58 below.
11 See para 6.59 below.
12 See para 6.60 below.

6.53   *Payment on account.* The lease should provide for the current rent to continue to be payable from the review date[1] pending the reviewed rent being ascertained.[2] It should be made clear that the current rent is being paid *on account* of the revised rent. This should ensure that if counter-inflation restrictions[3] were introduced restricting rent to that payable when the legislation came into effect, the rent would be frozen at the revised figure rather than the previous figure, because it would be the revised figure that was *payable* (although not then determined) on the date upon which the freeze took effect.

1 See *Torminster Properties Ltd v Green* [1983] 2 All ER 457, [1983] 1 WLR 676, CA; *South Tottenham Land Securities Ltd v R & A Millett (Shops) Ltd* [1984] 1 All ER 614, [1984] 1 WLR 710, CA.
2 For examples, see 22 Encyclopaedia of Forms and Precedents (5th edn) Forms 22 (see para 3.1), Rosscastle Letting Conditions (Appendix 1, Form No 1 below) Condition 7.3:1. This is unless an interim rent is intended – see para 6.56 below. As an alternative to an interim rent as such, the draftsman could provide for there to be paid on account the current rent increased by a specified percentage (although inevitably selected somewhat at random) but care should be taken to avoid the problems experienced in *Panavia Air Cargo Ltd v Southend-on-Sea Borough Council* [1988] 1 EGLR 111, [1988] 01 EG 60. See 22 Encyclopaedia of Forms and Precedents (5th edn) Form 121.
3 See para 6.58 below.

6.54 *Payment of shortfall.* The clause will then indicate that, as soon as the reviewed rent has been ascertained, there will be payable the difference between what rent would have been due had the reviewed rent been determined at the review date and the amount actually paid on account.[1] Exactly when this payment is to be made can vary from lease to lease – upon ascertainment of the rent, within a defined period of the ascertainment or on the next rent day are all adopted.[2]

1 See para 6.53 above.
2 For examples, see 22 Encyclopaedia of Forms and Precedents (5th edn) Forms 22 (Second Schedule para 4), 117 (clause 4(c)) and 118 (para 6), Rosscastle Letting Conditions (Appendix 1, Form No 1 below) Condition 7.4:3.1.

6.55 *Protection of the landlord: interest.* It is now common practice for interest to be payable on the shortfall and the landlord's arguments seem to have won the day.[1] They suggested that they were 'entitled' to the reviewed rent on all the rent days from the review date, and that as the tenant has had the use of the shortfall in the meantime (and thus the landlord has in effect made a loan to the tenant), the tenant should pay interest on that shortfall for the period from when it was due to the date on which it was paid after the revised rent had been agreed or determined. The counter-argument was that it is unreasonable to require the tenant to pay interest as he never requested the loan and, in any event, interest is only due on a sum that is both payable and exigible.[2] Against this, it has to be conceded that the tenant, having taken the advice of his surveyor, could usually make a reasonable estimate of what the revised rent might be. He could then pay into a deposit account each rent day the difference between the current rent and the estimated revised rent, thereby having available the rent and interest to pay over to the landlord, as and when the rent was ascertained.[3] Landlords are, of course, concerned that the lack of a provision to pay interest could persuade some tenants to be tardy in agreeing the revised rent, and perhaps to negotiate in less than good faith, in order to obtain this interest free loan from the landlord. Even if tenants concede the principle,[4] there are two points of detail that need consideration:
(a) landlords sometimes provide for interest to be payable on (all) the shortfall from the review date to the date that the shortfall is paid. That is unfair when more than one rent day has passed – the interest should be

calculated on an instalment basis, so that the tenant pays interest on the shortfall due on each rent day for the period from that rent day to the date that the shortfall is paid;[5]

(b) the rate of interest should be less than that provided in the lease in cases of default by the tenant.[6]

1   A fact recognised by the Joint Committee of the Law Society/RICS in the Background Notes to their model form of Rent Review Clause – see 22 Encyclopaedia of Forms and Precedents (5th edn) Form 117 p 506.

2   See *Trust House Forte Albany Hotels Ltd v Daejan Investments Ltd* (1980) 256 Estates Gazette 915.

3   In fact this is unlikely to be true because the tenant would no doubt have to pay tax on the interest earned, and so only the net rather than the gross amount would be available for the landlord.

4   If it is agreed that interest will not be paid on the shortfall but where a lease contains a general provision for interest to be due on any payments that are not promptly made, the subject of interest on the shortfall when the revised rent is determined after the review date should not be omitted altogether, because this leaves open the question that interest may be payable even without any express provision. The landlord may argue that since rent is payable (in one sense of the word) even when it is not ascertained, interest should be paid on the shortfall as soon as the amount of the new rent has been ascertained after the review date. There is a strong argument, however, that this is incorrect as interest should only be due upon a sum which is not only payable but also exigible (see footnote 2 above). Nevertheless, with high rents and interest rates it would be as well for this point specifically to be dealt with where it had been agreed that no interest was to be payable on the shortfall.

5   For an example that deals with this concern, see Rosscastle Letting Conditions (Appendix 1, Form No 1 below) Condition 7.3:3.2.

6   Perhaps Base Rate itself rather than the several percentage points above Base that is adopted for the panel rent.

6.56   *Protection of the landlord: 'interim rent'.* Recently some landlords have become dissatisfied with receiving only the interest on the shortfall and have developed the concept of an 'interim rent' on a rent review.[1] By this, the tenant pays a provisional reviewed rent from the review date and, when in due course the reviewed rent itself is ascertained, there is a reconciliation – if the ascertained rent exceeds the provisional rent the tenant pays the shortfall[2] and if it does not the landlord refunds the over-payment.[3] The vital question is how is the provisional rent to be determined? Clearly any procedure by which a third party decides in the absence of agreement defeats the object of the clause which is to arrive at the provisional rent quickly and prior to the review date, and yet the tenant must be protected from a dishonourable landlord who, by fixing a ridiculously high provisional rent, could in effect obtain a loan from his tenant. Five safeguards are worth considering:

(a) provide for the provisional rent to bear the same proportion to the current rent as a standard index for the month prior to the review date bears to that index as at the previous review date or, when appropriate, the commencement of the term – in other words, link the provisional rent to inflation during the review period[4]

(b) provide for the provisional rent to be the sum certified by a surveyor as being his reasonable estimate of the revised rent. There may very well be some reluctance on the part of a surveyor to accept this, however, because he would apparently be liable to the tenant for a negligent certification. Nevertheless, the parties to the lease are entitled to rely upon the landlord's surveyor as a professional man to exercise an independent judgment[5]

(c) provide for the provisional rent to be a specific percentage of the sum determined under (a) or (b) above on the basis that an interim rent ordered when a lease is being renewed under the 1954 Act is likely to be only a proportion of the open market rent[6]

(d) further limit the provisional rent by limiting the amount by which it can exceed the current rent

(e) provide that the landlord will pay interest to the tenant when he refunds any over payment at a rate that exceeds the rate that he would pay for a loan.[7]

The tenant's best protection, however, is to resist the inclusion in the rent review clause of an interim rent provision.

1 For a precedent, see 22 Encyclopaedia of Forms and Precedents (5th edn) Form 132. The term 'interim rent' has clearly been borrowed from the renewal of a tenancy under the 1954 Act: see para 14.15 below.
2 No doubt together with interest: see para 6.55 above.
3 See sub-para (e) and footnote 7 below.
4 See para 6.64 below.
5 *Concorde Graphics Ltd v Andromeda Investments SA* (1982) 265 Estates Gazette 386.
6 See para 14.15 below.
7 Perhaps 6% over the base rate. It would appear that the question of a penalty and the possibility of the provision being void (see para 7.31 below) could not arise because this is not a penal rate of interest being charged on a party in default but rather a contractual commitment to pay at a high rate.

6.57 *Counter-inflation legislation.* Rents of business premises were once statutorily restricted.[1] This was before the presumption was established that time was not of the essence on the procedural aspect of rent review clauses.[2] Landlords were concerned that they would lose altogether a review which fell during the time when the counter-inflation legislation was in force and that, upon the expiry of the legislation, they would have to wait for the next rent review date (if there was one) before becoming entitled to any increase. It is perhaps unlikely that counter-inflation legislation will ever be reintroduced, but landlords will no doubt continue to seek the reassurance of a clause which permits the rent to be reviewed after the counter-inflation legislation ceases to apply in cases where a review date has occurred while the legislation was in force.[3] Tenants should insist that the landlord has only a relatively short period after the legislation ceases in which to invoke the clause, otherwise the landlord could delay until a favourable time. In any event, tenants need to be aware that these clauses generally give to the landlord the advantage of being able to substitute a deferred valuation date for the one set out in the lease.

1 See the Counter-Inflation Act 1973, s 11 (repealed) and *London Transport Executive v Gray Bros (East Finchley) Ltd* (1981) 259 Estates Gazette 629.
2 See paras 6.6–6.12 above.
3 See 22 Encyclopaedia of Forms and Precedents (5th edn) Forms 22 (Second Schedule para 5) 118 (clause 7) Rosscastle Letting Conditions (Appendix 1, Form No 1 below) Condition 7.4. As to the effect of the existence of a rent freeze on a rent review see *Compton Group Ltd v Estates Gazette Ltd* (1977) 36 P & CR 148, CA.

6.58 *Review of the rent review.* The expiry of a lease contains an element of risk for both parties. The tenant might find that the landlord has statutory grounds[1] for opposing his application for a new lease, while the landlord will be worried about a void period and a less satisfactory tenant if the tenant does not wish or cannot afford to renew. Thus, in certain circumstances, a long term may be attractive to both parties. The landlord, however, will remember that landlords suffered (or, more precisely, failed to take the benefits that were there) by granting in the 1950s and 1960s long leases without rent review clauses. He may, therefore, be worried that a rent review clause consistent with modern practice may be out of date in say 20 years, when there may be perhaps another 25 or 30 years of the term left to run. Thus, a landlord contemplating the grant of a lease for a long term should consider providing in the lease for the rent review provision itself to be reviewed. There are essentially two options: the lease can provide for a review of the whole of the clause or of only the rent review period.[2] The landlord would no doubt prefer it to be solely at his option as to whether and when this review of the review provision operated – the tenant, hoping that in 20 years review clauses will be more generous, would want the clause either to operate automatically or to be at the option of either party. Where this is the case, the landlord ought to insert the equivalent of an 'upwards only' clause: it may be that in 20 years the market will be back to perhaps seven or ten year review periods as the norm. If the lease provided for reviews every five years, the landlord would no doubt prefer this to remain in operation.

1   See para 14.29 below.
2   For a precedent, see 22 Encyclopaedia of Forms and Precedents (5th edn) Form 133.

6.59   *Memorandum and documentation.* A memorandum of the reviewed rent should be attached to the original and counterpart lease;[1] whether or not the lease itself so provides.[2] Such memoranda will not only preclude further argument between the parties[3] but will also serve to provide evidence as to the reviewed rent to the parties' successors in title.[4] Where there has been an arbitration award or an expert determination the memoranda should say so. Copies of all directions, submissions, counter-submissions and other documentation used in any determination or arbitration together with the determination or award itself should be kept with the title deeds by both parties as a prudent purchaser of either party's interest will wish to inspect them.[5]

1   For precedents, see 22 Encyclopaedia of Forms and Precedents (5th edn) Forms 134 and 135 and Form 117 p 507.
2   Where a reviewed rent has been agreed, care should be taken to refer to the fact that the increased rent has been agreed pursuant to the provisions for rent review contained in the lease in order to avoid the possibility of the memorandum being stampable ad valorem as a new agreement varying the rent payable. See (1980) 124 Sol Jo 118. The lease should refer to the need for a memorandum: see 22 Encyclopaedia of Forms and Precedents (5th edn) Forms 22 (Second Schedule para 2.5) 117 (clause 4(c)) and 118 (clause 9), Rosscastle Letting Conditions (Appendix 1, Form No 1 below) Condition 7.2:9.
3   And thereby avoid the problems seen in *Esso Petroleum Co Ltd v Anthony Gibbs Financial Services Ltd* (1983) 267 Estates Gazette 351, CA. As to the dangers of an incorrectly completed memorandum, see *Equity and Law Life Assurance Society Ltd v Coltness Group Ltd* (1983) 267 Estates Gazette 949.
4   Where the reviewed rent has been agreed the memoranda may be the only evidence of such agreement.
5   The principle of issue estoppel applies to arbitrations: *Fidelitas Shipping Co Ltd v V/O Exportchleb* [1966] 1 QB 630: 'There are strong dicta which suggest that the decision by the arbitrator on this point of law will constitute an issue estoppel which will prevent a different arbitrator taking a different view of the point of law on future reviews': *Lucas Industries plc v Welsh Development Agency* [1986] 1 EGLR 147 per Sir Nicolas Browne Wilkinson V-C at 148 c; and see *Arnold v National Westminster Bank plc* [1989] Ch 63, [1988] 3 All ER 977. It is suggested that issue estoppel cannot apply to rent reviews concluded by agreement or expert determination but this is undecided.

6.60   *Tenant commercial concerns.* There are two matters that the tenant needs to consider. They have become so standard in leases that tenants may have been persuaded that the dangers involved are minimal. This need not be the case, and even if the tenant cannot succeed in persuading the landlord to accept amendments,[1] the following are points that might encourage him to require a shorter term, notwithstanding the disadvantages, so that the potential for problems is confined to perhaps only one or two reviews:

6.60:1 *Upwards only.* Leases today virtually without exception provide that the revised rent will never be less than that being paid as at the review date, even where open market rents have fallen during the review period. Indeed, this represents one of the great attractions of investing in property – the return can never decrease during the term[2] of the lease so long as there is an 'upwards only' rent review clause and a clear lease.[3] Where rents have decreased during the period, an 'upwards only' review will mean that the tenant will be paying an inflated rent. This not only affects him directly, but means that it will be difficult to dispose of the lease, and in order to do so he may have to pay a reverse premium. When market forces permit, the tenant should consider amending the draft lease so that the rent can be reviewed both ways, and for the market rent to be payable from the review date, whether it be more or less than the existing rent.[4]

6.60:2 *Inability to terminate on review.* Alternatively (or perhaps even in addition to such a provision) the tenant should consider making an amendment giving him the right to terminate the lease in the event of the rent being raised on a review to a level that he cannot afford.[5] In support of this, he can rely upon s 35(2) of the 1954 Act which gives the tenant the right to refuse a new lease within fourteen days of the terms being fixed by the court after an application has been made for a lease to be renewed under Part II of the 1954 Act.[6] At the time of the 1954 Act, rent reviews were virtually unknown and the tenant generally knew what his rent commitment would be for the whole of the term of the lease. He knew too that, if the rent was increased at the end of the term to a level that he could not afford, he need not take up the renewed lease. Rent reviews without a break clause mean, however, that a tenant could be committed for perhaps another fifteen or twenty years to rents that his particular business will never be able to afford, and it may well prove very difficult to dispose of such a lease.[7]

1 It is certainly true that the value of the landlord's development will be reduced if parts of it are let on leases containing amendments of the nature discussed below.
2 At least in the absence of the tenant's insolvency but even this can be protected by insisting upon a guarantor; see paras 5.5–5.13 above.
3 See para 11.1 below.
4 For precedents, see 22 Encyclopaedia of Forms and Precedents (5th edn) Form 117.
5 For a precedent, see ibid Form 136.
6 See para 14.16 below.
7 See Robert Lyons 'Rent Reviews: theory and malpractice' (1983) 265 Estates Gazette 451 (discussed by Ronald Bernstein QC et al 'Raising the efficiency and lowering the cost of Rent Review' (Blundell Memorial Lecture 1983)) and John Marples and Robert Lyons: 'Rent Reviews in shopping developments' (1984) 271 Estates Gazette 515 and 606 (Abridged Blundell Memorial Lecture 1984).

J ALTERNATIVE METHODS OF RENT REVIEW

6.61 *Introduction.* A periodic review to the market rent demands that a potentially expensive and time consuming process is undertaken every few years. The parties are likely to incur professional fees even in the most straightforward and non-contentious cases, and these may be considerable where disputes arise that can only be resolved by arbitration or litigation. Even the successful party in such proceedings will not be able to recover all his expenditure from the other, and neither party will be reimbursed for all the management time that is likely to be involved. Such concerns prompt the question of whether or not there is a viable alternative? If the parties are seeking some form of 'automatic' method of arriving at the market rent, the answer is clearly that there is not but four topics should be considered: short leases,[1] premium rents,[2] indexation[3] and turnover/subleases rental leases.[4]

1   See para 6.62 below.
2   See para 6.63 below.
3   See para 6.64 below.
4   See para 6.65 below.

6.62   *Short leases.* Superficially the way to avoid rent reviews is to grant leases the terms of which are no longer than the current review period for that type of property. Short leasess are common elsewhere in the world but generally the tenant has no security of tenure, and so there is an open market negotiation at the end of the term. Assuming the tenant in England and Wales requires a further lease, the parties will then be involved in a renewal under the 1954 Act which may be even worse than a rent review.[1] In any event, the tenant will often require greater security than three/five years while the institutional landlord is looking for at least twenty-five year terms for investment reasons.

1   See Chapter 14 below.

6.63   *Premium rents.* A premium rent arises where the tenant pays an inflated rent in return for a longer period than would be normal without a rent review. Thus, rather than a ten year lease with a review after five years, the lease would provide for the same rent to be payable throughout the term but that rent would be fixed at perhaps 10 or 15% above the market rent at the start of the lease. This would be to compensate the landlord for the 'loss' that he will suffer towards the end of the term when (in theory) market rentals will have risen above the inflated figure. So by way of example, a landlord, instead of receiving five years rent at £50,000 per annum and then (after a conventional rent review) a further five years at £60,000, will on a premium rental receive ten years rent at £55,000 per annum. He will thus receive some payment in advance, which he will no doubt be able to put to good use, while the tenant, providing he can survive the early years, will be paying less than the market rent towards the end of the lease. Both parties will have been saved the trouble and expense of a rent review. The same principle could apply on a long lease where, in return for rent reviews every ten years (rather than the normal five) the tenant agreed to pay 20% more than the open market rent on each review date. The revised rent would thus be expressed in the rent review clause to be a certain specified percentage in excess of the open market rent on the review date which would be determined in the usual way. The problem, of course, with premium rents is that men of property are no more able than anyone else to predict the future, and such an arrangement would seem a gamble by both parties, potentially for very high stakes, and with very little form to rely upon bearing in mind that the dramatic rise in (at least some) commercial rental values is a comparatively recent phenomenon and one subject to considerable regional and industry variations. It is virtually impossible to foresee the economic future with any certainty and it is this difficulty that has produced the conventional rent review clause by which the parties fix the rent only for a few years and establish a mechanism by which it can be determined thereafter in the light of subsequent developments. The principle of premium rents, by which rents are to be fixed for long periods, cannot accurately reflect the changes in the economic environment. The market rent of the premises may rise quickly and dramatically, in which event the 'premium' will not adequately compensate the landlord, or remain constant or even fall, in which event it is the tenant who will be penalised. Both parties would be on much safer ground – although perhaps fortunes are not made by playing safe – by providing for the rent to be reviewed by the conventional method, however troublesome rent reviews may be, and as such it is hard to believe that the concept of premium rents will ever widely be adopted as a deliberate conveyancing device[1] especially as the majority of landlords and tenants are likely to be essentially cautious corporations and individuals.

1   There are many older commercial leases granted in the 1950s and 1960s where the review periods are longer than the current 'norm', and where the valuers have to grapple with the problem on reviews under such leases and determine, in effect, a premium rent, although note the uncertainty on this point created by the decision of *Lear v Blizzard* [1983] 3 All ER 662. See para 6.4:4 above.

6.64   *Index-linked rents.* Another means of avoiding a conventional rent review is to link the rent to an index.[1] By this method, it is possible for the rent to be reviewed on every rent day and not just every three or five years. Nevertheless, there are fundamental concerns that could work to the advantage or disadvantage of either party. Any form of indexation of rent to an index other than one of comparable local rents, that will probably not exist,[2] ignores the fact that the rate of increase or decrease in the market rent of the premises may differ in the future from the way in which the index[3] moves, even if until that date they had moved in tandem. Indexation also ignores the effect that purely local phenomena can have on the market rent of premises.[4] These factors would be taken into account in determining the revised rent on a conventional rent review. If the rent is indexed, it will rise in line with the index and such matters will be irrelevant.[5] There can also be practical problems in the collection of an index-linked rent. The effect of the rent being linked with an index is that it will almost certainly vary every time it is payable. This may be exaggerated by changes in the indices brought about by seasonal variations. The effect of these constant changes can be mitigated by suitable drafting, for example, by providing in the lease that the rent is only altered if the index varies by more than a specified number of points, or by fixing the rent for the whole year by reference to the index for a particular month, or by providing for a fixed rent to be paid on every rent day and for the landlord to produce a statement at the end of the year, showing the actual amount that is due, and for this sum to be payable on demand. Provisions should also be included dealing with the possibilities of the base upon which the index is calculated being changed or the index itself ceasing to exist.[6] It must be stressed, however, that indexation is not a means of determining the market rent for the premises in question – indeed it does not even pretend to do this. Instead it ensures that the rent increases in line with general inflation.

1 See eg *Blumenthal v Gallery Five Ltd* (1971) 220 Estates Gazette 31. For precedents, see 22 Encyclopaedia of Forms and Precedents (5th edn) Forms 137 and 138. Form 138 as it originally appeared is not correct. Clause 2.2. (following the advice of Hoffman J in *London Regional Transport v Wimpey Group Services Ltd* [1986] 2 EGLR 41, 280 Estates Gazette 898) should read: 'The revised rent for any Review Period shall be determined by multiplying the Initial Rent by the index for the month preceding the Review Date at the beginning of the Review Period and then dividing the result by the Base Figure'. Clause 1.4 of Form 138 should be deleted. As to the meaning of the word 'proportion' in rent review clauses, see *Stylo Barratt Properties Ltd v Legal and General Assurance Society Ltd* [1989] 31 EG 56.

2 As to the property indices that do exist see Clarke and Adams *Rent Reviews and Variable Rents* (2nd edn, 1984) p 315.

3 The index most frequently used is the General Index of Retail Prices (RPI) which measures the monthly changes in the retail prices of goods and services purchased by United Kingdom households. The prices of some 350 goods and services are used and some 150,000 separate price quotations are utilised each month in compiling the index. The current index is based on the price levels at January 1974. RPI is essentially domestic, reflecting the prices of food, alcoholic drink, tobacco, housing, fuel and light, durable household goods, clothing and footwear, transport and vehicles and various miscellaneous goods and services. The criticism of using RPI is that it relates to domestic life and therefore need not be related to the rent of commercial premises. A possible alternative would be to use the Producer Price Index (formerly the Wholesale Prices Index). This is calculated from the price movements of about 11,500 closely defined materials and products representative of goods purchased and manufactured by industry in the United Kingdom. There are individual figures dealing with materials and fuel purchased by selected broad sectors of industry, but a draftsman wishing to use this index should use the combined figures dealing with materials and fuel purchased by all manufacturing industry. All these indices appear in press notices issued by the Department of Trade and Industry, in the monthly digest of statistics published by the Central Statistical Office, and in British Business published weekly by the Department of Trade and Industry.

4 A shop's trade could have been decimated as the result of a new one-way traffic system or the opening of a supermarket nearby.

5 Thus the tenant can find himself paying an index-linked rent that exceeds the open market rent and it will probably be able to assign only if it pays a reverse premium.

6 See 22 Encyclopaedia of Forms and Precedents (5th edn) Form 137 Second Schedule.

6.65 *Turnover and sublease rents.* These are similar, the tenant paying by way of rent a percentage of either the turnover of the business carried on at the premises[1] or the rental income received by the tenant from subletting the premises.[2] The circumstances in which either of these alternatives would be viable are inevitably limited,[3] but given good drafting they do have certain attributes and, although not common in the United Kingdom, apparently work effectively elsewhere.[4] Nevertheless, the parties need to recognise that they represent an entirely different approach to that adopted in a periodic review to market rent, involving almost an element of partnership between the landlord and the tenant, and are not a trouble-free way of determining the market rent.[5]

1 For a precedent, see 22 Encyclopaedia of Forms and Precedents (5th edn) Forms 139 & 140.

2 For a precedent, see ibid Form 141. For a fuller discussion of turnover and sublease rents, see ibid paras 96 & 97, Kim Lewison: *Drafting Business Leases* Longmans (3rd edn, 1989) Chapter 4, and D N Clarke and J E Adams: *Rent Reviews and Variable Rents* Longmans (2nd edn, 1984) Chapter 16. As to reservation of rent calculated by reference to the price of a commodity such as gold or to the value of the pound: see *Treseder-Griffin v Co-operative Insurance Society Ltd* [1956] 2 QB 127, [1956] 2 All ER 33, CA; *Multiservice Bookbinding Ltd v Marden* [1979] Ch 84, [1978] 2 All ER 489.

3 In many commercial premises, no turnover is created (for example administrative offices or warehouse/distribution centre) while it is only in a headlease of a building where multi-occupation is contemplated (for example a shopping centre) that a rent geared to sublease rents could be reserved.

4 Although generally in countries where business tenants have no security of tenure or rights to a new lease.

5   Indeed sometimes a turnover or sublease rent is reserved in addition to a market rent, the tenant paying perhaps 75% of the market rent (that is reviewed in the conventional way) and in addition the turnover rent. So here the turnover rent is used as well as and not instead of a conventional rent review. As to turnover rents generally, see Bob Walsh 'Shopping centres: why are turnover rents not more popular' (1988) 13 Estates Gazette 20.

Chapter 7

The tenant's covenants

A ALIENATION

7.1 *Introduction and concerns*. In the absence of restrictions in the lease, a tenant with a fixed term or periodic business tenancy can deal with the whole or part of the premises, by means of assignment, underletting, charging or otherwise, and may permit any person to use or occupy the whole or part of them, as he thinks fit and without reference to the landlord. It is, however, a rare lease which does not restrict the tenant's freedom in this respect.[1] Restrictions on alienation generally take the form of covenants on the part of the tenant prohibiting certain types of dealing.[2] Such prohibitions may be 'absolute',[3] 'qualified'[4] or 'fully qualified'[5] in form. The parties have various concerns when they consider what prohibitions should be inserted in the lease:

7.1:1 *Assignment*. Other than in exceptional circumstances, for example when there is a special relationship between the landlord and tenant or where the duration of the lease is extremely short, the *tenant* will need to ensure that he will be able to dispose of the lease in the future. At some point during the term, he may no longer need the premises, either because he ceases to need premises at all, or because the particular premises become unsuitable for his purposes.[6] If, in such circumstances, he is unable to dispose of the lease[7] quickly and easily (or indeed at all) his business may be prejudiced. The tenant's main concern will be to ensure that he has the ability to rid himself of day to day liability under the lease,[7] but he should also remember that circumstances might arise in which he does not want simply to dispose of the lease, but to dispose of the lease to a particular person,[8] and that, on disposal, he might like to be able to realise any enhancement of the value of the premises which has resulted from his efforts and expenditure.[9] The *landlord* will wish to retain control over the disposal of the premises, as the identity of the tenant for the time being is of great importance to him, essentially for economic reasons. The assignee will be the person to whom the landlord will look, primarily, for payment of the rent reserved by, and compliance with the covenants contained in, the lease. An assignee of doubtful financial standing is more likely to be unable to pay that rent, and perform those covenants. Even though the original tenant will usually remain liable following assignment[10] the landlord could suffer loss because of the cost and inconvenience of enforcement, and because of the adverse effect that such a tenant could have on the value of the reversion.[11] The assignee will also frequently be the person who will be in occupation of the premises, and the landlord may have estate management reasons for objecting to a particular tenant as, for example, when his proposed user[12] conflicts with that of adjoining premises belonging to the landlord. There may, however, be

162

many other reasons why the landlord requires control,[13] whether economic, practical or personal.

7.1:2   *Underletting.* Why should a *tenant* who is able to assign the premises be concerned about the ability to underlet? There are a number of reasons. Although preferring to dispose of the lease, the tenant might not be able to assign. It could be that, because of changes in the market coupled with an upwards-only rent review clause,[14] the rent payable under the lease is so high that no assignee can be found, even if offered a reverse premium. Subletting at a lower rent will enable the tenant to cut his losses. Alternatively, the only prospective assignees in the market might be of a relatively low financial standing, with the result that a landlord might be prepared to consent to an underlease but not an assignment. Sometimes, even if the tenant can find a suitable assignee, he might prefer to sublet. He will remain liable for the rent reserved by, and under the covenants contained in, the lease following assignment,[15] and may therefore prefer to grant a sublease which will enable him to 'keep an eye' on the position and retain control over such matters as rent review and further alienation. The ability to sublet is also useful for a tenant who does not need the premises, or at least the whole of the premises, for a temporary period, as it will give him the chance to use himself only premises that he needs and to obtain an income from premises for which he has no use. So far as the *landlord* is concerned, he should bear in mind that the greater the number of interests in the premises, whether at the same, or on different, levels,[16] the greater the administrative and management problems which will be caused. To a certain extent this will be the case anyway, but it will most affect the landlord if, as is possible, the tenant were to drop out of the picture in the future.[17] Because of this possibility, and because the subtenant will usually be the person in occupation of the premises, the identity of a subtenant is important to the landlord for much the same reasons as the identity of an assignee is important.[18]

7.1:3   *Other restrictions.* There may be circumstances in which the tenant would like to part with the possession of the whole or part of the premises, or allow some third party to occupy them, but does not want to assign or sublet. For example, he might want to allow a prospective purchaser into possession prior to completion, or to share occupation of the premises with a business associate or group company. As a general rule, because of the way in which this would dilute his control over the ownership and occupation of the premises, the landlord will find this unacceptable, although he may permit alienation short of assignment or subletting in limited circumstances.[19]

7.1:4   *Additional concerns.* Naturally both landlord and tenant should bear in mind the effect which the alienation provisions of the lease may have on the rent. Generally, a lease which contains wide alienation provisions will command a higher rent both initially, on rent review[20] and under any new lease granted on the determination of the lease pursuant to the 1954 Act,[21] than a lease which contains restrictive alienation provisions. Another general point of interest to both parties is that a landlord who has himself a leasehold interest will need to ensure that any restraints on assignment by subtenants imposed by his own lease are included in the lease.

1   Restrictions on alienation contained in a lease are valid. An assignment or subletting in breach of such a restriction is, however, effective, subject to the landlord's rights in respect of the breach (see, for example, *Williams v Earle* (1868) LR 3 QB 739).

2   When considering alienation, however, the parties should not forget its relationship with user. Restrictions on the purpose for which the premises may be used (see paras 7.8–7.18 below) will limit the class of people who are able to occupy the premises, and thus the number of potential assignees or subtenants. Indeed, tight restrictions on user can in practice prevent dealing altogether. The parties should remember that there is little point, for example, in inserting alienation provisions in the lease which enable the tenant to assign with the consent of the landlord, such consent not to be unreasonably withheld, if the premises can only be used for the purpose of the narrowly defined business conducted by the original tenant.

3   An absolute prohibition takes the form, for example, of a covenant 'not to assign part of the premises' or 'not to charge the whole or any part of the premises'. It is absolute, in that it does not provide for the possibility of the landlord consenting to the relevant dealing.

4   Such a prohibition takes the form, for example, of a covenant 'not to underlet the whole or any part of the premises without the consent of the landlord. It is qualified, in that the relevant dealing may be permitted by the landlord.

5   A fully qualified prohibition takes the form, for example, of a covenant 'not to grant any underlease of any part of the premises without the consent of the landlord, such consent not to be unreasonably withheld'. It is fully qualified, in that the landlord's consent to be relevant dealing is not to be unreasonably withheld.

6   For example, his business may expand, develop or contract, it may become preferable to operate from a different area, or the premises may become too expensive as a result of market demands.

7   The tenant will not usually be released from future liability for the rent reserved by, and under the covenants contained in, the lease by assignment (see note 10 below), but will as a practical matter be relieved of day to day responsibility so long as the assignee complies, and will generally have an indemnity not only from his immediate assignee, but also from the tenant for the time being, in the event of non-payment or other breach.

8   For example, if the tenant is disposing of the business which he operates at the premises, he may be unable to find a purchaser, or realise as good a price, if he is unable to include the premises in the sale.

9   For example, a tenant who has carried out improvements, installed fixtures and fittings, or built up goodwill, might be able to obtain a premium for these on assignment because they are not reflected in the rent payable under the lease: as a general rule, the value of such items is disregarded on rent review (see paras 6.30–6.40 above).

10   For the current law, and proposals for changing the same, see paras 5.5 and 5.14–5.16 above. As the law currently stands, the liability of the original tenant in contract continues notwithstanding assignment. His contract is not merely one of suretyship and will not, therefore, be affected by any variation of the lease, such as the surrender of part of the premises (*Baynton v Morgan* (1888) 22 QBD 74, CA). He will also be liable to an assignee of the reversion (*Arlesford Trading Co Ltd v Servansingh* [1971] 3 All ER 113, [1971] 1 WLR 1080, CA).

11   Notwithstanding the continuing liability of the original tenant: see *Ponderosa International Developments Inc v Pengap Securities (Bristol) Ltd* [1986] 1 EGLR 66, 277 Estates Gazette 1252.

12   For a discussion of the landlord's concerns in relation to the user of the premises, see para 7.11 below. Whether or not it is necessary for the landlord to consider these, not only in the context of the user provisions, but also in the context of the alienation provisions, of the lease will depend on the strictness of the user provisions. On the question of whether or not it will be reasonable, in the case of a lease containing a fully qualified prohibition against a particular disposal, (see para 7.5 below) for a landlord to refuse consent to that disposal on the grounds of the proposed user of the disposee when that user is permitted by the lease, see *International Drilling Fluids Ltd v Louisville Investments (Uxbridge) Ltd* [1986] Ch 513, [1986] 1 All ER 321, CA.

13   For example, a landlord who is letting part of premises occupied by himself may not want to be in close proximity to a rival or competitor; a landlord might be concerned about assignment to a person who will obtain security of tenure (as to whether or not, in the case of a lease containing a fully qualified prohibition against a particular disposal, a landlord would be reasonable (see para 7.5 below) in refusing consent to assignment in such circumstances, see Woodfall's *Law of Landlord and Tenant* para 1–1182).

14   See para 6.60:1 above.

15   See para 7.1:1, and in particular note 10, above.

16   A number of interests at the same level may be created, for example, if the tenant is given the unfettered ability to sublet part, as he may grant subleases of part to a number of different subtenants. A number of interests at different levels may be created, even when the tenant is

only able to sublet the premises as a whole, if there is nothing to prevent a subtenant subletting to a subundertenant, a subundertenant to a subsubundertenant, and so on.

17 The tenant may drop out of the picture in a number of ways. First of all, the headlease might be forfeited. This would bring both the lease and any sublease to an end, but the subtenant might obtain relief from forfeiture, with the result he would become a tenant rather than a subtenant. Alternatively, the lease might be disclaimed. This does not bring the lease, nor any sublease, to an end, although the tenant will drop out of the picture. In such a case, the subtenant may apply for a vesting order in respect of the lease and, if successful, would become the tenant. Thirdly, the tenant might not apply for a new lease under the 1954 Act (see Chapter 14 below) on the determination of the term of the lease and a subtenant in occupation may do so. If the subtenant is successful in such circumstances the landlord will be forced to grant a new lease of the sublet premises to the subtenant, thus rendering him a tenant. If the tenant is not in occupation of any part of the premises, he will have no right to apply for a new tenancy, but if he is in occupation of part of the premises and applies for a new lease of that part, the landlord is entitled to refuse to grant him a new lease unless he takes a new lease of the whole of the premises comprised in the original lease (see para 14.3 below). In the circumstances set out in s 30(1)(e) of the 1954 Act (see para 14.29 below), the landlord will be able to oppose an application for a new lease by a subtenant.

18 See para 7.1:1 above.

19 See para 7.7:4 below.

20 As to rent review generally, see Chapter 6. Rent review clauses usually provide for the revised rent to be assessed on the basis of a hypothetical letting of the premises on the same terms as the lease itself, and otherwise in accordance with reality, with the result that the terms of the lease, including the alienation provisions, may have a substantial effect on the revised rent – see para 6.18:3 above. For the reasons mentioned, in particular in para 7.1:1 and 7.1:2, restrictive alienation provisions will reduce the number of hypothetical tenants who would be prepared to take the hypothetical lease and the rent which any hypothetical tenant would be prepared to pay, and thus the revised rent. It is possible for the landlord to avoid this disadvantage by providing in the rent review clause that the hypothetical lease is to contain wider alienation provisions than the actual lease, but few tenants would be prepared to accept this, in the absence of very special circumstances.

21 As to the tenant's rights to a new lease generally, see Chapter 14. As a general rule, the user provisions of the new lease will reflect those of the existing lease, although the court has a discretion and may order different terms if that would be fair – see paras 14.56–14.60 below. The rent awarded by the court under s 34 of the 1954 Act will be determined by ascertaining the rent which a hypothetical tenant in the open market would pay for the premises on a letting on the terms of the new tenancy. It is not possible for the landlord to avoid this by drafting, as it is on rent review (see note 20 above).

7.2 *Statutory provisions.* There are a number of statutory provisions that may affect the operation of the prohibitions on alienation contained in a lease:

7.2:1 *Section 19(1)(b) of the Landlord and Tenant Act 1927* provides that 'a covenant condition or agreement against assigning, under-letting, charging or parting with possession of demised premises or any part thereof without licence or consent' contained in a lease[1] 'for more than forty years . . . made in consideration wholly or partially or the erection, or the substantial improvement, addition or alteration of buildings' is deemed to be subject to a proviso to the effect that no consent or licence shall be required to any assignment, under-letting, charging or parting with the possession by the tenant or any under-tenant (whether immediate or not) effected more than seven years before the end of the term if notice of the transaction is given to the landlord within six months. This is the most sweeping of the provisions affecting prohibitions on alienation, in that, in cases where it applies, the tenant is simply relieved of the necessity to seek consent.

7.2:2 *Section 19(1)(a) of the Landlord and Tenant Act 1927*[2] provides that 'a covenant condition or agreement against assigning, under-letting, charging or parting with possession of demised premises or any part thereof without licence or consent' contained in any lease[1] is 'deemed to be subject to a proviso to the effect that such licence or consent is not to be unreasonably withheld'. This is the provision affecting prohibitions on alienation which is most frequently called in aid by tenants. It converts many qualified prohibitions on alienation to fully qualified prohibitions, and also affects the operation of fully qualified prohibitions, whether the relevant proviso is express or implied by the sub-section. Where this sub-section applies, it not only affects the ability to impose conditions on the granting of consent, but also the ability to withhold consent. It is discussed in detail below.[3]

7.2:3 *Section 144 of the Law of Property Act 1925*[4] provides that unless the lease contains an express provision to the contrary,[5] 'any covenant, condition or agreement against assigning, underletting, or parting with the possession, or disposing of the land or property leased without licence or consent' contained in it is 'deemed to be subject to a proviso to the effect that no fine or sum of money in the nature of a fine[6] shall be payable for or in respect of such licence or consent'.[7] Unlike s 19(1)(a), this provision does not affect the ability to withhold or delay consent, but only the ability to impose conditions on its grant. Nonetheless, a refusal to give consent save on payment of a fine will relieve the tenant from the necessity of obtaining consent and entitle him to effect the relevant disposition without consent or seek a declaration from the court.[8] As a result, a landlord who imposes a condition in contravention of this section may lose his rights and incur cost.

7.2:4 *Race and sex.* With one minor exception, s 24 of the Race Relations Act 1976[9] renders it unlawful to discriminate against another on grounds of colour, race, nationality or ethnic or national origins by withholding licence or consent to a disposal of the whole or part of any premises comprised in a tenancy. Section 31 of the Sex Discrimination Act 1975 contains similar provisions with regard to discrimination on grounds of sex.

1 Section 19(1) does not apply to agricultural holdings and, in addition, s 19(1)(b) does not apply to mining leases or to any lease if the landlord is 'a Government department or local or public authority, or a statutory or public utility company'. See also s 30(5) of the Leasehold Reform Act 1976.
2 See also s 89 of the Law of Property Act 1925: if a licence to assign is required on a sale by a mortgagee it must not be unreasonably withheld.
3 Together with the Landlord and Tenant Act 1988: see paras 7.5–7.6 below.
4 Replacing s 3 of the Conveyancing Act 1892. Certain of the authorities referred to below concern this section rather than s 144 of the Law of Property Act 1925.
5 This section is unusual, in that it can be excluded by agreement.
6 It seems that this may include any valuable consideration in the nature of a fine (see s 205(1)(xxiii) of the Law of Property Act 1925 and *Waite v Jennings* [1906] 2 KB 11, CA; *Gardner & Co v Cone* [1928] Ch 955), but that compensation is not a fine (see *Sheldrake v Chesterman* (1925) 69 Sol Jo 327), nor perhaps the requirement that a prospective assignee gives direct covenants to the landlord (see the comments to this effect in *Waite v Jennings*, above, although they were obiter, and the court was not unanimous on the point). The section expressly provides that payment of 'a reasonable sum' may be required 'in respect of any legal or other expense incurred in relation to' the licence or consent.
7 Caselaw on the operation of s 144 and its predecessor indicates that there is nothing illegal about such a payment (*Waite v Jennings*, above; *Andrew v Bridgman* [1908] 1 KB 596, CA): once paid, generally, it cannot be recovered (see *Andrew v Bridgman*, above). Furthermore, it establishes that a covenant to pay such a fine is enforceable (*Waite v Jennings*, above) but not, perhaps, an undertaking which is not under seal, as there will have been a failure of consideration (see *Waite v Jennings*, above; *Comber v Fleet Electrics Ltd* [1955] 2 All ER 161, [1955]

1 WLR 566). It will be apparent that this section has been substantially superseded by
s 19(1)(a) of the Landlord and Tenant Act 1927 (see para 7.2:2 above). For the possible effect
of the Landlord and Tenant Act 1988 on these rules, see para 7.6 below.
8   *Andrew v Bridgman*, above; *West v Gwynne* [1911] 2 Ch 1, CA.
9   Replacing in amended form provisions of the Race Relation Acts 1965 and 1968.

7.3   *Absolute prohibitions.* It is generally accepted that none of these statutory
provisions[1] applies to an absolute prohibition against any particular dealing.[2]
Naturally, the landlord may waive such a restriction, but a tenant holding
under a lease containing an absolute prohibition against a particular dealing,
and who wants so to deal with the premises, will be at the mercy of his
landlord, who will generally be able to consider or ignore, and approve or
reject, any application by the tenant in his absolute discretion. The effect of
such a prohibition on the landlord and the tenant will vary according to the
circumstances. So, for example, a tenant holding under a lease containing an
absolute prohibition against subletting part of the premises could encounter
serious problems during the term, whilst as a general rule the rent awarded on
rent review will be reduced, if the premises demised consist of a large office
block, but not if they consist of a small lock-up shop. From a practical point of
view, the parties should bear in mind that if a prohibition on dealing is
absolute, any waiver granted will constitute a variation of the lease, which
should be effected by deed.[3]

1   Or rather those referred to in paras 7.2:1–7.2:3 above although it is possible to envisage
circumstances in which those referred to in para 7.2:4 might apply.
2   In *Property and Bloodstock Ltd v Emerton* [1968] Ch 94 Danckwerts LJ indicated (at 119) that he
was 'by no means convinced' that s 19(1)(a) of the Landlord and Tenant Act 1927 (see para
7.2:2 above) did not apply to such a covenant, and reserved his opinion on the point. Although
the possibility was rejected by Megaw LJ in *Bocardo SA v S & M Hotels Ltd* [1980] 1 WLR 17 at
22, CA, the reasoning behind that rejection has been doubted (see para 7.4 note 3 below).
Nonetheless, the words of the statute seem clear, and the generally accepted view has been
accepted by the courts. For the Law Commission's proposals in this respect see its Report on
Covenants Restricting Dispositions Alterations and Change of User: (1985) Law Com No 141.
3   See 22 Encyclopaedia of Forms and Precedents Vol 22 p 556 para 4. As an absolute
prohibition on alienation may not always run with the land, the landlord would be wise to
require appropriate direct covenants as a condition of waiver.

7.4   *Qualified prohibitions.* In the majority of cases a prohibition against dealing
contained in a lease, which takes the form of a qualified prohibition, will be
converted, by s 19(1)(a) of the Landlord and Tenant Act 1927, to a fully
qualified prohibition.[1] There may, however, be prohibitions restricting
alienation to which the sub-section does not apply. For example, it seems that
it will not apply to a covenant 'not to permit a third party to occupy the
premises without consent',[2] which will remain merely a qualified prohibition.
Accordingly, it is always wise, when drafting, to insert words to the effect that
any requisite consent should not be unreasonably withheld as a matter of
course when this is intended. In the case of a prohibition which remains
qualified, the general rule[3] is that the person from whom consent is required
may decide whether or not to consider the granting of consent, whether or not
to grant or refuse consent, and whether or not to impose conditions on the
granting of consent, at his absolute discretion[4] although, of course, even if
s 19(1)(a) does not apply, more limited protection may still be given by other
of the statutory provisions mentioned in para 7.2 above. In the case of a
qualified prohibition, the landlord's consent may be written or oral, and need
be in no particular form, unless the lease provides to the contrary.[5]

1   See para 7.2:2 above.
2   See para 7.7:4 below. It seems that it will also not apply to a prohibition on granting consent without approval (see para 7.6 note 19 below), nor to a covenant given, for example, by an undertenant to the landlord in a licence to underlet.
3   It has been suggested (see, for example, the dictum of Megaw LJ in *Bocardo SA v S & M Hotels Ltd* [1979] 3 All ER 737 at 741 with regard to a covenant not to assign without consent) that the words 'such consent not to be unreasonably withheld', or words to similar effect, should be implied in any qualified covenant as a matter of course, but see *Price v Bouch* [1986] 2 EGLR 179 (no general rule of law that such words should be implied); *Guardian Assurance Co Ltd v Gants Hill Holdings Ltd* (1983) 267 Estates Gazette 678 (no such words implied in covenant against change of use without consent); *Pearl Assurance plc v Shaw* [1985] 1 EGLR 92 (no such words implied in covenant against applying for planning permission without consent); but see also *Cryer v Scott Bros (Sunbury) Ltd* (1986) 55 P & CR 183, CA, in which it was held that there was no rule of law either way, and whether or not such words should be implied depends on the circumstances of the particular case. In the special circumstances of that case, the words were implied in a covenant concerning the approval of works.
4   With the result that, subject as mentioned below, he will have as much control in the case of a qualified prohibition as he does in the case of an absolute prohibition. One would also think that he would have the same detriment on rent review, (see para 7.1:4 above) but this may not be the case. Valuers may consider that the addition of the words 'without consent', or the equivalent, is an indication that the landlord may more readily consider the granting of consent.
5   To ensure that there is a record of dealings, and to avoid dispute or error, many landlords and tenants prefer the lease to specify that any consent given must be in writing. Such a prohibition is not affected by an oral licence in the absence of fraud or waiver.

7.5   *Fully qualified prohibitions: general law and s 19(1).* Such prohibitions[1] contain a proviso, express or implied by statute[2] to the effect that consent[3] to a particular dealing will not be unreasonably withheld. The courts have construed such a proviso, not as imposing a covenant on the part of the landlord not to withhold consent unreasonably, but as qualifying the tenant's covenant, with the result that if consent is unreasonably withheld, the tenant is relieved of the necessity of obtaining consent.[4] The proviso places the tenant under an obligation to seek consent. If he fails to do so, whether by inadvertence or otherwise, he will be in breach of covenant, even if it is established that consent could not have been reasonably withheld.[5] Consent will be considered to have been unreasonably withheld for the purposes of such a proviso in a case where it would be reasonable for consent to be given, not only if the landlord refuses consent, but also if he does not respond to the tenant's application within a reasonable time.[6] In addition, it is generally accepted that consent will be considered to have been unreasonably withheld if an unreasonable condition is imposed on its grant.[7] Until the enactment of the Landlord and Tenant Act 1988,[8] if the tenant believed that consent was being unreasonably withheld, he had only two remedies.[9] The first was to proceed without consent and to defend any action for breach of covenant that the landlord might bring on the ground that consent had been unreasonably withheld.[10] The second was to seek a declaration from the court to the effect that consent was being unreasonably withheld, and that the transaction should proceed.[11] The inadequacy of these remedies[12] meant that in many cases the tenant suffered loss and was left without recourse, whilst the landlord had little incentive to be either quick or reasonable.[13] The way in which the 1988 Act has attempted to improve the tenant's position with regard to these two remedies, and has created new remedies, is discussed below.[14] The courts have developed certain principles on which to decide whether, in any particular case, consent has been unreasonably withheld.[15] Naturally, the landlord's idea of reasonableness may not always correspond with that of the courts. The extent of control which the landlord will have over alienation is, accordingly, substantially diluted by a proviso to the effect that the consent is not to be unreasonably withheld.[16] Any attempt to exclude or limit s 19(1)(a) of the Landlord and Tenant Act 1927 is ineffective. If the sub-section applies to a particular prohibition,[17] whether that prohibition is expressed as a fully qualified prohibition, or converted to a fully qualified prohibition by the sub-section,[18] consent cannot be unreasonably withheld in accordance with the principles applied by the courts.[19] Accordingly, any attempt by the parties to limit its effect by setting out in the lease that which is to be considered reasonable, is ineffective.[20] On the other hand, the sub-section does not prevent the parties from including further restrictions on the ability to withhold consent.[21]

1   See para 7.1 note 4 above.
2   See para 7.2:2 above.
3   As to form which the consent must take, see para 7.4 above.
4   *Treloar v Bigge* (1874) LR 9 Exch 151, in which it was made clear that, under the usual form of fully qualified covenant, because the proviso imposes no covenant on the part of the landlord, the tenant had no right to claim damages for failure to grant consent where reasonable. It has, of course, always been possible expressly to impose a covenant on the landlord. In *Ideal Film Renting Co v Nielsen* [1921] 1 Ch 575, it was held that such a covenant not only gave the tenant a right to damages for breach but also qualified the tenant's covenant. Although, it is submitted, the Landlord and Tenant Act 1988 (see para 7.6 below) does not affect the law in this respect, it does now give the tenant a claim in damages – not for breach of covenant, but for breach of statutory duty.
5   See *Eastern Telegraph Co v Dent* [1899] 1 QB 835, CA; *Barrow v Isaacs & Son* [1891] 1 QB 417, CA; *Creery v Summersell and Flowerdew & Co Ltd* [1949] Ch 751.
6   Such a reasonable time must be given: *Wilson v Flynn* [1948] 2 All ER 40; *Lewis and Allenby (1909) Ltd v Pegge* [1914] 1 Ch 782 (in which the landlord was considered to have withheld his consent by failing to respond within 11 days, although the court made it clear that the relevant period, in any particular case, would depend on the circumstances).
7   See, for example, the Law Commission's views: Law Com No 141 para 8.52. For the reasons mentioned above in connection with s 144 of the Law of Property Act 1925 (see para 7.2:3 note 7 above), consideration given in compliance with an unreasonabe condition will not, it seems, be recoverable, although for the possible effect of the Landlord and Tenant Act 1988 on this, see para 7.6 below.
8   See para 7.6 below.
9   It is submitted that these are still available – see para 7.6 below.
10 This has not proved a particularly satisfactory remedy from the tenant's point of view, mainly because of the risk involved. In many cases it is difficult for a tenant to be sure whether or not consent is being unreasonably withheld, and/or that he will be able to establish unreasonableness to the satisfaction of the court. Prior to the enactment of the Landlord and Tenant Act 1988 (see para 7.6 below) this was particularly the case, because the landlord was under no obligation to respond to the tenant's application. Even if he did respond, he was under no obligation to give reasons for a refusal of consent (*Young v Ashley Gardens Properties Ltd* [1903] 2 Ch 112, CA, although failure to give reasons might weaken the landlord's position), or for the imposition of conditions, and even if he gave reasons, he was entitled to rely on other reasons at the hearing (*Sonnenthal v Newton* (1965) 109 Sol Jo 333, CA). In addition, if the question as to whether or not consent had been unreasonably withheld arose in proceedings for damages or forfeiture by the landlord for breach of covenant, the burden was on the tenant to establish prima facie that it had been (the same applied in proceedings brought by the tenant for a declaration: see *Shanly v Ward* (1913) 29 TLR 714, CA). The extent to which the 1988 Act has changed the position in these respects is discussed below (see para 7.6). Because of this uncertainty, tenants have generally been reluctant to proceed with the transaction without consent, because if the tenant does so, and it should subsequently be determined by the court that the landlord had not been given a reasonable time to consider the application, that it was, or would have been, reasonable for the landlord to refuse consent, or that the conditions imposed by the landlord were reasonable, the tenant will be in breach, which breach may give rise not only to damages, but also to forfeiture under a normally drafted lease. This is the case, even though the problem arose because the landlord simply failed to respond and, prior to the enactment of the Landlord and Tenant Act 1988 (see para 7.6 below), the landlord was not liable for any loss caused by such failure.

Furthermore, it has generally been the case that, even if the tenant is prepared to take the risk of proceeding without consent, any third party (such as a prospective assignee) involved will not be prepared to do so and, generally, the tenant will not be able to obtain specific performance in such circumstances (*Re Marshall and Salt's Contract* [1900] 2 Ch 202; *Lipman's Wallpaper Ltd v Mason and Hodghton* [1969] 1 Ch 20, [1968] 1 All ER 1123; *Property and Bloodstock v Emerton*, above).

11 For the form of declaration, see *Woolworth & Co Ltd v Lambert* [1937] Ch 37, [1936] 2 All ER 1523, CA; *Re Town Investments Underlease* [1954] Ch 301, [1954] 1 All ER 585. Whilst it is obviously safer for the tenant to seek a declaration than to proceed without consent, this has also proved a far from satisfactory remedy, mainly because of the delay involved. It may take months for an application to be heard, and even if the tenant can afford to wait this length of time, most prospective assignees or subtenants will not be prepared to do so, and will seek accommodation elsewhere. The incentive to incur the cost and delay involved in applying for a declaration is still further reduced by the uncertainty as to whether or not it will ultimately be granted, arising from the fact that it is often difficult for the tenant and prospective disposee to know whether or not consent has been unreasonably withheld, or whether or not they will be able to establish unreasonableness (see note 10 above). Furthermore, until the enactment of the Landlord and Tenant Act 1988 (see para 7.6 below) if the landlord failed to respond, but it was later determined, when the facts were known, that he would have been reasonable in withholding consent, the tenant and disposee received no compensation for the delay and cost incurred.

12 See notes 10 and 11 above.

13 Although, if the landlord behaved unreasonably, he ran the risk of losing his rights and incurring cost, he knew that, in the vast majority of cases, this would not occur. He knew that, save in exceptional circumstances, the tenant would not risk proceeding without consent and that, therefore, he risked nothing more than the costs of an action for a declaration, which the tenant was unlikely to bring.

14 See para 7.6 below.

15 For examples of the way in which the courts have applied the 'reasonableness' test, see Woodfall's *Law of Landlord and Tenant* para 1–1181 et seq; Hill & Redman's *Law of Landlord and Tenant* para [2599] et seq. The basic principles to be applied were restated in *International Drilling Fluids Ltd v Louisville Investments (Uxbridge) Ltd* [1986] Ch 513 (discussed in Hill & Redman's *Law of Landlord and Tenant* at para [2616]). See also *Orlando Investments Ltd v Grosvenor Estate Belgravia* [1989] EGCS 58, CA; *Warren v Marketing Exchange for Africa Ltd* [1988] 2 EGLR 247; *Deverall v Wyndham* [1989] 1 EGLR 57; *Venetian Glass Gallery v Next Properties Ltd* [1989] 30 EG 92. Section 19(1)(a) expressly provides that it does not preclude the right of the landlord to require payment of a reasonable sum in respect of any legal or other expense incurred in connection with the licence or consent. For the possible effect of the Landlord and Tenant Act 1988 on the reasonableness test, see para 7.6 below.

16 Legally, although in practice this has often not been the case because of the reluctance of tenants to pursue the remedies available (see notes 10, 11 and 13 above). There is little doubt that the Landlord and Tenant Act 1988 will render this statement closer to the truth in practice.

17 As mentioned (see para 7.4 above) there are circumstances in which the sub-section will not apply to convert a qualified prohibition to a fully qualified prohibition and, in similar circumstances, it seems that it will not apply to affect the operation of a prohibition which is expressly fully qualified. So, for example, the comments in para 7.5 will not, if it is submitted, apply to a fully qualified prohibition against sharing occupation with a third party.

18 See paras 7.2:2 and 7.4 above.

19 See note 15 above.

20 See *Creery v Summersell and Flowerdew & Co Ltd*, above (in which the words: '. . . save that the lessor reserves the right not to give his consent if in his opinion the proposed . . . sub-lessee is for any reason in his discretion undesirable . . .' were considered by the court to be attempting to reserve rights to the landlord which were invalid as going beyond s 19(1)(a)); *Re Smith's Lease, Smith v Richards* [1951] 1 TLR 254 (in which the proviso was followed by the words: '. . . Provided always that any refusal by the lessor to consent . . . shall not be deemed to be an unreasonable withholding . . . by reason only that the lessor . . . at the time of intimating any such refusal may offer to accept from the lessee a surrender . . .' and it was held that the parties could not themselves decide what was or was not reasonable and so restrict the operation of the section). One would imagine, therefore, that if a fully qualified prohibition against a particular dealing is inserted in the lease any other provisions in the lease which purport to restrict the tenant's ability to effect that particular dealing will be valid only if they satisfy the 'reasonableness' test. There are cases, however, which indicate that whether or not an additional restriction will be so vulnerable will depend on the drafting of the lease. In *Adler v Upper Grosvenor Street Investment Ltd* [1957] 1 All ER 229, [1957] 1 WLR

227 a covenant not to assign or underlet without consent was expressed to be subject to the proviso that if the tenant wanted to assign or underlet he had first to offer to surrender the lease, and it was held that this did not contravene s 19(1)(a) because the proviso imposed a condition precedent to the coming into operation of the covenant. Although the correctness of this was doubted in *Greene v Church Comrs for England* [1974] Ch 467, [1974] 3 All ER 609, CA (*per curiam*, as the provision in that case was void for want of registration as a land charge), the decision was approved by the Court of Appeal in *Bocardo SA v S & M Hotels Ltd* [1979] 3 All ER 737, [1980] 1 WLR 17 and accepted to be correct in *Allnatt London Properties Ltd v Newton* [1981] 2 All ER 290 (in which it was held, however, that the agreement resulting from the landlord's acceptance of the offer to surrender was void by virtue of s 38(1) of the Landlord and Tenant Act 1954: see para 7.7 footnotes 59 and 60 below). There are, therefore, two possible views on additional restrictions imposed on dealings which are the subject of a fully qualified prohibition to which s 19(1)(a) of the Landlord and Tenant Act 1927 applies. The narrower view is that they are not subject to the 'reasonableness' test only if they are pre-conditions to the coming into operation of the prohibition against dealing. The wider view is that they are only vulnerable if they are drafted in such a way as expressly to purport to specify what will or will not be considered to be reasonable, or when the landlord will or will not be considered to be unreasonably withholding consent. In view of the uncertainty, the tenant should ensure that he is happy with any additional restrictions imposed, or that he inserts provisions to the effect that they will only apply if and to the extent reasonable, whilst the landlord should give careful thought to the drafting of those of such restrictions about which he is particularly concerned, and should bear in mind that they might be subject to the reasonableness test notwithstanding.

21   In *Moat v Martin* [1950] 1 KB 175, [1949] 2 All ER 646, CA the lease contained the proviso that 'such consent will not be withheld in the case of a respectable and responsible person', and it was held that, if the proposed assignee was respectable and responsible, consent could not be withheld even on other reasonable grounds. For the effect of the Landlord and Tenant Act 1988 on such provisions, see (1987) Law Com No 161 Explanatory Notes para 5.

7.6   *Fully qualified prohibitions: the Landlord and Tenant Act 1988.* The 1988 act applies to any lease,[1] granted before or after the Act,[2] containing a fully qualified prohibition[3] against assigning, underletting, charging or parting with possession of the whole or part of the premises comprised in the lease.[4] Briefly, it provides that any person[5] whose consent[6] is required under such a fully qualified prohibition is under a duty[7] to respond[8] to the tenant's[9] application[10] for consent within a reasonable time,[11] notifying him whether or not consent is given, if consent is given subject to conditions, the conditions, and if consent is withheld the reasons why it is withheld.[12] He is also under a duty[13] to give consent within a reasonable time,[14] unless it is reasonable[15] for him not to give consent. Similar duties[16] are owed by a landlord[17] to a subtenant[18] with regard to any approval required under a fully qualified prohibition[19] which prevents the tenant from consenting to any assignment, underletting, charging or parting with possession of the whole or part of the premises comprised in the subtenancy without the landlord's approval. The 1988 Act provides[20] that if any question arises[21] whether any such notification was given within a reasonable time, whether any condition imposed was reasonable, whether any withholding of consent or approval was reasonable, or whether consent or approval was given within a reasonable time, it is for the person whose consent or approval was required to show that it was. A further duty[22] is imposed on the landlord,[23] and any person whose consent is required to any particular transaction, to take reasonable steps to ensure that any other person from whom he believes consent is required[24] receives a copy of any application received within a reasonable time.[25] A tenant who considers that he has suffered loss as a result of any breach of the duties imposed by the Act, may bring a claim in tort for damages for breach of statutory duty.[26] The Act came into force on 28 September 1988, implementing some of the proposals put forward in the Law Commission's Report on Covenants Restricting Dispositions Alterations and Change of User,[27] with the purpose of speeding up the process of conveyancing.[28] In the further Report[29] to which the draft bill was appended, the Law Commission made it clear that it was not intended to affect substantive rights, but merely to improve the means of enforcing existing rights.[30] In the light of differing views expressed by commentators,[31] and in the absence of judicial guidance, the following comments are put forward only as suggestions on the likely effect of the Act:

7.6:1 *Additional remedies.* It seems that the existing remedies that the tenant has[32] if the landlord unreasonably refuses consent, fails to respond within a reasonable time, or imposes unreasonable conditions on the grant of consent, remain,[33] but that a further remedy, in the form of a right to damages for breach of statutory duty,[34] is given in these and other circumstances:

(a) A person whose consent or a landlord whose approval or consent is required is under an obligation to give a *decision*, one way or another, within a reasonable time.[35]

(b) A person whose consent or a landlord whose approval or consent is required is under a duty to give *consent or approval* within a reasonable time unless it is reasonable not to do so.[36]

(c) A person whose consent or a landlord whose approval or consent is required is under a duty to give *reasons* for withholding consent or approval within a reasonable time.[37] Although the contrary view has been expressed, it seems that this may have the effect of preventing the landlord from raising reasons other than those given within a reasonable time later on during proceedings.[38]

(d) A person whose consent is required is under a duty *to pass on applications* to others from whom they believe consents are required.[39]

So how does this affect the position of the parties? Where the tenant, as a result of the landlord's failure to respond, or unreasonable withholding or conditions, *decides not to pursue* an application any further, because he, or the prospective disposee, is not prepared to take the risk of proceeding without consent,[40] or to incur the delay involved in applying for a declaration,[41] the tenant previously had no recourse against the landlord. Now the landlord may be liable in damages. Where the tenant *does pursue* the application further, it seems that he could sometimes resort to more than one remedy. For example, a tenant whose landlord fails to respond to his application might apply for a declaration and claim damages for breach of statutory duty. Even if it transpires that the landlord would have been reasonable in withholding consent, he will presumably still be liable for any loss suffered by the tenant as a result of the delay. Similarly, there seems to be no reason why, for example, a tenant whose landlord unreasonably refuses consent should not complete the transaction if he is sufficiently confident, and also claim damages for statutory duty. Indeed, in the past once the transaction had completed (whether because the tenant simply proceeded without consent or because the landlord gave consent) the landlord was free from concern, no matter how unreasonably he had behaved beforehand. Under the 1988 Act, as soon as a person unreasonably withholds consent, either wholly or by imposing unreasonable conditions, he is in breach of statutory duty. It is assumed, therefore, that even if the person later gives the consent, or withdraws the conditions, the tenant will be able to bring an action against him for loss suffered as a result of that breach in the interim, whether or not the relevant transaction subsequently will be, or has been, effected.

7.6:2 *Affect on existing law.* It may be that the Act has affected the law relating to the recoverability of moneys paid, or the enforcement of covenants given, in compliance with an unreasonable condition.[42] It could be argued that, if an unreasonable condition is imposed, which is either immediately or eventually complied with, the tenant will be able to claim for any loss caused by the imposition of that condition either before or after the relevant transaction is effected. Suppose, for example, that a landlord consents to the grant of a sublease on the (unreasonable) condition that the tenant pays him £1,000. In order to ensure that the transaction takes place quickly, the tenant pays the money and completes the sublease. Is he then able to make a claim against the landlord for loss suffered as a result of the condition imposed? If so, will his loss include the £1,000? Naturally, as no duty is owed to the subtenant, he would be unable to make a claim if the money had been by him, but would the landlord be entitled to keep money paid as a result of his breach of duty? Similarly, if the tenant had covenanted to pay money, or if the subtenant had given a covenant, would the landlord be entitled to enforce such covenants obtained as a result of his breach of statutory duty?

7.6:3 *Burden of proof.* One evident change made by the Act, is that the burden of proof is on the landlord.[43] There seems to be no reason why the relevant sub-sections should only apply when the tenant is claiming damages for breach of statutory duty, and it is submitted that they will also apply in proceedings brought by the landlord for damages or forfeiture for breach of the relevant prohibition, or in proceedings brought by the tenant for a declaration.

7.6:4 *Advice to landlords and tenants.* It was said that the purpose of the Act, in making landlords liable in damages, 'is not to encourage litigation but, in effect, to encourage good practice and quicker conveyancing by giving some "leverage" to vendor-tenants'.[44] A landlord 'would be stupid to run the risk of incurring this liability; and solicitors and other advisers would be failing in their duty if they did not advise him to act in such a way as to avoid it.'[45] Those advising the landlord on the grant of a lease should draw his attention to the liabilities which now attach to the inclusion of certain fully qualified prohibitions against alienation and, if any are to be included, they should advise him to ensure that a system is set up at the outset to enable him to deal with applications quickly and efficiently.[46] This will probably involve the preparation of standard forms of response,[47] and will mean that the landlord must be fully conversant with and/or have ready access to professional assistance on the question of what is, and what is not, reasonable in any particular case, and the way in which responses should be served. Indeed, because of the importance of the landlord's response, many landlords may simply send copies of all applications received immediately to their professional advisers to deal with. Similar considerations apply to those advising tenants, in order that they do not inadvertently lose their rights by, for example, failing to serve a proper application, or failing to challenge unreasonable conditions.

1   It applies to any lease or other tenancy, including a subtenancy and an agreement for a tenancy (s 5(1)), but not to a secure tenancy (s 5(3)). For discussion of the Act, see David N Levy 'Landlord and Tenant Act 1988' [1988] Gazette 2 Nov 35, Stephen Shaw 'Breaking the commercial lease deadlock: a sign of things to come' (1988) 138 NLJ 918, John Austin: 'Landlord and Tenant: the 1988 Act' [1988] 12 Estates Gazette 55.
2   Section 5(1).
3   Ie any covenant condition or agreement. The Act is evidently intended to apply to all fully qualified prohibitions, whether the proviso that consent is not to be unreasonably withheld is express, or included by statute (see para 7.2:2 above).

4 Section 1(1).

5 This may be the landlord, a superior landlord, a mortgagee, or any other person whose consent is required.

6 In the Act 'consent' includes licence (s 5(1)).

7 Section 1(3)(b).

8 By service of notice in writing (s 1(3)(b)). For service, see s 5(2). Although it was originally recommended ((1985) Law Com No 141 para 8.128 et seq) that the landlord's response should be in a prescribed form, forming a separate part of a prescribed form of application, this recommendation was not implemented (see (1987) Law Com No 161 para 2.4).

9 Where the tenancy is affected by a mortgage and the mortgagee proposes to exercise his power of sale, 'tenant' includes the mortgagee (s 5(1)).

10 The application should be in writing and the original, or a copy, should be served on the person whose consent is required. Although it was originally recommended that there should be a prescribed form of application ((1985) Law Com No 141 para 8.128 et seq) this recommendation was not implemented (see (1987) Law Com No 161 para 2.4). Disputes may arise as to whether or not a particular communication constitutes an 'application' for the purposes of the 1988 Act. Whilst it seems possible that any written communication which evinces the desire to effect a dealing will suffice, and that it will be for the recipient to request further information by means of imposing conditions in his response, the applicant would be advised to make the communication as clear, and give as much information, as possible. The Act applies only to applications for consent or approval served after its coming into force (s 5(4)).

11 Although it was originally recommended that a period of 28 days should be given as a general, though variable, guideline as the time within which it would be reasonable for a decision, one way or the other, to be given ((1985) Law Com No 141 para 8.125) it was decided that this recommendation should not be implemented (see (1987) Law Com No 161 para 2.5), and that no guideline should be specified. See also para 7.5 note 6 above.

12 Section 1(3)(b). There is no specific duty to give reasons for conditions imposed. Perhaps it is arguable that, in the same way as the imposition of an unreasonable condition constitutes unreasonable withholding (see para 7.5) above and s 1(4)), the imposition of a condition on the grant of consent is an element of withholding consent, and that, therefore, a duty to give reasons for the imposition of conditions is included in the duty to give reasons for withholding consent. It is noticeable that, whilst the 1988 Act makes it clear that whether or not consent is reasonably withheld for the purposes of the statute will depend on whether or not it is reasonable in accordance with the 'reasonableness' test developed by the courts (see para 7.5 note 15 above and note 15 below), the reference to 'any condition that is not a reasonable condition' is not so linked with that test. The intention that it should be is, however, evident.

13 Section 1(3)(a).

14 See note 11 above.

15 There has been some debate about the meaning of s 1(5): see for example D N Levy 'Landlord and Tenant Act 1988' [1988] Gazette 2 Nov 35, Stephen Shaw 'Breaking the commercial lease deadlock: a sign of things to come' (1988) 138 NLJ 918, H W Wilkinson 'Unreasonably withholding consent to sub-let' (1989) 139 NLJ 413, Hill & Redman's *Law of Landlord and Tenant* (18th edn) para 2599, footnote 10A. At first sight s 1(5) appears to limit greatly the circumstances in which consent might be reasonably withheld, for it says that for the purposes of the Act it is reasonable for a person not to give consent to a proposed transaction only in a case where, if he withheld consent and the tenant completed the transaction, the tenant would be in breach of a covenant. *Leasehold Conveyancing* (1987), Law Com No 161 that made the proposal, however, said that it covers only the case 'where the lease itself specifies what is or is not a good reason for withholding consent . . . such as a provision that consent will always be given provided that the proposed assignee is a respectable person'. Thus if the proposed assignee is respectable the landlord cannot refuse consent even if there are other valid reasons for refusing it. Thus it was intended that s 1(5) should deal only with a lease by which the landlord, in effect, excludes his right to withhold consent to an assignment where the assignee falls within a defined group: for example, respectable or responsible persons (see *Moat v Martin* [1950] 1 KB 175, [1949] 2 All ER 646, CA); a partnership in which at least one of the original tenants is a partner; or solicitors. Section 1(5) was intended to mean no more than in such a case it would be unreasonable for a landlord to withhold consent for an assignment to an assignee who falls within the group. See footnote 30 below.

16 Section 3(2).

17 By virtue of s 5(1) 'landlord' includes any superior landlord, but not third parties.

18 Despite the contrary view expressed in the Explanatory Notes ((1987) Law Com No 161 Explanatory Notes para 8), these duties do not appear to be owed to the tenant.

19 See para 7.4 note 2 above with regard to such prohibitions. The 1988 Act does not purport to alter the substantive law: 'The Landlord and Tenant Act 1927, s 19 does not apply to such covenants but the covenant itself may state that landlord may not unreasonably withhold his approval.' – (1987) Law Com No 161 Explanatory Notes para 8.

20 Section 1(6); s 3(4).

21 Although they state that the burden of proof is on 'the person who owed any duty' under it, the relevant sub-sections do not appear to be limited in application to proceedings brought by the tenant for damages for breach of any such duty.

22 Section 2(1).

23 Even if the landlord's own consent is not required. See also note 17 above.

24 Unless he believes that the person has received the application or a copy of it. Although there is apparently no duty on a person whose consent or approval of consent is required to pass a copy of the application to any person whose approval of consent is required, it is assumed that failure to do so would constitute a breach of his duty under ss 1(3) or 3(2).

25 It was originally recommended that fourteen days should be specified as a general, though variable, guideline to the time within which it would be reasonable for applications to be passed on ((1985) Law Com No 141 para 8.125), but this recommendation was not implemented.

26 Section 4. For the reasons why the 1988 Act imposes a statutory duty, rather than implying a statutory covenant, see (1987) Law Com No 161 paras 2.1–2.3.

27 (1985) Law Com No 141. It should be noted that the 1988 Act only applies to certain fully qualified prohibitions affecting dispositions. In other cases, a tenant who would like to give himself more effective remedies than those provided by the general law (see para 7.5 above) will need to make express provision in the lease.

28 'The failure of a landlord to give consent to a transaction can be a considerable source of delay in conveyancing. The Law Society has long pressed for reform in this area. The Conveyancing Standing Committee decided that it wished to encourage implementation of this part of our report as part of its work to make conveyancing quicker.' – (1987) Law Com No 161 para 1.3.

29 (1987) Law Com No 161.

30 But see Woodfall's *Law of Landlord and Tenant*, para 1179/1: 'The Act is expressed in convoluted language and it is not a simple matter, on a first consideration of it, to appreciate how widely it strikes. The Act does not purport directly to alter the general law expressed in paras 1–1180 et seq, post, which has evolved from decided cases on the construction of covenants and on reasonableness . . . but indirectly it may have that effect or even render it otiose.' It is rather concerning that, after so dire a warning, there follows no explanation of how, or why, this should be the case! See footnote 15 above.

31 See notes 30 above and 38 below.

32 See para 7.5 above.

33 'The two remedies provided by the present law in the case of unreasonable withholding – proceeding without consent; and obtaining a declaration from the court – should of course be retained.' (1985) Law Com No 141 Para 8.111.

34 Section 4.

35 Section 1(3)(b); s 3(2)(b).

36 Section 1(3)(a); s 3(2)(a).

37 Section 1(3)(b)(ii); s 3(2)(b)(ii).

38 'If the landlord advances a ground in his reasons and a different ground at the hearing, this will not of itself make any difference, as it is presumably still the case that a landlord is not confined to the reasons he advances at the time of refusing consent . . .' (Commercial Leases, Vol 2 Issue No 10: Landlord and Tenant Act 1988). In support of this view, the Act does not specifically provide that failure to give any particular reason within a reasonable time will prevent the landlord from relying on that reason (cf Housing Act 1980, s 37A) and, as it is clear that this was not the case prior to the enactment of the Act (see para 7.5 notes 10 and 11 above), one would have thought that, if the Act intended to change the position, it would have made this clear. On the other hand, it is arguable that the old rule that the landlord could produce in proceedings reasons which he did not put forward at the time of refusing consent was a necessary result of the rule that the landlord was under no obligation to give any reasons at all and, under the 1988 Act, the landlord is under a duty to give reasons at the time of refusing consent. Furthermore, s 1(3)(b)(ii) of the 1988 Act does not simply provide that the landlord is to give reasons, but that he is under a duty to give '*the* reasons for withholding' consent. Finally, the purported purpose of the 1988 Act is to speed up conveyancing and, whilst the fact that the existence of a right to damages for breach of statutory duty will presumably encourage the landlord to give all his reasons, if the tenant could rely entirely on the reasons given, and thus make an informed decision as to whether or not the landlord was being reasonable, this purpose would be better achieved. Even if the Act

does not directly achieve this position, it seems that it may be achieved indirectly. Suppose, for example, that the landlord refuses consent, giving a reason which is obviously unreasonable, and the tenant then proceeds with the transaction. It is arguable that the tenant is entitled to rely on the reason, given as it was pursuant to a statutory duty, and that the landlord will be estopped from putting forward other reasons in proceedings for damages or forfeiture for breach of the prohibition. Even if estoppel does not apply, it is possible that any damages awarded to the tenant for breach of statutory duty would include damages awarded to the landlord for breach of covenant, and it is equally possible that a court of equity would give serious consideration to granting relief against forfeiture to a tenant against a landlord in breach of statutory duty.

39 Section 2.
40 See para 7.5 note 10 above.
41 See para 7.5 note 11 above.
42 It will be remembered (see para 7.2:3 note 7 and para 7.5 note 7 above) that, although s 144 of the Law of Property Act 1925 and s 19(1)(a) of the Landlord and Tenant Act 1927 renders payment of a fine, or compliance with an unreasonable condition, unnecessary, it does not make it unlawful, and that any money paid or covenant given is enforceable. However, before the 1988 Act, the landlord was under no *obligation* to be reasonble (see para 7.5 note 3 above) whereas, as a result of the 1988 Act, a person who imposes an unreasonable condition on the grant of consent is now in breach of statutory duty.
43 See notes 20 and 21 above.
44 (1987) Law Com No 161 para 2.3.
45 (1985) Law Com No 141 para 8.108.
46 Even before the enactment of the 1988 Act, it was advisable for the landlord to have such a system set up. Although the risk of challenge was small (see para 7.5 above), a landlord who behaved in a dilatory or unreasonable way could lose rights and incur cost. As a result of the 1988 Act it seems, however, that the risk of challenge, and the loss which the landlord could incur, are substantially increased.
47 It seems possible that the Act will result in the disappearance of the type of licences to assign, underlet, etc currently in use, as the landlord's response to the tenant's application will constitute a refusal, a consent, or a consent subject to conditions. Presumably, even if one of the conditions subject to which consent is granted involves the giving of a covenant by an assignee or other person, this can be dealt with in a short separate deed. It is submitted that, if this is the case, it will contribute greatly to reducing delays in conveyancing resulting from the need to obtain consent.

7.7   *Drafting.* There are a number of points which the parties should bear in mind when drafting alienation provisions:

7.7:1   *General.* There are numerous ways in which the tenant is able to part with the ownership and/or use and occupation of the premises and a prohibition against one particular type of dealing may not restrain another.[1] It has been held that a covenant against assignment will not prevent underletting,[2] a covenant against assignment or underletting will not prevent the tenant from parting with possession of the premises to a purchaser prior to completion,[3] and a covenant against parting with possession will not prevent the tenant from permitting others to use and occupy the premises.[4] The lease should deal with each different type of disposal separately,[5] and make it clear in each case whether or not that type of disposal is permitted.[6] Although a prohibition against one particular type of dealing will not necessarily prevent another, the various expressions used are not mutually exclusive. It has been held that a covenant against parting with possession will restrain assignment[7] so that a fully qualified covenant against assignment will conflict with an absolute covenant against parting with possession. The parties should ensure that no ambiguities are created in this way. So, in the example given, they should ensure that the absolute prohibition against parting with possession is qualified by the words 'otherwise than by means of a permitted assignment', or words to similar effect.[8] The parties must remember, when dealing with each different type of disposal, to deal with both a disposal of the whole of the premises and a disposal of part: a covenant 'not to underlet the premises', for example, will not prevent an underletting of part of the premises.[9]

7.7:2 *Assignment.*[10] Leases today generally contain an absolute[11] prohibition against the assignment of part of the premises,[12] and a fully qualified[13] prohibition against the assignment of the whole of the premises.[14] In addition, they frequently contain an additional requirement[15] to the effect that any assignee will covenant direct with the landlord to pay the rent reserved by, and perform and observe the covenants contained in, the lease during the residue of the term.[16] There are two main reasons why landlords impose such a requirement: the first is to ensure that there is no question of the assignee arguing that he is not bound by a particular covenant because it does not touch and concern the land,[17] and the second is to give the assignee an incentive not to assign to a person of poor financial standing, by rendering the assignee liable following further assignment.[18] Often in the case of an assignment to a limited company there is a requirement that at least two of the directors will give guarantees, if the landlord so requires.[19]

7.7:3 *Underletting.*[20] Save where there is a headlease which dictates otherwise,[21] a lease will usually contain a fully qualified prohibition[22] against underletting the whole of the premises[23] and, in the case of premises capable of sub-division, it will often also contain a fully qualified prohibition[22] against underletting part of the premises. If the landlord is prepared to permit underletting, there are a number of matters which he should bear in mind[24] and, because of these, leases frequently contain a number of additional restrictions:[25]

7.7:3.1 *Underletting of part.* The sub-division of the premises may cause the landlord problems of management, administration and control,[26] which would be exacerbated if the tenant dropped out of the picture[27] in such a way as to render the landlord the immediate landlord in respect of the sub-divided premises.[28] In addition, landlords are frequently concerned that the sub-division of the premises, if taken too far, will result in their deterioration. Usually, therefore, even when underletting of part is permitted, the part or parts which can be underlet are specified. So, for example, in the case of a large office block, the tenant will often not be permitted to grant underleases of anything other than a whole floor, or whole floors, excluding service areas such as lobbies. This is generally achieved by defining those areas which can be underlet separately as 'Permitted Areas'. Often, if the landlord is reluctant to allow the sub-division of the premises either at all, or in units smaller than the Permitted Areas, he may agree to do so to some extent provided that the relevant underleases are excluded from the protection of the 1954 Act.[29]

7.7:3.2 *Guarantors.* As in the case of assignment, the landlord will often want the lease to specify that guarantors should be provided on underletting, and the same arguments apply.[30] If there is such a requirement, it should relate to the giving of guarantee covenants to the tenant and not the landlord.[31]

177

7.7:3.3 *Rent.* The landlord is concerned about the rent to be reserved by any underlease[32] and, accordingly, the lease will almost invariably impose some requirements in this respect. Often it will provide that no underlease is to be granted at a fine or premium, and that any underlease should reserve not less than either the open market rent for the premises to be underlet, or the rent payable under the lease (or the relevant proportion thereof in the case of an underletting of part), whichever is the greater.[33] The tenant should consider such a provision carefully. The first point relates to such matters as fixtures and fittings.[34] Should the open market value of the premises to be underlet include the existence of such items as fixtures and fittings installed by the tenant, or should the tenant be able to take the value from the undertenant in the form of a premium? Secondly, when dealing with the requirement that there should be no fine or premium, it would be as well for the lease to make it clear that this does not include a reverse premium if this is intended. Thirdly, the tenant should consider whether he might, for example, want to underlet to a company within the same group, or to a business associate, at a concessionary rent. The landlord might be prepared to allow this, subject to certain conditions.[35] Finally, most tenants will not find it acceptable for a lease to require that an underlease, particularly an underlease of the whole of the premises, should be granted at the higher of the open market rent and the rent reserved by the lease.[36] Such a requirement would render the premises unlettable in the event of a fall in market rents, which is one of the times when a tenant might find the ability to underlet most useful.[37]

7.7:3.4 *Other terms.* So far as the other terms of any underlease are concerned, landlords attempt to retain control over these[38] in a variety of different ways. Some leases provide that any sublease should contain similar covenants to those in the headlease.[39] Others spell out in more or less detail the way in which certain aspects of the sublease, which are of particular concern, should be drafted.[40] Others require any sublease to contain a covenant by the subtenant to observe and perform the lessee's covenants in the headlease, so far as they relate to the underlet premises.[41] Others simply require any sub-lease to be in a form approved by the landlord.[42] There is no easy formula by which a lease can be converted into an underlease and accordingly each of these methods has its drawbacks,[43] with the result that it is probably best for the landlord to adopt a combination of these approaches. The tenant should check the requirements carefully: whilst there are good reasons why the landlord is concerned about the terms of any sublease,[38] requirements which are unnecessary and unduly onerous will detract from, and perhaps extinguish, the tenant's ability to underlet, as no undertenant, especially one with a short term, will be willing or, perhaps, able to comply with them. The tenant should also consider asking the landlord to agree to allow any underlease to be granted on less onerous terms, provided that certain conditions are complied with.[44]

7.7:3.5 *Direct covenants.* There is no privity of contract or estate between the landlord and a subtenant and the landlord will, accordingly, be unable to take proceedings against the subtenant direct for breaches of covenants contained in the headlease or underlease, except in very limited circumstances.[45] Landlords accordingly often require direct covenants from undertenants.[46]

7.7:3.6   *Enforcement.* Although direct covenants are useful, the landlord will often not want to be involved in the time and expense of policing and enforcing the subtenant's obligations while breach of a direct covenant will not give rise to a right to forfeiture which is often the only satisfactory remedy. As a result, the landlord should always place the tenant under an obligation to enforce the subtenant's obligations.[47]

7.7:4   *Other restrictions: group companies.* A prohibition against assigning or underletting will not restrain the tenant from parting with the possession of the premises in some other way,[48] and the lease will, therefore, usually contain an absolute prohibition[50] against parting with possession of the whole or any part of the premises otherwise than by means of a permitted assignment or sublease.[51] A covenant against suffering any other person to use or occupy the premises[49] is wider than a covenant against parting with possession, and many leases contain an absolute prohibition[50] against permitting any person, other than a permitted assignee or undertenant, to use or occupy any part of the premises.[51] It is quite standard, however, for there to be an exception to this absolute prohibition, which permits the tenant to share occupation, if he so requires, with members of the same group of companies.[52] The lease usually provides that the right is only to subsist in relation to any company whilst it is a member of the group, that no relationship of landlord and tenant is to be created between the tenant and any such company, and that the tenant is to give notice to the landlord of the identity of any company let into occupation. Some leases also provide for a maximum number of occupiers, whether the tenant, subtenants or mere occupiers. Landlords should not, however, permit sharing with group companies without thought. For example, a landlord who is letting part of a building occupied by himself, and who is concerned about being close to a rival or competitor, should bear in mind that the tenant could acquire a subsidiary falling within the category of companies to which the landlord would object even if he does not have one at the time of the letting. If, as may well be the case, the landlord is concerned about occupiers, for this or any other reason, he should make provision for it, for example by limiting the right to particular members of the group or by prohibiting sharing with group companies without his consent, such consent not to be unreasonably withheld. From the tenant's point of view, it should be remembered that the ability to share with group companies is now so standard a requirement that, if possible, he should obtain the right for assignees, and the right to permit undertenants, to do so. Naturally, in such a case, the landlord is even more likely to require some control over the identity of the group companies allowed into occupation. Finally, most leases nowadays contain an absolute prohibition[50] against creating a legal or equitable charge over part of the premises,[53] and an absolute,[50] or fully qualified,[54] prohibition against creating a legal or equitable charge over the whole of the premises.[55] Although in many cases a commercial lease, at a rack rent, with the usual proviso for re-entry, will not constitute particularly attractive security to a lender, a tenant should retain the right to create a charge over the whole of the premises, and indeed the right to permit a subtenant to create a charge over the whole of the sublet premises, if possible.[56]

7.7:5   *Registration.* At common law, there is no obligation on a tenant, assignee or subtenant to give notice of any dealing with or devolution of the premises to the landlord and, accordingly, such an obligation is invariably included in the lease.[57] Historically the clause often required the tenant to produce the original deed or document relating to the dealing or devolution to the landlord or his solicitors, but nowadays it invariably refers to a certified copy.[58] The tenant should ensure that, in the case of dealings or devolutions in which he will not be directly involved, the obligation applies only if and to the extent that he is aware of the relevant dealing or devolution, and is able to obtain a certified copy of the relevant deed or document.

7.7:6   *Surrender-back clauses.* Landlords are sometimes attracted by the concept of being able to obtain a surrender of the lease when the tenant no longer requires the premises, and insert clauses by which the tenant has to offer to surrender the lease and can assign or underlet only if the landlord declines that offer.[59] The agreement that comes into being if the landlord accepts the tenant's offer to surrender is, however, void in the case of a business tenancy.[60] Without a surrender-back clause the tenant may be able to assign or underlet at a premium[61] or underlet at a rent higher than it is paying under the headlease. The tenant's advisers should resist a surrender-back clause. It could be difficult to market premises where the tenant does not know for certain if it will be able to assign the lease to a third party. Where the landlord insists on such a clause, the tenant must be in a position to receive from the landlord a sum equal to the premium that it would have received from an assignee on the open market. But there are problems in attempting to provide for this in the lease. It is easy to state that the surrender will be at 'the open market premium value (if any) of this lease' or 'the premium (if any) for which the tenant might reasonably be expected to assign this lease in the open market' in both cases for the unexpired residue of the term as at the date of the tenant's offer to surrender, and then to provide for this to be fixed by a third party acting as an expert or arbitrator if the parties are unable to agree upon the sum. In the open market, however, that premium may well be higher where the assignee proposes to carry on at the premises the same business as that undertaken by the tenant/assignor. An alternative to avoid this might be to provide that with the offer to surrender the tenant could provide details of a genuine proposed sale to a third party and the landlord could accept the surrender for the same premium as that offered by the third party. This has the advantage of being (on the face of it) the best possible evidence of what the premium value really is, but would be open to abuse. User would not be a problem where the lease contained a wide user covenant, for example, for use of offices and would be unlikely to be one where the landlord could not unreasonably refuse consent to a change of trade. The difficulty, however, is where the user is narrow, so that most assignees would require consent to a change of use, and where the covenant is absolute and therefore the landlord could unreasonably refuse that consent. It would appear that that valuer would not be able to assume that the landlord would give consent for a reasonable change of use,[62] thus producing uncertainty and probably a low premium valuation.

1   For the ambit of prohibitions against assignment, underletting, parting with possession, sharing occupation, etc, see Woodfall's *Law of Landlord and Tenant* para 1–1190 et seq; Hill & Redman's *Law of Landlord and Tenant* para [2571] et seq.
2   See *Sweet and Maxwell Ltd v Universal News Service Ltd* [1964] 2 QB 699, [1964] 3 All ER 30, CA.
3   See *Horsey Estatee Ltd v Steiger* [1899] 2 QB 79, CA; *Eastern Telegraph Co v Dent* [1899] 1 QB 835, CA.
4   See *Lam Kee Ying Sdn Bhd v Lam Shes Tong* (1975) AC 247, [1974] 3 All ER 137, PC.

5   Most leases nowadays refer to assigning, underletting, charging, parting with or sharing possession or occupation and holding on trust for another, see for example 22 Encyclopaedia of Forms and Precedents (5th edn) Form 22 clause 5.9, Rosscastle Letting Conditions (Appendix 1, Form 1 below) Condition 3.7.

6   If the landlord wants to restrict free alienation by the tenant the burden lies on him to express this in clear terms so that there is no doubt, as the alienation provisions will be construed against him: see *Russell v Beecham* [1924] 1 KB 525, CA; *Marks v Warren* [1979] 1 All ER 29; *Sweet and Maxwell Ltd v Universal News Service Ltd*, above.

7   See *Abrahams v MacFishers Ltd* [1925] 2 KB 18.

8   See 22 Encyclopaedia of Forms and Precedents (5th edn) Form 22 clause 5.9:1, Rosscastle Letting Conditions (Appendix 1, Form 1 below) Condition 3.7:1.

9   See *Cook v Shoesmith* [1951] 1 KB 752, CA, although a covenant not to assign or underlet *any part* of the premises restrains an assignment or underletting of whole (*Field v Barkworth* [1986] 1 All ER 362, [1986] 1 WLR 137).

10 See note 1 above. Note that a prohibition against assignment will generally restrict only voluntary assignment (see Woodfall's *Law of Landlord and Tenant* para 1–1203 et seq; Hill & Redman's *Law of Landlord and Tenant* para [2581]).

11 See para 7.3 above.

12 See 22 Encyclopaedia of Forms and Precedents (5th edn) Form 22 clause 5.9:2, Rosscastle Letting Conditions (Appendix 1, Form 1 below) Condition 3.7:2.

13 See para 7.5 above.

14 See ibid Form 22 clause 5.9:3 and ibid Condition 3.7:3. It is possible, though unlikely, that this practice will change as a result of the additional burdens placed on the landlord in the case of fully qualified prohibitions by the Landlord and Tenant Act 1988 (see para 7.6 above): see the Law Commission Report to which the draft bill was annexed ((1987) Law Com No 161 para 1.4): 'In that Report . . .' (Report on Covenants Restricting Dispositions Alterations and Change of User: (1985) Law Com No 141) '. . . we suggested that implementation of this recommendation might make fully qualified covenants slightly less attractive to landlords and might lead to some movement towards absolute covenants if they were to remain valid. However we believe that the risk is small because absolute covenants against dispositions are not generally acceptable to tenants, and we doubt whether it would be possible for many landlords to impose such covenants. If we are wrong in this and there is any move towards absolute covenants, this would be an additional reason for the remainder of our Report to be implemented.'

15 It is in this way that the landlord will deal with any particular concerns which he may have (see, for example, those mentioned in para 7.1:1 above). For the validity of any such requirement in the case of a fully qualified prohibition, see para 7.5 note 20 above.

16 See 22 Encyclopaedia of Forms and Precedents (5th edn) Form 22 clause 5.9:4, Rosscastle Letting Conditions (Appendix 1, Form 1 below) Condition 3.7:4. As to whether or not, in the absence of an express requirement, this would be a fine for the purposes of s 144 of the Law of Property Act, see para 7.2:3 above and, in particular, note 6 and, as to whether or not, in the case of a fully qualified prohibition, the courts would consider it unreasonable for a landlord to require such a covenant as a condition to the granting of his consent, see *Evans v Levy* [1910] 1 Ch 452 and *Balfour v Kensington Gardens Mansions Ltd* (1932) 49 TLR 29. Although it would usually seem reasonable for a tenant to resist the insertion of such a requirement, it is very rare for a landlord to encounter any objection to it.

17 In the absence of any contractual obligation, an assignee will be liable, by virtue of privity of estate, only for breaches of covenants touching and concerning the land. On the other hand, it may well be that other, personal, covenants should not bind an assignee.

18 In the absence of any contractual obligation, an assignee will be liable, by virtue of privity of estate, only for breaches which are committed during his interest in the premises. An assignee bound only by privity of estate can, therefore, avoid future liability under the lease by assignment to a pauper. On the other hand, this is unlikely to be of concern nowadays, because the lease will almost invariably provide that the landlord's consent is required to any assignment. If a direct covenant is given, it is effective to render the assignee liable following assignment, even though a number of subsequent assignees also give such covenants (see *J Lyons & Co Ltd v Knowles* [1943] 1 KB 366, [1943] 1 All ER 477, CA).

19 See 22 Encyclopaedia of Forms and Precedents (5th edn) Form 22 clause 5.9:5, Rosscastle Letting Conditions (Appendix 1, Form 1 below) Condition 3.7:5. In the case of a fully qualified prohibition, the tenant will usually attempt to resist such an additional requirement, arguing that whether or not guarantees are given should be determined in accordance with the 'reasonableness test' (see para 7.5 above) when the circumstances of a particular assignment are known. If it is accepted, the tenant should ensure that the landlord is only allowed to require guarantees if and to the extent reasonable. The lease should not

specify that guarantees should be given by directors – in many cases, the directors of a company may simply be, in effect, employees of the company, in which case it might be more appropriate for a guarantee to be given by a parent company or principal shareholder. The parties should also give thought to the form of guarantee which may be required, to avoid future dispute. Is it to subsist beyond further assignment? Is it to relate simply to the rent and covenants, or is it, for example, to place an obligation on the guarantor to take a new lease on forfeiture, or to apply for a vesting order on disclaimer? Sometimes, the parties consider it wise to include an agreed form of guarantee in the lease to avoid future dispute, although others prefer to leave the matter more open, on the grounds that it will depend on the circumstances of the particular assignment. Landlords should bear in mind that the form of guarantees required by landlords has developed, with developments in the law, substantially in recent years and may continue to do so.

20   See note 1 above.

21   See para 7.1:4 above.

22   See note 13 above.

23   See 22 Encyclopaedia of Forms and Precedents (5th edn) Form 22 clause 5.9:3, Rosscastle Letting Conditions (Appendix 1, Form 1 below) Condition 3.7:3.

24   See para 7.7:3 below.

25   It is in this way that the landlord will deal not only with the general concerns discussed below, but also any particular concerns which he might have (see para 7.1:2 above). For the validity of such requirements in the case of a lease containing a fully qualified prohibition against underletting, see para 7.5 above.

26   See para 7.1:2 above.

27   For a discussion of the ways in which this might happen, see para 7.1:2 note 17 above.

28   This is only likely to happen if the subtenant successfully applies for a new lease under the Landlord and Tenant Act 1954 and the tenant fails to do so.

29   See notes 27 and 28 above.

30   See para 7.7:3.5, and in particular note 19, above.

31   Save in respect of direct covenants, if appropriate: see para 7.7:3(e) below.

32   The existence of an underlease at a low rent may adversely affect the landlord in the following circumstances: (a) On rent review: if the existence of an underlease at a low rent is taken into account it will reduce the revised rent (see para 6.19:1 above). Even if it is disregarded it may be put forward as a comparable (see para 6.42 above), both on a rent review under the lease and under leases of other properties belonging to the landlord. (b) On any future sale mortgage or letting: a prospective purchaser or mortgagee of the premises may consider the underlease rent evidence of the market value of the premises and assume that the tenant is paying 'over the odds'. It may also be regarded as a comparable by intending tenants of other premises belonging to the landlord. (c) If the headlease rent is in arrears: the landlord may be unable to recover the full amount of arrears under the Law of Distress Amendment Act 1908. (d) If the tenant drops out of the picture (for the various ways in which this might happen, see para 7.1:2 note 17 above): the only likely reason why the landlord should be adversely affected by a low underlease rent if the tenant drops out of the picture is if the undertenant's tenancy continues by virtue of the Landlord and Tenant Act 1954 and the tenant's does not, because in assessing any interim rent to be awarded pursuant to s 24A of the Act the court is to have regard (inter alia) to the rent payable under the current tenancy (and see *Charles Follett Ltd v Cabtell Investments Co Ltd* [1987] 2 EGLR 88, CA). For a discussion of some of these disadvantages, and of whether or not the landlord would be reasonable, in the case of a fully qualified prohibition against underletting, in refusing consent to an underletting at a rent below the market value, or below the rent payable under the lease, see *Re Town Investments Ltd Underlease, McLaughlin v Town Investments Ltd* [1954] Ch 301, [1954] 1 All ER 585; *Balfour v Kensington Gardens Mansions Ltd* (1932) 49 TLR 29.

33   See 22 Encyclopaedia of Forms and Precedents (5th edn) Form 22 clause 5.9:6, Rosscastle Letting Conditions (Appendix 1, Form 1 below) Condition 3.7:6. In order to preserve the position after the grant of the lease, the lease often contains requirements relating to the drafting of the rent review clause (see para 7.7:3.4 below), and also the operation of that clause (see Form 22 clause 5.9:9, Rosscastle Condition 3.7:9).

34   The tenant may also have carried out improvements, or built up goodwill.

35   For example, provided that the underlease is disregarded on rent review, that the tenant and subtenant provide a document declaring that the rent is below the market rent and explaining why and, perhaps, that the lease is excluded from the protection of the Landlord and Tenant Act 1954. See note 32 above.

36   Tenants may find themselves paying a higher rent than the market rent between review dates if market rents fall, and even after a subsequent review if, as is usual, the lease contains an upwards-only rent review clause. They may also find themselves paying such a rent if the rent review clause is drafted so as to remove the hypothetical letting from reality. Most tenants would consider it 'adding insult to injury' if in such circumstances they are unable to underlet the whole of the premises at the market rent.

37 See para 7.1:2 above.

38 There may be restrictions binding on the landlord, either in a superior lease or in a separate contract, breach of which by a tenant, subtenant or subundertenant will render the landlord liable. The landlord will inevitably ensure that he is able to prevent, and that he does not suffer loss as a result of the tenant's breach by including similar restrictions, or an obligation on the part of the tenant to comply with such restrictions, in the lease, together with an indemnity in the event of breach. He will also, however, want to ensure that he is able to prevent, and does not suffer any loss as a result of, breach by any subtenant. There may be other restrictions which the landlord has imposed on the tenant in the lease, for estate management or other reasons, with which he would also like any subtenant or subundertenant to comply. As a general rule, a subtenant is under no obligation to comply with covenants binding on the landlord or tenant, even the covenants on the part of the tenant in the lease. Certain restrictions might be binding on him, and enforceable by injuction, in accordance with the equitable rules relating to restrictive covenants (see Megarry & Wade: *Law of Real Property* pp 741, 770 et seq), but it should be remembered that (a) these rules are limited and, in particular, that a subtenant only has constructive notice of his own landlord's lease, and that an assignee of the subtenant and a subundertenant will not even have notice of that lease (see s 44 of the Law of Property Act 1925) and (b) that some restrictions in the lease may be drafted in such a way that they are only breached by acts of the tenant, and will not therefore be breached by acts of a subtenant or subundertenant, even if they would otherwise be bound by them. In some cases, even if a subtenant or subundertenant is not bound by a restriction, breach by them will constitute a breach of the lease, with the result that the landlord may be able to obtain damages from the tenant or enforce compliance by forfeiture, but this will depend on the drafting of the restriction in the lease: again, it may be drafted in such a way that it is only breached by the acts of the tenant, in which case the landlord will have no recourse. As a result, it is essential for the landlord that such restrictions are dealt with in any underlease or subunderlease. As common law, the tenant is under no obligation to impose in a sublease covenants as strict as those in the lease (*Prothero v Bell* (1906) 22 TLR 370) and it seems that even if he is under an obligation not to permit any particular act, matter or thing, failure to insert an appropriate restriction in an underlease may not constitute a breach. Accordingly, the landlord should ensure that the tenant is under an obligation to insert in any underlease, and to procure that there is inserted in any subunderlease, an obligation on the part of the undertenant or subundertenant to comply with all such restrictions, together with an indemnity in favour of the landlord, where appropriate. Another point which the landlord should bear in mind, is that the tenant might drop out of the picture (see para 7.1:2 note 17 above for the ways in which this could occur) and, in certain circumstances, he could become the subtenant's immediate landlord on the terms of the underlease. This would happen where the tenancy created by the underlease continued by virtue of the 1954 Act, (see Chapter 14) but the tenancy created by the lease determined. Whilst such a situation would only subsist for a limited period, if the undertenant successfully applied for a new lease under the 1954 Act, the new lease would be granted by the landlord and, under s 35 of the 1954 Act, (see paras 14.56–14.60 below) the court is to have regard to the terms of the existing tenancy in determining the terms of any new tenancy. For this reason the landlord will want to be sure that the lessor's covenants in any underlease are no more onerous, and the lessee's covenants no less onerous, than those in the lease. As mentioned above, the tenant is under no obligation to ensure that this is the case at common law, and the lease should accordingly contain such an obligation.

39 See *Williamson v Williamson* (1874) 9 Ch App 729: this allows the tenant to use the provisions of the headlease as models and to make proper alterations of names and other matters. Whilst it is advisable for the provisions of the underlease to be based on those of the lease, this formula is not, however, adequate alone. For example, if the lease contains a prohibition against assigning without the consent of the landlord, the landlord will want any underlease to contain a prohibition against assigning without the consent not only of the lessor, but also the superior lessor. Leases, especially complex modern leases, will require more than formal amendments to result in an underlease which effectively protects the landlord. Such a formula will also not require the tenant to make changes to accommodate developments in the law or drafting practice, or, for example, to impose more restrictive alienation provisions than in the lease (see note 40 below).

40 Such as those relating to restrictions and indemnities (see note 38 above), alienation and rent review. Most landlords will want the alienation provisions of any underlease to be more restrictive than those in the headlease. For example, a landlord may be happy to allow the tenant to underlet, but may not be prepared to allow any further underletting (see para 7.1:2

above and 22 Encyclopaedia of Forms and Precedents (5th edn) Form 22 clause 5.9:6.4, Rosscastle Letting Conditions (Appendix 1, Form 1 below) Condition 3.7:6.3). In addition, most landlords will want any underlease to provide for the rent to be reviewed at similar intervals, and on similar terms, as the rent under the headlease (see EPP Form 22 clause 5.9:6.1, Rosscastle Condition 3.7:6.3). The landlord would, however, be unwise to leave the remaining terms of the underlease to the tenant's discretion, unless it is to be excluded from the protection of the 1954 Act (see note 38 above).

41 Such a covenant is traditionally included in underleases, but is not very satisfactory from the point of view of landlord, tenant or undertenant, as there may be many clauses in the lease to which it should not apply and, in the case of a relatively complex modern lease, it is likely in any event to cause uncertainty and difficulties of interpretation: see EFP Form 144, footnote 11.

42 Although it is time-consuming, the only way in which a landlord can ensure that an underlease is drafted in such a way as to protect his position is to approve the draft. It is unwise, however, for the lease to give the tenant no guidance on the terms which are to be included, as this is likely to cause delay and dispute.

43 See notes 39–42 above.

44 For example, provided that the landlord is protected in against breaches of restrictions, that further underletting is absolutely prohibited, and that the lease is excluded from the protection of the 1954 Act (see note 38 above).

45 As mentioned above (see note 38), the landlord may bring an injunction against the subtenant for breach of a restriction which is binding on him in equity, and may bring forfeiture proceedings against the tenant if the subtenant's acts or omissions constitute a breach of the lease, which will also bring the sublease to an end subject to the subtenant's right to relief. In addition, the landlord may distrain against the sub-tenant for non-payment of rent due under the lease subject to the operation of the Law of Distress Amendment Act 1908. It seems that, depending on the drafting of the relevant clause, a landlord may be able to enforce covenants in the underlease, which were inserted for his benefit and at his stipulation, by virtue of s 56 of the Law of Property Act 1925 (see *Drive Yourself Hire Co (London) Ltd v Strutt* [1954] 1 QB 250, [1953] 2 All ER 1475, CA; *Beswick v Beswick* [1968] AC 58, [1967] 2 All ER 1197, HL; *White v Bijou Mansions Ltd* [1938] Ch 351, [1938] 1 All ER 546, CA).

46 Landlords sometimes require a covenant from the undertenant to comply with the covenants in the lease, so far as they relate to the underlet premises. There are the same arguments against such a covenant as against a covenant to the same effect given to the tenant in the underlease (see note 41 above). Although it is more time-consuming, it is more satisfactory for both landlord and undertenant if the landlord ensures that the underlease is correctly drafted and obtains a covenant from the undertenant in respect of the underlease covenants. On the question of whether or not, in the case of a fully qualified prohibition against underletting, a requirement that an undertenant should give direct covenants is reasonable, see *Balfour v Kensington Gardens Mansions Ltd* (1932) 49 TLR 29.

47 See 22 Encyclopaedia of Forms and Precedents (5th edn) Form 22 clause 5.9:8, Rosscastle Letting Conditions (Appendix 1, Form 1 below) Condition 3.7:8. Such obligations may be implied: see *Drive Yourself Hire Co (London) Ltd v Strutt*, above, but the landlord should insert them in any event.

48 See para 7.7:1 above.

49 See para 7.7:1 note 1 above.

50 See para 7.3 above.

51 See 22 Encyclopaedia of Forms and Precedents (5th edn) Form 22 clause 5.9:1, Rosscastle Letting Conditions (Appendix 1, Form 1 below) Condition 3.7:1.

52 See EFP Form 22 clause 5.9:11.

53 See EFP clause 5.9:2, Rosscastle Condition 3.7:2.

54 See para 7.5 above.

55 See EFP clause 5.9:3, Rosscastle Condition 3.7:3.

56 Lenders frequently take a floating charge over the assets of a company, which will include the premises. In many cases, the premises are an important part of the security because, although they may not be valuable in themselves, a purchaser would not be prepared to buy the other assets of the company, or pay as much, if he were unable to continue to operate from the premises.

57 See EFP Form 22 clause 5.9:10, Rosscastle Condition 3.7:10. Despite the existence of such an obligation in the lease, landlords frequently have difficulty in procuring compliance. As a result, some landlords attempt to insert provisions, in the lease or in the relevant licence, rendering consent to the relevant dealing void in the event of non-registration within a certain period. The effect of such provisions is dubious but, in any event, it must be said that they provide a cure worse than the disease and should not be accepted by the tenant.

58 An obligation to produce the original could interfere with stamping and registration at HM Land Registry and give rise to the risk of loss.

59 See 22 Encyclopaedia of Forms and Precedents (5th edn) Form 74. Such a provision is an estate contract and will not bind a successor in title to the original tenant unless registered under the Land Charges Act 1972 s 2(4) (37 Halsbury's Statutes (4th edn) REAL PROPERTY) as a land charge class C (iv) (*Greene v Church Comrs for England* [1974] Ch 467, [1974] 3 All ER 609, CA) or (where the tenant's interest is registered at HM Land Registry) unless a notice, restriction or caution has been registered. See *Adler v Upper Grosvenor Street Investment Ltd* [1957] 1 All ER 229, [1957] 1 WLR 227; *Bocardo SA v S & M Hotels Ltd* [1979] 3 All ER 737, [1980] 1 WLR 17, CA (neither case decided under the 1954 Act).

60 Ie where the tenancy is subject to the 1954 Act (ss 23–46): *Joseph v Joseph* [1967] Ch 78, [1966] 3 All ER 486, CA and see *Allnatt London Properties Ltd v Newton* [1981] 2 All ER 290; affd [1984] 1 All ER 423, CA where the tenant offered to surrender in accordance with the clause and the landlord subsequently accepted the offer, but the tenant then withdrew his offer. It was held that as the agreement to surrender, if carried out, would preclude the tenant from applying at the end of his tenancy for a new tenancy under the Landlord and Tenant Act 1954 Pt II (ss 23–46), the agreement was void under ibid s 38(1) and the landlord could not therefore enforce the agreement. Nevertheless to guard against the mischief envisaged by ibid s 38(1) it was sufficient for only the actual agreement to surrender to be struck down as void. The clause remained valid, and the tenant was still required to offer to surrender the lease before he could obtain the landlord's consent to an assignment. It seems therefore that the tenant can either remain as tenant or dispose of its lease by completing the surrender, assuming the landlord accepts the surrender. Suggestions have been made by landlords in an attempt to make the agreement to surrender enforceable eg providing that the surrender-back clause will operate only when the tenant is not occupying the demised premises for the purposes of its business. This would presumably be effective where a business tenant had ceased to occupy premises but see *Morrison Holdings Ltd v Manders Property (Wolverhampton) Ltd* [1976] 2 All ER 205, [1976] 1 WLR 533, CA, but it is submitted that one could not be confident that a tenant who served such a notice while in occupation would be estopped from subsequently taking the point. In any case (assuming the lease permitted assignment with consent where the landlord did not take up the offer of surrender) a tenant in occupation could point out to the landlord that it was in occupation and therefore the surrender-back clause did not apply and then apply for a licence. Another suggestion is that the provision refers, not to surrender, but to assignment of the lease to the landlord or its nominee. This, it is argued, neither precludes the tenant from making an application under the 1954 Act (ss 23–46) nor provides for the termination or surrender of a tenancy in the event of such an application being made. It is submitted that there are all too many examples of courts looking at substance rather than form to be confident that this approach would succeed. For a further method see 22 Encyclopaedia of Forms and Precedents (5th edn) Form 75.

61 In so far as these comments apply to tenancies generally it should be noted that the Rent Act 1977 s 120 (23 Halsbury's Statutes (4th edn) LANDLORD AND TENANT) prohibits the charging of a premium in relation to the granting or assigning of a tenancy to which that Act applies. A premium may also be payable where the current rent has been determined (on a rent review or on a renewal under the Landlord and Tenant Act 1954 Pt II (ss 23–46) (23 Halsbury's Statutes (4th edn) LANDLORD AND TENANT)) on the basis that improvements should be disregarded when they would be regarded in determining the rent on an open market letting.

62 See *Plinth Property Investments Ltd v Mott, Hay and Anderson* (1978) 249 Estates Gazette 1167, CA.

B USER

7.8 *Introduction.* Leases generally contain provisions, in the form of covenants on the part of the tenant, which specifically limit the purposes for which the premises can be used.[1] Such covenants are usually contained in what is referred to as the 'user clause'. It is not only the user clause, however, which restricts the use of the premises and, as the nature and variety of the purposes for which the premises can be used can have a substantial effect on the interests of both the landlord and tenant, the parties and their advisors should give *all* matters affeccting the use to which the premises can be put considerable thought.

1   See 22 Encyclopaedia of Forms and Precedents (5th edn) Form 22 Third Schedule para 2.1, Rosscastle Letting Conditions (Appendix 1, Form 1 below) Conditions 3.8 and 3.9. As to the discharge and modification of restrictions of use, see Woodfall, para 1–1225; *Hill & Redman* p A587 para A [1328].

7.9   *Unavoidable limitations.* Unavoidable limitations on the use to which the premises can be put may already exist. That use may be restricted by legislation,[1] by the common law,[2] by restrictions affecting the freehold or a superior leasehold interest, or by other obligations binding on the landlord.[3] As a practical matter, the physical nature of the premises,[4] and their location, may limit the range of uses to which they can be put. These unavoidable limitations are relevant to the landlord for several reasons. He should check that, in the light of these limitations and the prospective tenant's proposed user, the prospective tenant is suitable. He should ensure that certain of these unavoidable limitations are reflected in general covenants on the part of the tenant in the lease.[5] Thus, the prudent landlord will want the lease to contain a general covenant from the tenant to comply with legislation, and perhaps further covenants requiring compliance with particular legislation,[6] together with covenants not to use the premises for any illegal or unlawful purpose,[7] or in such a way as to cause a nuisance.[8] He should also ensure that all obligations binding on him are disclosed to the tenant prior to any agreement for lease,[9] and that the lease contains covenants on the part of the tenant in respect of them. Finally, the landlord should bear in mind that these limitations already exist when considering what, if any,[10] further restrictions on use should be included in the lease. These unavoidable limitations are relevant to the tenant in two ways. He must check that, in the light of them, and his proposed use and general concerns about user, the premises are suitable. Secondly, he, just as much as the landlord, should bear in mind that these limitations already exist when considering what, if any, further limitations on use should be included in the lease.

1   That legislation which is most obviously relevant is planning legislation, which may affect the use to which the premises can be put not only directly, but also indirectly, by regulating the tenant's ability to adapt the premises physically to a particular use.
2   An obvious aspect of the common law which might affect the use of the premises is the law relating to nuisance. It is frequently thought that this might only affect the manner in which a use is conducted from the premises, but it can also affect the purpose for which the premises are used – see *Harris v James* (1876) 35 LT 240; *Winter v Baker* (1887) 3 TLR 569; *Jenkins v Jackson* (1888) 40 Ch D 71; *Tetley v Chitty* [1986] 1 All ER 663. It may also affect user by restricting the tenant's ability to carry out works of physical adaptation.
3   The landlord may be under an obligation to other tenants, such as an obligation not to let nearby premises for a competing user – see, for example, *A Lewis & Co (Westminster) Ltd v Bell Property Trust* [1940] Ch 345, [1940] 1 All ER 570; *Labone v Litherland UDC* [1956] 2 All ER 215, [1956] 1 WLR 522; *Connswater Properties Ltd v Wilson* (1986) 16 CSW 928 – although generally there is no implied obligation on the part of the landlord not to grant leases to competitors, nor will doing such a thing render the landlord in derogation from grant (*Port v Griffith* [1938] 1 All ER 295). See also para 7.18:2 below and paras 9.4–9.6 below.
4   And their potential for adaptation. See also notes 1 and 2 above and para 7.18:1 below.
5   This is because (a) Not all obligations binding on the landlord will be binding on the tenant without express provision (as to those which will, see Megarry and Wade *The Law of Real Property* (5th edn) pp 724–727; for an example of those which will not, see note 3 above), and yet breach by the tenant may render the landlord liable. (b) Even if the tenant is bound by unavoidable limitations, the fact that he is liable under statute (or to a third party) for breach will not give the landlord rights and yet, as he may be adversely affected by breach, the landlord will want to be in a position either to prevent the implementation or continuance of the use by injunction or forfeiture, or to claim damages from the tenant for loss suffered. As well as a potential liability in contract, the landlord may be adversely affected because he may be placed under obligations, and incur liability, as a result of the tenant's breach of

legislation; acts of the tenant constituting a nuisance may render the landlord liable for nuisance, and/or in breach of a covenant for quiet enjoyment and/or in derogation from grant in relation to leases of other property in the vicinity (*Hilton v James Smith & Sons (Norwood) Ltd* (1979) 251 Estates Gazette 1063, CA; *Sampson v Hodson-Pressinger* [1981] 3 All ER 710, CA); the value of the premises might be adversely affected because a licence for a profitable use is lost by the tenant's breach (see para 7.11 below); or the value of the landlord's adjoining premises may be reduced by the tenant's nuisance. (c) The insertion of such covenants might assist in preventing the lease from being held to be void and/or unenforceable because entered into for an illegal purpose (see *Best v Glenville* [1960] 3 All ER 478, [1960] 1 WLR 1198, CA), and was of assistance in preventing the landlord from being held liable for the tenant's nuisance in *Smith v Scott* [1973] Ch 314, [1972] 3 All ER 645, and (d) Failure to insert covenants in respect of obligations binding on the landlord might constitute breach of an obligation by the landlord to a third party not to permit a particular use (see para 17.15 note 3 below).

6   See 22 Encyclopaedia of Forms and Precedents (5th edn) Form 22 clauses 5.7 and 5.12, Rosscastle Letting Conditions (Appendix 1, Form 1 below) Conditions 3.11 and 3.13.

7   See 22 Encyclopaedia of Forms and Precedents (5th edn) Form 22 clause 5.10.2, Rosscastle Letting Conditions (Appendix 1, Form 1 below) Condition 3.8:4. A covenant against illegal user is also implied.

8   See 22 Encyclopaedia of Forms and Precedents (5th edn) Form 22 clause 5.10.1, Rosscastle Letting Conditions (Appendix 1, Form 1 below) Condition 3.8:3. In a lease, the word 'nuisance' probably bears its technical meaning (*Walter v Selfe* (1851) 4 De G & Sm 315; *Harrison v Good* (1871) LR 11 Eq 338). Such a covenant does not import any implied term that the landlord will enforce similar covenants against other tenants (*O'Leary v London Borough of Islington* (1983) 9 HLR 83) because the tenant has his own remedies in tort, but see note 5 above.

9   The discovery of undisclosed onerous covenants will entitle the tenant to withdraw from the transaction and the landlord will be unable to obtain specific performance of the contract (*Darlington v Hamilton* (1854) Kay 550).

10 Sometimes the landlord is prepared for the premises to be used for *any* purpose for which planning permission is obtained (or in respect of which planning permission is not needed), although the landlord also needs to be sure that the premises are not used in breach of other unavoidable limitations (see para 7.9 above). In such a case, there is no need for the lease to contain a user clause at all, provided that the usual general covenants (ie those referred to in para 7.9 above and, possibly, those referred to in para 7.18:1) are included. The landlord should bear in mind that planning, like other legislation, may change, rendering the permitted user far wider than originally envisaged. See also para 7.14:1 below.

7.10   *The tenant's concerns*. In assessing the suitability of the premises, and what (if any) further limitations on use should be included in the lease, the tenant will generally have three main concerns:

7.10:1   *Accommodate business needs*. The tenant's first consideration will be the property needs of his business. In addition to ensuring that the premises can be used for the purposes for which he is *initially* proposing to use them, he should also take into account the possible future expansion and development of his business. For example, a factory tenant would want to be free to vary the products manufactured, while a retailer should recognise that he may want to extend the range of goods which he sells. The nature of the tenant's business may also change because of commercial demands[1] or technological advances.[2] Particularly if the lease is for a relatively long term, or if the tenant considers it possible that he may apply for a new lease[3] at the end of a short term, the tenant will want to be in a position to use the premises for any use that he might reasonably require without having to seek the landlord's consent.

7.10:2   *Disposal*. The tenant must recognise that he may want to dispose of the lease in the future, for example because the expansion or development of his business renders the premises physically unsuitable for his use, because it becomes preferable to operate from a different area, or because his business contracts. If he is unable to dispose of the lease quickly and easily, his business may be prejudiced. Generally, it can be said that the wider the nature of use and/or range of uses to which the premises can be put, the easier it will be to find a suitable assignee. Again, therefore, the tenant will be concerned to ensure, if possible, that the user restrictions are not so narrow that he will be saddled with an expensive white elephant in the future.

7.10:3 *Rent review implications.* The above concerns might lead the tenant to believe that it is in his interests for the user provisions in the lease to be as wide as possible. There is, however, a conflicting concern. The greater the flexibility of use attaching to premises, the more attractive they will be to tenants because this will enable them to accommodate changes in their business and make the premises easier to assign. They will also be more desirable to a greater number of tenants, some of whom may want to use the premises for a more profitable use than that to which the tenant puts them. This means that premises let subject to a wide user covenant will generally command a higher rent both initially, on rent review[4] and under any new lease granted in the determination of the lease pursuant to the 1954 Act.[5] Indeed it is sometimes said that nowadays it is the tenant, and not the landlord, who attempts to obtain narrow user provisions in a lease, in the hope that these will result in his having to pay a lower rent on rent review or lease renewal. The tenant should certainly bear this concern in mind, but it would be unwise to take it too far. There may be occasional situations in which the tenant is not affected by the points mentioned above,[6] with the result that he will sensibly attempt to obtain the most restrictive user provisions he can, but these will be rare. The tenant should generally balance the conflicting considerations, by attempting to obtain a lease which gives him sufficient flexibility in respect of use as he needs, but no more, and in particular try to ensure that the premises could not be used for a use that is unnecessary from his point of view and that would commend a higher rent.[7] Even if this is of no consequence initially, because the rent has been agreed on the basis of the tenant's actual user, the rent subsequently payable on a rent review or lease renewal could be increased because the rent here will generally be that obtainable from a hypothetical tenant proposing to use the premises for the highest rental-producing use available.[7] The worst position of all for the tenant is a narrow user clause in the actual lease, and a broad one in the hypothetical lease.[8] This can be achieved by assuming that the hypothetical lease contains a wide clause,[9] or by directing that actual restrictions on the user be disregarded.[10] The tenant's advisers should strive to prevent their client being forced to accept such a position.

1   Words used in a covenant are construed in the sense that they were used at the time – see the examples given by Stephen Tromans in 'Commercial leases: what's the use?' Law Society's Gazette 84 (22) p 1725 at 1727. See also *St Marylebone Property Co Ltd v Tesco Stores Ltd* [1988] 2 EGLR 40, [1988] 27 EG 72 in which the lease which was the subject of the court's consideration was granted in the 1950s, and permitted user for the trade or business 'of grocers provisions wine spirit and beer merchants'. It was accepted by the court that, since the date the lease was granted, food retailing had changed, with modern retailers of grocery products also selling a wide range of non-food items. Hoffmann J was satisfied that the trade of the traditional grocer was virtually obsolete, but nonetheless held that the covenant had to be construed as permitting user for that purpose only. As has been pointed out (Legal Notes [1988] 30 Estates Gazette 63) a use which is quite commonplace today may have disappeared tomorrow.

2 Consider, for example, the current development of some businesses towards the new 'high-tech' uses, for a discussion of which see Robert Bushnell 'High-technology building requirements: a user view' (1985) 273 Estates Gazette 836 and, for a working example of the way in which a new type of use may, or may not, be accommodated by existing leases, Tony Jorden and Jane Rigler: 'Rent Reviews: B1 and hi-tech buildings' (1988) 20 Estates Gazette 20.

3 As to the tenant's rights to a new lease generally, see Chapter 14. As a general rule, the user provisions of the new lease will reflect those of the existing lease, although the court has a discretion and may order different terms if that would be fair – see para 14.52 below.

4 As to rent review generally, see Chapter 6. Rent review clauses usually provide for the revised rent to be assessed on the basis of a hypothetical letting of the premises on the same terms as the lease itself, and otherwise in accordance with reality, with the result that the terms of the lease, including the user provisions, may have a substantial effect on the revised rent – see para 6.18:3(a) and the cases referred to in para 7.16:1 notes 4 & 10 and para 7.17 notes 3, 4, 8 and 9 below.

5 See note 3 above and the cases referred to in note 7 and para 14.52 below.

6 See paras 7.14:2 and 7.16:3 below and, for an example of this problem on rent review, see Stephen Tromans 'Commercial-leases and the new use classes order: part 2' Law Society's Gazette 14 13 April 1988 p 35 at 37 and the article by Tony Jorden and Jane Rigler referred to in note 2 above.

7 See *Aldwych Club Ltd v Copthall Property Co Ltd* (1962) 185 Estates Gazette 219; *Giannoukakis v Saltfleet Ltd* [1988] 1 EGLR 73, [1988] 17 EG 121 and para 14.52 below.

8 Rent review: see para 6.17:1 above.

9 See para 6.18:3 above.

10 See para 6.30 above.

7.11 *The landlord's concerns.* There are many reasons why a landlord may be concerned to limit the use to which premises can be put. For example, it may be that a particular company landlord is only empowered to invest in particular types of property, or in a variety of different types of property in particular proportions, or that an individual landlord has conscientious objections to owning property used to perpetuate certain businesses. Generally, however, the landlord will be influenced mainly by economic considerations. He will want to ensure that the use to which the premises are put produces the maximum profit for him, both from the premises themselves and other premises which he may own in the vicinity. Accordingly, in deciding what (if any) further restrictions on use should be included in the lease, the landlord has three main concerns:

7.11:1 *Prevent adverse effect on value.* Unless the landlord controls the use to which the premises are put, they may be used for a purpose which adversely affects their value. For example, the value of the premises may depend largely on the existence of planning permission for a profitable use,[1] or on goodwill which has been built up by previous occupiers. The landlord will want to be sure that he is able to veto any proposed change of use[2] which might result in the loss of such valuable attributes,[3] and which might accordingly reduce the rent obtainable on rent review,[4] on lease renewal,[5] or when he re-lets the premises after the existing tenant vacates. Similarly, the landlord may want to be able to prevent use of the premises in such a way as to give the tenant or a subtenant security of tenure, or which might make the whole or part of the premises subject to statutory rent control.[6]

7.11:2 *Near-by property.* If the landlord has other property in the vicinity his desire for control may be greater, as the use to which the premises are put could adversely affect the value of that other property as well as the value of the premises themselves. For example, the use of the premises may conflict with the use of adjoining premises (as would, for example, a butcher's shop adjacent to a vegetarian restaurant), or may compete with it.[7] It may be advisable for all parts of a building to be put to similar office use, or for all premises in a particular area to be used as shops. In a shopping centre, it may be advisable to preserve a 'good mix' of uses.[8]

7.11:3 *Rent review.* Were it not for the implications on rent, a landlord might decide to impose in all his leases the most restrictive user provisions possible, thus giving himself the right to consider at his leisure, and accept or reject in his absolute discretion, any request which the tenant might make in the future for permission to change the use. The landlord has, however, the same conflicts as the tenant – premises available for a wide user, or for a wide range of uses, will generally command a higher rent and, conversely, premises affected by tight restrictions on user will generally command a lower rent initially, on rent review and on lease renewal.[9] Furthermore, changes in commercial demand, and thus the market, or in the area in which the premises are situated, may render a once profitable use less profitable, or even virtually obsolete,[10] or may render profitable a previously unprofitable or unknown use for which the premises are ideally suited.[11] The landlord has to weigh up these competing considerations, and will have to be sure that the benefit which he will obtain from particular restrictions on user will justify any rental diminution which may result.

1 A similar point may arise with regard to a gaming, liquor, or other similar licence for a profitable use.
2 Or that he is able to obtain compensation as a condition of giving consent. Even if the user covenant is qualified, s 19(3) of the Landlord and Tenant Act 1927 (see para 7.16:2 below) does not preclude the landlord from requiring a reasonable sum in respect of any damage to or diminution in the value of the premises or of any neighbouring premises which belong to him.
3 If premises have planning permission, or a special licence, for a particular use, and the use is changed, it may be impossible to re-implement the previous use without a new licence or further planning permission. The fact that premises have previously had the benefit of a licence or planning permission does not necessarily mean that it will be granted again.
4 On rent review, the revised rent is usually assessed on the basis of a hypothetical letting corresponding with reality (see paras 6.1, 6.2, 6.17:1 and 6.18:3 above) and accordingly, if no licence or planning permission for a particular use is in existence, none will be assumed. The valuer must exclude from consideration the possibility of future illegal use although he can take into account the 'hope' value of obtaining planning permission (see *Compton Group Ltd v Estates Gazette Ltd* (1977) 244 Estates Gazette 799, CA; *Sixth Centre Ltd v Guildville Ltd; Badouraly Jeanamod-Karim v Guildville Ltd* [1988] NPC 33). It would be possible for the landlord to avoid this disadvantage if he was able to ask for an amendment to the rent review clause as a condition of the granting of his consent to the change of use, as he could then insert an appropriate assumption in the clause (see para 6.17:1 *Bovis Group Pension Fund Ltd v G C Flooring & Furnishing Ltd* (1984) 269 Estates Gazette 1252, CA; *Daejan Investments Ltd v Cornwall Coast Country Club* [1985] 1 EGLR 7; *Ritz Hotel (London) Ltd v Ritz Casino Ltd* [1988] EGCS 142). Care should be taken when drafting assumptions removing the hypothetical letting from reality – see para 6.17:1.
5 The rent awarded on lease renewal will reflect reality (see para 14.50, *Cardshops Ltd v Davies* [1971] 2 All ER 721, [1971] 1 WLR 591), and it is not possible to alter this by assumptions in the lease.
6 The most obvious example is a covenant in a business lease which prevents residential use (see 22 Encyclopaedia of Forms and Precedents (5th edn) Form 22 clause 5.10:3, Rosscastle Letting Conditions (Appendix 1, Form 1 below) Condition 3.8:2) so as to avoid the application of the Rent Acts. The recent case of *Deverall v Wyndham* [1988] NPC 58, from which it appears that a landlord will not always be reasonable in refusing consent to a subletting on the grounds that the subtenant would be entitled to Rent Act protection, will

render landlords more anxious to ensure that such a covenant is included in the user clause. Sometimes the user clauses of business leases are carefully drafted to correspond with the exceptions set out in s 43 of the Landlord and Tenant Act 1954 in the hope of excluding the protection of that Act from the tenancy. This is unobjectionable, but will have no effect if a sham.

7 For example, see *Atwal v Court Garages* [1989] 07 EG 78, CA, discussed [1989] 10 EG 119.
8 Indeed, it is in leases of retail shops that one most frequently finds tighter user clauses contrary to the modern trend (see para 7.11:3 below), because of the landlord's desire to maintain a balance in a centre or parade.
9 Para 7.10:3 above.
10 See para 7.10 note 1 above.
11 See para 7.10 note 2 above.

7.12 *Key questions.* If as usual the parties decide that there should be specific restrictions on the user of the premises in addition to those limitations that already exist,[1] there are then five questions that they need to consider:
(a) should the uses that are permitted be defined, perhaps in conjunction with uses that are prohibited?[2]
(b) should the user clause make reference to the Use Classes Order?[3]
(c) is the obligation to be positive or negative?[4]
(d) is the obligation to be absolute, qualified or fully qualified?[5]
(e) is the proposed use peculiar to the tenant?[6]

1 See para 7.9 above.
2 See para 7.13 below.
3 See para 7.14 below.
4 See para 7.15 below.
5 See para 7.16 below.
6 See para 7.17 below.

7.13 *How is the use to be defined?* One approach to the drafting of the user clause is to define the uses which are prohibited, whilst another is to define the uses which are permitted. It is inadvisable simply to define prohibited uses, as undesirable uses may be inadvertently omitted, and further undesirable uses may come into existence after the grant of the lease.[1] Leases usually, therefore, adopt a combination of the two approaches, permitting a particular use or range of uses, and also prohibiting certain undesirable uses which could fall within the permitted user. Care should be taken in combining the two approaches,[2] and the parties must ensure that it is absolutely clear what is permitted, and what is prohibited. Whilst the clause should be concise, there seems no reason for the reluctance traditionally shown by draftsmen to use more than half a dozen words to define so important a matter as the permitted user and, if the words and expressions first considered are not self-explanatory,[3] they should be expanded. The draftsman should give some thought to the specifying of prohibited uses, as a covenant permitting only one particular use will not be breached by tenant carrying on a different use, provided that that use is ancillary.[4] If it is intended that the tenant should not be permitted to do, or sell, or manufacture, a particular thing on the premises then this should be clearly stated, as a covenant which prohibits the tenant from carrying on the business of doing something may not prevent the doing of that thing as *part* of a different business.[5]

1 But see para 7.18:1 note 13 below for one way in which this disadvantage may be mitigated.
2 See, for example, *Forte & Co Ltd v General Accident Life Assurance Ltd* [1986] 2 EGLR 115; *J T Sydenham & Co Ltd v Enichem Elastomers Ltd* [1986] NPC 52.
3 For examples of the problems of construction which can arise from using everyday

descriptions which are not terms of art, like 'butcher' or 'nursery furniture and goods', with no further explanation, see the cases referred to in Hill & Redman pp A583, A584 paras [A1308]–[1318] footnote 10.

4   This is a question of fact and degree – see *St Marylebone Property Co Ltd v Tesco Stores Ltd* [1988] 2 EGLR 40, [1988] 27 EG 72, in which Hoffmann J conceded that the tenant would still be carrying on the trade of a grocer if the sale of non-grocery items was ancillary to a grocery business, but did not think that this could be the case where (as here) the sale of non-grocery items accounted for about half the shop's turnover.

5   A covenant against the carrying on of a particular trade or business prohibits the carrying on of any part of that trade or business (see, for example, *Errington v Birt* (1911) 105 LT 373) whether or not ancillary to a permitted trade or business, but not as part of a permitted trade or business (see, for example, *Stuart v Diplock* (1889) 43 Ch D 343, CA (sale of items usually sold by a ladies' outfitter did not constitute the carrying on of the business of ladies' outfitter); *Labone v Litherland UDC* [1956] 2 All ER 215, [1956] 1 WLR 522 (covenant not to allow adjacent premises to be used for the trade or business of 'bread and confectionery' was held not to be broken by a grocery business selling bread and confectionery as part of its trade); *A Lewis & Co (Westminster) Ltd v Bell Property Trust Ltd* [1940] Ch 345, [1940] 1 All ER 570 (sale of cigarettes in a restaurant/tea shop was not a breach of covenant against use 'for the purposes of the business of the sale of tobacco cigars and cigarettes')).

7.14   *Should the user make reference to the Use Classes Order?* This has been a very popular practice in recent years, and user clauses in many current leases make reference to the Town and Country Planning (Use Classes) Order 1972 for example by permitting use for any purpose within a particular class,[1] or by authorising a particular use and then permitting that use to be changed to any other use within the same class with the consent of the landlord.[2] Here landlords and tenants were attempting to find a compromise between a wide and a narrow permitted use, by permitting a range of similar uses. This approach had the added advantage that the range of similar uses did not have to be spelled out in the lease, that in many cases it meant that the permitted use in the lease corresponded with the planning permission affecting the premises, and that problems in construing words and expressions used[3] were reduced. The revocation of the 1972 Order, and implementation of the Town and Country Planning (Use Classes) Order 1987,[4] has alerted the property world to certain problems affecting leases referring to the 1972 Order.[5] As these could also affect leases referring to the 1987 Order, it has been suggested that the practice of referring to the current Use Classes Order in user clauses may be inadvisable, or at least the parties should not draft a user clause with reference to the 1987 Order without considering two points:

7.14:1   *Subsequent amendments to the Order.* The parties must decide, and make it clear in the lease, whether or not they are referring to the 1987 Order as enacted at the date of the grant of the lease or as subsequently modified. This will depend on the function which they want the Order to perform. If they are intending to refer to the Order as enacted, they are simply using the reference to the Order as shorthand to incorporate in the lease the list of uses comprised in a particular class or particular classes of the Order at that time. This does have drawbacks. As any subsequent modification of the Order will not affect the permitted user, one or more of the uses permitted by the lease may subsequently become 'sui generis'[6] or in a different class of the Order than other permitted uses. Thus, depending on the drafting of the user clause, the tenant may be able to change the use of the premises to a use which is sui generis, or in a different class from the other permitted uses, without reference to the landlord.[7] Similarly, a use subsequently included in the relevant class or classes by a modification of the Order would not be permitted by the lease, which may be to the disadvantage of either the landlord or the tenant.[8] But these consequences are no different than those which would follow if the parties actually spelled out their own list of permitted uses in the user clause. If, on the other hand, the parties are intending to refer to the Order as modified, or even re-enacted, from time to time, different problems could arise. Here, they are using the Order to define the permitted use, with the result that it will be Parliament which sets the parameters of the use or uses permitted by the lease from time to time. Relying on the changing nature and continued existence of a creature of statute to define the use permitted by a lease at any time may be thought at best arbitrary, and at worst dangerous. For example, the Order may be modified so as to exclude the actual use from the class referred to in the lease, or in such a way as substantially to widen or narrow the permitted user. What happens when the 1987 Order is revoked? The replacement Order may have no class corresponding with that referred to in the lease, or there may be no replacement Order.[9]

7.14:2 *All or only some of the uses within each class.* Do the parties want all, or only some of the uses included in a particular class to be permitted?[10] For example, reference to Class B1 of the 1987 Order could enable the tenant to convert office premises to light industrial use which the landlord might not want, whilst a tenant using premises for light industrial use might be horrified at having to pay an office rent on rent review or lease renewal.[11]

1   See 22 Encyclopaedia of Forms and Precedents (5th edn) Form 23 Clause 1.8.
2   See 22 Encyclopaedia of Forms and Precedents (5th edn) Form 22 Clause 1.8.
3   See para 7.13 above.
4   The Town and Country Planning (Use Classes) Order 1987 (SI 87/764) came into force on 1 June 1987, revoking the Town and Country Planning (Use Classes) Order 1972. On the same date consequential amendments were made to the General Development Order by the Town and Country Planning General Development (Amendment) (No 2) Order 1987 (SI 87/765).
5   See Ian Gatenby, Blundell Memorial Lectures 1988, Current Problems in Property Law 'The effect of the Use Classes Order 1987 on existing leases and on future leasing' the article by Stephen Tromans referred to in para 7.10 note 6 above; *Brett v Brett Essex Golf Club Ltd* [1986] 1 EGLR 154, CA; and *Brewers Co v Viewplan plc* [1989] EGCS 78.
6   For a recent example, see *London Residuary Body v Secretary of State for the Environment* [1988] JPL 637, in which it was held that the primary use of County Hall was for the exercise of local government statutory functions, and that to use the building as offices would constitute a material change of use for planning purposes. See also *Wolff v Enfield London Borough Council* [1987] 1 EGLR 119, 281 Estates Gazette 1320, CA.
7   As pointed out by Ian Gatenby in the lecture referred to in note 5 above, it might not be easy to move back into the class, with the result that the value of the premises could be adversely affected.
8   See the article by Tony Jorden and Jane Rigler referred to in para 7.10 note 2 above.
9   The main problems discussed in relation to leases referring to the 1972 Order concern this point – see the lecture and article referred to in note 5 above and consider the assumption as to use contained in the rent review clause of the lease which was the subject of the court's consideration in *Wolff v Enfield London Borough Council* [1987] 1 EGLR 119, 281 Estates Gazette 1320: 'for use for any purpose within Class III of the Town and Country Planning (Use Classes) Order 1972 or any other class or classes of the said order within which falls the use or uses of the demised premises permitted by the planning authority from time to time.' In fact, in that case, planning permission had been obtained for a 'sui generis' use which did not fall within any class, with the result that such use was not included by virtue of the assumption. Leaving that aside, however, how should the second limb of the assumption be interpreted now that the 1972 Order has been revoked? Even if, in the second limb of that assumption, no particular Order had been referred to, problems could still arise from referring to 'use class or classes' as legislation may change and 'use classes' cease to exist. The same point applies to any other creature of statute such as, for example, 'planning permission'. Consider, for example, the user clause in the lease mentioned above: 'not to use

the premises . . . otherwise than for light industrial purposes . . . or for such other purpose for which planning permission shall have been obtained . . .' If planning legislation changes and 'planning permission' ceases to exist, will no other purpose be permitted?
10 See the lecture by Ian Gatenby referred to in note 5 above: 'There is no reason why a series of definitions prepared for planning purposes should correspond even approximately to a definition of use designed to protect a landlord's investment'.
11 See the articles referred to in para 7.10 note 6 above.

7.15 *Is the obligation to be positive or negative?*:

7.15:1 *Negative*. The most normal form of covenant is negative, taking the form: 'not to use the premises otherwise than . . .'[1] As such a covenant will not give the landlord rights against the tenant in the event of user in breach by, for example, a subtenant[2] the landlord will want to extend the restriction to permitting[3] or suffering[4] the premises to be used otherwise than for the permitted use. Sometimes landlords go further, inserting an absolute covenant that the premises will not be used otherwise than for the particular purpose.[5] Landlords should remember that a negative covenant will not be breached by non-user, but only by user for a purpose other than that permitted.[6]

7.15:2 *Positive*. It is in leases of retail premises that landlords most frequently require a positive obligation on the part of the tenant to use the premises for the permitted use, because of the damage which closure of the premises might cause to the premises, or to other premises in a parade or centre.[7] Tenants frequently object to such provisions. They do not want to be under an obligation to keep the premises in use if this has become unprofitable, or impracticable.[8] It seems likely that, because of the possible disadvantages to the tenant, a positive user obligation could have a depressing effect on rent on rent review[9] and on lease renewal.[10] A landlord wanting the tenant to be under an obligation to use the premises for the permitted user can achieve this either simply by means of a positive obligation in the user clause, or by means of a negative obligation in the user clause coupled with a separate obligation to use the premises for the permitted user.[11] As the former method gives rise to drafting problems[12] and other disadvantages,[13] it is advisable for the landlord to adopt the latter. In any event, the tenant should ensure that provisions are inserted permitting the premises to be closed in some defined circumstances, for example repair and staff training.[14]

1 Such a covenant is of advantage to the landlord, because it can be enforced by injunction and in that a subtenant will have constructive notice of the restriction – cf a positive obligation as to which see para 7.15 note 13 below.
2 Although the landlord may have rights against the subtenant.
3 It seems that this means either giving leave for something to be done or abstaining from taking reasonable steps (such steps being within the power of the covenantor) to prevent it being done (provided that it was reasonably forseeable) – see *Berton v Alliance Economic Investment Co* [1922] 1 KB 742, CA; *Tophams Ltd v Earl of Sefton* [1967] 1 AC 50, [1966] 1 All ER 1039, HL; *Norton v Charles Deane Productions Ltd* (1969) 214 Estates Gazette 559. Whether or not the tenant is under an obligation to embark on litigation to prevent an act being done appears to depend on the likely outcome of that litigation (*Berton v Alliance* (above); *Atkin v Rose* [1923] 1 Ch 522). It has been held that the grant of an underlease without any restriction on use is not a breach of a covenant not to permit a particular use (*Prothero v Bell* (1906) 22 TLR 370) and although dicta in *A Lewis & Co (Westminster) Ltd v Bell Property Trust Ltd* [1940] Ch 345 at 351 cast doubt on this, it seems to be consistent with the approach of the courts in construing such a covenant.
4 It has been said that 'suffer' is wider than 'permit' (*Barton v Reed* [1932] 1 Ch 362 at 375) but the words have been treated as synonymous.

5 This is effective – see *Prothero v Bell* (above). It may be achieved by a general interpretation provision, such as 'any covenant by the tenant not to do any act matter or thing shall include a covenant that such act matter or thing shall not be done.'

6 *Doe d Marquis of Bute v Guest* (1846) 15 M & W 160. Cf a positive obligation – see para 7.15:2.

7 Whilst such a covenant is particularly relevant to retail premises in a parade or centre, landlords may attempt to obtain one in leases of other property to avoid the increased risk of vandalism, deterioration of the premises from unattended damage and general deterioration of the area which might result from vacant premises. Although it has been held that such covenants are not enforceable by injunction (see para 7.15 note 13 below), it seems that substantial damages may be awarded to a landlord whose reversion is adversely affected by breach – see the recent case of *Costain Property Developments Ltd v Finlay & Co Ltd* [1989] 1 EGLR 237, [1988] NPC 93 in which the landlord received damages of £147,000 plus interest. In addition, it is thought that if a tenant has stopped trading in breach of such an obligation, he is unlikely to be entitled to a new lease under the 1954 Act even if he is still technically in occupation for business purposes.

8 For example, the premises may have become too small and the tenant may have found alternative, larger premises but may not have found a suitable assignee. Should he have to leave the new premises empty and operate from premises which have become too cramped?

9 See para 7.10 note 4 above.

10 See para 7.10 note 5 above.

11 See para 7.18:2 below.

12 Wording which would appear to impose a positive obligation may well not have the desired effect. For example, it has been said that the words 'to use the premises only as . . .' (see Bernstein & Reynolds *Handbook of Rent Review* para 5.14) and the words 'to use as business offices only' (see Hill & Redman p A582 para A[1306] and p A584 paras A[1308–1318] footnote 11) are in substance negative, but that the words 'to use for (permitted user) only' (see D N Clarke and J E Adams: *Rent Reviews and Variable Rents*, 2nd edn, p 204) impose a positive obligation. In *Levermore v Jobey* [1956] 2 All ER 362, [1956] 1 WLR 697, CA a covenant that the tenant would 'use and occupy the demised premises and permit them to be used and occupied as and for the trade or business of a news vendor . . . only' was held to impose a positive obligation, while in *Edler v Auerbach* [1950] 1 KB 359, [1949] 2 All ER 692 a covenant 'to use and occupy the premises for professional purposes and not otherwise' was conceded to be negative in substance. See also *J T Sydenham & Co Ltd v Enichem Elastomers Ltd* [1989] 1 EGLR 257. A further problem relates to the question of whether or not other uses are allowed – it appears that a restriction prohibiting other uses may be implied (see *Kehoe v Marquess of Lansdowne* [1893] AC 451, HL; *Abbey v Gutteres* (1911) 55 Sol Jo 364), but the covenant in *Levermore v Jobey* (above) permitted residential use.

13 Unlike a negative obligation (see note 1 above), a positive obligation will not be enforceable by way of injunction (*F W Woolworth plc v Charlwood Alliance Properties Ltd* [1987] 1 EGLR 53) nor will a subtenant have constructive notice or it. Furthermore, it is possible that, if user in compliance with a positive obligation becomes illegal, the covenant will be discharged, whilst a negative covenant will not. Accordingly, because a positive covenant may not imply a corresponding restrictive covenant (see note 12 above) the landlord should take a negative covenant from the tenant whether or not he also imposes positive obligations.

14 See 22 Encyclopaedia of Forms and Precedents (5th edn) Form 22 Third Schedule para 3.2, Rosscastle Letting Conditions (Appendix 1, Form 1 below) Condition 3.9:4.

7.16 *Is the obligation to be absolute, qualified or fully qualified?*:

7.16:1 *Absolute.* An absolute obligation takes the form: 'not to use the premises otherwise than as . . .' or 'to use the premises as . . .' followed by a specified use, and makes no provision for this to be changed. As a result, a tenant who wants to change the use will be at the mercy of his landlord, who will be able to consider or ignore, and approve or reject, the tenant's application in his absolute discretion. Depending on the width of the specified user, this could cause great problems to the tenant who wants to alter or develop his use or assign,[1] and to the landlord on rent review and lease renewal.[2] The landlord should bear in mind that the valuer, on rent review, cannot take into account the possibility of relaxation of the user clause[3] and the landlord will not be able, unilaterally, to widen the user provisions.[4] In addition, the court may well not permit the landlord to widen the user clause on lease renewal.[5]

7.16:2 *Qualified.* Such an obligation takes the form, for example, of a covenant 'not to use the premises otherwise than as . . . without the consent of the landlord'. In the case of covenants, conditions or agreements against assigning, subletting, charging or parting with possession of the premises without consent, or against making improvements to the demised premises without consent, statute generally intervenes to deem such covenant condition or agreement subject to a proviso that such consent is not to be unreasonably withheld.[6] There is no similar statutory intervention with regard to covenants conditions or agreements against changing the use of the premises without consent.[7] Instead, s 19(3) of the Landlord and Tenant Act simply deems any such covenant condition or agreement to be subject to the proviso that no fine, or similar sum, is to be payable for such consent.[8] It has been suggested that the words 'such consent not to be unreasonably withheld' should be implied in any event[9] but it is now clear that this is not generally the case.[10] Accordingly, the landlord has an unfettered right to refuse consent arbitrarily, which means that he has the same amount of control as he does with an absolute prohibition.[11] It would seem that he should also have the same disadvantages on rent review and lease renewal as in the case of an absolute covenant[12] but this may not be the case.[13]

7.16:3 *Fully qualified.* Such a covenant specifically provides that the landlord's consent to a change of use, either to any other use or to any other use within a specified class of uses[14] is not to be unreasonably withheld. The extent of control which the landlord will have over the use to which the premises are put will, of necessity, be diluted by the addition of such words, as it will ultimately be the courts which decide whether or not the landlord is, in any particular case, acting unreasonably. Naturally, the landlord's idea of reasonableness may not always correspond with that of the courts. The majority of cases in which the test of reasonableness has been considered by the courts concern covenants against assigning or underletting without consent, but it seems that the same principles will apply.[15] The landlord should bear in mind that if, having applied to the landlord,[16] the tenant considers that consent is being unreasonably withheld he may either seek a declaration from the court to that effect, or he may simply proceed without consent.[17] In addition, an unreasonable delay,[18] or the imposition of unreasonable conditions, will constitute unreasonable withholding. Accordingly, if such a qualified covenant is included in the lease, it is advisable for the landlord to ensure that a system is set up at the outset to enable him and his advisors to make quick and informed decisions on applications submitted by the tenant, as unreasonable withholding could cause the landlord to incur cost, and lose rights.[19] There are a few points which the tenant should consider:
(a) The landlord is under no obligation to give reasons for his refusal of consent,[20] or the imposition of conditions. In the absence of such reasons, it is difficult for the tenant to be able to assess the likelihood of his succeeding in obtaining a declaration, or of his being held to have been in breach of covenant by proceeding without consent. Accordingly, the tenant should consider inserting an obligation on the part of the landlord to give reasons.

(b) There is no duty on the landlord not unreasonably to withhold his consent, which means that a tenant who is prejudiced by the landlord's unreasonable withholding of consent has no claim in damages.[21] The tenant might like to consider remedying this by means of a covenant on the part of the landlord.[22]

(c) The landlord is under no obligation to notify the tenant of a refusal of consent within a reasonable time[23] and, again, the tenant might like to attempt to obtain an appropriate covenant from the landlord.

Such qualified user provisions enable the landlord to retain an element of control while still permitting a sufficiently wide range of uses to give the tenant flexibility and prevent the landlord from being adversely affected on lease renewal and rent review.[24] As the valuer on rent review and lease renewal will be entitled to value the premises on the basis of the most profitable use for which consent could not be unreasonably withheld[25] it will often be advisable for the tenant to ensure that the class of uses within which changes can be made is limited so far as possible without losing him the flexibility he needs.[26].

1   See paras 7.10:1 and 7.10:2 above.

2   See para 7.11:3.

3   See *Plinth Property Investments Ltd v Mott, Hay and Anderson* (1978) 249 Estates Gazette 1167, CA.

4   See *C & A Pensions Trustees Ltd v British Vita Investments Ltd* (1984) 272 Estates Gazette 63. It is suggested by D N Clarke and J E Adams (*Rent Reviews and Variable Rents*, 2nd edn, p 209) that the landlord might insert in the lease a provision which would allow him to waive user restrictions at his discretion, and which would enable him to relax the user restrictions in the lease immediately prior to a review date so as to avoid a lower rent. It is true that this would allow the landlord to wait and see whether or not the tenant is sufficiently well advised at rent review to argue for a lower rent on the basis of a restrictive user clause. In the majority of cases, however, it will simply result in a deferring of the evil moment when the landlord has to decide whether his priority is control or income. It would normally be extremely imprudent for a tenant to accept such a provision. Indeed, perhaps the greatest argument against this suggestion is that a tenant in so weak a position, or so badly advised, as to accept such a provision would probably also be prepared to accept an assumption, in the rent review clause, rendering the user clause in the hypothetical lease wider than that in the actual lease (see para 6.17:1), which would normally be preferable from the landlord's point of view.

5   See para 14.52 below. A request by the landlord to widen a user clause was rejected by the court in *Charles Clements (London) Ltd v Rank City Wall Ltd* (1978) 246 Estates Gazette 739.

6   Landlord and Tenant Act 1927, s 19(1)(a) and s 19(2).

7   The position may change, however – see the Law Commission's Report on Covenants Restricting Dispositions Alterations and Change of User (1985) Law Com No 141, Part VI para 6.2.

8   Provided that the proposed change of use does not involve any structural alteration to the premises. Section 19(3) does not apply to mining or agricultural leases. The proviso does not preclude the landlord's right to require a reasonable sum in respect of any damage to, or diminution in the value of, the premises or neighbouring premises belonging to him, and of any legal or other expenses incurred in connection with such consent. The effect of the section is a little odd – why should entitlement depend on structural alterations which will be regulated by other provisions in the lease, and possibly by statute, anyway? If the new use is more profitable, or wider, than the existing use, the change may render the lease more valuable from the tenant's point of view. Why should the landlord be unable to receive payment, or have to wait for the next rent review or lease renewal to receive payment, for that benefit? The section could work to the tenant's disadvantage. If a landlord is under no obligation to consider the tenant's application for change of use and cannot ask for payment for granting consent, what incentive does he have to consider the tenant's application at all? For remedies in the event of breach of s 19(3) see Woodfall Para 1–1221; Hill & Redman p A568 para A[1283] and p A569 paras [1284]–[1294] footnote 13 – the landlord should beware that once he demands a sum by way of compensation in respect of which the tenant can seek a declaration from the court, he will be under an

obligation to grant the licence subject to payment of the sum determined by the court to be reasonable. As to a contract for payment of a sum in breach of the section, see *Comber v Fleet Electrics Ltd* [1956] 2 All ER 161, [1955] 1 WLR 566.

9   See, for example the dictum of Megaw LJ in *Bocardo SA v S & M Hotels Ltd* [1979] 3 All ER 737 at 741, CA with regard to a covenant not to assign without consent.

10   See *Price v Bouch* [1986] 2 EGLR 179 (no general rule of law that such words should be implied); *Guardian Assurance Co Ltd v Gants Hill Holdings Ltd* (1983) 267 Estates Gazette 678 (no such words implied in covenant against change of use without consent); *Pearl Assurance plc v Shaw* [1985] 1 EGLR 92 (no such words implied in covenant against applying for planning permission without consent); but see also *Cryer v Scott Bros* (1986) 55 P & CR 183, CA, in which it was held that there was no rule of law either way, and whether or not such words should be implied depends on the circumstances of the particular case. In the special circumstances of that case, the words were implied in a covenant concerning the approval of works.

11   See para 7.16:1 above.

12   See para 7.16:1 above, or indeed even greater disadvantages – see note 8 above.

13   Valuers may consider that the addition of the words 'without consent', or the equivalent, is an indication that the landlord may more readily consider a change of use – see the comments of Peter Gibson J in *Forte & Co Ltd v General Accident Life Assurance Ltd* [1986] 2 EGLR 115: 'The decision in the *Plinth* case in my view turned on the particular wording of the particular lease which permitted only one form of user. It does not follow that the decision applies to a case where the lease expressly contemplates that other forms of user might be authorised. Of course it would be open to the arbitrator to say that the possibility of the superior lessors acting arbitrarily, as they are entitled to do, when asked for their authority has the effect in valuation terms that the rental value has to be assessed on the footing that the specified forms of user are the only permitted forms of user. But equally, in my judgment, if he were to say that the hypothetical lessee would pay more for a lease which expressly contemplated the possibility of change of use, I do not see that he could be faulted.'

14   For an example of the latter, see 22 Encyclopaedia of Forms and Precedents (5th edn) Form 22 clause 1.8.

15   See Woodfall para 1–1221 and para 7.5 above. The basic principles to be applied were recently restated in *International Drilling Fluids Ltd v Louisville Investments (Uxbridge) Ltd* [1986] Ch 513, [1986] 1 All ER 321, CA. For cases concerning user, see *Anglia Building Society v Sheffield City Council* (1982) 266 Estates Gazette 311, CA; *Tollbench Ltd v Plymouth City Council* [1988] 1 EGLR 79. The landlord should bear in mind that views on acceptability may change, because of changes in the neighbourhood of the premises, or with the climate of opinion. For example, it has been suggested that the 1987 Use Classes Order and accompanying planning guidance notes from the Department of the Environment are intended to introduce a new climate of opinion on changes of use, which may affect views on what is reasonable.

16   If the tenant does not ask for consent he will be in breach, even though the landlord's consent could not have been withheld – see *Eastern Telegraph Co Ltd v Dent* [1899] 1 QB 835, CA.

17   See Woodfall para 1–1221. The latter is obviously a more risky method of proceeding, and is likely to be unacceptable to any third party involved. The effect of unreasonable withholding is to release the tenant from his covenant (*Treloar v Bigge* (1874) LR 9 Exch 151).

18   Tenants often prefer this to be expressed, by inserting the words 'or delayed' after the words 'not to be unreasonably withheld'.

19   This is particularly the case if the tenant's amendments suggested in paras 7.16:3(a)–(c) are agreed. In practice, without such amendments, tenants are generally reluctant to pursue the remedies available to them in the event of the landlord's unreasonableness, because of the delay and expense, or risk, involved. The landlord should, however, bear in mind the possibility that statute will intervene in the future to impose obligations on the landlord in respect of user similar to those imposed in respect of alienation by the Landlord and Tenant Act 1988 – see para 7.6 above and the Law Commission's proposals (Report on Covenants Restricting Dispositions Alterations and Change of User (1985) Law Com No 141).

20   Cf the position on alienation by virtue of the Landlord and Tenant Act 1988 – see para 7.6 above. It has been said that if the landlord gives no reason for refusing consent the court will more readily imply that the withholding was unreasonable – see *Frederick Berry Ltd v Royal Bank of Scotland* [1949] 1 KB 619 at 623; *Tollbench Ltd v Plymouth City Council* [1988] 1 EGLR 79 at 81.

21   See *Treloar v Bigge* (1874) LR 9 Exch 151 and cf the position on alienation by virtue of the Landlord and Tenant Act 1988 (see para 7.6 above). Implementation of the Law Commission's proposals (Report on Covenants Restricting Dispositions Alterations and Change of User (1985) Law Com No 141) in this respect was given encouragement by Dillon

LJ in *Equities Ltd v Bank Leumi (UK) Ltd* [1986] 1 WLR 1490 at 1494, CA: 'One of the difficulties that arose in this case and arises in many cases where there is a sale of leaseholds subject to landlords' consent to assign is that neither the vendor nor the purchaser has any real leverage on the landlords to give their consent or even to act speedily in going through any necessary formalities. What so often happens is that landlords take a very long time before giving their minds to the matter. Surveyors or managing agents have other things to do and are in no hurry. Ultimately the matter is passed to the landlords' solicitors to prepare a formal deed of licence or consent, and rather a large meal is made of it over a considerable period of time at the expense ultimately of the vendor or purchaser of the leasehold interest.' Such comments remain valid in the case of changes of use.

22   See *Ideal Film Renting Co v Nielsen* [1921] 1 Ch 575.
23   Cf the position on alienation by virtue of the Landlord and Tenant Act 1988. See para 7.6 above.
24   See paras 7.10 and 7.11 above.
25   See para 7.10 note 8 above.
26   See para 7.10 note 7.

7.17   *What if the proposed use is peculiar to the tenant?* It is, generally, quite easy to select the type of use to be specified in the user clause. For example, in the case of the letting of retail premises, the user clause may refer to a retail shop for the sale of goods of the nature which the tenant is intending to sell, or simply to a retail shop, or it may make reference to the relevant class of the Use Classes Order. But there are circumstances in which the tenant's proposed use of the premises is 'sui generis'[1] or not entirely clear at the date of the grant of the lease.[2] In such circumstances, the parties may well be tempted to define the use by reference to the tenant's business. From both parties' point of view, there are potential problems with such an approach. The first problem is one of clarity. If reference is made to the original tenant by name,[3] it should be made clear whether the reference is to the business conducted by him at the date of the grant of the lease, or from time to time. If reference is made to 'the tenant's business' it should be made clear whether the reference is to the actual business conducted by the original tenant, the actual business conducted by the tenant for the time being, business of a similar nature to that conducted by the original tenant, or business of a similar nature to that conducted by the tenant for the time being.[4] If the clause is intended to refer to the business of the original tenant, it should again be made clear whether it means the business conducted by the original tenant at the time of the grant of the lease or from time to time. Depending on the alternative selected, the landlord may lose control[5] and suffer on rent review and lease renewal,[6] and the tenant may find himself unable to develop his business at the premises and with an inalienable lease,[7] and may also suffer on rent review and lease renewal.[8] Accordingly, both parties will normally consider it advisable to avoid any reference in the user clause to the tenant or the tenant's business whenever possible. If it is not possible, the above problems should be borne in mind. Although the solution in each case will depend on the particular circumstances, as a general rule both parties will normally consider it advisable to ensure that the clause is expressed to refer to the actual business conducted by the original tenant at the date of the grant of the lease, and that the development of that business, and an alternative use or alternative uses, are permitted with the landlord's consent, such consent not to be unreasonably withheld.[9]

1   See para 7.14 note 6 above.
2   See *Wolff v Enfield London Borough Council* [1987] 1 EGLR 119, 281 Estates Gazette 1320, CA.
3   A restriction in the lease requiring the premises to be used by the original tenant in person is valid (*Law Land Co Ltd v Consumers' Association Ltd* (1980) 255 Estates Gazette 617, CA). In such

a case the tenant will be unable to assign or underlet (*Granada TV Network Ltd v Great Universal Stores Ltd* (1963) 187 Estates Gazette 391).

4   It seems that, in the absence of contrary provision, it will be construed as the business of the tenant for the time being, particularly if 'tenant' is expressly defined in the lease as including its successors in title – see *Plinth Property Investments Ltd v Mott, Hay and Anderson* (1978) 249 Estates Gazette 1167, CA (offices in connection with the lessee's business of consulting civil engineers); *SI Pension Trustees Ltd v Ministerio de Marina de la Republica Peruana* [1988] 1 EGLR 119 (offices in connection with the lessee's business of mortgage finance and insurance consultants). Following the reasoning in *Cramas Properties Ltd v Connaught Fur Trimmings Ltd* [1965] 2 All ER 382, [1965] 1 WLR 892, HL a case concerning the words 'tenant's business' in para 5(1) of Schedule 9 to the Landlord and Tenant Act 1954, it will be construed as the actual business of the tenant. Thus, if the user clause only refers to the 'tenant's business', the landlord will lose control over user otherwise than by virtue of other restrictions in the lease (see para 7.9 above and para 7.18:1 below) and the tenant will be able to assign (subject to other restrictions), but not underlet.

5   See note 4 above.

6   See *Plinth Property Investments Ltd v Mott, Hay and Anderson* (1978) 249 Estates Gazette 1167, CA.

7   See note 4 above and note 8 below.

8   See *Sterling Land Office Developments Ltd v Lloyds Bank plc* (1984) 271 Estates Gazette 894 in which the use was 'not . . . for any purpose other than as a branch of Lloyds Bank Ltd' Harman J accepted that this meant that the premises were, in effect unassignable. It was held that, on rent review, the user clause in the hypothetical lease should be considered to read 'the demised premises shall not be used otherwise than as . . .' only to be completed when the hypothetical tenant's business or name was known. Although the revised rent would reflect the fact that the premises would be unassignable by the hypothetical tenant, it would not reflect reality, because the user was open – Harman J said: '. . . Here, if the letting is to a hypothetical tenant, there is, until the business is known, no definition whatsoever of the use to which the premises may be put. It could be used as a shop, a bank or an office; and the rents payable could vary substantially . . . The result of there being a lease of these premises on offer, with no defined user clause, is that any lawful user of the premises may be a bidder for them, and his offer would be relevant in arriving at the market price. It is possible that user as a bank branch would provide a narrower market and perhaps thereby a lower level of rental competition than a market open to all lawful users. To that extent Lloyds Bank may have to pay a higher rent than if the market were confined to bank branches . . .'

9   As was intended in *James v British Crafts Centre* [1986] 1 EGLR 117; *Wolff v Enfield London Borough Council* (above). In such circumstances, it may be appropriate to include provisions in the rent review clause removing the hypothetical letting from reality to some extent – see para 6.17:1 – but this will not assist the landlord on lease renewal.

7.18   *Inter-relationships.* In considering the question of user, the parties should not forget the inter-relationship between the user clause and other negotiable provisions of the lease:

7.18:1   *Other clauses.* Other negotiable provisions of the lease may limit the use to which the premises can be put:

(a)   covenants inserted by the landlord, which reflect unavoidable limitations, have already been discussed – these covenants often go further than strictly necessary and, for example, prohibit any disagreeable,[1] dangerous,[2] noxious or offensive[3] or immoral[4] use, or any use which might cause an annoyance or inconvenience[5] to the landlord, his other tenants or others;

(b)   leases often contain covenants on the part of the tenant concerning waste, which can restrict changes in use;[6]

(c)   covenants which restrict the tenant's ability to apply for, or implement, planning permission, or to carry out development[7] will limit the use to which the premises can be put but, as with user clauses,[8] the extent of the limitation will depend greatly on the strictness of the covenants, which may be absolute,[9] qualified[10] or fully qualified;[11]

(d) provisions in the lease restricting the tenant's ability to carry out alterations may limit the use to which the premises may be put;[12]

(e) it seems that covenants restricting alienation can limit changes in use;[13]

(f) there may be other provisions in the lease which limit the use to which the premises can be put, and all the provisions should be checked carefully. For example, would a covenant requiring the premises to be kept open during the normal business hours of a shopping centre[14] prevent user as a bank, or a clause prohibiting the exhibition of signs prevent use as a shop?

7.18:2 *Ancillary.* Having established for what purpose, or range of purposes, the premises can be used without further reference to the landlord, the parties need to consider if there are any ancillary matters which should be dealt with in the lease. For example, certain uses will by statute require to be licensed by the local authority or some other body,[15] and the landlord may want covenants from the tenant in respect of any such licence, as the value of the premises may be adversely affected by its loss.[16] If the premises are a shop, the landlord may want a covenant from the tenant to keep open,[17] or to dress the windows properly,[18] and the tenant may want a covenant from the landlord in respect of competing uses in adjoining premises.[19] Both parties should ensure that a standard form precedent is suitably adapted to the permitted use or uses.[20]

1 See *Wauton v Coppard* [1899] 1 Ch 92.

2 Dangerous user will not necessarily breach a covenant against 'noisome or offensive' uses (*Hickman v Isaacs* (1861) 4 LT 285).

3 This will depend on the purpose for which the premises are used, the way in which the use is conducted, the locality of the premises and whether or not the particular use was being conducted at the time of the grant of the lease – see *Gutteridge v Munyard* (1834) 7 C & P 129; *Duke of Devonshire v Brookshaw* (1899) 81 LT 83; *Nussey v Provincial Bill Posting Co and Eddison* [1909] 1 Ch 734, CA.

4 Such a covenant is probably not implied. Some of the comments in para 7.9 note 5 above apply to immoral, as well as illegal, use and, accordingly, it is advisable for the landlord to insert such an express covenant.

5 Thus extending the prohibition beyond nuisance – see *Tod-Heatly v Benham* (1888) 40 Ch D 80, CA (hospital an 'annoyance'); *Errington v Birt* (1911) 105 LT 373 (fried fish shop not a nuisance but an 'annoyance or inconvenience') and Aldridge *Leasehold Law* para 4.147.

6 See 22 Encyclopaedia of Forms and Precedents (5th edn) Form 22 clause 5.5:1.1. Waste consists of any act which alters the nature of land, whether for better or worse. Four types of waste are recognised: ameliorating, permissive, voluntary and equitable. Since 1267 statute has provided that a tenant for a fixed term of years is liable for both voluntary and permissive waste unless there is a contrary agreement. Accordingly, the tenant may be prohibited from effecting a change of use if it alters the character of the premises – see *Marsden v Edward Heyes Ltd* [1927] 2 KB 1, CA. Whilst covenants against waste may have been appropriate at one time, it is difficult to see what function they perform in the context of modern leases, with their detailed and complex provisions as to repair, alterations and user. To avoid problems, the tenant should ask for any covenant against waste to be fully qualified.

7 The latter has a more restrictive effect. For an example of the former, see 22 Encyclopaedia of Forms and Precedents (5th edn) Form 22 clause 5.12:2. Subject to certain exceptions, permission is needed for the carrying out of any development of land by virtue of the Town and Country Planning Act 1971 and 'development' is defined in that Act as including 'the making of any material change in the use of buildings or other land'. Both landlords and tenants relying on such covenants to restrict the purposes for which the premises can be used (see paras 7.10 and 7.11 above) either alone or in conjunction with the user clause should, however, bear in mind that even an absolute covenant may not have as restrictive an effect as may initially appear, for five reasons: (a) No planning permission is needed for non-material changes of use, as they do not constitute development. In the lecture referred to in para 7.14 note 5 above, Ian Gatenby pointed out that the mere fact that uses fall within two separate classes of the use classes order does not mean that a change from one to the other will be material. He suggests that an office falling within Class A2 of the 1987 Order may not be

materially different from one falling within Class B1, with the result that, notwithstanding covenants such as these, the tenant could move the premises from one use class to another. He also points out that it might not be easy to move back. (b) Planning permission is not needed for the alteration and implementation of ancillary uses. (c) Certain uses of land are specifically excluded from the definition of 'development', the most significant being changes in use from one purpose to another within one of the use classes specified in the use classes order, with the result that no permission is needed. (d) Even where permission is needed, it may be granted otherwise than on application to the local planning authority, for example, by special or general development order. The General Development Order grants permission for various classes of development, including development consisting of certain changes from one class to another in the 1987 Use Classes Order. (e) Planning legislation and subordinate legislation may be changed at some time or times throughout the term, with the result that the covenants may have a less restrictive effect than originally intended. Such provisions may also restrict changes of use indirectly, by regulating alterations to the premises – see paras 7.9 and 7.18:1(a), (b) and (d) above.

8   See para 7.16 above.
9   Eg a covenant not to apply for planning permission. See para 7.16:1 above.
10 Eg a covenant not to apply for planning permission without consent. See para 7.16:2. It is believed that s 19(3) of the Landlord and Tenant Act 1954 will not apply to such a covenant, despite the fact that it may have the effect of preventing a change of use, because it does not technically constitute a covenant 'against the alteration of the user of the demised premises without licence or consent'.
11 Eg a covenant not to apply for planning permission without consent, such consent not to be unreasonably withheld. See para 7.16:3 above.
12 See paras 7.18:1(a), (b) and (c) above and 7.22:1 below.
13 It has been held that the landlord may withhold consent to an assignment if he reasonably objects to the proposed use of the prospective assignee, even if such use is not prohibited either by the lease or by any other restriction affecting the premises (*Re Spark's Lease, Berger v Jenkinson* [1905] 1 Ch 456; *Bates v Donaldson* [1896] 2 QB 241, CA) but see *International Drilling Fluids v Louisville Investments* (above), in which Balcombe LJ indicated that the principle applied where the user clause only prohibited certain types of use, and not where the clause permitted only one specific type of use.
14 See 22 Encyclopaedia of Forms and Precedents (5th edn) Form 22 Third Schedule para 3 and para 4.3.
15 For example, a public house will require a liquor licence; a casino will require a gaming licence.
16 See para 7.11:1 above and 22 Encyclopaedia of Forms and Precedents (5th edn) Form 25 Fourth Schedule paras 1.6–1.9.
17 See paras 7.15:2 and 7.18:1(f).
18 See 22 Encyclopaedia of Forms and Precedents (5th edn) Form 22 Third Schedule para 4.
19 See para 7.9 note 3 above and paras 9.4–9.6 below.
20 See 22 Encyclopaedia of Forms and Precedents (5th edn) Preliminary Note, para 3, page 277, explaining the way in which standard form leases can be amended to suit the particular use permitted, by adopting the 'Shop Covenants', 'Office Covenants' or 'Industrial Covenants'.

C ALTERATIONS

7.19 *Introduction.* Commercial leases almost invariably contain restrictions, in the form of covenants on the part of the tenant, which specifically limit the tenant's ability to carry out alterations to the premises demised by the lease.[1] These are usually contained in that which is generally referred to as the 'alterations clause'. It is not only the alterations clause, however, which imposes restrictions on the tenant's ability to carry out alterations. There may be unavoidable limitations resulting from factors outside the lease,[2] and even in the absence of specific covenants in the alterations clause, limitations will, or may, arise from the lease, either by virtue of other of its provisions or by virtue of the relationship of landlord and tenant.[3]

1 See 22 Encyclopaedia of Forms and Precedents (5th edn) Form 22 clause 5.5, Rosscastle Letting Conditions (Appendix 1, Form 1 below) Condition 3.5.
2 See para 7.20 below.
3 See para 7.21 below.

7.20 *Restrictions outside the lease.* It will be remembered that the tenant's ability to change the use of the premises is affected by factors outside the lease.[1] These same factors also affect the tenant's ability to carry out works of alteration, which may be limited by legislation,[2] by the common law,[3] by restrictions affecting the freehold or a superior leasehold interest in the premises and/or by other obligations binding on the landlord.[4] In addition, adverse rights affecting the premises[5] and such practical matters as the nature of the premises and their method of construction may interfere with, or reduce the viability of, their physical adaptation. The reasons why the *landlord* should be aware of these limitations have already been discussed.[1] He should ensure that, bearing in mind these limitations and the prospective tenant's proposals for the premises, the prospective tenant is suitable and that certain of the limitations are reflected in general covenants in the lease.[6] Thus the prudent landlord will ensure that the lease contains covenants on the part of the tenant to comply with legislation,[7] and perhaps further covenants in respect of particular legislation,[8] together with covenants prohibiting acts which might cause a nuisance to the landlord, his other tenants, or otherwise.[9] The landlord will also ensure that all obligations binding on him are disclosed to the tenant prior to any agreement for lease,[10] and that the lease contains corresponding obligations and appropriate indemnities on the part of the tenant. The landlord should also bear in mind that these unavoidable limitations exist when deciding what (if any) other limitations on the tenant's ability to carry out works should be included in the lease. From the *tenant's* point of view, these limitations should be borne in mind when considering whether or not, in the light of his proposals for the premises and his general concerns about alterations,[11] the premises are suitable. He should also, like the landlord, bear them in mind when considering what, if any, further limitations should be imposed in the lease on his ability to carry out alterations. Finally, of course, the tenant should consider these limitations if he is being asked to enter into any obligation to carry out works in the lease or any agreement for lease.

1 See para 7.9 above.
2 Such as legislation relating to planning, building and fire precautions.
3 The most obvious aspect of the common law which might affect the tenant's ability to carry out works of alteration is perhaps the law relating to nuisance. For common law restrictions arising by virtue of the lease, see para 7.21 below.
4 Such restrictions may, for example, be contained in agreements with the local authority or with a statutory undertaker, or in other leases granted by the landlord.
5 Such as rights of way, or rights of light.
6 For examples of the reasons why such covenants should be inserted, see para 7.9 note 5.
7 See 22 Encyclopaedia of Forms and Precedents (5th edn) Form 22 clause 5.7, Rosscastle Letting Conditions (Appendix 1, Form 1 below) Condition 3.11.
8 See EFP Form 22 clause 5.12, Rosscastle Condition 3.13.
9 See para 7.9 note 8.
10 See para 7.9 note 9.
11 See para 7.22 below.

7.21 *Limitations contained in or arising from the lease.* There may be other limitations on the tenant's ability to carry out alterations, quite apart from those contained in the covenant against alterations. For example:

7.21:1   *Waste.* Waste is generally referred to as any act which changes the nature of the premises.[1] There are four types of waste: ameliorating, voluntary, permissive and equitable. Generally, ameliorating waste improves the land,[2] voluntary waste is any act which tends to the destruction of the premises or changes their nature, permissive waste is any omission whereby damage results to the premises, and equitable waste is any act of extreme damage (in effect, aggravated voluntary waste). It seems that alterations to the premises which alter their nature may render a fixed term or periodic tenant liable, in tort, for voluntary, ameliorating or equitable waste.[3] There are, however, three points to bear in mind. First of all, it has been said that waste must alter the permanent character of the premises.[4] Secondly, although ameliorating waste may be a breach of the tenant's obligations in respect of waste[5] it will often be a breach without a penalty, because it seems that, unless there is a substantial alteration in the character of the premises, the courts will not give relief in the form of an injunction,[6] nor accept it as a ground for forfeiture. In addition, of course, if the works increase the value of the premises there will be no liability in damages. Thirdly, although the tenant's liability for waste is not excluded by express covenants dealing with the same matter, waste can be sanctioned by the landlord.[7]

7.21:2   *Repair.* Alterations to the premises will generally constitute a breach of the tenant's covenant to repair, in that this involves a duty not to destroy the premises in whole or part, unless the alterations are expressly or impliedly authorised by the lease.[8]

7.21:3   *Duty to use the premises in a tenant-like manner.* It is the duty of every tenant to use the premises in a tenant-like manner and yield them up so used at the end of the tenancy.[9] The precise nature[10] and extent of this obligation is unclear, but it is clear that if the tenant carries out structural alterations to the premises which alter their character he will be in breach[11] unless, again, such alterations were authorised.

7.21:4   *Other covenants.* Covenants inserted by the landlord which reflect unavoidable limitations have already been discussed. These covenants often go further than strictly necessary, however, and, for example, prohibit acts which are dangerous or which cause an annoyance,[12] disturbance or inconvenience to the landlord or others.[13] Other provisions of the lease may prevent the tenant from carrying out alterations to the premises – for example, leases often contain provisions which restrict the tenant's ability to affix signs, canopies or aerials to the premises,[14] or to stop up or obstruct windows and doors.[15]

7.21:5   *Planning permission.* Covenants in leases which restrict the tenant's ability to apply for, or implement, planning permission[16] will curtail the tenant's ability to carry out alterations although, of course, the extent to which it will be curtailed will depend on whether the obligation is absolute, qualified or fully qualified.[17]

---

1   Whether for better or worse, but see note 5 below. For a discussion of the law of waste, see Megarry and Wade's *Law of Real Property* (5th edn) p 96 et seq.
2   Or, perhaps, its value.

3   As to the liability of tenants for waste, see Megarry and Wade's *Law of Real Property* (5th edn) pp 702, 703. In addition, some leases contain what appear to be absolute covenants in respect of waste (see, for example, 22 Encyclopaedia of Forms and Precedents (5th edn) Form 22 clause 5.5). In the case of a lease containing detailed provisions relating to repair and alterations, the reason for this is difficult to ascertain. It seems that the tenant's tortious liability for waste is not excluded by express covenants dealing with the same matter, such as repairing covenants, although the provisions of the lease will affect that liability (see note 7 below). See Rosscastle Letting Conditions (Appendix 1, Form 1 below) Condition 3.5:6.

4   See *West Ham Central Charity Board v East London Waterworks Co* [1900] 1 Ch 624.

5   There appears to be some confusion as to whether or not alterations which benefit the reversion constitute waste. It has been said that there is no waste if the reversion is not injured (see *Jones v Chappell* (1875) LR 20 Eq 539) and yet it is clear that there is such an animal as ameliorating waste.

6   No injunction will be granted in the case of trivial or ameliorating waste (see *Doherty v Allman* (1878) 3 App Cas 709, HL).

7   Authority for the execution of alterations may be implied from the permitted user (*Meux v Cobley* [1892] 2 Ch 253 so that even damage resulting from the use of the premises in a reasonable and proper manner having regard to the class of tenement is not waste – see *Saner v Bilton* (1878) 7 Ch D 815) and, perhaps, from the fact that the lease is drafted in such a way that the parties clearly envisaged that alterations would be carried out (*Jones v Chappell*, above).

8   In construing the covenant regard must be had to what was contemplated by the parties at the time of the lease as permissible conduct on the part of the tenant. So, again, regard should be had to the permitted user (see *Hyman v Rose* [1912] AC 623, HL; revsg *Rose v Spicer; Rose v Hyman* [1911] 2 KB 234, CA) and to whether or not the lease is drafted in such a way that the parties clearly envisaged that alterations would be carried out.

9   See *Marsden v Edward Heyes Ltd* [1927] 2 KB 1, CA.

10 It seems that it is an implied covenant to repair, excluded if the lease contains an express repairing obligation, but it may be a separate, independent common law obligation (see *Regis Property Co Ltd v Dudley* [1959] AC 370, [1958] 3 All ER 491, HL).

11 See *Marsden v Edward Heyes Ltd*, above, in which it was also said that the alteration of the character of the premises would constitute a breach. In *Warren v Keen* [1954] 1 QB 15, [1953] 2 All ER 1118, CA it was said that this imposed a duty on the tenant not to damage the premises wilfully or negligently.

12 A trellis has been held to constitute an 'annoyance' (*Wood v Cooper* [1894] 3 Ch 671).

13 See 22 Encyclopaedia of Forms and Precedents (5th edn) Form 22 clause 5.10:1, Rosscastle Letting Conditions (Appendix 1, Form 1 below) Condition 3.8:3.

14 See EFP Form 22 clause 5.6, Rosscastle Condition 3.10.

15 See EFP Form 22 clause 5.16:1, Rosscastle Condition 3.17. For other examples, see para 7.25 below. The tenant should check all the provisions of the draft lease with this in mind. For example, some leases prohibit the tenant from doing any act matter or thing which will or might increase the landlord's tax liability. Most tenants will find this objectionable, on the ground that the parameters of their freedom of action should not be set by the landlord's tax position. From the point of view of alterations, however, would such a clause effectively prevent the tenant from carrying out any alterations which increased the rental value of the premises, on the basis that this would increase the landlord's liability to Capital Gains Tax if he disposed of his reversion?

16 See EFP Form 22 clause 5.12, Rosscastle Condition 3.13. Tenants often object to the need to apply to the landlord for consent to apply for planning permission. They argue that, if planning permission is granted, this will involve duplication (under many leases, the tenant first has to apply to the landlord for consent to apply for planning permission, then to apply to the landlord for approval of any planning permission granted and for consent to the relevant alterations), whilst, if planning permission is not granted, the application for consent will have been unnecessary. Landlords are, however, sometimes concerned to retain control over planning applications made. An application by the tenant might cause concern amongst the landlord's other tenants and, if the application is refused (perhaps because it is not pursued efficiently by the tenant), the existence of a refusal might reduce the value of the reversion.

17 See para 7.24 below and para 7.18:1(c) above.

7.22   *The tenant's concerns.* In assessing the suitability of the premises and the alterations provisions of the lease, the tenant will generally have three main concerns.

7.22:1 *Business needs.* The tenant's first consideration will be the property needs of his business. If the premises are not exactly as he needs them to be, he must ensure that he is able to carry out initial works of fitting out and adaptation. The extent to which he is concerned about the ability to carry out works beyond this will depend on the nature of his business, the nature and state of the premises, and the length of the term. Usually, unless the lease is for a very short term and the tenant has no intention of attempting to obtain a new lease on its determination,[1] he will also want to be able to carry out works to up-date the premises and adapt to the changing needs of his business throughout the term, whether those needs change as a result of the development of the business, technological advances or otherwise. The tenant should bear in mind the effect which the alterations clause can have on user. Onerous restrictions on alterations could prevent the tenant from using the premises for a different permitted use, because he is unable to adapt them physically so as to be suitable for that use.[2]

7.22:2 *Disposal.* Again, unless the lease is for a very short term, the tenant will bear in mind that he may need to dispose of it, or underlet, in the future.[3] Any assignee or underlessee will usually want to carry out initial works of fitting out and to adapt the premises to the needs of his business, and will be reluctant to acquire premises if he himself will be unable to carry out works to up-date and adapt to the changing needs of his business throughout the term. Onerous restrictions on alterations could impede the tenant's ability to dispose of the lease, or grant underleases, not only for this reason, but also by reducing the number of potential assignees or underlessees by preventing their adaptation so as to be suitable for a different permitted use.[4]

7.22:3 *Rent.* Generally,[5] for the reasons mentioned above, the greater the tenant's ability to carry out alterations to the premises, the higher the rent which the premises will command, both initially, on rent review[6] and on lease renewal.[7] A tenant who considers that he himself will not want to carry out works which will realise the full potential of the premises, nor have problems in disposing of the lease if necessary without the ability so to do, may therefore want the lease to contain relatively onerous restrictions on alterations for this reason, but should not attempt to pursue this course of action unless he is very confident indeed.

1 As to the tenant's rights to a new lease generally, see Chapter 14 below. As a general rule, the alterations provisions of the new lease will reflect those of the existing lease, although the court has a discretion, and may order different terms if that would be fair (see paras 14.56–14.60 below).
2 For reasons why the tenant might want to change the use of the premises, see para 7.10:1 above.
3 See para 7.1:1–7.1:3 above.
4 See para 7.10:2 above.
5 This is, however, a matter of valuation depending on the circumstances, and in particular on the state of the premises, their potential for adaptation and their use.
6 As to rent review generally, see Chapter 6. Rent review clauses usually provide for the revised rent to be assessed on the basis of a hypothetical letting of the premises on the same terms as the lease itself, with the result that the alterations clause may have an effect on the revised rent (see paras 6.1, 6.2, 6.17:1 and 6.18:3). It is possible for the lease to provide that the hypothetical letting is to be on more generous terms than those contained in the lease (see paras 6.17:1 and 6.18:3 above) but few tenants would be prepared to accept this.
7 See note 1 above. The rent awarded by the court under s 34 of the 1954 Act will reflect reality (see paras 14.50–14.55), and it is not possible to alter this by directions in the lease, as it is on rent review.

7.23 *Landlord's concerns.* In deciding what, if any, further restrictions to impose on the tenant's ability to carry out works to the premises, there are a number of concerns which the landlord might have. In *Lambert v F W Woolworth & Co Ltd (No 2)*[1] MacKinnon LJ, when considering the reasons why a landlord might object to works to which the tenant requested consent, expressed the view[2] that he might attempt to justify his refusal '. . . on aesthetic, artistic, or sentimental grounds . . . that the alterations would damage the demised premises or diminish their value . . . that the alterations would damage his neighbouring premises, or diminish their value . . .' or '. . . that, as the alteration would not add to the letting value of the premises, he would have to undo it and reinstate the old conditions at the end of the term.' For similar reasons,[3] the landlord will often want to retain the right to prevent the tenant from carrying out alterations.[4] On the other hand, of course, the landlord will want to be able to obtain as high a rent as possible both initially, on rent review[5] and on lease renewal,[6] and onerous restrictions on the tenant's ability to carry out alterations may reduce the rent obtainable.[7] He will therefore have to balance these conflicting concerns, retaining as much control as he needs, but no more.

1   [1938] Ch 883, [1938] 2 All ER 664, CA.
2   At p 911.
3   And, indeed, for other reasons. For example, a landlord who is letting the premises for a relatively short period and who intends to occupy the premises himself on the departure of the tenant might want them to be left exactly as they are.
4   Or particular alterations, or at least the right to impose conditions on the grant of consent to alterations.
5   See para 7.22:3 note 7 above.
6   See para 7.22:3 and in particular note 6 above.
7   See para 7.22:3 above.

7.24 *Form of prohibition.* There are four basic types of covenant:

7.24:1 *Absolute prohibitions.* An absolute prohibition takes the form, for example, of a covenant not to carry out any structural alterations to the premises. It is absolute, in that it does not provide for the possibility of any alterations being permitted by the landlord. As has been mentioned in connection with absolute prohibitions against alienation[1] and change of use,[2] the generally accepted view is that, although the existence of an absolute prohibition does not prevent the tenant from applying for consent to particular alterations, as it will then be open to the landlord to waive the prohibition, it does mean that the landlord will be free to decide whether or not to consider the tenant's application, whether or not to grant consent, and what conditions to impose on the grant of consent, at his absolute discretion. It has been explained that absolute prohibitions against alienation[1] and change of use[2] can cause problems for both the landlord and tenant. The same is true of absolute prohibitions against alterations,[3] subject to statute. Part I of the Landlord and Tenant Act 1927, as modified by Part II of the Landlord and Tenant Act 1954[4] entitles tenants of business premises to compensation for improvements[5] made by them or their predecessors in title on quitting the premises. Briefly, in order to fall within the statute, the improvements must add to the letting value of the holding at the end of the tenancy, they must not be trade or other fixtures which the tenant is by law entitled to remove, they must be reasonable and suitable to the character of the holding, they must not diminish the value of any other property belonging to the landlord or superior landlord and they must not be made in pursuance of a contract made for valuable consideration. In order to be entitled to compensation the tenant must comply with a statutory procedure at the time of the making of the improvement and must also adopt the correct procedure subsequently when making a claim for compensation. It is generally accepted that the Act provides not only a means by which the tenant can obtain compensation for certain improvements, but also a means by which the tenant is able either to obtain authority to carry out improvements despite restrictions[6] in the lease, or to have such improvements carried out by the landlord in return for an increase in rent. Other statutes give the court power to set aside or modify covenants which prevent the tenant from making alterations necessary for compliance with certain statutes.[7] As a result, it is impossible for the landlord to maintain absolute control over alterations to the same extent as he can with alienation and user.[8]

7.24:2 *Qualified prohibitions.* Such a prohibition takes the form, for example, of a covenant not to carry out any non-structural alterations without consent. By virtue of s 19(2) of the Landlord and Tenant Act 1927[9] '. . . a covenant condition or agreement against the making of improvements[10] without licence or consent . . . shall be deemed . . . to be subject to a proviso that such licence or consent is not to be unreasonably withheld'. It specifically provides that the proviso 'does not preclude the right to require as a condition of such licence or consent the payment of a reasonable sum in respect of any damage to or diminution in the value of the premises or any neighbouring premises belonging to the landlord and of any legal or other expenses properly incurred in connection with such licence or consent'.[11] In addition, it does not preclude the right to require as a condition of such licence or consent 'an undertaking on the part of the tenant to reinstate the premises in the condition in which they were before the improvement was executed' but only 'in the case of an improvement which does not add to the letting value' of the premises, and 'where such a requirement would be reasonable'. Works must, of course, go beyond repair to constitute improvements.[12] 'Improvements' have been held to be alterations which improve the premises from the tenant's point of view, by increasing their value or usefulness to the tenant.[13] In the light of this interpretation, it is perhaps difficult to envisage alterations which the tenant will want to carry out which will not constitute improvements. To avoid uncertainty, however, many tenants prefer the words 'such consent not to be unreasonably withheld or delayed' to be inserted in prohibitions against alterations. If these words are not inserted, and s 19(2) does not apply to any particular alterations, with the result that the prohibition remains merely qualified so far as those alterations are concerned, it is generally accepted that the landlord has the same control as he would have with an absolute prohibition.[14]

7.24:3 *Fully qualified prohibitions.* Such a covenant takes the form, for example, of a covenant not to erect, alter or remove partitioning without the consent of the landlord, such consent not to be unreasonably withheld. It is fully qualified, in that it contains a proviso, either express or implied by statute[15] to the effect that the landlord's consent is not to be unreasonably withheld. The construction, effect and operation of fully qualified prohibitions have already been discussed in connection with fully qualified covenants against alienation.[16] It will be remembered that the landlord's control is substantially diluted in the case of a fully qualified prohibition, because it will ultimately be the courts which decide whether or not the landlord is being reasonable in any particular case, and the court's view of reasonableness will not always correspond with that of the landlord. Although the majority of cases in which the courts have considered reasonableness concern covenants against alienation, it seems that the same principles apply.[16] As with other fully qualified prohibitions,[17] it is advisable, if a fully qualified prohibition against alterations is included in the lease, for the landlord to ensure that a system is set up at the outset to enable him and his advisors to make quick and informed decisions on applications submitted by the tenant, as unreasonable withholding could cause the landlord to incur cost, and lose rights.[18] It will be remembered that, in the case of certain fully qualified prohibitions against alienation, because of the application of s 19(1) of the 1927 Act, any attempt in the lease to specify what would, and would not, be considered to constitute reasonableness is invalid.[19] In the case of fully qualified covenants against alterations, s 19(2) of the 1927 Act[15] applies in the same way with regard to improvements. The Landlord and Tenant Act 1988,[20] which affects the operation of certain fully qualified prohibitions against alienation, does not, however, apply to fully qualified prohibitions against alterations or improvements. Because of this, there are a few points which the tenant should consider:

(a) The landlord is under no obligation to give reasons for his refusal of consent,[21] or the imposition of conditions. In the absence of such reasons, it is sometimes difficult for the tenant to be able to assess the likelihood of his succeeding in obtaining a declaration, or of his being held to have been in breach of covenant by proceeding without consent. Accordingly, the tenant should consider inserting an obligation on the part of the landlord to give reasons.

(b) There is no duty on the landlord not unreasonably to withhold his consent, which means that a tenant who is prejudiced by the landlord's unreasonable withholding of consent has no claim in damages.[22] The tenant might like to consider remedying this by means of a covenant on the part of the landlord.[23]

(c) The landlord is under no obligation to notify the tenant of a decision, whether consent or refusal of consent, within a reasonable time[24] and, again, the tenant might like to attempt to obtain an appropriate covenant from the landlord.

A fully qualified prohibition against alterations enables the landlord to retain an element of control while still permitting works to a sufficient extent to give the tenant flexibility and prevent the landlord from being adversely affected on lease renewal and rent review.[25]

1   See para 7.3 above.
2   See para 7.16:1 above.
3   For the reasons set out in paras 7.22 and 7.23 above.
4   For a detailed discussion of the provisions, and operation, of this statute, see Hill & Redman's *Law of Landlord and Tenant*, paras B[20]–[46] and [321]–[430] and for a concise summary, see 22 Encyclopaedia of Forms and Precedents (5th edn) Preliminary Note, para 59. It does not apply to certain leases, such as mining leases or leases of agricultural holdings. For improvements to agricultural holdings, see the Agricultural Holdings Act 1986.
5   See para 7.24:3 below.
6   With the exception of certain specified restrictions, such as those imposed for naval or military purposes – see s 3(4).
7   Certain statutes which require the execution of alterations give the court the right to modify the terms of the lease, and also to apportion the cost of the alterations between the parties. For examples, see Aldridge: *Leasehold Law* para 4.226.

8   See notes 1 and 2 above. The court will not authorise works which will involve trespass. In order to prevent the tenant from increasing the height of any building forming part of the premises, or building on open space forming part of the premises, some landlords exclude the airspace above and around the building. Most tenants will find this objectionable, even if the lease specifically grants them such rights over the airspace as they need to comply with their covenants, because of the uncertainty, and because of unforeseen problems which might arise in the future. Such an exclusion would, for example, prevent the tenant from installing an aerial or small satellite dish on the premises, even if this should become necessary in order for the tenant to conduct his business.

9   Section 19(2) does not apply to mining leases or leases of agricultural holdings.

10   Section 19(2) applies to a prohibition against making alterations without consent, to the extent that alterations to which the tenant requests consent constitute improvements (*Woolworth & Co Ltd v Lambert* [1937] Ch 37, [1936] 2 All ER 1523, CA; *Lambert v FW Woolworth & Co Ltd (No 2)* [1938] Ch 883, [1938] 2 All ER 664, CA; *Haines v Florensa* [1989] EGCS 86, CA).

11   Where the landlord demands a sum in respect of damage, it is for the tenant to produce sufficient evidence to prove that the landlord is being unreasonable, and if he fails to do so the landlord will be taken not to be so.

12   For the distinction between repair and renewal on the one hand, and improvement on the other, see *Morcom v Campbell-Johnson* [1955] 1 QB 106, [1955] 3 All ER 264, CA and a recent consideration of the distinction can be found in *Rich Investments Ltd v Camgate Litho Ltd* [1988] EGCS 132.

13   Notwithstanding the fact that they actually diminish the value of the premises from the point of view of the landlord or a third party: *Balls Bros Ltd v Sinclair* [1931] 2 Ch 325; *Lambert v FW Woolworth & Co Ltd (No 2)*, above. In the latter case, alterations which involved the amalgamation of the premises with adjoining premises which did not belong to the landlord were held to be improvements for the purposes of s 19(2). See also *National Electric Theatres Ltd v Hudgell* [1939] Ch 553, [1939] 1 All ER 567, a case concerning compensation for improvements (see para 7.24:1 above) in which the demolition of the existing building forming part of the premises, and the construction of a new building, was held to be an improvement.

14   As in the case of other qualified prohibitions unaffected by statute: see para 7.4 and in particular notes 3 and 4.

15   Para 7.24:2 above.

16   See para 7.5 above. It should be remembered, however, that the Landlord and Tenant Act 1988 (see para 7.6 above) does not apply to alterations or improvements as it does to alienation. As to the tenant's remedies in the event of unreasonable withholding, see also Woodfall's *Law of Landlord and Tenant* para 1–1260.

17   Such as those relating to alienation and user, see paras 7.5, 7.6 and 7.16:3 above.

18   See para 7.6:4 note 46 and, for example, *Lambert v FW Woolworth & Co Ltd*, above. This will particularly be the case if the tenant's amendments suggested below are included. See also note 20 below.

19   See para 7.5.

20   See para 7.6. The landlord should bear in mind that statute might well intervene in the future to impose obligations on the landlord in respect of improvements similar to those imposed in respect of alienation by the 1988 Act – see the Law Commission's proposals (Report on Covenants Restricting Dispositions Alterations and Change of User (1985) Law Com No 141) and also (1988) Law Com No 161 para 1.3.

21   See para 7.5 note 10. Cf the position on alienation by virtue of the Landlord and Tenant Act 1988 – see para 7.6. It seems that if the landlord gives no reason for a refusal of consent the burden of proof is transferred to the landlord, and the court will more readily imply that the withholding was unreasonable.

22   See para 7.5. Cf the position on alienation by virtue of the Landlord and Tenant Act 1988 – see para 7.6.

23   See *Ideal Film Renting Co v Nielsen* [1921] 1 Ch 575.

24   See para 7.5 note 10 above. Cf the position on alienation by virtue of the Landlord and Tenant Act 1988 – see para 7.6 above.

25   See paras 7.22 and 7.23 above.

7.25   *Drafting*. Assuming that, as is usual, the parties decide that covenants in respect of alterations should be included in the lease, their next concern is the drafting of the alterations provisions. There are a number of points which they might like to consider:

7.25:1 *Inspection.* Often, the only guidance which the parties' solicitors will have when considering the alterations clause is a brief two-line extract from the heads of terms. To avoid future problems they should, if possible, inspect (or at the least obtain a photograph of) the premises, and discuss their construction and potential for adaptation and their client's proposals and concerns with their respective clients and the surveyors involved. It is only in this way that, for example, the landlord's solicitor will be alerted to the need to prohibit absolutely the erection of any new building on an open area of the premises which the landlord would like retained as such, to the futility of prohibiting the maiming of main timbers in the case of premises constructed almost entirely of concrete, steel and glass, or to the need to include provisions concerning an awning or canopy at the front of the premises.

7.25:2 *Usual form of covenant.* Ideally, the alterations clause should be drafted in such a way as to prohibit all works save those expressly permitted, and should then specifically authorise the class of works which is to be permitted with consent, and that (if any) which is to be permitted without the need for consent.[1]

7.25:3 *Definition of alteration.* The parties should be aware of the way in which the courts have construed prohibitions against 'alterations',[2] with the result that if the landlord wants to retain control over the external appearance of the premises, the layout of the premises, etc, specific provision will have to be made.

7.25:4 *Definition of structure.* In the past many leases distinguished between external and internal alterations, although nowadays most leases maintain a distinction between structural and non-structural alterations.[3] The reason for this is clear, but unfortunately, without more specific drafting such a distinction may cause confusion and operate in an arbitrary fashion. For this reason, many landlords now consider it advisable to insert a definition of 'structure' in the lease prepared with the specific building in mind and then to distinguish in the alterations clause between alterations to the structure (as defined) and other alterations.[4]

7.25:5 *Minor works.* Even leases which contain restrictive provisions will often permit the tenant to carry out minor works, such as the installation, alteration and removal of partitioning,[5] without reference to the landlord. This is because it would be time-consuming and costly for the landlord to be approached for consent each time, and because, provided that certain conditions are complied with, the execution of such minor works cannot adversely affect the landlord. In such cases, the lease will usually contain certain conditions as to the execution of works,[6] a requirement that the tenant notifies the landlord of the execution of such works and supplies plans of works carried out, and an obligation on the part of the tenant to reinstate the relevant works at the end of the term.[7]

7.25:6 *General conditions.* Whenever it is possible that the tenant will carry out works, it is always advisable for the lease to contain certain general conditions[8] relating to their execution. So, for example, the lease may provide that any works should be carried out in a good and workmanlike manner, with new and proper materials, in accordance with planning and other legislation, so as not to cause a nuisance to neighbours, to the satisfaction of the landlord's surveyor,[9] etc and that they should be completed as soon as reasonably possible. It will usually also contain a right of entry for inspection and/or supervision and an indemnity in favour of the landlord in respect of any loss arising from the execution of such works. These conditions will then apply, not only to the execution of works which the tenant is entitled to carry out without prior reference to the landlord, but also in the case of works for which the landlord's consent is required, thereby saving time and cost by reducing the length of (or, in straightforward cases, avoiding the need for) a formal licence, and preventing the possibility of inadvertent omission of standard requirements from a formal licence. In the case of leases containing a qualified[10] or fully qualified[11] prohibition against alterations, the lease may specify additional conditions which should be complied with when the tenant applies for consent to works. So, for example, the lease will often specify the number of sets of plans which the landlord will need,[12] and provide for the tenant to pay the landlord's costs, whether or not consent is granted or the application is proceeded with.[13] The landlord should remember, however, that unless the works are straightforward, there may well be many other requirements which it will be desirable for him to impose on the grant of consent. He should therefore ensure that he does not preclude his right to impose further requirements in an appropriate case.[14] From the tenant's point of view, he should ensure that the general conditions imposed are all reasonable and acceptable.

7.25:7   *Absolute prohibitions where some work permitted.* If the lease permits the execution of a certain class of works without reference to the landlord, or contains a qualified[10] or fully qualified[11] prohibition against a particular class of alterations, there may be certain works falling within that class about which the landlord is particularly concerned, and which he wants absolutely[15] to prohibit. These will vary with the circumstances but, for example, he may want to prohibit the demolition of the existing building forming part of the premises and/or the erection of a new building,[16] the amalgamation of the building forming part of the premises with adjoining premises,[16] works which interfere with the air conditioning or other system serving the premises or which affect conduits other than those exclusively serving the premises, works which might render more onerous the performance of his own repairing obligations, building on an open space included in the premises, the erection of signs, aerials, canopies, etc,[17] or works which stop up or darken windows or doors.[18]

7.25:8   *Cutting main walls.* Landlords almost invariably insert, in the alterations clause, an absolute prohibition[15] against cutting or maiming the main walls or timbers of the premises. The landlord is obviously concerned to retain control over the supporting walls, etc of the premises, but such a prohibition could effectively prohibit absolutely[15] relatively innocuous alterations, simply because they involve the cutting of a main wall. The tenant should attempt to ensure that, if certain alterations are permitted with consent, any specific restriction along these lines is qualified in the same way.

7.25:9 *Reinstatement.* Some leases contain a general condition[8] obliging the tenant to reinstate all alterations made before or at the end of the term[19] if so required by the landlord. This is done for two reasons – it is an attempt by the landlord to avoid any possible argument as to whether or not a reinstatement obligation is reasonable at the time when a tenant applies for consent under a fully qualified covenant,[11] and also, many landlords admit that they impose such an obligation so as to avoid the need to pay compensation for alterations when the tenant quits the premises.[20] A landlord imposing such an obligation should bear in mind that such a general obligation could have the effect of reducing the rent obtainable both initially, on rent review and lease renewal,[21] and that, if the obligation is included in an attempt to avoid the need to pay compensation, it may not be effective.[22] A well-advised tenant will resist the inclusion of such a general obligation, save in exceptional circumstances. If it is included, he should ensure that he will only be under an obligation to reinstate if, and to the extent, reasonably required, and only if he actually quits the premises.[23]

7.25:10 *Compulsory alterations.* Leases almost invariably contain obligations on the part of the tenant to carry out certain alterations. Most leases place the tenant under an obligation to carry out works required by statute,[24] or required by certain authorities pursuant to statutory powers[25] and others go further, by referring to works such as those required by insurers.[26] Some leases, or agreements for lease, also contain obligations in respect of initial works of fitting out or adaptation.[27] Both landlord and tenant should be aware of the way in which such works will be treated on rent review and lease renewal.[28] The landlord should consider the tax implications of the imposition of obligations in respect of initial works,[29] and the tenant should consider the potential cost and inconvenience of obligations concerning statutory works[30] and the fact that no compensation will be payable to him under the 1927 Act in respect of works carried out pursuant to an obligation given in pursuance of a contract for valuable consideration when he quits the premises at the end of the term.[31]

1 To avoid any doubt, it should be made clear that both prohibitions and authorities apply not only to the tenant, but also to permitted undertenants, if this is intended. See para 7.15:1.

2 See *Joseph v LCC* (1914) 111 LT 276 ('alteration' referred to an alteration in the fabric of the premises and not in their appearance); *Bickmore v Dimmer* [1903] 1 Ch 158, CA (in which Stirling LJ and Vaughan Williams LJ indicated that a prohibition against alterations was limited to alterations which would affect the form and structure of the premises, Stirling LJ that there must be excluded from the covenant not only those things absolutely essential to the carrying on of the tenant's business, but also things fixed to the premises for the purposes of carrying on that business in a reasonable, ordinary and proper way, and Vaughan Williams LJ that it excluded acts which are convenient and usual for a tradesman to do in the ordinary conduct of his business).

3 See 22 Encyclopaedia of Forms and Precedents (5th edn) Form 22 clause 5.5.

4 As to problems with the use of the word 'structure', see para 8.6 above. For an example of a more detailed approach, see Rosscastle Letting Conditions (Appendix 1, Form 1 below) Condition 3.5.

5 Where the landlord is prepared to allow the installation, alteration and removal of partitioning without reference to him, the tenant might consider asking for a similar right in respect of such matters as ancillary electrical works. In many buildings, any alteration to partitioning will also necessitate an alteration to electrical and telephone sockets.

6 See para 7.25:6 above.

7 An obligation to reinstate minor works, such as partitioning works, which the tenant is entitled to carry out without reference to the landlord, should be contrasted with a general obligation to reinstate – see para 7.25:9 above.

8 For the validity of additional requirements imposed in the case of alterations which are the subject of a fully qualified prohibition, see para 7.24:3 above.

9 In *Hunt v Bishop* (1853) 8 Exch 675, the court considered an obligation on the part of the defendant to carry out works under the direction, and to the satisfaction, of the plaintiff's surveyor. It was held that the appointment of a surveyor was a condition precedent to the performance of the defendant's obligations. In *Doe d Baker v Jones* (1848) 2 Car & Kir 743, where the tenant was under an obligation to carry out repairs to the satisfaction of the landlord's surveyor, the court held, in an action for ejectment brought by the landlord because his surveyor was not satisfied with the repairs, that if the court thought that the surveyor ought to have been satisfied then that was sufficient.

10 See para 7.24:2 above.

11 See para 7.24:3 above.

12 He may need extra sets for his agents, solicitors, a superior landlord or mortgagee.

13 The tenant will usually limit this obligation to costs incurred reasonably and properly, and will often specifically exclude costs incurred if the landlord unreasonably withholds consent in circumstances where that consent should not be unreasonably withheld.

14 See 22 Encyclopaedia of Forms and Precedents (5th edn) Form 22 clauses 5.5:2.4 and 5.5:4, Rosscastle Letting Conditions (Appendix 1, Form 1 below) Condition 3.5:4, although the tenant should ensure that such an obligation is limited to reasonable requirements.

15 See para 7.24:1 above.

16 See para 7.24:2 note 13 above and EFP Form 22 Clause 5.5:1, Rosscastle Condition 3.5:1.

17 See EFP Form 22 clause 5.6 and Third Schedule para 2.7, Rosscastle Conditions 3.9 and 3.10.

18 See EFP Form 22 clause 5.16:1, Rosscastle Condition 3.17.

19 See EFP Form 22 clause 5.5:4, Rosscastle Condition 3.5:4. Such a general obligation should be contrasted with more limited requirements which may be reasonable, such as those relating to the removal of signs, etc (see EFP Form 22 clause 5.17:3, Rosscastle Condition 3.26:3). It should be remembered that, although the tenant has the right to remove tenant's fixtures, he is under no obligation to remove them (unless the lease provides otherwise) although he is under an obligation to make good any damage caused by removal. Nevertheless, landlords seem to require the protection of provisions like EFP 5.5:4 and Rosscastle 3.5:4.

20 See para 7.24:1 above.

21 See paras 7.22 and 7.23 above.

22 Section 9 of the 1927 Act as amended by s 49 of the 1954 Act prohibits contracting out. See also *James v Hutton and J Cook & Sons Ltd* [1950] 1 KB 9, [1949] 2 All ER 243, CA and Rosscastle Letting Conditions (Appendix 1, Form 1 below) Condition 3.5:4 and footnote 55.

23 Ie not if his tenancy continues and/or is renewed by virtue of the 1954 Act – see Chapter 14.

24 This goes beyond the obligation, discussed in para 7.28, to comply with statutes. See EFP Form 22 clause 5.7:1, Rosscastle Condition 3.11. Leases also often contain an obligation on the part of the tenant to execute works which are required as a condition of any planning permission granted in respect of the premises prior to the end of the term (see EFP Form 22 clause 5.12:5.1, Rosscastle Condition 3.16:6). The tenant should attempt to limit this obligation to apply only to a planning permission implemented by him, and only so far as is reasonable.

25 Such as the fire authority.

26 The tenant should ensure that any such obligation is limited to reasonable requirements.

27 See EFP Form 22 Third Schedule para 1.

28 See para 7.26 below.

29 Section 34(2), (3) of the Income and Corporation Taxes Act 1988 (formerly s 80(2) of the Income and Corporation Tax Act 1970) provides that when a lease not exceeding fifty years imposes an obligation on the tenant to carry out any work to the premises, there shall be deemed to have been paid a premium. This, however, applies only to work covenanted to be done by the tenant *at the time of the grant of the lease* and is thus not relevant to improvements that the tenant wishes to undertake during the term and where there is no covenant in the lease to carry them out.

30 We live in an age of great safety awareness and this type of covenant would, for example, impose on the tenant an obligation to carry out work needed to be done by virtue of any safety legislation passed during the term. Thus, if a sprinkler system or some other fire fighting or alarm equipment, or fire exit, was required by law in properties such as the demised premises, it would fall to the tenant to carry out the relevant works. These works could, of course, prove extremely expensive, and it should be borne in mind that, if the requirement arises towards the end of the term of the lease, the responsibility will still be that of the tenant, even if he knows that the landlord is proposing to oppose the grant of a new lease under the 1954 Act on the ground that he would like to occupy the premises himself! (see para 14.29).

31 See para 7.24:1 note 7 above. An apportionment of the cost may, however, be made by the court in certain circumstances – see para 7.24:1 note 8 above. A well-advised tenant will, however, attempt to obtain a contractual right to compensation for works which he is under an obligation to execute, where appropriate. See, for example, EFP Form 96.

7.26 *Relationship with rent review*[1] *and lease renewal.*[2] Whenever it is possible that the tenant will carry out works[3] both parties should give thought to the way in which those works will be treated on rent review and lease renewal. Usually, the rent review clause will contain a disregard of improvements carried out by the tenant other than those carried out pursuant to an obligation to the landlord[4] although it is possible for other provisions to be made.[5] On lease renewal, the 1954 Act[6] provides for the rent to be determined disregarding any effect on rent of an improvement carried out by a person who was the tenant at the time it was carried out, provided that it was carried out otherwise than in pursuance of an obligation to the landlord and provided that either it was carried out during the current tenancy, or certain further conditions are satisfied.[7]

1 As to rent review generally, see Chapter 6 above.
2 As to lease renewal generally, see Chapter 14 below.
3 As to which, see para 7.24:1 above.
4 See para 6.36:3 above.
5 For example, although improvements carried out by the tenant or its predecessors pursuant to an obligation to the landlord are usually taken into account on rent review, it is becoming quite usual for tenants to insist on a disregard of statutory works (see paras 6.36:3 and 6.36:5 above). The parties should give consideration to whether or not initial works of fitting out or adaptation should be taken into account or disregarded (see para 6.36:4 above).
6 Section 34. See paras 14.50–14.55 below.
7 See paras 6.34–6.43 above and 14.55 below. Contrary to the position on rent review where the disregards can be varied, it is not possible for s 34 to be altered by agreement.

D OTHER COVENANTS

7.27 *To pay rates, taxes, etc.* A tenant of business premises today will be requied to pay all rates, taxes, assessments,[1] duties, outgoings, impositions or charges[2] imposed on the demised premises at the time of or subsequent to the grant of the lease.

1 A covenant confined to 'rates, taxes and assessments' will apply only to matters of a recurring nature and not to expenses representing a permanent improvement: *Wilkinson v Collyer* (1884) 13 QBD 1; *Lyon v Greenhow* (1892) 8 TLR 457. If the covenant is wider, and includes words such as 'duties', 'outgoings' etc, the effect is to carry the tenant's liability beyond actual assessments and to make the tenant liable to pay all sums of money payable in respect of the demised premises notwithstanding that they are expenses of permanent improvement: *Sweet v Seager* (1857) 2 CBNS 119; *Thompson v Lapworth* (1868) LR 3 CP 149; *Budd v Marshall* (1880) 5 CPD 481, CA; *Brett v Rogers* [1897] 1 QB 525; *Farlow v Stevenson* [1900] 1 Ch 128, CA; *Villenex Co Ltd v Courtney Hotel Ltd* (1969) 20 P & CR 575.
2 As to construction see 27 Halsbury's Laws (4th edn) para 338 et seq. See 22 Encyclopaedia of Forms and Precedents (5th edn) Form 22 clause 5.2:1, Rosscastle Letting Conditions (Appendix 1, Form 1 below) Conditions 3.2:1 and 3.2:2. As to VAT, see paras 2.23–2.29 above.

7.28 *To comply with statute.* Having ensured that the tenant will be responsible for all payments due in respect of the demised premises,[1] the landlord will require the tenant to carry out all work called for by the local or any other authority pursuant to a statute.[2] Such a covenant is not limited to circumstances where the tenant is in breach of a statutory requirement but would extend to any new requirements.[3] Therefore, if a sprinkler system or other fire fighting or alarm equipment became compulsory in properties such as the premises, it would fall to the tenant to install it. Moreover, in the case of a typical rent review clause, any increase in rental value as a result of this work will not be disregarded on the reviews, because such work will have been carried out 'in pursuance of an obligation to the landlord'.[4] At least during the term of the lease, it will be possible to remove this unfairness by expressly providing in the clause that any such work is disregarded,[5] but it will not be when the lease falls to be reviewed under the 1954 Act.[6]

1   See para 11.1 below.
2   See EFP Form 22 clause 5.7, Rosscastle Condition 3.11.
3   There is no recent authority on the point but it is possible that, notwithstanding such a covenant, a tenant may be able to obtain from the landlord a contribution towards the costs incurred in carrying out such works. Many of the Acts under which such work would be ordered contain a provision to the effect that, where as a result of the provisions of the Act an occupier of premises has to make structural alterations, it may apply to the county court alleging that the whole or part of the expenses should be borne by the owner of the building, and that the court should make such order as to the expenses and their apportionment as it considers just and equitable eg the Offices, Shops and Railway Premises Act 1963 s 73(2) (19 Halsbury's Statutes (4th edn) HEALTH AND SAFETY AT WORK); Fire Precautions Act 1971 s 28 (35 Halsbury's Statutes (4th edn) PUBLIC HEALTH). It might be thought that a clear and unequivocal covenant by the tenant to carry out such work as its own expense would preclude an application to the court under the above sections but in *Horner v Franklin* [1905] 1 KB 479, CA it was acknowledged that a party on whom the responsibility lay by virtue of the lease might obtain a contribution from the other party to the letting. It is probably fair to say that it is unlikely that a court would today depart from the express wording of the covenant where the expenditure was such as might have reasonably been in the contemplation of the parties when they entered into the lease. On the other hand, it is submitted that a court might take the view that it was not just and equitable for a tenant to bear the full expense of some very major work, especially near the end of the tenancy.
4   See para 6.36:3 above.
5   See para 6.36:5 above.
6   Ie because the wording of s 34 cannot be varied: see para 14.50 below.

7.29   *To reimburse the landlord for upkeep of shared items.* Where the premises are such that the landlord will be required to undertake recurring expenditure to enable the tenant to use and enjoy them, the lease should provide for the payment of a service charge.[1] There will be many lettings, however, where any such expenditure by the landlord will be infrequent, for example in relation to the maintenance of a private road or sewer used by the tenant and other tenants of the landlord, but where the landlord would still wish to be able to recover from the tenants any expenditure that he does incur. As with service charges, the question arises as to how the tenant's share should be determined. It is suggested that in most instances the tenant should be required to reimburse 'a fair proportion' of the expenses incurred by the landlord.[2] This seems preferable to setting out an exact share because it provides for flexibility, which may be valuable where, for example, the work is needed as a result of some form of misuse by an individual tenant, or where the properties using the sewer or road vary during the terms of the lease. The clause should provide how the share is to be determined. It is suggested that the lease should provide for the share to be determined by a third party (perhaps the landlord's surveyor) acting as an expert and not as an arbitrator.[3] There will not generally be implied a covenant by the landlord to undertake the work in question,[4] and therefore the tenant should seek an express covenant.[5]

1 See Chapter 11 below.
2 See EFP Form 26 fourth schedule para 1.1. Appendix 1, Form 4 below clause 4.1 and paras
   11.2–11.3 below.
3 See para 11.5 below.
4 See paras 11.2–11.3 below.
5 See Appendix 1 Form 4 below clause 5.

7.30 *Normal hours.* Leases, especially of shops and offices, often contain a covenant forbidding the tenant from using the premises outside 'normal business hours'.[1] This can be justified only in a letting of part of a building where there are access, security and services implications. No tenant should accept such a restriction where the premises are self-contained. Where there is to be such a provision in a lease of a suite of offices, the tenant must ensure that the specified hours are such that the normal working day and conventional 'overtime' are included. Over and above this, the tenant should press for special arrangements to be made for access outside normal office hours.[2] For example, these may require the tenant to notify the landlord when such working will be required, agree to pay the overtime to the caretaker, indemnify the landlord against any loss suffered as a result of such access, and acknowledge that no services need to be provided (although this may not be required as the landlord's obligation to provide services such as heating and hot water is often expressed to apply only to 'normal office hours'). In the case of a lease of a unit in a shopping development, there may be little that can be done where the centre itself is closed after business hours but the tenant will need to be satisfied that arrangements adequate to its needs are made for access to the premises for the delivery or collection of goods as well as for staff training and dressing the shop.

1 See for example, 22 Encyclopaedia of Forms and Precedents (5th edn) Form 31 clause 1.9,
   Fifth Schedule para 1.3. The same situation can be achieved by indirect means eg the
   limitation on the right of the tenant to use the common parts in Form 29 Second Schedule para
   1 may deny the tenant access to the shop outside certain hours.
2 The tenant should insist that these arrangements are set out in the lease itself, rather than in a
   side-letter, which may not bind the landlord's successor in title and may mean that they would
   not be included in a renewed lease under the 1954 Act Pt II: see *G Orlik (Meat Products) Ltd v
   Hastings and Thanet Building Society* (1974) 29 P & CR 126, CA, para 14.43 below.

7.31 *Interest.* Leases today generally provide for interest to be payable by the tenant on any late payment of rent, and any other sums due under the lease, such as the service charge and (the proportion of) the insurance premium.[1] It is difficult for a tenant to resist the principle because by so doing it is seeking to absolve itself from a breach of covenant. The more profitable course is likely to be for the tenant to argue for amendments of detail to be made in order to mitigate the effect of the principle such as the rate of interest[2] to be reduced, interest to be payable only after a certain time has elapsed from the due date, so as to ensure that interest is not payable when some minor administrative problem or postal delay has caused payment to be a day or two late, or interest to be payable only after the landlord has served a notice and then only from the date of the notice (or better still so far as the tenant is concerned a short time afterwards) and not from the date on which the payment was due. It is important from the tenant's point of view to ensure that the landlord will be sending out rent demands. Strictly speaking, no demand is needed because the lease itself makes the tenant aware of the amount and the dates for payment. As a practical matter, however, it is often difficult for a large organisation to make any payment other than against an invoice that can be passed for payment. Landlords should, therefore, be persuaded always to send a demand.[3]

1   See 22 Encyclopaedia of Forms and Precedents (5th edn) Form 22 clause 5.18, Rosscastle Letting Conditions (Appendix 1, Form 1 below) Condition 3.22. But interest can become payable on arrears even when there is no covenant in the lease: Supreme Court Act 1981 s 35A as inserted by the Administration of Justice Act 1982 (11 Halsbury's Statutes (4th edn) COURTS). See also *Allied London Investments Ltd v Hambro Life Assurance Ltd* [1985] 1 EGLR 45, 274 Estates Gazette 148, CA.
2   The rate will generally be fixed in relation to the base lending rate of the landlord's bank. It is submitted that landlords would be unwise to require a rate of interest significantly in excess of the rate payable on a loan from the bank, or to insert a minimum rate of interest, in case during the term rates drop and this minimum comes to represent an excessively high rate. The danger is that a high rate could be held to amount to a penalty and therefore be void: see *Dunlop Pneumatic Tyre Co Ltd v New Garage and Motor Co Ltd* [1915] AC 79, HL.
3   Whenever there is an interest provision in a lease containing a rent review clause, the question of interest on the difference between the rent paid on account and the revised rent where the same was fixed only after payment of rent during the period should be specifically dealt with: see para 6.55 above.

7.32   *Landlord's legal fees.* The Costs of Leases Act 1958[1] provides that, in the absence of agreement in writing to the contrary, each party to a lease bears its own solicitor's costs.[2] Those acting for the tenant in the negotiations should always resist the suggestion that the tenant should pay the landlord's costs. As always, the law of supply and demand will apply, and there will be cases where the tenant finds that he has no option but to agree to the principle, but, even when this is conceded, there are many matters of detail to be considered. The amount of the landlord's solicitor's costs will depend in part on the time spent on the matter,[3] which in turn will be related to the number of points that the tenant's solicitor raises in connection with the draft lease, and the force with which he presses them. If the draft lease is returned approved as drawn, the work of the landlord's solicitor (and therefore his 'proper charges') will be reduced. Where the landlord's solicitor submits a most unreasonable lease, the tenant who has agreed to pay the landlord's solicitor's costs is in the most unfortunate position of not only having to pay its own solicitor to resist the lease, but also the landlord's solicitor for advancing it. This can be avoided if at the time of the commercial negotiations it is agreed that the tenant will pay a specified sum which is fixed at that time and irrespective of the amount of work actually done. Such a sum may, according to the negotiations, represent either a nominal contribution, or a serious and realistic attempt by the parties to arrive at what the legal fees could be, if the matter proceeds 'normally', or some figure midway between the two. When this is not accepted the tenant's solicitor should:

(a)   amend the clause in the draft lease if it could be construed as including costs other than the landlord's solicitor's cost and disbursements. Landlords tend to like expressions such as 'all costs and expenses incurred by the landlord' which could be taken to include the fees of the various other professionals incurred by the landlord in relation to the letting;[4] or

(b)   as the matter nears completion, agree the charges with the landlord's solicitor and provide for this figure to be inserted in the lease.[5]

1   Ie the Costs of Leases Act 1958, s 1.
2   For solicitor's charges see the Solicitors' Remuneration Order 1972/1139 and two Law Society publications *The Expense of Time* (4th edn) and *An approach to non-contentious costs.* As to the landlord's costs on a lease being renewed under the 1954 Act see *Cairnplace Ltd v CBL (Property Investment) Co Ltd* [1984] 1 All ER 315, [1984] 1 WLR 696, CA, para 14.62 below.

3 An interesting point arises on a lease, eg of a unit on an industrial estate or in a shopping centre. The landlord's solicitor may well have spent only some 5 or 6 hours on that particular letting but have spent very much longer in drafting the 'master lease' for the estate or centre. Where a letting has been negotiated on the basis that a tenant pays the landlord's legal fees, is the landlord entitled to include in each letting a proportion of the time spent in drafting the master lease and, if so, what proportion, ie should it be shared equally amongst all the units (so that the larger units pay no more than the smaller) or on a specific area basis? This is even more relevant in small but complicated developments eg the addition of a quarter of the time spent in drafting the master lease for a four-shop high street development may serve to double the time spent on each matter. There is no real answer to this, which represents a further argument in favour, so far as the tenants are concerned, of lettings being agreed on the basis that they will pay a fixed sum for the landlord's legal fees rather than the sum actually incurred.

4 See 22 Encyclopaedia of Forms and Precedents (5th edn) Form 22 clause 5.26 post.

5 See EFP Form 93.

7.33 *General points for the tenant.* The tenant should seek to avoid absolute covenants and to qualify them by inserting, whenever practical, terms such as 'reasonable' or 'use best endeavours'. Such changes (where accepted) will generally mean that the tenant will not be in breach of a covenant where the failure to comply was due to circumstances beyond his control. The tenant's covenants in some draft leases grant to the landlord and others rights of access to the premises. The tenant should ensure that there is a limitation on when these can be exercised[1] and an obligation on the landlord to make good.[1] Whenever the landlord's consent is required, the tenant should qualify this by providing that such consent is not to be unreasonably withheld or delayed.[2] The tenant must insist that it is provided with a copy of any document the terms of which it will be required to observe, for example the insurance policy[3] or any regulations.[4]

1 See EFP Form 54, Rosscastle Letting Conditions (Appendix 1, Form 1 below) Conditions 3.6:1 and 4.2.

2 As to when this would be implied see the Landlord and Tenant Act 1927, s 19 and paras 7.2:1, 7.2:2, 7.5, 7.16:2, 7.24:2.

3 See EFP Form 22 clause 7.8.

4 See eg EFP Form 27 fourth schedule para 9.

Chapter 8

Repairing covenants

A FUNDAMENTALS

8.1 *Meaning of 'repair'.* A party who seeks guidance from his lawyer as to the meaning of a repairing covenant, and in particular the extent of the work that might be required by virtue of the covenant, could sometimes be disappointed by the lack of definitive advice. There is no absence of authorities, and the general principles are clear. The problem is the practical one of applying those principles to particular work required to a specific building. Inevitably, in cases of dispute, a judge will have to decide. He will, no doubt, be 'appropriately and carefully referred to the plethora of authorities'[1] including, almost certainly, the following well-known passages:

> 'However large the words of the covenant may be, a covenant to repair . . . is not a covenant to give a different thing from that which the tenant took when he entered into the covenant.'[2]

> 'Repair is restoration by renewal or replacement of subsidiary parts of a whole. Renewal, as distinguished from repair, is reconstruction of the entirety, meaning by the entirety not necessarily the whole but substantially the whole.'[3]

> 'The true test is, as the cases show, that it is always a question of degree whether that which the tenant is asked to do can properly be described as a repair, or whether on the contrary it would involve giving back to the landlord a wholly different thing from that which he demised.'[4]

> 'It seems to me that the correct approach is to look at the particular building, look at the state which it is in at the date of the lease, look at the precise terms of the lease, and then come to a conclusion whether, on a fair interpretation of those terms in relation to that state, the requisite work can be fairly called repairs. However large the covenant it must not be looked at in vacuo.'[5]

Thus if the work in question looked at in this way, involves a reconstruction of substantially the whole, or giving back to the landlord a wholly different thing from that demised, then the party who has covenanted to repair will not be required to undertake that work. Sachs LJ continued:[6]

> 'Quite clearly this approach involves in every instance a question of degree . . . and I would in this behalf echo the words of Sir Raymond Evershed MR in *Wales v Rowland*[7] when dealing with an analogous problem relating to repairs. After setting out two plain examples, he said:
>
>> "Between the two extremes it seems to me to be largely a matter of degree, which in the ordinary case the county court judge could decide as a matter of fact applying a common-sense man-of-the-world view."
>
> . . . In the upshot . . . it is "the good sense of the Agreement" that has to be ascertained – a phrase conveniently quoted from the 1842 judgment of Tyndall CJ [in] *White v Nicholson*.'[8]

The particular form of words may not matter providing the covenant plainly expresses the intention that the premises are to be repaired, kept in repair and yielded-up in repair, although there is a powerful dissenting view. In *Anstruther-Gough-Calthorpe v McOscar*[9] Scrutton LJ felt[10] there was no substantial difference in construction between to keep 'in repair', 'in good repair', 'in sufficient repair' or 'in tenantable repair', while Bankes LJ attached 'no importance to the particular form of words used in the covenant' providing they disclose an intention to repair.[11] Atkin LJ, however, said:[12]

> 'I see no reason for construing the words of covenants in leases dealing with obligations to repair in any other way than that in which one would construe any other covenant. Effect should be given if possible to every word used by the parties: see per Moulton LJ, in *Lurcott v Wakely and Wheeler* [1911] 1 KB 905 at 915. It does not appear to me useful to refer to such covenants as the usual covenants to repair, or general repairing covenants, and then consider only what is the meaning of "repair". It appears to me still less useful to take a number of terms which may be found in different leases, treat them all as synonymous, and so impute to all of them a special meaning attached by authority to one of them.'

The addition of 'renew' has been held to add nothing to a covenant to repair.[13] Nevertheless there is clearly nothing to prevent the covenant imposing a greater obligation on the tenant,[14] providing 'much stronger and more specific words' are used.[15]

1 *Brew Bros Ltd v Snax (Ross) Ltd* [1970] 1 QB 612, [1970] 1 All ER 587 per Sachs LJ at 602. But even these may be unhelpful – 'the citation of a plethora of illustrative authorities, apart from being time and cost consuming, presents the danger of so blinding the court with case-law that it has difficulty in seeing the wood of legal principle from the trees of paraphrase': *Lambert v Lewis* [1981] 1 All ER 1185 per Lord Diplock at 1189. The remarks, however, were not directed to repairing covenants.

2 *Lister v Lane and Nesham* [1893] 2 QB 212 per Lord Esher MR at 216. Tenant covenanted to 'well, sufficiently and substantially repair, uphold, sustain, maintain, amend and keep' 100-year-old premises. Near the end of the term, a wall's timber foundations had rotted and subsided. Property condemned and had to be demolished. Held: tenant not liable to repair because such work would lead to an entirely new and different house. Note also *ACT Construction Ltd v Customs and Excise Comrs* [1982] 1 All ER 84, [1981] 1 WLR 1542 in which the House of Lords held that the construction of additional foundations to underpin buildings in order to correct subsidence and comply with modern building regulations involved a radical and fundamental alteration that would extend the life of the building, and could not be classed as 'repair and maintenance' within note 2 to Group 8 of the Finance Act 1972.

3 *Lurcott v Wakely and Wheeler* [1911] 1 KB 905 per Buckley LJ at 924. Tenant covenanted 'well and substantially to repair and keep in thorough repair and good condition' the premises. Just before expiry of term, local authority served a dangerous structure notice requiring the front wall of the 200-year-old house to be demolished. Landlord complied with the notice and rebuilt the wall with concrete foundations, footings and a damp-proof course in accordance with local byelaws etc. Held: tenant liable to rebuild the wall as merely a subsidiary portion of the premises.

4 *Ravenseft Properties Ltd v Davstone (Holdings) Ltd* [1980] QB 12, [1979] 1 All ER 929 per Forbes J at 937. See footnote 3 to para 8.14 below.

5 *Brew Bros Ltd v Snax (Ross) Ltd* [1970] 1 QB 612, [1970] 1 All ER 587, per Sachs LJ at 602. Year after commencement of 14-year lease, flank wall began to tilt because its foundations had been undermined by seepage of water from drains. Neighbouring owners brought an action in nuisance against the landlord, who in turn claimed to be indemnified by the tenant, under repairing covenant. To rectify, the foundations had to be underpinned, the drains replaced and the tilting wall rebuilt. Work would cost £8,000 and after rebuilding the premises would be worth an estimated £7,500 to £9,500. Held to be a renewal and thus tenant not liable. For recent applications of this approach see *Halliard Property Co Ltd v Nicholas Clarke Investments Ltd* (1983) 269 Estates Gazette 1257; *Elmcroft Developments Ltd v Tankersley-Sawyer* (1984) 270 Estates Gazette 140; *Post Office v Aquarius Properties Ltd* [1985] 2 EGLR 105, 276 Estates Gazette 923 (in fact the analysis here may not have been necessary: see [1987] 1 All ER 1055); *Elite Investments Ltd v TI Bainbridge Silencers Ltd* [1986] 2 EGLR 43, 280 Estates

Gazette 1001; *McDougall v Easington District Council* [1989] 1 EGLR 93; *Plough Investments Ltd v Manchester City Council* [1989] 1 EGLR 244. For a slightly different approach involving a landlord's covenant, see *Smedley v Chumley and Hawke Ltd* (1981) 44 P & CR 50, 261 Estates Gazette 775, CA.

6 [1970] 1 All ER 587 at 603.
7 [1952] 1 All ER 470 at 477, CA.
8 (1842) 4 Man & G 95 at 98.
9 [1924] 1 KB 716, [1923] All ER Rep 198, CA.
10 At 203.
11 At 200.
12 At 204.
13 *Collins v Flynn* [1963] 2 All ER 1068. Parts of the Judgment of Sir Brett Cloutman VC, QC were criticised by Forbes J in *Ravenseft* (see note 4 above) at p 936. See also *Norwich Union Life Insurance Society v British Railways Board* [1987] 2 EGLR 137, 283 Estates Gazette 846.
14 See para 8.11 below. 22 Encyclopaedia of Forms and Precedents (5th edn) Form 56.
15 See note 13 above at p 1074.

8.2 *Standard of repair.* The standard of repair that is required is a quite separate question from the meaning of 'repair'. Essentially the tenant must undertake work that, having regard to the age, character and locality of the property, would make it reasonably fit for the occupation by a reasonably minded incoming tenant of the class who would be likely to take it.[1] A deterioration in the class of tenants likely to require the property during the term of the lease does not operate to reduce the standard of repair.[2]

1 *Proudfoot v Hart* (1890) 25 QBD 42, CA; *Lurcott v Wakely and Wheeler* [1911] 1 KB 905, CA; *Anstruther-Gough-Calthorpe v McOscar* [1924] 1 KB 716, [1923] All ER Rep 198, CA.
2 *Calthorpe* – see note 1 above.

8.3 *The need for disrepair.* The Court of Appeal has given two reminders recently that the meaning of the repairing obligation[1] and the standard of repair[2] are not the only issues and that a further question must be considered. The plaintiff will also have to show that a state of *disrepair* exists because, unless it does, there is nothing to *repair* and thus the proper construction of the obligation is irrelevant.[3] In *Quick v Taff-Ely Borough Council*,[4] a council house had been rendered virtually uninhabitable by condensation caused by the lack of insulating materials in the windows and sweating from the metal windows. The tenant argued that the landlord was in breach of the statutory covenant to repair the structure and exterior of the property[5] and was required to undertake the various steps proposed to alleviate the problem, for example installing timber or UPVC window frames and facings of installation material on the window lintels. The Court of Appeal held that, as there was no disrepair to the structure and exterior of the property, the landlord was not in breach of the covenant and did not have to undertake the work.[6] This approach was followed in *Post Office v Aquarius Properties Ltd*.[7] A defect in the structure of a newly constructed office building had caused flooding in the basement for some five years until the water table receded and the basement became dry. The issue was whether the tenant was required to remedy the defect by virtue of his covenant 'to keep in good and substantial repair . . . the demised premises'. Work costing between £86,000 and £175,000 would have been required and Hoffmann J held that this would have involved structural alterations and improvements and not repairs.[8] The Court of Appeal agreed that the tenant did not have to undertake the work but based this view upon different reasoning. There was no evidence that the flooding had caused damage to the demised premises. Therefore, said the court, there was no disrepair and thus no obligation to repair.[9]

1 See para 8.1 above.
2 See para 8.2 above.
3 The court has hinted that this question is sometimes overlooked: 'The first question, accordingly, is whether it has been proved that the building was out of repair so as to give rise to an obligation under the covenant to put it into repair. The second question, *which appears to have been treated as the main, if not the only, question at the trial*, is whether, assuming the building to be in a state of disrepair by reason of the existence of the defect, any of the schemes of treatment put forward for curing the defect were capable of being regarded as work of repair as opposed to being structural alterations and improvements' *Post Office v Aquarius Properties Ltd* [1987] 1 All ER 1055 per Ralph Gibson LJ at 1057, CA. The emphasising is the author's.
4 [1986] QB 809, [1985] 3 All ER 321, CA.
5 Formerly Housing Act 1961, s 32 now Landlord and Tenant Act 1985, ss 11–16, as amended by the Housing Act 1988, s 116.
6 If the work suggested by the tenant had been carried out to all the local authority landlord's houses the cost would have been in the region of £9m. The tenant was re-housed between the trial and the appeal.
7 [1987] 1 All ER 1055, CA.
8 [1985] 2 EGLR 105, 276 Estates Gazette 923.
9 The court accepted that the facts of the case, and in particular the lack of damage, were highly unusual: 'When the water entered by reason of the original defects, damage might have been done to the premises, whether to plaster on walls, or to the flooring, or to electrical or other installations. But no such damage was proved. If such damage is done, the authorities show that the resulting state is a condition of disrepair: see *Ravenseft Properties Ltd v Davstone (Holdings) Ltd* [1980] QB 12, [1979] 1 All ER 929, and *Elmcroft Developments Ltd v Tankersly-Sawyer* (1984) 270 Estates Gazette 140' per Ralph Gibson LJ at 1063, CA. See para 8.14 below.

B DEFINITIONS – 'DEMISED PREMISES', 'INTERIOR', 'STRUCTURE', 'STRUCTURAL REPAIRS', 'INHERENT DEFECTS'

8.4 *The demised premises.* A number of expressions that need careful consideration are likely to appear in the covenant to repair. For example the covenant will frequently relate to '*the demised premises*', and so there is a need to refer elsewhere in the lease to establish the definition of this term and thus the extent of the covenant. If the draft lease does not define with absolute certainty the extent of the premises to be let, then clarifications must be proposed.[1] This will be particularly true when the demised premises form part of a larger building, and the draft fails to deal precisely with the boundaries in 'shared' walls, floors, and ceilings, and in exterior walls.[2] If the proposed lease is of part of a larger building, and the repairing covenant is not limited to the interior, it will only be when the definition of the demised premises has been established, that the tenant's solicitor will be able to see the extent of the repairing covenant.

1 See Chapter 3 above.
2 See paras 3.11–3.17 above.

8.5 *The interior of the premises.* Alternatively the covenant may specify the extent of the premises to which it applies by requiring the tenant to repair the *interior* of the demised premises. Such wording could, however, be dangerously vague. The walls and floors of a modern building consist of various layers[1] and the word 'interior' could mean either those parts of the walls that are not part of the exterior facing, those parts that are neither the exterior facing nor form part of the structure of the building, or purely the interior decorative finishes of the walls. A tenant's solicitor would always argue that the last interpretation is the correct one, but it would seem desirable, for the avoidance of doubt, to use an expression such as 'interior decorative finishes of walls ceilings and floors' in the lease, in preference to 'interior'.

1 See paras 3.11–3.16 above.

8.6   *Structure and structural repairs.* After tough negotiating, the tenant's advisers may have persuaded the landlord to accept some liability for repair. This may prove less advantageous than was hoped if the landlord's covenant contains words like '*structure*' or '*structural repairs*' because these permit disputes as to their interpretation. In construing any contract, the court always wishes to give effect to the intention of the parties at the time the contract is made, and where the landlord has covenanted in a lease to maintain the structure or undertake structural repairs, and in the absence of any assistance from the document itself, it would seem that the parties may have intended one of three widely differing meanings:

(a) the *broad* approach of Vaisey J who held[1] that structural repairs meant repairs of or to a structure, thereby dividing all repairs into structural or decorative. Thus a landlord who had so covenanted would be obliged to carry out all repairs needed to the premises other than decorative repairs, or

(b) a *narrow* interpretation limiting the landlord's responsibility to the load-bearing elements essential to the strength and stability of the building and the load-bearing parts of the roof, or

(c) a position *midway* between (a) and (b) where any 'serious repair' was to be the responsibility of the landlord.[2]

There is a world of difference between these alternatives. For example, a court asked to construe a covenant to maintain the structure of a conventional brick-built building, may decide that the parties did not intend the approach of Vaisey J and construe the structure as including the roof, foundations, load-bearing walls (other than decorative finishes) and the beams.[3] On the other hand, a typical modern office building consists of a structural framework of steel columns and beams. The pre-cast concrete floors are laid on the beams, and the exterior walls of the building are in fact, a number of small individual walls built on each floor up to the underside of the floor above. If these walls were in need of serious repair, a failure to undertake this work would not affect the basic stability of the building, as they do not form part of the structural framework of the building. Thus, it could be said, they are not part of the 'structure', at least by one interpretation of the word. When the landlord does agree to accept responsibility for repairs to the structure, it is, therefore, essential for this term to be defined in the lease, for example 'roof[4] foundations beams and load bearing walls'.[5] In many cases, the parties' property advisers would have little difficulty in agreeing a definition in relation to the building in question, although there may well be some items that could be disputed.[6] Whether these are to be included in the definition then becomes a matter for negotiation between the parties. How much better it is for the definition of the structure to be established as part of the negotiation of the terms of the lease, rather than when a specific dispute has arisen during the term and urgent work is needed. When a definition has been agreed between the parties, this can either be set out in the repairing covenant itself or as a further defined term in the definitions clause.

1 *Granada Theatres Ltd v Freehold Investment (Leytonstone) Ltd* [1958] 2 All ER 551, [1958] 1 WLR

845. See also *Blundell v Obsdate Ltd* [1958] EGD 144; *Campden Hill Towers v Gardner* [1977] QB 823, [1977] 1 All ER 739; and *Douglas-Scott v Scorgie* [1984] 1 All ER 1086, [1984] 1 WLR 716, CA.

2 For example including all or some of the external non load-bearing walls, the cladding thereto, internal walls (excluding plaster surfaces), screeds on the floors etc. As to the term 'external walls' see *Goldfoot v Welch* [1914] 1 Ch 213 and *Pembery v Lamdin* [1940] 2 All ER 434, CA. Note also *Plough Investments Ltd v Manchester City Council* [1989] 1 EGLR 244.

3 But even this is not comprehensive – are the floor boards included?

4 But does a skylight form part of the roof? See *Taylor v Webb* [1937] 2 KB 283, [1936] 2 All ER 763; revsd (on other grounds) [1937] 2 KB 283, [1937] 1 All ER 590, CA and note 5 below.

5 But are windows (ie glass and frames) part of the main walls? When both the landlord and the tenant undertake certain repairing obligations the question of the responsibility for the windows should specifically be dealt with because there is no general rule as to whether or not they form part of the main walls. Lord Evershed MR felt that a correct statement of the law was 'It would appear that windows in the outer wall of a building may, in certain contexts and for certain purposes, be regarded as part of the walls' – *Holiday Fellowship Ltd v Hereford* [1959] 1 All ER 433 at 436. See also *Boswell v Crucible Steel Co* [1925] 1 KB 119; *Ball v Plummer* (1879) 23 Sol Jo 656, CA and *Taylor v Webb* – see note 4 above.

6 For example, the walls of the building referred to in paras 3.13–3.17 above.

8.7 *Inherent defect.* In those cases where the landlord of a new building is prepared to accept at least some liability for inherent defects,[1] it would seem wise expressly to state in the lease that it means (if that be the case) a defect existing but not visible at the commencement of the term that is the result of defective design,[2] defective supervision of the construction of the property,[3] or defective workmanship or defective materials used during its construction.[4] Another potential dispute would be the extent of the application of any covenant relating to inherent defects – for example, does it apply only to 'structural' defects that manifest themselves in the roof, foundations, load-bearing walls and beams, or does it extend to any defects including those of a decorative nature? This point too should be dealt with.

1 See para 8.14 and Additional Clauses A & B (Appendix 1 below).

2 In *Jackson v Mumford* (1902) 51 WR 91; affd (1904) 52 WR 34 Kennedy J held at 91 that the term 'latent defect in the machinery' did *not* include defects in design.

3 The covenant in *Smedley v Chumley and Hawke Ltd* (1981) 261 Estates Gazette 775 (see para 8.18 below) omitted reference to defective design or supervision. The landlord's argument that this omission was material failed in that case but the tenant should not leave this to chance and should insist upon the broadest definition being expressly set out.

4 As to further judicial comment on latent defects, see *Yandle & Sons v Sutton* [1922] 2 Ch 199 per Sargant J at 210 and *Sanderson v National Coal Board* [1961] 2 QB 244, [1961] 2 All ER 796 per Holroyd Pearce LJ at 799 and 251, CA.

C THE LANDLORD'S CONSIDERATIONS

8.8 *Repair: straightforward buildings.* Market forces are such that virtually every commercial letting is negotiated today on the footing that the tenant will bear the ultimate responsibility for the cost of repairing the premises. Which party actually does the work will depend upon the nature of the building. Where a detached building is being let, the landlord's solicitor will no doubt be instructed to impose upon the tenant a covenant to repair the premises – a full repairing lease.[1] In lettings of parts of properties in multi-occupation – for example, a suite in an office block, a factory unit forming part of a larger building, or a shop in a shopping centre – the tenant's obligations to undertake work are more likely to be limited to the interior of his premises, with the landlord carrying out such repairs and maintenance as are needed to the structure of the whole building. The leases will provide for the landlord to be

225

fully reimbursed by the tenants for the costs that he has incurred in carrying out the work either by a detailed service charge provision[2] or by a covenant by the tenant to pay the landlord a proportion of the costs of such work, as and when incurred.[3]

1   The landlord must consider if he will require a right of entry to the demised premises in order to repair etc other parts of the property that could only be reached from there – ie the reverse of the right referred to in para 4.8 above.
2   See paras 11.4–11.29 below.
3   See paras 11.1–11.3 below.

8.9   *Repair: the hybrid building.* It is the case mid-way between the detached property and the small part of the large building that needs careful consideration by the landlord and his advisers, such as a factory that is to be let as two or three units, or a shop being let separately from the residential or office accommodation on the floors above.[1] The temptation is to grant full repairing leases so that each tenant will be responsible for those parts of the building that fall within his demise. This, however, could cause practical difficulties if major repairs are needed because any loss will be suffered 'where it falls'. For example, a problem may be limited to one wall and thus only the tenant or tenants who have part of that wall included in their demise(s) would be affected. This would be so even where a failure to repair promptly could cause further damage to the building. In addition, where any significant repairs were needed, co-operation between two and more tenants whose premises include the part of the structure involved would be essential – there would have to be agreement between them that action was needed, and as to the nature of the work that was required, by whom, how and when it was to be undertaken. There could be disagreement between the tenants on any of these points, or worse still, a total refusal by one tenant to participate. Here the landlord would be involved almost as a referee attempting to enforce the repairing covenants contained in the leases. It is suggested that there will be many instances where it would be preferable for the landlord to covenant to repair the structure of the whole of the building, on the basis that the costs incurred in so doing are reimbursed by the tenants, by means either of a service charge or a reimbursement covenant. The landlord would then be in the satisfactory position of having direct control of the work. There can be no firm rules that would apply to all such lettings but, before preparing a full repairing lease of part of a building, the landlord's solicitor must satisfy himself in conjunction with his client's architect, engineer or surveyor that such arrangements for the repair of that particular building would be practical.

1   For a precedent, see the 2nd edition of this work, Form P5. The same situation can arise on a sub-let of part of premises demised by a lease.

8.10   *More extensive repairing obligations.* The landlord's advisers should also consider if this is a letting where it would be appropriate to impose obligations on the tenant greater than the general covenant to repair, by virtue of which the tenant may even be required to re-build the premises,[1] and to undertake other very substantial work. There is no reason why the lease should not impose a greater burden on the tenant but on a rent review the tenant is likely to argue for a discount from the market rent on the grounds that his obligations are more onerous than the norm.[2]

1   This may not be that unreasonable where the term of the lease exceeds the likely life of the building. See 22 Encyclopaedia of Forms and Precedents (5th edn) Form 56.

2 See *Norwich Union Life Insurance Society v British Railways Board* [1987] 2 EGLR 137, 283 Estates Gazette 846.

D   THE TENANT'S CONSIDERATIONS

8.11 *Points to consider.* The tenant's solicitor needs to consider a number of points in relation to the repairing covenant contained in the draft lease – for example:

(a) is it what was previously agreed between the parties 'subject to lease'?[1]
(b) will it work in practice?[2]
(c) are there any features to that particular letting that ought to be reflected in the repairing covenant – for example the age of the building or the length of the letting?[3]
(d) are there suitable exclusions from the covenant to repair?[4]
(e) are what might be called the 'procedural matters' in order?[5]
(f) has the relationship with the other parts of the lease been considered?[6]

1 As to 'subject to lease', see para 1.8–1.12 above. For example, does the covenant as drafted by the landlord's solicitor go further than 'repair': see para 8.10 above.
2 See para 8.9 above. It is worth noting that few leases contain repairing covenants that cover all eventualities. A covenant by the tenant to repair the interior of the demised premises, coupled with a comprehensive covenant by the landlord to maintain the structure of the demised premises or the building of which the premises form part (no doubt at the expense of the tenant) goes a long way towards achieving the satisfactory position of covenants that, taken together, cover *all* the work that could be required to the building. This is not always the case – for example, a tenant's covenant in a full repairing lease will not cover work that would involve reconstructing the whole or giving back to the landlord a different thing from that which he demised (see para 8.1 above). Thus, in the absence of any specific covenant from the landlord to do *all* the work that was required to the premises that is not (on a proper construction of the tenant's repairing covenant) the responsibility of the tenant, the unsatisfactory position could result in which the tenant is not obliged to do work and the landlord refuses to do it.
3 As to old buildings, see paras 8.12 and 8.13, as to new buildings, see paras 8.14 and 8.16. In a short letting, the tenant's solicitor should argue that the tenant's liability should be limited to the interior of the premises, on the grounds that it is unreasonable for a tenant, who has only a brief occupancy of the premises, to run the risk of incurring any greater liability. Against this, so far as the landlord is concerned, is the possibility that the lease might be renewed by the tenant or an assignee under the 1954 Act, and since *O'May v City of London Real Property Co Ltd* [1983] 2 AC 726, [1982] 1 All ER 660, HL (see para 14.58 below) it would be very difficult for a landlord to obtain on a renewal (at least where another short term is contemplated) a full repairing lease where the current tenancy limited the tenant's obligations to the interior. An answer might be to exclude from the letting the security of tenure provisions of the 1954 Act, although the tenant would in such circumstances have to be satisfied that his need for that property was short-term.
4 There should be excluded from the tenant's repairing covenant disrepair due to an insured risk (see Rosscastle Letting Conditions (Appendix 1, Form No 1 below) Condition 3.4:1) and, in the light of *Eyre v Johnson* [1946] KB 481, [1946] 1 All ER 719 (a decision doubted by Goff J in *Sturcke v S W Edwards Ltd* (1971) 23 P & CR 185), the tenant should be absolved from non-performance where this is prevented by an inability to obtain the necessary consents etc (see ibid Additional Clause A). Note too *Wright v Lawson* (1903) 19 TLR 203.
5 Are the premises properly defined, are any terms that are used either clear in themselves or adequately defined (see para 8.3 above), will the tenant require to enter adjoining property of the landlord in order to carry out repairs (see for example Appendix 1, Form No 5 below, clause 1.5:3).
6 For example, the suspension of rent proviso: see para 10.23 below.

8.12 *Old buildings: the problems.* The tenant and his advisers need to be particularly cautious when the lease of an old building is contemplated because 'if on a true view of the facts the works required were *"repairs"* within the *meaning of the covenant, it matters not . . . that the property was in these respects in a defective state at the time of the demise*.[1] As Lord Esher MR said in *Proudfoot v Hart*[2]

> 'What is the true construction of a tenant's contract to keep and deliver up premises in "tenantable repair"?[1] Now, it is *not* an express term of that contract that the premises should be put into tenantable repair, and it may therefore be argued that, where it is conceded, as it is in this case, that the premises were out of tenantable repair when the tenancy began, the tenant is not bound to put them into tenantable repair, but is only bound to keep them in the same repair as they were in when he became the tenant of them. *But it has been decided – and, I think, rightly decided – that, where the premises are not in repair when the tenant takes them, he must put them into repair in order to discharge his obligation under a contract to keep and deliver them up in repair. I am of opinion that under a contract to keep the premises in tenantable repair and leave them in tenantable repair, the obligation of the tenant, if the premises are not in tenantable repair when the tenancy begins, is to put them into, keep them in, and deliver them up in tenantable repair.*'

Nevertheless, the covenant will be construed in the light of the principles set out in para 8.1 above and thus the tenant will not be required to reconstruct substantially the whole or give back a wholly different thing from that demised. The disrepair may have been caused by old age,[3] by an inherent defect in the building,[4] or perhaps even by some outside event.[5] Drafting cannot entirely protect the tenant[6] – even assuming the landlord is prepared to accept something less than a full repairing lease – and the tenant must realise that a structural survey is as important when leasing as when purchasing a freehold. He should think long and hard before entering into a lease of premises that his surveyor advises may require significant repairs during or at the end of the letting. A freehold-repairer will at least benefit from repairs and may not even have to carry them out, if the disrepair does not hinder his use or the sale of the property. A tenant's repairs may be entirely for the benefit of the landlord – perhaps even carried out or paid for after the lease has expired – and yet the tenant can be compelled to undertake them.

1   *Brew Bros v Snax (Ross) Ltd* [1970] 1 QB 612, [1970] 1 All ER 587 per Harman LJ at 594, CA.
2   (1890) 25 QBD 42 at 42, CA. The emphasis is the author's. See also *Foster v Day* (1968) 208 Estates Gazette 495, CA.
3   For example *Lurcott v Wakely and Wheeler* [1911] 1 KB 905, CA (wall); *Elite Investments Ltd v T I Bainbridge Silencers Ltd* [1986] 2 EGLR 43, 280 Estates Gazette 1001 (roof).
4   For example *Lister v Lane and Nesham* [1893] 2 QB 212, CA (wooden foundations); *Pembery v Lamdin* [1940] 2 All ER 434, CA (no damp course); *Sotheby v Grundy* [1947] 2 All ER 761 (no foundations); *Elmcroft Developments Ltd v Tankersley-Sawyer* (1984) 270 Estates Gazette 140, CA (damp course wrongly positioned).
5   For example *Brew Bros Ltd v Snax (Ross) Ltd* [1970] 1 QB 612, [1970] 1 All ER 587, CA (war-time bomb, defective drains and cutting down tree produced water seepage that caused foundations of a wall to shift – work required held to be not within tenant's repairing covenant).
6   See para 8.13 below.

8.13 *Old buildings: drafting.* The various alternatives seek by one means or another to absolve the tenant from major repairs. They suffer from the same two weaknesses. A major disrepair (for which the tenant is not responsible) may require the carrying out by the tenant of minor repairs or, worse still, make these repairs pointless. Thus, for example, a tenant may quite literally have to plaster over cracks and redecorate where the cracks are the result of a major problem with the structure of the building. Secondly, the premises could become unfit for use as a result of a disrepair for which the tenant was not responsible. This would merely produce an 'impasse' with the lease, and thus the tenant's liability to pay rent, remaining in being.[1] Not only, therefore, does he require the extent of his covenant to be reduced, but ideally the tenant also needs either the landlord to accept liability for all other repairs that may be needed, or to be able to terminate the lease if the premises are unfit for use as a result of a disrepair for which he is not responsible. There are three ways in which the tenant's obligations can be reduced:

8.13:1 *Limiting extent.* Here the repairing covenant is expressed to apply, for example, only to the internal decorations of the premises.

8.13:2 *Schedule of Condition.* By this approach a Schedule is prepared and agreed on behalf of both parties that describes the condition of the premises at the time of the lease. A proviso is then added to the tenant's repairing covenant to the effect that 'the Premises need not be maintained in any better state or condition than that evidenced by the annexed Schedule of Condition.' It is important, however, that the lawyers involved in the letting review the Schedule to satisfy themselves that it would fulfil its purpose. For example, statements like 'defective guttering on front wall'[2] or 'crack on front wall'[3] leave great uncertainty. They should be expanded so that they more accurately identify the limitation of the tenant's liability.

8.13:3 *Fair wear and tear.* By this alternative a proviso is added to the tenant's repairing covenant to the effect that he does not have to deal with disrepair caused by fair wear and tear.[4] In the words of Talbot J in *Haskell v Marlow*[5] which have been approved by the House of Lords:[6]

> 'The meaning of (the exception for fair wear and tear) is that the tenant is bound to keep the house in good repair and condition, but is not liable for what is due to reasonable wear and tear. That is to say, his obligation to keep in good repair is subject to that exception. If any want of repair is alleged and proved in fact, it lies on the tenant to show that it comes within the exception. Reasonable wear and tear means the reasonable use of the house by the tenant in the ordinary operation of natural forces. The exception of want of repair due to wear and tear must be construed as limited to what is directly due to wear and tear, reasonable conduct on the part of the tenant being assumed. It does not mean that if there is a defect originally proceeding from reasonable wear and tear the tenant is released from his obligation to keep in good repair and condition everything that it may be possible to trace ultimately to that defect. He is bound to do such repairs as may be required to prevent the consequences flowing originally from wear and tear from producing others which wear and tear would not directly produce.'

The proviso of fair wear and tear is not often seen in commercial lettings, although it does seem that it would be a useful, and not unreasonable, protection for the tenant of an old building, in that it would absolve him from liability to carry out major repairs due to the age of the building, although one must accept that construing what repairs fall within the proviso could well not prove easy.

1 Because the mere fact that the premises are unfit for the tenant's use will serve to bring the lease to an end only if it is frustrated – see paras 10.13 and 10.15 below – and that will only happen very rarely.
2 The tenant, therefore, does not have to repair the guttering but the position is uncertain if the defect gives rise to consequential damage.
3 Apparently, therefore, the tenant does not have to fill in the crack, but what if it is merely the first manifestation of something more serious?
4 The conventional wording is 'damage by fair wear and tear excepted'. Perhaps 'disrepair'

would be preferable to 'damage' in the light of the current emphasis on disrepair: see para 8.3
above.
5 [1928] 2 KB 45.
6 *Regis Property Co Ltd v Dudley* [1959] AC 370, [1958] 3 All ER 491.

8.14 *New buildings: the problem of inherent defects.* The original tenant of a new
building held under a full repairing lease can find himself in the invidious
position of having to make good defects in the design or construction of the
property. It was once thought that a covenant to repair could never oblige the
covenantor to remedy disrepair caused by an inherent defect, let alone to
remedy the defect itself.[1] It is now clear that this is not the case.[2] Disrepair
caused by an inherent defect is no different from any other type of disrepair,
and the normal principles apply.[3] Moreover, compliance with a repairing
covenant will involve the remedy, not only of the disrepair caused by an
inherent defect, but also of the defect itself, if this is 'the only realistic way of
effecting the relevant repairs'.[4] Again however the normal principles apply,
and if the remedial works, taken as a whole, would involve more than 'repair',
they will fall outside the scope of a covenant to repair.[5] The mere existence,
however, of an inherent defect does not in itself constitute a state of disrepair
and where the defect has not caused any disrepair, the remedying of the defect
does *not* fall within a covenant to repair.[6] This is because 'there must be
disrepair before any question arises as to whether it would be reasonable to
remedy a design fault when doing the repair'[7] and 'a state of disrepair . . .
connotes a deterioration from some previous physical condition'.[8] Thus where
the inherent defect has simply existed, and there has been no damage to the
building since the original construction, there is no deterioration or disrepair.[9]

1   As to what constitutes an 'inherent defect', see eg *Brew Bros Ltd v Snax (Ross) Ltd* [1970] 1 QB
    612 at 640, CA per Sachs LJ: 'Things which can be easily recognised are not always susceptible
    of simple definition. Indeed the only observation I need offer is to reject the submission that if
    "inherent nature" or "inherent defects" have to be considered, they are confined to a state of
    affairs due to the age of the premises or to defects that originated when the building was
    erected'. See also *Post Office v Aquarius Properties Ltd* [1987] 1 All ER 1055 at 1063, CA per Ralph
    Gibson LJ: 'The reasoning of the court in *Quick's* case [see note 6 below] is equally applicable
    whether the original defect resulted from error in design, or in workmanship, or from
    deliberate parsimony or from any other cause'. It should be noted that 'inherent defects' are
    not confined to *new* buildings: an application of the principles referred to in this paragraph and
    in para 8.1 above can mean that a covenant to repair can require the remedying of an 'inherent
    defect' in an *old* building: see eg *Elmcroft Developments Ltd v Tankersley-Sawyer* (1984) 270 Estates
    Gazette 140. It should also be noted that the definition of 'inherent defect' suggested in para
    8.7 above is probably more restrictive in scope than 'inherent defect' (or its near synonyms) as
    used in the authorities.
2   *Ravenseft Properties Ltd v Davstone (Holdings) Ltd* [1980] QB 12, [1979] 1 All ER 929. This case
    was 'cited to this court in *Elmcroft Developments Ltd v Tankersely-Sawyer* (1984) 270 Estates
    Gazette 140 and clearly approved. It was not cited to this court in *Wainwright v Leeds City Council*
    (1984) 270 Estates Gazette 1289, CA. In the latter case counsel for the tenant seems to have
    based his unsuccessful submissions on social rather than legal grounds. I am satisfied that the
    approach of Forbes J in the *Ravenseft* case was right': *Quick v Taff-Ely Borough Council* [1985]
    3 All ER 321 at 328, CA per Lawton LJ.
3   See para 8.1 above. Some concern was expressed at the decision in *Ravenseft* (see note 2 above)
    by which the tenant was required to lay-out some £55,000 in remedying an inherent defect, but
    it is important to note that Forbes J did not say that remedying an inherent defect would *always*
    fall within the tenant's covenant. What he did say was that there was no principle that such
    repairs could *never* be the responsibility of the tenant. A covenant to repair would not require a
    tenant to remedy a defect (inherent or otherwise) that would amount to either a reconstruction
    of substantially the whole of the premises (see *Lurcott v Wakely and Wheeler* [1911] 1 KB 905 at
    924, CA per Buckley LJ – see para 8.1 above), or giving back to the landlord a wholly different
    thing from that demised (*Lister v Lane and Nesham* [1983] 2 QB 212 at 216, CA, per Lord Esher –
    see para 8.1 above). See also *Rich Investments Ltd v Camgate Litho Ltd* [1988] NPC 100.

4   *Quick v Taff-Ely Borough Council* [1985] 3 All ER 321 at 329, CA per Neill LJ. The circumstances
    in which compliance with a repairing covenant will involve the remedy of an underlying defect
    have been variously characterised in the authorities: see eg the judgments of Stocker LJ and Sir
    John Arnold P in *Stent v Monmouth District Council* [1987] 1 EGLR 59, 282 Estates Gazette 705,
    at 64 and 65, 712 and 715, CA. Although the principle is clear, its practical application may
    sometimes be less so. With *Elmcroft Developments Ltd v Tankersley-Sawyer* (1984) 270 Estates
    Gazette 140, contrast *Mullaney v Maybourne Grange (Croydon) Management Co Ltd* [1986] 1 EGLR
    70, 277 Estates Gazette 1350 and *Murray v Birmingham City Council* [1987] 2 EGLR 53, 283
    Estates Gazette 962, CA.
5   *Elmcroft Developments Ltd v Tankersley-Sawyer* (1984) 270 Estates Gazette 140; *Stent v Monmouth
    District Council* [1987] 1 EGLR 59, 282 Estates Gazette 705, CA. See para 8.1 above, and note 3
    above.
6   *Quick v Taff-Ely Borough Council* [1986] QB 809, [1985] 3 All ER 321, CA; *Post Office v Aquarius
    Properties Ltd* [1987] 1 All ER 1055.
7   *Quick v Taff-Ely Borough Council* [1985] 3 All ER 321 at 329, CA per Lawton LJ.
8   *Post Office v Aquarius Properties Ltd* [1987] 1 All ER 1055 at 1065, CA per Slade LJ.
9   It is of course open to the parties to the lease to provide expressly that one or other of them will
    be liable to remedy defects in the premises, even in circumstances where to do so would go
    beyond 'repair'.

8.15   *New buildings: drafting.* The tenant of a new building would ideally want
the landlord to covenant to repair any disrepair caused by defective design or
poor workmanship. The tenant would no doubt advance 'consumerism'
arguments – he would suggest that he is entitled to a building of 'merchantable
quality' and an obligation from the landlord to put it into that condition if it is
not, or to reimburse the tenant the cost of so doing.[1] He would probably add
that the landlord ought not to suffer financially because he should be able to
recover any sums spent on remedying inherent defects from, for example, the
contractor or architect by means of a claim for breach of contract or
negligence.[2] The landlord will not welcome these proposals – he will be
looking to let the property on a full repairing or clear lease,[3] and for there to be
no risk of him having to spend any of the rent that he receives on repairing the
property. As ever, the final form of the lease will depend upon the negotiating
strengths of the parties, and there are a number of compromises worth
exploring, although it is vital, if the lease is to deal in any way with this topic,
for the defects in question to be defined.[4] The compromises worth considering
are:

8.15:1   *Latent defects.* In many ways, 'latent defect' is a more appropriate term
to describe what is involved, conveying as it does the concept that the defect is
neither apparent nor foreseeable at the commencement of the lease. It would
seem reasonable for any provision that shifts the responsibility for these defects
from the tenant to the landlord to be confined to defects that would not have
been apparent from an inspection of the property and, perhaps, the drawings
and specification for it.[5]

8.15:2   *Time.* The value of an investment will be adversely affected if some
parts of it are let on leases that are not 'institutionally acceptable' and this is
frequently why landlords are so reluctant to accept *any* repairing obligations
(or, more accurately, obligations the cost of which will not be reimbursed by
the tenant). A compromise might be for the landlord to accept liability for any
latent defect that manifests itself within the first few years of the term.[6] The
obligation would then lapse, and the lease revert to a tenant's full repairing
lease, thereby confining the valuation implications to those initial years. The

tenant will obviously require professional advice as to the period during which latent defects are likely to come to light.[7]

8.15:3 *Involve the tenant in the building work.* Some leases for new buildings appear for the first time in a schedule to a draft agreement by which the landlord agrees to erect a building to an agreed specification and then to grant a lease in an agreed form.[8] If building work has not (or has hardly) begun, that agreement could give the tenant's advisers the right to inspect first the drawings and specification and then the work as it progresses, and to report any defects that they see to the landlord's architect so that they can be remedied.[9] In practice, this can mean that the landlord's and the tenant's architects work together. In addition, the tenant could insist upon entering into Duty of Care Agreements with the contractor and the landlord's professional team to provide him with a contractual remedy should their negligence cause defects that the tenant has to remedy under the terms of the lease.[10]

8.15:4 *Landlord to pursue remedies.* Very much as a last resort where the above proposals are either rejected or impractical, the tenant should seek to persuade the landlord to enter into a supplemental deed by which the landlord makes a claim against a third party under any rights that he may have in relation to inherent defects that the tenant has remedied under the tenant's repairing covenant. The landlord then accounts to the tenant with any sums recovered, less costs.[11]

1 Although in fact no warranty is implied that business premises are or will remain physically fit for the use contemplated: see Hill & Redman's *Law of Landlord and Tenant* (18th edn) para A1001.
2 Or perhaps, for example, the local authority.
3 See paras 8.8 above and 11.1 below.
4 See para 8.7 above and Appendix 1 below, Additional Clause C. This applies whether or not the 'latent proviso' is included: see para 8.15:1.
5 See ibid, Additional Clause C, proviso.
6 See ibid, Additional Clauses D–F.
7 The pessimist would point out that some of the old building repairing cases (for example those referred to in footnote 4 to para 8.12 above) concern disrepair caused by latent defects that only manifested themselves many years later. It is to be hoped that modern building control would prevent such defects today.
8 See, for example, 22 Encyclopaedia of Forms and Precedents (5th edn) Form No 13.
9 Ibid, Fourth Schedule para 7.
10 See, for example, 22 Encyclopaedia of Forms and Precedents (5th edn) Forms No 19 and 20.
11 Ibid, Form No 21. The parties could consider effecting insurance against latent defects. 'Building Insurance', as it is known, is available in the United Kingdom through the subsidiaries of a few overseas insurers – apparently UK insurers experience so little demand that they cannot write a sufficient portfolio of businesses to get an adequate spread of risk. Consultants appointed by the insurers are involved during the planning and construction of the building. The policy runs for ten years from the date of practical completion and any latent defects that manifest themselves during that period are remedied at the insurer's expense. Presumably the insurer is then subrogated to the rights that the insured would have, for example against the contractors or the professional team. See Property Director (1989) Issue No 12 p 19 (published by the Institute of Directors).

8.16 *Service charges.* A tenant contemplating a lease that contains a comprehensive service charge will need to consider the extent of work that the landlord will be entitled to undertake at the tenant's expense. Typical questions that arise are would the landlord be entitled to include in the service charge the cost of, for example, improving the property, of which the demised premises form part, or remedying major disrepairs due, for example, to old age or inherent defects?[1]

1 See para 11.18:3 below.

E   BREACH OF TENANT'S REPAIRING COVENANT

8.17 *Statutory limitation on enforcement.* Where property[1] is held on a lease for seven years or more of which three years or more remain unexpired, the Leasehold Property (Repairs) Act 1938 (referred to in this chapter as 'the 1938 Act') provides that the landlord cannot enforce a right to damages for a breach of a covenant to repair unless he has served[2] on the tenant a notice of the breach under section 146(1) of the Law of Property Act 1925 not less than one month before the commencement of the action.[3] The notice must contain a statement, in characters not less conspicuous than those used in any other part of the notice:
(a) to the effect that the tenant is entitled to serve counter-notice, and
(b) specifying the time within which and the manner in which a counter-notice may be served, and the name and address for service of the landlord.[4]

1 Other than an agricultural holding.
2 Ie in accordance with the Law of Property Act 1925, s 196 and the 1938 Act, s 7(2).
3 The 1938 Act, ss 1(1), 7(1), the 1954 Act, s 51(1), (2).
4 The 1938 Act, s 1(4). See *Sidnell v Wilson* [1966] 2 QB 67, [1966] 1 All ER 681, CA; *Middlegate Properties Ltd v Messimeris* [1973] 1 All ER 645, [1973] 1 WLR 168, CA; *BL Holdings Ltd v Marcolt Investments Ltd* (1978) 249 Estates Gazette 849.

8.18 *Statute not apply.* These provisions of the 1938 Act do not apply, however, to covenants
(a) to put premises into repair upon taking possession or within a reasonable time thereafter,[1]
(b) to cleanse the premises,[2] even where this forms part of the repairing covenant, nor
(c) to pay the landlord's costs of taking steps under s 146 of the Law of Property Act 1925, even where arising from a breach of the repairing covenant.[3]

1 The 1938 Act, s 3, the 1954 Act, s 51(2). *National Real Estate and Finance Co Ltd v Hassan* [1939] 2 KB 61, [1939] 2 All ER 154, CA.
2 *Starrokate Ltd v Barry* (1982) 265 Estates Gazette 871, CA.
3 *Bader Properties Ltd v Lindley Property Investment Ltd* (1968) 19 P & CR 620; *Middlegate Properties v Gidlow Jackson* (1977) 34 P & CR 4, CA; *Hamilton v Martell Securities Ltd* [1984] Ch 266, [1984] 1 All ER 665; *Colchester Estates (Cardiff) v Carlton Industries plc* [1986] Ch 80, [1984] 2 All ER 601; *Elite Investments Ltd v T I Bainbridge Silencers Ltd (No 2)* [1987] 2 EGLR 50, 283 Estates Gazette 747. (Note the conflicting cases of *Swallow Securities v Brand* (1983) 45 P & CR 328, 260 Estates Gazette 63; *SEDAC Investments Ltd v Tanner* [1982] 3 All ER 646, [1982] 1 WLR 1342.)

8.19 *Procedure.* Where, within twenty-eight days of the service of a notice of breach of covenant to repair, a tenant[1] serves[2] a counter-notice to the effect that he claims the benefit of the statutory provisions as to leasehold repairs, the landlord may not commence proceedings for re-entry or forfeiture, or for damages, without the leave of the Court.[3] If the landlord has obtained leave to commence proceedings against the tenant, however, and the tenant subsequently assigns the lease, the landlord may bring an action against the assignee without obtaining fresh leave.[4] Leave will not be granted unless the landlord proves:

(a) that the breach has substantially diminished the value of the reversion, or will do so unless immediately remedied;[5] or

(b) that the immediate remedying of the breach is necessary to comply with any enactment, byelaw or other provision having effect under an enactment, or to comply with any court order or requirement of any authority under such enactment, byelaw or other provision;[6] or

(c) where the tenant is not in occupation of the whole premises, that the immediate remedying of the breach is required in the interests of the occupier of the premises or of part of them;[7] or

(d) that the immediate remedying of the breach would be much less expensive than if the repair were postponed;[8] or

(e) that there are special circumstances which, in the opinion of the court, render it just and equitable that leave should be given.[9]

1 But not a tenant's mortgagee: *Church Comrs for England v Ve-Ri-Best Manufacturing Co Ltd* [1957] 1 QB 238, [1959] 3 All ER 777.
2 See note 3 for para 8.17 above.
3 The 1938 Act, s 3(1). The prohibition ceases to apply where there are less than three years of the term to run: *Baker v Sims* [1959] 1 QB 114, [1958] 3 All ER 326, CA. 'Court' means the county court except where the action for which leave is sought would have to be begun in the High Court: Leasehold Property (Repairs) Act 1938, s 6(1).
4 *Kanda v Church Comrs for England* [1958] 1 QB 332, sub nom *Church Comrs for England v Kanda* [1957] 2 All ER 815, CA.
5 The 1938 Act, s 1(5)(a).
6 The 1938 Act, s 1(5)(b); the 1954 Act, s 51(2).
7 The 1938 Act, s 1(5)(c), the 1954 Act, s 51(2).
8 The 1938 Act, s 1(5)(d).
9 The 1938 Act, s 1(5)(e).

8.20   *Granting or refusing leave.* In granting or refusing leave the court may impose such terms and conditions on the lessor or the lessee as it may think fit.[1] These conditions are alternatives, and leave may be given if the landlord shows a prima facie case ('or perhaps a bona fide arguable case')[2] that one of the conditions is fulfilled,[3] by adducing evidence in the normal way.[4] The court has a discretion to refuse leave, even if the landlord has made out such a case, but this discretion should only be exercised so as to exclude the landlord from pursuing his rights under the lease if the court is clearly convinced that leave should be refused.[5]

1 The 1938 Act, s 1(6).
2 *Land Securities plc v Metropolitan Police District Receiver* [1983] 2 All ER 254 at 258 per Megarry V-C. See also *Associated British Ports v C H Bailey plc* [1989] 1 EGLR 69.
3 *Phillips v Price* [1959] Ch 181, [1958] 3 All ER 386; *Sidnell v Wilson* [1966] 2 QB 67, [1966] 1 All ER 681, CA, Land Securities – see note 2 above.
4 *Jackson v Charles A Pilgrim Ltd* (1975) 29 P & CR 328, CA.
5 *Re Metropolitan Film Studios Ltd v Twickenham Film Studios Ltd* [1962] 3 All ER 508, [1962] 1 WLR 1315, *Land Securities* – see note 2 above.

8.21   *Registration.* A landlord who has made an application to the Court under the 1938 Act (or indeed who has commenced any action for forfeiture) should register this as a pending land action, because the object of such an application is to terminate the legal estate vested in the tenant.[1] Where the lease is registered at HM Land Registry an assignee will not be bound even if he was aware of the application where there is no registration.[2] An assignee of an unregistered lease who has actual notice will, however, be bound even without registration.[3]

1 *Selim Ltd v Bickenhall Engineering Ltd* [1981] 3 All ER 210, [1981] 1 WLR 1318 – see appendix 3 below.
2 Land Registration Act 1925, s 59(6).
3 Land Charges Act 1972, s 5(7).

8.22 *Statutory limitation on damages during lease.* Section 18(1) of the 1927 Act limits damages for a breach of a covenant to keep or put premises in repair *during the currency of a lease* to the amount, if any, by which the value of the reversion (whether immediate or not) in the premises is diminished owing to the breach of that covenant. The reversion to be considered is that expectant upon the existing lease and not that expectant on a reversionary lease to take effect on a future day.[1] In practice the damages will generally be the amount by which the saleable value of the premises has been diminished by reason of the non-repair of the premises.[2] If the damages are claimed during the subsistence of the term the amount of the diminution depends in part upon the length of the unexpired term;[3] but where the term is forfeited by reason of the breach of covenant the damages are assessed as if the term had expired, so that the acceleration of the landlord's reversion by reason of the forfeiture does not reduce or discount the damages then recoverable.[4] Where the landlord is the freeholder, and is entitled to the reversion free from any liability on his part, the proper measure of damages will be the diminution caused to the saleable value of his estate.[5] Where the landlord is himself a tenant, the reversion may only be notional, but this does not prevent it from being valued and damages from being assessed.[6] If the landlord has covenanted with his superior landlord to repair, and the tenant has notice of the existence of a headlease, the landlord's liability under the covenant in the headlease must be taken into account in assessing the damages.[7] Thus where an underlease is being granted, it should always be described as such.

1 *Terroni and Necchi v Corsini* [1931] 1 Ch 515; *Hanson v Newman* [1934] Ch 298 at 304, CA.
2 *Smith v Peat* (1853) 9 Exch 161; cf *Metge v Kavanagh* (1877) IR 11 CL 431.
3 *Turner v Lamb* (1845) 14 M & W 412; *Ebbetts v Conquest* [1895] 2 Ch 377, CA; affd sub nom *Conquest v Ebbetts* [1896] AC 490, HL: *Smiley v Townshend* [1950] 2 KB 311 at 332, CA.
4 *Hanson v Newman* [1934] Ch 298, CA.
5 *Ebbetts v Conquest* [1895] 2 Ch 377 at 386, CA.
6 See *Lloyds Bank Ltd v Lake* [1961] 2 All ER 30, [1961] 1 WLR 884; distinguishing *Espir v Basil Street Hotel Ltd* [1936] 3 All ER 91, CA.
7 *Ebbetts v Conquest* [1985] 2 Ch 377, CA; affd sub nom *Conquest v Ebbetts* [1896] AC 490, HL. *Williams v Williams* (1874) LR 9 CP 659.

8.23 *Statutory limitation on damages or termination.* After a lease has *terminated*, the landlord may bring an action on the covenant to yield up the premises in repair, but here again section 18(1) of the 1927 Act limits the damages to the amount if any by which the value of the reversion (whether immediate or not) in the premises is diminished as a result of the breach of the covenant. No damages will be recovered for a breach of the repairing covenant or at the termination of a lease if it is shown that the premises, in whatever state of repair they might be, would at or shortly after the termination of the tenancy have been or be pulled down, or such structural alterations made to them as would render valueless the repairs covered by the covenant.[1] The tenant, however, must show that at the termination of the lease the landlord had formed a definite intention to demolish or reconstruct the premises.[2] At common law the measure of damages was the sum which it would take to put the premises in the state of repair in which the tenant ought, under the covenant, to leave them.[3] The proper cost of repairs is still prima facie evidence of the extent of the damage to the reversion[4] but the tenant may be able to show that this cost exceeds the diminution in value of the landlord's reversion at the termination of the lease.[5]

1 Landlord and Tenant Act 1927, s 18(1).
2 *Cunliffe v Goodman* [1950] 2 KB 237, [1950] 1 All ER 720, CA. See also *Hibernian Property Co Ltd v Liverpool Corpn* [1973] 2 All ER 1117, [1973] 1 WLR 751; *Mather v Barclay's Bank plc* [1987] 2 EGLR 254. The material time is the date of the termination of the lease, and it does not matter if the landlord abandons his intention to demolish at some subsequent date: *Salisbury v Gilmore* [1942] 2 KB 38, [1942] 1 All ER 457, CA; *Keats v Graham* [1959] 3 All ER 919, [1960] 1 WLR 30, CA.
3 *Joyner v Weeks* [1891] 2 QB 31 at 43, CA; *Morgan v Hardy* (1886) 17 QBD 770; affd (1887) 35 WR 588, CA, per Lord Esher MR; affd sub nom *Hardy v Fothergill* (1888) 13 App Cas 351, HL); *Anstruther-Gough-Calthorpe v McOscar* [1924] 1 KB 716, CA. As to the landlord's loss while repairs being carried out, see *Woods v Pope* (1835) 6 C & P 782; *Birch v Clifford* (1891) 8 TLR 103.
4 *Jones v Herxheimer* [1950] 2 KB 106, [1950] 1 All ER 323, CA; *Smiley v Townshend* [1950] 2 KB 311, [1950] 1 All ER 530, CA; *Drummond v S & U Stores Ltd* (1980) 258 Estates Gazette 1293.
5 *Portman v Latta* [1942] WN 97; *London County Freehold and Leasehold Properties Ltd v Wallis-Whiddett* [1950] WN 180. As to date upon which damages should be assessed, see *Associated Deliveries Ltd v Harrison* (1984) 272 Estates Gazette 321, CA.

8.24 *Damage to the reversion.* In assessing the damages to the reversion it has been held irrelevant that:

(a) the premises can immediately be re-let without any substantial expenditure due to a shortage of housing although it would seem that if premises can be sold at the same price, whether or not in disrepair, there can be no diminution in the value of the reversion,[1] and

(b) the landlord has taken a covenant from a new tenant to put the premises into repair, while agreeing to pay over to him any damages for dilapidations recovered from the previous tenant.[2]

Nevertheless Glidewell J held in *Drummond v S & U Stores Ltd*[3] that a landlord was not entitled to recover damages for want of decoration to the interior of a shop on the grounds that any incoming tenant would fit out and decorate the shop according to his own requirements and accordingly there was no damage to the reversion. Apparently the landlord is entitled, as part of his damages, to a sum for loss of rent during the time the repairs are being effected, as long as this sum and the cost of repairs do not exceed the diminution in the value of the reversion,[4] but the cost of drawing up a schedule of dilapidations is not recoverable, unless (as today would usually be the case) this is provided for in the lease.[5] If the landlord has, during the term, already recovered damages for breach of covenant to keep in repair, these will be deducted from the sum which the tenant would otherwise pay as damages for breach of the covenant to leave in repair.[6] If the landlord has re-entered for breach of the covenant to repair, the damages to which he is entitled will not be diminished by the fact that he has obtained possession of the premises at an earlier date than if the lease had run its full period – here the proper measure of damages is the difference in value between the premises as they were at the time of re-entry and the condition in which they would have been had the covenant been performed.[7]

1 *Landeau v Marchbank* [1949] 2 All ER 172; *Smiley v Townshend* [1950] 2 KB 311, [1950] 1 All ER 530, CA; *Haviland v Long* [1952] 2 QB 80, [1952] 1 All ER 463, CA; *Jaquin v Holland* [1960] 1 All ER 402, [1960] 1 WLR 258, CA; *Mather v Barclays Bank plc* [1987] 2 EGLR 254. See also *Family Management v Gray* (1979) 253 Estates Gazette 369, CA, as to the effect of a right to a new tenancy under the 1954 Act.
2 *Haviland v Long* [1952] 2 QB 80, [1952] 1 All ER 463, CA.
3 (1980) 258 Estates Gazette 1293.
4 See *Woods v Pope* (1835) 6 C & P 782; *Birch v Clifford* (1891) 8 TLR 103.
5 *Maud v Sandars* [1943] 2 All ER 783; *Lloyds Bank Ltd v Lake* [1961] 2 All ER 30, [1961] 1 WLR 884.
6 *Henderson v Thorn* [1893] 2 QB 164; *Ebbetts v Conquest* (1900) 82 LT 560.
7 *Hanson v Newman* [1934] Ch 298, CA.

F LANDLORD'S COVENANT TO REPAIR

8.25 *Drafting.* The property market is such that the landlord's repairing covenants are unusual today at least other than where the costs incurred by the landlord in complying with the covenant are to be reimbursed by the tenant in the form of a service charge. Even a 'compromise' to deal with inherent defects in a new building is hardly commonplace. Where a landlord is prepared to undertake responsibility for the structure, the tenant's advisers should ensure that the wording is comprehensive.[1]

1 In *Smedley v Chumley and Hawke Ltd* (1981) 44 P & CR 50, 261 Estates Gazette 775, CA, it was argued for the landlord that there was a significant omission from the covenant, lacking as it did a reference to foundations. On the construction of the lease in question, the Court of Appeal did not feel able to agree that the landlord would be relieved of his obligation if the walls and roof became unsafe because of problems with the footings or foundations. Nevertheless the tenant's solicitor should not leave so important a matter to chance.

8.26 *Tenant's remedies for landlord's breach.* Where the landlord does covenant to carry out repairs, there will be an implied condition that the tenant must give notice of want of repair before the landlord's obligation arises[1] although where the landlord has actual notice from some other source, notice by the tenant is apparently no longer required.[2] The fact that the landlord has a right of entry upon the premises does not relieve the tenant of the obligation to give such notice before he can hold his landlord liable for breach of covenant.[3] As soon as the landlord has been given notice or he (or his agent) has knowledge of the defect, he must, if permanent repair is not immediately possible, take immediate steps to render the premises temporarily safe.[4] Prima facie the measure of damages for a breach by the landlord of his covenant to repair is the difference in value to the tenant of the premises, from the date of the notice to repair down to the date of the assessment of damages, between the premises in their condition at the time of assessment and their value if the landlord, on receipt of the notice, had fulfilled the obligations of his covenant.[5] The tenant is also entitled to recover damages for personal injuries and for damage to his chattels during the same period caused by the landlord's default in repairing.[6] In assessing such damages, damage due to defects which the landlord is not bound to remedy must be excluded, and consideration of the question whether the execution of the repairs is to the commercial advantage or disadvantage of the landlord is irrelevant.[5] The tenant will not necessarily disqualify himself to damages by continuing to use the premises pending the carrying out of repairs,[7] but he will not be entitled to damages if he prevents the landlord from doing the necessary work.[8] A tenant of part of premises is entitled to recover from the landlord the cost of carrying out work required to the whole building under the landlord's covenant, and this will not be reduced to reflect the fact that the tenant is not in possession of the whole building.[9]

1 *Makin v Watkinson* (1870) LR 6 Exch 25; *Torrens v Walker* [1906] 2 Ch 166 and *O'Brien v Robinson* [1973] AC 912, [1973] 1 All ER 583, HL, but note *McGreal v Wake* (1984) 269 Estates Gazette 1254, CA; *Calabar Properties Ltd v Stitcher* [1983] 3 All ER 759, [1984] 1 WLR 287, CA; *Chiod's Personal Representatives v De Marney* (1988) 21 HLR 6, [1988] 2 EGLR 64, CA. See too H W Wilkinson: 'Breach of Landlord's Covenant to Repair' (1984) 134 NLJ 379, Apr 20.

2 *Griffin v Pillet* [1926] 1 KB 17; *O'Brien v Robinson* [1973] 1 All ER 583 at 589, HL, per Lord Morris; *Dinefwr Borough Council v Jones* [1987] 2 EGLR 58, 284 Estates Gazette 58, CA; *Hall v Howard* [1988] 2 EGLR 75, [1988] 44 EG 83, CA.

3 *McCarrick v Liverpool Corpn* [1947] AC 219, [1946] 2 All ER 646, HL. If the part of the property which becomes defective is not in the exclusive possession of the tenant, there may be no necessity for the notice as where the defect is in a sea wall over which the landlord keeps control: *Murphy v Hurly* [1922] 1 AC 369, HL.

4 *Griffin v Pillet* [1926] 1 KB 17.

5 *Hewitt v Rowlands* (1924) 93 LJKB 1080, CA but note *Calabar Properties Ltd v Stitcher* [1983] 3 All ER 759 and *McGreal v Wake* (1984) 269 Estates Gazette 1254, CA. See Nic Madge: 'Damages for breach of repairing obligations' [1988] Gazette 17 July 20.

6 *Griffin v Pillet* [1926] 1 KB 17; *Porter v Jones* [1942] 2 All ER 570, CA. See also the Defective Premises Act 1972, s 4, para 8.28 below.

7 *Porter v Jones* [1942] 2 All ER 570, CA; and see *Greene v Chelsea Borough Council* [1954] 2 QB 127, [1954] 2 All ER 318, CA.

8 *Granada Theatres Ltd v Freehold Investment (Leytonstone) Ltd* [1959] Ch 592, [1959] 2 All ER 176, CA.

9 *Marenco v Jacramel Co Ltd* (1964) 191 Estates Gazette 433, CA. As to the subject generally, see D W Williams: 'Tenants' Remedies for Disrepair' [1984] Gazette 9 May 1269.

8.27 *Alternatives to a claim for damages.* There are, however, various alternatives to suing the landlord for damages that the tenant should consider, for example:

(a) undertaking the repairs himself and then deducting the costs from future rent due to the landlord. In *Lee-Parker v Izzet*[1] Goff J held that tenants were entitled to do this to the extent that the repairs were within the express or implied covenants of the landlord;

(b) setting off against future rent an unliquidated claim for damages, a course approved by Forbes J in *British Anzani (Felixstowe) Ltd v International Marine Management (UK) Ltd.*[2] Since this case, however, landlords have tended expressly to prevent the tenant from setting off against rent damages in respect of claims against the landlord.[3]

(c) seeking specific performance although this is only likely to be granted 'where there has been a plain breach of a covenant to repair and there is no doubt at all what is required to be done to remedy the breach';[4]

(d) suing in nuisance;[5]

(e) avoiding the lease on the grounds that it has been frustrated.[6]

1 [1971] 3 All ER 1099, [1971] 1 WLR 1688.

2 [1980] QB 137, [1979] 2 All ER 1063, see also *Melville v Grapelodge Developments Ltd* (1978) 39 P & CR 179. See also Andrew Waite: 'Repairs and Deduction from Rent' [1981] Conv 199 and 'Disrepair and Set-off of Damages Against Rent' [1983] Conv 373 and D W Williams: 'Tenants's Remedies for Disrepair' [1984] Gazette 9 May 1269.

3 See for example Rosscastle Letting Conditions (Appendix 1, Form 1 below) Condition 3.1:4, and see *Gilbert Ash (Northern) Ltd v Modern Engineering (Bristol) Ltd* [1974] AC 689, [1973] 3 All ER 195, HL, per Lord Diplock at 717.

4 *Jeune v Queens Cross Properties Ltd* [1974] Ch 97, [1973] 3 All ER 97 per Pennycuick V-C.

5 *Brew Bros Ltd v Snax (Ross) Ltd* [1970] 1 QB 612, [1970] 1 All ER 587, CA.

6 *National Carriers Ltd v Panalpina (Northern) Ltd* [1981] AC 675, [1981] 1 All ER 161, HL. See para 10.15 below.

8.28 *Statutory obligations.* In the absence of an express covenant, a landlord gives no warranty that the premises are or will remain physically fit for the use contemplated[1] and is not liable to do any repairs other than those imposed on him by common law[2] or statute.[3] Neither impose any specific obligations on a landlord of business premises towards his tenant purely because of the relationship of landlord and tenant,[4] although he should never lose sight of Section 4 of the Defective Premises Act 1972. This imposes upon a landlord who has covenanted to maintain or repair premises a duty to all persons who might be affected by defects in the state of the premises. The duty is to take such care as is reasonable in all the circumstances to see that such persons are reasonably safe from personal injury or from damage to their property caused by a 'relevant defect' which is defined as a defect which constitutes a breach of the landlord's repairing obligations. The landlord is liable from the moment that he 'reasonably ought to know' of the want of repair or from the date of the lease. Section 4(4) serves to extend the section by providing that, where the landlord has a right to enter premises to carry out maintenance or repair, he shall be treated for the purposes of Section 4 as if he were under an obligation to the tenant for that description of maintenance or repair.[5] When there are common parts the Factories Act 1961[6] and the Offices Shops and Railway Premises Act 1963[7] will as and when they apply impose certain duties on the landlord in relation to floors passages and stairs.

1 *Cheater v Cater* [1918] 1 KB 247, CA; *Edler v Auerbach* [1950] 1 KB 359, [1949] 2 All ER 692. See Hill & Redman's *Law of Landlord and Tenant* (18th edn) para A1001.
2 Implied covenant by landlord of a furnished house that it is fit for immediate habitation: *Smith v Marrable* (1843) 11 M & W 5; *Wilson v Finch Hatton* (1877) 2 Ex D 336; *Collins v Hopkins* [1923] 2 KB 617.
3 Landlord and Tenant Act 1985, s 11 as amended by the Housing Act 1988, s 116. See D W Williams: 'Implied repairing obligations' [1988] Gazette 32 Feb 3; *Brikom Investments Ltd v Seaford* [1981] 2 All ER 783, [1981] 1 WLR 863, CA. But note covenant for quiet enjoyment and derogation from grant etc – see Hill and Redman's *Law of Landlord and Tenant* (18th edn) paras A935–1000.
4 *Arden v Pullen* (1842) 10 M & W 321.
5 This Act is generally thought of as one protecting third parties, but see *Smith v Bradford Metropolitan Council* (1982) 126 Sol Jo 624, 44 P & CR 171, CA – para 8.29 below. This related to a council house but the same principles would apply to business premises.
6 Section 28.
7 Section 16. See also Occupiers Liability Act 1957, s 3.

8.29 *Other obligations imposed by the courts.* There have, however, been several cases in recent years where courts have held a landlord of *residential* premises liable to the tenant outside the express terms of the lease, either in negligence or by implying a term into the lease, and commercial conveyancers and their litigation colleagues need to be aware of them, and to consider if they could have any application to business premises. For example:

(a) In *Liverpool City Council v Irwin*,[1] the House of Lords held that where there was no covenant in the lease to maintain the common parts (in this case the stairs, lifts and rubbish chutes of a tower block) there should be implied an obligation on the landlord to take reasonable care to maintain them in a state of reasonable repair and efficiency.

(b) In *Smith v Bradford Metropolitan Council*[2] the tenant of a council house was injured because of the condition of the property. The Court of Appeal held that, although there was no covenant by the Council to repair, the Council was liable to the tenant under s 4 of the Defective Premises Act 1972 because the tenancy agreement required the tenant to 'give the council officers agents contractors and workmen reasonable facilities for inspecting the Premises and their state of repair and for carrying out repairs'.

(c) In *Rimmer v Liverpool City Council*,[3] the tenant of a maisonette, while negotiating a toy-strewn corridor tripped, and in the course of his fall put his hand through a glass panel. The Court of Appeal held the local authority landlord, being their own architect and builders, liable in negligence – the fact that thin and unwired glass was used was dangerous and an accident of this kind was always likely to happen. Nevertheless, the Court of Appeal felt that[4] 'the (trial) judge formulated the duty too widely so as to include a bare landlord as well as the builder-owner. It may be that to impose a duty on all landowners who let and sell their land and dwellings, whether or not they are their own designers or builders, would be so great a change in the law as to require legislation'.

(d) In *Ryan v Camden London Borough*[5] a six-month-old baby wriggled off a bed, fell against exposed heating pipes, and was badly burned. Her father, the tenant of the flats sued the landlord, and although failing on the facts on the basis that the accident could not reasonably have been foreseen, the defendants and the Court of Appeal appear to have accepted that a duty of care was owed by the landlord in such circumstances.

(e) In *Barrett v Lounova (1982) Ltd*[6] the tenant was obliged to repair the interior of a dwelling house. There were no express obligations imposed upon the landlord[7] and the Court of Appeal upheld the decision of the County Court Judge who applied the business efficacy and officious bystander test,[8] and held that there was an implied covenant by the landlord to repair the exterior. Frequently, however, courts have been more reluctant to imply repairing obligations.[9]

1 [1977] AC 239, [1976] 2 All ER 39.
2 (1982) 126 Sol Jo 624, 44 P & CR 171. See also *King v Liverpool City Council* [1986] 1 EGLR 181, 278 Estates Gazette 516, CA; *Stockley v Knowsley Metropolitan Borough Council* [1986] 2 EGLR 141, 279 Estates Gazette 677, CA.
3 [1985] QB 1, [1984] 1 All ER 930, CA. See also *McNerny v Lambeth London Borough Council* (1988) 21 HLR 188, [1989] 1 EGLR 81, CA.
4 Per Stephenson LJ at 322.
5 (1983) 13 Fam Law 81, CA and see (1983) 267 Estates Gazette 169.
6 [1988] 2 EGLR 54, [1988] 36 EG 184, CA.
7 The provisions now contained in the Landlord and Tenant Act 1985, s 11 (as amended by the Housing Act 1988, s 116) did not apply to tenancies created before 24 October 1961.
8 *Reigate v Union Manufacturing Co (Ramsbottom) Ltd* [1918] 1 KB 592 at 605; per Scrutton LJ; *Shirlaw v Southern Foundries (1926) Ltd* [1939] 2 KB 206, [1939] 2 All ER 113 at 227 and 124 per MacKinnon LJ.
9 *Duke of Westminster v Guild* [1985] QB 688, [1984] 3 All ER 144, CA. Note also *Tennant-Radient Heat Ltd v Warrington Development Corpn* [1988] 1 EGLR 41, [1988] 11 EG 71, CA especially the comments of Dillon LJ at 43c.

Chapter 9

Landlord's covenants

A INTRODUCTION

9.1 *Topics dealt with elsewhere.* The shortest part of a lease will generally be the landlord's covenants, and as such, the length of this chapter is no coincidence. Its brevity is emphasised by the inclusion elsewhere of various topics that can be the subject of a covenant from the landlord, such as repairs,[1] upkeep of shared items,[2] services,[3] insurance,[4] and those matters relevant to underleases.[5]

1 See paras 8.25–8.26 above.
2 See paras 11.1–11.7 below.
3 See paras 11.8–11.37 below.
4 See Chapter 10 below.
5 See Chapter 13.

B QUIET ENJOYMENT

9.2 *Against whose actions is the tenant protected?* The covenant for quiet enjoyment as it appears in the draft lease[1] will generally be qualified and restricted to the landlord and 'all persons claiming under him'.[2] The effect of this is that the covenant would not extend to the acts of a person claiming by title paramount[3] and thus, would not protect the tenant from the acts of a superior landlord,[4] or a predecessor in title of the landlord.[5] A subtenant's solicitor should require the protection given by the covenant to be extended so that the covenant is expressed also to apply to the acts of all persons rightfully claiming by title paramount.[6]

1 In the absence of an express covenant for quiet enjoyment, one will be implied: *Markham v Paget* [1908] 1 Ch 697; *Kenny v Preen* [1963] 1 QB 499, [1962] 3 All ER 814, CA.
2 See Rosscastle Letting Conditions (Appendix 1, Form 1 below) Condition 4.1.
3 For more detailed discussion, see 27 Halsbury's Laws (4th edn) para 322, Hill and Redman's *Law of Landlord and Tenant* (18th edn) para A935.
4 Except by accident: see *Queensway Marketing Ltd v Associated Restaurants Ltd* [1988] 2 EGLR 49, [1988] 32 EG 41, CA where 'the Landlord' was defined as including superior lessors.
5 *Celsteel Ltd v Alton House Holdings Ltd (No 2)* [1987] 2 All ER 240, [1987] 1 WLR 291, CA.
6 This is all the more important where title has not been deduced (see paras 2.9 and 2.10 above) because the sub-tenant will be bound by restrictive covenants in the headlease or affecting the freehold. Thus, in the absence of an absolute covenant for quiet enjoyment or a warranty from the landlord, the subtenant would have no guarantee that his intended use is permitted.

9.3 *Nature of the covenant.* The covenant for quiet enjoyment has been described as a covenant to secure title and possession, rather than a guarantee to the tenant that he may use the land for all purposes not expressly prohibited,[1] but this statement presents too narrow a view of the covenant. It

241

is in every case a question of fact whether the quiet enjoyment of the property has or has not been interrupted. Where the ordinary and lawful enjoyment of the demised premises is substantially interfered with by the acts of the landlord or those lawfully claiming under him (or where the covenant is absolute, by anybody claiming under title paramount) the covenant is broken, although neither the title to the property nor the possession of the land may be otherwise affected.[2] A landlord does not commit a breach of the covenant for quiet enjoyment merely by asserting that the tenant's title and right to possession has been validly determined, at any rate if the landlord believes the assertion to be true, nor does he commit a breach by threatening proceedings.[3] It has been said that the alleged breach must consist in some actual physical interference with the premises or the tenant's enjoyment thereof;[4] but a course of conduct involving threats of physical eviction and removal of tenant's belongings, in a deliberate effort to drive the tenant out, with substantial physical interference by knocking at the door and shouting threats is a breach.[5] The breach may be the result of acts done off the premises, for example, flooding a mine;[6] erecting adjacent buildings so as to cause chimneys of the demised buildings to smoke;[7] overheating the demised premises;[8] failure to keep in repair a culvert on adjoining land, belonging to the successors in title of the landlord, by which as assignee of the lease suffered damage by erosion;[9] erecting and maintaining scaffolding for eleven days before a lock-up shop obstructing access to tenant's shop window and door.[10] But, where the interference could not have been reasonably foreseen to be the result of the acts complained of, there is no breach.[11] A temporary inconvenience which does not interfere with the estate or title or possession is not a breach of this covenant;[12] nor is an act which merely affects the amenities or comfortable enjoyment of the premises let.[13]

1   *Dennett v Atherton* (1872) LR 7 QB 316 at 326, Exch.
2   *Williams v Gabriel* [1906] 1 KB 155. As to the absolute covenant see para 9.2 above.
3   *Kenny v Preen* [1963] 1 QB 499, [1962] 3 All ER 814, CA.
4   *Browne v Flower* [1911] 1 Ch 219; *Sampson v Floyd* [1989] 33 EG 41, CA.
5   *Kenny v Preen* [1963] 1 QB 499, [1962] 3 All ER 814, CA.
6   *Shaw v Stenton* (1858) 2 H & N 858.
7   *Tebb v Cave* [1900] 1 Ch 642; *Davis v Town Properties Investment Corpn Ltd* [1903] 1 Ch 797, CA.
8   *Robinson v Kilvert* (1889) 41 Ch D 88, CA.
9   *Booth v Thomas* [1926] Ch 397, CA.
10   *Owen v Gadd* [1956] 2 QB 99, [1956] 2 All ER 28, CA; see para 4.13 above.
11   *Harrison, Ainslie & Co v Muncaster* [1891] 2 QB 680, CA.
12   *Manchester, Sheffield and Lincolnshire Rly Co v Anderson* [1898] 2 Ch 394 at 401, CA.
13   *Browne v Flower* [1911] 1 Ch 219.

C   RESTRICTING USE OF ADJOINING PROPERTY

9.4   *Competing user.* The fact that a lease contains a covenant by the tenant to use the demised premises only for one particular business does not put the landlord under an implied obligation not to let adjoining property for the purpose of carrying on the same business.[1] In order to prevent the use of adjoining premises for a particular business, the landlord should be required to covenant not only that he will not carry on or permit to be carried on that business on adjoining premises, but also that he will on any conveyance or lease of these premises insert a similar restriction binding the purchaser or lessee and will join in enforcing it. If the landlord covenants merely that he will not:

(a) let the adjoining premises for a particular business, the tenant may have no remedy if those premises are in fact used for the business by a lessee to whom they have been let for another purpose,[2]

(b) cause or permit the adjoining premises to be used for a particular business, it seems that he will not be liable for breach of the covenant merely because he sells the premises with knowledge that they will be used for that business by the purchaser[3] – the position may be different if the landlord lets the premises knowing that they will be so used because he does not by a lease part with his whole interest.[4]

In *Holloway Bros Ltd v Hill*,[5] where the landlord covenanted that he would not suffer a particular business to be carried on upon specific premises, and subsequently let the premises for such a business, the tenant obtained a declaration against the landlord and an injunction restraining the lessees of the premises (who were held to have constructive knowledge of the restriction) from carrying on the business.

1   *Port v Griffith* [1938] 1 All ER 295.
2   *Kemp v Bird* (1877) 5 Ch D 974, CA; *Ashby v Wilson* [1900] 1 Ch 66; but cf *Fitz v Iles* [1893] 1 Ch 77, CA; see also *Brigg v Thornton* [1904] 1 Ch 386, CA; *Palliser v Dover Corpn* (1914) 110 LT 619.
3   *Tophams Ltd v Earl of Sefton* [1967] 1 AC 50, [1966] 1 All ER 1039, HL.
4   *A Lewis & Co (Westminster) Ltd v Bell Property Trust Ltd* [1940] Ch 345 at 351, [1940] 1 All ER 570 at 575; *Tophams Ltd v Earl of Sefton*, above at 64, 68 and at 1042, 1045, respectively.
5   [1902] 2 Ch 612.

9.5   *Registration.* A covenant or agreement restrictive of the user of land but made between a lessor and lessee is not registrable as a restrictive covenant under s 2(5) Class D (ii) of the Land Charges Act 1972 nor, in the case of registered land, does it fall within the provisions of s 50(1) of the Land Registration Act 1925 which relate to the entry of notice of restrictive covenants on the register. If steps are thought to be necessary to bring the position to the knowledge of any person acquiring an interest in the adjoining premises affected by the covenants, a suitable endorsement on the lessor's title deeds may be considered or, in the case of registered land, a caution or a restriction may be registered on the lessor's title to the adjoining premises under s 54 or s 58 of the Land Registration Act 1925.

9.6   *RTP.* When a covenant restricting the use of land is inserted, two parties to an agreement are accepting restrictions, but this will not of itself make the lease registrable under the Restrictive Trade Practices Act 1976. Limitation of freedom of trade effected by covenants in a lease would only in most exceptional circumstances (and then only where there was some trading nexus between the parties) constitute restrictions that would fall within the Act.[1]

1   *Re Ravenseft Properties Application Ltd* [1978] QB 52, sub nom *Ravenseft Properties Ltd v Director General of Fair Trading* [1977] 1 All ER 47. As to covenants in restraint of trade, see *Esso Petroleum Co Ltd v Harper's Garage (Stourport)* [1968] AC 269, [1967] 1 All ER 699, HL and *Alec Lobb (Garages) Ltd v Total Oil GB Ltd* [1983] 1 All ER 944, [1983] 1 WLR 87.

Chapter 10

Insurance

A FUNDAMENTALS

10.1 *Who insures – usually the landlord.* The first question that has to be resolved as the landlord's solicitor approaches the insurance provisions of the lease[1] is which party will insure the property? There are some cases where the landlord has to insure – for example it would obviously not be practical for each tenant to insure his unit in a building that was in multi-occupation. Even where the demised premises are such that either party could insure, for example, a detached commercial building in single occupation, the current practice is for insurance to be undertaken almost invariably by the landlord. No doubt landlords prefer to rely upon the efficiency of their own organisations, and are worried by the nightmare of premises let on a tenant's insuring lease being destroyed at a time when the insurance had lapsed. If the tenant did not have funds of his own with which to reinstate the premises, the landlord would have lost his investment.[2] In this age of the 'clear lease', however, it will be the tenant who pays for the insurance effected by the landlord.[3]

1 It is suggested that it is helpful to collect together in the one clause all the insurance provisions: see for example 22 Encyclopaedia of Forms and Precedents (5th edn) Form 22 clause 7, Rosscastle Letting Conditions (Appendix 1, Form 1 below) Condition 6.
2 For an example of the consequences of the *landlord* not insuring where he had covenanted to do so, see *Naumann v Ford* [1985] 2 EGLR 70, 275 Estates Gazette 542.
3 See para 11.1 below.

10.2 *Key provisions.* Assuming that the landlord is to insure,[1] his solicitor would do well to consider the provisions that he should insert in the lease under the following broad headings:
(a) the sum for which insurance will be effected[2]
(b) the risks against which the property will be insured[3]
(c) what issues would arise if the property was damaged by an insured risk, and in particular what would the situation be if the damage was so extensive that the property could not be used by the tenant[4]
(d) procedural matters.[5]
As in so many areas, the landlord's solicitor will probably not be helping his client by producing a draft that does not provide the reasonable safeguards that any prudent tenant would require.

1 For examples of the provisions required when the landlord is to insure, see those referred to in footnote 1 to para 10.1 above.
2 See section B, paras 10.4–10.9 below.
3 See section C, paras 10.10–10.12 below.
4 See section D, paras 10.13–10.24 below.
5 See section E, paras 10.25–10.29 below.

244

10.3 *Tenant to insure.* In those rare instances in which the tenant is to insure, the landlord's solicitor will need to consider basically the same issues, but amended to reflect the reversal of roles.[1]

1 See section F, paras 10.30–10.31 below.

B THE SUM INSURED

10.4 *Basic concepts of insurance.* It is helpful to recall the basic concepts of insurance before considering the sum for which the property should be insured.[1] A contract of insurance is one in which the insurer agrees, in return for a premium, to pay a sum of money to the insured on the happening of a certain event, or to indemnify the insured against loss caused by a risk that has been insured against. It is fundamental, therefore, that the insured cannot recover, or retain for his own benefit, more than his actual loss. As Brett LJ said in *Castellain v Preston*:[2]

'In order to give my opinion upon this case, I feel obliged to revert to the very foundation of every rule which has been promulgated and acted on by the courts with regard to insurance law. The very foundation, in my opinion, of every rule which has been applied to insurance law is this, namely that the contract of insurance contained in a marine or fire policy is a contract of indemnity, and of indemnity only, and that this contract means that the assured, because of a loss against which the policy has been made, shall be fully indemnified but shall never be more than fully indemnified. That is the fundamental principle of insurance, and if ever a proposition is brought forward which is at variance with it, that is to say which either will prevent the assured from obtaining a full indemnity, or which will give to the assured more than a full indemnity, that proposition must certainly be wrong.'

The indemnity is generally based on the market value of the property insured rather than the cost of reinstatement, and this will be so in the absence of an express provision to the contrary in the policy.

1 For insurance generally see 25 Halsbury's Laws (4th edn).
2 (1883) 11 QBD 380 at 386, CA.

10.5 *Property: the three alternatives.* Forbes J has pointed out[1] that there are in fact three alternatives on which that indemnity can be based:
(a) market value of the property;
(b) cost of building an equivalent modern replacement; or
(c) cost of reinstating the building in its existing form.
As a general rule the insured will require the insurance moneys, in the event of total destruction, to rebuild the property[2] and as such should effect insurance on a reinstatement basis.[3] Further, the cost of removing the debris should be made recoverable, and a 'public authorities clause' inserted in the policy by which the insurance is extended to include additional costs of reinstatement incurred in complying 'with Building or other Regulations under or framed in pursuance of any Act of Parliament or with Bye-Laws of any Municipal or Local Authority'.[4]

1 In *Reynolds v Phoenix Assurance Co Ltd* [1978] 2 Lloyds Rep 22, CA.
2 Alternatively, the landlord may wish to redevelop rather than rebuild.
3 The policy will thus include a reinstatement memorandum along the following lines: 'In the event of the building insured under the within policy being destroyed or damaged the basis

245

upon which the amount payable in respect of such property is to be calculated shall be the reinstatement of the property destroyed or damaged, subject to the following special provisions and subject also to the terms and conditions of the policy except in so far as the same may be varied hereby . . .'. *Leppard v Excess Insurance Co Ltd* [1979] 2 All ER 668, [1979] 1 WLR 512, CA illustrates the dangers of not insuring on a reinstatement basis.

4   Obviously such additional costs are recoverable only up to the sum insured.

10.6   *'Average' policies*. There is a further point to be considered in relation to all 'fire policies', whether the indemnity is expressed to be on a market value or reinstatement basis. Such policies will rarely be valued policies, that is where the insurer agrees that where a total loss occurs, a sum representing the agreed value is recoverable by the insured, even though it exceeds his actual loss. The agreed valuation will be conclusive and the insurers will be unable to claim, in the absence of misrepresentation or non-disclosure,[1] that the insured's value was not the true value[2] unless the overvaluation was so excessive as to amount to a wager.[3] Virtually no property insurance is undertaken on a valued basis and thus disputes as to the insured's 'actual loss' are always a possibility. It is thus more accurate to say that, under an unvalued policy, the insurers are liable to pay, in the event of total destruction, the sum insured or the actual loss suffered by the insurer, whichever is the lesser. As Forbes J said:[4]

> 'In a standard fire policy, the sum for which the buildings stand insured serves only three purposes, all for the benefit of the insurers:
> (a) upon which to base premiums
> (b) the maximum the insurers may be called upon to pay
> (c) upon which, if appropriate "average"[5] may be applied.'

1   'In policies of insurance, whether marine insurance or life insurance, there is an understanding that the contract is *uberrimae fidei* that if you know any circumstances at all that may influence the underwriter's opinion as to the risk he is incurring and consequently as to whether he will take it or what premium he will charge if he does take it, you will state what you know. There is an obligation there to disclose what you know; and the concealment of a material circumstance known to you, whether you thought it material or not, avoids the policy': per Lord Blackburn in *Brownie v Campbell* (1880) 5 App Cas 925, HL. 'Insurance is a contract of the utmost good faith and it is of the gravest importance to commence that that position should be observed': per Scrutton LJ in *Greenhill v Federal Insurance Co* [1927] 1 KB 65, CA. See also *Woolcott v Sun Alliance and London Insurance Ltd* [1978] 1 All ER 1253, [1978] 1 WLR 493 and *Reynolds v Phoenix Assurance Co Ltd* (1978) 122 Sol Jo 161, CA. (NB The insurance company appealed against the decision of Forbes J not on a question of the basis of indemnity – see [1978] 2 Lloyds Rep 22 – but on the grounds that the insureds failed to disclose, before entering the policy, that one of them has been convicted of an offence for which he had been fined.)

2   *Bruce v Jones* (1863) 1 H & C 769.

3   *Lewis v Ruckel* (1761) 2 Burr 1167.

4   In *Reynolds v Phoenix Assurance Co Ltd* [1978] 2 Lloyds Rep 22, CA.

5   Fire policies generally contain an average clause, for example: 'Whenever a sum insured is declared to be Subject to Average, if the property covered thereby shall at the breaking out of any fire or at the commencement of any destruction of or damage to such property by any other peril hereby insured against be collectively of greater value than such sum insured, then the Insured shall be considered as being their own insurers for the difference and shall bear a rateable share of the loss accordingly.' The operation of such a clause is seen on a partial destruction. Assume the sum insured is £400,000 but the value is £600,000. Thus the owner has insured two-thirds of the value and is 'his own insurer' for one-third. Where damage valued at £400,000 arises, the insurers will be liable, where the policy is expressed to be subject to average, for two-thirds of this (£266,667). Had the policy not been subject to average the insurers would have been liable for the full £400,000. See *Acme Wood Flooring Co Ltd v Marten* (1904) 90 LT 313.

10.7   *Full replacement value*. Policies effected on the basis of reinstatement should, therefore, always be read with this qualification in mind. The landlord (and, where applicable, the tenant) will need to consider with their property and insurance advisers the question of full replacement value, because the market value, meaning the sum of money that the freeholder could reasonably expect to receive for the sale of the building on the open market, is not directly relevant. There should be few difficulties in the case of a modern building where it would be possible to construct a replacement building substantially the same as the original. There may well have to be some alterations necessitated by changes in building techniques or materials, or by some slight change in the appropriate regulations, but it is unlikely that these will have a significant impact on the cost of replacing the building. The problems arise where it would, in practice, be impossible to replace the building with anything similar, for example an old building being used as offices. Furthermore, not only would it be impossible to reconstruct such a building, but it might be equally difficult to anticipate the attitudes of the planning and other authorities to the type of building that they would permit to be rebuilt on the site. There is no general answer to the question – all that one can ask is that the parties, their advisers and insurance brokers are alerted to the problem so that due consideration can be given to each case.

10.8 *Cost of reinstating – when?* Forbes J also held in *Gleniffer Finance Corpn Ltd v Bamar Wood and Products Ltd*,[1] that 'full cost of reinstatement' should be construed as covering the cost which might properly be expected to be incurred *at the time when reinstatement takes place*, as opposed to the cost calculated as at the date on which each annual insurance premium was paid. The judge found that it would take, in that particular case, at least nine months to demolish the remains of the building, to prepare plans, to obtain all necessary consents, and obtain competitive tenders for the works and a further nine months to rebuild. As such the minimum period, if the landlord was covered for the full cost of reinstatement, was at least eighteen months from the date of the destruction, which could occur on the last day of the period covered by the annual insurance premium. Reinstatement could therefore be completed two-and-a-half years from the date on which the annual premium was payable, and as a result the landlord was entitled to insure for an estimate of the cost that he might properly expect the reinstatement to be two-and-a-half years after the date on which the premium was due. In many cases where a more complex building was involved, these period could be longer.

1   [1978] 2 Lloyds Rep 49.

10.9 *Advice needed.* It follows that a commercial landlord (and indeed any other property owner) needs to obtain advice, not on the value of his property in the open market, but on the likely cost of rebuilding it, and on what allowance to make for inflation in respect of building costs. He should make a reasonable estimate of the time that it would take to demolish and be ready to rebuild and for the rebuilding itself, and he should then make another reasonable estimate of the full cost of reinstatement *at that time*. Clearly, in the light of *Finchbourne*,[1] the landlord could not pick a random period but would have to approach the whole question of insurance in a fair and reasonable manner. In all but the simplest case, the landlord would be prudent to obtain professional insurance advice on the arrangements of the insurance cover.

1   *Finchbourne Ltd v Rodrigues* [1976] 3 All ER 581, CA and see para 11.26 below.

C   RISKS

10.10   *Why insured risks relevant to the tenant.* Where the landlord insures, the tenant's solicitor needs to review the risks against which the landlord covenants to insure in conjunction with the repairing covenant and the proviso for the suspension of rent if the premises become unfit for use. The repairing covenant should exclude from the tenant's liability for repair damage caused by an insured risk and, if it does not, the tenant's solicitor should propose a suitable amendment.[1] If the landlord does not covenant to insure against all reasonably foreseeable risks but only, for example, 'fire and such other risks as the Landlord shall from time to time decide', the tenant would remain liable under the repairing covenant to repair damage due to storm, tempest, flood etc where the landlord has decided not to insure against these risks. Furthermore, if the proviso for cesser of rent is expressed to operate only where the damage is due to an insured risk, the tenant would remain liable for rent where the premises have been rendered unfit for use by a risk against which the landlord has not insured.[2] If the tenant's solicitor is unable to obtain an amendment to the proviso, the question of insurance must be considered. There are essentially two alternatives. The tenant could either propose that the landlord's covenant is widened to include all normal risks, in which event the tenant would obtain protection under the repairing covenant and cesser of rent proviso, or the tenant could leave the lease as drafted, but take out insurance of his own in respect of any liability under the repairing covenant to repair or reinstate as a result of damage or destruction to the premises caused by an insurable risk against which the landlord has not insured, and any liability to pay rent for a time during which he is unable to occupy the premises.[3] The latter option appears at first sight to have some advantages, because, as the tenant would not be insuring pursuant to the lease, there would be no restrictions on where the insurance was placed, and therefore he would be able to insure through his own agency and thus obtain some financial benefit. On the other hand, it seems undesirable for the same premises to be insured twice[4] and it would appear that the most sensible practical step is to impose upon the landlord a covenant to insure against all normal risks. If the landlord is minded to accept the principle, he needs protection as it may prove at some stage during the term of the lease impossible to obtain insurance for that building in respect of one of the specified risks, and then the landlord himself would be liable in the event of damage being caused by this risk. The landlord should always state that his covenant to insure against any particular risk is 'subject to the availability of insurance cover against such risks and to the extent that and subject to such conditions as insurance cover against any such risk is generally available'.

1   See para 8.11(d) and footnote 4 above.
2   As would nearly always be the case: see para 10.23:2.
3   This will leave unanswered the question of uninsurable risks.
4   Although, despite the two policies, there would not be dual insurance because the insured perils would be different.

10.11   *Loss of rent – period.* The period during which loss of rent is insured should be a considered and reasonable estimate by the landlord (no doubt on the advice of his surveyor) of the time that it would take to demolish, prepare plans and obtain the necessary consents, and rebuild.[1]

1   The period should be the same as the one used for calculating the date upon which the cost of reinstatement would be due – see para 10.8 above

10.12 *Loss of rent – rent review.* When the lease contains a rent review clause, there will be times during the term when the period during which rent is insured will extend beyond the next rent review date. A well-drawn rent review clause will provide that the rent is to be reviewed disregarding any damage or destruction. Here the landlord will need the advice of his surveyor as to what the rent is likely to be *after* the review before effecting the loss-of-rent insurance for such a period. The fashion used to be to insure to the fixed percentage of the value of the premises for architects' and surveyors' fees. It seems more desirable for the landlord to avoid a percentage, because such fees may vary unpredictably over the years and to provide for 'an *appropriate percentage* for *professional fees* to be incurred in rebuilding or reinstatement'. The landlord should recognise that there may be professions other than architects and surveyors involved and it seems not unreasonable that these fees should be insured against.

D DAMAGE OR DESTRUCTION OF THE DEMISED PREMISES BY AN INSURED RISK

10.13 *Legal background.* In this vital area, the law can be both unfair and uncertain – for example:

(a) there is no simple principle of law to the effect that a landlord is bound to use the insurance moneys to reinstate the premises,[1]

(b) the general rule is that rent continues to be payable even if the premises cannot be used by the tenant,[2]

(c) although it may seem unlikely that the premises could ever be reinstated, the lease will probably not be terminated, and the circumstances in which the law would regard the lease as terminated are far from clear,[3] and

(d) where reinstatement is not possible, there could well be uncertainty as to which party is entitled to the insurance moneys.[4]

1 See para 10.14 below.
2 See para 10.15 below.
3 See para 10.15 below.
4 See para 10.16 below.

10.14 *No general obligation to reinstate.* There is no general obligation imposed upon the Landlord to use the insurance moneys to reinstate. True, s 83 of the Fires Prevention (Metropolis) Act 1774 provides that where a loss has occurred by fire which is covered by insurance, either the occupier or the owner, as the case may require, is entitled to call upon the insurance company to apply the policy moneys so far as the same will go, in rebuilding, instead of paying them to the insured. This Act applies generally throughout England and Wales and is not limited to London or other cities, but generally the application must be made *before* the insurance office has paid the sum involved to the insured. In *Mumford Hotels Ltd v Wheler,*[1] Harman LJ (sitting as an additional judge of the Chancery Division) held that 'on the true construction' of a lease containing no covenant by the landlords to reinstate, the landlords were bound to put the insurance moneys received by them towards reinstatement, because the landlord's obligation to keep the demised premises 'adequately insured against comprehensive risks' was undertaken at the tenant's expense, and was 'an obligation intended to ensure for the benefit of both the landlords and the tenant'. Thus the tenant in this case succeeded in compelling the landlords to use the insurance moneys for reinstatement, although this was a decision, not recognising the existence of a general principle of law, but in the construction of a particular lease.

1 [1964] Ch 117, [1963] 3 All ER 250.
2 So in order to avoid uncertainty, the tenant should always require a specific covenant from the landlord: see paras 10.18–10.22 below.

10.15 *Rent continues and lease not terminated.* Rent continues to be payable notwithstanding the fact that the premises cannot be used by the tenant because of a fire or some other catastrophe, in the absence of any express provision in the lease to the contrary.[1] This may seen most unfair to the tenant, but the logic is that where a lease consists of buildings and land (even if the only land is that beneath the building) the land remains after the destruction of the building, and thus the subject matter of the lease has not ceased to exist.[2] The only possible exception to the general rule would be that the lease had been frustrated but until recently the question of whether the doctrine of frustration applied to a lease remained unanswered. In *Cricklewood Property and Investment Trust Ltd v Leighton's Investment Trust Ltd*[3] Viscount Simon LC and Lord Wright had indicated that they felt that the doctrine of frustration *could* apply to leases, although in very rare circumstances (for example, as Viscount Simon suggested, if 'some vast convulsion of nature swallowed up the property altogether or buried it in the depths of the sea'). But Lords Russell and Goddard believed that the doctrine of frustration did *not* apply to leases.[4] The question was not resolved until *National Carriers Ltd v Panalpina (Northern) Ltd*[5] when the House of Lords held that *the doctrine of frustration was capable of applying to a lease* so as to bring the lease to an end where an event occurred duing the term such that no substantial use permitted by the lease and contemplated by the parties remained possible to the tenant. Their lordships stressed, however, that the circumstances when the doctrine would apply were exceedingly rare. Coastal erosion was suggested as one example.[6] Lord Simon felt that the 'vast convulsion of nature' statement of Viscount Simon LC in *Cricklewood* 'puts the matter too catastrophically even in the case of a long lease . . . and in the case of a short lease something other than such natural disaster (the sort of occurrence, for example, that has been held to be the frustrating event in a charter party) might in practice have a similar effect on parties to a lease. Take the case of a demise-chartered oil tanker lying alongside an oil storage tank leased for a similar term, and an explosion destroying both together'.[7] Lord Roskill did 'not think any useful purpose would presently be served by attempting to categorise those cases where the doctrine might be successfully invoked and those where it might not. Circumstances must always vary infinitely'.[8] Lord Simon suggested that the test was 'in the light of the quantitative computation[9] and of all other relevant factors (from which I would not entirely exclude executed performance), would outstanding performance in accordance with the literal terms of the contract differ so significantly from what the parties reasonably contemplated at the time of execution that it would be unjust to insist on compliance with those literal terms?'[10]

1 *Matthey v Curling* [1922] 2 AC 180, HL; *Cleveland Shoe Co Ltd v Murrays Book Sales (Kings Cross) Ltd* (1973) 229 Estates Gazette 1465, CA.
2 But what of a lease of a suite of offices on say the third floor of a building – here there would be no land included in the demise.

3   [1945] AC 221, [1945] 1 All ER 252, HL.
4   Lord Porter expressed no view on the general issue.
5   [1981] AC 675, [1981] 1 All ER 161. Lord Russell (as had his father in *Cricklewood*) believed that the principle could not generally apply to leases. The only exception, in his view, would be 'the frustration of a commercial adventure when, as merely incidental to the overall commercial adventure and a subordinate factor, a lease has been granted'. The doctrine of frustration can apply to agreements for lease – see *Denny Mott and Dickson Ltd v James B Fraser & Co Ltd* [1944] AC 265, [1944] 1 All ER 678; *Rom Securities Ltd v Rogers (Holdings) Ltd* (1967) 205 Estates Gazette 427.
6   At 168 and 175.
7   At 175 and 176.
8   At 188.
9   Ie what relation does the likely period of interruption bear to the outstanding period of performance?
10   At 180.

10.16   *Insurance moneys when rebuilding impossible.* There is no general principle of law dealing with the ownership of the insurance moneys if rebuilding is prevented. There have been two cases on the point, but both turned very much on their own facts, and in particular the conduct of the parties *after* construction. The lease of a factory in *Re King*[1] contained a covenant by the tenant to insure the premises in the joint names of the landlord and the tenant and to reinstate, making-up herself any shortfall in the cost of so doing. The premises were destroyed by fire in 1944. Wartime restrictions made immediate rebuilding impractical, and in 1945 the insurance moneys were invested in the joint names of the landlord and the tenant, the parties agreeing that the sums should stand charged with the tenant's liability to perform the covenants under the lease. In 1955, and before rebuilding had been commenced, a compulsory purchase order was made for the acquisition of the premises by the local authority. Upjohn and Diplock LJJ held that, as the purpose of investing the insurance moneys in joint names was that they should stand as security for the reinstatement of the premises by the tenant in pursuance of the covenants under the lease, the tenant became entitled to the investments on such performance becoming impossible, because the tenant had paid the premiums on the policy, and because the agreement between the parties relating to the investment of the insurance money had said nothing to the contrary. Lord Denning MR dissented – he felt that the moneys should be divided proportionately to the value of the interests of the landlord and tenant in the property at the time of destruction. Twenty years later, the Court of Appeal adopted Lord Denning's approach although on rather different facts. Indeed, Browne-Wilkinson LJ stressed that if the principle in *Re King*[1] had been applied, the same conclusion would have been reached. In *Beacon Carpets Ltd v Kirby*[2] a warehouse had been let in 1972 on a fourteen year tenant's full repairing lease that contained covenants by the landlord to insure the premises in the joint names of the landlord and the tenant, and in the event of destruction to reinstate. The tenant agreed to reimburse the landlord for the cost of such insurance. The premises were destroyed in 1977 and a planning application to reinstate the premises was refused on the grounds that part of the property might be needed for road widening. Planning permission was subsequently obtained for a smaller building,[3] but the tenant indicated that this would be too small for him. The insurance moneys were paid into a joint account in the names of the parties' solicitors. There was no agreement as to the basis on which this sum was to be held, although two years later the tenant agreed to release half of it to the landlord. Then the lease was surrendered. The Court of Appeal held:

(a) The landlord was not in breach of the covenant to reinstate because the tenant had never suggested that the landlord should rebuild – agreeing to the unconditional release to the landlord of half of the insurance moneys was inconsistent with a claim that the insurance moneys should be used in rebuilding.

(b) The landlord had not committed an anticipatory breach of covenant by refusing to rebuild because there was no evidence that the landlord had ever told the tenant that he would not rebuild.

(c) The tenant was entitled to the nominal damages of £2 awarded by the Judge for the admitted failure by the landlord to insure in the full value.

(d) The basic right of both the landlord and the tenant was to have the insurance moneys applied in rebuilding for their respective benefits, although they had released the right to have the moneys applied in rebuilding without agreeing how to deal with the moneys. These belonged to the landlord and the tenant in shares proportionate to their respective interests in the premises. The only explanation for the parties' conduct was that they both assumed that the property would not be rebuilt and were, in default of agreement, treating the moneys as standing in place of the property.

(e) In default of agreement, there should be valuations of the freehold with vacant possession (£x) and the leasehold interest (£y), both valuations to be made as at the date of the fire and on the basis that there was unconditional planning permission for the premises. The insurance moneys would then be multiplied by a fraction, the numerator[4] of which was y and the denominator[5] x, and this proportion of the insurance moneys would be paid to the tenant (plus the interest actually received on the sum so paid) the balance, to the extent that he had not already received it, going to the landlord.

1 [1963] Ch 459, [1963] 1 All ER 781, CA.
2 [1985] QB 755, [1984] 2 All ER 726, CA.
3 The planning permission applied only for 8 years.
4 Ie above the line.
5 Ie below the line.

10.17   *Draftsman to create fairness and certainty.* It is suggested that in the light of the unfairness and uncertainty of the general law,[1] there should be included in every lease:

(a) a covenant by the landlord to insure in the joint names of the landlord and the tenant[2] and, where this is not practical, a covenant by the landlord to reinstate,[3]

(b) a suspension of rent proviso,[4] and

(c) a termination clause, to be exercisable if reinstatement proves impossible, and that deals, amongst other things, with the ownership of the insurance moneys.[5]

1 See paras 10.13–10.16 above.
2 See para 10.18 below.
3 See paras 10.19–10.22.
4 See para 10.23 below.
5 See para 10.24 below.

10.18   *Insurance in joint names.* Where the draft lease provides for the insurance to be effected by the landlord, there would rarely be any point in the tenant's solicitor amending this to provide for insurance by the tenant, as it must be assumed that the landlord has made this policy decision prior to the preparation of the draft lease. One exception might be if the tenant would be able to benefit from special terms that would not be available to the landlord. Whenever practical, however, the tenant's solicitor should propose that the premises be insured in the joint names of the landlord and the tenant. This will mean that both parties will be informed before the policy lapses and that any insurance money will be paid jointly to the landlord and tenant (who will no doubt have to open a joint account in which to deposit the money) which will give the tenant control over the spending of the insurance moneys, and thus the reinstatement of the premises. Insuring in the joint names will also avoid problems in the event of the landlord going into liquidation, and will prevent the insurers from exercising their rights of subrogation against the tenant, in relation to damage caused or contributed to by the tenant. Normally, an insurer who has paid out under a policy stands in the insured's shoes in so far as any claim that the insured may have had against a third party. Thus where premises were destroyed through some act or omission of the tenant, in circumstances in which the landlord would have had a claim against the tenant, there was concern that the insurers would be able to bring the claim against the tenant in the name of the landlord.[1] Where, however, the premises are insured in the joint names of the landlord and the tenant, there can be no subrogation as the tenant is one of the insured parties. This point will be of no great concern to the landlord but where he will suffer from the insurance being in joint names is that he will lose control of the insurance moneys. Even here, the actual loss may not be all that great because a prudent tenant will not permit the landlord to have unfettered control over the insurance money – if insurance in joint names is refused or impractical the tenant will require the protections referred to in the next paragraph. Where, however, the landlord accepts the principle of insurance in joint names, he should insist that the covenant is drafted in such a way as to permit insurance also in the name of 'such other person as the Landlord may reasonably require'. A mortgagee of the landlord may require his name to be added, and yet it has been held that a covenant to insure in the joint names of the landlord and the tenant is broken by the addition of a further name.[2]

1   In fact it now seems that the insurers would probably not have a right of subrogation against the tenant where the tenant had paid for the insurance: see *Mark Rowlands Ltd v Berni Inns Ltd* [1986] QB 211, [1985] 3 All ER 473, CA but see footnote 1 to para 10.19 below.
2   *Penniall v Harborne* (1848) 11 QB 368.

10.19   *Covenant to reinstate.* There will, however, be cases in which insurance in the joint names of the landlord and tenant is not practical for example where the demised premises form part of a larger building. In these circumstances, the tenant's solicitor should insist upon the landlord covenanting to reinstate and that a note of the tenant's interest is endorsed on the policy because when this has been done, the insurers *should* give notice to the tenant of any lapse in the policy. Also where this has been done, and it can be shown that the tenant is responsible for the insurance premium under the terms of the lease, it is even more likely that the insurers would not be able to exercise subrogation rights against him, although it would still be as well for the tenant to seek from the insurers a specific waiver of subrogation.[1]

1   In fact the insurers may have no right of subrogation: see *Mark Rowlands Ltd v Berni Inns Ltd* [1986] QB 211, [1985] 3 All ER 473, CA but this case turned on construction and no general statement of principle: see Stephen Tromans: 'Commercial Lease insurance obligations' [1988] Gazette 26 June 8 at 27. Note also *Sella House Ltd v Mears* [1989] 1 EGLR 65, CA.

10.20   *Shortfall.* What if the landlord covenants to reinstate but the insurance moneys are insufficient to pay for the reinstatement? Where the covenant is to 'lay out all moneys received in respect of such insurance' in reinstatement (as opposed simply 'to reinstate') it would seem that the landlord would *not* have to complete the work at his own expense[1] – he would have complied with his covenant by laying out all the insurance moneys received. Thus the tenant should call for a specific covenant from the landlord to make up any shortfall.[2] Clearly the tenant needs this protection in order to prevent a situation in which the landlord refused to complete the rebuilding. This would be of particular concern if the suspension of rent proviso was expressed to operate for a limited period, because on the expiry of such period[3] the tenant would become liable for rent.[4] The tenant should argue most strongly for the inclusion of an obligation compelling the landlord to reinstate. Such a provision might mean that the landlord wishes to increase the sum for which the premises are insured and, as the tenant is generally responsible for (his share of) the insurance premium, some extra expense may fall to the tenant. The additional premium involved in increasing the sum insured, however, from a conservative to a generous estimate of the full reinstatement value is unlikely to be large, when expressed as a percentage of the total premium.

1   Except where the tenant could establish that the landlord was in breach of his covenant to insure 'for the cost of reinstatement' (or whatever expression is used in the lease) by underinsuring, hence the shortfall – see *Mumford Hotels Ltd v Wheler* [1964] Ch 117, [1963] 3 All ER 250.
2   See words in square brackets at the end of clause 7.6:2 of 22 Encyclopaedia of Forms and Precedents (5th edn) Form 22.
3   See para 10.23:5 below.
4   Unless he could satisfy the court that the lease had been frustrated – see para 10.15 above.

10.21   *Increasing building costs.* If the landlord accepts an obligation to reinstate, he should consider one safeguard. Building costs increase dramatically annually, and if rebuilding was delayed it may well be that the insurance monies would be insufficient. If the delay was the fault of the landlord he clearly deserves no protection but if, for example, obtaining the permission and consents required before rebuilding proves impossible he deserves protection. The possibility of this situation arising is a strong argument for an unlimited suspension of rent provision,[1] and for giving the tenant the option to terminate the lease if the premises are not made fit for use within a certain period after a catastrophe.[2]

1   See para 10.23:5 below.
2   See para 10.24 below.

10.22   *Qualified covenant to reinstate.* There will, however, be circumstances in which the landlord will not wish to be committed to reinstate,[1] especially where old premises are involved, or at least not to have to reinstate in the same form.[2] He may have redevelopment in mind, at some future and undefined date, and would wish to be able to bring that date forward if some 'unfortunate' catastrophe was to destroy the premises, and thus achieve for the landlord at least part of the demolition that would be required as the first step for any future development. In addition, the landlord would have the insurance moneys to put towards that development. Even where new, or relatively new, premises are involved the landlord might wish to have this option where a lease for a long duration is being contemplated. A tenant should, of course, resist such a provision. If the landlord is adamant a compromise might be for the landlord to be relieved from his covenant to reinstate during the last few years of the term, but in any event the tenant should require a clause to be inserted by which the tenant will receive from the landlord, in such circumstances, a share of the insurance money payable equal to the value of the tenant's interest. This, however, may not compensate the tenant for the loss that his business may suffer as a result of having to vacate that particular location.

1   See for example 22 Encyclopaedia of Forms and Precedents (5th edn) Form 68. Any clause by which a landlord can terminate a lease of business premises must be considered in the light of the 1954 Act: see para 10.24 below.
2   See ibid, 67.

10.23   *Suspension of rent proviso.* The tenant should insist upon a proviso being inserted by which the payment of rent is suspended if the premises become unfit for use.[1] This is an important provision and careful consideration needs to be given to certain aspects of the drafting:

10.23:1   '. . . *the Rent or a fair proportion of the Rent according to the nature and the extent of the damage sustained shall be suspended . . .*'. Landlords by a variety of drafting mechanisms frequently provide that only the actual rent is suspended and any other payments due to the landlord under the lease such as the service charge and (a proportion of) the insurance premium continue to be payable. If there has been total destruction of the entire development, the point is of no practical concern to tenants because in the absence of a property there would be no services or insurance. What is of concern is the case where a fire renders unfit for use, for example, several suites of offices in an office building, or more likely one or two shop units in a shopping centre while business carries on as usual in the remainder of the building. Thus the landlord is providing exactly the same services and effecting the same insurance as he would have done if all the units had been in use, and in fact the landlord may incur greater expenditure under both of these heads until the damaged part has been reinstated. The tenant should argue for the suspension of rent proviso to apply to all sums due from him under the lease – the principle behind the clause, he would argue, is that it is inequitable for a tenant to pay rent when he is unable to use or occupy his premises and this principle applies equally well to other payments. Suffice to say that this inevitably will depend upon the relative strengths of the parties at the time the lease is negotiated and whichever party is unsuccessful should investigate the situation so far as insurance is concerned.

10.23:2   '. . . *by fire or any other risk insured against by the Landlord . . .*'. Care must be taken in providing for the circumstances in which the cesser will operate because the words will be strictly construed. Thus where rent was to be suspended if the premises were destroyed or damaged by 'fire storm or tempest', and the building collapsed as a result of one of the floors being overloaded, it was held that the suspension did not operate.[2] As such, the limitation to an insured risk means that the cesser of rent provision will not operate, and therefore the rent will remain payable, where the damage is due to a risk against which the landlord is *not insured*. The tenant's solicitor should resist this on the basis that it is of no concern to the tenant whether or not there

255

in insurance against that particular risk – the fact remains that the tenant is unable to occupy the premises and therefore it is only fair that the rent should cease.[3] If the powers of persuasion of the tenant's solicitor are unsuccessful, he should then either insist that the landlord insures against *all* practical risks, or should advise his client to take out his own insurance against rent paid while the premises are unfit as a result of a risk against which the landlord had not insured.[4] It seems undesirable to have two insurance policies in existence in relation to the same premises, and so it appears preferable for the landlord to insure against the full range of risks in that, as the lease will provide for the tenant to reimburse him for the premiums, this should be of no great concern to the landlord. This would then merely leave the question of uninsurable risks, such as subsidence.

10.23:3   '. . . *unless the insurance of the demised premises or the Building shall have been vitiated by the act neglect default or omission of the Tenant . . .*'. There can be no objection in principle to this provision, although one can make the somewhat pedantic observation that it should only apply where the premises were rendered unfit for occupation by a risk that would have been covered by insurance had the tenant not vitiated the policy. In other words a counter-proposal might be: 'except where the risk that caused the destruction or damage was insured against by the Landlord but such insurance was vitiated by the act neglect default or omission of the Tenant'.

10.23:4   '. . . *the amount of such proportion to be determined by the Landlord's surveyor . . .*'. It is not unreasonable for there to be a mechanism by which the proportion may be determined, although if there is an arbitration provision in the lease the tenant's solicitor should provide for: 'the amount of such proportion to be determined in default of agreement between the parties under clause . . .' specifically referring by number to the arbitration clause. When there is no arbitration clause, the tenant could provide for determination by some third party, for example: 'the amount of such proportion to be determined in default of agreement between the parties by a surveyor (acting as an expert and not as an arbitrator) nominated by the parties or in default of agreement as to the said nomination appointed by the President for the time being (or his duly appointed duputy) of the Royal Institution of Chartered Surveyors'.

10.23:5   '. . . *or until the expiration of . . . whichever is the shorter*'. This is a most significant provision and should be resisted by the tenant's solicitor on the basis that it is equitable that no rent be payable *for so long as it takes to make the premises fit for occupation again*. If this is not accepted by the landlord, the tenant's solicitor should consider two amendments. He should certainly insist that a period of time is inserted that more than adequately covers the time that it will probably take to rebuild the premises. The landlord may well require that he insures the loss of rent for this period, and as the tenant will have covenanted to be responsible for the insurance premium, this will therefore be at the expense of the tenant, but even this is more acceptable than having a short period inserted. If the landlord refuses to do even this, then the tenant should once again consider insuring against rent paid after the expiry of the 'rent-free' period until the premises are ready for occupation. The tenant's solicitor should then consider the situation of the premises not being ready for occupation after the 'rent-free' period because rebuilding has either been prevented or frustrated, or delayed through a failure by the landlord to comply with the terms of his covenant to reinstate. If the landlord had covenanted to reinstate and had defaulted, it would seem that no court would permit the landlord to recover rent where the tenant was not in occupation as a result of this breach by the landlord and if the landlord were to sue for rent, the tenant would counterclaim alleging breach of covenant. The problem, however, is where rebuilding had been prevented, for example because of an inability to obtain all the consents, permissions and approvals needed in order to start rebuilding.[5]

1   For the reasons set out in paras 10.13(b) & (c), 10.15 and 10.17(b) above.
2   *Manchester Bonded Warehouse Co v Carr* (1880) 5 CPD 507.
3   Except where this is due to a failure by the tenant to observe the provisions of the lease.
4   See para 10.10 above.
5   See para 10.24 below.

10.24   *The right to terminate when reinstatement prevented.* The effect of most leases where the landlord insures the premises is that the landlord covenants to reinstate provided he can obtain the planning and other permissions and consents that are required. Some leases go further, and provide that the landlord wil not be required to reinstate if prevented by other circumstances beyond its control. Such clauses could, however, lead to uncertainty because their effect would seem merely to suspend the landlord's covenant to reinstate, rather than to discharge it, so that if the landlord was prevented from reinstating and the parties were unable to arrive at a mutual solution, both would have to wait to see if the circumstances preventing reinstatement would pass. Thus the landlord would not be able to use the insurance money[1] while the tenant would not know when, or if, it would be able to use the premises again. Moreover, if the suspension of rent proviso were limited in time, the tenant would become liable again to pay rent.[2] It is submitted, therefore, that a termination clause that is fair to both parties should be inserted in every lease to deal with this uncertainty.[3] Any clause by which a landlord can terminate a lease of business premises must be considered in the light of the 1954 Act,[4] which provides that a tenancy to which it applies does not come to an end unless terminated in accordance with the provisions of the Act.[5] If the Act is to apply, the tenant must show that he was continuing in occupation of the premises for the purposes of a business carried on by him or, if events over which he had no control have led it to absent itself from the premises, that he had continued to exert and claim his right of occupancy.[6] In the case of the latter, it is a question of fact whether the tenant had made it clear that it was his intention to maintain its right of occupancy and to resume physical occupation as soon as the landlord had reinstated the premises.[5] If the Act does apply, the landlord will additionally have to serve a notice terminating the tenancy[7] and will be able to oppose the tenant's application for a new tenancy only if he can establish one of the grounds permitted by the Act.[8]

1   See para 10.16 above.
2   See para 10.23:5.
3   See 22 Encyclopaedia of Forms and Precedents (5th edn) Form 22 clause 7.6 and Forms 70–72 and Rosscastle Letting Conditions (Appendix 1, Form 1 below) Conditions 6.5:1–6.5:6.
4   See Chapter 14.
5   Ie under ibid ss 25–28: see paras 14.6–14.21 below.

6   *Morrison Holdings Ltd v Manders Property (Wolverhampton) Ltd* [1976] 2 All ER 205, [1976] 1 WLR 533, CA.
7   See 1954 Act, s 25 and para 14.7 below.
8   See ibid s 30(1) and paras 14.29–14.39 below.

E   PROCEDURAL MATTERS

10.25   *Tenant to reimburse premium.* In every commercial lease in which the landlord covenants to insure, there will be a reciprocal provision by which the tenant covenants to reimburse the landlord for the premiums paid for such insurance. The landlord will generally reserve this as rent because a lease can be forfeited for non-payment of rent (subject to any relief against forfeiture that the tenant may obtain) without the landlord having to serve notice under s 146(1) of the Law of Property Act 1925.[1] Where the insurance policy covers the whole of the building of which the demised premises form part, the tenant's covenant will provide for him to pay the proportion of the insurance premium attributable to the demised premises. The tenant's solicitor needs to satisfy himself that the amount that will be allocated to the tenant is calculated on an equitable basis and related to the tenant's risks alone. In the event of the draft lease providing a fixed percentage, the tenant's solicitor should enquire as to how this percentage has been calculated.[2] There are circumstances in which a fixed percentage may be undesirable, if it were possible for an occupier of other premises in the building to have a high fire risk, for example, because his business is more hazardous and highly rated from a fire insurance point of view. It is hard to see how this could apply in relation to an office building but it is conceivable in the case of a light industrial building divided into several units each forming separate fire risks. Where this is so, a share of the premium representing the same percentage as the area of the demised premises forms of the total area of the building would not seem an equitable way of dealing with the matter and wording such as 'a reasonable proportion to be determined by the landlord's surveyor acting as an expert and not as an arbitrator' would seem preferable.

1   But note para 11.7 below.
2   Generally on the basis of the net usable floor area.
3   For a detailed discussion of the related problem of how individual tenant's shares of the landlord's cost of providing the services should be determined, see paras 11.8–11.11 below.

10.26   *Who is entitled to commission?* Where the landlord covenants to insure he will usually do so with an agency that he has with one of the major companies.[1] He may therefore be receiving some commission probably in the form of a deduction from each premium. The question therefore arises of whether the tenant is responsible under his covenant to reimburse the landlord for the tenant's share of the 'quoted' insurance premium or that amount less the discount. The landlord would argue that the benefit of the discount should accrue to the landlord, because it is only by virtue of the landlord's other property commitments that such a discount is available. On the other hand, it is arguable that applying the principle of *Finchbourne Ltd v Rodrigues*,[2] the landlord must pass on this discount to the tenant in order to obtain the most 'fair and reasonable' premium. Perhaps a distinction should be drawn between commission (to which the landlord would be entitled) and premium discount (which the benefits should accrue to the party responsible for the premium).

1 In *Bandar Property Holdings Ltd v J S Darwen (Successors) Ltd* [1968] 2 All ER 305, it was held that there was no obligation on the landlord, who was insuring at the expense of the tenant, to 'shop around' for the most economic insurance.
2 [1976] 3 All ER 581, CA: see para 11.19 below.

10.27 *Where insurance effected.* As well as who should effect the insurance policy, the parties will need to consider with whom that insurance must be effected. It is in both parties' interests for that insurer to be reputable, but the landlord may prefer to have no limitations in the lease, leaving him entirely free to make his decision each time the policy comes up for renewal. The tenant, however, should seek some protection – the term 'reputable insurer' is frequently used, or even 'publicly quoted insurance company'. In the case of the latter (or any variation that refers only to an insurance company or insurance office) 'or with Lloyd's underwriters' should be added.

10.28 *Tenant request details when lease submitted.* The tenant's solicitor should always apply as soon as the draft lease is submitted for a copy of the insurance policy and the latest memoranda endorsed thereon. He will then be able to ensure that the cover is properly arranged, that correct principles have been used in arriving at the sum insured, and that the cover complies with the terms of the lease. Indeed, it is in the landlord's interests for the tenant to be supplied with a copy of the policy in that the tenant's attention should be drawn to any warranties and special conditions in the policy and, if necessary, confirmation obtained from the tenant that he is able to comply with them.

10.29 *Tenant to satisfy himself.* It is only reasonable for the tenant to have the right to satisfy himself that the landlord is maintaining the insurance in accordance with the provisions of the lease, for example the basis of cover, the insured risks, sum insured etc. A landlord, however, should avoid committing himself to supplying a copy of the insurance policy itself as this may relate to other properties, and the landlord may regard it as a confidential document and not wish to disclose this information. He should propose that, as an alternative to the policy and the latest premium receipt, he should be able to provide 'reasonable evidence from the insurers of the terms of the policy and the fact that the same is subsisting in effect.'

F INSURANCE BY THE TENANT

10.30 *Similar issues arise.* Where the landlord wishes the tenant to insure, the landlord's solicitor should adopt similar language to that used in the landlord's covenant, substituting 'landlord' for 'tenant'. In particular the landlord's solicitor should insist upon insurance in joint names[1] although even with this safeguard, perhaps he should enquire of his client *why* he wishes the tenant to insure, in those circumstances where insurance could very easily be effected by either party.[2] The same points arise – should there be an absolute covenant to reinstate (or just to 'lay out the insurance moneys') and should the tenant covenant to make up any shortfall. It really is no solution for the tenant's solicitor simply to delete the covenant to make up the shortfall.[3] There is, however, one possible compromise and that is to provide for the sum for which the premises will be insured either to be specified by the landlord's surveyor (and in the light of *Finchbourne*[4] this would have to be a serious attempt by him to arrive at 'the full cost of reinstatement' or whatever term was used in the lease) or to be agreed between the parties, with perhaps some provision for resolving disputes. By either method, the landlord would then be able to ensure that the property was not underinsured by the tenant, and as such it would seem reasonable for the tenant to be absolved from any liability to make up the shortfall. Further it could be suggested that such liability should be imposed on the landlord. In other words, in return for being able to control the amount for which the premises are insured, the landlord accepts liability for any error in that figure. This should certainly be the case where the tenant would not have the right to terminate the lease if the premises remain unfit for use.[5]

1   See para 10.18 above.
2   See para 10.1 above.
3   For the reason set out in para 10.20 above.
4   [1976] 3 All ER 581, CA and see paras 10.26 above and 11.19 below.
5   See para 10.24 above.

10.31   *Where insurance effected.* Where the lease provides for insurance by the tenant, the tenant's solicitor should ensure his client will either be entitled to insure with any company or at Lloyd's or (at worst) with a company approved by the landlord, 'such approval not to be unreasonably withheld'. This will mean that the tenant should then be free to insure the premises through the company that handles all its property insurance and this should produce some financial benefit to the tenant in view of the agency arrangements that it will probably have there. It seems unreasonable for the landlord to specify that insurance by the tenant will be through a particular insurance office, and even in some cases through the landlord's agency, because the landlord is then 'getting the best of both worlds' – he is not having the administrative problems and expense of insuring, and yet is receiving the agency benefit.

G   OTHER INSURANCE

10.32   *Inform insurers of new property.* Finally it is worth remembering that the tenant will maintain employers' liability and public liability policies. A condition of these such policies will be that the insurers are notified of all premises at which the tenant is carrying on business. The tenant's solicitor should therefore remind his client to inform his insurers on the acquisition of any new premises.

Chapter 11

Service charges

A PHILOSOPHY

11.1 *Clear leases.* We live in an age in which landlords of business premises generally succeed in providing that no part of the rent that they receive from their tenants has to be spent on the upkeep, maintenance or insurance of the demised premises, or the developments of which they form part. They achieve this broadly in one of three ways:

(a) Where the demised premises do not form part of a larger unit[1] a full repairing covenant will be imposed upon the tenant.[2]

(b) There will be instances where the tenant, in order to occupy the demised premises, will require to use some item such as a private road or sewer belonging to the landlord and used by the landlord and perhaps his other tenants. Where the items in question are such that no regular expenditure is envisaged, and that in all likelihood many years will pass during which no work will be required, the tenant will be invited to enter into a covenant by which he agrees to reimburse the landlord for any expenditure incurred by the landlord in the upkeep and maintenance of the shared items.[3] If the landlord does not use the item in question for his own purposes (and sometimes even where he does) he will aim to provide for total reimbursement by all the tenant-users.

(c) Where the landlord will have ongoing and recurring work, a provision will be included in the lease by which each tenant pays a service charge representing a share of the costs incurred by the landlord in undertaking this work. Thus the landlord's total expenditure is reimbursed by the tenants. This is standard today in leases of suites of offices[4] and shops in shopping centres[5] and fairly normal in industrial estates, at least where there are extensive common parts and landscaped areas, and for example, estate roads that have to be lit as well as maintained.[6] Tenants, however, need to be alert to the fact that their obligation to reimburse the landlord will generally extend far beyond expenditure incurred on 'services', by any conventional meaning of the word – they will usually have to pay for the maintenance of the structure of the building or development of which demised premises form part.[7] These then are the 'clear leases' defined by Lord Wilberforce in *O'May v City of London Real Property Co Ltd*[8] as 'leases in which the tenants bear all the costs and risks of repairing maintaining and running the building of which their demised premises form part, so that the rent payable reaches the landlord clear of all expenses and overheads'.

In all three cases, the tenant will in addition always bear the financial responsibility of the insurance.[9]

1 As to when a full repairing covenant would not be practical see para 8.9 above.
2 As to repairing covenants see Chapter 8 above.

3 See para 11.2–11.3 below.
4 At least in new lettings but not upon renewals under the 1954 Act – see *O'May v City of London Real Property Co Ltd* [1983] 2 AC 726, [1982] 1 All ER 660, HL. As to a precedent see appendix 1 Form 6 below and 22 Encyclopaedia of Forms and Precedents (5th edn) Form 31.
5 See ibid Form 29.
6 See ibid Form 30. A simpler form appears in Appendix 1, Form 5 below.
7 See Appendix 1 Form 6 below, clause 7.
8 [1982] 1 All ER 660 at 671, HL.
9 See Chapter 10 and in particular para 10.1 above.

B   REIMBURSEMENT AS AND WHEN INCURRED

11.2   *Covenant by the tenant.* Where no regular maintenance will be required from the landlord in relation to shared items, then the 'simple' solution referred to in subpara 11.1(b) above can be adopted. The tenant should be required to reimburse 'a fair proportion' of the expenses incurred by the landlord'[1] This seems preferable to setting out an exact share because it provides for flexibility that may be valuable where, for example, the work is needed as a result of some form of misuse by one individual tenant, or where the properties using the sewer or road vary during the terms of the lease.[2] The clause should provide how the share is to be determined – for example by the landlord's surveyor.[3]

1 See Appendix 1, Form 4 below, clause 4.1.
2 See para 4.5 above.
3 Or when using the Rosscastle Letting Conditions (Appendix 1, Form 1 below) the Qualified Expert: see Condition 9 and Form 4, clause 4.1.

11.3   *Covenant by the landlord: unlikely to be implied.* The tenant must insist that the landlord covenants to carry out the work in question.[1] Where there is no covenant, the question arises of whether the court would assist a tenant, who had covenanted to contribute towards the costs incurred by the landlord in carrying out certain work, where the landlord refused to carry out work that was required. At first sight, there appears to be an argument that if the want of repair was so bad that it was preventing the tenant from enjoying a right granted by the lease, the landlord would be derogating from his grant, and the tenant would have a remedy. For example, a lease of a factory on an industrial estate may contain rights of way over the estate roads and rights of drainage through the private sewers of the estate. If the condition of the road had so deteriorated that effectively the right of way could not be enjoyed, or the pump broke down preventing the use of the sewer, then (so the tenant's argument goes) the landlord would have derogated from his grant. Such an argument would, however, be unlikely to succeed because derogation is essentially a *negative* doctrine – it entails that the grantor shall *not do* (as opposed to refrain from doing) anything on his retained property which would render the demised premises unfit for carrying on business in the way in which it is ordinarily carried on.[2] Until recently there were two cases that lent some weight to the tenant's argument that in the absence of an *express* covenant there should be *implied* into the lease a covenant by the landlord to carry out the work.[3] These were considered in the *Duke of Westminster v Guild*,[4] in which the Court of Appeal held that a landlord was not responsible for the repair of a drain when there was no covenant to this effect in the lease, although the tenant had covenant to reimburse the landlord a fair proportion of expenses incurred by the landlord in repairing the drain in question. Slade LJ pointed out that *Barnes*[5] was a much stronger case than the present, if only because the obligation of the tenants to pay the rent for the particular service was an unqualified obligation to pay a definite periodic amount in respect of that service, the obligation to pay not being expressed so as to be conditional on the provision of the service or on the service of notice requesting payment' and continued:

'We do not question the correctness of these two decisions on their particular facts or doubt that in some instances it will be proper for the court to imply an obligation against a landlord, on whom an obligation is not in terms imposed by the relevant lease, to match a correlative obligation thereby expressly imposed on the other party. Nevertheless we think that only rather limited assistance is to be derived from these earlier cases where obligations have been implied. The general rule is, in our judgment, correctly stated in *Woodfall's Landlord and Tenant*[6] at para 1–1465:

"In general there is no implied covenant by the lessor of an *unfurnished* house or flat, or of land, that it is or shall be reasonably fit for habitation, occupation or cultivation, or for any other purpose for which it is let. No covenant is implied that the lessor will do any repairs whatsoever . . ."

On occasions special facts may no doubt justify a departure from the general rule. However, the decision of the Court of Appeal in *Sleafer v Lambeth Borough Council*[7] well illustrates that, though the provisions of a lease may indicate the parties' contemplation that in fact and in practice the landlord will do repairs, and indeed may confer express rights on him to enter the demised premises for this purpose, it does not follow that any contractual obligation to do the repairs is to be implied against him.'[8]

The court then considered the criteria for implying terms and in particular the test formulated by Lord Cross in *Liverpool City Council v Irwin*:[9]

'Sometimes, however, there is no question of laying down any *prima facie* rule applicable to all cases of a defined type but what the court is being in effect asked to do is to rectify a particular – often a very detailed – contract by inserting in it a term which the parties have not expressed. Here it is not enough for the court to say that the suggested term is a reasonable one the presence of which would make the contract a better or fairer one; it must be able to say that the insertion of the term is necessary to give – as it is put – "business efficacy" to the contract and that if its absence had been pointed out at the time both parties – assuming them to have been reasonable men – would have agreed without hesitation to its insertion.'

Applying this test, the court found itself unable to imply into the lease in question a covenant by the landlord to maintain the sewer. The second limb of the tenant's submissions was that the failure to repair the drain amounted to a breach of the landlord's duty of care[10] but the court took the view that this could only apply where there had been an escape of some dangerous noxious or unwelcome substance from the landlord's premises onto the demised premises as a result of the landlord's failure to maintain for example a drain. The lesson of these cases is clear. As Slade LJ said:[11]

'We think that the present case well illustrates that a tenant who contemplates that his landlord shall carry out repairs to property retained by the landlord over which the tenant is granted easements will ordinarily be well advised to demand an express covenant to this effect.'[12]

1 See Appendix 1, Form 4 below, clause 5.
2 See *Browne v Flower* [1911] 1 Ch 219.
3 *Barnes v City of London Real Property Co* [1918] 2 Ch 18: set of rooms was let at a yearly rent and

an additional and smaller rent for 'cleaning the rooms by the housekeeper appointed for the time being by the landlord'. Sargant J said: 'And if (which I do not think is the case) it were necessary for me to decide the point, I should, as at present advised, come to the conclusion that there was in these agreements imposed on the lessors an obligation corresponding to the obligation imposed on the lessees to pay them rent for the purpose of a particular service; and that not only could they not take or retain the rent without performing the services, *but that they were bound to perform the service*'; *Edmonton Corpn v W M Knowles & Son Ltd* (1961) 60 LGR 124: lease contained a covenant by the tenant to pay the Council the cost of painting with two coats at least of good oil paint, in a workmanlike manner, every third year of the term, all the outside wood and metal work, and other exterior parts of the demised premises. McNair J considered that on the proper construction of the clause there was an implied obligation on the Council to carry out this work.

4   [1985] QB 688, [1984] 3 All ER 144, CA but note *Barrett v Lounova (1982) Ltd* [1989] 1 All ER 351, [1988] 2 EGLR 54, CA.
5   See footnote 3 above.
6   28th edn.
7   [1960] 1 QB 43, [1959] 3 All ER 378.
8   See for example at 56–57 per Morris LJ.
9   [1977] AC 239 at 258, HL.
10   See *Hargroves, Aronson & Co v Hartopp* [1905] 1 KB 472 and *Cockburn v Smith* [1924] 2 KB 119, CA.
11   *Duke of Westminster v Guild* (1983) 267 Estates Gazette 763 at 768. Note also *Tennant Radiant Heat Ltd v Warrington Development Corpn* [1988] 1 EGLR 41, [1988] 11 EG 71, CA.
12   The Court of Appeal did not rule out the possibility that, on particular facts, it would be possible for the court to imply an obligation against the landlord (see for example *Barrett v Lounova (1982) Ltd* [1989] 1 All ER 351, [1988] 2 EGLR 54). Where this arises, the covenant is likely to be in absolute terms, and that being so, the landlord might have been better advised to include a rather more qualified express covenant in the lease.

C   SERVICE CHARGE – INTRODUCTION

11.4   *Components*. Whenever it is contemplated that the landlord will be providing services on an ongoing basis, the type of 'reimbursement as and when incurred' clause referred to in the proceeding two paragraphs will not be appropriate and the lease needs to provide for a service charge. There are six distinct components of such a provision that must be considered by the landlord and his advisers:

(a)   the nature of the service charge: should it be reserved as rent or dealt with by means of a covenant by the tenant to pay?[1]
(b)   how is each tenant's share to be determined?[2]
(c)   how is the tenant to pay the service charge?[3]
(d)   what does the landlord covenant to do?[4]
(e)   what are the services that the landlord must or may provide?[5]
(f)   should a sinking fund be set up?[6]

1   See para 11.7 below.
2   See paras 11.8–11.11 below.
3   See paras 11.12–11.13 below.
4   See paras 11.14–11.16 below.
5   See paras 11.17–11.20 below.
6   See paras 11.21–11.29 below.

11.5   *The landlord's surveyor and accountant (and the Qualified Expert[1]): their roles.* There is an important preliminary issue to be considered before any service charge provisions are drafted. The operation of these clauses frequently call for day-to-day decisions to be made, and significant roles are often given to the landlord's surveyor and accountant. The landlord wants these decisions to be final and the lease very often states this and provides that in performing these roles, the individual will be acting as an expert and not as an arbitrator.[2] This, however, will not always achieve finality. A third party can make 'first instance'[3] determinations or can determine disputes *where the issues involve questions of fact*. What is 'fair and reasonable' or 'a fair proportion' are questions of fact.[4] There can probably be no appeal to the court on these determinations unless they reveal an error of law, and the chance of this happening is unlikely because the third party rarely gives the reasons for his determination.[5] What will be ineffective, however, is a clause that provides for the landlord's surveyor or accountant to determine a dispute to which he is a party,[6] or *to make final decisions involving questions of law*, such as the proper contruction of the lease. The latter was illustrated in *Re Davstone Estate Ltd's Leases*[7] where the leases of ten flats contained identical provisions to the effect that the tenants would pay the landlord the sum of £15 as a contribution towards the expenses incurred by the landlord in performing the landlord's covenants set out in the lease. The tenant further covenanted in each lease that if one tenth of the expenses actually incurred by the landlord in any year, 'as certified by the surveyor for the time being to the lessor . . . whose certificate shall be final and not subject to challege in any matter whatsoever', exceeded £15 then each tenant would pay to the landlord the excess. The landlord covenanted to keep the building (apart from the parts demised by the leases) and the roof and drains in good repair and 'to defray such other costs as may be necessary to maintain the building as good class residential flats and garages.' Considerable work arising out of defective workmanship was done to the building by the landlord, the cost of which was certified by the landlord's surveyor. The tenants refused to pay on the grounds that the work in question did not fall within the landlord's covenant and thus the tenants were not liable to contribute towards it. Ungoed-Thomas J held that whether the work in question was covered by the terms of the lease was a question of construction, and thus one of law. As such, the proviso was void, as being contrary to public policy in so far as it applied to questions of law because parties cannot purport to take the law out of the hands of the courts. This point must be addressed in the drafting of any certification or determination provision where questions of law could be involved, otherwise the whole clause could fail.[8] Thus, for example, the lease may provide for the landlord to prepare an account setting out the expenses and outgoings in relation to the services 'and upon such account being certified by the Accountant this will be conclusive evidence for the purposes of this Lease of all matters of fact referred to in the account'.[9] This almost certainly[10] would prevent the tenants from disputing whether expenditure had been incurred, and the extent of it, but the tenant could still bring before the court allegations that reimbursement was being claimed for items that the landlord was not entitled to recover, having regard to the terms of the lease.[11]

1   See Appendix 1, Form 1 below, Rosscastle Letting Conditions Condition 9.
2   See ibid, Conditions 9.1:2, 9.2.
3   Essentially there are two types of determination – those that are made as the first and only step and, more commonly, those that are made after the parties have failed to agree, and by way of resolving a dispute as was the case, for example, in *Concorde Graphics Ltd v Andromeda Investments SA* (1982) 265 Estates Gazette 386.
4   *In Concorde Graphics Ltd v Andromeda Investments SA* (1982) 265 Estates Gazette 386 new managing agents had been appointed and the service charge trebled as they 'put in hard substantial works to bring the estate up to a proper standard'. The tenant sought declarations as to the nature of the expenditure and the due proportion of it payable by each tenant. Vinelott J said (at 390): 'The matters in dispute are eminently matters for the exercise of the judgment of an expert'. But see footnote 7 below.

5 See para 6.45(c) and especially footnotes 5 & 6 above.

6 *Concorde Graphics Ltd v Andromeda Investments SA* (1982) 265 Estates Gazette 386.

7 *Re Davstone Estate Ltd's Leases, Manprop Ltd v O'Dell* [1969] 2 Ch 378, [1969] 2 All ER 849. See also *Coventry Trading Estates Ltd v Ford Motor Co Ltd* (3 December 1979, unreported); *Secretary of State for Employment v Assciated Society of Locomotive Engineers and Firemen* [1972] 2 QB 443, [1972] 2 All ER 853; *Rapid Results College Ltd v Angell* [1986] 1 EGLR 53, 277 Estates Gazette 856, CA. It seems that Vinelott J might have been suggesting in *Concorde Graphics Ltd v Andromeda Investments SA* (1982) 265 Estates Gazette 386 a rather narrower definition of a question of law (see footnote 4 above) and that he may have been prepared to permit a third party expert to determine issues verging on what Ungoed-Thomas J would have regarded as matters of law.

8 In *Davstone* (see footnote 7 above) the judge was not prepared to sever the objectionable part of the proviso because the 'part ousting the jurisdiction of the court on questions of law is not separately expressed so as to be severable and leave the unobjectionable parts unaffected. The same words which make the certificate final on questions of law make it final on all other questions too, including those on which its finality is free from objection. The result is that the objectionable aspects cannot be separated from the unobjectionable aspects by severance but only by remoulding the proviso, ie by remoulding the agreement between the parties; and this is not within the province of the courts' per Ungoed-Thomas J at 855.

9 The practice has grown up in recent years of adding 'save in the case of manifest error'. This must inevitably introduce some uncertainty (what is 'manifest' is to some extent in the eyes of the beholder) but is a compromise that the hard pressed negotiator (whose client is anxious to complete) will often concede.

10 See para 6.45(c) footnote 6 above.

11 Ie because this is a question of law that can be finally determined only by the courts: see footnote 7 above.

11.6 *The landlord's surveyor and accountant (and the Qualified Expert): their status.* There are two questions of status that require consideration. The first is that, unless the lease provides otherwise, these persons must be separate from the landlord. In *Finchbourne Ltd v Rodrigues*[1] a tenant of a flat was required to contribute 'a yearly sum equal to 4 percentum of the amount which the landlord shall from time to time have expended in maintaining and running the block of flats as a whole'. The amount of the contribution was to be 'ascertained and certified by the managing agents acting as experts and not as arbitrators'. It was found, however, that the purported managing agents and the landlord were in effect the same person and the Court of Appeal held that as the lease intended the managing agents to be separate from the landlord, no valid certificate had been issued by the managing agents. Thus the landlord's solicitor should provide that the terms 'Accountant' and 'Surveyor' should be capable of applying to employees of the landlord,[2] otherwise a landlord who manages his properties in-house could well be in difficulties in the light of this decision. A tenant must question how independent an employee of the landlord can be. The tenant's solicitor should always provide that these individuals must be members of the relevant professions.[3] There is perhaps only a slight risk of the landlord looking for outside advice and services from the unqualified – the real reason for the tenant's concern is the over-zealous employee of the landlord who is performing accountancy or surveying tasks in connection with the property, but who is not qualified in the relevant professions, and who is not supervised by a qualified person. The tenant is entitled to the protection of the third party needing to balance the fact that he is retained by the landlord with the standards and ethics of his profession.[4]

1 [1976] 3 All ER 581. See also *New Pinehurst Residents Association (Cambridge) Ltd v Silow* [1988] 1 EGLR 227, CA.

2 See 22 Encyclopaedia of Forms and Precedents (5th edn) Form 90. The same applies to a Qualified Expert (see Appendix 1, Form 1 below, Rosscastle Letting Conditions, Condition 9.1) although it was felt that an employed Qualified Expert would be in too 'delicate' a position (see footnote 4 below). An outsider is preferable and thus the provision has been omitted from Condition 9.1.

3 See ibid, Condition 9.1:1.

4 'His position [the landlord's surveyor] will be one of some delicacy. Although he is the landlord's agent he must act impartially and hold the balance equally between the landlord and the tenant notwithstanding that the landlord is his principal and paymaster. He must not simply obey the instructions of the landlord. But his position is no more delicate than the position of an architect required to issue certificates under the standard RIBA contract. As in the case of the architect the parties to the lease are entitled to rely upon him as a professional man to exercise an independent judgment.' *Concorde Graphics Ltd v Andromeda Investments SA* (1982) 265 Estates Gazette 386 per Vinelott J at 389.

D THE NATURE OF THE SERVICE CHARGE

11.7 It is common to reserve the service charge as rent. The advantages are that the remedy of distress[1] will be available to recover arrears and the fact that a lease can be forfeited for non-payment of rent without the landlord having to serve a notice under s 146(1) of the Law of Property Act 1925.[2] The latter, of course, would be required where the tenant was in breach of a *covenant* to pay the service charge. Distress, however, may well not be considered to be a practical remedy and in any event would not be available if there was any dispute as to the amount of service charge due[3] while the right to forfeiture is subject to the provisions as to relief set out in the Common Law Procedure Act 1852. The advantages of a covenant by the tenant to pay the service charge are that a very short period under the Section 146 Notice would probably be held to be reasonable and if the landlord then achieves re-entry by action or where permissible peaceful retaking, forfeiture is then complete and the tenant is not entitled to any relief.[4] At least one distinguished commentator prefers this latter approach.[5]

1 As to distress, see Hill and Redman *Landlord and Tenant* (18th edn) chapter 4 and Alexander Hill-Smith: '*Distress and Execution*' [1983] Conv 444. Such service charge rents are now disregarded by the Controller of Stamps in the calculation of stamp duty unless exceptionally a single sum is reserved as rent both for the demised premises and the services – see [1981] Gazette 27 May 604.

2 See para 12.2 below.

3 *Concorde Graphics Ltd v Andromeda Investments SA* (1982) 265 Estates Gazette 386.

4 Ie because the Common Law Procedure Act 1852 permits a tenant to obtain relief for six months after the judgment re forfeiture for arrears of rent but s 146(2) of the Law of Property Act 1925 does not permit where forfeiture for breach of covenant after re-entry or judgment – see paras 12.2 and 12.3 below. As to the taxation implications, see Hill & Redman's *Law of Landlord and Tenant* (18th edn) para G494.

5 J E Adams [1979] Conv 320. I am indebted to Professor Adams for his permission to use in preparing this chapter material presented by him at The 1983 Service Charges and Replacement Funds in Commercial Properties Symposium organised by Professional and Executive Seminars in February 1983 and for his helpful suggestions after reviewing this chapter (before it appeared in the 2nd edition) in draft.

E THE TENANT'S SHARE

11.8 *Two approaches*. The draftsman needs to turn now to the most significant question of how the share of the landlord's expenditure on services for which each tenant is to be responsible should be determined. In broad terms there are two alternatives – the lease can either set out a formula for establishing that share, or indicate that the tenant's contribution will be a *fair proportion* of the expenditure incurred by the landlord.[1] The various formulae approaches all have their individual strengths and weaknesses[2] but their overall advantage is certainty. The disadvantage is that they need not reflect the amount by which the tenant in question has used or enjoyed the services. That flexibility can be provided with the *fair proportion* approach enabling there to be taken into account all relevant circumstances including the user of the services. Its disadvantage is that it does give tenants the potential to dispute the apportionment. As a matter of law it it possible, given good drafting,[3] to limit severely the rights of appeal against such a determination, which of itself is significant, but that need not prevent there being considerable correspondence and discussion between the landlord or the managing agents and the individual tenants. If the lease had provided that each was to pay a fixed share then there would have been no scope for such arguments.

1   A provision will generally be added indicating how that proportion is to be determined, generally by the landlord's surveyor.
2   See para 11.9 below.
3   See paras 11.5 and 6.45(c) above.

11.9   *Various formulae.* There are basically three formulae that can be used in order to determine the tenant's share:

11.9:1   *A fixed percentage.* The lease provides that the tenant will pay a defined percentage of the total expenses and outgoings incurred by the landlord in providing the services. In arriving at the percentages to be set out in the leases, the landlord will no doubt have used either the rateable value or the floor area approach set out below.[1] This form, of course, provides the most certain determination of all because there is nothing that can be the subject of a dispute.[2] Its certainty, however, may rebound on a landlord who acquires additional land on which he extends the office building, shopping centre or industrial estate. The landlord would almost certainly wish to operate the extension as part of the original development, and provide the same services in relation to the enlarged area. And yet, unless he has either made specific provision for this in the lease or all the original tenants give their consent to such a variation, he will probably[3] not be able to do this where the tenants are contributing a fixed share relating to the defined original development. Instead there would have to be an apportionment between the original and the extended areas and the tenants of the former would pay 'their' percentage of the apportioned figure. Thus the landlord's solicitor should ensure that the term 'the Estate', 'the Centre' or 'the Building' is defined in such a way as to include any extension,[4] or provide for the percentage to be varied should such extension take place.[5]

11.9:2   *Rateable values.* In this case, the lease providing that 'the proportion of the Landlord's expenditure attributable to the Premises shall bear to the Landlord's expenditure the proportion that the rateable value of the Premises bears to the aggregate of the rateable values of all the premises in respect of which the Services are provided'. The advantage of this system is that there is a certain amount of flexibility, and as such there is no need to provide specifically for the development being extended,[6] because as and when any additional units are created they would automatically fall within the term the 'premises for which the Services are being provided'.[7] There is a further element of certainty here because rateable values are specific items of information that are readily available and (unlike floor areas)[7] do not lend themselves to disputes, although it is vital for the draftsman to specify the date upon which the rateable values are to be taken.[8] It is assumed that a draftsman who adopts this approach would wish to use a current date, because if he wanted the shares to be fixed according to the rateable values prevailing at the commencement of the lettings, then he may as well have established these, made the appropriate calculations himself, and provided in the lease for the shares to be on a fixed percentage basis.[8] Thus the clause should refer to 'rateable values in force at the end of the appropriate Financial Year'.[9] The disadvantage[10] of this approach is that rateable values can change, for example where the user of a property changes, while the demand on the services for that particular unit remains unaffected. Furthermore well advised tenants on an estate may successfully have appealed against the rateable values where others have not. Thus identical units could find themselves paying different service charges. There is also the uncertainty of how rateable values are determined, while any draftsmen who historically have preferred this method on the grounds that rateable values are periodically reviewed, and thus by this means the system for apportioning shares amongst the tenants is kept up to date, should remember that Part V of the Local Government, Planning and Land Act 1980 abolished the statutory requirement for quinquennial revisions of rateable values.[11] Finally there is the problem of when will rateable values be determined on a new development – this may be after the time when the first leases have been granted. The drafting can deal with this, but potential tenants may well not welcome the uncertainty.

11.9:3 *Floor areas.* Here the lease provides that 'the proportion of the Landlord's expenditure attributable to the Premises shall bear to the Landlord's expenditure the proportion which the net lettable area of the Premises bears to the aggregate net lettable area of all the lettable areas for the time being comprised in the area for which the Services are provided'. This again provides flexibility but, while having the inevitable disadvantage of any formula approach,[10] has the added potential for disputes of the measuring of the areas involved.[12] The draftsman should also provide that the aggregate net lettable area of all the lettable areas comprised in the development, being a question of fact, shall be finally certified by his surveyor.[13] Once more there is a need to provide the date upon which the proportion is to be determined – presumably the first or last day of the financial year.[9]

1 See paras 11.9:2 and 11.9:3. The floor area approach is the more likely, because at the time draft leases are being submitted, the rateable values may well not have been determined.
2 Ie there can be no arguments as to floor areas or rateable values – see paras 11.9:2 and 11.9:3.
3 It could perhaps be argued in view of the decision of the Court of Appeal in *Pole Properties Ltd v Feinberg* (1981) 43 P & CR 121 that in such circumstances either party would in the absence of an express provision in the lease be able to apply to the Court to determine a fair and reasonable percentage of the landlord's expenditure for the tenant to pay in view of the enlarged area.
4 For example by providing that the expression 'the Centre' (assuming this to be the defined term for the shopping centre of which the unit that is being let is part) 'includes where the context so admits any adjoining land and buildings acquired by the landlord and that are intended to form part of the centre'.
5 See 22 Encyclopaedia of Forms and Precedents (5th edn) Form 29 Sixth Schedule para 8.2.
6 As there is when a fixed percentage is used – see para 11.9:1.
7 See para 11.9:3.
8 Or where the lease is drafted in this way the Computing Date as defined in clause 7.2(a). For an example of consequences of not providing date upon which the rateable values to be taken see *Moorcroft Estates Ltd v Doxford* (1979) 254 Estates Gazette 871.
9 Or Computing Date – see footnote 8 above.

10   The general concern with any formula determination is that it makes no attempt to reflect accurately each tenant's user of the services – see para 11.10 below.

11   A more significant consequence of this is that it led to the Landlord and Tenant Act 1954 (Appropriate Multiplier) Regulations 1981 – see para 14.40 below. Note too the valuation problems that can arise in determining rateable values: see *K Shoe Shops Ltd v Hardy (Valuation Officer) and Westminster City Council* [1983] 3 All ER 609, [1983] 1 WLR 1273, HL.

12   It is suggested that a provision be inserted to the effect that all measurements should be in accordance with the then current edition of the 'Code of Measuring Practice' produced jointly by the Royal Institution of Chartered Surveyors and the Incorporated Society of Valuers and Auctioneers (2nd edition published in 1987). At first sight, the total lettable areas of the demised premises and the whole building (as at the time that the initial leases are being granted) should be set out in the lease but note *National Westminster Bank plc v Arthur Young McCelland Moores & Co* [1985] 2 All ER 817, [1985] 1 EGLR 61, CA.

13   See para 11.5 above.

11.10   *Concern with formulae: exclude certain work.* The concern with any of these approaches is that they make no attempt to reflect the amount of the services used or enjoyed by the individual tenants. There are, perhaps, two ways in which this situation can be improved. The modern type of service charge generally provides that the maintenance of the structure of the development of which the demised premises form part is one of the services for which the tenants are liable for reimbursement.[1] Thus if a structural repair is needed to one particular unit, possibly as a result of the negligence of the tenant or some third party at or near the demised premises expressly or impliedly with the tenant's consent, the cost of such work would be shared amongst all the tenants.[2] There seems something fundamentally wrong with this because were this a detached unit it would almost certainly be let subject to a full repairing lease which would impose upon the tenant the liability for such repairs.[3] Thus there would seem merit in inserting a provision where any formulae are being used to the effect that the whole cost of any work or anything affecting only the demised premises (or any part of the walls roofs or floors of the development enclosing only the demised premises)[4] should be attributed to the demised premises, although this may be argued to be unfair where the work is required in the absence of any fault on the part of the tenant.

1   See Appendix 1, Form 6 below clause 6.1:1.

2   It may very well be that the other tenants would be able to recover from the negligent party the extra service charges so incurred (one tenant on an estate would presumably owe a duty of care to the others) but in practice this would only be of assistance when a large sum was involved. Otherwise, the expenditure might not appear as a separate item in the accounts (and thus the other tenants may never learn of it) and anyway it may not be worthwhile seeking to recover a small sum.

3   As to where a full repairing covenant will not be practical, see para 8.9 above.

4   There needs to be a reference to the walls etc enclosing the demised premises where the demised premises are defined as in Appendix 1, Form 6 below clause 1.2 in such a way that excludes from the demise the walls etc.

11.11   *Concern with formulae: different categories.* Alternatively, in some instances it might be possible to arrive at a more equitable arrangement, without moving away from the certainty that a formula approach involves, by dividing the services up into several categories with the tenants paying a different percentage of each category. Take, as an example, an industrial estate comprising four buildings each divided into five individual units. If the landlord was prepared to categorise his services and record them in such a way that he would be able to establish the expenditure on the estate roads and landscaped areas on the one hand, and the expenditure in relation to each individual building on the other, the lease could then provide that each tenant would be responsible for say one twentieth of the cost of maintaining the estate roads and landscaped areas and one fifth of the costs incurred in relation to the particular building of which his unit forms a part. A similar arrangement could be devised in an office block to deal with the upkeep of the lift, to meet the ground floor tenants' complaints that they have to pay the same share for the lift they never use as the tenants of the higher floors. Thus there would be in effect two service charges, one for the lift which would be shared in some way relative to user,[1] the other for all the other expenses that would be apportioned according to one of the formulae. The disadvantage of such a method is, of course, that it involves more administrative work for the managing agents (for which obviously the tenants will be paying as part of the service charge[2]) and it may in practice simply not prove possible to apportion the expenditure between the various aspects of the development.[3]

1   For example in the case of a four storey office building with four units of equal size on each floor the tenants on the first floor each pay one fortieth of the lift expenditure, on the second floor two fortieths on the third floor three fortieths and on the fourth floor four fortieths. But note *Campden Hill Towers Ltd v Marshal* (1965) 196 Estates Gazette 989 for a contrary view.
2   See for example Appendix 1, Form 6 below clause 7.1:2.3.
3   Where this arises, it may prove possible to determine the shares of expenditure on non-differential works on the basis of the formula related to other items.

F   PAYMENT OF THE SERVICE CHARGE

11.12   *Procedure.* There must be a mechnanism for establishing the sum due, and this will nearly always involve an action by the landlord's accountant or surveyor, for example the certifying of the landlord's accounts by the former[1] or the latter determining the amount due. It is only then that the actual liability of the tenants will be determined but a well drawn clause will provide that they pay throughout the year with the rent a quarterly payment in effect on account of the service charge.[1] The initial 'Provisional Service Charge' should be set out in the lease,[1] that should also provide how the provisional charge for future years will be determined.[2] This can be, for example, the amount of the previous year increased by a fixed percentage (or alternatively the rate of inflation that has prevailed during the year) or determined by the landlord's surveyor, his estimate being based on a forecast of the landlord's likely expenditure during the year in question. Then finally there has to be a reconciliation procedure so that the difference between the provisional amount and the actual amount can be dealt with. Landlords generally provide that any shortfall should be payable forthwith, but that any overpayment should, instead of being refunded to the tenant, be retained by the landlord and credited to the tenant against the next quarterly payment of rent and service charge.[2] Where large sums might be involved, the tenant would not be unreasonable in insisting upon an immediate refund of any overpayment and failing this to be credited on the next rent day with not only any overpayment but also interest at the current deposit rate.

1   In the absence of an express provision for payments on account, it seems unlikely that one would be implied: *Daiches v Bluelake Investments Ltd* [1985] 2 EGLR 67, 275 Estates Gazette 462. See Appendix 1, Form 6 below clause 1.17. Where the tenant is being granted a lease of an existing building, he should obtain copies of the accounts for the previous 3–5 years.
2   See ibid, clause 7.2.

11.13   *Tenant's amendments.* There are two important matters that the tenant's advisers should consider. There should be inserted an obligation on the landlord's part to pay into his 'service charge account' the service charge due in respect of any parts of the development that are unlet. Secondly the tenant should seek to extend the proviso for the suspension of rent to include the service charge as well.[1] The landlord will no doubt provide that the cesser of rent would be limited to rent per se and by one means or another would ensure that any other sums reserved as rent such as the service charge or proportion of the insurance premium would not be suspended. There are arguments both ways. The landlord would say that in the event of total destruction he will be incurring no expenditure on services and thus no reimbursement in the form of the service charge will be due. Where however there has only been partial destruction and part of the development remains operating then he will still be providing services and incurring expenditure and thus will be entitled to reimbursement. Indeed additional services may be needed as a result of this partial destruction. The tenant's likely response is that it is inequitable for him while his premises are unfit for use to have to pay for services that he is unable to use or enjoy. As is so often the case there is no 'answer' and the relative negotiating strengths of the parties will no doubt prevail.

1   The service charge would not be suspended, for example, in Appendix 1, Form 6 below.

G   THE LANDLORD'S COVENANT

11.14   *The parties' objectives.* The effect of a typical service charge clause is that the landlord *must* provide certain services and *may* provide others.[1] The latter are those non-essential 'services' for which the landlord would want to be reimbursed if he chose to (or was forced by outside circumstances to) undertake them, but that he would not want to be committed to provide. The tenant requires a covenant from the landlord[2] to perform the essential services, giving him a clause to sue upon should they not be provided. Not only might the lack of services adversely affect the ability of the tenant to use and gain access to the demised premises and the marketability of the premises (because the availability of these services may well have been reflected in the rent) but in certain circumstances it could mean that the tenant was committing an offence under the Offices Shops and Railway Premises Act 1963 containing provisions as it does for securing and maintaining cleanliness,[3] a reasonable temperature,[4] ventilation,[5] sanitary conveniences,[6] washing facilities.[7] On the other hand, no landlord could reasonably be expected to give an absolute covenant, so as to be liable for any non-performance even where due to circumstances beyond his control. There are breakdowns and failures in the best run systems, and indeed a company owning the freehold of an office block and occupying it for its own business could never guarantee that it could provide itself a constant supply of services. The problem is to draft a covenant that strikes a fair balance between the landlord and the tenant. An approach frequently adopted is that the covenant provides that the landlord will perform the services but he will not be liable for any failure or interruption due to circumstances beyond his control.[8] The tenant's advisers should require two amendments:

(a)   there should be added what is, in effect, a proviso to this proviso by which the landlord shall be absolved from liability only if the failure or interruption could not reasonably have been prevented or shortened by the landlord, and only for so long as the landlord uses his best endeavours to restore the service;

(b) consideration should be given to extending the covenant 'to perform'. At one level, it is no doubt true that bad or inadequate performance amounts to non-performance, but it is suggested that the tenant would be strengthening his position by calling for performance 'in an efficient manner in accordance with the principles of good estate management'. The effect of these words is like to be limited to the actual performance of the work because the standard to which the work has to be done will, in a well-drafted lease, be included in the definition of the services.

1 There are various ways of achieving this. One is to divide the services into two groups and provide that the tenant will reimburse the landlord for the costs incurred (a) in complying with an absolute (or nearly absolute) covenant to perform the essential ones and (b) in providing any of the other services that the landlord may provide. For an example see Philip Freedman and Eric Shapiro *Service Charges – Law & Practice* (Henry Stewart Publications, 1986) page 88 (note the proviso on page 95). Alternatively all the services can appear together, but in defining some of them an indication can be included that they are discretionary: see 22 Encyclopaedia of Forms and Precedents (5th edn) Form 29 (note sixth schedule para 16 and 17). For further precedents and commentary see Hill & Redman's *Law of Landlord and Tenant* (18th edn) paras G365–G1195.
2 Sometimes the covenant by the landlord to perform the services is expressed to be subject to the payment by the tenant of the service charge. The sanction is unlikely to be effective because, as the services apply to all the tenants, the landlord would only be able to withdraw the services if all the tenants were in arrears and note *Yorkbrook Investments Ltd v Batten* [1985] 2 EGLR 100, 276 Estates Gazette 545, CA.
3 Office Shops and Railway Premises Act 1963, s 4.
4 Ibid, s 6.
5 Ibid, s 7.
6 Ibid, s 9.
7 Ibid, s 10.
8 See Appendix 1, Form 6 below, clause 6.2.

11.15 *Negligence of landlord's employees.* Landlords frequently go further, however, and seek to exclude in the service charge provision or elsewhere[1] any liability on their part for any act omission or negligence of any porter or other employee of the landlord. They argue that this is to cover any 'unfortunate accident' and that, as the tenant would have insurance against this in any event, the absence of such a provision would mean that the landlord would have to effect insurance himself and recover the premium from the tenants by virtue of the insurance and/or service charge provisions. Thus, says the landlord, the tenant would be paying the premium for the landlord's insurance so that the tenant who would have effected such insurance himself would be carrying double insurance. In fact, as is all too often the case, the clause goes rather further than it needs even to achieve the landlord's aim, at least, as will nearly always be the case, where the landlord is a corporation. A corporate landlord can only act through its agents and thus many of the landlord's covenants in the lease and virtually all of the service charge covenants, will be performed by 'porters attendants or other employees'. It would be an absurd position if the landlord were to argue that this clause relieved him of liability for an obvious breach of the service charge covenant on the basis that such breach was brought about by some act omission or negligence of the employee of the landlord who should have attended to the matter. The argument raised as to insurance should be carefully checked out with the tenant's insurance advisers but as an absolute minimum if the provision is to remain in the lease a proviso must be added to ensure that it is not to be construed as relieving the landlord from liability for breach of any of the landlord's covenants contained in the lease.

1 For example by inserting clauses such as 'The Landlord will not be responsible to the Tenant or to anyone at the Centre expressly or by implication with the Tenant's authority for any accident or injury suffered or for any damage to or loss of any chattel sustained in or near the Centre'.

11.16 *Exclusion of liability for negligence.* In fact, this clause by the landlord seeking to absolve himself from negligence amounts to an exclusions clause which raises a rather more fundamental point. The Unfair Contract Terms Act 1977 ('UCTA') prevents a party from excluding his liability for death or personal injuries due to his negligence and provides that he can only exclude liability for any other loss due to negligence subject to the test of reasonableness.[1] UCTA does not apply, however, to any contract 'so far as it relates to the creation or transfer of an interest in land'.[2] The correct interpretation of these words is uncertain, although most relevant to exclusion clauses of this type. If construed widely, so as to apply to *every* part of any contract dealing with land, UCTA would not apply to a lease. If construed narrowly, as meaning that the Act does not apply only to those parts of the contract that deal specifically with the creation or transfer of the interest in land (ie the 'pure conveyancing') then the provisions of the Act could apply to the remainder of the lease. Thus such an exclusion clause would be ineffective in absolving the landlord from liability for negligence causing death or personal injuries and would be effective elsewhere only if it was held to be reasonable. It is suggested that UCTA should apply to exclusions clauses of this nature. This was the view taken by the Minister when the Bill was before Parliament[3] while *Regis Property Co Ltd v Redman*[4] gives support to the view that a lease containing a service charge provision can be divided into two parts – 'pure conveyancing' and a separate contract by the landlord to provide services. The tenant's solicitor may be tempted to deal with this point by adding a proviso to the exclusions clause that 'the provisions of the Unfair Contract Terms Act 1977 shall be deemed to apply to this clause', although it is perhaps unlikely that any landlord would ever accept such a suggestion.

1 Unfair Contract Terms Act 1977, ss 2(1), 2(2), 11(2) and Sch 2.
2 Ibid, para 1(b) of Sch 1.
3 [1977] Gazette 6 October 836. As to admissibility of Hansard as an aid to construction, see *Hadmor Productions Ltd v Hamilton* [1983] 1 AC 191, [1982] 1 All ER 1042, HL; *R v Secretary of State for Trade, ex p Anderson Strathclyde plc* [1983] 2 All ER 233. See Correspondence (1983) 133 NLJ 506 3 June, (1983) 133 NLJ 633 15 July.
4 [1956] 2 QB 612, [1956] 2 All ER 335, CA.

H THE SERVICES THEMSELVES

11.17 *The parties' objectives.* The landlord's aim will be simple – he will want the service charge provision to be drafted in such a way that he can recover from the tenants *all* the expenditure that he incurs in connection with the building,[1] and yet be entirely free to decide what work is needed and how it should be undertaken. The tenant, in the ideal world, would like his liability to be limited to reimbursing the landlord for basic 'services'[2] and for the costs recoverable even on these to be limited, for example, to reasonable amounts. There is, of course, no presumption or general entitlement by which the landlord can claim reimbursement for every expenditure – each item will depend upon the wording of the lease in question.[3]

1 Or the shopping centre or industrial estate.
2 Ie those referred to in para 11.18:1 below.
3 See for example *Embassy Court Residents' Association Ltd v Lipman* (1984) 271 Estates Gazette 545, CA; *Rapid Results College Ltd v Angell* [1986] 1 EGLR 53, 277 Estates Gazette 856, CA; *Mullaney v Maybourne Grange (Croydon) Management Co Ltd* [1986] 1 EGLR 70, 277 Estates Gazette 1350.

11.18 *Categories of service.*[1] It is possible to divide the services into four categories:

11.18:1 *Conventional services.* These are the items the cost of which anyone contemplating taking a lease of a part of a building or larger development, would recognise that he would have to pay a share – for example maintaining the common parts (and any equipment or apparatus in them)[2] and the conducting media used by more than one tenant, providing heating and hot water to the common parts, collection of refuse etc.

11.18:2 *People costs.* The landlord will often have some people permanently working at the building (such as receptionists, porters and caretakers[3]) and others working in connection with the building – for example, collecting the rent and managing the property[4] and performing the roles of landlord's surveyor and accountant as provided in the lease. Sometimes other professional help will be needed. The landlord will require reimbursement in relation to all these people, whether they are his employees[5] or outsiders.[6] The tenant should note that provisions concerning staff are frequently dangerously vague. Where there is a requirement for the tenant to reimburse the landlord's costs for employing staff, it is hoped that the court would construe such provisions as applying only if, or to the extent that, staff are engaged in performing the services referred to in the lease. It would be unfair for a landlord to be able to recover from tenants all the salary and national insurance payments paid to an employee of the landlord who was engaged for part of the time on other duties elsewhere. Nevertheless, to avoid any uncertainty over construction, the tenant's solicitor should insert after any reference to the employment of staff 'to the extent that the staff are performing the Services and other duties referred to in this Lease.' Terms such as 'incidental expenditure' in relation to that staff should also be deleted and replaced with a list of the actual expenses that the landlord is entitled to include. The description of the duties of the staff is often inadequate and the tenant should clarify these in the Lease. If, for example, there is to be a porter or a caretaker then this should be specifically stated.[3] The point could have a practical effect, in that the nature of the reception and security arrangements at the main door of the building may well have a bearing on the arrangements that the tenant feels obliged to make in relation to his premises.

11.18:3 *The structure of the building.* The landlord would like to be able to recover all sums that he spends on the building, whether it be for 'general maintenance', to remedy a latent defect or simply to improve the building. This is one of the most contentious and concerning aspects of any lease that provides for a service charge. The basic concept is not unreasonable, at least in an age when all lettings of business premises are on the basis that the tenant will be responsible for repairs. A tenant taking a lease of an entire building will expect to be liable for repairing that building so a tenant taking a lease of part of a building should expect to be collectively liable with the other tenants for the repairs that have to be carried out to the building. The problem, however, is that all too often, the service charge provision imposes a greater burden on the tenant of part of a building – not only does he not have control of the work (the landlord is in effect spending the tenant's money), but often he can find himself paying for more than repairs. A typical 'landlord's clause' might permit recovery by the landlord of sums incurred on 'maintaining, repairing, amending, improving, altering, rebuilding, renewing and reinstating' the building or development of which the demised premises form part. The precise extent of such terms (and in particular questions such as whether the landlord could rebuild the whole or a large part of the development, where this was practical, at the cost of the tenants) would no doubt have to be determined in a specific instance by the court but two points can be made, both of concern to the tenant. Such wording would permit the landlord to recover the cost of repairing the consequence of a latent defect in the building[7] and, if this is the only practical way of dealing with the point, of remedying the inherent defect itself.[8] Secondly, such wording is very much wider than a simple covenant 'to repair'[9] and it would enable the landlord to carry out work that he would not be required to undertake by virtue of such a covenant, either because of its extent[10] or because it was an alteration or improvement rather than a repair. The tenant's solicitor must press for amendments here and, if they cannot be achieved, be quite certain that his client understands the extent of these provisions. The tenant should propose that they be excluded from the service charge provisions repairs (or at least major repairs) required as a result of an inherent defect and require the landlord to carry out such work, not as part of the services, but at his own expense.[11] Where the landlord refuses, a slight reassurance to the tenant in the case of the former might be to provide that the landlord must before including the item in the service charge have used his best endeavours to recover the item from the builder or the relevant member of the landlord's professional team. Over and above this, the only advice to a potential tenant is that he has a thorough survey of the whole building undertaken in order to ensure that the landlord is not likely to be forced to undertake costly work of this nature in the future . . . costly, that is, to the tenants. In order to do this, the tenant's surveyor may well need access to other parts of the building but it is suggested that it would be an unreasonable landlord who refused this. A more serious concern arises, for example, in a letting of a small shop unit in a major shopping development. The professional fees involved in undertaking a survey of the whole centre would be prohibitive and out of all proportion to the rent to be paid. As such, a shop tenant is unlikely to proceed with such a survey. It follows too that when such a survey is practical, the landlord should be asked to make available to the tenant's surveyor or engineer the specifications and drawings for the development. Over and above this, the tenant should reduce the width of the provision and, if possible, limit it to repairing by deleting all the additional words (ie amending, improving, altering, rebuilding, renewing and reinstating).

11.18:4 *Any other expenditure.* Finally, the landlord will want to be free to incur any expenditure on the building, even if it is not expressly mentioned, that he believes would be appropriate. Thus landlords include a mopping-up clause that they hope will permit this.[12] At one level, this is not unreasonable, because it is virtually impossible to draft a comprehensive list, and it would be unfair if the tenant could refuse to pay his share of the cost of work that is clearly a 'service' by any normal meaning of the word, simply because reference to it had been omitted from the clause. Nevertheless the tenant should ensure that the clause is not too widely drawn,[13] while the landlord should still provide as comprehensive as possible a list of items, because there will inevitably be some uncertainty in the contruction of these clauses.[14]

1   For detailed precedents, see 22 Encyclopaedia of Forms and Precedents (5th edn) Forms 29 (shopping centre), 30 (light industrial or warehouse unit) and 31 (suite of offices). For an alternative suite of offices, see Appendix 1, Form 6 below.

2   The common parts may be outside (eg roads and landscaped areas of industrial estate) or inside (eg reception area of office building in multi-occupation).

3   In the light of *Russell v Laimond Properties Ltd* (1983) 269 Estates Gazette 947 and *Posner v Scott-Lewis* [1987] Ch 25, [1986] 3 All ER 513, care must be taken in the drafting of any provision dealing with porters, caretakers, receptionists, etc if the landlord would not wish to be obligated to provide them throughout the term.

4   It would seem that in a commercial letting the cost of management could only be recovered if it is specifically provided for (*Cleve House Properties Ltd v Schildof* [1980] CLY 1641) and that the decision in *Embassy Court Residents' Association Ltd v Lipman* (1984) 271 Estates Gazette 545, CA is based on the fact that the provider of the services was a management company (who could only obtain funds from the tenants) rather than a landlord who would have funds of its own.

5   The lease should specifically provide that the landlord can be reimbursed where the management is provided in house: *Parkside Knightsbridge Ltd v Horwitz* (1983) 268 Estates Gazette 49, CA.

6   The tenant should seek to qualify any reference to professional fees with terms such as 'reasonable' or 'properly incurred'.

7   It is a daunting thought that if the building in *Ravenseft Properties Ltd v Davstone (Holdings) Ltd* [1980] QB 12, [1979] 1 All ER 929 (see para 8.14 above) had been in multi-occupation, each of the tenants would have had to pay a proportion of the cost of the remedial work. Moreover this expense would have fallen in one, or at most, two financial years thereby dramatically increasing the service charge payable in those years. Thus a tenant holding a lease for a term of only a few years – or assigning a lease for a longer term after only a few years – could find himself paying a share of the expense of this major work that would accrue to the benefit of the building and the subsequent tenants long after his lease may have expired or been assigned.

8   See para 8.14 above.

9   See paras 8.1 and 8.10 above.

10   Ie it goes beyond the tests set out in para 8.1 above.

11   Landlords seek to justify imposing the liability for inherent defects on to the tenant on the need to create a clear lease, (see para 11.1 above) but as has been pointed out (Hill & Redman's *Law of Landlord and Tenant* (18th edn) para G378): 'It seems doubtful whether that is correct or, if it is, whether it justifies such a transfer of liability. The "clear lease" is an income concept. The building is provided (for profit) by a developer usually acting in conjunction with a funding institution. The rent paid by the tenant is the return for the landlord (whether he is the developer or institution or a subsequent purchaser) on his capital investment. The tenant pays for the use (ie occupation) of the landlord's capital (ie the building): he is not expected to replace it. Looked at in this way, it is no more incompatible with a clear lease that the landlord should himself meet the cost of eg design defects inherent in the building than that the landlord should accept depreciation in the relative value of the building itself as it ages. . . . Furthermore – and perhaps most importantly – the landlord is quite likely to have remedies against the persons directly responsible eg the developer, the contractor, or the architect. Where these remedies are based in contract, they will extend to economic loss even where there is no physical damage. The tenant's remedies are in many cases likely to be severely limited'.

12   See for example Appendix 1, Form 6 below clause 7.1:2.16.

13   Perhaps by adding to the landlords 'Any other services provided by the Landlord from time to time and not expressly mentioned above' words such as 'which shall at any time during the term be (a) capable of being enjoyed by the occupier of the Property (b) reasonably calculated to be for the benefit of the Tenant in conjunction with other tenants of the Building or be reasonably necessary for the maintenance upkeep or cleanliness of the Building and (c) in keeping with the principles of good estate management'.

14   A mopping-up clause cannot remedy a clear omission from one of the services: *Mullaney v Maybourne Grange (Croydon) Management Co Ltd* [1986] 1 EGLR 70, 277 Estates Gazette 1350; *Boldmark Ltd v Cohen* [1986] 1 EGLR 47, 277 Estates Gazette 745; *Sella House Ltd v Mears* [1989] 1 EGLR 65, [1989] 12 EG 67, CA.

11.19 *Implied terms.* The landlord's solicitor needs to be aware that certain terms may be implied, unless they are specifically excluded, and in one instance there is some doubt as to how effective any exclusion will be. Unless the lease provides otherwise it is likely that the landlord would be entitled to recover only costs that were fair and reasonable. In *Finchbourne Ltd v Rodrigues*,[1] Cairns LJ said:[2]

> '. . . there has been no valid certificate within the meaning of the eighth schedule, and that is an end of the plaintiff's case. However, I will express my opinion briefly on the second point. Is there an implication that the costs claimed are to be "fair and reasonable"? It is contended that no such implication is necessary to give business efficacy to the contract. Passages from the speeches in the House of Lords in the recently decided case of *Liverpool City Council v Irwin*[3] are referred to as the most recent statement of the principles on which terms can be implied. *Taking the strictest of tests on that matter, I am of opinion that such an implication must be made here.* It cannot be supposed that the plaintiffs were entitled to be as extravagant as they chose in the standards of repair, the appointment of porters etc. Counsel for the plaintiffs said that there would come a point without any implied term where the costs might be so outlandish as not to come within the description of the seventh schedule at all. In my opinion, the parties cannot have intended that the landlords should have an unfettered discretion to adopt the highest conceivable standard and to charge the tenant with it.'

The Court of Appeal agreed with the county court judge that, even if the certificates had been valid,[4] the landlords would only have been able to recover costs that were fair and reasonable.[5] Thus the landlord's solicitor will no doubt provide that the redecoration of the common parts will be 'to such standard as the Landlord may from time to time consider adequate' and the provision of any plants, shrubs, trees etc will be 'at the Landlord's absolute discretion'.[6] The tenant's solicitor should seek to reinstate the concept of reasonableness and provide for 'a reasonable standard' or 'that are reasonably required'. Thus it would always be up to the tenants in such circumstances to bring an action against a landlord on the basis, for example, that his redecoration of the common parts was not to a reasonable standard. A compromise that may commend itself to the landlord would be to provide that what was reasonable in all these various instances would be determined by a surveyor acting as an expert and not as an arbitrator. As such the landlord ought to be able to keep such disputes out of the courts[7] although a surveyor separate from the managing agents should be appointed to make such determinations.[8] Section 13 of the Supply of Goods and Services Act 1982 provides that 'in a contract for the supply of a service where the supplier is acting in the course of a business, there is an implied term that the supplier will carry out the service with reasonable care and skill.' It would seem that a landlord providing services to the tenants of a building in multi-occupation would fall within this section. Section 16 of the Act provides that this implied term can be excluded or varied by express agreement, by the course of dealing between the parties or by usage, but that to exclude or vary the right is subject when applicable to the Unfair Contract Terms Act 1977. There is, of course, some doubt as to whether this Act applies to service charge provisions in leases.[9] So if the landlord seeks to exclude his obligation to carry out the services with reasonable care and skill, the tenant may be able to argue that this would only be effective if it satisfies the reasonableness test of the Unfair Contract Terms Act 1977.[9]

1 [1976] 3 All ER 581. Note also *Firstcross Ltd v Teesdale* (1982) 265 Estates Gazette 305.

2   At 586, 587.

3   [1977] AC 239, [1976] 2 All ER 39, HL.

4   See para 11.5 above.

5   Not that the awareness that such an implication will probably be made will necessarily assist the parties' advisers in deciding what would be considered to be fair and reasonable in any particular case because this is a difficult phrase to apply to a specific situation. Dictionaries (for example Chambers *Twentieth Century Dictionary* (1972)) include 'reasonable' as a definition of 'fair' but it is suggested that two separate concepts are involved when the words are used in this context. (See *Re Stuart, ex p Cathcart* [1898] 2 QB 201, CA per Lord Esher MR at 204, 205.) In the middle of the last century a direction to a jury that 'if "reasonably" meant anything else than "in good faith", it meant "according to his reason" as contra-distinguished from "caprice" . . .' was approved (*Booth v Clive* (1851) 10 CB 827) although today perhaps a higher standard would be demanded – possibly the individual would have to be acting according to a reason that he genuinely believed that he could justify. What is reasonable has to be looked at in the light of all the relevant circumstances (*Re A Solicitor* [1945] KB 368, [1945] 1 All ER 445, CA) and the commercial purpose of the contract (*Fraser v B N Furman (Productions) Ltd* [1967] 3 All ER 57, CA per Diplock LJ at 62, 63). It is suggested that 'fair' should be applied as meaning just and equitable between the parties in all the relevant circumstances. Thus what is fair may not be reasonable, and what is reasonable may not be fair. See correspondence [1983] Gazette 2 Nov 2724. For an expenditure to be fair and reasonable, it does not necesarily have to have been the cheapest option open to the landlord, although it is not clear from the report of the case if the tenant's argument in *Manor House Drive Ltd v Shahbazian* (1965) 195 Estates Gazette 283, CA was one of construction, or an allegation that the landlord's expenditure was unreasonable and therefore could not be recovered. The landlord had covenanted to 'maintain repair and decorate the main structure and roof of the building' and the tenant was under an obligation to pay a proportion of the costs of the works. There were problems with the roof and the landlord having received the advice of a surveyor undertook comprehensive repair work and then called upon the tenants to pay their proportion of the cost. The tenants argued that this item should be disallowed because the landlord could have undertaken work costing less than a quarter of the amount claimed, although this would only have lasted for some three years or so, and further 'patching up' would have been needed frequently thereafter. The Court of Appeal allowed the landlord's claim for the full amount apparently on the basis that the temporary repairs were not reasonable or even proper in view of the surveyor's advice. See also *Bandar Property Holdings Ltd v J S Darwen (Successors) Ltd* [1968] 2 All ER 305.

6   See for example Appendix 1, Form 6 below clauses 6.1:3, 6.1:6, 6.1:13.

7   See para 11.5 above.

8   See *Concorde Graphics Ltd v Andromeda Investments SA* (1983) 265 Estates Gazette 386.

9   See para 11.16 above.

11.20   *Consultation.* One concept that is likely to be missing altogether from any service charge provision is that of *consultation* between the landlord and his tenants. There are instances in relation to residential property where consultation must take place as a matter of law[1] and there are clearly many office buildings in multi-occupation and shopping centres where there is a happy working relationship between the landlord and his tenants. One can well understand the desire of the landlord to be unfettered in relation to the performance of the services in that, realistically speaking, it is rarely possible to have regard to everybody's wishes when more than a few people are involved. Nevertheless, this concept is one worth canvassing for the consideration of commercial landlords and tenants in the future. If wording was ever needed, one would simply propose 'the Landlord shall wherever practical have regard to the wishes of [the representatives of] the tenants'. One hesitates to suggest the principle of a 'tenants' association' in commercial letting, but, on the other hand, in a large building containing numerous lettings there may be room for such an organisation representing to the landlord the tenants' views so far as services and other matters are concerned.[2]

1   Housing Act 1988.
2   In *CIN Properties Ltd v Barclays Bank plc* [1986] 1 EGLR 59, 277 Estates Gazette 973, CA a
failure by the landlord to observe a proviso in the lease by which estimate would not be
accepted without them being submitted to and approved by the tenants disbarred the landlord
from being entitled to be reimbursed for the work in question. See J E Adams: 'Shopping
Centres: Tenants' associations in Centres' [1988] 15 EG 24.

I   SINKING FUNDS

11.21   *Objectives.* Essentially there are two types of sinking fund. The first
would better be called 'a recurring expenditure equalisation fund'. Its object is
to avoid wide fluctuations in the amount of the service charge payable each
year. Thus, as an alternative to asking the tenants to pay every five years for a
recurring expenditure such as the decoration of the exterior and the common
parts of a major office building, the landlord makes an estimate of the likely
cost in advance, and collects this sum by means of five equal instalments over
the years preceding the work. In many ways, this is much fairer because if
tenants change during the period, each pays a share proportionate to his
period of ownership. The other is a replacement fund, by which the landlord
aims to build up over many years a fund to pay for the replacement of major
items of plant and equipment such as lifts and the air-conditioning system
when they have outlived their useful lives. This can, of course, be extended to
the replacement of the building itself, and is another aspect of the clear lease[1] –
not only does the landlord expect all his day-to-day expenditure to be
reimbursed, but he sees no reason why the tenants should not pay to have the
building and its components replaced as they wear out. Landlords tend to
prefer simple provisions enabling them, for example, to recover as part of the
service charge 'such provision (if any) for anticipated expenditure in respect of
any of the Services as the Landlord shall in its absolute discretion consider
appropriate'. There are, however, a number of safeguards that the tenant
should insist upon.[2] The sinking fund must be kept separate from the
landlord's own money to ensure that such fund does not form part of the
landlord's assets on a bankruptcy or liquidation.[3] The purpose of the fund
must be set out clearly together with the circumstances in which the landlord
must resort to the fund. Otherwise the landlord could maintain a fund and at
the same time recover all the expenditure incurred each year by means of the
service charge for that year, perhaps leaving the fund available for other
purposes of the landlord.[2] An attempt should be made to provide that the
landlord would be entitled to recover only anticipated expenditure that was
reasonable, and for the tenant to have a basis for resisting an unreasonable
operation of the clause.[2]. The anticipated expenditure must be limited to the
term of the lease and the clause should be drafted so as to prevent the landlord
building up, by means of a sinking fund, a sum that will enable it to rebuild the
property at the end of the term.[2] When the tenant comes to assign the lease, he
may be tempted to try to recover from the assignee the contributions that it has
made to the sinking fund, on the basis that it will be the assignee (and perhaps
subsequent assignees) who will benefit from these payments rather than the
assignor. The assignee could well resist, arguing that the contributions to the
sinking fund are merely payments required in order to occupy the premises
and, as such, are not recoverable. In addition, if the sinking fund is (at least in
part) an 'expenditure equalisation fund', the assignor may have derived some
benefit from the fund.

1 See para 11.1.
2 See 22 Encyclopaedia of Forms and Precedents (5th edn) Form 92.
3 In very limited cases where the landlord has maintenance a separate account and has not regarded the money as his own property, this may be implied: see *Re Chelsea Cloisters Ltd (in liquidation)* (1980) 41 P & CR 98, CA.

11.22 *Taxation concerns.* A person contemplating taking a lease of a suite of offices may find it difficult to accept that, over and above the rent, the landlord will be reimbursed by the tenants for all the expenditure that he incurs in relation to the building and the plant and machinery installed in it. Once he comes to terms with this, there is much to commend the concept of a sinking fund.[1] It should prevent the occasional very high service charge in those years when major work or replacements have to be undertaken. Moreover, where there has been an assignment during the period, a fund is a fairer way of ensuring that every tenant for the time being pays a share, instead of the entire burden of the cost of the work attributable to the premises in question falling on the party who has the misfortune to be the tenant in the year in question. It is, therefore, a matter of concern that the taxation uncertainties and complications are such that sinking funds are rarely operated in commercial premises. A landlord contemplating inserting a sinking fund provision in the lease or a tenant confronted with one in a draft needs the most detailed advice from tax specialists. Ironically, it is the trust aspects that make the sinking fund more acceptable in the 'commercial' sense that cause the greatest fiscal problems.[2] It seems impossible if the conventional format is used to make the fund tax effective, while complications can arise in the tenant's own tax affairs in respect of payments made into the trust fund. There is no place in this book which is essentially a work on drafting for any detailed analysis and what follows is only intended to be a brief over-view.

1 Providing the details are properly dealt with: see para 11.21 above.
2 See para 11.21 above. I am indebted to Erica Stary for her assistance with these and other taxation issues.

11.23 *Where the service charge including the sinking fund is payable to the landlord as rent.*[1] In this case the landlord is taxed under Schedule A[2] in the same way as rent.[3] He can deduct his expenditure in accordance with the Schedule A rules,[3] that is expenditure incurred during the accounting period in question, or an unrelieved expenditure incurred in a previous accounting period. A sinking fund payment, however, is a sum received on account of future anticipated expenditure and is not deductible under Schedule A rules.[4] Thus a landlord will have an income tax liability on a sinking fund. When the expenditure is made in respect of which the sinking fund has been accrued, the landlord will be able to deduct the cost against the rent and service charge (including sinking fund contributions) for that year, and carry any excess forward against income in future years. The landlord will not, however, be able to set off any excess of expenditure over income against the income for previous years.[5] This is of real concern in the case of a sinking fund – the first expenditure out of the fund might be, for example, in the fifth year of the term and this could not be set off against the sum received by the fund during the first four years when there would have been nothing to set off against such income.

1 See para 11.7 above.
2 Ie the Schedules of Income contained in the Income and Corporation Taxes Act 1988 ('Taxes Act 1988'). Corporation Tax is charged on the profits which include both income and

chargeable gains of any company resident in the UK (Taxes Act 1988, s 6) and in general terms these are computed according to the principles used for income tax (Taxes Act 1988, s 9(1)) and capital gains tax (Taxes Act 1988, s 345).

3   Taxes Act 1988, s 15.
4   See Taxes Act 1988, ss 25–31 which in essence restrict deductions to expenditure actually incurred.
5   Taxes Act 1988, s 25(3), (4) provides that sums spent on an allowable expenditure are deductible from the rents receivable during that period in respect of those premises or subsequent periods so long as the same lease continues. In other words, expenditure can be claimed forward against future rents, but not backwards. Section 28 likewise provides in relation to receipts other than rent that allowable expenditure actually incurred may be deducted. The rules in effect provide that the deduction for the expenditure is allowed first for the year when the payment is made, if that income was insufficient to absorb it then it can be set against the year when the payment fell due, and finally if the payment is still not completely absorbed carried forward. There is, however, one major caveat. Where there is a change of landlord, the Revenue might take the view that the repairs were reflected in the price paid for the property so as to prevent any deduction at all – see *Odeon Associated Theatres Ltd v Jones* [1973] Ch 288, [1972] 1 All ER 681, CA. Also the rules in Schedule A prevent the carry forward for deduction against income of a later lease of expenditure found to be incurred during a period when the landlord claiming deduction was not the landlord, was in owner occupation, or (unlikely in commercial properties) had granted either lease at an uneconomic rent, taking one year with another.

11.24   *Where the service charge including the sinking fund is payable to the landlord other than as rent.*[1] Here the position in practice will be very similar to that set out in the preceeding paragraph. The service charge would be payable to the landlord not 'by virtue of his ownership of an estate or interest in land', but for Revenue purposes the landlord would probably be considered to be carrying on a trade (ie the provision of the services) and would be assessable under Schedule D, Case I.[2] In one respect, this could be more or less satisfactory from the landlord's point of view, depending on his circumstances, because a Schedule A loss can only be carried forward against future Schedule A income, whereas a Schedule D loss can be set against all profits of the year of the loss and of the previous period, as well as carried forward against future income of the same trade.[3]

1   See para 11.7 above.
2   Taxes Act 1988, s 18.
3   Taxes Act 1988, ss 380, 382 & 385 (for individuals) and s 393 (for companies).

11.25   *Where the landlord (or a third party) receives the sinking fund as a trustee.*[1] The trust is a separate entity, and thus the sinking fund should not affect the landlord's tax position.[2] Trustees are liable to income tax on trust income received by them including that received as a result of investing the fund, with no relief for the expenses incurred in managing the trust. Where the tenants are companies the trust will generally be a discretionary trust.[3] When the fund incurs expenditure, deductions can be made subject to the limitations referred to in para 11.24 above.

1   See para 11.21 above.
2   There is, perhaps, the somewhat forced argument that the money ought not to be regarded as being subject to the trust until the landlord pays it into the sinking fund and thus it has been received by the landlord and should be taxed in his hands under paras 11.23 and 11.24 above. It is difficult to see how this could prevail especially where the drafting makes it quite clear that the sinking fund is paid to the landlord as trustee.
3   See Inheritance Tax Act 1984, ss 58, 59.

11.26 *Capital allowances.* The landlord may well have incurred capital expenditure on the plant and machinery installed in the building, and be entitled to allowances under the Finance Act 1971, ss 41 and 46. If the sinking fund provision is drawn in such a way that it appears that the trust will be reimbursing the landlord for such expenditure the landlord will be prevented from claiming these allowances.[1] To keep his allowance, the provision must be drafted in such a way that it is clear that the landlord incurs the expenditure and the trust or the tenant cannot be found to have made a capital contribution.[2]

1   Capital Allowances Act 1968, s 85 and Finance Act 1971. Sch 8, para 15(6).
2   Capital Allowances Act 1968, s 84(2)(b) and Finance Act 1971, Sch 8, para 15(5).

11.27 *The tenant's position.* To turn to the position of the tenant:
(a) *Where the service charge is payable as additional rent,* it will be deductible in the same way as rent.[1]
(b) *Where the service charge is payable to the landlord other than as additional rent,* it will be deductible in the same way as rent, as it will be paid pursuant to an obligation undertaken to obtain the use of business premises.[1]
(c) *Where a sinking fund is payable to either the landlord or a third party as trustee,* the position is unclear. The tenant would argue that the payment should be deductible because it is paid pursuant to the terms of the lease whereas the Revenue may take the view that the tenant is not entitled to relief on money not actually laid out or expended. This would be a very real danger when the lease was drafted in such a way that the trust fund would be returned to the tenants if not utilised. If the latter view prevailed, the expenditure would not be regarded as being incurred by the individual tenants until the year in which the money was actually laid out by the fund, and this would be a most unsatisfactory situation from the tenant's point of view.

1   See Taxes Act 1988, s 74(a). The expenditure must be wholly exclusively laid out or expended for the purpose of the tenant's trade profession or vocation.

11.28 *Inheritance tax ('IHT').* There could also be significant IHT implications where the landlord (or for that matter a third party) holds the sinking fund on trust because such a trust would probably amount to a settlement for IHT purposes.[1]

11.28:1 *Creation.* The tenant would clearly argue that there would be no IHT implications on the creation of the fund because there was no gratuitous intent[2] in making the payments into it because they were required to do by the provisions of the lease. That is, the transaction was made at arm's length between persons not connected with each other, or, if connected, the transaction is like one which unconnected persons would make at arm's length. The position is unclear and, if this argument were not accepted, the IHT position on the creation of the settlement will depend on whether the settlement has an interest in possession (ie the trust is for the benefit of the tenants for the time being) or is a discretionary trust. In the former case, the creation of the trust will not give rise to an immediate liability to IHT but instead will be a PET (potentially exempt transfer),[3] with, presumably, the tenant being regarded as the settlor.[4] This means that in the event of the tenant dying within seven years of the contribution or ceasing to have an interest, the potential exemption ceases and the funds will be caught for IHT.[5] Where the trust is a discretionary trust, IHT is chargeable on creation in the usual way.[6] There is a further complication because the tenant retains an interest in the funds he has transferred to the settlement. The result is that if he dies whilst still retaining an interest or within seven years of relinquishing his interest, his contributions to the trust fund will be caught for tax on death with a credit for the tax payable on creation (where the trust was a discretionary trust) if any.[7]

11.28:2   *Assignment.* If the tenant has an interest in possession there is a potential liability to IHT when he disposes of his lease. This will bring about a cessation of his interest in possession which will generate a potential liability to IHT on the difference between the disposal proceeds of the interest and the underlying value of the assets in the settlement attributable to his interest.[8] There should be no potential tax charge if the tenant ensures that when he sells his lease he attributes the appropriate proportion of the price to the disposal of his interest in the sinking fund so that there is no transfer of value.[9] Further, in most cases the disposal of the lease will be a transaction at arm's length between persons not connected with each other where there is no gratuitous intent so that the likelihood of any liability to IHT arising, actually or potentially, is very low.[10]

11.28:3   *Discretionary trust.* Where the trust is a discretionary trust, and if the sinking fund were to be held for ten years or more, an IHT charge would arise on every tenth anniversary of the creation of a trust, based on the value of the trust fund on the anniversary in question plus the settlor's cumulative total for IHT the day before settlement was made.[11] If – as would appear to be the case – the part attributable to each tenant were to be regarded as a separate settlement,[12] no liability to IHT would arise unless the amount attributable to any individual tenant exceeds the nil rate band.

1   Within Inheritance Tax Act 1984, s 43. Potential IHT liability will apply to individuals (including partnerships) and close companies (through participators), IHTA ss 2, 94. It is doubtful if it could be argued that, because there is no element of bounty, there is no settlement, *IRC v Plummer* [1980] AC 896, [1979] 3 All ER 775, HL; this would involve applying income tax principles to IHT which the courts might be reluctant to do.
2   IHTA 1984, s 10.
3   Ibid, ss 3A, 7.
4   Ibid, s 44(1).
5   Finance Act 1986, s 101, Sch 19.
6   IHTA 1984, s 7.
7   Finance Act 1986, s 102, Sch 20.
8   IHTA 1984, ss 50–53.
9   IHTA 1984, s 3.
10   Ibid, s 10.
11   Ibid, ss 61–69.
12   Ibid, s 44(2).

11.29   *Management company.* The solution as to the provision of services that generally works effectively for residential property is likely to be of little assistance where commercial premises are involved. In the former, a management company is frequently incorporated, that relies upon the principle of mutuality to ensure that any profits (that in this case would be any element of sinking fund paid by the tenants) are free from tax.[1] Each tenant in the development has a share in the company and provision is made for these to be transferred to the assignee on an assignment. The company covenants, either by being made a party to the lease or in a separate deed, to perform the services, including the maintenance of the structure of the building, and the tenants covenant to reimburse their appropriate share. Mutuality occurs where a defined group of people combine for a purpose and contribute towards expenses in such a way that their contributions can only be expended for that common purpose or returned to them.[2] The principle applies even though the contributions are made to a separate legal entity such as a company,[3] so long as the company exists simply for the convenience of its members, and as an instrument obediant to their mandate. Two problems arise, however, when seeking to apply this approach to commercial property:

(a) A landlord of a block of flats who plans to dispose of all the flats by means of long leases at premiums is very anxious to limit his involvement in the property in the future and to find a third party who will take on the 'landlord-type duties'. As such, he welcomes handing over the responsibility for providing the services to, in effect, a consortium of tenants. A landlord of a commercial development, however, who will let the units by means of leases at rack rents is very anxious to keep control of the services because he knows that poor management could cause the value of his investment to deteriorate. He could not tolerate a situation in which the standards could be allowed to drop at the whim of the majority of the tenants. This is why landlords go to considerable lengths to be in absolute control of the provision of the services.[4] And yet the landlord could not be a member of the management company (unless and for so long as he retained a part of the development) because that would destroy the mutuality ie *all* the members would not have a common purpose.[5]

(b) There is authority for saying that the exemption from tax afforded by mutual dealings does not operate to prevent contributions being claimed as deductions in computing the taxable income of the contributor.[6] On the other hand, this merely establishes the general principle – whether or not a deduction could be made would depend upon the circumstances of the individual case. The question of deduction of payments made to a management company does not arise in the case of individuals who are tenants of residential flats, because service charges are not deductible in computing their personal tax liability. Service charges are, however, deductible by business tenants[7] but it seems unlikely that a management company would overcome the potential problem mentioned in para 11.27(c) above, and that the Revenue would still be in a position to argue that contributions made to a sinking fund operated by a management company should be regarded for the purposes of deduction as being made not in the year in which the tenant paid them to the comany but in the year in which the company expended them.

1 *Carlisle and Silloth Golf Club v Smith* [1913] 3 KB 75, CA.
2 See per Lord Normand in *English and Scottish Joint Co-operative Wholesale Society Ltd v Assam Agricultural Income Tax Comr* [1948] AC 405 at 419, [1948] 2 All ER 395 at 400, PC; *IRC v Eccentric Club Ltd* [1924] 1 KB 390, CA, and Finlay J in *National Association of Local Government Officers v Watkins* (1934) 18 TC 499 at 506. But note Taxes Act 1988, s 486 and *IRC v Ayrshire Employers Mutual Insurance Association Ltd* [1946] 1 All ER 637 at 640, HL.
3 Per Rowlatt J in *Thomas v Richard Evans & Co Ltd* [1927] 1 KB 33 at 47, CA.
4 See paras 11.14 and 11.19 above.
5 *New York Life Assurance Co v Styles* (1889) 14 App Cas 381, HL; *Fletcher v Income Tax Comr* [1972] AC 414, [1971] 3 All ER 1185, PC.
6 *Thomas v Richard Evans & Co Ltd* [1927] 1 KB 33, CA.
7 See para 11.27(a) and (b) above.

Chapter 12

Provisos

A FORFEITURE

12.1 *Re-entry*. A breach of covenant gives no right of re-entry unless a proviso for re-entry is included in the lease.[1] It must provide that the right to enter for non-payment of rent applies whether formally demanded or not, in order to avoid the common law requirement that an actual demand has to be made.[2] If the landlord elects to determine the lease he must do so by re-entry[3] which he may effect by physically entering the premises with the intention of determining the tenancy[4] or by the issue and service[5] of proceedings for the recovery of possession. If the writ in such proceedings contains an unequivocal demand for possession[6] the service of the writ operates as a final election to determine the term whether judgment is obtained or not.[5] The Law Commission has suggested that the law of forfeiture is unnecessarily complicated, is no longer coherent and gives rise to injustices and has recommended that it be totally replaced by a new system.[7] There have been no public indications by the government as to whether it proposes to introduce legislation implementing the Law Commission's recommendations.

1   See Rosscastle Letting Conditions (Appendix 1, Form 1 below) Condition 10.1.
2   *Doe d Chandless v Robson* (1826) 2 C & P 245; *Hill v Kempshall* (1849) 7 CB 975; *Jackson & Co v Northampton Street Tramways Co* (1886) 55 LT 91. The demand must be made upon the land, and, if there is a house on the premises, at the front door: Co-Litt 201b, 202a. In the absence of the tenant it may be made upon the occupier (*Doe d Brook v Brydges* (1822) 2 Dow & Ry KB 29), but it is effective even if no one is on the premises (Co Litt 201b). The demand must be only of the sum due for rent for the last period for payment (*Scot v Scot* (1587) Cro Eliz 73; *Fabian v Winston* (1589) Cro Eliz 209; *Doe d Wheeldon v Paul* (1829) 3 C & P 613), and must be made before sunset on the last day of payment, and continued until sunset (Co Litt 202a; *Wood d Chivers* (1573) 4 Leon 179; *Doe d Wheeldon v Paul*, supra; *Acocks v Phillips* (1860) 5 H & N 183; and see 1 Wms Saund (1871 edn) 434–440; *Doe d Darke v Bowditch* (1846) 8 QB 973). The condition is fulfilled by tender of the rent to the person who is to receive it on any part of the land at any time on the last day of payment: Co Litt 202a.
3   Where the premises are in the possession of an underlessee, a reletting of the premises to him by the landlord is a sufficient re-entry to avoid the lease (*Baylis v Le Gros* (1858) 4 CBNS 537), but it has been held to be otherwise when he relets to a stranger to whose entry the underlessee objects (*Parker v Jones* [1910] 2 KB 32). See also *London and County (A & D) Ltd v Wilfred Sportsman Ltd* [1971] Ch 264, [1970] 2 All ER 600, CA. As to whether there has been peaceable re-entry of the headlease where possession obtained with the co-operation of the subtenant, see *Ashton v Sobelman* [1987] 1 All ER 755, Law Notes (1987) 282 Estates Gazette 1135.
4   As to the need for intention to effect a forfeiture, and the circumstances in which an apparent re-entry by the landlord may not determine the lease, see *Relvok Properties Ltd v Dixon* (1972) 25 P & CR 1, CA, applying the earlier test, in relation to the question whether a landlord's acts amounted to the acceptance of a surrender, in *Oastler v Henderson* (1877) 2 QBD 575, CA.
5   *Canas Property Co Ltd v KL Television Services Ltd* [1970] 2 QB 433, [1970] 2 All ER 795. CA; *Elliott v Boynton* [1924] 1 Ch 236, CA. See also *Jones v Carter* (1846) 15 M & W 718; *Kilkenny Gas Co v Somerville* (1878) 2 LR Ir 192; *Scarf v Jardine* (1882) 7 App Cas 345, HL; *Serjeant v Nash, Field & Co* [1903] 2 KB 304, CA. As to the consequences of a landlord going into possession pursuant to a court order that is reversed on appeal, see *Hillgate House Ltd v Expert Clothing Service and Sales Ltd* [1987] 1 EGLR 65, 282 Estates Gazette 715.

6   Where the writ contains a claim for a permanent injunction, it is not an unequivocal election by the landlord to determine the lease on the ground of forfeiture: *Calabar Properties Ltd v Seagull Autos Ltd* [1969] 1 Ch 451, [1968] 1 All ER 1, discussing *Moore v Ullcoats Mining Co Ltd* [1908] 1 Ch 575 and *Wheeler v Keeble (1914) Ltd* [1920] 1 Ch 57. The landlord is entitled at the trial to abandon his claim for possession and proceed with his claim for an injunction upon the basis that the lease is still afoot. A claim for a declaration of title to possession will operate as a forfeiture although the writ does not claim an order for possession: *Cohen v Donegal Tweed Co Ltd* (1935) 79 Sol Jo 592, CA.

7   Report on Forfeiture of Tenancies (1985) Law Com No 142. The report recommended the replacement of the present law which allows landlords to terminate leases by re-entry and forfeiture by a scheme of termination orders for which landlords could apply, and which would be supplemented by a parallel scheme for orders available to tenants.

12.2   *A 'Section 146 Notice' and relief.* Before a right of re-entry of forfeiture under any proviso in a lease[1] for breach of a covenant or condition may be enforced,[2] the landlord must, except where the breach is non-payment of rent or certain other exceptions,[3] serve on the tenant a notice under s 146(1) of the Law of Property Act 1925 specifying the breach of which complaint is made and if it is capable of remedy, requiring the tenant to remedy it,[4] and in any case requiring the tenant to make compensation for the breach. If the tenant fails within a reasonable time after service of the notice to remedy the breach, if it is capable of remedying, and to make reasonable compensation to the satisfaction of the landlord, the landlord may either re-enter or begin an action to recover possession. The requirement of a notice is not confined to cases where the tenant has broken a specific provision of the lease and thus subject to statutory exceptions[5] a notice is required before a forfeiture on the grounds of the bankruptcy of the tenant, or on the grounds of the bankruptcy of a guarantor.[6] The notice of breach of covenant must be so distinct as to direct the tenant's attention to the particular things of which the landlord complains in order that the tenant may have an opportunity of remedying them before the forfeiture is enforced.[7] It must also be sufficient to inform the tenant of what is complained of but it need not identify every defect or amount to a detailed specification of the work to be done,[8] nor will the notice be invalid because, in attempting to enumerate the specific breaches, it includes some that have not been committed[9] nor because, in referring to covenants which do exist, it refers to one that does not.[10] It is not necessary that the notice should require payment of compensation[11] nor where the breach is incapable of remedy[12] need the notice require it to be remedied,[13] although if the breach is capable of remedy and the notice fails to require it to be remedied the notice will be insufficient.[14] If there is any doubt as to whether the breach is or is not capable of remedy it is sufficient in the notice to require remedy of the breach 'if it is capable of remedy'.[14] The notice may state a time within which the breach is to be remedied but the landlord will not be entitled to re-enter at the end of that period unless the time is in fact reasonable[15] and even if the time is incapable of remedy, a reasonable time must be given to the tenant between the service of the notice and the commencement of proceedings against him.[16] The service of a notice under s 146(1) of the Law of Property Act 1925 and default under it must have taken place before the landlord brings proceedings to enforce the forfeiture but thereafter the tenant may apply to the court for relief under the Law of Property Act 1925 s 146(2),[17] although the application must be made before the landlord has actually re-entered.[18] Where relief is granted, it may be on such terms, if any, as to costs expenses damages compensation penalty or otherwise including an injunction against a further like breach as the court in the circumstances of each case shall think fit.[17] The Leasehold Property

(Repairs) Act 1938 imposes further requirements on the landlord and confers benefits on the tenant where a breach of the tenant's covenant to repair is involved,[19] while s 147 of the Law of Property Act 1925 empowers the court to grant relief against forfeiture where the breach of covenant relates to internal decorative repairs, provided the tenant was not required to put the premises into a decorative state of repairs. Where the tenant or occupier of premises has been convicted of permitting the premises to be used as a brothel, the Sexual Offences Act 1956, s 35(1) entitles the landlord to require the tenant to assign the lease to some person approved by the landlord, such approval[20] not to be unreasonably withheld. If the tenant fails to do so within three months, the landlord is entitled to determine the lease.[21]

1 The statutory provisions as to service of a notice on the tenant and the tenant's right to apply to the court for relief against forfeiture cannot be avoided by disguising what is in truth and substance a forfeiture as some other form of transaction: *Plymouth Corpn v Harvey* [1971] 1 All ER 623, [1971] 1 WLR 549; *Richard Clarke & Co Ltd v Widnall* [1976] 3 All ER 301, [1976] 1 WLR 845, CA. However, the statutory provisions do not apply where the re-entry is by operation of law and not under a proviso or stipulation in a lease: see *Warner v Sampson* [1958] 1 QB 404, [1958] 1 All ER 44. For helpful over-views of when a landlord may successfully take forfeiture proceedings against a tenant, and the procedural requirements that he must follow, see 'Mainly for Students: Forfeiture of Leases' (1987) 281 Estates Gazette 1335 and Delyth Williams: 'Current problems in forfeiture' (1985) 275 Estates Gazette 860.

2 Ie by action of peaceable entry: *Re Biggs, ex p Lovell* [1901] 2 KB 16 at 20. See also *Howard v Fanshawe* [1895] 2 Ch 581.

3 As to the inspection etc of books and right to enter the mine in a mining lease (s 146(8)(ii)) and in certain circumstances on bankruptcy – see s 146(9) and (10) and para 12.4 below.

4 Certain breaches of covenant are, by their very nature, irremediable; see *Rugby School Governors v Tannahill* [1935] 1 KB 87, CA (use of house for immoral purposes); *Egerton v Explanade Hotels, London Ltd* [1947] 2 All ER 88 (hotel used as brothel); *Hoffmann v Fineberg* [1949] Ch 245, [1948] 1 All ER 592 (use as gaming house); *Borthwick-Norton v Romney Warwick Estates Ltd* [1950] 1 All ER 798, CA (sub-let flat used as brothel); *Bickerton's Aerodromes Ltd v Young* (1958) 108 L Jo 218 (breaches of licensing laws); *Ali v Booth* (1966) 110 Sol Jo 708, CA (conviction under food and drugs regulations); *Scala House and District Property Co Ltd v Forbes* [1974] QB 575, [1973] 3 All ER 308, CA (breach of covenant not to assign, sub-let or part with possession of the demised premises); *D R Evans & Co v Chandler* (1969) 211 Estates Gazette 1381 (use of premises so as to give them a stigma or bad name which would last well beyond the cessation of the use; but note *Expert Clothing Service and Sales Ltd v Hillgate House Ltd* [1986] Ch 340, [1985] 2 All ER 998, CA); *Dunraven Securities Ltd v Holloway* (1982) 264 Estates Gazette 709, CA (shop used as sex shop, tenant failing to show cause why material should not be forfeited under Obscene Publications Act 1959, s 2); *British Petroleum Pension Trust Ltd v Behrendt* [1985] 2 EGLR 97, 276 Estates Gazette 199, CA (prostitute using flat); and *Ropemaker Properties Ltd v Noonhaven Ltd* [1989] 34 EG 39 where relief against forfeiture was granted where premises used for prostitution. Whether the breach of a covenant not to suffer distress is remediable depends upon the particular circumstances of the case; if the landlord has sustained no undue injury, and no undue notoriety has attached to the premises, the breach may be remediable on payment of the rent due and the costs of the landlord's distress: *Hartley v Larkin* (1950) 66 (Pt 1) TLR 896; *Glass v Kencakes Ltd* [1966] 1 QB 611, [1964] 3 All ER 807. See also Delyth Williams: 'Irremediable breaches of covenant' (1985) 275 Estates Gazette 308.

5 See para 12.4 below.

6 *Halliard Property Co Ltd v Jack Segal Ltd* [1978] 1 All ER 1219, [1978] 1 WLR 377.

7 *Fletcher v Nokes* [1897] 1 Ch 271, where a notice that the tenant had broken the covenants of repair, without giving any details of the want of repair, was held to be insufficient; *Re Serle, Gregory v Serle* [1898] 1 Ch 652; *Jolly v Brown* [1914] 2 KB 109, CA; affd sub nom *Fox v Jolly* [1916] 1 AC 1, HL; *Davenport v Smith* [1921] 2 Ch 270. However, the notice need not specify the particular acts which the tenant must do: *Piggott v Middlesex County Council* [1909] 1 Ch 134 at 147.

8 *Fox v Jolly* [1916] 1 AC 1, HL, where the notice concluded 'and note that the completion of the items mentioned in this schedule does not excuse the execution of other repairs if found necessary'. It was held that the notice was not thereby invalidated, but that the landlord had merely reserved his rights if he later discovered a further breach.

9 *Matthews v Usher* [1900] 2 QB 535, CA; *Pannell v City of London Brewery Co* [1900] 1 Ch 496, followed in *McIlvenny v McKeever* [1931] NI 161 (NI CA); *Blewett v Blewett* [1936] 2 All ER 188, CA. However, the notice will be invalid if it claims in respect of special covenants to repair

which are not in fact contained in the lease (*Guillemard v Silverthorne* (1908) 99 LT 584), or refers to the wrong covenant (*Jacob v Down* [1900] 2 Ch 156).

10 *Silverster v Ostrowska* [1959] 3 All ER 642, [1959] 1 WLR 1060, where a notice to remedy a breach of covenant to repair also referred to a breach of a non-existing covenant against subletting.

11 *Lock v Pearce* [1893] 2 Ch 271, CA; *Civil Service Co-operative Society v McGrigor's Trustee* [1923] 2 Ch 347; *Rugby School Governors v Tannahill* [1935] 1 KB 87, CA.

12 See note 4 above.

13 *Rugby School Governors v Tannahill* [1935] 1 KB 87, CA.

14 *Hoffman v Fineberg* [1948] 1 All ER 592; *Glass v Kencakes Ltd* [1966] 1 QB 611, [1964] 3 All ER 807 at 819.

15 *Horsey Estate Ltd v Steiger* [1899] 2 QB 79 at 92, CA; *Civil Service Co-operative Society v McGrigor's Trustee* [1923] 2 Ch 347, where fourteen days was held to be sufficient notice. A three months' notice will usually be reasonable (see *Penton v Barnett* [1898] 1 QB 276, CA; *Gulliver Investments v Abbott* [1966] EGD 299); but where the notice applies to all the premises and a longer period is necessary in respect of part, it must be allowed in respect of the whole (*Hopley v Tarvin Parish Council* (1910) 74 JP 209).

16 *Horsey Estate Ltd v Steiger* [1899] 2 QB 79, CA; *Scala House and District Property Co Ltd v Forbes* [1974] QB 575, [1973] 3 All ER 308, CA. In such a case the purpose of allowing to the tenant a period of time is so that he will have an opportunity to consider his position generally and in particular to consider such matters as whether he should apply for relief and offer compensation to the landlord. In *Horsey*, two days was held not to be a reasonable time. In *Scala*, fourteen days was held to be sufficient.

17 For examples of the court's attitude to granting relief, see *Hoffmann v Fineberg* [1948] 1 All ER 592; *Central Estates (Belgravia) Ltd v Woolgar (No 2)* [1972] 3 All ER 610, [1972] 1 WLR 1048, CA; *Tulapam Properties Ltd v De Almeida* (1981) 260 Estates Gazette 919; *Ropemaker Properties Ltd v Noonhaven Ltd* [1989] 34 EG 39.

18 *Rogers v Rice* [1892] 2 Ch 170, CA; *Lock v Pearce* [1893] 2 Ch 271 at 274, CA; *Scott v Matthew Brown & Co Ltd* (1884) 51 LT 746.

19 See paras 8.17–8.21 above – the 1938 Act applies where lease was for seven years or more and at the date of the service of the notice three years or more remain unexpired.

20 Sexual Offences Act 1956, s 35(2).

21 Sexual Offences Act 1956, Sch 1, paras 2 and 3.

12.3 *Non payment of rent.* Section 146(11) provides that the section does not affect the law relating to re-entry or forfeiture or relief in case of non-payment of rent. Thus no notice has to be served by the landlord in relation to forfeiture for non-payment of rent although the tenant will be entitled to relief against forfeiture upon payment of the rent and any expenses incurred by the landlord[1] providing the landlord and any other interested person as can be put in the same position as before.[2] It is only in exceptional circumstances that relief will not be granted on payment of the rent in arrear[3] even where there are other breaches of covenant.[4] Section 212 of the Common Law Procedure Act 1852 provides that if the landlord has brought an action to recover possession then at any time before the trial, and providing the rent is six months in arrear,[5] the tenant or his assigns may pay or tender to the landlord or pay into court all the rent in arrear together with costs whereupon all further proceedings will be stayed, and the tenant or his assigns will hold the premises under the lease without the need for any new lease.[6] Even after trial and judgment for recovery of possession, the tenant will still be entitled to relief, but he must apply within six months of the date upon which judgment is executed – after that time relief is barred.[7] Nevertheless if he applies within the period and obtains relief he holds the demised premises under the original lease, again without the need for a new lease.[8] Where the landlord has re-entered peaceably without bringing proceedings the statutory six month time limit for an application for relief does not apply, and the court may grant relief under its equitable jurisdiction outside the limit.[9]

1 The original jurisdiction to grant relief against forfeiture for non-payment of rent arose from the practice of the old Court of Chancery: see *Popham v Bampfeild* (1682) 1 Vern 79; *Grimston v*

Lord Bruce (1707) 1 Salk 156. Later the equitable intervention which originally extended to all breaches, was confined to non-payment of rent: *Hill v Barclay* (1810) 16 Ves 402. For modern discussions of the historic basis of relief, see *Belgravia Insurance Co Ltd v Meah* [1964] 1 QB 436, [1963] 3 All ER 828, CA; *Shiloh Spinners Ltd v Harding* [1973] AC 691, [1973] 1 All ER 90, HL. Statute intervened to restrict the time within which relief could be granted to six months after execution of a judgment, first by the Landlord and Tenant Act 1730 and then by the Common Law Procedure Act 1852, of which s 210 remains the statutory basis of relief where the tenant seeks relief after a judgment for possession. Relief in favour of underlessees is also available under the Law of Property Act 1925, s 146(4). Where the landlord enters without a judgment for possession, relief may still be obtained apart from statute under the old equitable jurisdiction. As to granting of relief under statute, see *Gill v Lewis* [1956] 2 QB 1 at 16, [1956] 1 All ER 844 at 853, CA, per Hodson LJ; *Wadman v Calcraft* (1804) 10 Ves 67; *Howard v Fanshawe* [1895] 2 Ch 581 at 588; *Dendy v Evans* [1910] 1 KB 263 at 270, CA; *Di Palma v Victoria Square Property Co Ltd* [1986] Ch 150, [1985] 2 All ER 676, CA: see para 12.4 below. Where the lease contains a provision allowing the landlord to determine the lease on giving a period of notice following a breach of covenant by the tenant, the court may grant relief against the operation of the clause after non-payment of rent: *Richard Clarke & Co Ltd v Widnall* [1976] 3 All ER 301, [1976] 1 WLR 845, CA. It is the same whether there is a proviso for re-entry or whether the lease is conditioned to be void on non-payment of rent: *Bowser v Colby* (1841) 1 Hare 109 at 128. If the order granting relief fixes a time-limit for compliance with the conditions, there is power to extend the time: see *Chandless-Chandless v Nicholson* [1942] 2 KB 321, [1942] 2 All ER 315, CA; *Starside Properties Ltd v Mustapha* [1974] 2 All ER 567, [1974] 1 WLR 816, CA.

2 *Stanhope v Haworth* (1886) 3 TLR 34, CA; *Chandless-Chandless v Nicholson* [1942] 2 KB 321, [1942] 2 All ER 315, CA.

3 An example of an exceptional case where relief was refused in spite of the arrears being paid was *Public Trustee v Westbrook* [1965] 3 All ER 398, [1965] 1 WLR 1160, CA, where no rent had been paid for twenty-two years. See also *Stanhope v Haworth* (1886) 3 TLR 34, CA. The payment of the arrears is a statutory condition of relief: *Barton, Thompson & Co Ltd v Stapling Machines Co* [1966] Ch 499, [1966] 2 All ER 222. See also *Howard v Central Board of Finance of the Church of England* (1976) 244 Estates Gazette 51, DC.

4 *Gill v Lewis* [1956] 2 QB 1, [1956] 1 All ER 844, CA; *Silverman v AFCO (UK) Ltd* [1988] 1 EGLR 51, [1988] 14 EG 67, CA. However, in *Piccadilly Estates Hotels Ltd v Total Property Investments Ltd* (1974) 232 Estates Gazette 590, relief against forfeiture was given for non-payment of rent but on terms that the tenant remedied other breaches of covenant.

5 *Standard Pattern Co Ltd v Ivey* [1962] Ch 432, [1962] 1 All ER 452. But where the Common Law Procedure Act 1852 does not apply (ie rent not six months in arrears) see Supreme Court Act 1981, s 38.

6 Common Law Procedure Act 1852, s 212. In order that an assignee may obtain relief against an order for possession, it is necessary that he should pay or tender not only the amount due from him but also the amount of rent due from the original lessee, his assignor: *Barratt v Richardson and Cresswell* [1930] 1 KB 686. It appears that arrears which are statute barred need not be paid: see *Re Howell's Application* [1972] Ch 509, [1972] 3 All ER 662. A mortgagee is entitled to relief on the same terms as the tenant: *Doe d Whitfield v Roe* (1811) 3 Taunt 402. The relief protects sub-tenants: *Shine v Gough* (1811) 1 Ball & B 436.

7 See the Common Law Procedure Act 1852, s 210; *Vesey v Bodkin* (1830) 4 Bli NS 64, HL. The fact that after judgment has been obtained against him the tenant signs an agreement by which he undertakes to give up possession will not necessarily deprive him of the right to relief: *Nance v Naylor* [1928] 1 KB 263, CA. However, relief cannot be spelled out of the conduct of the parties without any application for relief or order: see *Smith v Odder* [1949] WN 249, CA, where an order for possession in default of appearance had been set aside and the tenant continued in possession without any further order. As to rent accruing due after judgment where the tenant is restored to possession, see *Wilson v Burne* (1889) 24 LR Ir 14, CA.

8 Supreme Court Act 1981, s 38 (formerly Supreme Court of Judicature (Consolidation) Act 1925, s 46).

9 *Thatcher v C H Pearce & Sons (Contractors) Ltd* [1968] 1 WLR 748 and see note 1 above. See too Supreme Court Act 1981, s 38.

12.4 *Re-entry on bankruptcy.* A tenant seeking to raise finance will find that potential lenders are unlikely to be impressed with the offer of a mortgage of his leasehold business premises as security. Initially there is the valuation concern – an item can only constitute worthwhile security if it has a realisable value and special circumstances will need to be present for a lease to have any real value when at an open market rent and with a rent review pattern in keeping with the current norm[1] Then lenders need to be satisfied that the item being offered as security will remain in being on the bankruptcy or liquidation of the borrower. Leases of business premises invariably contain a proviso for re-entry upon the bankruptcy or liquidation of the tenant, although statute modifies this in two important ways:

(a) In practice, the provisions of s 146(1) of the Law of Property Act 1925 will apply in most instances[2] either for the period of one year from the bankruptcy or liquidation, or until the tenant's interest is sold, in which event they will apply indefinitely.[3] Thus the landlord will be required to serve a notice[4] and the tenant (via the trustee in bankruptcy or liquidator) entitled to apply for relief.[5]

(b) Where a landlord is proceeding by action or otherwise to enforce a right of re-entry or forfeiture, the court may[6] on the application of an underlessee of the whole or part of the demised premises make an order vesting in the underlessee the property comprised in the headlease, for the whole (or a shorter) term of the lease, upon such conditions as to the execution of any deed or other document, payment of rent, costs, compensation, security or otherwise as the court in the circumstances of the case thinks fit.[7] The court under this provision has power to grant relief to an underlessee upon forfeiture on the bankruptcy of the head-tenant,[8] and a mortgagee of leaseholds by sub-demise is an underlessee within the meaning of the Act and thus entitled to relief.[9] An equitable mortgagee who has the right to call for the execution of a legal charge or mortgage is a person having an agreement for an underlease and is thus entitled to seek relief,[10] as is a mortgagee where the charge is by way of legal mortgage,[11] because he is entitled to the same protection powers and remedies as if a sub-term less by one day than the term vested in the mortgagor had been created in his favour.[12] Where a mortgagee obtains relief, a new term is vested in him but it is held as a substituted security, and the mortgagor has a right to redeem that security although the original lease has been forfeited.[13]

These are, however, complex statutory provisions necessitating applications to the court and involving their fair share of time, trouble, expense[14] and uncertainty. As such, when acting for a client who may wish to mortgage his leased business premises, the tenant's solicitor should consider introducing into a lease a limitation on the rights of the landlord to forfeit the lease on the bankruptcy or liquidation of the tenant.[15]

1 Ie would the tenant be able to assign at a premium? He would be, for example, towards the end of a review period if there had been a sharp rise in rents, if other traders were willing to 'buy their way in' to the development in question, or if the rent had been determined disregarding significant improvements.

2 The Law of Property Act 1925, s 146(9) provides that s 146 does not apply to a condition for forfeiture on bankruptcy (by virtue of s 205(1)(i) of the LPA this includes liquidation of a company) of the tenant, or on the taking in execution of the tenant's interest if contained in a lease of agricultural or pastoral land, or of mines or minerals, or of a house used or intended to be used as a public house or beer shop, or of a house let as a dwelling house with the use of furniture and other chattels not being in the nature of fixtures, or of any property with respect to which the personal qualifications of the tenant are of importance for the preservation of the value or character of the property, or on the ground of neighbourhood to the landlord or any person holding under him. See *Bass Holdings Ltd v Lewis* [1986] 2 EGLR 40, 280 Estates Gazette 771, CA.

3 The Law of Property Act 1925, s 146(10). The provisions of the Law of Property Act 1925, s 146(9) & (10) are comprehensive in respect of relief against forfeiture arising out of the tenant's bankruptcy and any inherent equitable jurisdiction to grant relief has been ousted:

Official Custodian for Charities v Parway Estates Developments Ltd [1985] Ch 151, [1984] 3 All ER 679, CA.
4 Ie under Law of Property Act 1925, s 146(1), see para 12.2 above.
5 Ie under Law of Property Act 1925, s 146(2), see para 12.2 above.
6 Law of Property Act 1925, s 146(4). As to the right of a mortgagee to claim relief against forfeiture, see Legal Notes (1986) 277 Estates Gazette 1256 and (1987) 282 Estates Gazette 1263.
7 The underlessee must pay the costs of obtaining relief (*London Bridge Buildings Co v Thomson* (1903) 89 TL 50), including the costs of an enquiry necessary to determine the new rent (*Ewart v Fryer* (1902) 86 LT 676), the estate so vested is a new estate (*Serjeant v Nash, Field & Co* [1903] 2 KB 304 at 313, CA), the rent may be increased (*Ewart v Fryer* above, *Wardens of Cholmeley School, Highgate v Sewell* [1894] 2 QB 906 at 913) and relief may be restricted to part of the land originally leased (*London Bridge Buildings Co v Thomson* – see above – and *Gray v Bonsall* [1904] 1 KB 601, CA). Where the headlease is forfeited, a subtenant can apply for relief even though the sub-lease had expired if the sub-tenancy is within the 1954 Act and no action had been taken under the 1954 Act to bring the sub-tenancy to an end (*Cadogan v Dimovic* [1984] 2 All ER 168, [1984] 1 WLR 609, CA). Note also *Abbey National Building Society v Maybeach Ltd* [1985] Ch 190, [1984] 3 All ER 262; *Official Custodian for Charities v Mackay (No 2)* [1985] 2 All ER 1016, [1985] 1 WLR 1308; *Ladup Ltd v Williams & Glyn's Bank plc* [1985] 2 All ER 577, [1985] 1 WLR 851; *Hill v Griffin* [1987] 1 EGLR 86, 282 Estates Gazette 85, CA; *Smith v Metropolitan City Properties Ltd* [1986] 1 EGLR 52, 277 Estates Gazette 753.
8 *Wardens of Cholmeley School Highgate v Sewell* – see above.
9 *Egerton v Jones* [1939] 2 KB 702, [1939] 3 All ER 889, CA; *Grangeside Properties Ltd v Collingwoods Securities Ltd* [1964] 1 All ER 143, [1964] 1 WLR 139, CA.
10 In the Law of Property Act 1925, s 146(5) an 'underlease' includes an agreement for an underlease where the underlessee has become entitled to have his underlease granted. See *Re Good's Lease, Good v Wood* [1954] 1 All ER 275, [1954] 1 WLR 309.
11 *Grand Junction Co Ltd v Bates* [1954] 2 QB 160, [1954] 1 WLR 309.
12 Law of Property Act 1925, s 87(1).
13 *Chelsea Estates Investment Trust Co Ltd v Marche* [1955] Ch 328, [1955] 1 All ER 195.
14 See note 7 above. Where the document creating the mortgage was drafted as an absolute assignment, the mortgagee was ordered to pay only two-thirds of the Landlord's party and party costs: *Grangeside Properties Ltd v Collingwoods Securities Ltd* [1964] 1 All ER 143, [1964] 1 WLR 139, CA.
15 See 22 Encyclopaedia of Forms and Precedents (5th edn) Form 80.

12.5 *Take advantage of or waive forfeiture.* The landlord has the option whether or not to take advantage of the forfeiture and if he elects not to do so the forfeiture is waived. Such election may be either expressed or implied and it is implied when after the cause of forfeiture has come to his knowledge[1] the landlord does any act by which he recognises that the relationship of landlord and tenant is still continuing.[2] This will arise and thus the right to forfeiture will be waived:

(a) by the landlord bringing an action for rent which had accrued since the cause of forfeiture[3] or the mere demand for or receipt of such rent[4] – the fact that the landlord by accepting rent had no intention of waiving the breach does not prevent his action amounting to a waiver,[5] nor can the landlord prevent the waiver by demanding or accepting rent 'without prejudice',[6] while an acceptance of rent in error by a managing agent's clerk will bind the landlord and constitute waiver.[7] If the landlord, however, has already shown a final determination to take advantage of the forfeiture,[8] no subsequent act will operate as waiver.[9] Forfeiture is not waived by acceptance of rent accrued due before the cause of forfeiture[10] unless at the same time the landlord recognises the tenancy as subsisting, for example by describing the tenant as such in the receipt;[11]

(b) by the landlord distraining for rent which accrued due before or after the forfeiture[12] unless the object of the distress is such that the distress does not imply a recognition of the tenancy for example where it is levied for the purpose of escaping the requirement of a formal demand of the rent,[13] or

(c) by the landlord agreeing to grant a new lease to commence from the expiry of the existing lease.[14]

1   Waiver implies knowledge: see *Pennant's Case* (1596) 3 Co Rep 64a, sub nom *Harvey v Oswald* (1596) Cro Eliz 553 at 572; *Roe d Gregson v Harrison* (1788) 2 Term Rep 425; *Atkin v Rose* [1923] 1 Ch 522; *London and County (A & D) Ltd v Wilfred Sportsman Ltd* [1971] Ch 764, [1970] 2 All ER 600, CA; *Central Estates (Belgravia) Ltd v Woolgar (No 2)* [1972] 3 All ER 610, [1972] 1 WLR 1048, CA; *Chrisdell Ltd v Johnson* [1987] 2 EGLR 123, 283 Estates Gazette 1553, CA. See also Mark Pawlowski: 'Waiver of a tenant's breach of covenant' (1985) 273 Estates Gazette 364, and H W Wilkinson: 'Acceptance of Rent as a Waiver' (1988) 138 NLJ 95.

2   *Ward v Day* (1864) 5 B & S 359 at 362, Ex Ch; *Re Garrud, ex p Newitt* (1881) 16 Ch D 522 at 533, CA; *Official Custodian for Charities v Parway Estates Developments Ltd* [1985] Ch 151, [1984] 3 All ER 679; *Expert Clothing Service and Sales Ltd v Hillgate House Ltd* [1986] Ch 340, [1985] 2 All ER 998, CA. See also *Green's Case* (1582) Cro Eliz 3; *Doe d Sore v Eykins* (1824) 1 C & P 154. A reference in a reversionary lease granted to a third person to the effect that it was granted subject to and with the benefit of another lease then liable to be forfeited is not a waiver of the right to forfeit that other lease as it was an ordinary conveyancing practice and did not amount to an unequivocal recognition of the existence of the other lease: *London and County (A & D) Ltd v Wilfred Sportsman Ltd* [1971] Ch 764, [1970] 2 All ER 600, CA. overruling *Davenport v Smith* [1921] 2 Ch 270.

3   *Roe D Crompton v Minshall* (1760) Bull NP 96; *Dendy v Nicholl* (1858) 4 CBNS 376; *Penton v Barnett* [1898] 1 QB 276. CA. If the landlord takes advantage of the forfeiture he will recover the equivalent of the rent as mesne profits. When proceedings for possession have been begun in the High Court the landlord may apply by summons for an interim in respect of the tenant's continuing occupation of the land: see RSC Order 29, r 18. The taking of other proceedings which imply the continuance of the tenancy will also operate as a waiver of the forfeiture: see *Pellatt v Boosey* (1862) 31 LJCP 281; *Evans v Davis* (1878) 10 Ch D 747. However, there appears to be no objection to commencing proceedings in which a claim for possession on the ground of forfeiture is joined with a claim, in the alternative, for a permanent injunction to restrain breaches of covenant: *Calabar Properties Ltd v Seagull Autos Ltd* [1969] 1 Ch 451, [1968] 1 All ER 1.

4   As to demand, see *Doe d Nash v Birch* (1836) 1 M & W 402 at 408; *Toleman v Portbury* (1872) LR 7 QB 344; *Segal Securities Ltd v Thoseby* [1963] 1 QB 887, [1963] 1 All ER 500; *Central Estates (Belgravia) Ltd v Woolgar (No 2)* [1972] 3 All ER 610, [1972] 1 WLR 1048; *David Blackstone Ltd v Burnetts (West End) Ltd* [1973] 3 All ER 782, [1973] 1 WLR 1487; *Welch v Birrane* (1974) 29 P & CR 102. As to receipt etc, see *Pennant's Case* (1596) 3 Co Rep 64a at 64b; *Whitchcot v Fox* (1616) Cro Jac 398; *Goodright d Walter v Davids* (1778) 2 Cowp 803; *Arnsby v Woodward* (1827) 6 B & C 519; *Doe d Griffith v Pritchard* (1833) 5 B & Ad 765; *Doe d Gatehouse v Rees* (1838) 4 Bing NC 384; *Pellatt v Boosey* (1862) 31 LJCP 281; *Miles v Tobin* (1867) 17 LT 432; *Clifford v Reilly* (1869) IR 4 CL 218. This is especially so if the landlord has also required repairs to be done: *Griffin v Tomkins* (1880) 42 LT 359. Payment into the landlord's bank account, if usual, may operate as a waiver, even if the landlord has instructed the bank not to receive it: *Pierson v Harvey* (1885) 1 TLR 430. It is sufficient if payment is accepted from a sub-tenant (*Price v Worwood* (1859) 4 H & N 512) or other person in satisfaction of the rent (*Pellat v Boosey*, supra). Acceptance from an assignee prior to the completion of the assignment will not enable the assignee to make a good title when he has failed to comply with a notice of dilapidations: *Re Martin, ex p Dixon (Trustee) v Tucker* (1912) 106 LT 381. On the other hand, where a lease was at the date of assignment voidable on the ground of breach of covenant to repair, the defect of title was cured by the acceptance of rent from the assignee by the landlord after the assignment: *Butler v Mounview Estates Ltd* [1951] 2 KB 563 at 568, [1951] 1 All ER 693 at 698. The rule applies to a Crown lease: *Bridges v Longman* (1857) 24 Beav 27.

5   *Windmall Investments (London) Ltd v Milano Restaurant Ltd* [1962] 2 QB 373, [1962] 2 All ER 680; *Legal and General Assurance Society Ltd v General Metal Agencies Ltd* (1969) 20 P & CR 953; *Central Estates (Belgravia) Ltd v Woolgar (No 2)* [1972] 3 All ER 610, [1972] 1 WLR 1048, CA; *David Blackstone Ltd v Burnetts (West End) Ltd* [1973] 3 All ER 782, [1973] 1 WLR 1487. The statement of Harman J in *Creery v Summersell and Flowerdew & Co Ltd* [1949] Ch 751 at 761 that the effect of a demand for or acceptance of rent depends on the intent with which the act was done is probably no longer correct – see para 12.7 below.

6   *Segal Securities Ltd v Thoseby* [1963] 1 QB 887, [1963] 1 All ER 500 (demand); *Windmill Investments (London) Ltd v Milano Restaurant Ltd* [1962] 2 QB 373, [1962] 2 All ER 680 (acceptance); *Matthews v Smallwood* [1910] 1 Ch 777; *Oak Property Co Ltd v Chapman* [1947] KB 886, [1947] 2 All ER 1, CA. The insertion in the lease of a provision that, to be binding on the landlord, the waiver must be in writing does not prevent the acceptance of rent being a waiver: *R v Paulson* [1921] 1 AC 271, PC.

7   *Central Estates (Belgravia) Ltd v Woolgar (No 2)* [1972] 3 All ER 610, [1972] 1 WLR 1048, CA. Cf *Creery v Summersell and Flowerdew & Co Ltd* [1949] Ch 751. However, a mechanical acceptance of rent by a computer was held not to constitute a waiver in *Legal and General Assurance Society Ltd v General Metal Agencies Ltd* (1969) 20 P & CR 953.

8   For example by commencing an action to recover possession.

9   For example receipt of rent – see *Doe d Morecraft v Meux* (1824) C & P 346; *Toleman v Portbury* (1872) LR 7 QB 344 at 351, Ex Ch; *Evans v Enever* [1920] 2 KB 315; where Lord Coleridge said the bringing of an action to recover possession is an irrevocable election to determine the lease; *Civil Service Co-operative Society v McGrigor's Trustee* [1923] 2 Ch 347. However, receipt of rent may be evidence of a new tenancy from year to year on such of the former terms as are applicable: *Evans v Wyatt* (1880) 43 LT 176; *Grimwood v Moss* (1872) LR 7 CP 360; and see *Kilkenny Gas Co v Somerville* (1878) 2 LR Ir 192.

10   *Greens' Case* (1582) Cro Eliz 3; *Price v Worwood* (1859) 4 H & N 512.

11   *Greens' Case* – see note 10 above.

12   *Green's Case* – see note 10 above; *Pennant's Case* (1596) 3 Co Rep 64a; *Doe d Flower v Peck* (1830) 1 B & Ad 428; *Doe d David v Williams* (1835) 7 C & P 322; *Shepherd v Berger* [1891] 1 QB 597, CA. As, apart from statute, the landlord may only distrain during the continuance of the tenancy, it makes no difference whether the arrears accrued due before or after the forfeiture. In ordinary cases of determination of tenancy, distress may be made within six months after the determination under the Landlord and Tenant Act 1709, but this does not apply where the tenancy is determined by forfeiture: *Grimwood v Moss* (1872) LR 7 CP 360 at 365; *Kirkland v Briancourt* (1890) 6 TLR 441; cf *Ward v Day* (1864) 5 B & S 359, Ex Ch. But the continuing in possession of a distress levied before the forfeiture is not a waiver: *Doe d Taylor v Johnson* (1816) 1 Stark 411.

13   See the Common Law Procedure Act 1852, s 210; *Brewer d Lord Onslow v Eaton* (1783) 3 Doug KB 230; *Thomas v Lulham* [1895] 2 QB 400, CA.

14   *Doe d Weatherhead v Curwood* (1835) 1 Har & W 140; *Ward v Day* (1864) 5 B & S 359, Ex Ch. See also Nicholas Nardecchia 'Acceptance of Rent' [1981] Gazette 1 April 359.

12.6   *Continuing breach.* Where the breach of covenant which gives the right of re-entry is a continuing breach there is a continually recurring cause of forfeiture.[1] The demand for or acceptance of rent (or distraining for rent)[2] which is payable in arrear is only a waiver of breaches which have occurred up to the date upon which the rent is due,[3] and where the rent is payable in advance, is a waiver only of those breaches which at the time of the demand or acceptance are known to be continuing, and operates only for such period as it is definitely know that they will continue.[4] The landlord, therefore, is not precluded from taking advantage of a subsequent continuation of the breach.[5]

1   For example a covenant to use premises as a private residence only (*Segal Securities Ltd v Thoseby* [1963] 1 QB 887, [1963] 1 All ER 500), a covenant to repair (*Fryett d Harris v Jeffreys* (1795) 1 Esp 392; *Coward v Gregory* (1866) LR 2 CP 153; *Penton v Barnett* [1898] 1 QB 276, CA) a covenant to insure (*Doe d Flower v Peck* (1830) 1 B & Ad 428; *Doe d Muston v Gladwin* (1845) 6 QB 953). In the case of a covenant against assigning or underletting or permitting a third person to occupy the premises, it is not a continuing breach to allow an underlessee to remain in possession (*Walrond v Hawkins* (1875) LR 10 CP 342), although user of premises by the underlessee contrary to a covenant in the headlease may be a continuing breach of that covenant on the part of the tenant (*Lawrie v Lees* (1880) 14 Ch D 249 at 262, CA; affd (1881) 7 App Cas 19 at 30, HL; contra *Griffin v Tomkins* (1880) 42 LT 359). A failure to pay rent is a once and for all and not a continuing breach: *London & County (A & D) Ltd v Wilfred Sportsman Ltd* [1971] Ch 764, [1970] 2 All ER 600, CA. In *Cooper v Henderson* (1982) 263 Estates Gazette 592, the landlord continued to accept rent and even renewed the lease knowing that, in breach of his covenant to use the premises for business purposes only, the tenant was living there. But the Court of Appeal held that the landlord was entitled to forfeit because the breach of a user covenant is a continuing one.

2   *Doe d Hemmings v Durnford* (1832) 2 Cr & J 667.

3   *Doe d Ambler v Woodbridge* (1829) 9 B & C 376. *Doe d Baker v Jones* (1850) 5 Exch 498.

4   *Segal Securities Ltd v Thoseby* [1963] 1 QB 887, [1963] 1 All ER 500.

5   *Penton v Barnett* [1898] 1 QB 276, CA, where a three months' notice to repair was served under what is now the Law of Property Act 1925, s 146, on 22 September 1896 and on 14 January

1897, no repairs having been done, an action was brought claiming the rent due on 25 December and possession. It was held, overruling *Bevan v Barnett* (1897) 13 TLR 310, that the claim for rent was not a waiver of the breach of the covenant to repair continuing after 25 December. This case was followed in *New River Co v Crumpton* [1917] 1 KB 762, in which some doubt was cast on the correctness of the decision in *Guillemard v Silverthorne* (1908) 99 LT 584, where a landlord was held to have waived the breach, notwithstanding that it was continuing, by the acceptance of rent while negotiations for a new lease were proceeding and after some repairs had been undertaken. Note *Downie v Turner* [1951] 2 KB 112, [1951] 1 All ER 416, CA: where the breach of one covenant (for example not to underlet) necessarily involves breach of another covenant (for example to use the premises as a single dwelling house), waiver of a breach of the first covenant, even though that breach is not a continuing breach, necessarily waives the continuing breach of the second covenant.

12.7 *Drafting cannot avoid waiver.* Draftsmen have sought to avoid the severity of the general law in relation to waiver. Landlords argue that the principle may well have been not unreasonable where landlords were individuals or small corporate bodies, but suggest that it imposes an unreasonable requirement upon the institutional landlord with many hundreds of properties, where the collection of rent is handled on an administrative basis or 'by the computer' rather than by the individual who is responsible for the day-to-day estate management matters, and who will be aware of the failings of the individual tenants. They suggest that is unfair on the landlord to lose his right of re-entry where a rent demand has been sent out, or some other action taken in the event of non-payment, where in fact the tenant is in breach of another covenant of the lease and where those who have responsibility for such matters within the landlord or his agents are in contact with the tenant in connection with this.[1] As such, leases frequently include a proviso to the effect that the landlord's right to forfeit the lease shall remain in force 'notwithstanding the acceptance of or demand for rent by the Landlord or its agent with knowledge of a breach of any of the covenants on the part of the Tenant herein contained'.[2] It is suggested that such clauses are ineffective, and that a landlord cannot by means of a provision in the lease protect himself from waiving forfeiture by 'inadvertently' demanding or accepting rent.[3] The judgment of Lord Mansfield in *Doe d Cheny v Batten*[4] is sometimes relied upon by those who argue that the clause should be effective, but this was a case in which it was contended that the receipt of rent waived a notice to quit and these cases are governed by different principles from those relating to waiver of forfeiture. Further support may be obtained from the judgment of Harman J in *Creery v Summersell and Flowerdew & Co Ltd*[5] where it was held that a routine demand for rent sent out by a clerk in ignorance of the matters giving rise to waiver did not waive it but this aspect of the decision has been consistently criticised and cannot now be regarded as good law.[6]

1 But see note 7 to para 12.5 above.
2 In view of the criticisms of the clause set out below some landlords go further in an attempt to make it more reasonable and add words to the effect that 'provided that this provision [ie acceptance of rent etc shall not amount to waiver] shall have effect in relation only to any acceptance of or demand for rent made during such period (if any) as may in all the circumstances be reasonable for enabling the Landlord to conduct negotiations with the Tenant for remedying the breach which shall have been commenced by either party upon the Landlord becoming aware of the said breach'.
3 *Davenport v R* (1877) 3 App Cas 115, PC; *R v Paulson* [1921] 1 AC 271, PC.
4 (1775) 1 Cowp 243.
5 [1949] Ch 751 – see note 5 to para 12.5 above.
6 See *David Blackstone Ltd v Burnetts (West End) Ltd* [1973] 3 All ER 782, [1973] 1 WLR 1487.

B BREAK CLAUSE

12.8 *Option to determine.* Leases can, but today rarely do, confer on the tenant an option[1] to purchase the landlord's reversion[2] or to review the lease.[3] An option by which the tenant[4] can determine the lease is, however, rather more common.[5] If the lease has been assigned, the option is exercisable by the person in whom the term is for the time being legally vested.[6]

1 The terms of the option usually require that it is to be exercised in writing but this requirement, even where not expressed, is implied, as is the intention that the resulting contract is to be binding on both parties. *Birmingham Canal Co v Cartwright* (1879) 11 Ch D 421 at 434 per Fry J, but see *Beatson v Nicholson* (1842) 6 Jur 620 and *Gardner v Blaxill* [1960] 2 All ER 457, [1960] 1 WLR 752 affd on another point [1961] Ch 105, [1961] 1 All ER 90, CA. Subject to any provision in the lease to the contrary, an option constitutes an offer which the landlord is contractually precluded from withdrawing so long as it remains exercisable: *Beesly v Hallwood Estates Ltd* [1960] 2 All ER 314, [1960] 1 WLR; affd on another point [1961] Ch 105, [1961] 1 All ER 90, CA.

2 See 22 Encyclopaedia of Forms and Precedents (5th edn) paras 73.1 and 73.3 and Form 82.

3 See ibid, paras 73.2 and 73.3 and Form 83.

4 Such options are generally only exercisable by the tenant and if the lease is silent as to the person who is to exercise it, it may be exercised by the tenant only: *Dann v Spurrier* (1803) 3 Bos & P 399. If the lease gives the landlord the right to terminate the lease, he will in addition have to comply with the requirements of the 1954 Act (see Chapter 14) and be required to grant the tenant a new lease unless he can establish one of the grounds under s 30(1) (see paras 14.29–39 below).

5 See Appendix 1 below Additional Clause G. A provision by which a landlord of business premises can determine the lease as to part of the premises should be avoided because of the technical difficulties associated with the service of a notice under the 1954 Act, s 25: see *Southport Old Links Ltd v Naylor* [1985] 1 EGLR 66, 273 Estates Gazette 767, CA, but note *Moss v Mobil Oil Co Ltd* [1988] 1 EGLR 71, [1988] 06 EG 109, CA. Two separate leases should be granted, one of the part that may be determined and the other of the remainder of the premises. Whenever a *landlord* proposes to exercise a right granted to it in a lease of business premises to terminate the tenancy, it needs to consider the implications of the 1954 Act and will need to follow the statutory procedure for termination contemplated under the 1954 Act as well: see Chapter 14.

6 It may not, therfore, be exercised by an equitable assignee: *Seaward v Drew* (1898) 67 LJQB 322, or by a beneficiary of the person in whom the term is legally vested: *Stait v Fenner* [1912] 2 Ch 504, unless the beneficiary was duly authorised for that purpose: *Jones v Phipps* (1868) LR 3 QB 567 and note *Re Knight and Hubbard's Underlease, Hubbard v Highton* [1923] 1 Ch 130.

12.9 *Conditions precedent to the exercise of the option.* Any matters which by the terms of the option are made conditions precedent to the exercise of the option must be strictly observed.[1] Therefore the notice exercising the option must be given within the specified period[2] and must comply with any other relevant provisions of the lease.[3] The exercise of the option is sometimes made subject to the tenant having paid the rent and complied with the terms of the lease.[4] Where this is the case, the tenant should seek some protection, for example by making the exercise of the option subject to reasonable[5] performance of the covenants,[6] so that the right of the option is not lost by a minor breach of covenant, and by clearly providing that it is the expiry of the notice exercising the option on which there has to have been compliance with the terms of the lease, rather than at the date when the notice was served.[7] A bold tenant will suggest that all such conditions precedent should be deleted on the basis that, to the extent that the landlord has suffered loss as a result of any breaches there may have been, he will have all the normal remedies against the tenant that can be enforced quite separately from the exercise of the option.

1 *Finch v Underwood* (1876) 2 Ch D 310, CA; *West Country Cleaners (Falmouth) Ltd v Saly* [1966] 3 All ER 210, [1966] 1 WLR 1485, CA; *Bassett v Whiteley* (1983) 45 P & CR 87, CA; *Kitney v Greater*

London Properties Ltd (1984) 272 Estates Gazette 786. Generally, when there have been past breaches of covenant which have been remedied, the right to the option will not be lost: *Robinson v Thames Mead Park Estates Ltd* [1947] Ch 334, [1947] 1 All ER 366.

2   For a form of notice exercising the option see 22 Encyclopaedia of Forms and Precedents (5th edn) Form 205. In the case of an option time is of the essence of the contract (*Lord Ranelagh v Melton* (1864) 2 Drew & Sm 278) and see *United Scientific Holdings Ltd v Burnley Borough Council* [1978] AC 904, [1977] 2 All ER 62, HL where rent review clauses were distinguished as not being true options so that in respect of those clauses time was not of the essence. See also *Wheatley v Burrell Enterprises Ltd* (1963) 186 Estates Gazette 259, CA; *Page v Mallow Investments Ltd* (1974) 29 P & CR 168. The landlord may, however, by its conduct waive the delay: *Pegg v Wisden* (1852) 16 Beav 239.

3   *Hankey v Clavering* [1942] 2 KB 326, [1942] 2 All ER 311, CA where notice given to expire on 21 December instead of 25 December was held to be invalid. See, however, *Carradine Properties Ltd v Aslam* [1976] 1 All ER 573, [1976] 1 WLR 442 where it was held that, if the meaning of a notice would be quite clear to a reasonable person reading it, the notice is valid even if it contains a clerical error. See also *Manorlike Ltd v Le Vitas Travel Agency and Consultancy Services Ltd* [1986] 1 All ER 573, CA.

4   This may be a condition precedent to the purchase of the freehold, the grant of a new lease or the determination of a lease.

5   As to 'reasonable' in this context see *Gardner v Blaxill* [1960] 2 All ER 457, [1960] 1 WLR 752; *Bassett v Whiteley* (1983) 45 P & CR 87. CA.

6   As to the meaning of 'duly paid his rent' see *Starkey v Barton* [1909] 1 Ch 284.

7   *Simons v Associated Furnishers Ltd* [1931] 1 Ch 379; *Multon v Cordell* [1986] 1 EGLR 44, 277 Estates Gazette 189. If the drafting is otherwise, a breach eg of the tenant's covenant to repair and to decorate existing at the date of service of the notice (even if remedied by the time the notice expired) could mean that the right to exercise the option was lost. An alternative might be to provide that the right would be lost only if the landlord had served a notice under the Law of Property Act 1925 s 146(1) (37 Halsbury's Statutes (4th edn) REAL PROPERTY) in relation to that breach.

C   ARBITRATION

12.10   *Basic principle.* A contract that purports to deny the right of one or both parties to submit questions of law to the courts is contrary to public policy and therefore void.[1] An arbitration agreement, however, by which contracting parties provide that before legal proceedings are taken questions of law and fact shall be decided by a private tribunal is not a contract to oust the jurisdiction of the courts but is valid and is enforceable. If in breach of its terms one of the parties commences legal proceedings against the other the latter will almost invariably obtain an order from the court staying those proceedings.[2]

1   See *Thompson v Charnock* (1799) 8 Term Rep 139 and *Lee v Showmen's Guild of Great Britain* [1952] 2 QB 329, [1952] 1 All ER 1175, CA.

2   See *Scott v Avery* (1856) 5 HL Cas 811 and the Arbitration Act 1950, s 4(1).

12.11   *General advantages of arbitration.* Parties to a contract can therefore agree that any dispute arising out of that contract should be determined by arbitration, and this will be controlled by the Arbitration Acts 1950 and 1979. Following the award of an arbitrator, an appeal is possible in certain very limited circumstances to the High Court and then to the Court of Appeal.[1] The aim of the 1979 Act, however, was to introduce greater finality into arbitration awards and the Act and the subsequent cases have very significantly reduced the prospects of an appeal to the courts being permitted.[1] Once arbitration proceedings have been commenced, it is possible for the parties to agree to exclude an appeal to the court altogether.[2] An arbitration agreement can, therefore, be included as a proviso in a lease of commercial premises. There are advantages in providing for arbitration in certain contracts. For example, where any disputes are likely to concern technical matters, an arbitrator can be selected or appointed who has the appropriate qualifications and experience and this could be particularly helpful where numerous findings of fact will have to be made.[3] Arbitrations are held in private and so the parties need not be concerned with the disclosure of confidential information. With the agreement of the parties the arbitration may be conducted by means of written representations but, even where there is to be a hearing, the arrangements should be flexible with the arbitrator being prepared to sit at a venue and a time to suit the parties and should be shorter as an arbitrator is expected to study the documents in advance.

1   See para 6.46 above. As to determination by the court of a preliminary point of law, see para 6.47 above.
2   See 1979 Act, s 3(6).
3   But as to when arbitrator entitled to act on his own knowledge, see note 2 to para 6.45 above.

12.12   *But how relevant to leases?*   These advantages, however, appear of little relevance in leases. So many disputes between landlord and tenant are likely to involve points of law and thus it seems more sensible to go straight to the court and have these determined by a judge rather than by an arbitrator who is unlikely to be a judge or even a lawyer. Although the likelihood of an appeal to the court following an arbitrator's award has become less likely since 1979,[1] it remains the case that an unsuccessful party to an arbitration may apply to the court for leave to appeal and if this should be forthcoming, then there would have to be two or even three (if the application for leave to appeal is heard at a different time from the appeal itself) 'first instance' decisions. Confidentiality is unlikely to be crucial, nor are cases involving construction likely to be very long, and the length of trials is a factor that has prompted many to seek other ways of resolving their differences. Arbitrations under a commercial lease are unlikely to be significantly cheaper than litigation, which is a further factor often canvassed in favour of arbitration unless perhaps the parties agree to written representations. Counsel's fees tend to be the same in either event and at least in litigation the court fees remain fairly modest and the parties do not have to pay for the hire of a court room or a fee to the judge.[2]

1   See para 6.46 above.
2   Nevertheless, for those who see advantages in arbitrations, a clause is included (Appendix 1 below, Additional Clause I).

Chapter 13

Underleases

A INTRODUCTION

13.1 *Terminology*. Most leases of business premises give to the tenant a qualified right to sublet the demised premises.[1] In this chapter such a lease will be called a 'headlease', the landlord will be called 'the superior landlord', the tenant will be called 'the sublessor', and the undertenant will be called 'the sublessee'.

> 1 See for example Rosscastle Letting Conditions (Appendix 1, Form 1 below) Conditions 3.7:3, 3.7:6–3.7:8.

13.2 *The superior landlord's concern*. The grant of an underlease by the sublessor creates no privity either of contract or estate between the superior landlord and the sublessee.[1] Nevertheless, the superior landlord should recognise that such privity could arise in the future and take steps to ensure that both the sublessee and the terms of the underlease are suitable. Privity between the superior landlord and the sublessee may arise, for example, on a successful application by the sublessee for relief against forfeiture of the headlease,[2] or, in certain circumstances, upon a renewal of the sublessee's lease under the 1954 Act.[3] If the sublessor underlets all the premises demised by the headlease so that he is no longer in occupation for business purposes, he will cease to be the competent landlord[4] of the sublessee, who will on the expiry of the underlease have rights of renewal directly against the superior landlord. Even if the sublessor retains part of the demised premises for business use, the superior landlord will be in a similar position if the sublessor chooses not to renew the headlease. Thus the headlease is likely to require the superior landlord's consent and also to contain provisions, for example, that underleases must be at the open market rent and subject to similar review dates and periods as the headlease; that the sublessee should enter into direct covenants with the superior landlord to observe the covenants in the headlease; and that the sublessor must not waive any covenant given by the sublessee in the underlease. The headlease will also regulate the form of the alienation covenant to be inserted in the underlease.[5]

> 1 Thus the sublessee is not personally liable to the superior landlord for the payment of rent or the performance of covenants in the headlease. It may, however, become liable to pay its rent to the superior landlord by virtue of a notice in lieu of distress given to it: see 13 Halsbury's Laws (4th edn) para 260.
> 2 Law of Property Act 1925, s 146(4). See paras 12.2–12.4 above.
> 3 Ie under the 1954 Act, ss 23–46. See Chapter 14 below.
> 4 See paras 14.19–14.21 below.
> 5 See for example Rosscastle Letting Conditions (Appendix 1, Form 1 below) Condition 3.7:6.3.

13.3 *Types of underlease*. Underlettings generally arise in one of four situations:

299

13.3:1   *Freehold not available*. Institutions acquire commercial properties for investment purposes. Generally they prefer the freehold but that is not always available. There were, for example, many local authorities who, in days before the Town and Country Planning legislation, felt that a way of maintaining some control over the shops in the high street was to let them on 99 year (or even longer) 'ground leases' at what are now nominal rents, and subject to terms that, by modern standards, are not particularly onerous. Where the tenant is the occupier of the shop, he holds under this lease, but if an investor has acquired the property, then the 'occupational' lease between the investor and the trader will be an underlease, the investor having acquired the lessee's interest under the ground lease from the local authority that becomes a headlease.

13.3:2   *Underlettings of part always intended*. In many cases, the sublessor will have taken the headlease with a view to the grant of underleases and with no occupational requirement of its own, for example in the case of a developer of an industrial site or shopping centre. Here the sublessor will have no special objectives, except the need to maximise rental income and minimise estate management difficulties.

13.3:3   *Currently surplus to requirements*. A business with leasehold premises larger than it currently requires may wish to grant an underlease of its excess space. The term is likely to be relatively short so that the premises will be available if required in the future. The sublessor would be well advised to exclude the protection of the 1954 Act[1] because otherwise he will only be able to recover possession of the sublet premises if he can meet one or more of the strict statutory requirements.[2]

13.3:4   *Disposal but with control*. The doctrine of privity of contract poses a considerable danger both for original tenants and assignors of long leases.[3] As a result, the grant of an underlease of the whole of the originally demised premises to the sublessor can be a safer alternative to outright assignment.[4] The sublessor may be willing to accept the estate management responsibilities involved in the grant of an underlease as a small price to pay for the retention of control over the property which would otherwise be lost by assignment. In these circumstances, the sublessor will need to ensure that it is indemnified by the sublessee in respect of any service charge payments or insurance premiums due to the superior landlord and can at all times recover at least the amount of the rent payable under the headlease. It will also wish to reserve the widest possible powers to enter the demised premises to view their condition and remedy breaches of covenant.

1   Ie the 1954 Act, ss 24–28: see para 14.5 below.
2   Ie the requirements of ibid, s 30(1): see paras 14.29–14.39 below.
3   See paras 5.5, 5.14 and 5.16 above.
4   See para 5.15:5 above.

B   DRAFTING

13.4   *General*. Subject to any specific requirements of the headlease, the draftsman of an underlease is not bound to follow the precise form or content of the headlease and he may well feel that there is scope for improving upon its terms or using his own standard form with minor adjustments. The only constraint on the draftsman is the need to ensure that the underlease is consistent with the headlease and that no rights are given to the sublessee which are not granted in the headlease. It will also be necessary to incorporate general provisions relating the underlease to the headlease.[1] It is common to see in underleases a general covenant by the sublessee to observe and perform the covenants on the part of the sublessor contained in the headlease so far as they affect the underlet premises and subject to an indemnity for breach.[2] No sublessee should accept such a covenant without a careful examination of the headlease, particularly when taking an underlease of part where the need to apportion the obligations between the different parts of premises demised by the headlease could give rise to problems of interpretation. A further danger is the incorporation of a general covenant by the sublessor to observe and perform the terms of the headlease 'so far as the Tenant is not liable . . . in this Underlease . . .' If the sublessee's covenant is similarly limited by the extent of the sublessor's obligation, the circularity of the obligations will render both ambiguous. A more satisfactory approach is to ensure that any relevant obligations on the sublessor in the headlease are passed on in the underlease and the sublessee gives covenants to do nothing which would constitute a breach of the terms of the headlease.[3]

1   See for example Rosscastle Letting Conditions (Appendix 1, Form 1 below) Condition 8.
2   See ibid, Condition 8.2:1.
3   See ibid, Condition 8.2:2.

13.5   *Specific types of underlease.* The reason for and nature of the underletting will influence the drafting, and in particular how closely the underlease must follow the headlease:

13.5:1   *Freehold not available.*[1] Where the headlease is a ground lease, the underlease to the trader will probably follow the form that the sublessor/ investor would adopt were he the freeholder with the addition of the general underlease provisions.[2]

13.5:2   *Underlettings of part always intended.*[3] Here the headlease will deal with extensive property of which the premises to be demised by the underlease represent a very small part, and where it was never intended that the tenant would occupy the premises. An example of this will arise where the funding is such that a lease of the whole completed development[4] is granted to one party, who is then responsible for subletting the various units.[5] Here the draftsman will no doubt use his standard form of lease for the type of premises in question,[6] but will need to include in it certain of the general underlease provisions.[7] The headlease, as such, will not be particularly relevant to the drafting of the underlease, except if, as is often the case with such leases, it contains provisions regulating the form of the underleases.[8]

13.5:3   *Surplus to requirements or control.*[9] In these instances, the headlease will have been drafted on the basis that the tenant will be in occupation, and will deal either with only the premises that are to be demised by the underlease, or with these and other adjoining and similar premises. Here the draftsman will probably rely upon the headlease as the basis for his draft underlease and should incorporate into it such of the general underlease provisions as are relevant.[10]

1   See para 13.3:1 above.
2   See Rosscastle Letting Conditions (Appendix 1, Form 1 below) Condition 8.
3   See para 13.3:2 above.
4   For example a shopping centre or office building.
5   For example the individual units or floors/suites.
6   See for example 22 Encyclopaedia of Forms and Precedents (5th edn) Forms 29–31. Appendix 1, Form 6 below.
7   See Rosscastle Letting Conditions (Appendix 1, Form 1 below) Condition 8.
8   See for example ibid, Condition 3.7:6.3.
9   See paras 13.3:3 and 13.3:4 above.
10 See Rosscastle Letting Conditions (Appendix 1, Form 1 below) Condition 8.

13.6   *Term*. The sublessor should retain a reversion of at least one day, as a demise of the entire term of the headlease will almost invariably be construed as an assignment.[1] If rent reviews under the underlease are to coincide with those under the headlease, the draftsman should be careful to ensure that the review dates are not linked to the term of the underlease in a way which would defeat this purpose.[2]

1   See *Lewis v Baker* [1905] 1 Ch 46; *Milmo v Carreras* [1946] KB 306, [1946] 1 All ER 288, CA; cf *William Skelton & Son Ltd v Harrison and Pinder Ltd* [1975] QB 361, [1975] 1 All ER 182; 27 Halsbury's Laws (4th edn) para 121.
2   Indeed this may cause difficulties in agreeing the commercial terms of an underlease granted eg 2 years before a next review date in the headlease. The sublessee may well not accept a review in 2 years.

13.7   *Rent review*. Usually, the only link between rent reviews under the headlease and the underlease is a common review date. It is sometimes desirable, however, to link the two reviews more closely, particularly in an underlease of the whole where the sublessor wishes to ensure that there is not at any time a difference between the rent payable under the two leases or at least that any such difference is in its favour. Occasionally the underlease may provide that the rent will be the rent payable from time to time under the headlease, which will have the effect of an indemnity. From the point of view of the sublessee, such a provision is undesirable as it gives the sublessee no control of the review procedure under the headlease and gives no incentive to the sublessor to negotiate a true market rent. Before accepting such a provision, the sublessee should require, as a minimum protection, a covenant by the sublessor not to agree a new rent without the sublessee's consent, and to opt for independent determination of the rent if such consent if not forthcoming. Alternatively, the underlease may contain a standard review procedure with a provision that the same valuer shall be appointed for an independent determination of the rent under both leases, should this be necessary. This method may produce practical difficulties and the draftsman should take great care to ensure that the rent review machinery and procedures in the two leases are consistent.

13.8   *Renewal of underlease of part of the premises*. Sublessors of part of the premises should also beware of the danger inherent in the 1954 Act[1] when the time comes for a renewal of both the headlease and the underlease. For estate management reasons, the superior landlord may call upon the sublessor to take a new lease of all the premises demised by the headlease subject to the underlease.[2] The rent payable under both the headlease and the underlease will be determined pursuant to the 1954 Act.[3] An improvement carried out by the sublessee will be disregarded for the purposes of the underlease.[4] It will not, however, be disregarded in arriving at an open market rent of the headlease because it will not have been carried out by a person who at the time it was carried out was the tenant.

1 Ie the 1954 Act, s 34(1)(c).
2 See ibid s 32(2).
3 Ie pursuant to ibid s 34.
4 Ie by virtue of ibid s 34(1)(c).

13.9 *Repairing obligations.* Most underleases contain the same or similar repairing covenants as those in the headlease. It should not be assumed, however, that this will necessarily impose the same obligation. The extent and nature of a covenant to repair is partly determined by the state of the demised premises at the commencement of the lease,[1] and this could make a significant difference to a sublessor granting an underlease in the twentieth year of its own term. The sublessee's advisers should be aware, however, that, if the underlease contains a general covenant and indemnity, the sublessee's repairing obligation will be construed by reference to the repairing obligation in the headlease. On the grant of an underlease of part of the premises, the draftsman should take care to ensure that the underlet part is adequately defined and the repairing obligations as between the sublessor and the sublessee made clear.

1 See *Brew Bros Ltd v Snax (Ross) Ltd* [1970] 1 QB 612, [1970] 1 All ER 587, CA.

13.10 *Service charge.* The simplest method of dealing with service charge payments in an underlease of the whole premises is to provide for an effective indemnity by the sublessee so that the sublessor can merely pass on service charge demands to the sublessee. In an underlease of part of the premises, the parties may agree a division of payment fixed at the outset as a percentage based on the relative floor areas of the sublet and the retained premises or on some other basis. However, if the sublessor is simply passing on service charge demands, it may have little incentive to query them and the sublessee may wish to ensure that the sublessor takes steps to challenge such demands if they are unreasonable. If the sublessor has given a covenant to take reasonable steps or use its best endeavours[1] to enforce the covenants of the headlease,[2] it may feel that this is sufficient protection to the sublessee. The sublessee should resist any attempt by the sublessor to make the sublessee responsible for the cost of enforcement,[2] since any such action will be for the benefit of the sublessor, even if the sublessee may in consequence benefit indirectly.

1 See para 13.1 footnote 2 below.
2 See Rosscastle Letting Conditions (Appendix 1, Form 1 below) Condition 8.3:2.

13.11 *Insurance.* If insurance is effected by the superior landlord,[1] the sublessor will usually provide for payment of premiums by the sublessee either wholly or in part corresponding to payments made by the sublessor under the headlease for this purpose. In view of the importance of the insurance covenant, however, many sublessees insist that the sublessor additionally covenants to use its best endeavours[2] at all times to ensure that the superior landlord complies with the insurance covenant in the headlease and the obligation to reinstate. The sublessee will also wish to ensure that its interest is noted on the superior landlord's policy[1] and that it can obtain details of such policy when reasonably required.[1] The draftsman must ensure that the proviso for suspension of rent in the underlease is consistent with the terms of the headlease and that it does not, for example, agree to the suspension of rent in circumstances where its own rent would continue to be payable.[1]

1   See Appendix 1 Form 7 below.
2   The extent of the duty to use best endeavours depends upon the facts in each case: see *Monkland v Jack Barclay Ltd* [1951] 2 KB 252, [1951] 1 All ER 714, CA; *Terrell v Mabie Todd & Co Ltd* [1952] 2 TLR 574, CA; *NW Investments (Erdington) Ltd v Swani* (1970) 214 Estates Gazette 1115. In the light of *IBM United Kingdom Ltd v Rockware Glass Ltd* [1980] FSR 335, CA, it may be that there is little practical difference between a covenant to use best endeavours, a covenant to use reasonable endeavours and a covenant to take all reasonable steps. Where a 'best endeavours' covenant is given by a sublessor, there would appear to be no grounds for suggesting that the best endeavours obligations falls short of enforcement proceedings by the sublessor against the superior landlord under the terms of the headlease. Thus such a covenant adds little to an express covenant to enforce the provisions of the headlease.

13.12   *Break options exercised by the sublessor.* There may be two kinds of break option in the headlease: the superior landlord may have retained an option to determine the headlease during the term on specific grounds;[1] and the headlease may provide options in favour of either party or both, exercisable either at specified times or if the demised premises are destroyed or badly damaged by an insured risk. A surrender by the sublessor does not affect the interest of the sublessee. The interest of the sublessor is deemed to pass to the superior landlord subject to the rights of the sublessee.[2] There is some doubt, however, as to whether the exercise of a break option by a sublessor operates as a surrender.[3] It can be argued that surrender is a consensual act, whereas a break clause operates unilaterally to end the sublessor's term. In that case, the underlease will terminate with the headlease.[4] Unless the sublessor has included in the underlease a corresponding break option, it will find that its exercise of the option terminating the headlease will have the effect of ending its sublessee's term and exposing it to an action by the sublessee on the covenant for quiet enjoyment.

1   See eg the 1954 Act, s 30(1)(f), (g) paras 14.29–14.39 below and 22 Encyclopaedia of Forms and Precedents (5th edn) Form 85.
2   See the Law of Property Act 1925, s 139 (37 Halsbury's Statutes (4th edn) REAL PROPERTY).
3   See *Phipos v Callegari* (1910) 54 Sol Jo 635 and 27 Halsbury's Laws (4th edn) para 115 note 4, para 451 text and note 1.
4   Ie under common law principles because the sublessee will not have the protection of the Law of Property Act 1925, s 139.

13.13   *Break options exercised by superior landlord.* The exercise of a break option by the superior landlord will have the effect of terminating the underlease.[1] However, this will not generally give rise to an action by the sublessee under the covenant for quiet enjoyment unless the covenant itself includes not only the acts of the sublessor but also those of any person with title paramount.[2]

1   See *Keith Bayley Rogers & Co v Cubes Ltd* (1975) 31 P & CR 412 and 27 Halsbury's Laws (4th edn) para 485.
2   The landlord's covenant for quiet enjoyment will generally be qualifed ie relate to conduct by

the landlord or any person claiming under or in trust for the landlord. When an underlease is being negotiated, the tenant should always seek to add 'or by title paramount' so that it would have an action against its landlord for any interruption or disturbance. See para 9.2 above.

13.14 *Break options; the sublessee's position.* Whatever the position may be under common law following the exercise of a break option in the headlease, most commercial underleases will have the protection of the 1954 Act. Thus, on the termination of the underlease, a subtenancy will continue as against the competent superior landlord.[1] This may, however, be small consolation to a sublessee whose fixed term has been replaced by a statutory right of renewal which may be costly and, if the superior landlord establishes statutory grounds,[2] even unsuccessful. There are two lessons to be learned from these principles by the draftsman of the underlease and the solicitor acting for the sublessee. The first is that, wherever the headlease contains a break option of any kind, it it always wise to include a corresponding break clause in the underlease.[3] The second is that the sublessee should always insist upon seeing a full copy of the headlease, of whose contents it will be deemed to have constructive notice. It should not compromise by accepting an extract showing the landlord and tenant covenants, as break options will appear in other parts of the headlease. In the face of persistent refusal by the sublessor, the sublessee should at the least insist that the covenant for quiet enjoyment in the underlease is extended to include title paramount.[4]

1 See the 1954 Act, ss 24, 44. See Chapter 14 below.
2 Ie grounds under ibid s 30(1): see paras 14.29–14.39 below.
3 The sublessee may wish to ensure that the option in the underlease is exercisable only on the exercise of the option under the headlease. Its advisers should seek the insertion of a proviso: 'provided that the power contained in this underlease by the Landlord to determine this underlease shall be exercisable only in the event of the superior lessor exercising the option to determine the headlease contained in the headlease'.
4 See para 13.13 note 2 above.

Chapter 14

Renewal of business leases

A INTRODUCTION

14.1 *Right to a new tenancy.* Part II of the Landlord and Tenant Act 1954 gives a tenant of business premises the right to a new tenancy[1] providing he complies with the formalities of the Act,[2] and assuming he can afford to pay the open market rent,[3] except where the landlord can establish certain specified grounds.[4] The 1954 Act provides that every business tenancy continues until determined in accordance with the provisions of the Act.[5] If the landlord can establish a ground of opposition,[4] the tenant will receive compensation where the ground involves no fault on the part of the tenant.[6] Where there is no successful opposition, the tenant will be granted a new tenancy upon terms either agreed between the parties or determined by the court in accordance with ss 32–35 of the 1954 Act.[7] As such the negotiation of the terms of a lease being renewed under the 1954 Act will be conducted against a background of what the court would be likely to order under these sections if agreement cannot be reached between the parties.[8]

1 The 1954 Act, s 29, except where the provisions of ss 24–28 of the 1954 Act have been excluded: see para 14.5 below.
2 The 1954 Act, ss 25–28, see sections B and C below.
3 The 1954 Act, ss 34, see section J below.
4 The 1954 Act, s 30(1), see section F below.
5 The 1954 Act, ss 24, 64(1), see section B below.
6 The 1954 Act, s 37, except when excluded: see section G below.
7 See sections H–K below.
8 This chapter has been based in part upon material created for, but then not used in, 22 Encyclopaedia of Forms and Precedents (5th edn). I am, therefore, indebted to my fellow contributors to that volume for their input then, particularly to Andrew Campbell and David Hayward for their work in what are now sections C and E.

14.2 *History and reform.* The 1954 Act came into force on 1 October 1954 and was based upon the final report of a committee under the chairmanship of Lord Justice Jenkins.[1] A number of detailed amendments were made by the Law of Property Act 1969[2] following a report by the Law Commission.[3] In August 1984 the Department of the Environment announced that it was carrying out a review of the working of the Act and invited representations.[4] This prompted considerable interest amongst practitioners, views were expressed[5] and representations made but in due course the Department announced that it did not propose to seek legislative changes because the comments received 'support the view that Part II of the Act still works satisfactorily and that the balance of rights between both parties to business lettings ... is being maintained.'[6] The Law Commission has recently published a working paper in which it makes some proposals for improving the working of the Act and canvasses views on them.[7]

1 Cmd 7982.
2 For example, s 24 (amended), 24A (added), 27 (amended), 30(3) (added), 31A (added), 32 (amended), 34 (amended), 37 (amended), 38 (amended and added s 38(4)), 41 (amended), 41A (added), 42 (amended), 43(3) (amended), 43A (added), and 44(1) (amended). There have been a number of minor amendments from time to time and note the amendment of sub-s (2) and the addition of sub-ss (8) and (9) to s 37 – see para 14.40 below.
3 'Report on the Landlord and Tenant Act 1954, Part II' (1969) Law Com No 17.
4 The review was commissioned 'with particular reference to its effect on small business tenants'.
5 See for example Steven Fogel and Philip Freedman: '1954 Act – some thoughts on reform' (1985) 275 Estates Gazette 118 and 227, John Sweetman: 'Business Tenancies: Statutory Reform' (1985) 129 Sol Jo 493, 512 and 534, William Wells and David Neuberger: 'Part II of the Landlord and Tenant Act 1954 – Abolish, Amend or Leave it alone?' (abridged Blundell Memorial Lecture) [1985] Gazette 11 Sept 2498.
6 Richard Tracey, Parliamentary Under Secretary, Department of the Environment, Hansard (HC) 20 November 1985, Vol 87, Written Answers, col 245.
7 Part II of the Landlord and Tenant Act 1954 (1988) LCWP No 111. Amongst the topics examined are: the effect of time limits for applications for a new tenancy, which mean that tenants have to take legal proceedings in many cases which go no further than the initial step; the stalemate created by lease clauses requiring the tenant to surrender the property back to the landlord before assigning, as a result of which the contract created by accepting the offer is void but the tenant is nevertheless not authorised to assign; and the lack of sanction to support the statutory obligations to provide necessary information.

14.3 *Tenancies to which the Act applies.* Section 23 of the 1954 Act provides that the Act applies to any tenancy where the property comprised in the tenancy is or includes premises which are occupied by the tenant for the purposes of a business carried on by him.[1] Since 1954 every aspect of this section has been considered by the court. A licence is not a *tenancy* and will not be covered by the Act – the general law has to be applied to the circumstances of each case to establish if a tenancy or licence is involved.[2] *'Premises'* includes land with no buildings on it[3] but does not apply to a letting of a right-of-way or other easement or incorporeal hereditament.[4] As the tenant must be *occupying* the premises, it follows that a tenant loses his rights under the Act altogether by subletting all the premises[5] or by granting a licence,[6] or simply by vacating the premises.[7] Where the tenant has sublet part of the premises comprised in the lease, the tenant loses his right to renew the sublet part, although the landlord may require him to take a lease of all premises including the part sublet.[8] The occupation of premises by a company in the same group as the tenant is sufficient occupation for the purposes of the Act.[9] A business tenant can 'occupy' residential accommodation used by its students[10] or employees.[11] The term *'business'*[12] includes a trade, profession[13] or employment and any activity[14] carried on by a body of persons whether corporate or unincorporate.[15]

1 1954 Act, s 23(1).
2 As to whether transaction a lease or licence see *Street v Mountford* [1985] 2 All ER 289, [1985] 1 EGLR 128, HL; *Bretherton v Paton* (1986) 18 HLR 257, 278 Estates Gazette 615, CA; *Ashburn Anstaldt v Arnold (No 2)* [1988] 1 EGLR 64, [1988] 23 EG 128, CA; *Brooker Settled Estates v Ayers* (1987) 54 P & CR 165, 282 Estates Gazette 325, CA; *Hadjiloucas v Crean* [1987] 3 All ER 1008, 284 Estates Gazette 927, CA; *Crancour Ltd v Da Silvaesa* (1986) 278 Estates Gazette 618, 733, CA; *Dresden Estates Ltd v Collinson* (1987) 55 P & CR 47, 281 Estates Gazette 1321, CA; *London and Associated Investment Trust plc v Calow* [1986] 2 EGLR 80, 280 Estates Gazette 1252; *Dellneed Ltd v Chin* [1987] 1 EGLR 75, 281 Estates Gazette 531; *Smith v Northside Developments Ltd* (1987) 55 P & CR 168 283 Estates Gazette 1211, CA; *Essex Plan Ltd v Broadminster* [1988] 2 EGLR 73, [1988] 43 EG 84; *A G Securities v Vaughan, Antoniades v Villiers* [1988] 3 All ER 1058,

2 EGLR 78; *Nicolaou v Pitt* [1989] 1 EGLR 84, CA; *Stribling v Wickham* (1989) 21 HLR 381, CA. Note in relation to gallops *Bracey v Read* [1963] Ch 88, [1962] 3 All ER 472 distinguished in *University of Reading v Johnson-Houghton* [1985] 2 EGLR 113, 276 Estates Gazette 1353. See Sandi Murdoch: 'Landlord and Tenant: the Lease/Licence distinction' [1989] 11 EG 22.

3 See *Gardiner v Sevenoaks RDC* [1950] 2 All ER 84 and *Bracey v Read* [1963] Ch 88, [1962] 3 All ER 472. See also *Edicron Ltd v William Whiteley Ltd* [1984] 1 All ER 219, [1984] 1 WLR 59, CA.

4 *Land Reclamation Co Ltd v Basildon District Council* [1979] 2 All ER 993, [1979] 1 WLR 767, CA. Disputes as to extent and nature of property can also arise under s 30(1)(g) of the 1954 Act – ie meaning of word 'holding' see para 14.35 below. See *Nursey v P Currie (Dartford) Ltd* [1959] 1 All ER 497, [1959] 1 WLR 273, CA; *Method Developments Ltd v Jones* [1971] 1 All ER 1027, [1971] 1 WLR 168, CA and *Cam Gears Ltd v Cunningham* [1981] 2 All ER 560, 258 Estates Gazette 749, CA.

5 Unless he is back in occupation by the time his lease expires.

6 *Hancock and Willis v GMS Syndicate Ltd* (1982) 265 Estates Gazette 473, CA. As to situation where tenant ceases to use the premises for the purposes of his business, see *Morrison Holdings Ltd v Manders Property (Wolverhampton) Ltd* [1976] 2 All ER 205, [1976] 1 WLR 533, CA; *Teasdale v Walker* [1958] 3 All ER 307, [1958] 1 WLR 1076, CA; *Pulleng v Curran* (1980) 44 P & CR 58, CA; *Aspinall Finance Ltd v Viscount Chelsea* [1989] 1 EGLR 103, [1989] 09 EG 77: if events over which the tenant has no control cause him to absent himself from the premises, he must continue to exert and claim his right to occupancy.

7 *Aspinal Finance Ltd v Viscount Chelsea* [1989] 09 EG 77.

8 1954 Act, s 32(2). See para 14.42 below.

9 1954 Act, s 42 but note *Cristina v Seear* [1985] 2 EGLR 128, 275 Estates Gazette 898, CA and *Nozari-Zadeh v Pearl Assurance plc* [1987] 2 EGLR 91, 283 Estates Gazette 457, CA in which the tenant who was a shareholder failed in his application for a new tenancy on the grounds that the companies of which he was a shareholder were carrying on the business and thus the premises were not occupied for the purpose of a business carried on by the applicant.

10 In *Groveside Properties Ltd v Westminster Medical School* (1983) 267 Estates Gazette 593, the Court of Appeal held that a medical school occupied for the purposes of a business a flat consisting of four study bedrooms, kitchen, sitting room, bathroom and lavatories, and thus the 1954 Act applied.

11 *Linden v Department of Health and Social Security* [1986] 1 All ER 691, [1986] 1 EGLR 108: tenancy of eight self contained flats managed by a Health Authority and occupied by employees of the National Health Service held by Scott J to fall within the 1954 Act.

12 The word 'business' extends to all cases where work is done for payment: *Doe d Bish v Keeling* (1813) 1 M & S 95; *Kemp v Sober* (1851) 1 Sim NS 517; *Hobson v Tulloch* [1898] 1 Ch 424; *Thorn v Madden* [1925] Ch 847; *Barton v Reed* [1932] 1 Ch 362; *Westripp v Baldock* [1939] 1 All ER 279, CA; *Tendler v Sproule* [1947] 1 All ER 193, CA; or even without payment where the result is in effect the same as if a charge were made: *Rolls v Miller* (1884) 27 Ch D 71, CA; *Town Investments Ltd v Department of the Environment* [1978] AC 359, [1977] 1 All ER 813, HL but note *Lewis v Weldcrest Ltd* [1978] 3 All ER 1226, [1978] 1 WLR 1107, CA. The making of profit is not essential to constitute a business, nor, on the other hand, does payment necessarily constitute one: *Rolls v Miller*, above; *Portman v Home Hospitals Association* (1879) 27 Ch D 81n. A Sunday school carried on for one hour each Sunday without reward is not a business: *Abernethie v A M and J Kleiman Ltd* [1970] 1 QB 10, [1969] 2 All ER 790, CA. See too *Bell v Alfred Franks and Bartlett Co Ltd* [1980] 1 All ER 356, [1980] 1 WLR 340, CA.

13 The term profession, in the words of Scrutton LJ in *IRC v Maxse* [1919] 1 KB 647 at 657, CA, involves the idea of an occupation requiring either purely intellectual skill, or of manual skill controlled, as in painting and sculpture, or surgery, by the intellectual skill of the operator, as distinguished from an occupation which is substantially the production or sale or arrangements for the production or sale of commodities.

14 As to 'activity', see *Hillil Property and Investment Co Ltd v Naraine Pharmacy Ltd* (1979) 252 Estates Gazette 1013, CA in which the 1954 Act held not to apply to dumping ground for waste material – the word 'activity' connoted some general use and not casual operation. Note also *Botterill and Cheshire v Bedfordshire County Council* [1985] 1 EGLR 82, 273 Estates Gazette 1217, CA – see para 14.33, footnote 8.

15 This includes a lawn tennis club carried on by a society registered under the Industrial and Provident Societies Act 1965: *Addiscombe Garden Estates Ltd v Crabbe* [1958] 1 QB 513, [1957] 3 All ER 563, CA; and the provision of accommodation, equipment and staff by a landlord company for another body: *Willis v Association of Universities of the British Commonwealth* [1965] 1 QB 140, [1964] 2 All ER 39, CA; and the business of letting apartments – *Lee-Verhulst (Investments) Ltd v Harwood Trust* [1973] QB 204, [1972] 3 All ER 619, CA but note *Jones v Jenkins* [1986] 1 EGLR 113, 277 Estates Gazette 644, CA and *Bagettes Ltd v G P Estates Co Ltd*

[1956] Ch 290, [1956] 1 All ER 729, CA (see cases referred to in footnotes 10 and 11 above) but it does not include a Sunday school carried on by an individual with the aid of assistants: *Abernethie v A M and J Kliman Ltd* [1970] 1 QB 10, [1969] 2 All ER 790, CA. But it does not follow that, whenever the tenant is a body of persons (incorporated or unincorporated), the 1954 Act will apply. The premises still have to be occupied for business purposes: see *Lewis v Weldcrest Ltd* [1978] 3 All ER 1226, [1978] 1 WLR 1107, CA; *Chapman v Freeman* [1978] 3 All ER 878, [1978] 1 WLR 1298, CA; and *Cheryl Investments Ltd v Saldanha; Royal Life Saving Society v Page* [1979] 1 All ER 5, [1978] 1 WLR 1329, CA. Note too *Groveside Properties Ltd v Westminster Medical School* (1983) 267 Estates Gazette 593, CA and *Linden v Department of Health and Social Security* [1986] 1 All ER 691, 277 Estates Gazette 543. (See footnotes 10 and 11 above.)

14.4   *Tenancies to which the Act does not apply.* The 1954 Act does not apply to:
(a)   agricultural holdings[1] and mining leases.[2]
(b)   a tenancy protected by the Rent Act, or excluded from it only because of the low rent.[3]
(c)   licensed premises as such but hotels, restaurants, and other places of entertainment, where a substantial proportion of the business consists of transactions other than the sale of intoxicating liquor, come within the Act. The test is the proportion of the receipts attributable to alcoholic drinks.[4]
(d)   a tenancy granted in writing to an employee for so long as he remains in the landlord's employment.[5]
(e)   a tenancy at will.[6]
(f)   a tenancy granted for a term certain not exceeding six months unless the tenancy contains a provision for renewing the term or for extending it beyond six months from its beginning, or the tenant has been in occupation for a period which, together with any period during which any predecessor in the business was in occupation, exceeds twelve months.[7] This therefore allows the grant of two tenancies totalling slightly less than twelve months providing there is no provision for renewal in the first tenancy.

1   1954 Act, s 43(1)(a).
2   1954 Act, s 43(1)(b).
3   1954 Act, s 43(1)(c) as amended by Sch 23, para 18 of the Rent Act 1977. As to 'tenancy at a low rent' see Rent Act 1977, s 5(3). As to the effect of former business use or mixed residential and business use, see *Cheryl Investments Ltd v Saldanha* [1979] 1 All ER 5, [1978] 1 WLR 1329; *Pulleng v Curran* (1980) 44 P & CR 58; *Russell v Booker* (1982) 263 Estates Gazette 513, CA; *Wagle v Trustees of Henry Smith's Charity Kensington Estate* [1989] 2 WLR 609, sub nom *Henry Smith's Charity Trustees v Wagle* [1989] 1 EGLR 124, CA; and Rent Act 1977, s 24 as amended by the Housing Act 1988.
4   1954 Act, s 43(1)(d). See *J G Swales & Co H S Mosley* [1968] CLY 2187; *Grant v Gresham* (1979) 252 Estates Gazette 55, CA; *Ye Olde Cheshire Cheese Ltd v Daily Telegraph plc* [1988] 3 All ER 217, [1988] 2 EGLR 107.
5   1954 Act, s 43(2).
6   *Wheeler v Mercer* [1957] AC 416, [1956] 3 All ER 631, HL; *Manfield & Sons Ltd v Botchin* [1970] 2 QB 612, [1970] 3 All ER 143; *Hagee (London) Ltd v AB Erikson and Larson* [1976] QB 209, [1975] 3 All ER 234, CA. In *Cardiothoracic Institute v Shrewdcrest Ltd* [1986] 3 All ER 633, [1986] 2 EGLR 57 the landlord was contemplating redevelopment and had granted three short leases, all with the 1954 Act contracted-out (see para 14.5 below). The last lease expired but the tenant remained in possession, rent being paid and accepted. Knox J found that it was understood by both parties that until a court order had been obtained under s 38(4) there would be no binding agreement and that either party was at liberty to resile from the negotiations and held that this was a classic case of the circumstances that created a tenancy at will. See Legal Notes (1986) 278 Estates Gazette 1485.
7   1954 Act, s 43(3).

14.5   *Contracting out of the 1954 Act.* The Law of Property Act 1969, s 5 added a new sub-s (4) to s 38 of the 1954 Act. Upon the joint application[1] of the parties to a proposed letting business tenancy for a term of years certain,[2] the court[3] may authorise an agreement excluding from that tenancy the provisions of ss 24–28 of the 1954 Act.[4] Such a tenancy will end by effluxion of time on the contractual expiry date and the tenant will have no rights under the 1954 Act to a new tenancy.[5] The agreeent must be contained in or endorsed on the lease.[6] The court may also authorise an agreement for the surrender of an existing business tenancy.[7] Previously both such agreements would have been void as purporting to preclude an application or request for a new tenancy under the 1954 Act.[8]

1   For precedents of an originating application for an order authorising the exclusion of the 1954 Act and the order itself, see 22 Encyclopaedia of Forms and Precedents (5th edn) Forms 212 and 213.
2   It is sometimes suggested that the reference to 'a term of years certain' could preclude an application to the court in respect of a lease that contained a break clause. The Law Commission doubts this and provisionally regards the matter as sufficiently clear that no amendment clarifying the point is needed ((1988) LCWP No 111, para 3.5.7). They refer to *Scholl Manufacturing Co Ltd v Clifton (Slim-Line) Ltd* [1967] Ch 41, [1966] 3 All ER 16, CA a case concerning the interpretation of s 69(1): 'A tenancy with a break clause is a tenancy for a term of years certain within the meaning of the Act of 1954 . . .' per Diplock LJ at 51.
3   The 1954 Act, s 63 (as amended), *Practice Direction* [1971] 2 All ER 215, [1971] 1 WLR 706; *Practice Note* [1973] 1 All ER 796, CCR 1981 Ord 43 ris (2).
4   Section 38(4)(a). As to ss 24–28, see section B below. The application must be made before the grant of the lease: see *Essexcrest Ltd v Evenlex Ltd* [1988] 1 EGLR 69, [1988] 01 EG 56, CA.
5   As to 'holding over' after the expiry of a tenancy where the 1954 Act is excluded, see *Cardiothoracic Institute v Shrewdcrest Ltd* [1986] 3 All ER 633, [1986] 2 EGLR 57, para 14.4 above, footnote 6.
6   For a precedent, see 22 Encyclopaedia of Forms and Precedents (5th edn) Form 211.
7   Section 38(4)(b), *Tarjomani v Panther Securities Ltd* (1982) 46 P & CR 32.
8   Section 38, *Joseph v Joseph* [1967] Ch 78, [1966] 3 All ER 486, CA; *Allnatt London Properties Ltd v Newton* [1984] 1 All ER 423, CA. See para 7.7:6 above.

B   TERMINATION OF A BUSINESS TENANCY AND THE PROCEDURE OF RENEWAL

14.6   *The basic concept.* Section 24(1) of the 1954 Act provides that a tenancy to which the Act applies[1] does not come to an end unless terminated in accordance with the provisions of ss 25–28 of the Act – in other words a business tenancy will not automatically[2] end by effluxion of time on the expiry date of the contractual term or as a result of a landlord's notice to quit,[3] as would be the case at common law. The only exceptions are forfeiture,[4] or notice to quit given by the tenant or surrender, provided the notice is given or the surrender executed after the tenant had been in occupation as tenant for at least a month.[5] Subject to this, a tenancy to which the 1954 Act applies will only come to an end if terminated by a notice from the landlord,[6] if the tenant requests a new tenancy,[7] if the tenant gives notice that he does not require a new tenancy,[8] or if the parties agree upon the terms of a new tenancy.[9]

1   See paras 14.3–14.5 above.
2   A business tenancy will only end on the contractual expiry date where the termination procedures of ss 25–28 have been operated in such a way that the tenancy is thereby terminated on the contractual expiry date.
3   Ie where the lease gives the landlord the right to terminate the tenancy by notice.
4   Including forfeiture of a superior tenancy: 1954 Act, s 24(2). As to effect of forfeiture on an application for a new tenancy, see *Meadows v Clerical, Medical and General Life Assurance Society*

[1981] Ch 70, [1980] 1 All ER 454; *Cadogan v Dimovic* [1984] 2 All ER 168, [1984] 1 WLR 609, CA.

5 Ibid, s 24(2). A joint application to the court can be made, however, in order to make an agreement to surrender enforceable: see para 14.5 above.
6 Ibid, s 25: see paras 14.7–14.8 below.
7 Ibid, s 26: see paras 14.9–14.10 below.
8 Ibid, s 27: see para 14.17 below.
9 Ibid, s 28: see para 14.18 below.

14.7 *Termination by the landlord.* The most common way by which a business tenancy is terminated is the service of a notice by the landlord[2] (referred to throughout as a 'Section 25 Notice'). The Section 25 Notice must:
(a) be in the prescribed form,[3] or in a form substantially to the like effect,[4]
(b) specify the date on which the landlord requires possession, such date not being more than twelve, nor less then six, months from the date of service of the notice,[5] nor earlier than the date of the expiry of the contractual term[6] or the date upon which the landlord could have terminated the tenancy by contractual notice[7] – thus if the landlord has not served the notice six months before the expiry date, the tenancy will be extended until six months have elapsed from the date upon which the notice is finally served,
(c) require the tenant within two months to notify the landlord in writing whether or not at the date of termination specified in the notice the tenant will be willing to give up possession,[8]
(d) state whether the landlord would oppose an application to the court for the grant of a new tenancy, and if so on which ground,[9]
(e) relate to the whole of the premises demised by the lease[10] unless the lease can be read as two separate and independent leases.[11]
If the requirements of s 25 are not followed, the notice will be invalid and, by virtue of s 24, the tenancy will continue.[9]

1 In accordance with the 1954 Act, s 66(4) and the Landlord and Tenant Act 1927, s 23.
2 1954 Act, s 25. As to when a landlord who is not the freeholder will be the competent landlord and thus entitled to serve a Section 25 Notice on a subtenant, see section C below. As to the steps landlord should take to ensure notice served on correct party see paras 14.20–14.21 below. As to service generally, see *Price v West London Investment Building Society Ltd* [1964] 2 All ER 318, [1964] 1 WLR 616, CA; *Chiswell v Griffon Land and Estates Ltd* [1975] 2 All ER 665, [1975] 1 WLR 1181, CA; *Italica Holdings SA v Bayadea* [1985] 1 EGLR 70, 273 Estates Gazette 888. As to Section 25 Notice being withdrawn by a superior landlord, see para 14.20 below.
3 Ie prescribed by regulations made by the Lord Chancellor by statutory instrument: 1954 Act, s 66(1). The current are the Landlord and Tenant Act 1954 Part II (Notices) (Amendment) Regulations 1989 amending in the case of forms number 1, 3, 13 and 15 the Landlord and Tenant 1954, Pt II (Notices) Regulations 1983. As to when the form is incorrectly completed, see *Bolton's (House Furnishers) Ltd v Oppenheim* [1959] 3 All ER 90, [1959] 1 WLR 913, CA; *Tennant v LCC* (1957) 121 JP 428, CA; *Sunrose Ltd v Gould* [1961] 3 All ER 1142, [1962] 1 WLR 20, CA; *Falcon Pipes Ltd v Stanhope Gate Property Co Ltd* (1967) 204 Estates Gazette 1243; *Stidolph v American School in London Educational Trust Ltd* (1969) 211 Estates Gazette 925, CA; *Morrow v Nadeem* [1987] 1 All ER 237, [1986] 2 EGLR 73, CA; *Yamaha-Kemble v ARC Properties Ltd* [1989] NPC 5. As to an inaccurate description of the property in the notice, see *Safeway Food Stores Ltd v Morris* (1980) 254 Estates Gazette 1091; *Herongrove Ltd v Wates City of London Properties plc* [1988] 1 EGLR 82, [1988] 24 EG 108.
4 By virtue of Regulation No 4 (see footnote 3 above) a form substantially to the like effect to that prescribed may be used. Nevertheless no prudent landlord will use anything but the prescribed form. As to consequences of an out-of-date form see *Sun Alliance and London Assurance Co Ltd v Hayman* [1975] 1 All ER 248, 233 Estates Gazette 927, CA; *Morris v Patel* [1987] 1 EGLR 75, 281 Estates Gazette 419, CA; or lack of marginal notes, see *Tegerdine v Brooks* (1977) 245 Estates Gazette 51, CA. As to whether tenant subsequently estopped from disputing validity, see *British Railways Board v A J A Smith Transport Ltd* (1981) 259 Estates Gazette 766; but as to whether tenant has waived an error in the completing of the form, see

Norton v Charles Deane Productions Ltd (1969) 214 Estates Gazette 559; *Morrow v Nadeem* [1987] 1 All ER 237, [1986] 2 EGLR 73, CA. See also footnote 9 below.

5 In *Hogg Bullimore & Co v Co-operative Insurance Society Ltd* (1984) 50 P & CR 105 Whitford J held that a notice served on 2 April 1984 specifying the date of termination as 2 October 1984 was valid.

6 1954 Act, s 25(4). See *Castle Laundry (London) Ltd v Read* [1955] 1 QB 586, [1955] 2 All ER 154; *Commercial Properties Ltd v Wood* [1968] 1 QB 15, [1967] 2 All ER 916, CA; *Ladyman v Wirral Estates Ltd* [1968] 2 All ER 197; *Central Estates (Belgravia) Ltd v Webster* (1969) 209 Estates Gazette 1319.

7 Ibid, s 25(3).

8 Ibid, s 25(5).

9 1954 Act, s 25(6). A notice may sufficiently state the ground of opposition without setting out verbatim the words of the appropriate paragraph of s 30(1) (see below). Indeed the courts have allowed landlords considerable latitude in satisfying the requirements of s 25(6) providing the notice is not deceptive or misleading and makes clear which of the grounds it is relying on: *Biles v Ceasar* [1957] 1 All ER 151, [1967] 1 WLR 156, CA; *Bolton's (House Furnishers) v Oppenheim* [1959] 3 All ER 90, [1959] 1 WLR 913, CA; *Marks v British Waterways Board* [1963] 3 All ER 28, [1963] 1 WLR 1008, CA (a case on s 26(6)); *Housleys Ltd v Bloomer-Holt Ltd* [1966] 2 All ER 966, [1966] 1 WLR 1244, CA; *Philipson-Stow v Trevor Square Ltd* (1980) 257 Estates Gazette 1262. But note *Barclays Bank Ltd v Ascott* [1961] 1 All ER 782, [1961] 1 WLR 717 (distinguished in *Lewis v M T C Cars Ltd* [1975] 1 All ER 874, [1975] 1 WLR 457, CA) in which it was held that a notice that did not specify any ground of opposition mentioned in s 30(1) (see below), and did not give the tenant sufficient information to enable her to deal with the situation arising from the notice, was ineffective – the words of Barry J in *Ascott* that 'provided that the notice gives the real substance of the information required, then the mere omission of certain details or the failure to embody in the notice the full provisions of the section of the Act referred to will not in fact invalidate the notice' were approved by the Court of Appeal in *Tegerdine v Brooks* (1976) 36 P & CR 261, CA. See also *Carradine Properties Ltd v Aslam* [1976] 1 All ER 573, [1976] 1 WLR 442; *Germax Securities Ltd v Spiegal* (1978) 250 Estates Gazette 449, CA. The ground(s) of opposition cannot subsequently be amended (s 25(6) ibid) but note *Hutchinson v Lamberth* (1983) 270 Estates Gazette 545, CA.

9 1954 Act, s 24. See para 14.6 above.

10 *Southport Old Links Ltd v Naylor* [1985] 1 EGLR 66, 273 Estates Gazette 767, CA illustrated a deficiency in the 1954 Act (but note footnote 11 below). The lease contained a resumption clause by which the landlord could recover possession of part of the demised premises (the golf course but not the clubhouse). When exercising that clause, the landlord served a Section 25 Notice, but the Court of Appeal held that ss 23(1), 23(3), 24(1), 24(5), 29(2), 32(1) and 34 contemplate that what is terminated by the Section 25 Notice is the tenancy of the holding and that there is no provision in the Act for the termination of part of the holding. Thus the intention of the lease was defeated. Unless and until the 1954 Act is amended, the parties should obviously deal with the situation contemplated here by means of two leases. As to when the reversion has been severed, so that there are different landlords for various parts of the demised premises, see *Dodson Bull Carpet Co Ltd v City of London Corpn* [1975] 2 All ER 497, [1975] 1 WLR 781; *William Skelton & Son Ltd v Harrison and Pinder Ltd* [1975] QB 361, [1975] 1 All ER 182.

11 *Moss v Mobil Oil Co Ltd* [1988] 1 EGLR 71, [1988] 06 EG 109, CA: Kerr LJ and Eastham J distinguished *Dodson* and *Southport* (see above).

14.8 *Tenant's counter-notice and court application.* A tenant who has been served with a Section 25 Notice is entitled to a new tenancy (unless the landlord establishes a ground of opposition)[1] if, within two months of the landlord's notice he serves a written notice on the landlord to the effect that he is unwilling to give up possession on the date prescribed in the landlord's notice,[2] and if he applies to the court for a further tenancy not less than two, nor more than four, months after the landlord's notice.[3] Where the rateable value of the property to be comprised in the new tenancy does not exceed £5,000, the application should be made to the county court for the area in which the property is located, and where this figure is exceeded, to the High Court.[4] By agreement between the parties, any application can be transferred to the High Court, or from it to a specified county court.[5] If the counter-notice has not been served and proceedings commenced within the relevant periods, then unless an agreement has been entered into with the landlord by which the four month period is extended[6] the tenant will have lost his rights under the Act, and the landlord may recover possession of the premises on the date specified in the Section 25 Notice.[7]

1   1954 Act, s 30(1), see section F below.
2   1954 Act, ss 25(5) and 29(2) – see *Smale v Meakers* [1957] JPL 415, 169 Estates Gazette 287; *Chiswell v Griffon Land and Estates Ltd* [1975] 2 All ER 665, [1975] 1 WLR 1181, CA. There is no prescribed form for this but for a precedent, see 22 Encyclopaedia of Forms and Precedents (5th edn) Form 217. The Court of Appeal held in *Lewington v Trustees of the Society for the Protection of Ancient Buildings* (1983) 266 Estates Gazette 997 that the tenant's negotiations to purchase the freehold made it clear that she was unwilling to give up possession, and thus her rights were not defeated by the lack of a formal notice. Waller LJ said that s 29(2) 'does not require a particular form of notice . . . the only thing which is required is that the tenant should, in writing, notify the landlord whether or not he or she is willing or unwilling to give up possession . . . the letters show that [the tenant] had no intention whatever of giving up possession . . .'. In *Mehmet v Dawson* (1983) 270 Estates Gazette 139, CA, however a tenant whose proposed purchase of the freehold was at an altogether earlier stage was unsuccessful and the lesson is clear – a tenant ought to leave nothing to doubt and serve a formal notice.
3   1954 Act, s 29(3). As to computation of the four month period, see *Dodds v Walker* [1981] 2 All ER 609, [1981] 1 WLR 1027, HL; *EJ Riley Investments Ltd v Eurostile Holdings Ltd* [1985] 3 All ER 181, [1985] 1 WLR 1139, CA and *Manorlike Ltd v Le Vitas Travel Agency and Consultancy Services Ltd* [1986] 1 All ER 573, [1986] 1 EGLR 79, CA. Note *Evans Constructions Co Ltd v Charrington & Co Ltd* [1983] QB 810, 264 Estates Gazette 347, CA where proceedings were commenced against a party who was not the landlord and *Bar v Pathwood Investments Ltd* [1987] 1 EGLR 90, 282 Estates Gazette 1538, CA where premises were incorrectly described in the application to the court and the tenant sought to amend this after the four month period had expired.
4   1954 Act, s 63(2) as amended by the Administration of Justice Act 1973, s 6 and Sch 2. RSC Ord 97 CCR 1981 Ord 43.
5   1954 Act, s 63(3).
6   See para 14.11 below.
7   Virtually all potential reformers of the 1954 Act (see para 14.02 above, especially footnotes 5 & 7) address the undesirability of having to commence proceedings in every case in which the terms of the rent lease have not been agreed within four months when in fact only a very small percentage of such proceedings are contested. Usually the terms are in due course agreed. The most often canvassed solutions are to delete the 'automatic' requirement to apply to the court and replace it either by giving the right to either party to apply to the court at any time after (or at any time say two months after) the service of the counter-notice; by giving the landlord the right to serve a further notice after the counter-notice has been served requiring the tenant to apply to the court in say two months; or to leave the automatic requirement but to give statutory force to the fact that the period can be extended by agreement: see para 14.11 below. As to computation of damages against solicitors who have not commenced proceedings in time see *Jolliffe v Charles Coleman & Co* (1971) 219 Estates Gazette 1608.

14.9   *Tenant's request.* A tenant's request for a new tenancy must be made by a notice in the prescribed form[1] otherwise it is of no effect[2] and the tenant must state in his request:
(a)   the property to be comprised in the new tenancy;[3]
(b)   the date from which such tenancy is to commence. This date must be not more than twelve, nor less than six, months after the making of the request, and not earlier than the date on which, apart from the Act, the current tenancy would come to an end by effluxion of time (or could be brought to an end by notice to quit given by the tenant);[4]
(c)   the duration of the term asked for;[5]
(d)   the rent to be payable and the other terms.[5]
The tenant cannot take the initiative by requesting a new tenancy unless his current tenancy was granted for a term certain exceeding one year, or for a term of years certain, and thereafter from year to year.[6] Nor can the tenant

serve a Section 26 Request if a Section 25 Notice has been served on him.[7] If the landlord wishes to oppose an application to the court for the grant of a new tenancy following a request from the tenant, the landlord must give notice to the tenant to this effect within two months of the tenant's request.[8] The landlord must specify the ground or grounds upon which he can oppose the tenant's request. If within four months of the tenant's request the new lease has not been agreed, the tenant must apply to the court[9] for a new tenancy.[10] If he does not, he loses his rights under the Act in the same way as if he had not made an application to the court following a Section 25 Notice,[11] unless an agreement has been entered into to extend the period.[12]

1 1954 Act, s 26(3). See footnotes 3 and 4 to para 14.7 above.
2 But see *Bristol Cars Ltd v RKH (Hotels) Ltd* (1979) 251 Estates Gazette 1279, the tenant's request specified a date for the commencement of the new term that was too early but the Court of Appeal held that the landlords had waived the defect.
3 1954 Act, s 26(3).
4 1954 Act, s 26(2).
5 1954 Act, s 26(3), see *Sidney Bolsom Investment Trust Ltd v E Karmios & Co (London) Ltd* [1956] 1 QB 529, [1956] 1 All ER 536, CA.
6 1954 Act, s 26(1).
7 1954 Act, s 26(4).
8 1954 Act, s 26(6). There is no prescribed form but for a precedent, see 22 Encyclopaedia of Forms and Precedents (5th edn) Form 220.
9 1954 Act, s 63(2) (as amended by the Administration of Justice Act 1973, s 6 and Sch 2) and s 63(3). See para 14.8 above.
10 1954 Act, s 29(3).
11 If the tenant serves a request under s 26, the current tenancy expires the day before the date upon which the new tenancy is expressed to commence. Thus a tenant who fails to apply to the court within four months cannot simply serve a second notice under s 26 and purport to withdraw the first one – see *Stile Hall Properties Ltd v Gooch* [1979] 3 All ER 848, [1980] 1 WLR 62, CA and *Polyviou v Seeley* [1979] 3 All ER 853, [1980] 1 WLR 55, CA. As to computation of four months period, see *Dodds v Walker* [1981] 2 All ER 609, [1981] 1 WLR 1027, HL.
12 See para 14.11 below.

14.10 *Significance of s 26.* It may be wondered why a tenant would ever apply for a new tenancy in view of the fact that, if the landlord has overlooked the matter and failed to serve a Section 25 Notice, the Act provides that the existing tenancy continues beyond the term referred to in the lease, and thus the tenant will continue to pay the rent reserved by the old lease that would presumably be below the market rent.[1] Sometimes, however, the tenant will require certainty as to his future, because by doing nothing he leaves himself in a position in which the landlord could at any time serve a Section 25 Notice indicating that he would oppose an application to the court by the tenant for a new tenancy. Further, if the tenant can serve his notice before the landlord,[2] he may be able to extend the length of the existing tenancy. The tenant can require a new tenancy to commence 'not more than twelve nor less than six months' after his request. So if the landlord has failed to serve a Section 25 Notice[2] as the tenancy moves into its last year, the tenant can, at any time until the landlord serves a Section 25 Notice,[2] request a new tenancy to begin a year after his notice . . . and in the meantime the current tenancy will continue until that new tenancy commences. Where the term of a business lease is to expire on say 25 December, the landlord may believe that, providing he serves his Section 25 Notice by 24 June, nothing can prevent him from bringing the tenancy to an end on the contractual term date.[3] If, however, he delays and plans to serve his Section 25 Notice only a day or two before 24 June, he runs the risk that the tenant will serve a Section 26 Request in perhaps early June requesting a new tenancy to commence in June the following year.[4] Providing that date is not more than twelve months from the request, the current tenancy will thereby have been extended by nearly six months beyond the expiry of the contractual term.[5] The simple answer, of course, is for the landlord to deny the tenant the potential for benefiting from s 26 by serving his Section 25 Notice as soon as the current tenancy has only a year left to run. And yet this may not always be possible, or desirable, for other reasons – that far in advance, the landlord may not know whether or not he will be in a position successfully to oppose the grant of a new tenancy under s 30(1)[6] of the 1954 Act, while he may prefer to delay opening negotiations for the new rent (that will inevitably follow the service of a notice) until as late as possible on the grounds that the rent will be higher if negotiated later.

1 Where the lease contains a rent review clause, the rent being paid at the end of the term would be that determined or agreed on the last review. In fact, the last review can sometimes be at the end of the term (see paras 6.4:3 above and 14.15 below) and where this is the case the rent at this stage need not be below the market rent.
2 The 1954 Act, s 26(4) provides that if the landlord has served a Section 25 Notice, the tenant cannot request a new tenancy under s 26. The converse is also true.
3 Ie because his Section 25 Notice need give not less than six months notice.
4 And yet, in the unlikely event of the landlord totally overlooking the contractual expiry of the tenancy, the tenant would be in a worse position by serving his request. Without it, the tenancy would continue until six months after the landlord woke up to the situation and served a Section 25 Notice, which may (in the above example) be later than the following June.
5 Section 24A of the 1954 Act (see para 14.15 below) will be of no assistance to the landlord because the first date upon which an interim rent can be payable is the date upon which the current tenancy is expressed to be brought to an end, and it is that date that the tenant has postponed.
6 See section F below.

14.11 *Agreement to extend time limits.* Until 1981, the great majority of practitioners apparently believed that the period during which proceedings must be commenced by the tenant under the 1954 Act could *not* be extended by agreement and this had prompted various attempts, all of them unsuccessful, to amend the law by relaxing the strict time limits.[1] But a note from the Standing Committee of the Law Society on Land Law and Conveyancing[2] suggested a way in which this could apparently[3] be done.[4]

1 See [1981] Gazette 11 February 142.
2 [1981] Gazette 29 July 853. Reproduced with the permission of the Law Society in Appendix 3.
3 Despite the authority cited by the Law Society, there has always been unease in some quarters as to whether a court that does not have jurisdiction (because a statutory time limit has expired) can be given jurisdiction by the agreement of the parties. See [1989] Gazette 30 August 10.
4 In order to bind a purchaser of the reversion, because in the absence of legal proceedings there can be no registration unless such an agreement was held to be an estate contract (see para 14.13 below), it is suggested that the agreement is expressed to bind the landlord's successors and that the agreement (or a memorandum of it) is endorsed on the counterpart lease.

14.12 *Service of proceedings.* There is a further time limit that the tenant and his advisers must not overlook – after the proceedings have been commenced, the relevant documents must be served upon the landlord within the period prescribed by the County Court Rules or the Rules of the Supreme Court.[1] Both Rules give the court power to extend the time for service[2] but it is clear that this descretion will be used sparingly[3] although the latest County Court Rules may have made it easier for tenants to obtain an extension.[4]

1   Ie within two months of date of issue CCR 1981, Ord 7 r 20, Ord 43, r 6(3). RSC Ord 6, r 8(1), Ord 97, r 6. As to service of an application for an interim rent (see para 13.2:10 below) see *Texaco Ltd v Benton and Bowles (Holdings) Ltd* (1983) 267 Estates Gazette 355.
2   CCR 1981 Ord 13, r 4, RSC Ord 6, r 8(12).
3   *Battersby v Anglo American Oil Co Ltd* [1945] 1 KB 23, [1944] 2 All ER 387, CA; *Heaven v Road and Rail Wagons Ltd* [1965] 2 QB 355, [1965] 2 All ER 409; *Re Chittenden* [1970] 3 All ER 562, [1970] 1 WLR 1618; *Lewis v Wolking Properties Ltd* [1978] 1 All ER 427, [1978] 1 WLR 403, CA; *Joan Barrie Ltd v GUS Property Management* (1981) 259 Estates Gazette 628, CA.
4   Compare *Robert Baxendale Ltd v Davstone (Holdings) Ltd* [1982] 3 All ER 496, CA (a case under CCR 1936, Ord 8 r 35) with *Ali v Knight* (1983) 272 Estates Gazette 1165, CA. If the case goes that far, the tenant must appeal in time: *Rawashden v Lane* [1988] 2 EGLR 109, [1988] 40 EG 109, CA.

14.13   *Registration of an application or agreement for a new tenancy.* If a tenant's application for a new tenancy is a pending action, a purchaser of the reversion would only be bound if he had express notice of the application, in the absence of registration. The Standing Committee of the Law Society on Land Law and Conveyancing has provided guidance,[2] and in the light of Megarry VC's decision in *Selim Ltd v Bickenhall Engineering Ltd*,[3] the tenant should protect himself by registration. The fate of the tenant[4] in *R J Stratton Ltd v Wallis Tomlin & Co Ltd*[5] highlighted the fact that the position is the same when the landlord and tenant have agreed the terms of the new letting. Here the landlord's receiver sold the reversion shortly after the agreement had been reached and before the new lease had been granted. In the absence of registration, the Court of Appeal held that the purchaser of the reversion was not bound by the agreement and, because there had been an agreement, the court had no jurisdiction to grant the tenant a new tenancy.[6] It seems arguable that such an application or agreement is in the case of registered land, an overriding interest, so long as the tenant is in actual occupation of the land and does not fail to disclose the application or agreement upon enquiry.[7] Nevertheless, the prudent solicitor acting for a tenant should put the matter beyond doubt by registering but the inability of the tenant to require the landlord to deduce his title can make any such registration difficult.[8] The landlord's solicitor may be prepared to indicate whether or not his client's title is registered at HM Land Registry and, if it is, the title number. Where the landlord's title is registered and the title number known, a caution should be registered against that title.[9] If it is not registered, a pending action should be registered against the landlord at HM Land Charges Registry, and a caution against first registration at HM Land Registry. If however, the landlord's solicitor will not disclose this information (although it is difficult to see how his client could be prejudiced by so doing) all the tenant's solicitor can do is make a map index search. Where the landlord is the freeholder or headlessee, the result should provide the relevant information, but where there have been numerous sublettings, this may not be the case.

1   Land Charges Act 1972, ss 5(1)(a), 17(1).
2   [1982] Gazette 13 January 30. Reproduced with the permission of the Law Society in Appendix 3.
3   [1981] 3 All ER 210, [1981] 1 WLR 1318.
4   And perhaps the tenant's solicitors, although May LJ left open the question of whether reasonable solicitors would have registered: [1986] 1 EGLR 106 at F. See 'Points in practice' (1987) 131 Sol Jo 1245.
5   [1986] 1 EGLR 104, 277 Estates Gazette 409, CA.
6   By virtue of the 1954 Act, s 28. See para 14.18 below.
7   Land Registration Act, s 70(1)(g).
8   See para 2.10 above.
9   Land Registration Act 1925, s 59(1) and (5).

14.14 *Extension of the tenancy.* The service of a Section 25 Notice brings the contractual tenancy to an end on the date that is specifies,[1] and the service of a Section 26 Request for a new tenancy brings the tenancy to an end on the date before the date which the request proposes for the commencement of the new tenancy.[2] Assuming, however, that an application is made by the tenant to the court within the prescribed period,[3] the tenancy is extended until three months after the final disposal of that application.[4] The three months starts to run from the expiry of the time for appealing, or further appealing, unless the application is withdrawn[5] or an appeal abandoned, in which case it is the date of the withdrawal or abandonment.

1 1954 Act, s 25(1).
2 Ibid, s 26(6).
3 Ie not less than two nor more than four months after the Section 25 Notice or Section 26 Request: 1954 Act, s 29(3). Moreover, where the application is made in consequence of a Section 25 Notice, the tenant must have notified the landlord within two months of the Section 25 Notice that he will not be willing to give up possession: 1954 Act, s 29(2), *Chiswell v Griffon Land and Estates Ltd* [1975] 2 All ER 665, [1975] 1 WLR 1181, CA.
4 1954 Act, s 64. See *Covell Matthews & Partners v French Wools Ltd* [1977] 2 All ER 591, [1977] 1 WLR 876 and *Re No 20 Exchange Street, Manchester, Austin Reed Ltd v Royal Insurance Co Ltd (No 2)* [1956] 3 All ER 490, [1956] 1 WLR 1339.
5 As to when an application can be discontinued, see para 14.16 below.

14.15 *Interim rents.* Until 1969 the rent under the original contractual tenancy continued unaltered until the new tenancy came into effect. This provision could operate most unfairly for landlords where delays either on the part of the tenant, or in obtaining a hearing date, could mean that a considerable time had elapsed between the expiry of the Section 25 Notice and the date of the hearing. Section 3 of the Law of Property Act 1969 added s 24A to the 1954 Act which provides that a landlord who has either given a Section 25 Notice, or received a Section 26 Request, may apply to the court[1] to determine the rent that would be reasonable for the tenant to pay while the current tenancy continues. This rent is referred to in RSC Ord 97, r 9(a) as 'an interim rent' and, although this expression is used neither in the 1954 Act nor the County Court Rules, it has come to be generally applied. The interim rent runs from the later of the dates specified in the Section 25 Notice to terminate the current tenancy (or in the Section 26 Request as the commencement date for the new tenancy), or the date of commencement of the proceedings for determination of the interim rent.[2] Accordingly the landlord should apply promptly for an interim rent to be fixed. Section 24(A)(3) provides that: 'in determining a rent under this section the court shall have regard to[3] the rent payable under the terms of the tenancy,[4] but otherwise subsections 1 and 2 of section 34 of this Act shall apply to the determination' on the basis that the whole of the premises were being let on a new tenancy from year to year. Thus the interim rent is to be determined on the hypothetical basis of a yearly tenancy and this lack of security has led to interim rents being lower than the open market rent of the premises for the new tenancy.[5] There are conflicting authorities on the interpretation and significance of the words directing the court to have regard to the rent payable under the terms of the existing tenancy, especially as s 34(1) contains the opposite direction.[6] In *Fawke v Viscount Chelsea*[7] the Court of Appeal held that in arriving at an interim rent the court could have regard to the state of repair of the premises and determine a differential interim rent with a reduced rent initially until the necessary works of repair had been carried out, and from this it would seem to follow that a 'step' in an interim rent could be made to be conditional upon any other circumstances. It is felt, especially by landlords, that s 24A has not satisfactorily dealt with the problem of the rent paid during the sometimes lengthy statutory extension of the contractual term.[8] There remain uncertainties and inconsistencies in the approach adopted by the courts[9] while the principle of the tenant paying an interim rent that is less than the open market rent,[10] especially where the landlord is not opposing the grant of a new tenancy, concerns landlords, many of whom seek to avoid the need to rely upon s 24A by providing for a rent review at the end of the contractual term.[11]

1   Note particularly that an application for an interim rent can be made as soon as the Notice (s 25) or Request (s 26) has been given or received – there is no need to wait until proceedings have been commenced by the tenant under s 29(3). As to the dangers to the tenant's advisers of overlooking the fact that an application for an interim rent has been made, see *Teasdale v Williams & Co* (1983) 269 Estates Gazette 1040, CA. As to the effect of the tenant withdrawing his application when the landlord has issued a counter summons for interim rent, see *Artoc Bank and Trust Ltd v Prudential Assurance Co plc* [1984] 3 All ER 538, [1984] 1 WLR 1181. As to time for service of summons for interim rent, see *Texaco Ltd v Benton and Bowles (Holdings) Ltd* (1983) 267 Estates Gazette 355. As to how rent determined and when the Court of Appeal should order a new trial, see *Halberstam v Tandalco Corpn NV* [1985] 1 EGLR 90, 275 Estates Gazette 393, CA.
2   1954 Act, s 24A(2). See *Stream Properties Ltd v Davis* [1972] 2 All ER 746, [1972] 1 WLR 645; *Victor Blake (Menswear) Ltd v City of Westminster* (1978) 249 Estates Gazette 543 and *Thomas v Hammond-Lawrence* [1986] 2 All ER 214, [1986] 1 WLR 456, CA. Where delay in serving summons re application for interim rent, see *Texaco Ltd v Benton and Bowles Holdings Ltd* (1983) 267 Estates Gazette 355.
3   See *Regis Property Co Ltd v Lewis and Peat Ltd* [1970] Ch 695, [1970] 3 All ER 227.
4   In *Charles Follett Ltd v Cabtell Investment Co Ltd* [1987] 2 EGLR 88, 283 Estates Gazette 195 the Court of Appeal (while recognising that it was an exceptional case) upheld Mr T L G Cullen QC (sitting as a deputy judge of the Chancery Division) who had reduced the interim rent that he had calculated on the usual basis (ie in the way indicated in the cases cited in footnote 5 below) by 50% (to £40,000) having regard to the high increase over the rent currently being paid (£13,500 to £80,000). Mr Cullen had then declined to order *any* interim rent, accepting instead an undertaking by the tenant to pay £25,000 a year. The Court of Appeal however held that the judge could only make one of two orders – £13,500 or £40,000, and awarded the latter, referring to *English Exporters (London) Ltd v Eldonwall Ltd* [1973] Ch 415 per Megarry J at 432H and *Bloomfield v Ashwright Ltd* (1983) 266 Estates Gazette 1095, CA per Lawton LJ. It has been suggested that *Charles Follett* will encourage tenants to argue for more substantial discounts than previously: (1987) 283 Estates Gazette 319. To avoid these difficulties, see para 6.4:3 above (end of term rent reviews).
5   *Janes (Gowns) Ltd v Harlow Development Corpn* (1979) 253 Estates Gazette 799; *Ratners (Jewellers) Ltd v Lemnoll Ltd* (1980) 255 Estates Gazette 987; *UDS Tailoring Ltd v BL Holdings Ltd* (1981) 261 Estates Gazette 49; *Charles Follett Ltd v Cabtell Investment Co Ltd* [1986] 2 EGLR 76, 280 Estates Gazette 639. As to effect on application for interim rent of sale of reversion, see *Bloomfield v Ashwright Ltd* (1983) 266 Estates Gazette 1095, CA. As to the attitude of the Court of Appeal to judical calculations of interim rents, see *Halberstam v Tandalco Corpn NV* [1985] 1 EGLR 90, 274 Estates Gazette 393, CA.
6   See *Regis Property Co Ltd v Lewis and Peat Ltd* [1970] Ch 695, [1970] 3 All ER 227 and *English Exporters (London) Ltd v Eldonwall Ltd* [1973] Ch 415, [1973] 1 All ER 726. 'The legislative purpose of the requirement that regard should be had to the old rent was, where appropriate, to cushion the tenant against that shock': *Charles Follett Ltd v Cabtell Investments Ltd* [1987] 2 EGLR 88, 283 Estates Gazette 195 per Nourse LJ at 90 G. See also *Conway v Arthur* [1988] 2 EGLR 113, [1988] 40 EG 120, CA.
7   [1980] QB 441, [1979] 3 All ER 568, CA. See also *Woodbridge v Westminster Press Ltd* [1987] 2 EGLR 97, 284 Estates Gazette 60.
8   See for example the criticisms made in the articles referred to in para 14.2, footnote 5 above.
9   As is indicated by the cases referred to in this paragraph.
10 Ie because it is calculated on the basis of a tenancy, from year to year and because the interim rent apparently can be further significantly reduced where the open market rent is considerably higher than the current rent – see footnote 4 above.
11 See para 6.4:3 above.

14.16   *Revoking the court's order for the grant of a new tenancy and discontinuance of an application.* On an application made by the tenant following a Section 25 Notice[1] or a Section 26 Request[2] the court[3] shall make an order to the grant of a new tenancy comprising such property,[4] at such a rent[5] and on such other terms[6] as are provided for in ss 32–35 of the 1954 Act[7] unless the landlord has grounds for opposing the application under s 30(1).[8] A tenant, in whose favour the court makes an order for the grant of a new tenancy, has the right to apply to the court within fourteen days for the order to be revoked.[9] This provision is there to protect a tenant who finds the terms of the tenancy determined by the court to be unacceptable. Here the original contractual tenancy will be extended for such period that the parties may agree, or the court determines, to be necessary to give the landlord a reasonable opportunity to re-let or otherwise dispose of the premises. If the landlord and tenant agree in writing on the grant of a new tenancy, the current tenancy terminates on the date specified in the agreement.[10] An application for a new tenancy in the County Court can be discontinued at any time without agreement from the other party and without leave. Leave was required in the High Court although it has been suggested[11] that this is no longer required by virtue of recent amendments to the Rules of the Supreme Court.[12]

1   See paras 14.2–14.3 above.
2   See para 14.4 above.
3   See para 14.8 above.
4   See 1954 Act, s 32, see section H below.
5   Ibid, s 34, see subsection J below.
6   As to duration, see ibid, s 33 (section I below) and other terms, see ibid, s 35 (section K below).
7   Ibid, s 29(1).
8   See section F below.
9   1954 Act, s 36(2). As to costs where tenancy revoked, see 1954 Act, s 36(3) and *Re 88 High Road Kilburn, Meakers Ltd v DAW Consolidated Properties Ltd* [1959] 1 All ER 527, [1959] 1 WLR 279.
10   1954 Act, s 28.
11   [1983] Gazette 2 November 2732 but see (1983) 4 PLB 47.
12   RSC (Amendment No 3) 1982 (SI 1982/1786). As to applications for leave, see *Ove Arup Inc v Howland Property Investments Co Ltd* (1981) 42 P & CR 337; *Lloyds Bank Ltd v London City Corpn* [1983] Ch 192, [1983] 1 All ER 92, CA; *Fribourg and Treyer Ltd v Northdale Investments Ltd* (1982) 263 Estates Gazette 660; *Artoc Bank and Trust Ltd v Prudential Assurance Co plc* [1984] 3 All ER 538, [1984] 1 WLR 1181.

14.17   *Tenant's notice of non-continuance.* A tenant on whom the landlord serves a Section 25 Notice[1] and who does not require a new tenancy, will generally fail to comply with the procedural steps required by the section[2] so that the tenancy ends on the date specified in the notice, and is not extended by virtue of the 1954 Act.[3] Without a Section 25 Notice, however, the tenancy would not terminate, and so s 27 provides that a tenant[4] may, not later than three months before the contractual expiry date, give to his immediate landlord a notice[5] that the tenant does not desire his tenancy to be continued, whereupon the Act will not apply and the tenancy will end on that date.[6] When no such notice has been served by a date three months before the contractual expiry date, the tenant may at any time thereafter give not less than three months' notice[5] to bring the tenancy to an end on any quarter day.[7]

1   See paras 14.7 and 14.8 above.
2   See para 14.8 above.
3   Ie the 1954 Act, s 24. In *Long Acre Securities Ltd v Electro Acoustic Industries Ltd* [1989] EGCS 125 the Court of Appeal held that the tenant could serve a notice under s 27 after the landlord has

served a notice under s 26. This is relevant where the landlord has delayed and extended the term beyond the contractual date and the tenant's requirements.

4 Under a tenancy granted for a term of years certain: ibid, s 27.

5 In writing but no prescribed form: ibid, s 27. For a precedent, see 22 Encyclopaedia of Forms and Precedents (5th edn) Form 218 (at least three months of the contractual term remains unexpired) and 219 (less than three months unexpired).

6 Ibid, s 27(1).

7 Ibid, s 27(2).

14.18 *Renewal of tenancies by agreement.* Section 28 of the 1954 Act provides that, where the landlord[1] and the tenant agree[2] the terms of a new tenancy of the demised premises (or of demised premises with other land), the current tenancy continues until the date upon which it has been agreed that the new tenancy shall commence. If the parties have agreed the terms of the new tenancy, the court has no jurisdiction to grant a tenancy under the Act.[3]

1 *Bowes-Lyon v Green* [1963] AC 420, [1961] 3 All ER 843, HL.

2 The agreement must be in writing: 1954 Act, s 69(2).

3 Clearly the parties should make it quite clear when the terms are agreed and the tenant should then seek to register the agreement as an estate contract to avoid the problems experienced in *R J Stratton Ltd v Wallis Tomlin & Co Ltd* [1986] 1 EGLR 104, 277 Estates Gazette 409, CA.

C THE COMPETENT LANDLORD

14.19 *With whom should the tenant renew?* The landlord who serves a Section 25 Notice,[1] or on whom the tenant serves a Section 26 Request[2] must be the competent landlord as defined by the Act.[3] The immediate landlord will be the competent landlord if he is the freeholder or, where a tenant himself, if his tenancy will not expire within fourteen months, and, if it is such a tenancy, no notice has been served to terminate the tenancy within that period. When the immediate landlord does not comply with these criteria, the competent landlord will be the next most immediate landlord who does comply. There can be only one competent landlord at any time. Where there has been a subletting, one of two situations must subsist:

(a) The immediate landlord does *not* occupy for business purposes any part of the premises demised by his lease. Here the Act will not apply[4] to the immediate landlord's lease that will be brought to an end by effluxion of time or by notice to quit. If the immediate landlord's reversion is less than fourteen months, the next most immediate landlord with such a reversion becomes the subtenant's competent landlord.[5] If the reversion is fourteen months or longer, the immediate landlord will be the subtenant's competent landlord,[6] until less than that period remains, when the identity of the competent landlord will change.

(b) The immediate landlord *does* occupy for business purposes part of the premises demised by his lease and thus the immediate landlord's tenancy will continue until terminated in accordance with the Act.[7] Here the immediate landlord will generally[8] be the subtenant's competent landlord[6] until the service of a notice under ss 25 or 27 or a request under s 26 in relation to the immediate landlord's tenancy, whereupon the superior landlord becomes the subtenant's competent landlord.[9] Thus the 'competence' of a landlord who has sublet part of his premises but remains in occupation of the remainder for business purposes will depend upon whether or not he has been served with a Section 25 Notice or himself served a Section 26 Request or a Notice under s 27.

It follows that the identity of the competent landlord may change so that procedures and litigation may have to be continued by or against different parties.[10] When the term of the subtenant's renewed lease as agreed or determined by the court will extend beyond the interest of the immediate landlord, the court has power to order the grant of a new tenancy until the expiry of the immediate landlord's interest and such reversionary tenancy or tenancies as may be required to make up the term.[11]

1   See para 14.7 above.
2   See para 14.9 above.
3   1954 Act, s 44(3) and Sch 6 (para 1). As to the consequences of tenant serving wrong party, see *Re 55 and 57 Holmes Road, Kentish Town, Beardmore Motors Ltd v Birch Bros (Properties) Ltd* [1959] Ch 298, [1958] 2 All ER 311.
4   1954 Act, s 23. An intermediate landlord, who has sublet all of the premises demised to him and retained a reversion of less than two months will never be competent (because his term must expire within fourteen months by the time it would have become possible for him to serve and be served with notices and proceedings under the 1954 Act) unless, although not then in occupation, he later acquires possession of and occupies for business purposes part of the premises let to him.
5   1954 Act, s 44(1)(b) as amended by the Law of Property Act 1969, s 14(1).
6   But the superior landlord will be able to override any Section 25 Notice that the immediate landlord may serve: see para 14.20 below.
7   1954 Act, s 24; *Bowes-Lyon v Green* [1963] AC 420, [1961] 3 All ER 843, HL; *Cornish v Brook Green Laundry Ltd* [1959] 1 QB 394, [1959 1 All ER 373, CA.
8   The only exception is the circumstances referred to in s 25(3)(b) and where the date specified in the Section 25 Notice is fourteen months or more after the giving of the Notice in which case the intermediate landlord will remain the competent landlord until such date as is fourteen months before the date so specified.
9   1954 Act, s 44(1)(b).
10 *Diploma Laundry Ltd v Surrey Timber Co Ltd* [1955] 2 QB 604, [1955] 2 All ER 992, CA; *XL Fisheries Ltd v Leeds Corpn* [1955] 2 QB 636, [1955] 2 All ER 875, CA; *Wimbush & Son Ltd v Franmills Properties Ltd* [1961] Ch 419, [1961] 2 All ER 197; *Rene Claro (Haute Coiffure) Ltd v Halle Concerts Society* [1969] 2 All ER 842, [1969] 1 WLR 909, CA; *Shelley v United Artists Corpn* [1989] EGCS 120, CA discussed [1989] 09 EG 83. Indeed, where the property has been let, underlet, subunderlet etc, a tenant in occupation under for example a subsubunderlease of part can find that different parties can become his competent landlord for very short periods. For example, freeholder A has let to headlessee B who has in turn sublet to sublessee C, retaining a nominal one day reversion, and C has himself created subunderleases. It is possible that B may become the competent landlord of the subunderlessees for that one day alone. If one of those subunderlessees were to serve a counter-notice (see para 14.8 above) on A or C on that day, it would be ineffective, and unless another effective notice was subsequently served, the sub-underlessee would lose his rights under the 1954 Act.
11 1954 Act, Sch 6 para 2. There can, however, at any one time be only one competent landlord. As to severed reversions, see *William Skelton & Son Ltd v Harrison and Pinder Ltd* [1975] QB 361, [1975] 1 All ER 182; *Dodson Bull Carpet Co Ltd v City of London Corpn* [1975] 2 All ER 497, [1975] 1 WLR 781; *Nevill Long & Co (Boards) Ltd v Firmenich & Co* (1983) 268 Estates Gazette 572, CA.

14.20   *Action to be taken relating to service/receipt of notice/request.* There are certain steps that the various parties should take in contemplation of, or following the service or receipt of a Section 25 Notice[1] or Section 26 Request:[2]

14.20:1   *By immediate landlord when he is the competent landlord.* If the contractual term of his tenancy expires less than sixteen months after the date of service or receipt, he must send a copy of the Section 25 Notice or Section 26 Request to the superior landlord[3] who by serving a notice in the prescribed form[4] has the right to withdraw the Section 25 Notice if he becomes the competent landlord within two months of the service of the Section 25 Notice.[5] The new competent landlord may or may not then serve a Section 25 Notice, as he chooses. The greatest possible care should be exercised where a landlord who is himself a 'business' tenant has sublet part and remains in occupation of the remainder, because his 'competence' may depend entirely on whether or not he is served with a Section 25 Notice or himself serves a Section 26 Request or a Notice under s 27. Thus a landlord in occupation of part should ensure that he serves a Section 25 Notice on his tenant before he himself is so served, otherwise he runs the risk that the new competent landlord may not serve his tenant, and so leave him in a rent shortfall trap. Similarly landlords serving Section 25 Notices should always serve tenants before subtenants.

14.20:2   *By the superior landlord when he is the competent landlord.* Where the superior landlord is not himself the freeholder, he must in the circumstances envisaged in para 14.20:1 above, send a copy to his landlord[3] who will have a similar right to withdraw a Section 25 Notice and to serve a new one himself.[5] He will also need to serve a Section 25 Notice upon his immediate tenant who is in occupation for business purposes of part before he seeks to serve a Section 25 Notice upon the subtenant.[6]

14.20:3   *By the tenant.* A Section 25 Notice served upon a tenant by an immediate landlord who is not the freeholder may be withdrawn,[7] and may not even be valid. To assess the risk of the former and to establish the latter, the tenant should serve on his immediate landlord a notice under s 40(2) of the Act[8] adding in the covering letter accompanying such notice a request for a copy of any Section 25 Notice received by such landlord terminating his current tenancy. Section 40(2) Notices should then be served with similar covering letters on the superior landlord or landlords until one is reached who will be competent for the period that the renewal is expected to take.

1   See para 14.7 above.
2   See para 14.9 above.
3   1954 Act, Sch 6, para 7.
4   Ie prescribed by the Landlord and Tenant Act 1954 Part II (Notices) Regulations 1983, Form No 12.
5   1954 Act, Sch 6, para 6.
6   He will also need to consider ibid, Sch 6, paras 3 and 4: in essence, the superior/competent landlord has power to bind the immediate landlord (and any supervening parties) in relation to Section 25 Notices that he gives to the subtenant in possession, and the terms of any renewed tenancy agreed with the subtenant, but if the competent landlord acts without the consent of the immediate landlord and any supervening parties (and such consent may not be unreasonably refused) he is liable to pay compensation.
7   See subparas (a) and (b) above.
8   See para 14.21 below.

14.21   *Notices requesting information.* Section 40(1) provides that a tenant who receives a notice in the prescribed form from his landlord or a superior landlord,[1] must indicate within one month if he occupies the premises or any part of them wholly or partly for business purposes and whether he has sublet and, if so, he must provide information about the subletting.[2] Sections 40(2)–(4) enable the tenant to serve a notice[3] on his landlord or any superior landlord who must indicate if he owns the freehold, and if not who (to the best of his knowledge and belief) is his immediate landlord, and when his own tenancy will expire. Section 40 is however defective in three respects. The questions asked in the notices are insufficiently extensive to enable the server to establish all the relevant facts from the replies.[4] Secondly, the notices do not require the recipient to notify the server of any future change in relevant circumstances.[4] Thirdly, no sanction is prescribed for failure by the recipient to respond within the prescribed period of one month.[5] Prudence would appear to dictate that, except where a landlord or tenant is absolutely sure of all the relevant facts,[6] notices under s 40 should be served either before or simultaneously[7] with all notices under ss 25, 26 and 27 of the 1954 Act.[8]

1   Prescribed by the Landlord and Tenant Act 1954 Part II (Notices) Regulations 1983 Form No 9.
2   Ie the premises sublet, the term of the letting, the rent, the subtenant's name and whether or not there has been a further subletting.
3   Must be in prescribed form (see note 1 above). Forms 10 and 11.
4   For a precedent of a supplemental tenant's information augmenting the prescribed form (ie Form 10) see 22 Encyclopaedia of Forms and Precedents (5th edn) Form 223.
5   It has been suggested that failure to respond may entitle the server of the notice to set up a waiver or estoppel of some kind preventing the defaulting party from taking advantage of such failure, eg a landlord may be estopped from pleading tenant's failure to serve a counter-notice within two months if the tenant is prevented from identifying the competent landlord on whom to serve it. Whether or not such an argument could apply to the suggested non-statutory forms is uncertain. Damages or mandatory injunctions have been suggested also as remedies.
6   Eg where the landlord is freeholder and tenant is a business tenant in occupation.
7   Serving s 40 information notices simultaneously with other notices can only be safely recommended where at least one month of the relevant period for service of the other notice remains; in case the reply should reveal that a different landlord is competent.
8   Unless perhaps it is felt that the service of a notice under s 40(2) by a tenant who was proposing to serve a Section 26 Request (see para 14.9 above) would alert a 'dormant' landlord into serving a Section 25 Notice.

D   SPECIAL CASES

14.22   *Business tenancies held on trust.* Where a tenancy is held on trust, occupation and the carrying on of a business by all or any of the beneficiaries is treated as occupation or the carrying on of a business by the tenant,[1] but it is the trustee, as the person in whom the legal estate is vested, who must make application to the court for a new tenancy,[2] albeit that he will hold any new tenancy upon the same trusts as he held the old tenancy. A change in the persons of the trustee is not to be treated as a change in the person of the tenant.[3] Where the landlord's interest is held on trust, the intention of the beneficiaries or any of them to occupy the holding for the purposes, or partly for the purposes, of a business, or as a residence, may be a ground on which an application for a new tenancy may be opposed.[4]

1   1954 Act, s 41(1). See *Teba Fabrics Ltd v Conn* (1958) 171 Estates Gazette 495.
2   Ibid, s 41A reversing (in the situations to which it applies). *Jacobs v Chaudhuri* [1968] 2 QB 470, [1968] 2 All ER 124, CA.
3   Ibid, s 41(1)(c). It is uncertain how far this will apply to a case where the business is carried on by a company controlled by the tenant: *Pegler v Craven* [1952] 2 QB 69, [1952] 1 All ER 685, CA.
4   1954 Act, s 41(2). By virtue of s 41(2) the ground of opposition to a new tenancy open to a landlord under s 30(1)(g) is extended to landlord/trustees whose beneficiaries have the necessary intention of occupying the holding (see para 14.35 below and *Frish Ltd v Barclays Bank Ltd* [1955] 2 QB 541 at 554, [1955] 3 All ER 185, CA). For the purposes of the 1954 Act, s 30(2) (the 'five year rule': see para 14.36 below), the reference to the creation of the landlord's interest includes the creation of a trust except in the case of a trust arising by will or on intestacy: s 41(2).

14.23   *Business tenancy held by partnership.* Special provisions apply where all of the following conditions are satisfied:

(a) a tenancy is held jointly by two or more persons;[1]
(b) the property comprised in the tenancy is or includes premises occupied for the purposes of a business;[2]
(c) the business, or some other business, was at some time during the existence of the tenancy carried on in partnership by all the persons who were then the joint tenants or by those and other persons, and the joint tenants' interest in the premises was then partnership property;[3]
(d) the business is carried on (whether alone or in partnership with other persons) by one or some of the joint tenants and no part of the property comprised in the tenancy is occupied for the purposes of a business carried on by the other or others.[4]

Any notice given by the business tenants[5] which, had it been given by all the joint tenants, would have been a Section 26 Request[6] or a notice terminating a fixed term[7] must be treated as such if it states that it is given by virtue of these provisions[8] and sets out the facts by virtue of which the persons giving it are the business tenants.[9] A Section 25 Notice given by the landlord to the business tenants which, had it been given to all the joint tenants, would have been a notice terminating the tenancy[10] must be treated as such a notice.[11] An application for a new tenancy[12] may, instead of being made by all the joint tenants, be made by the business tenants alone.[13] The business tenants are liable, to the exclusion of the other joint tenants, for the payment of rent and the discharge of any other obligation under the current tenancy for any rental period beginning after the date specified in the landlord's Section 25 Notice[14] or in the Section 26 Request[15] for a new tenancy.[16] Where the court makes an order for the grant of a new tenancy[17] on an application made by the business tenants it may order the grant to be made to them or to them jointly with the persons carrying on the business in partnership with them, and may order the grant to be made subject to the satisfaction, within a specified time, of such conditions as to guarantors, sureties or otherwise as appear to the court equitable, having regard to the omission of the other joint tenants from the persons who will be the tenant under the new tenancy.[18] The business tenants are entitled to recover any amount payable[19] by way of compensation.[20] These special provisions[21] do not avoid notices given to or requests or applications made by those persons who would ordinarily be regarded as the tenants notwithstanding that they are not the business tenants,[22] nor are they of any assistance unless all of the conditions referred to are satisfied.[23]

1   1954 Act, s 41A(1)(a).
2   Ibid, s 41A(1)(b).
3   Ibid, s 41A(1)(c).
4   Ibid, s 41A(1)(d).
5   In ibid, s 41A(3)–(7), those of the joint tenants who for the time being carry on the business are referred to as the business tenants and the others as the other joint tenants: s 41A(2).
6   See paras 14.9–14.10 above.
7   See para 14.17 above.
8   Ibid, s 41A(3).
9   Ibid, s 41A(3). References in ss 24A, 26, 27, are to be construed accordingly.
10 See paras 14.7–14.8 above.
11 Ibid, s 41A(4).
12 Ie under ibid, s 24(1).
13 Ibid, s 41A(5). Where an application is made by the business tenants alone, Part II has effect as if references to the tenant included references to the business tenants alone: s 41A(5)(a).
14 See paras 14.7–14.8 above.
15 See paras 14.9–14.11 above.
16 Ibid, s 41A(5)(b).
17 Ie under ibid, s 29(1).

18 Ibid, s 41A(6).
19 Ie under ibid, s 37 or s 39.
20 Ibid, s 41A(7).
21 Ie ibid, s 41A.
22 If partners choose not to rely upon the special provisions, then *Jacobs v Chaudhuri* [1968] 2 QB 470, [1968] 2 All ER 124, CA, will still apply, so that all of the original tenants must act conjointly in taking each step under the statutory procedure for renewing the tenancy.
23 It frequently occurs that all of the partners in whom the old lease was vested have retired, and that they hold the current tenancy as trustees for their successors in the partnership, either by reason of a declaration of trust or (more often) informally as a result of selling out their interest in the partnership to the continuing partners. In such circumstances, the special provisions as to trusts apply (see para 14.22 above) but the special provisions as to partnerships are of no assistance at all as the current partners in the business are not business tenants for the purposes of the 1954 Act.

14.24 *Business tenancy held by group of companies.* Where a tenancy is held by a member of a group[1] of companies, occupation and the carrying on of a business by another member of the group is treated[2] as equivalent to occupation or the carrying on of a business by the member of the group holding the tenancy.[3] An assignment of a tenancy from one member of the group to another is not to be treated as a change in the person of the tenant,[4] and for the purposes of the 'five year rule'[5] the purchase of an interest by one member of a group from another member, or the grant of a tenancy by one member of a group to another member, is to be disregarded.[6]

1 For this purpose two bodies corporate are taken to be members or a group if and only if one is a subsidiary of the other or both are subsidiaries of a third body corporate: 1954 Act, s 42(1). 'Subsidiary' has the meaning assigned to it for the purposes of the Companies Act 1985, s 736.
2 Ie for the purposes of ibid, s 23.
3 Ibid, s 42(2). In relation to a tenancy to which Part II (ss 23–46) applies by virtue of s 42(2), references (however expressed) in Part II to the business of, or to use, occupation or enjoyment by, the tenant, are to be construed as including references to the business of, or to the use, occupation or enjoyment by, the other member: s 42(2)(a).
4 Ibid, s 42(2)(c). Where the landlord's interest is held by a member of a group the reference in s 30(1)(g) (see paras 14.31, 14.32 and 14.35) to intended occupation by the landlord for the purposes of a business to be carried on by him must be construed as including intended occupation by any member of the group for the purposes of a business to be carried on by that member: s 42(3)(a); Law of Property Act 1969, s 10.
5 1954 Act, s 30(2). See para 14.36.
6 Ibid, s 42(3)(b); Law of Property Act 1969, s 10.

14.25 *Variations dependant upon identity of the landlord.* The rights of a tenant under the 1954 Act may be curtailed on the grounds of public interest when the tenant or a superior landlord is a government department, local authority, development corporation, statutory undertaker, Health Authority,[1] or the National Trust.[2] The appropriate Minister may certify that the premises are required for the purposes of the body in question and where this occurs, the tenant will not be granted a new tenancy for a term that extends beyond the date specified in the certificate.[2] In addition, where the landlord's interest is held by a government department, the Minister may certify that for reasons of national security it is necessary for the use or occupation of the property to be discontinued or changed, and this will preclude the grant of a new tenancy.[3] In both cases, a tenant who is precluded from obtaining a new tenancy, or a tenancy that extends beyond the date in the certificate, will in certain circumstances be entitled to compensation.[4] The rights of a tenant can also be modified where the landlord is the Minister of Technology or an Industrial

Estates Corporation and the premises are within a development area[5] or where the landlord, or a superior landlord, is the Welsh Development Agency,[6] the Development Board for Rural Wales[7] or the incumbent of a benefice.[8] The 1954 Act binds the Crown[9] and thus a tenant of the Crown including a government department is entitled to protection[10] as is a government department when itself a tenant.

1   Regional or Area.
2   1954 Act, s 57, see *R v Secretary of State for the Environment, ex p Powis* [1981] 1 All ER 788, [1981] 1 WLR 584, CA.
3   Ibid, s 58.
4   Ibid, s 59.
5   Or an intermediate area specified in Orders made under the Local Employment Act 1972: ibid, s 60.
6   Ibid, s 60A.
7   Ibid, s 60B.
8   Ibid, s 61.
9   Ibid, s 56. Note *Linden v Department of Health and Social Security* [1986] 1 All ER 691, [1986] 1 EGLR 108.
10   Subject to ss 57 and 58 (see above).

E   ASSIGNMENT OF A LEASE DURING THE RENEWAL PROCEDURE

14.26   *Continuation under ss 24 and 64.* A tenancy to which the Act applies continues after its contractual term until terminated as provided by the Act.[1] If a Section 25 Notice[2] or Section 26 Request[3] is served and the tenant applies to the court for a new tenancy, the current tenancy will not end until a date three months after the application is finally disposed of.[4] This statutory extension, unlike a statutory tenancy under the Rent Act, is a continuation of the tenancy itself, subject only to a variation as to the mode of its termination,[5] rather than the creation of some new interest. As such the tenant of such a tenancy clearly has a right to assign subject to the alienation provisions of the lease.[6]

1   Ie under the 1954 Act, s 24 – see para 14.6 above.
2   See paras 14.7–14.8 above.
3   See paras 14.9–14.10 above.
4   Ie under the 1954 Act, s 64 – see para 14.14 above.
5   See dicta of Denning LJ in *HL Bolton (Engineering) Co Ltd v TJ Graham & Sons Ltd* [1957] 1 QB 159 at 168, CA.
6   In the overwhelming majority of cases, landlords consent will be necessary. Where the covenant is qualified (see para 7.4 above) it is suggested in the absence of direct authority that it would not be possible for the landlord reasonably to withhold consent on the ground of the renewal itself unless the assignment would confer on the assignee a right to renew not possessed by the assignor. See *Lee v K Carter Ltd* [1949] 1 KB 85, [1948] 2 All ER 690, CA where a company tenant of a lease which fell within the Rent Acts was refused consent to assign to a director. Unlike the company, the director would have been able to claim protection as a statutory tenant and the refusal was thus held to be reasonable.

14.27   *Practical considerations and solutions.* The purchaser of a lease where the contractual term has expired will be wary of taking an assignment for a number of reasons:
(a)   If no notice has been served and the tenancy is continuing by virtue of s 24,[1] the landlord may at any time serve such notice[2] and oppose the grant of a new tenancy on grounds of which the purchaser had no knowledge.[3]

(b) If a Section 25 Notice has been served, a purchaser would be unwise to proceed until he had satisfied himself that the tenant had complied with the strict time limits for serving counternotice,[4] applying to the court[5] and serving the proceedings on the landlord.[6]

(c) Uncertainty over the terms of the new tenancy[7] will pervade all negotiations for the assignment. Although the landlord may be willing to indicate the basic terms he would be prepared to accept, such terms are usually subject to contract and formal lease. The assignee is thus taking on a negotiation and, possibly, a court application.[8] From the assignor's point of view, the uncertainty over rent and terms means that few purchasers will be prepared to offer more than a nominal premium for an assignment of the tenancy.

(d) The right of a tenant to renew is dependent upon the tenancy at all times during the renewal procedure conforming to the provisions of s 23 of the Act.[9] In particular, this requires continuous occupation of the premises by the tenant for the purpose of the business carried out by the tenant.[10] An assignee will, therefore be concerned to ensure that the assignor does not cease trading from the premises.[10]

1   See para 14.6 above.
2   Ie a Section 25 Notice (see paras 14.7–14.8 above). A landlord who has allowed a tenancy to continue under s 24 may be inefficient or may simply be waiting to establish grounds for opposition, for example to have formed the required 'intention' (see paras 14.31–14.32 below) or to have avoided the 'five year rule' (se para 14.36 below). In the case of the former, he is likely to be alerted to the termination of the contractual term by a request for consent to assign and serve his Section 25 Notice.
3   See 1954 Act, s 30(1) and section F below.
4   See para 14.8 above.
5   See paras 14.8–14.9 above.
6   See para 14.12 above.
7   And indeed in some case the extent of the premises themselves because if part of the premises in the current tenancy have been sublet, the landlord may wish to deal direct with the subtenants of the sublet part, or require the tenant to renew the lease of the entirely of the premises originally demised (1954 Act, s 32(2)).
8   1954 Act, s 29.
9   See para 13.1:2 above.
10 See *I and H Caplan Ltd v Caplan (No 2)* [1963] 2 All ER 930, [1963] 1 WLR 1247 and *Morrison Holdings Ltd v Manders Property (Wolverhampton) Ltd* [1976] 2 All ER 205, [1976] 1 WLR 533, CA. Whether the tenant continues in occupation for business purposes is a question of fact. Protection is not lost merely by the tenant ceasing physically to occupy the premises, but the thread of continuity of business must not be broken. Where occupation is impossible because of circumstances beyond the tenant's control, it is sufficient that the tenant continued to exert his right to occupy.

14.28   *The assignment.* Despite these uncertainties,[1] tenants can and do assign tenancies continuing under ss 24[2] and 64[3]. In many cases, the premiums payable on such assignments bear no relation to the intrinsic value of the tenancy but represent 'key money', or the desire of tenants to occupy a particular property, especially in profitable retail locations such as shopping centres and high streets. In most cases, provided that the landlord is satisfied with the prospective assignee, he will be prepared to agree a form of lease and give consent to the assignment. Completion will then take place through an assignment of the existing tenancy[4] and a simultaneous agreement for lease between the landlord and the assignee.[5] Alternatively the tenant may surrender the existing tenancy in consideration of the simultaneous grant of a new lease to the assignee and the payment by the assignee of the agreed premium.[6] There is, of course, nothing to prevent a tenant from entering into a new lease with the landlord and immediately assigning it with the landlord's consent. This method, however, imposes upon the tenant liability by privity of contract for the remainder of the new term and is unlikely to be an attractive proposition to him.[7]

1   Ie those set out in para 14.27 above.
2   See para 14.6 above.
3   See para 14.14 above.
4   For precedents of an agreement to assign and the assignment of a lease that is close to expiry or continuing under ss 24 and 64, see 22 Encyclopaedia of Forms and Precedents (5th edn) Forms 254 and 263.
5   For a precedent, see ibid, Form 1. Such an agreement brings to an end the current tenancy: see para 14.18 above.
6   The former is preferable, as any agreement to surrender will only be enforceable if sanctioned by the court under s 38(4)(b) of the Act: see para 14.5 above.
7   As to privity of contract, see paras 5.5 and 5.14–5.16.

F   OPPOSITION BY THE LANDLORD

14.29   *Grounds for opposition.* The seven grounds upon which the landlord may oppose the tenant's application for the grant of a new tenancy are:[1]
(a)   breach of the tenant's repairing obligations;[2]
(b)   persistent delay in paying the rent;[3]
(c)   substantial breaches of the tenant's other obligations, or any other reason connected with the tenant's use or management of the holding;[4]
(d)   the provision of suitable alternative accommodation;[5]
(e)   where the current tenancy is a subletting of part only of the property comprised in a headlease and the reversioner of that headlease can demonstrate that the property could, more economically, be let as a whole;[6]
(f)   that the landlord intends to demolish, re-construct or carry out substantial works of construction;[7]
(g)   that the landlord intends to occupy the premises for the purposes of a business carried on by himself (or a company which he controls) or as his residence although this ground is not available to a landlord who has purchased his interest in the property within the preceding five years.[8]
Even if the landlord makes out grounds under paragraphs (a), (b), (c) or (e) the court retains a general discretion – it must still consider whether the tenant ought not to be granted a new tenancy.[9] There is not such discretion under the other grounds.

1   1954 Act, s 30(1).
2   The discretion which is vested in the court means that the seriousness of the breach has to be considered, including, no doubt, the tenant's willingness and capacity to remedy the breach. The fact that the tenant proposes to sell his interest with the benefit of any new tenancy ordered is not a relevant consideration: *Lyons v Central Commercial Properties Ltd* [1958] 2 All ER 767, [1958] 1 WLR 869, CA. See also *Nihad v Chain* (1956) 167 Estates Gazette 139; *Eichner v Midland Bank Executor and Trustee Co Ltd* [1970] 2 All ER 597, [1970] 1 WLR 1120, CA; *Hutchinson v Lamberth* (1983) 270 Estates Gazette 545, CA.
3   The requirement of persistent delay means that there must have been more than one occasion involving one short delay in paying rent. Presumably the persistent delay may mean that one instalment of rent was in arrear for a significant period of time, or that instalments have persistently been paid late, or both. The inconvenience and expense that has been imposed on the landlord in recovering the rent is clearly a material factor to be considered by the court in deciding whether a new tenancy ought to be granted. See *Hopcutt v Carver* (1969) 209 Estates Gazette 1069, CA and *Horowitz v Ferrand* [1956] CLY 4843 (county court).

4 Any breach of any obligation under the current tenancy can be relied upon by the landlord but in exercising its discretion the court will consider the seriousness of the breach, proposals for its remedy and whether the landlord has acquiesced in it: see *Eichner v Midland Bank Executor and Truste Co Ltd* [1970] 2 All ER 597, [1970] 1 WLR 1120, CA. Paragraph (c) is not limited to matters concerned with the relationship between landlord and tenant: see *Turner and Bell v Searles (Stanford-le-Hope) Ltd* (1977) 33 P & CR 208, CA. In considering such a matter as this the court is entitled to consider the intended future use of the premises as well as the past use. See also *Beard (formerly Coleman) v Williams* [1986] 1 EGLR 148, 278 Estates Gazette 1087, CA. As to breaches of covenant against committing a nuisance or annoyance, see *Norton v Charles Deane Productions Ltd* (1969) 214 Estates Gazette 559. As to waiver, see *Jones v Christy* (1963) 107 Sol Jo 374, CA.

5 Note the application of Part IV of Sch 15 to the Rent Act 1977 dealing with suitable alternative accommodation and the criteria to be applied in determining whether the accommodation is suitable. See also *Singh v Malayan Theatres Ltd* [1953] AC 632, CA. A part of the premises can probably rank as alternative accommodation as is the case under the Rent Act 1977: see *Mykolyshyn v Noah* [1971] 1 All ER 48, [1970] 1 WLR 1217, CA.

6 Note *Greaves Organisation Ltd v Stanhope Gate Property Co Ltd* (1973) 228 Estates Gazette 725. This paragraph is frequently criticised (by landlords) as being too narrowly drafted – for example: (a) the ground is based upon a difference in rental values. This is often difficult to prove, forcing the landlord to grant a new lease to the former subtenant. This lease (being a lease of part of the building) may have to impose obligations on the landlord to manage the building and to provide services etc. Any new letting of other parts of the building might have to follow the same form. The former intermediate lease may have left the landlord with little or no management or maintenance responsibility, and letting the property in a number of parts in this way might well adversely affect the value of the landlord's reversion from an investment viewpoint, even if there were no diminution in the rental income. Thus it is suggested that the rental value should not be the sole possible ground of opposition – a wider test such as 'damage to the reversion' – should be substituted; (b) only the effect on the property comprised in the headlease can be considered and the landlord cannot invite the court to have regard to the effect on *other* properties – for example if the headlease had been of two floors and the sublease of one, it would not be possible to look at the building as a whole.

7 See paras 14.31–14.34 below.

8 See paras 14.31–14.32 and 14.35–14.37 below.

9 By the use of the words 'ought not to be granted' in these paragraphs: see for example *Hurstfell Ltd v Leicester Square Property Co Ltd* [1988] 2 EGLR 105, [1988] 37 EG 109, CA.

14.30 *Timing.* The question arises of the date at which the court must judge the issues under paragraphs (a), (b) and (c). The decision of the House of Lords in *Betty's Cafes Ltd v Phillips Furnishing Stores Ltd*[1] establishes that in respect of (f) and (g), the intention of the landlord has to be judged at the actual hearing. There is support in the speeches for the view that as regards paragraphs (a), (b) and (c) the court must likewise have regard to the factual situation at the date of the hearing, but may also consider the facts as at the date of the landlord's notice under ss 25 or 26(6). The landlord is restricted to those grounds of opposition that have been stated in his notice under ss 25 or 26(6).[2]

1 [1959] AC 20, [1958] 1 All ER 607. See also *Spook Erection Ltd v British Railways Board* [1988] 1 EGLR 76, [1988] 21 EG 73, CA.

2 See *Nursey v P Currie (Dartford) Ltd* [1959] 1 All ER 497, [1959] 1 WLR 273, CA (but see *Hutchinson v Lamberth* (1983) 270 Estates Gazette 545, CA). Section 30(1) reads 'the grounds on which a landlord may oppose . . . are such of the following grounds, as may be stated in the landlord's notice'. It is in principle possible that a landlord has in the past acted in such a way that he is estopped from relying on a particular ground of opposition, but, in accordance with the general principles of promissory estoppel, a clear and unambiguous promise or assurance on the part of the landlord must be established if the tenant is to rely on such a plea: see *Spence v Shell UK Ltd* (1980) 256 Estates Gazette 55, CA.

14.31 *Demolition or reconstruction (paragraph (f)): intention.* To succeed under paragraph (f) the landlord will have to show that he *intends* to demolish or reconstruct the premises. There are two elements of the concept of intention – a genuine desire that a particular result will come about, and a reasonable prospect of bringing about that result. The project must have moved out of the zone of contemplation – out of the sphere of the tentative, the provisional and the exploratory – into the valley of decision.[1] Most projects of development will require the approval of local or other authorities before they can be implemented. It is obviously preferable that the landlord has obtained the necessary permission by the hearing, but failure to do so will not be fatal since the test is whether there is a reasonable prospect of getting consent.[2] Providing the landlord can establish his intention as a matter of fact, his motive for carrying out the work is irrelevant. Thus it does not matter that the primary object of the landlord is to occupy the reconstructed premises himself.[3] Similarly an intention to demolish is not made ineffective by the fact that it is ancillary to an intention to incorporate the cleared land in an agricultural holding.[4] The landlord does not have to show that he will do the work with his own hands – it is enough if the work will be carried out by his employees or by contractors under a building contract, or through the medium of a building lease to be entered into.[5] The intention which has to be proved can, in the case of a corporate body, be proved by any relevant and admissible evidence. A resolution of the body, such as the board of directors of a company incorporated under the Companies Acts or by the council when the body is a local authority, is preferable from an evidential point of view but is not essential.[6] If the landlord intends merely to sell the premises for the purchaser to carry out the works he cannot rely upon paragraph (f) but can do so if he intends to carry out the redevelopment by means of a building lease.[7] A landlord, therefore, who is seeking to rely upon paragraph (f) should ensure that, if a corporation, there is a recent and appropriately worded resolution of the corporation, that any requisite consents and approvals (for example, planning permission or listed building consent) have been obtained, that plans and specifications have been prepared, that either a building contract has been entered into for the proposed works or at least that evidence is available that a contract will be entered into in good time,[8] that the necessary finance for the project is or can be made available, and that the project will not be held up by some impediment, such as a tenant of another part of the building who cannot be removed.

1   *Cunliffe v Goodman* [1950] 2 KB 237, [1950] 1 All ER 720, CA per Asquith LJ at 254 and 725. These observations were approved by the House of Lords in *Betty's Cafes Ltd v Phillips Funishing Stores Ltd* [1959] AC 20, [1958] 1 All ER 607, HL. See also *Fisher v Taylors Furnishing Stores Ltd* [1956] 2 QB 78, [1956] 2 All ER 78, CA; *Reohorn v Barry Corpn* [1956] 2 All ER 742, [1956] 1 WLR 845, CA (compare with *P F Ahern & Sons Ltd v Hunt* [1988] 1 EGLR 74, [1988] 21 EG 69, CA); *Fleet Electrics Ltd v Jacey Investments Ltd* [1956] 3 All ER 99, [1956] 1 WLR 1027, CA; *DAF Motoring Centre (Gosport) Ltd v Hutfield and Wheeler Ltd* (1982) 263 Estates Gazette 976, CA; *Europark (Midlands) Ltd v Town Centre Securities plc* [1985] 1 EGLR 88, 274 Estates Gazette 289; *A Levy & Son Ltd v Martin Brent Developments Ltd* [1987] 2 EGLR 93, 283 Estates Gazette 646; *Capocci v Goble* [1987] 2 EGLR 102, 284 Estates Gazette 230, CA.

2   *Gregson v Cyril Lord Ltd* [1962] 3 All ER 907, [1963] 1 WLR 41, CA. *Westminster City Council v British Waterways Board* (1983) 268 Estates Gazette 145. The 1954 Act did not contemplate the major redevelopment schemes of the type that are seen today. The 'development process' may be so long and complex that the landlord will be unable to satisfy the intended requirement when the first leases of properties falling parts of the site expire. His only option here is to argue that a short term or a break clause be inserted in the renewed lease – see para 14.47 footnote 5 below.

3   *Betty's Cafes Ltd v Phillips Furnishing Stores Ltd* [1959] AC 20, [1958] 1 All ER 607, HL; approving *Fisher v Taylors Furnishing Stores Ltd* [1956] 2 QB 78, [1956] 2 All ER 78, CA; see also *Town Tailors Ltd v Peacock's Stores Ltd* (1956) 167 Estates Gazette 292, CA. Observations to the

contrary in *Atkinson v Bettison* [1955] 3 All ER 340, [1955] 1 WLR 1127, CA are no longer good law.

4   *Craddock v Hampshire County Council* [1958] 1 All ER 449, [1958] 1 WLR 202, CA.

5   *Gilmour Caterers Ltd v St Bartholomew's Hospital Governors* [1956] 1 QB 387, [1956] 1 All ER 314, CA; *Reohorn v Barry Corpn* [1956] 2 All ER 742, [1956] 1 WLR 845, CA; *Bites v Caeser* [1957] 1 All ER 151, [1957] 1 WLR 156, CA; *P F Ahern & Sons Ltd v Hunt* [1988] 1 EGLR 74, [1988] 21 EG 69 (a decision criticised in (1988) 9 PLB 1).

6   *H L Bolton Engineering Co Ltd v T J Graham & Sons Ltd* [1957] 1 QB 159, [1956] 3 All ER 624, CA; *Fleet Electrics Ltd v Jacey Investments Ltd* [1956] 3 All ER 99, [1956] 1 WLR 1027, CA; *Betty's Cafes Ltd v Phillips Furnishing Stores Ltd* [1959] AC 20, [1958] 1 All ER 607, HL; *Poppett's (Caterers) Ltd v Maidenhead Borough Council* [1970] 3 All ER 289, [1971] 1 WLR 69, CA. As to when directors do not have adequate powers, see *A and W Birch Ltd v P B (Sloane) Ltd and Cadogan Settled Estates Co* (1956) 167 Estates Gazette 283. As to intention of regional manager, see *Manchester Garages Ltd v Petrofina UK* (1974) 233 Estates Gazette 509, CA.

7   Even where the transaction looked at as a whole was tantamount to an outright disposal: *Spook Erection Ltd v British Railways Board* [1988] 1 EGLR 76, [1988] 21 EG 73, CA. See also footnote 5 above.

8   *A J A Smith Transport Ltd v British Railways Board* (1980) 257 Estates Gazette 1257, CA.

14.32   *Demolition or reconstruction (paragraph (f)): time of intention and who must have it.* The intention of the landlord has to be established as at the date upon which the application is heard by the court.[1] In the view of the provisions for interim continuation,[2] the date of termination of the current tenancy cannot be assessed accurately at the hearing. However, apart from the possibility of an appeal the interim continuation will end approximately four and a half months after the decision of the court. As a matter of common sense, therefore, the landlord has to show an intention to start to carry out the work on which he relies at or shortly after a date which is four and a half months from the hearing. If he cannot establish his intention at that date but can do so in relation to a date within the next year he will be able to invoke the provisions of s 31(2). It is the person who is the landlord at the date of the hearing as defined in s 44 who must establish the requisite intention. Thus if the predecessor in title of the landlord has served a notice under s 25 or s 26(6), the present landlord can rely upon that notice at the hearing.[3] The survivor of two joint tenants is the person with legal title to the land who must prove the intention.[4] An executor can give a notice and evidence of his intention prior to probate: probate must, however, be obtained before judgment is given.

1   *Betty's Cafes Ltd v Phillips Furnishing Stores Ltd* [1959] AC 20, [1958] 1 All ER 607, HL. See also *AD Wimbush & Son Ltd v Franmills Properties Ltd* [1961] Ch 419, [1961] 2 All ER 197; *Marks v British Waterways Board* [1963] 3 All ER 28, [1963] 1 WLR 1008, CA; *Rumsey v Owen, White and Catlin* (1976) 241 Estates Gazette 611. If a preliminary issue is heard as to whether the landlord can establish his ground of opposition the relevant date is the hearing of that issue: *Dutch Oven Ltd v Egham Estate and Investment Co Ltd* [1968] 3 All ER 100, [1968] 1 WLR 1483.

2   1954 Act, s 64. See para 14.14 above.

3   *AD Wimbush & Son Ltd v Franmills Properties Ltd* [1961] Ch 419, [1961] 2 All ER 197; *Marks v British Waterways Board* [1963] 3 All ER 28, [1963] 1 WLR 1008, CA.

4   *Biles v Caesar* [1957] 1 All ER 151, [1957] 1 WLR 156, CA.

14.33   *Demolition or reconstruction (paragraph (f)).* The words of the statute are: 'to demolish or reconstruct the premises comprised in the holding or a substantial part of those premises or to carry out substantial work of construction on the holding or part thereof and that the landlord could not reasonably do so without obtaining possession of the holding'.[1] To reconstruct means to rebuild[2] and involves substantial interference with the structure.[3] Reconstruction implies the demolition of some structure which was previously there, whereas construction connotes building from scratch or adding to what was there.[4] If the holding is mainly unbuilt upon, the 'premises' capable of being demolished or reconstructed will, of course, be such structures as do exist.[5] The proper approach to the question whether or not what is intended will amount to reconstruction of a substantial part of the holding is to look at the position as a whole and compare the result on the premises of carrying out the proposed work with the condition and state of the premises before the work is done.[6] Thus, an intention to change the character or identity of premises from a small shop with two storage rooms into part of a large hall intended to become an amusement arcade was held to be within paragraph (f)[3] but an intention to effect a change of identity by converting three floors which had been occupied separately into a self-contained unit with internal staircases was held not to be covered by the paragraph.[7] Matters such as the making of a road, the laying of concrete and the laying of pipes, cables and drains may be works or construction.[8] To succeed under paragraph (f) the landlord must show that he could not carry out the demolition or reconstruction 'without obtaining possession of the holding'. It follows that if the lease reserves to the landlord rights of entry sufficient to carry out the work, he will not succeed under paragraph (f).[9] The word possession means legal right to possession and not physical possession.

1   See 1954 Act, s 30(1)(f). A criticism of this paragraph is that the works have to be substantial, *and* the works have to be substantial in relation to the tenant's holding (see for example *Barth v Pritchard* [1989] EGCS 124, CA). This can cause problems in the case of a major refurbishment of, for example, an office building. The proposals may involve the modernisation of the plant and machinery in the building including the lifts, the installation of air conditioning and double glazing, the strengthening of floors, the raising of floors, the installation of suspended ceilings etc. Thus the work taken as a whole is clearly substantial. And yet it might well be that in relation to the particular holding in question, the works would be trivial. In such circumstances the landlord may have great difficulty in opposing the grant of a new lease. In order to deal with this, the landlord may undertake more comprehensive work than was in fact needed, and this is hardly in the public interest. It is, however, in the public interest that buildings should be renewed and modernised in order to meet the current demands of commerce and industry.

  Section 31A was introduced by the 1969 Act (see para 14.34 below). By this the court was permitted to grant a new tenancy where the tenant was prepared to accept terms giving the landlord access to carry out work or was prepared to accept a lease of an economically severable part of the holding. This is, however, of little assistance because it could only apply if the landlord *had* established a ground to oppose the tenancy under paragraph (f). The whole problem is that the situation referred to above the landlord will *not* have such grounds. There are several possible reforms: (a) an amendment could be introduced by which work that even if it was insubstantial in relation to the holding would still fall within paragraph (f) if it was part of a substantial scheme relating to the building of which the holding formed part, or (b) leave s 30(1)(f) unamended but give the court express powers to insert terms that would facilitate a refurbishment scheme and then provide, for example, for there to be a rent review so that the open market rent for the refurbished premises could be determined giving the tenant the right to surrender thereafter.

2   *Percy E Cadle & Co Ltd v Jacmarch Properties Ltd* [1957] 1 QB 323, [1957] 1 All ER 148, CA.

3   *Joel v Swaddle* [1957] 3 All ER 325, [1957] 1 WLR 1094, CA. See also *Morar v Chauhan* [1985] 3 All ER 493, 276 Estates Gazette 300, CA.

4   See per Ormerod LJ in *Cook v Mott* [1961] 178 Estates Gazette 637, CA.

5   *Housleys Ltd v Bloomer-Holt Ltd* [1966] 2 All ER 966, [1966] 1 WLR 1244, CA.

6   *Joel v Swaddle*, supra; *Bewlay (Tobacconists) Ltd v British Bata Shoe Co Ltd* [1958] 3 All ER 652, [1959] 1 WLR 45, CA. The substantiality both of the works and of the part of the premises concerned is a question of fact in each case: see *Palser v Grinling* [1948] AC 291 at 317, HL (construing a provision in the Rents Acts) referred to by Hodson LJ in *Atkinson v Bettison* [1955] 3 All ER 340, [1955] 1 WLR 1127, CA.

7   *Atkinson v Bettison*, supra.

8   *Housleys Ltd v Bloomer-Holt Ltd* [1966] 2 All ER 966, [1966] 1 WLR 1244, CA. In *Botterill and Cheshire v Bedfordshire County Council* [1985] 1 EGLR 82, 273 Estates Gazette 1217, the Court of

Appeal held that the removal of top-soil and clay, filling the excavated space with refuse and then covering it with a fresh layer of clay and top-soil and planting trees did not fall within s 30(1)(f) and thus the County Council landlord's opposition to grant of a new tenancy on these grounds failed.

9 *Heath v Drown* [1973] AC 498, [1972] 2 All ER 561, HL; *Price v Esso Petroleum Co Ltd* (1980) 255 Estates Gazette 243, CA; *Leathwoods Ltd v Total Oil (Great Britain) Ltd* (1984) 270 Estates Gazette 1083; affd [1985] 2 EGLR 237, CA.

14.34 *Demolition or reconstruction (paragraph (f)): landlord access or tenancy of part.* Section 31A of the 1954 Act[1] provides that where the landlord opposes an application by the tenant under paragraph (f),[2] the court shall not hold that the landlord could not reasonably carry out the proposed work without obtaining possession if the tenant:

(a) agrees to give access to the landlord and, given access, the landlord could reasonably carry out the work without obtaining possession and without interfering substantially with the use of the premises for the tenant's business,[3] and

(b) is willing to accept a tenancy of an economically separable part of the holding.

1 This section was inserted by the Law of Property Act 1969, s 7(1).
2 In *Heath v Drown* [1973] AC 498, [1972] 2 All ER 561 the House of Lords reiterated that s 31A has no application unless the landlord could establish under paragraph (f) that it was necessary for him to obtain legal possession. Thus s 31A was not relevant where the landlord could have carried out the works by virtue of a right of entry contained in the lease.
3 See *Redfern v Reeves* (1978) 37 P & CR 364, CA; *Price v Esso Petroleum Co Ltd* (1980) 255 Estates Gazette 243, CA; *Leathwoods Ltd v Total Oil (Great Britain) Ltd* (1984) 270 Estates Gazette 1083; affd [1985] 2 EGLR 237, CA; *Mularczyk v Azralnove Investments Ltd* [1985] 2 EGLR 141, 276 Estates Gazette 1064, CA; *Cerex Jewels Ltd v Peachey Property Corpn plc* [1986] 2 EGLR 65, 279 Estates Gazette 971, CA; *Blackburn v Hussain* [1988] 1 EGLR 77, [1988] 22 EG 78, CA. For discussion, see (1988) 9 PLB 1.

14.35 *Occupation by the landlord (paragraph (g)).* The intention under this paragraph must be a real, fixed and settled intention as under paragraph (f).[1] Consequently factors such as the availability of planning permission for the use proposed by the landlord when a permission is needed will be relevant.[2] A landlord can rely on paragraph (g) when his intention is to carry on business at the premises in partnership with someone else,[3] or if his intention is to occupy through a manager of the business.[4] In *Parkes v Westminster Roman Catholic Diocese Trustee*[5] it was held that landlords, a body of trustees, could intend to occupy premises through the agency of a parish priest, and the Board of Governors of a teaching hospital successfully opposed an application for a new tenancy on the ground that they intended to occupy the premises for the purpose of a business to be carried on there by them when their intention was to sell the premises to the Minister of Health and then to use the premises themselves for hospital purposes as they ran the rest of the hospital.[6] A landlord will not be prevented from succeeding under paragraph (g) if he shows that he proposes to use a part, but not the whole, of the holding for the purpose of his business, the remaining part remaining unused.[7] Where paragraph (g) is relied upon the landlord is often willing to give an undertaking to the court that he will occupy the premises, something which adds materially to the evidence of a genuine intention to do so.[8] Even so an undertaking is not conclusive evidence of the genuineness of the landlord's intention. It is one of the factors to be considered and the court is entitled to conclude that the landlord has not proved a genuine intention to occupy the premises notwithstanding any undertaking offered.[9] It seems that the intention to occupy must be to occupy for more than a minimal period.[10]

1   See paras 14.31–14.32 above. See *Cox v Binfield* [1989] 1 EGLR 97, [1989] 01 EG 69, CA.
2   *Gregson v Cyril Lord Ltd* [1962] 3 All ER 907, [1963] 1 WLR 41, CA; *Westminster City Council v British Waterways Board* [1985] AC 676, [1984] 3 All ER 737, HL.
3   *Clift v Taylor* [1984] 2 KB 394, [1984] 2 All ER 113, CA; *Re Crowhurst Park, Sims-Hilditch v Simmons* [1974] 1 All ER 991, [1974] 1 WLR 583.
4   See for example *Street v Powell-Sneddon* [1988] 2 EGLR 112, [1988] 40 EG 116, CA. There seems to be no limitation on the nature of the business. Thus for example a trader could acquire the freehold of a competitor's shop and (subject to the five year rule – see para 14.36 below – and paying compensation – see paras 14.40 and 14.41) to rely upon the fact that he intended to carry out the same business at the shop to oppose under ground (g).
5   (1978) 36 P & CR 22, CA.
6   *Hills (Patents) Ltd v University College Hospital (Board of Governors)* [1956] 1 QB 90, [1955] 3 All ER 365, CA.
7   *Method Developments Ltd v Jones* [1971] 1 All ER 1027, [1971] 1 WLR 168, CA; but compare with *Nursey v P Currie (Dartford) Ltd* [1959] 1 All ER 497, [1959] 1 WLR 273, CA in which the premises let were a number of buildings in a yard. It was held that the landlords could not rely on ground (g) when they intended to demolish the buildings and to use the site together with adjoining land as a petrol filling station. The Court of Appeal in *Cam Gears Ltd v Cunningham* [1981] 2 All ER 560, [1981] 1 WLR 1011 found some difficulty in understanding the reasoning in *Nursey v P Currie (Dartford) Ltd*, supra. In that case the premises consisted of a vacant site with a hardstanding used by the tenant for car parking, and it was held that when the landlord erected a prefabricated building covering about a third of the site to be used for vehicle testing, he had satisfied s 30(1)(g). In *J W Thornton Ltd v Blacks Leisure Group plc* [1986] 2 EGLR 61, 279 Estates Gazette 588 the Court of Appeal felt that *Nursey* could be distinguished and preferred the ratio decidendi of Willmer LJ in Nursey to that of Wynn-Parry J. See also *Leathwoods Ltd v Total Oil (Great Britain) Ltd* [1985] 2 EGLR 237, CA; *Jones v Jenkins* [1986] 1 EGLR 113, 277 Estates Gazette 644, CA. It has been suggested (by for example Messrs Fogel, Freedman & Sweetman, see para 14.2 footnote 5) that the requirement in s 30(1)(g) that he must intende to occupy the *whole* holding could be unreasonably onerous on a landlord – the whole or a substantial part would be fairer.
8   *Espresso Coffee Machine Co Ltd v Guardian Assurance Co* [1959] 1 All ER 458, [1959] 1 WLR 250, CA.
9   *Lightcliffe and District Cricket and Lawn Tennis Club v Walton* (1977) 245 Estates Gazette 393, CA; *Chez Gerard Ltd v Greene Ltd* (1983) 268 Estates Gazette 575, CA.
10   *Willis v Association of Universities of the British Commonwealth* [1965] 1 QB 140, [1964] 2 All ER 39, CA; *Chez Gerard Ltd*, supra.

14.36   *Paragraph (g) – where landlord purchased within five years.* Paragraph (g) is subject to the qualification that the landlord cannot rely upon it if his interest was purchased or created within the period of five years immediately preceding the termination of the current tenancy, and the holding has been the subject of a business tenancy since the creation or purchase of that interest. Where the intention to occupy is by a company in which the landlord has a controlling interest, the landlord can rely on the intended occupation of that company for the purpose of paragraph (g).[1] The paragraph refers to the interest of the landlord when it originally arose and not necessarily the interest under which the landlord currently holds.[2] It was said obiter in *Diploma Laundry Ltd v Surrey Timber Co Ltd*[3] that the landlord's interest means the interest as at the date of the Section 25 Notice or Section 26 Request. If this is correct, then a landlord can serve a Section 25 Notice and then sell his interest and the purchaser will be able to rely on paragraph (g) even though his interest was purchased recently. Such a result is curious, and may not be followed should the matter arise again. The word 'purchased' is used in its modern popular sense of buying for money, and it does not include a surrender by operation of law.[4] In order to establish whether an interest has been purchased, it is proper to look at the whole transaction involved including the contract which preceded the transfer.[5] The word 'created' means the creation of the landlord's interest not the landlord's title to that interest. If it were otherwise, the word 'purchased' would be wholly redundant.[5] Where the interest in question is a reversionery lease, it is created when the lease is granted not when the term is to commence.[6] In determining the date for the termination of the current tenancy, any period of interim continuation under s 64 is to be ignored: the words 'comprised in a tenancy or successive tenancies' mean the interest of a subtenant not that of the landlord before a subletting.[2]

1   See the 1954 Act, s 30(3) added by the Law of Property Act 1969 reversing the decision in *Tunstall v Steigmann* [1962] 2 QB 593, [1962] 2 All ER 417, CA. See also *Harvey Textiles Ltd v Hillel* (1978) 249 Estates Gazette 1063.
2   *Artemiou v Procopiou* [1966] 1 QB 878, [1965] 3 All ER 539, CA. In that case the landlord had acquired a leasehold interest and, on its expiry, had been granted a new lease. The subtenant from him alleged that s 30(2) applied since the new lease was the purchase or creation of an interest within the five-year period. It was held that the new lease did not bring the landlord's interest within s 30(2).
3   [1955] 2 QB 604 [1955] 2 All ER 992, CA; see also *George Akin Ltd v Ward* [1981] CLY 1510 (county court).
4   *H L Bolton (Engineering) Co Ltd v T J Graham & Sons Ltd* [1957] 1 QB 159, [1956] 3 All ER 624, CA. Note *Frederick Lawrence Ltd v Freeman Hardy and Willis Ltd* [1959] Ch 731, [1959] 3 All ER 77, CA; *Morar v Chauhan* [1985] 3 All ER 493, 276 Estates Gazette 300, CA.
5   *Frederick Lawrence Ltd v Freeman Hardy and Willis Ltd* [1959] Ch 731, [1959] 3 All ER 77, CA. Thus where a contract does precede the actual transfer the five-year period runs from the date of the contract. As to where the landlord transferred the property to trustees to be held in trust for himself, see *Morar v Chauhan* [1985] 3 All ER 493, CA.
6   *Northcote Laundry Ltd v Frederick Donnelly Ltd* [1968] 2 All ER 50, [1968] 1 WLR 562, CA.

14.37   *Landlord succeeds or fails but would succeed later.* If the landlord establishes one or more of the grounds of opposition, the court will refuse to make an order for a new tenancy[1] and the current tenancy will come to an end in accordance with the interim continuation provisions.[2] The question of compensation will then arise.[3] Where the landlord has opposed under paragraphs (d), (e) or (f), the court may be satisfied that where these grounds had not been established at the date of termination specified in the Section 25 Notice or the Section 26 Request, they would be satisfied by some date up to a year later.[4] When this arises, the court must make a declaration to this effect, stating the date. The tenant then has two options – he may do nothing, in which case it is as if the landlord had succeeded in his opposition, or he can within 14 days apply to the court to order that the new date is substituted for the actual date of termination.

1   1954 Act, s 31(1). Note the court's discretion under paragraphs (a), (b), (c) and (e): see para 14.29, especially footnote 9.
2   1954 Act, s 64. See para 14.6 above.
3   1954 Act, s 37: see section G below.
4   1954 Act, s 31(2). See *Accountancy Personnel Ltd v Worshipful Co of Salters* (1972) 222 Estates Gazette 1589, CA.

14.38   *Landlord does not oppose new tenancy or fails in his opposition.* Where the landlord does not oppose the grant of a new tenancy, or fails in his opposition,[1] and the terms of the new letting cannot be agreed, the court will determine them[2] in accordance with ss 32–35.[3]

1   Ie under 1954 Act, s 30(1).
2   Ibid, s 29(1).

3   Ibid, s 32 (premises to be demised: see section H below), s 33 (duration of term: see section I below), s 34 (rent: see section J below), and s 35 (alternations: see section K below).

14.39   *Landlord does not carry out intention.* What rights does a tenant have where the landlord has successfully opposed the grant of a new tenancy under paragraphs (f) or (g) but then does not implement his intention to redevelop or occupy? Section 55 of the 1954 Act[1] provides that if the court refuses an order for a new tenancy and the decision was induced by misrepresentation or concealment of material facts,[2] the court may order the landlord to pay the tenant compensation for any resulting damage or loss.[3] This section, however, has two deficiences so far as the tenant is concerned:

(a) it applies only if the tenant has applied to the court and the court has refused to grant the new tenancy – a tenant who accepts the landlord's word and does not apply to the court for a new tenancy will have no rights under s 55,[4] and

(b) it applies only where there has been misrepresentation or concealment – a tenant will have no rights if at the time the landlord genuinely believed that he would implement the redevelopment or occupancy – but then changed his mind or circumstances meant that it was not possible.[5]

1   See Appendix 3 below.
2   The tenant need not establish actual fraud: *Thorne v Smith* [1947] KB 307, [1947] 1 All ER 39, CA.
3   A misrepresentation made in evidence may constitute perjury. A tenant may also be able to sue for damages in the tort of deceit.
4   Until 1969 this deficiency also applied to compensation under the 1954 Act, s 37 – see paras 14.40–14.41 below. The Law of Property Act 1969, s 11, however, amended s 37(1) and since then a tenant is entitled to compensation under s 37 even if he does not apply to the court. The Law Commission ((1988) LCWP No 111 para 3.6.16) has suggested that the same approach ought to be adopted in s 55.
5   Whether this is a deficiency that requires amendment is, of course, a matter of policy – some might argue that an 'innocent' landlord, who had neither misrepresented nor concealed, ought not to have to pay compensation even if it so happens that the tenant has been 'wrongly' dispossessed. If change was felt desirable, no proposal for reform is without its complications. It is sometimes suggested that a restriction in the form of a restrictive covenant could be imposed on the land, but this would raise complex registration issues. Alternatively the landlord could be compelled in every instance to give an undertaking to the court to occupy or redevelop as appropriate. If this proved impossible, then the landlord could go back to the court and apply to be released from his undertaking. The court would examine the circumstances of the case and could award the tenant compensation if it was considered appropriate on the particular facts. The problem here, however, is that an application to the court would be required every time.

G   COMPENSATION

14.40   *Payable to the tenant.* If the court is precluded from ordering a new tenancy solely on one of the grounds set out in paragraphs (e), (f) or (g) of 30(1),[1] the tenant will be entitled to compensation. Initially that compensation was the rateable value of the demised premises,[2] unless the premises had been occupied wholly or partly for the purposes of a business carried on by the occupier (or his predecessor) for fourteen years, in which case the compensation was twice the rateable value.[3] This was increased, however, by the Local Government, Planning and Land Act 1980 and the Landlord and Tenant Act 1954 (Appropriate Multiplier) Regulations 1981,[4] and then (with effect from 7 May 1984[4]) by the Landlord and Tenant Act 1954 (Appropriate

Multiplier) Order 1984 '3 times the rateable value' being substituted for 'rateable value'.[5]

1 See section F above. Originally such compensation was only payable (in the absence of agreement, for which no express provision was made) where the court had made an order that it had precluded from granting a new tenancy, but the effect of amendments introduced by the Law of Property Act 1969 is that the tenant is also entitled to compensation if the Landlord Notice (under s 25 or 26(6)) specifies one or more of these grounds (and no others) and either the tenant does not apply to the court or withdraws his application.

2 1954 Act, s 37(3)(b).

3 1954 Act, s 37(2)(a). Some amendment was necessary in the light of the abolition of the statutory requirement for quinquennial revision of rateable values. Such compensation is not liable to capital gains tax: *Davis (Inspector of Taxes) v Powell* [1977] 1 All ER 471, [1977] 1 WLR 258; *Drummond (Inspector of Taxes) v Austin Brown* [1985] Ch 52, [1984] 2 All ER 699, CA.

4 *Department of the Environment v Royal Insurance plc* [1987] 1 EGLR 83, 282 Estates Gazette 208 discussed (1987) 283 Estates Gazette 852. As to when the 1981 Regulations took effect, see *Cardshops Ltd v John Lewis Properties Ltd* [1983] QB 161, [1982] 3 All ER 746, CA; *International Military Services Ltd v Capital and Counties plc* [1982] 2 All ER 20, [1982] 1 WLR 575; *Sperry Ltd v Hambro Life Assurance Ltd* (1982) 265 Estates Gazette 223. See generally *Re Crowhurst Park, Sims-Hilditch v Simmons* [1974] 1 All ER 991, [1974] 1 WLR 583; *Edicron Ltd v William Whiteley Ltd* [1984] 1 All ER 219, [1984] 1 WLR 59, CA.

5 So compensation currently is three times the rateable value or six times where the fourteen year rule applies.

6 But note *Re 14 Grafton Street, De Havilland (Antiques) Ltd v Certrovincial Estates (Mayfair) Ltd* [1971] Ch 935, [1971] 2 All ER 1.

14.41 *Exclusion of compensation by agreement.* The lease may provide for the tenant's right to compensation[1] to be excluded or modified[2] but such an agreement will be ineffective if on the date the tenant has to quit the premises they have been occupied:

(a) for the purposes of the business of the occupier for the preceeding five years or

(b) even where there has been a new occupier during that period, he was a successor to the business of the previous occupier such business being carried on (by the occupier or his predecessors) for the preceeding five years.

Landlords frequently insert a proviso in a lease by which the right to compensation is excluded.[4] This is of no direct concern to the original tenant, who will obviously be entitled to compensation at the end of the term if he is still in occupation[5] but should still be resisted because it may affect the marketability of the lease especially during the last five years.[6] And yet it could operate against the landlord on the last rent review as this could be a factor, be it a small one, that could bring about a slight reduction in the rent.

1 See para 14.39 above.

2 1954 Act, s 38(3).

3 Ibid, s 38(2).

4 For a precedent, see 22 Encyclopaedia of Forms and Precedents (5th edn) Form 210.

5 Unless the lease is for less than five years and the tenant (or the tenant and his predecessors) has (have) not been carrying on the same business for five years.

6 If, however, the assignee proposed to carry on the assignor's business, so that the business would have been carried on for five years by the expiry of the lease, the point would not arise because such a clause would not then be effective in excluding compensation.

H THE TERMS OF THE NEW TENANCY – THE PREMISES

14.42 *The statutory provision.* The Act deals with the terms of new tenancies ordered by the court under the headings of the premises, duration, rent and other terms. As to the premises the general rule is that the new tenancy is to be of the holding,[1] that is all the property comprised in the tenancy but excluding any part not occupied by the tenant or an employee of his.[2] There are three exceptions:

(a) the landlord can require that the new tenancy shall comprise all the premises within the current tenancy not just the holding,[3]

(b) there may be a new tenancy of an economically separable part of the holding where the landlord intends to develop the remainder,[4]

(c) the parties can always agree that the new tenancy shall comprise premises different from just the holding.

1 As to when the holding no longer exists, see *Aireps Ltd v City of Bradford Metropolitan Council* [1985] 2 EGLR 143, 276 Estates Gazette 1067, CA.
2 1954 Act, s 32.
3 1954 Act, s 32(2).
4 1954 Act, ss 31A(1), 32(1A).

14.43 *The tenant's rights.* Where the current tenancy includes rights enjoyed by the tenant in connection with the holding, these should be included in the new tenancy.[1] These, however, must be legal rights. In *G Orlik (Meat Products) Ltd v Hastings and Thanet Building Society*[2] the landlord's predecessor in title has permitted the tenant to park delivery vans on adjoining land owned by the landlord but no express right to do this was contained in the lease. The Court of Appeal held that the tenant under the lease did not have as against the landlord any right to park on this land[3] and refused to include a specific grant of such a right in the new lease. Thus when an additional right is granted during the term of a lease, the tenant should ensure that it is formally set out in a deed, and expressed to be additional to and forming part of the lease. Such a right would be enjoyed by the tenant in connection with the holding and would thus be included in the new tenancy.

1 1954 Act, s 32(3). This is a further reason for ensuring that the drafting of the lease leaves no uncertainty as to the rights that are included – see paras 4.2–4.9 above.
2 (1974) 29 P & CR 126. Note also *Nevill Long & Co (Boards) Ltd v Firmenich & Co* (1983) 268 Estates Gazette 572, CA.
3 The court was unwilling to imply a term into the lease to this effect, was not prepared to permit rectification where the original landlord had parted with the reversion, and held that, on the facts, estoppel did not apply. See also para 14.60 below. One could imagine situations in which the rigidity of these sections could give insufficient scope to reflect changes in the physical circumstances surrounding the tenancy. Fogel and Freedman (see para 14.2 above, footnote 5) refer to the fact that it is generally assumed that ss 32 and 35 do not give a court power to add to or alter the exceptions/reservations and that this could cause problems for a landlord who wanted, for example, to run conducting media through the demised premises, or to have access to the demised premises to carry out work to the common parts.

14.44 *Lapsed rights.* Furthermore the right in the current tenancy must still be subsisting. In *Kirkwood v Johnson*[1] the current tenancy had granted to the tenant an option to acquire the freehold that was exerciseable by notice given not less than nine months before the termination of the term. The Court of Appeal held that no such term should be included in the new lease because the option in the current tenancy had lapsed, but what would the position have been had there been no time limit on the exercise if the option in the current tenancy was left open?

1 (1979) 38 P & CR 392.

14.45 *'In connection with the holding'.* There is some uncertainty as to the proper construction of these words in s 32(3). In *Re No 1 Albemarle Street*[1] the current tenancy gave the tenant the right to maintain advertising signs on adjoining premises of the landlord. Upjohn J held that this was a personal right having no real connection with the property and thus could not be included under s 32(3). He did however include such a right in the new lease by virtue of s 35 of the 1954 Act and whether or not 'a right' that fails under s 32(3) can be included in the new lease by virtue of s 35,[2] is discussed in para 15.12:4 below. Upjohn J left open the question of whether or not 'in connection with the holding' should be construed as applying only to terms touching and concerning the demised premises or whether a wider construction was appropriate.[2]

1 [1959] Ch 531, [1959] 1 All ER 250.
2 At 254.

I THE TERMS OF THE NEW TENANCY – DURATION OF THE TERM

14.46 *The statutory provision.* The duration is to be such as the court considers reasonable in all the circumstances.[1] A periodic tenancy may be ordered. If, as usual, a tenancy for a term certain is ordered it must not be longer than fourteen years.[2]

1 1954 Act, s 33.
2 Notwithstanding this limitation, there is no reason why the parties should not agree any term they wish: *Janes (Gowns) Ltd v Harlow Development Corpn* (1979) 253 Estates Gazette 799. The limitation is somewhat unfortunate today where fourteen years terms are rarely granted in practice, and where five years is the normal review pattern.

14.47 *Relevant factors.* The court has a very wide discretion in fixing the length of the new tenancy – the duration of the old lease,[1] the length of time during which the tenant has held over under the old rent[2] and the question of comparative hardship between the parties[3] are all relevant factors. Where a tenant applies for a very short tenancy the court may order a longer term in order to give the landlord a chance to relet the premises.[4] A break clause may be ordered enabling the lease to be determined in certain circumstances.[5]

1 *Betty's Cafes Ltd v Phillips Furnishing Stores Ltd* [1959] AC 20, [1958] 1 All ER 607, HL; and *London and Provincial Millinery Stores Ltd v Barclays Bank Ltd* [1962] 2 All ER 163, [1962] 1 WLR 510, CA.
2 *London and Provincial Millinery Stores Ltd v Barclays Bank Ltd* [1962] 2 All ER 163; *Frederick Lawrence Ltd v Freeman Hardy and Willis Ltd* (1960) 176 Estates Gazette 11.
3 *Upsons Ltd v E Robins Ltd* [1956] 1 QB 131, [1955] 3 All ER 348, CA; *Amika Motors Ltd v Colebrook Holdings Ltd* (1981) 259 Estates Gazette 243, CA.
4 *Re Sunlight House, Quay St, Manchester* (1959) 173 Estates Gazette 311; but note *CBS United Kingdom Ltd v London Scottish Properties Ltd* [1985] 2 EGLR 125, 275 Estates Gazette 718; *Charles Follett Ltd v Cabtell Investment Co Ltd* [1986] 2 EGLR 76, 280 Estates Gazette 639.
5 *McCombie v Grand Junction Co Ltd* [1962] 2 All ER 65n, [1962] 1 WLR 581, CA; *Adams v Green* (1978) 247 Estates Gazette 49, CA; and *Amika Motors Ltd v Colebrook Holdings Ltd* (1981) 259 Estates Gazette 243, CA; *JH Edwards & Sons Ltd v Central London Commercial Estates Ltd* (1983) 271 Estates Gazette 697, CA; *Peter Millett & Sons Ltd v Salisbury Handbags Ltd* [1987] 2 EGLR 104, 284 Estates Gazette 784; *National Car Parks Ltd v Paternoster Consortium Ltd* [1989] EGCS 87.

14.48 *Possession not obtained under s 30(1).* Landlords who have failed to obtain possession under s 30(1) of the 1954 Act may be able to obtain relief under s 33. In *Upsons Ltd v E Robins Ltd*[1] the court ordered a new tenancy of only a limited duration where the landlord was unable to rely upon his intention to occupy the premises under s 30(1)(g) because he had acquired the premises within the previous five years.[2]

1 [1956] 1 QB 131, [1955] 3 All ER 348. See also *Peter Millett & Sons Ltd v Salisbury Handbags Ltd* [1987] 2 EGLR 104, 284 Estates Gazette 784.
2 See 1954 Act, s 30(2).
3 [1956] 2 All ER 742.

14.49 *Commencement of the new tenancy.* The term of the new lease commences on the coming to an end of the current tenancy and as a result the new lease ordered by the court will generally start upon the expiry of three months after the application is finally disposed of.[1] The problem is that there is always the possibility of an appeal and as such the court at first instance when it determines the length of the new tenancy cannot be certain as to when the application will finally be disposed of and when the new tenancy will begin. In order to meet this difficulty the Court of Appeal has indicated that the court of first instance should first determine the appropriate length of the new lease and that the order should specify the date upon which the new lease shall expire on the assumption that the term commences three months after the hearing at first instance.[2]

1 1954 Act, s 64. See para 14.9 above.
2 This solution devised by Wynn-Parry J in *Re 88 High Road, Kilburn, Meakers Ltd v DAW Consolidated Properties Ltd* [1959] 1 All ER 527, [1959] 1 WLR 279 was adopted by the Court of Appeal in *Chipperfield v Shell UK Ltd* (1980) 257 Estates Gazette 1042 and *Turone v Howard De Walden Estates Ltd* (1983) 267 Estates Gazette 440, CA. Note *Bradshaw v Pawley* [1979] 3 All ER 273, 253 Estates Gazette 693.

J THE TERMS OF THE NEW TENANCY – RENT

14.50 *The statutory provision.* The rent is to be the rent at which, having regard to the terms of the tenancy, the holding might reasonably be expected to be let[1] in the open market by a willing lessor.[2] Since the open market rent cannot be fixed until the terms of the tenancy are known (the terms obviously have a bearing on the rent) the sensible approach is to fix the terms of the tenancy first and then to fix the rent.[3] In fixing the open market rent four factors have to be disregarded:

(a) no regard is to be had to the fact that the tenant or his predecessors in title have been in occupation of the holding – thus the fact that a sitting tenant might outbid the rest of the market because of his special interest in remaining is to be ignored,[4]

(b) the effect of any goodwill attaching to the holding by reason of the tenant's business is to be ignored,[5]

(c) the effect of certain improvements is to be disregarded – the improvement must have been carried out by the tenant and during the current tenancy or, if not, carried out in the previous 21 years and the holding comprised in business tenancies (at the end of each of which the tenant did not quit) since the improvement was completed but the effect of an improvement is to be taken into account if it was carried out pursuant to an obligation owed to the immediate landlord,[6]

(d) any addition to the value of the holding due to a liquor licence where in the circumstances the benefit of the licence belongs to the tenant is to be disregarded.

The court may order the inclusion of a rent review clause, a course which has become much more frequent in inflationary times.[7]

1   A vital question is *when* is it to be assumed that the holding will be let? In *Lovely and Orchard Services Ltd v Daejan Investments (Grove Hall) Ltd* (1979) 246 Estates Gazette 651 it was held that a rent should be determined under s 34 as at the date of the hearing but having regard to matters relevant to the amount of the rent which can reasonably be expected to happen between that date and the date when having regard to the interim continuation under s 64 the new tenancy is likely to commence (as to commencement of new tenancy, see para 14.49 above). It follows, therefore, that the date upon which the contractual term expires, or that specified in the Section 25 Notice, is irrelevant and that the rent valuation date is postponed until the hearing. This can cause valuation difficulties.

2   1954 Act, s 34. As to the reference to 'willing lessor' and the omission of 'willing lessee' see paras 14.55 below and 6.22 above. It is interesting to compare s 34 with the type of detailed assumptions and disregards seen in rent review clauses today: see, for example Rosscastle Letting Conditions (Appendix 1, Form 1 below) Condition 7. In any future review of the 1954 Act, it would be worth considering if s 34 had become too simplistic and if further assumptions/disregards were required in order to give greater certainty – a point that, somewhat strangely, is not even discussed by the Law Commission in its latest review of the 1954 Act (1988) LCWP No 111.

3   *Cardshops Ltd v Davies* [1971] 2 All ER 721, [1971] 1 WLR 591, CA.

4   See paras 14.55 below and 6.32 above.

5   See paras 14.55 below and 6.33 above.

6   See paras 14.55 below and 6.34–6.43 above.

7   1954 Act, s 34(3).

14.51   *Evidence.* In determining the rent the court must act upon the evidence put before it in the usual way. Evidence will generally be given by a surveyor or valuer supported by evidence of comparable transactions and other market transactions from which the court is invited to deduce the open market rent of the premises.[1] Evidence of the rateable values of comparable premises may be some guide although these, of course, are determined on the assumption of an *annual* hypothetical tenancy whereas the rent to be determined under s 34 will be the term of the new letting. The Court of Appeal held in *W J Barton Ltd v Long Acre Securities Ltd*[3] that trading accounts should not generally be considered in determining the open market rent. The court recognised that in certain special cases such as hotels, filling stations, theatres or race courses where premises were 'peculiarly adapted', it might be appropriate for such evidence of turnover to be required as part of the evidence which the court might reasonably wish to see in order to assess the open market rental. Otherwise, especially where there were no special features and ample available comparables the evidence as to trading figures was not a matter with which the court should be concerned. In any event if such figures were to be adduced, they would have to be relevant to the particular application, and trading figures from other premises in quite a different type of area would not be relevant in any circumstances. The fact that there is a subtenancy protected by the Rent Act is a relevant circumstance to take into account in deciding the open market rent.[4]

1   The usual rules of evidence apply and there is no principle permitting hearsay in relation to comparable transactions: *English Exporters (London) Ltd v Eldonwall Ltd* [1973] Ch 415, [1973] 1 All ER 726; and *Rogers v Rosedimond Investments (Blakes Market) Ltd* (1978) 247 Estates Gazette 467, CA; *Town Centre Securities Ltd v Wm Morrison Supermarkets Ltd* (1981) 263 Estates Gazette 435. As to comments on valuation generally, see *GREA Real Property Investments Ltd v Williams* (1979) 250 Estates Gazette 651 (per Forbes J at 653); and *Ratners (Jewellers) Ltd v Lemnoll Ltd* (1980) 255 Estates Gazette 987 (per Dillon J at 989). For examples of the way in which the court

deals with comparables, see *Turone v Howard de Walden Estates Ltd* (1982) 262 Estates Gazette 1189, CA; *Newey & Eyre Ltd v J Curtis & Son Ltd* (1984) 271 Estates Gazette 891 (wholesale warehouse of electrical goods); *Oriani v Dorita Properties Ltd* [1987] 1 EGLR 88, 282 Estates Gazette 1001, CA (shop in a centre); Dr M J Russell ('Free commercial rent valuations' (1986) 279 Estates Gazette 492, (1986) 130 Sol Jo 153) has suggested that the County Courts Act 1984, s 63(1) would enable parties who are in dispute over the rent to be payable on the renewal of a business tenancy to obtain a rental valuation at public expense from an independent valuer. For an indication of the Court of Appeal's attitude to the calculations of rent by judges having heard conflicting expert evidence, see *Halberstam v Tandalco Corpn NV* [1985] 1 EGLR 90, 274 Estates Gazette 393, CA. As to lack of comparables, see *National Car Parks Ltd v Colebrook Estates Ltd* (1982) 266 Estates Gazette 810.

2   *Davis v Brighton Corpn* (1956) 106 L Jo 556 (county court case).
3   [1982] 1 All ER 465, [1982] 1 WLR 398. The Court of Appeal held in *Rogers v Rosedimond Investments (Blakes Market) Ltd* (1978) 247 Estates Gazette 467 that the court should not rely upon the opinions of traders as to rental values.
4   *Oscroft v Benabo* [1967] 2 All ER 548, [1967] 1 WLR 1087, CA.

14.52   *User covenant.* The fact that the rent has to be determined having regard to the terms of the tenancy will mean that the user covenant in the current tenancy is relevant.[1] There have been attempts to alter the user provision in the new lease with a view to influencing the open market rent. On an application to renew a lease in which the user was restricted to that of a golf course, the landlord sought the removal of that restriction since the consequences of the land being capable of being put to a more profitable use would justify a higher rent. The county court judge refused to permit the change.[2] Similarly in *Charles Clements (London) Ltd v Rank City Wall Ltd*[3] the existing lease contained an absolute restriction on user for any purpose other than that of retail cutler. The landlord proposed to relax this restriction in the new lease because this would be able to command a higher rent. The tenant was content with the existing restriction and objected to the higher rent and Goulding J declined to permit the relaxation of the restriction. The converse had been seen in *Aldwych Club Ltd v Copthall Property Co Ltd*[4] where the tenant wished to restrain even further the user restriction requiring the premises to be used only as a club by removing the words 'without the landlord's consent'. The tenant's sole purpose was to bring about a diminution in the rent as the premises were suitable for development as offices and could most advantageously be let as such. Pennycuick J held that it would be contrary to reasonable justice to impose a new restriction at the instance of the tenant which would have the effect of reducing the lettable market value of the premises. Similar issues concerning user can arise in leases being renewed under the 1954 Act as in rent reviews.[5]

1   *Gorleston Golf Club Ltd v Links Estates (Gorleston) Ltd* (1959) 109 L Jo 140 – a user covenant that is wide enough to permit a more lucrative user can be costly for the tenant: see for example *Giannoukakis v Saltfeet Ltd* [1988] 1 EGLR 73, [1988] 17 EG 121, CA.
2   For an example of the effect that a restrictive user covenant can have, see *UDS Tailoring Ltd v BL Holdings Ltd* (1981) 261 Estates Gazette 49.
3   (1978) 246 Estates Gazette 739.
4   (1962) 185 Estates Gazette 219.
5   See paras 14.55 below and 6.18:3(a) above.

14.53   *Variable rents.* The court has power under s 34(1) to order that the rent payable shall vary at different times during the course of the tenancy – for example where the premises are in a poor state of repair there might be fixed an initial low rent to be succeeded by a higher rent as and when the premises were put into better repair.[1] It would seem likely, however, that such differential rents will be appropriate in only a few cases – for example where the initial disrepair is of a very serious character.[2] Section 34(3) that was added by the Law of Property Act 1969, merely confirmed the previous law[3] that the inclusion of a rent review provision in the new lease is permitted. The frequency of review will be a matter for negotiation and in default of agreement determination by the court as will the exact form of the clause although in the case of the latter the Law Society/RICS model clause[4] has provided a useful standard that courts have used, although the order must deal with the various optional wordings that are contained in the clause. Where the court does order the inclusion of a rent review clause this may provide for the possibility of a downward as well as an upward review of the rent[5] although, of course, the former is virtually unheard of today in new lettings.

1 *Fawke v Viscount Chelsea* [1980] QB 441, [1979] 3 All ER 568, CA. There is no such power for an arbitrator under a conventionally worded rent review clause: *Clarke v Findon Developments Ltd* (1983) 270 Estates Gazette 426.
2 Per Brandon LJ in *Fawke* at 578.
3 A rent review clause had already been ordered, for example in *Re 88 High Road, Kilburn, Meakers Ltd v DAW Consolidated Properties Ltd* [1959] 1 All ER 527, [1959] 1 WLR 279.
4 See 22 Encyclopaedia of Forms and Precedents (5th edn) Form 117.
5 See *Stylo Shoes Ltd v Manchester Royal Exchange Ltd* (1967) 204 Estates Gazette 803; *Janes (Gowns) Ltd v Harlow Development Corpn* (1979) 253 Estates Gazette 799.

14.54 *Premises in disrepair.* There is some uncertainty as to the proper way of dealing under s 34 with cases where the premises are in a state of disrepair at the end of the current tenancy because of breaches of the repairing covenant by the tenant. Essentially there are two approaches and both have authorities in their favour. On the one hand it is said that the premises should be valued in their *actual unrepaired state* because there is nothing in s 34 to warrant the court making an assumption that the premises are in good repair.[1] This may result in a lower rent being determined, but the tenant would not benefit overall from his failure to comply with the repairing covenant contained in the current lease because the landlord would be entitled to recover from the tenant any diminution to the value of his reversion by way of a claim for damages for breach of covenant. The other view is that the court should make the *hypothesis that the tenant had complied with his repairing obligations.* In *Family Management v Gray*[2] the freeholder of shop premises claimed damages from the head tenant for failure to leave the premises in repair on the expiry of the headlease. The premises consisted of two shops, each being sublet with repairing covenants similar to the headlease and after the determination of the headlease the freeholder negotiated new full repairing leases of the shops with the existing subtenants. No application to the court was required. During his judgment in the Court of Appeal,[3] Shaw LJ said that the subtenants had not been entitled to rely upon their own default in carrying out repairs as something which reduced the rent to be determined under s 34.[4] In other words, Shaw LJ was assuming that the rents contained in the new leases agreed between the freeholder and the subtenants had not been discounted to reflect the state of disrepair that the premises were in. Thus the Court of Appeal held that, as the freeholder had let the premises at the open market rent, the value of the reversion had not been diminished by the head tenant's failure to comply with the repairing covenant in the headlease[5] and no damages were due.

1 This approach is supported by the decision of the Court of Appeal in *Fawke v Viscount Chelsea* [1980] QB 441, [1979] 3 All ER 568.
2 (1979) 253 Estates Gazette 369, CA. In *Harmsworth Pension Funds Trustees Ltd v Charringtons*

Industrial Holdings Ltd [1985] 1 EGLR 97, 274 Estates Gazette 588 (a rent review case), Warner J preferred the views expressed in *Family Management* partly on the basis that they were part of the ratio decidendi of the case, whereas the relevant passages from *Fawke* related to the failure of a landlord to carry out his obligations and so, as regards the breach of a tenant's covenant, were obiter dicta. See also *Hibernian Property Co Ltd v Liverpool Corpn* [1973] 2 All ER 1117, 228 Estates Gazette 334.

3   Ie judgment in the action between the freeholder and the head tenant re-breach of the repairing covenant of the headlease.

4   The landlord delayed commencing proceedings and the first instance hearing was nearly three and a half years after the expiry of the headlease and the underleases. It turned on expert evidence as to whether or not the rents in the new leases had been discounted and it is not clear why evidence did not appear to be available as to whether the rents in the new leases had *in fact* been reduced to reflect the state of the premises.

5   See the Landlord and Tenant Act 1927, s 18.

14.55   *Rent review.* Rent review clauses, based as the early ones were upon s 34 of the 1954 Act require similar assumptions and disregards to be made although they have become over the years rather more sophisticated than s 34. Nevertheless cases on the many matters that are common to both are relevant to both and to avoid duplication they are generally dealt with in Chapter 6.[1]

1   See for example, 'willing lessor' (para 6.22 above), 'occupation' (para 6.32 above), 'goodwill' (para 6.33 above), improvements generally (paras 6.34–6.43 above), disregarding 'any effect on rent of an improvement' (para 6.40), 'carried out otherwise than in pursuance of an obligation to his immediate landlord' (para 6.3:3 above) and status of the improver (para 6.36:2 above) while similar issues can arise as to user (para 6.18:3(a) above).

K   THE TERMS OF THE NEW TENANCY – OTHER TERMS

14.56   *Statutory provision.* As to the other terms, the court is given a wide discretion – regard must be had to all relevant circumstances and to the terms of the current tenancy.[1]

1   1954 Act, s 35.

14.57   *Relevant factors.* The Court of Appeal gave valuable early guidance in *Gold v Brighton Corpn*[1] Premises had been used for dealing in both new and secondhand clothes but the landlord wished to insert in the new lease a provision that would prohibit the sale of secondhand clothes except with the landlord's consent. This term was rejected and Denning LJ said:[2]

> 'The Landlord and Tenant Act 1954 plainly intends to protect the tenant in respect of his business . . . in as much as the tenant is to be protected in respect of his business the terms of the new tenancy should be such as to enable him to carry on his business as it is. They should not prevent him from carrying on an important part of it. At any rate, if he is to be prevented from using the premises in the future in a way in which he has used them in the past, it is for the landlord to justify the restriction and there ought to be strong and cogent evidence for this purpose. I find no such evidence here.'

In *Cardshops Ltd v Davies*[3] the landlord sought to impose upon the tenant a clause by which he would be obliged to offer to surrender the lease to the landlord in the event of him wishing to assign or underlet.[4] The Court of Appeal would not permit the provision on the basis that it put the tenant's goodwill at risk as no assignment could be made even to the most responsible person without first offering to surrender the tenancy. Furthermore, the proposed term was so markedly different from the current lease that such a departure required very cogent justification in view of the words of s 35 requiring the court to have regard to the terms of the current tenancy.

1   [1956] 3 All ER 442, [1956] 1 WLR 1291. See also *Re No 5 Panton Street, Haymarket* (1959) 175 Estates Gazette 49.
2   At 443.
3   [1971] 2 All ER 721, [1971] 1 WLR 591, CA.
4   As to the effect of such a clause in a lease of business premises see para 7.7:6 above.

14.58   *The O'May case.* In *O'May v City of London Real Property Co Ltd*[1] the court was asked to decide when a five year lease of the fifth floor of an office building in the City of London came up for renewal, if the landlord could impose upon the tenants via a service charge a share of the actual cost of structural repairs, lift maintenance and repair, and the provision of a sinking fund for the renewal of plant and equipment, or alternatively, if these burdens should be borne by the landlords who in return would receive a higher rent. To impose a variable service charge would have involved a change from the terms of the current lease that provided for the tenant to pay a fixed service charge. The marketability of its investment had prompted the landlord to seek the change. Evidence was given of the widespread practice in Central London lettings of landlords including a service charge of the type proposed so as to create 'clear leases'.[2] Further evidence was given to the effect that major investment purchasers were reluctant to purchase other than clear leases as it was only a clear lease that ensured that the rent would represent net income to the landlord, because the total expense of all repairs and renewals was passed to the tenant. Potential purchasers of the freehold could, therefore, easily evaluate their proposed investment. The House of Lords held:

(a) Under s 35 the court was required to have regard to the terms of the current lease and, as such, the burden of persuading the court to change those terms rested upon the party proposing the change.

(b) Although the court had wide discretionary powers to change the terms and impose new terms, the party proposing the change has first to show that the change is fair and reasonable in all the circumstances, having regard to the comparatively weak negotiating position of a sitting tenant requiring renewal at a time of scarcity of business premises.

(c) In particular a landlord has to show, not that if the change was made the reduction in rent was adequate compensation, but that it would be fair and reasonable for the change to be made and for a fluctuating burden of unpredictable service charges to be imposed on tenants against their will, instead of a fixed figure valid throughout the tenancy and calculated at the beginning of the tenancy.

(d) Since the proposed variation required the tenants to assume the risk of an unpredictable liability disproportionate to their interest as leaseholders, and because they would have no control over the work done for which they would have to pay in the form of service charges, the landlord in this particular case had not discharged its burden of showing that there should be a departure from the terms of the current lease in respect of the liability for repairs and maintenance, and thus the 'service charge provision' was not permitted.

1   [1983] 2 AC 726, [1982] 1 All ER 660, HL.
2   See para 11.1(c) above.
3   In *Hyams v Titan Properties Ltd* (1972) 116 Sol Jo 884, 24 P & CR 359 the Court of Appeal had

allowed a landlord to introduce a variable service charge into a new five year lease. The current tenancy provided that a fixed sum of £125 per annum should be paid and this was changed to one ninth of the actual cost incurred by the landlord in maintaining the structure of the building decorating common parts, heating etc. This case, although not mentioned in their Lordships' speeches in *O'May*, must be taken to have been wrongly decided, because it seems impossible to distinguish the two cases except perhaps to the extent that it can be said that the decision in *Hyams* is limited to 'housekeeping' items – ie day-to-day running costs that will be affected by inflation – and does not include 'risk' items such as structural work etc.

14.59 *The extent of O'May.* The application of *O'May*[1] is uncertain, and in particular the extent that it permits the lease to be modernised. In s 34 there is clearly no intention to protect the tenant from commercial reality so far as the rent is concerned,[2] and yet *O'May*[1] perhaps suggests that a tenant should be protected in relation to the other terms of the lease. The unusual aspect of *O'May*[1] was that the term of the renewed lease was to be only five years, and in these circumstances it may well have been inappropriate to impose upon the tenant an unpredictable liability for services. On the other hand, if the term had been for say 15 years or longer, it is suggested that there are no reasons of policy why the tenant should not be granted a lease in the form then being used for open market lettings of similar premises.[3] If the market norm[3] had shifted during the term of the existing lease, from fixed service charges to indefinite and unlimited ones, the tenant would experience this if he sought new premises. Surely it would be anomalistic for the principle not to apply if he decided instead to renew his existing lease?[4] *O'May*[1] does not specifically prevent this, but as the Law Commission has said:[5] 'Nevertheless, it may be that legislation should seek to clarify the position or change the balance between the parties. There is wide concern about this matter among landlords. This is understandable, because the value of substantial properties is greatly influenced by the acceptability of the lease terms to investment institutions. The landlords in the *O'May* case stood to increase the value of their building between £1m and £2m, had the leases of all the tenants been revised. The interests not only of landlords and tenants, but also of general policy towards commercial property, need to be balanced, and this is a topic which would repay detailed consideration.' It is suggested that the only fundamental term is that the tenant should not be prevented from carrying out his business or any substantial part of it.[6]

1 [1983] 2 AC 726, [1982] 1 All ER 660, HL and see para 14.58 above.
2 See section J above.
3 The term of such leases and the market norm would obviously be matters that would be dealt with at the hearing when there may well be differences between the parties.
4 It is suggested that it is preferable to grant a lease with an indefinite service charge when this would be standard for new lettings, rather than (because of *O'May*) to provide for a fixed service charge but to increase the rent, inevitably in some random way, to reflect the fact that in the open market a tenant (if ever given the chance) would pay a higher rent for a lease containing any term that was more favourable than the norm for similar open market lettings at that time.
5 Landlord and Tenant: Reform of the Law (1987) Law Com No 162.
6 See *Gold v Brighton Corpn* [1956] 3 All ER 442, [1956] 1 WLR 1291, CA and para 14.57 above.

14.60 *Additional rights.* It is an open question as to whether or not s 35 can serve to mitigate the severity of s 32(3). In *Re No 1 Albemarle Street*[1] the current lease granted to the tenant a licence to exhibit advertising signs on adjacent property belonging to the landlord. Upjohn J held that he could not include this right in the new lease under s 32(3) because it was not a right 'enjoyed by the tenant in connection with the holding'. Nevertheless he felt able to include the right in the new lease by virtue of the wide general provision contained in s 35. In *G Orlik (Meat Products) Ltd v Hastings and Thanet Building Society*[2] the tenant failed under s 32(3) because the court held that as against the landlords the tenant had no legal right to park on part of the landlord's land.[3] The tenant then relied upon the decision in *Re No 1 Albemarle Street*[1] as authority for the proposition that s 35 gave the court the widest possible discretion as to the terms to be included in the new tenancy and argued that the right to park vehicles on the landlord's land could be included by virtue of s 35. The argument was rejected by the Court of Appeal. Stamp LJ said:

> 'The object of Part II of the Act is to give security of tenure to business tenants by inter alia conferring power on the court to order a new tenancy of the property comprised in the holding, that is to say (see s 23(3)) of the property comprised in the existing tenancy excluding any part not used for business purposes and however widely expressed s 35 cannot in our judgment, consistently with the scheme found in Part II, be construed to enable the court to enlarge the holding, for example, by ordering the grant of an easement over the landlord's land or by conferring rights of the landlord's land not hitherto enjoyed'.

It does not, of course, necessarily follow that *Re No 1 Albemarle Street*[1] was wrongly decided[5] because the two cases are easily distinguishable – in *Albemarle Street* the tenant certainly had the right under the current lease that he sought to have included in the new lease, whereas in *Orlik* the tenant had no such right.

1 [1959] Ch 531, [1959] 1 All ER 250.
2 (1974) 29 P & CR 126, CA. Note also *Kirkwood v Johnson* (1979) 250 Estates Gazette 239, CA – see para 14.44 above.
3 See para 14.43 above.
4 At 183.
5 In *Orlik* Stamp LJ said that 'it is not necessary to comment on that decision (ie *Albemarle Street*) except to point out that (as indicated) above the two cases are easily distinguishable'.

14.61   *Can a guarantor be ordered under s 35?* This question was answered in the affirmative by the Court of Appeal in *Cairnplace Ltd v CBL (Property Investment) Co Ltd*[1] who approved the county court judge's order that the new lease of the premises should include a term requiring the tenant to provide two guarantors acceptable to the landlord (such acceptance not to be unreasonably withheld) within six months of the execution of the lease.

1 [1984] 1 All ER 315, [1984] 1 WLR 696.

14.62   *Payment of the landlord's costs on the grant of the lease.* The Court of Appeal also dealt in *Cairnplace Ltd v CBL (Property Investment) Co Ltd*[1] with the question of was the discretion under s 35 wide enough to permit the court to insert a term in the new lease to the effect that the tenant would pay the landlord's legal fees and the stamp duty on the counterpart lease where a similar provision had been inserted in the current lease? Here the court found in favour of the tenant, Cumming-Bruce LJ saying:

> 'In 1954 there was a custom that the tenant should pay the landlord's cost of preparing a lease which was a practice generally followed by conveyancing solicitors in the absence of express agreement in the Agreement for a lease. So when in 1972 the lease between the landlords [and the original tenant included a term to the effect that the tenant would pay the scale costs of the landlord's solicitors in respect of the

lease and the stamp duty on the counterpart thereof] the clause was consistent with the general practice and before the [Costs of Leasses Act 1958] came into operation there is no doubt that the court had the power to embody it as "another term" in the new lease pursuant to s 35 of the 1954 Act. But in 1958 Parliament relieved the tenant of the usual obligation which conveyancing custom and practice had imposed on tenants. Thereafter it was only if there was express agreement in writing whereby the tenant agreed to pay the landlord's costs of preparation of the lease that the tenant was under an obligation. Where Parliament has enacted a later Act designed to relieve tenants of a specific obligation, it is not in our view a correct exercise of judicial discretion to use the wide power conferred on the court by the general words of s 35 of the 1954 Act to deprive the tenant of the protection conferred on him by a later Act dealing specifically with this very obligation'.

As such, the landlord was not permitted to insert in the new lease a clause to the effect that the tenant would pay the landlord's reasonable legal costs. It is suggested that the court paid rather more attention to this Act than it receives from commercial conveyancers. No figures can ever be available but, in what must be a significant proportion of the leases of business premises granted since 1958, the terms of the Act have been varied by agreement, and tenants have paid landlords' legal fees.

1   [1984] 1 All ER 315, [1984] 1 WLR 696.

Chapter 15

After the lease has been agreed

A PREPARATION FOR COMPLETION AND COMPLETION

15.1 *The engrossment.* In due course the wording of the lease will be agreed and the parties can move towards completion.[1] The lease should be engrossed from the travelling draft and 'examined' in the sense of one person reading aloud the draft and the other checking that it complies with the engrossment.[2] There is much to be said for one of those persons to be the solicitor involved in the matter – the act of examining affords him one last chance to satisfy himself that the lease is in order, and acceptable to his client. He should check every cross-reference to ensure that any consequential re-numbering has been dealt with. He may also find that certain provisions that have been heavily amended do not 'quite' make sense and, although the meaning will be clear to all concerned at this stage, it may well be far from obvious when the parties (or perhaps their successors) turn to that provision many years in the future. The necessary corrections should be made.[3] Over and above this, however, the fact remains that, even at this late stage, the wording of the lease has not been finally agreed,[4] unless there has been a specific prior agreement, and if while examining the lease, a solicitor sees a crucial point that would seriously operate against his clients' interests that he had previously overlooked, he can raise it even at this eleventh hour. The other solicitor and his client, who both believed that the drafting and negotiating was over, may well not be very pleased, and indeed where the amendment that is proposed by the tenant's solicitor is subsequently accepted, he may have to agree to be responsible for the cost of any re-engrossing that may be necessary. The other solicitor's annoyance and these charges, however, are preferable to running the risk of the client suffering, or worse still, an action for professional negligence. The lease document will have to survive throughout the term. It should be engrossed upon thicker paper, and preferably typed on both sides. Fortunately the movement to standardise all legal documents to A4 size has considerably advanced over recent years. It is important for the pages of the lease to be securely stitched or bound together and desirable for stiffer covers to be attached to the front and back of the document for protection.

1　More precisely, the exchange of the lease and counterpart – see para 15.9 below.
2　Word processing has revolutionised this aspect of the conveyancing process so far as the landlord is concerned and now the preparation of the engrossment generally involves no more than amending the disk upon which the draft was prepared. It is suggested that *all* the document (and not just the amendments) should be examined. Occasionally the version on the disk does not (for whatever reason) quite correspond with the draft, a point that would be overlooked if the parties merely checked that the amendments made during the negotiations have been implemented accurately.
3　Clearly all changes, however minor, must be discussed with the solicitor to the other party, to obtain his approval and to ensure that the amendment is made on the document that he is examining.
4　See paras 1.8–1.12 above.

15.2 *Formalities: by deed.* The practical effect of ss 52 and 54 of the Law of Property Act 1925 is that leases taking effect in possession[1] for terms not exceeding three years, at the best rent that can be obtained and without a premium, may be under hand (or even oral) but where the term exceeds three years the lease must be by deed. The general rule is that corporations cannot make any disposition of their property otherwise than by deed, sealed with their Common Seal. Section 36 of the Companies Act 1985, however, provides that a company may demise lands by their directors or a committee of directors in writing or orally if the lease is for less than three years, and there is a similar provision in relation to corporations other than those incorporated under the Companies Act under s 1(1)(b) of the Corporate Bodies' Contracts Act 1960. Most leases, therefore, will be by deed and the requirements as to the execution of deeds will be simplified by the Law of Property (Miscellaneous Provisions) Act 1989. No seal will be needed when executed by an individual – he must simply sign it in the presence of an attesting witness and deliver it as a deed[2] either personally or by a person authorised to do so on his behalf.[3] A deed still has to be delivered and the somewhat archaic law relating to this – and the principle of the deed being delivered as an 'escrow' – could be a trap for the unwary and create a position where a party found itself bound by the terms of the lease, although lease and counterpart have not been exchanged.[4] Thus:

(a) a deed should never be sealed until that party has irrevocably decided that it wishes to proceed with the matter to which it relates, and

(b) if a deed is sealed at a time when there remain outstanding some matters of detail, a note or memorandum should be prepared (and inserted in the sealing book where a corporate party is involved) to the effect that the document has been sealed subject to these matters being resolved to that party's satisfaction.

1   If the term of the lease is to commence subsequent to the date of the lease, the lease must be by deed because it does not take effect in possession.

2   For example: 'signed as a deed by . . . in the presence of:'. As of August 1989 no date has been specified for the coming into force of these provisions.

3   Where a solicitor or licenced conveyancer, in the course of or in connection with a transaction involving land, purports to deliver an instrument as a deed on behalf of a party, it shall be conclusively presumed in favour of a purchaser that he is authorised so to deliver the instrument: Law of Property (Miscellaneous Provisions) Act 1989, s 1(5).

4   See *Beesley v Hallwood Estates Ltd* [1961] Ch 105, [1961] 1 All ER 90, CA; *Vincent v Premo Enterprises (Voucher Sales) Ltd* [1969] 2 QB 609, [1969] 2 All ER 941, CA; *Glessing v Green* [1975] 2 All ER 696, [1975] 1 WLR 863, CA; *Alan Estates Ltd v WG Stores Ltd* [1982] Ch 511, [1981] 3 All ER 481, CA; *Bentray Investments Ltd v Venner Time Switches Ltd* [1985] 1 EGLR 39, 274 Estates Gazette 43, and para 1.12 above. Note too P H Kenny: 'Dating and Escrow' [1982] Conv 409. In *Venetian Glass Gallery Ltd v Next Properties Ltd* [1989] 30 EG 92 Harman J held that the engrossment and sealing of a licence to assign constituted delivery.

15.3 *Final searches and enquiries: the questions.* Before the lease is completed, the tenant's solicitor will need to satisfy himself on four points, for reasons that are briefly explained in the following paragraphs:

(a) Are the premises that will be the subject of the lease mortgaged, and if so, will the consent of the mortgagee be required or will the proposed lease bind the mortgagee without any express consent?[1]

(b) Has a receiver been appointed?[2]

(c) Is a corporate-landlord in liquidation or has an Administration Order been made or an administrative receiver appointed?[3]

(d) Is an individual landlord bankrupt?[4]

1   See para 15.4 below.

2   See paras 15.5 and 15.6 below.
3   See para 15.6 below.
4   See para 15.7 below.

15.4   *Mortgagors/mortgagees: powers of leasing.* At common law, a mortgagor could grant a lease binding against the third party tenant but not the mortgagee who, if he did not consent to the grant of the lease, could invalidate it and evict the tenant as a trespasser. A tenant under an unauthorised lease, however, was permitted by equity to redeem the mortgage and thus to secure himself against eviction. The position at common law now has to be read subject to s 99 of the Law of Property Act 1925 that confers upon a mortgagor *in possession* a statutory right to grant the following leases that are binding on the mortgagee:

(a)   agricultural or occupation leases for any term not exceeding twenty-one years, or, if the mortgage was made on or after 1 January 1926, for any term not exceeding fifty years and

(b)   building leases, for any term not exceeding 999 years.[1]

Such a lease must be made to take effect in possession not later than twelve months after its execution, must reserve the best rent that can reasonably be obtained, must not provide for a fine to be paid,[2] and must contain a condition of re-entry in the event of rent being in arrears for 30 days.[3] Further the mortgagor is bound to deliver to the mortgagee within one month a counterpart of the lease executed by the lessee.[4] A mortgagee in possession has similar powers of leasing.[5] The problem with s 99, however, is that it only applies in so far as a contrary intention is not expressed in the mortgage deed, or otherwise in writing[1] and mortgagees frequently insist upon excluding the operation of the section or impose further conditions in the mortgage over and above those contained in the section. It follows, therefore, that a solicitor whose client is about to accept a lease of mortgaged premises needs to establish that the landlord is permitted to grant the lease either by virtue of s 99 (the application of which has not been excluded or varied) or by the provisions of the mortgage itself. If s 99 has been excluded or does not apply to the letting in question, and the mortgage itself does not grant the landlord adequate powers of leasing, the specific consent of the mortgagee to the grant of that lease will have to be obtained. Without this, the mortgagee would be able to invalidate the lease and evict the tenant as a trespasser.[6] The tenant's solicitor would be well advised to raise with the landlord's solicitor in good time the question of whether or not the premises that will be the subject of the lease are mortgaged, even in those cases where a search will in due course confirm the position.[1] This will serve to put the landlord and his solicitor on notice and, where the premises are indeed mortgaged, give them time to investigate the matter and thus avoid a delay that could arise where the fact that a mortgagee's consent was needed emerges only at the last moment.

1   Law of Property Act 1925, s 99(1), (3).
2   LPA 1925, s 99(5) and s 99(6).
3   LPA 1925, s 99(7).
4   LPA 1925, s 99(11).
5   LPA 1925, s 99(2).
6   Law of Property Act 1925, s 99(13). Where the mortgage excludes s 99 any lease made by the mortgagor after the mortgage (leases made before the mortgage bind mortgagor and mortgagee; see *Moss v Gallimore* (1779) 1 Doug KB 279) is in the same position as one made under a mortgage before 1822 governed by common law rules; see *Dudley and District Benefit Building Society v Emerson* [1949] Ch 707, [1949] 2 All ER 252, CA; *Bolton Building Society v Cobb* [1965] 3 All ER 814, [1966] 1 WLR 1. Such a lease is binding between the mortgagor and the lessee by estoppel, but is void against the mortgagee; see *Keech v Hall* (1778) 1 Doug KB 21; *Cuthbertson v Irving* (1860) 6 H & N 135; *Lows v Telford* (1876) 1 App Cas 414 at 425, HL, per Lord Selborne.

15.5   *Receiver*. Section 101(1)(iii) of the Law of Property Act 1925 empowers a mortgagee under a mortgage deed, when the mortgage-money has become due, to appoint a receiver of the income of the mortgaged property, unless such power is specifically excluded by the mortgage. The receiver may not be appointed until the mortgagee has become entitled to exercise the power of sale and the appointment must be in writing.[1] The appointment of a receiver *operates to vest the statutory powers of leasing in the mortgagee*, and not the mortgagor.[2] The receiver has no authority to demise the mortgaged property unless the mortgagee has in writing delegated his power of leasing to him. Thus if a receiver has been appointed, and the mortgagee has delegated the power of leasing to him, the receiver will need to be made a party to the lease which will be expressed to be granted by the landlord 'acting by the receiver'.[3] If a receiver has been appointed but the mortgagee has not delegated the power of leasing, then the lease should be granted by the mortgagee. A receiver appointed by the High Court to collect rent and manage property has no power to grant leases without the authority and direction of the court.[4]

1   Law of Property Act 1925, s 109(1). A mortgagee may remove a receiver and appoint a new one from time to time in writing: s 109(5). Apart from s 101, a receiver may be appointed by the court upon the application of the mortgagee (see 32 Halsbury's Laws (4th edn) para 839) or out of court by the mortgagor at the time of the mortgage and as part of the security, or by the mortgagee under an express power in the mortgage deed. A body corporate cannot be appointed as receiver for a company: Companies Act 1948, s 366 and *Portman Building Society v Gallwey* [1955] 1 All ER 227, [1955] 1 WLR 96. As to the receiver's position generally, see LPA 1925, s 109.
2   LPA 1925, s 99(19).
3   LPA 1925, s 99(19).
4   *Wynne v Lord Newborough* (1790) 1 Ves 164.

15.6   *Liquidator, administrator, administrative receiver*. The property of the company does not vest in the liquidator[1] or in an administrator[2] or administrative receiver.[3] Thus the company remains the landlord, but the circumstances giving rise to the appointment should be recited and the corporate seal attested by the liquidator, administrator or administrative receiver.

1   See Insolvency Act, 1986, Part IV.
2   See ibid, Part II.
3   See ibid, Part III. The powers of an Administrator and Administrative Receiver are set out in Sch 1 and the powers of a liquidator in Sch 4. See Peter Totty: 'Insolvency practitioners: in whose name should they sue and convey' (1988) 1 Insolvency Intelligence 17 and *Sowman v David Samuel Trust Ltd* [1978] 1 All ER 616, [1978] 1 WLR 22.

15.7   *Bankruptcy*. The property of a bankrupt vests on adjudication in his trustee-in-bankruptcy, and as such it is the trustee and not the bankrupt who should grant a lease.[1] A lease purportedly granted by the bankrupt himself would be void.

1   Insolvency Act 1986, ss 283, 306.

15.8   *But what searches?* Paragraph 15.3 sets out the points upon which the tenant's solicitor will require confirmation for the reasons set out in para 15.4–7. But how is he to obtain that confirmation? The immediate reaction is that searches should provide the information, as would be the case in the purchase of freehold land, but analysis shows that in certain circumstances he will have to rely upon the assurances given by the landlord's solicitor. The position in relation to searches is as follows:

(a) If the landlord is a company incorporated under the Companies Acts as search should be made at Companies Registry. The law-agents who undertake searches there on behalf of solicitors carry out what is known as a 'conveyancing search' which will provide the solicitor with an indication of whether or not there is a registered charge relating to a specified property, if an administrative receiver or administrator has been appointed, and if a resolution has been passed for winding up, or a winding-up order or petition served. Such a search will not inflict upon the tenant's solicitor all the other information on the company's file which is not relevant to his needs.

(b) If the landlord is an individual or individuals, a bankruptcy search should be made at the Land Charges Registry.

(c) If the landlord is the freeholder, and the freehold title has been deduced, then the same searches should be made as would be in the case of a purchase of the freehold – that is Land Charges searches against the estate owners for the period during which they owned the property (insofar as copies of these have not been deduced as part of the title) or where the title is registered a 94A or a 94B Land Registry Search against the landlord.

The fact remains, however, that there is no obligation on the landlord to deduce title,[1] nor is there any registry corresponding to the Companies Registry for private individuals. How, therefore, can a solicitor whose client is on the point of taking a lease from a private individual where title has not been deduced check if the premises are mortgaged, and if so whether the mortgagee's consent will be needed, or if a receiver has been appointed? The answer is that he cannot – he can only raise the points as requisitions and there seems no way in which a tenant can obtain absolute protection from being evicted as a trespasser by a mortgagee if a solicitor acting for a non-corporate landlord had wrongly indicated that no mortgagee's consent was needed. The tenant would always have a claim against the mortgagor-landlord in these circumstances but this may provide little assistance in practice. At first sight, s 44(5) of the Law of Property Act 1925 would seem to offer the tenant some assistance. This provides that 'where . . . an intending lessee . . . is not entitled to call for the title to the freehold . . . he shall not . . . deem to be affected by notice of any matter or thing which if he had contracted that such title should be furnished he might have had notice'. On the other hand, this section can apply only between the landlord and tenant and cannot purport to govern the relationship between the tenant and the landlord's mortgagee. This then is a further reason for the tenant to urge that the landlord's title be deduced, although it is fair to say that relatively few commercial leases are granted by private individuals.

1 See paras 2.9–2.10 above.

15.9 *Completion.* As completion approaches the tenant's solicitor must make his final report to his client[1] and make sure that his client is fully aware of, understands[2] and accepts the 'final' terms of the lease.[3] He must ensure too that all the licenses that may be required have been obtained.[4] Completion itself or more properly the exchange of the lease and counterpart, is usually something of an anti-climax with the tenant's solicitor sending to the landlord's solicitor, or handing to him, the counterpart executed by the tenant and such sums that the lease provides will be due on the granting of the lease. The landlord then provides the executed lease in exchange. The landlord's solicitor (or both solicitors when there is an actual exchange) should ensure that all the blanks in the document are completed. It is easy to assume that the date is the only matter that has to be inserted, as this would be the case in most deeds, but for example the commencement of the term may have also been left blank, perhaps because it had been agreed that the term would commence on the quarter day immediately preceding completion.[5] Both solicitors' thoughts should now turn to the post-completion matters.

1   Ie on the assumption that no prior agreement has been entered into.
2   See para 1.18 above.
3   For an excellent discussion of the problems involved in the tenant taking possession before completion (written by the late and much missed Iain Buist: see Preface above) see 22 Encyclopaedia of Forms and Precedents (5th edn) paras 239–245. See also Peter Sparkes: 'Occupation of business premises pending completion' [1987] Gazette 7 October 2850.
4   And, if the 1954 Act is being excluded, that the Order has been obtained: see para 14.5 above.
5   Here will be advantage of gathering together all the blanks at the beginning of the lease.

B   POST-COMPLETION

15.10   *Stamp duty.* The stamping of leases and agreements for leases is controlled by the Stamp Act 1891.[1] The duty is ad valorem on the amount of the rent[2] and depends upon the length of the term.[3] The stamp duty on the counterpart, or the document executed by the tenant and handed to the landlord, is 50p, or, in the rare instances when the duty on the lease is less than 50p, the same duty as is payable on the lease.[4] If the counterpart is executed by the landlord, it must either be stamped as the lease itself or else with a denoting stamp showing that the lease was properly stamped.[5] An agreement for a lease (whether or not for a term exceeding 35 years or for a periodic tenancy) is to be stamped as if it were a lease.[6] Where duty has been duly paid on an agreement for a lease and subsequent to that agreement, a lease is granted which is either in conformity with the agreement of relates to substantially the same property and term as the agreement, then the duty which would otherwise be charged on the lease is reduced (or, as the case may be extinguished) by the deduction from it of the duty paid on the agreement.[7] A lease for a term of seven years or more must be produced to the Commissioners of Inland Revenue by the tenant, who must furnish the required particulars of the transaction.[8] A lease is a conveyance within the provisions for relief from duty on transactions between associated companies.[9] A lease chargeable with ad valorem duty must be stamped before the expiration of thirty days after it is first executed.[10] If the opinion of the Commissioners has been required as to the amount of duty chargeable it must be stamped within fourteen days of assessment.[10] The absence of a proper stamp means that the instrument may not be put in evidence before a civil court or before an arbitrator or referee.[11] It is the duty of the judge (or arbitrator or referee) to take point of an insufficient stamp.[12] Furthermore it is an offence not to stamp a lease.[13]

1   As to the rates of duty, see the table in the Stamp Act 1891, Sch 1, as amended by the Finance Act 1963, s 56, Finance Act 1974, s 49 and Sch 11, Finance Act 1980, s 128 and reproduced in Hill and Redman's *Law of Landlord and Tenant* (18th edn) para A821. The law stationers produce helpful tables setting out stamp duties etc and no practitioner should be without one.
2   The ad valorem duty is chargeable on the rent where the amount of rent, although not specified in the lease, is immediately ascertainable: *Parry v Deere* (1836) 5 Ad & El 551. The Office of the Controller of Stamps has announced that following legal advice received by the

Board of Inland Revenue the office is changing its practice with regard to the treatment for stamp duty purposes of leases containing provisions for payment of a service rent. Such 'rents' will now be disregarded in the calculation of duty (unless, exceptionally, a single sum is reserved as rent both for the demised hereditament and the right to services) and a certificate of value will be admissible in respect of provisions where the occupation rent does not exceed £250 per annum – see [1981] Gazette 27 May 604.

3 A lease granted for a fixed term and thereafter until determined is for the purposes of stamp duty to be treated as if it were a definite term equal to the fixed term together with the period which will elapse before the earliest possible determination under the terms of the lease. Finance Act 1963, s 56(3).

4 Stamp Act 1891, s 72.

5 Counterparts (not executed by or on behalf of the landlord) of instruments chargeable as leases are exempted from the general application of the Stamp Act 1891, s 72 that requires the counterpart either to be stamped as an original instrument or to bear a denoting stamp showing that the proper duty has been paid on such instrument.

6 Stamp Act 1891, s 75(1) as amended by the Finance Act 1984, s 111.

7 Stamp Act 1891, s 75(2) as amended by the Finance Act 1984, s 111.

8 Finance Act 1931, s 28(1), Sch 2 amended by the Land Commission Act 1967 and the Finance Act 1985, s 89. Commonly known as P D stamping.

9 *Littlewoods Mail Order Stores Ltd v IRC* [1961] Ch 210, [1961] 1 All ER 195; affd [1961] Ch 597, [1961] 3 All ER 258, CA; on appeal sub nom *IRC v Littlewoods Mail Order Stores Ltd* [1963] AC 135, [1962] 2 All ER 279, HL.

10 Stamp Act 1891, s 15.

11 Stamp Act 1891, s 14. In practice an unstamped instrument will generally be allowed in evidence provided there is an undertaking to stamp it.

12 Stamp Act 1891, s 14.

13 Stamp Act 1891, s 15.

15.11 *Registration at HM Land Registry.* Two questions arise under the Land Registration Acts 1925–1971:

15.11:1 *When must a lease be registered?* The position is as follows:

(a) If the landlord's title is registered (whether or not the land is in an area of compulsory registration) then application for first registration of a lease or underlease granted for a term of more than twenty-one years and otherwise capable of substantive registration *must* be made if the tenant is to get a legal estate.[1]

(b) Where the land is in an area of compulsory registration leases or underleases granted for a term of not less than forty years *must* be registered if the tenant is to get a legal estate whether or not the landlord's interest is registered.[2]

(c) Where the land is in an area of compulsory registration a lease or underlease granted for a term of more than twenty-one years or having more than twenty-one years to run and otherwise capable of substantive registration *may* be registered even if the reversion is unregistered.[3]

(d) Where the land is not in an area of compulsory registration and the reversion is not registered no application will be entertained except that under notice of the Registrar applications for first registration in non-compulsory areas will be entertained where it is intended to develop land as a building estate comprising not less than twenty accommodation units provided certain conditions are fulfilled.

(e) A lease for any term or interest not exceeding twenty-one years granted at a rent without taking a fine is an overriding interest.[4]

15.11:2 *Which title and how to effect registration?* The tenant may be registered with:

(a) An absolute title[5] for which title both to the leasehold and the freehold and to any intermediate leasehold that may exist must be approved by the Registrar. This vests in the tenant the possession of the leasehold interest with all implied or expressed rights, privileges and appurtenances attached thereto and subject only to:

   (i) any implied and expressed covenants, obligations, liabilities incident to the registered land;

   (ii) the incumbrances and other entries if any appearing on the register; and

   (iii) such overriding interests (if any) as affect the registered land unless the contrary is expressed on the register.

(b) A good leasehold title[6] in which case the title to the leasehold interest only has to be approved. Such registration does not affect or prejudice the enforcement of any estate, right, or interest affecting, or in derogation of, the title of the landlord to grant the lease but apart from this, such registration has the same effect as registration with an absolute title.

(c) Possessory title.[7] This is unlikely to be relevant in the case of a recently completed commercial lease.

Thus the tenant's solicitor should argue strongly for the landlord to provide him with office copies of his title and to place the Land Certificate on deposit so that his client may be registered with title absolute. The tenant is not entitled to a sight of the freehold title[8] but it is hard to see, where that is registered, how the landlord can have any objection to producing office copy entries of his title, or failing this, supplying the tenant's solicitor with written authority to inspect the register, so that the tenant's solicitor can obtain his own copies. Every effort should always be made to register the tenant with title absolute. The registration of a lease is always a 'first registration' even where the landlord's title is registered and the relevant Land Registry forms are as follows:

- where the tenant is *not* a company or corporation
  3B – good leasehold title
  3F – absolute leasehold title;
- where the tenant *is* a company or corporation
  3E – good leasehold title
  3F (co) – absolute leasehold title.

1 Land Registration Act 1925, ss 19(2), 22(2). The tenant's solicitor should ask that the Landlord's Land Certificate be placed on deposit for the purposes of the tenant's application.
2 Ibid, s 123(1). The position is the same on an assignment of a lease with not less than 40 years to run.
3 Ibid, ss 19, 22.
4 Ibid, s 70(k).
5 Ibid, s 9.
6 Ibid, s 10.
7 Ibid, s 11.
8 See paras 2.9–2.10 above.

15.12 *Registration – with superior lessors and options.* Where an underlease is involved, the landlord's solicitor should refer to the headlease after completion because it will almost certainly contain a covenant by the tenant to give notice of any underlease to the landlord's solicitor and to pay a fee for the privilege. Where the lease contains an option, this must be protected by registration as a C(iv) Land Charge (estate contract) under the Land Charges Act 1972 or, in the case of registered land, by the registration of a notice, caution or restriction under the Land Registration Act 1925.

15.13 *The deeds.* At the end of it all, the landlord's solicitor will be left with the stamped counterpart and the tenant's solicitor will have a stamped lease or, when the lease has been registered, a Land Certificate and the registered lease. Either solicitor may have a standing arrangement with his client to be the custodian of his deeds. In this event, the deeds and any other relevant documents such as a copy of the headlease, planning permission, licences etc should be transferred to the strongroom or the safe and entered up into whatever system of indexing the solicitor operates in relation to the deeds that he is holding. It is good practice to place with the deeds all those documents that are likely to be relevant on any future dealing with the property, or when any points arise. Many solicitors no doubt have arrangements for storing long since 'dead' files away from their main office and as such it may take a little time, and perhaps inconvenience, to recover them. Accordingly it is most helpful to have in the deeds envelope (which should be instantly recoverable) all documents that are likely to be needed. If the client does not wish his solicitor to retain the deeds, they should be sent to him by registered post or delivered by hand, once again together with all relevant documents.[1] A schedule should be enclosed in duplicate and the client should be asked to acknowledge receipt by signing and returning a copy.

1 Where the tenant is a corporation that has charged all future property by way of a mortgage debenture, the client should be reminded of the debenture holder's right to possession of the title deeds.

15.14 *Report to client.* Each solicitor should also, either at this stage or immediately after completion, consider providing a summary for his client of the major terms of the tenancy.[1] There is likely to have been much correspondence about the terms of the letting prior to the grant, perhaps including in the case of the tenant a report from his solicitor on the terms of the draft lease as submitted, but most clients would welcome a brief statement setting out the final terms incorporated in the lease.[1]

1 Unless the client's administration is such that he would rather that this was prepared by his own Property Department. Clearly the solicitor will have reported on the terms of the lease and explained them to his client (see para 1.18 above) *before* the grant of the lease, and where this was done formally this document will probably provide the tenant with the summary that he needs.

Appendices

Appendix 1

Rosscastle Letting Conditions
by the Author and Richard W Castle[1]

CONTENTS *Page*

INTRODUCTION

The concerns

The Law Commission recently highlighted an issue of very great concern to everybody involved in letting premises when it wrote:[2]

> 'There have been many complaints both about the length of leases and about the difficulty of understanding their contents. A lease contains the terms of a bargain between the landlord and the tenant, and we consider it important that the parties should be able readily to understand the document to ascertain their rights and liabilities. Although they will generally be well advised to have professional assistance in the original negotiation of the terms, it should be possible later for the parties to understand the lease without assistance. Ideally, the document would be clear, succinct and comprehensive, yet not too lengthy to be daunting to ordinary property owners. Unfortunately, some of these objectives may turn out to be mutually incompatible.'

We began our examination of that statement by considering the objectives that a lease should be clear and succinct. Why are leases frequently difficult to understand? We felt that this was because of the pompous, wordy, and artificial style in which they are frequently drafted. We could see no reason why a lease should not be drafted in normal English, with the draftsman departing from this only when there was a good reason.[3] He should be aware that often the reasons put forward (for example, the need to be unambiguous) will be suspect. We believed that it ought to be possible to draft a lease with very few departures from normal English. We considered that many leases would be more succinct if the draftsman had thought more about the letting in question before he began drafting. If he had visualised (or even inspected) the property and therefore understood, for example, the rights that the parties, would require, he may well have realised that many provisions in the lease were not appropriate to that particular letting. If he had more critically reviewed the final draft, he may have seen other topics that needed to be included, but that could have been dealt with in fewer words. Thus we took the view that a thoughtful and competent draftsman, who was prepared to take time and trouble over his work and to depart from tradition, ought to be able to achieve these objectives. His draft would be made *clear* by adopting normal English and a modern format and would be *succinct* because it would deal in a few well chosen words with the topics that it includes, and omit all matters that are not relevant.

Comprehensive but manageable?

The more difficult objective to achieve, however, is to make a lease *comprehensive* while still maintaining a manageable length. There is no doubt that the average landlord today includes more provisions in his lease than was once the case. We felt that it was facile to suggest that this was purely the result of the word processor, which enables the draftsman to produce a standard lease (and no doubt a lengthy and comprehensive one) at the push of a button, and constantly to add to that draft as new points occur to him. If ease and low cost of production were the only factors, leases would have been over-long when labour was cheap in the nineteenth century, and would have increased in length with the advent of the typewriter. We would suggest that in recent years leases would have grown in length even if the computer had not been invented, although it certainly has facilitated the production of leases of the type that we see today.

It is, rather, the emergence of the institutional landlord, and the approach that he has brought to commercial conveyancing, that has been the principal cause of leases of business premises becoming more 'comprehensive'. Some of these landlords were historically in the business of lending money and were well used to protecting their investments by means of the terms included in loan agreements, debentures or mortgages. They adopted a similar approach to property investment, seeking to maintain and improve their investments, and to produce a good yield, by means of the leases by which their property was let. Institutional landlords retained able property managers whose performance was measured by the success or otherwise of these investments, and these managers had access to high-powered lawyers, surveyors and other advisers. The ever-increasing sums of money involved served to concentrate the minds. Points that arose in practice, or in an arbitration or reported case, were closely studied by the experts to see what lessons could be learnt for future lettings, while those with special foresight needed nothing to trigger their thoughts but were able to anticipate what could happen and to take preventive drafting action. With such professionalism being brought to bear on the subject, it was inevitable that new and extended provisions would appear in leases.

It is easy to suggest that this new drafting has come about purely to protect and enhance the landlord's investment and the clear lease is certainly an example of this.[4] In fact, the primary aim of many additional provisions has been to create *greater certainty*, although admittedly the previous uncertainty has tended to be resolved in the landlord's favour. Rent review clauses are certainly longer than was once the case, a fact much regretted by some.[5] And yet, so much of the rent review litigation today concerns clauses drafted before the current state of awareness that lack some aspect that we now recognise as being desirable or essential.[6] Some additional clauses have been developed merely to tidy up certain aspects of management.[7] Others simply provide landlord's surveyors with even stronger arguments for maximising the rental increase on each review.[8]

Institutional landlords have been the instigators of the comprehensive lease but their approach has tended to be adopted by all landlords who have realised that such leases are equally consistent with their business objectives. So the solicitor acting for a manufacturing company letting off premises that are in excess of its current operational requirements is likely to prepare an institutional type of lease, not only because this may benefit his client directly but also because it would help if the property was to be sold with the benefit of that lease.

Institutional landlords have not been slow to litigate when they believe that to do so would be in the interests of their shareholders, investors, beneficiaries or policy holders. They have been encouraged by the fact that hearings are generally short where the case involves only a question of construction, and thus little management time is involved. The proceedings are relatively inexpensive, at least compared with many other types of commercial litigation. Litigation has often prompted further increases in the length of leases – the courts' unwillingness to take a practical line has encouraged draftsmen to deal expressly (and perhaps in painful detail) with topics so that nothing is left to chance. Happily however there are now signs that the courts are more often prepared to adopt a purposive approach to construction.[9]

This belt and braces drafting can also be seen where the draftsman has sought to deny even the possibility of an argument to the other party. For example, C might be an inevitable consequence of A and B. In a pure academic environment, there may well be no need expressly to refer to C, as it could safely be assumed that the reader would recognise its inevitability. Practitioners, however, have much experience of the real world in which the other side (but never one's own client) is sometimes obtuse and puts forward bizarre and illogical interpretations. While recognising that such a stance may well find little favour with a court, parties sometimes adopt them for what might politely be called tactical or negotiating reasons. Draftsmen who have suffered in this way tend to feel in the future that they would be failing their clients if they did not specifically deal with C.

Compromises can lengthen a lease. Tenants and their advisers have also built up expertise and are frequently ready with counter-proposals on many of the provisions contained in the draft. Sometimes (but not very often) the landlord will agree to the deletion of the clause – more often he is prepared to accept some words of qualification or limitation, and some compromises arrived at by the parties can only be implemented by the inclusion in the lease of complex and lengthy additional provisions.

There are, of course, other influences which have combined to produce the over-long, complex and badly-written leases sometimes seen today. Clients themselves often resist change, because they have come to know their way about traditional style leases and have used them on numerous occasions while sometimes they require their advisers to produce complicated schemes that are prompted by no, or very few, conventional property considerations. Clauses dreamt up for this type of documentation have a habit of finding their way into the conventional lease. The legal profession too is conservative, while the fear of negligence claims and the real or apparent demands of insurers have lead to rigid procedures and the potential for the accumulation of irrelevant clauses. Writers of precedent books have not been blameless. In a desire to include everything and to provide a document suitable for many circumstances, precedents have often become long and complex.

Finally the type of buildings seen today have called for more involved leases – a unit in a shopping centre or a business park will inevitably raise issues that must be addressed in the lease that are not present in the letting of a high street shop or basic factory.

How to reduce length

The easiest way to reduce the length of any document is to delete material from it and we first asked ourselves if the problem of the length of leases could be resolved by prudent editing. Our views were:

(a) length is merely one aspect of producing a user-friendly document and there is ample scope, even on the part of institutional landlords, to draft leases in normal English and to present them in a way that assists their reader so that the length of the lease would become less relevant;

(b) clauses that can have no relevance to the letting in question are all too often included and any draft should be thoroughly reviewed before it is submitted so that any such provisions can be omitted;

(c) a few provisions currently seen in some leases could certainly be left out without either party suffering, but in general terms, *we did not believe that it was practical to propose large scale deletion of clauses that have come into being in the light of the various factors we have mentioned, and to revert to leases as they once were.*

We say that for two reasons. First, any attempt to produce such leases would not find favour with the institutional landlord and would therefore be rejected by a most significant part of the letting industry. Secondly, we believe that many additional provisions that have served to lengthen leases over recent years do have a function. Admittedly they are not always required, but often it will be impossible to predict at the beginning of each letting whether or not they will be relevant. Accordingly, the safe solution is to include them every time.

It is sometimes said that some form of abridged lease should be used where the property is modest or the term short. But the situations that these recently-developed clauses seek to cover can arise in any letting and they are often troublesome when the property is small. A dispute can occur during a short term, though inevitably the longer the term the more likely it is that a dispute will come about while the lease is running. Nor should it be overlooked that the parties may be defining their relationship for more years than they realise if the tenancy is renewed under the 1954 Act.[10] We therefore rejected the idea of wholesale discarding of clauses as a means to shorten leases.

We considered the three possible approaches put forward by the Law Commission[2] – key words, implied terms and standard terms. The Leases Act 1845 provided a series of key words for use in leases so that they would then be read as if the whole clause set out in the lease was included in the document.[11] Terms are implied into some lettings already, for example landlords' repairing obligations in short leases of residential property,[12] rights of entry to carry out repairs,[13] and secure tenants' rights to take in lodgers.[14] Key words and implied terms have two disadvantages – there is nothing in the document to indicate the existence or details of these rights and obligations, which does not achieve the objectives that the parties should be able readily to understand the terms of their bargain[15] and both would require legislation to amend. As the Law Commission states:[16]

> 'The danger of obsolescence is real. One of the complaints about leases as at present drafted is that they are not revised often enough; when a lease is renewed the new one repeats the language of the old, notwithstanding that eg the decorative techniques and materials to which it refers are not longer in use. Because of the length of time for which leases last, the regular revision of the legislation would itself create difficulties [for key words] . . . The objections of inflexibility and obsolescence which apply to covenants introduced by key words also apply [to implied terms]. No statutory implied covenant yet seems to have been revised but the time may have come when this will be necessary and the appropriate procedure will have to be considered.'

The Law Commission's third alternative was to standardise the terms of the lease:[17]

> 'The wording would appear in the lease but always in the same form. That form could be prescribed by statute, or adopted voluntarily from authoritative recommendations . . . Standardisation seems immediately attractive. It could introduce the use of simple language, making documents easier to understand. It could save a great deal of professional time, and therefore expense, consumed in drafting and negotiating leases and then subsequently interpreting them. However, there are obvious difficulties in devising standard forms for the very wide variety of situations covered by leases. The more exceptions it will allow, the fewer the benefits of standardisation. Here again, there would be a problem of obsolescence.'

Conclusions on standardisation

Our thoughts on standardisation were:
(a) We agreed that there was much to commend it.
(b) We did not believe that it was realistic to seek 'total' standardisation. We felt that any attempt to impose one standard lease on the property market was doomed to failure and would produce a document that would be as neglected as the Leases Act 1845.
(c) If by their comment that 'the more exceptions that were allowed, the fewer the benefits of standardisation' the Law Commission was suggesting that anything that fell short of total standardisation were not worthwhile, then we disagreed. Standardisation of a significant part of a lease was likely, we felt, to be better than no standardisation at all.
(d) What we felt was needed was some form of standard document that could easily be varied so that topics already covered in the document could be dealt with in a different way, and new topics could be included.
(e) We did not see that there was any point in expressly setting out in each lease the standard wording. Not only did this seem unnecessary, but it would mean that the tenant's solicitor would have to examine the lease against the approved standard in order to ensure that the draftsman had not made amendments.
(f) We noted that the overwhelming majority of contracts for the sale of freehold or leasehold land incorporate either the Law Society's or the National Conditions of Sale. These generally work well. Practitioners are aware of the contents and effect of these conditions but do not have to study them in great detail when drafting and negotiating each contract.
(g) Most well drawn leases deal with virtually the same topics in virtually the same way – the variations arise only in the drafting. We agreed with the views of the Royal Commission on Legal Services (our emphasis):[18]

> 'We consider that efforts should also be made to standardise the provisions of a lease, particularly residential property. At the moment a lease, whether of residential property or commercial property, may be around forty or fifty pages and will contain provisions which are similar to, but not identical with, the provisions of other leases . . . If any problem arises, the particular wording of each lease must be studied, argued about, construed by the parties who may not be the original landlords or the original tenants, submitted to solicitors and counsel who probably had nothing to do with the original draft and finally if necessary construed by the court . . . *We doubt, however, whether the need for flexiblity requires liberty to invent a new form for each transaction'.*

(h) Although we did not believe that any of these commonly found provisions should be omitted from the standard document, we felt strongly that it should be drafted using a contemporary vocabulary and style and avoiding legalese and antique English.

Letting conditions

We concluded that what was needed was a set of letting conditions that would be used in conjunction with a document that would be similar to a conventional lease which would enable the draftsman easily to vary or add to the conditions.[19] We are not suggesting that these documents will enable leases to be granted without the parties or their advisers having to read or consider the detailed terms. A landlord's solicitor today must consider if all the provisions of the document upon which he proposes to base his draft – be it his own standard lease or a published precedent – are appropriate for the letting in question. His task will be the same if he decides to use the conditions and the tenant's solicitor will still have to consider the draft to see if its provisions are acceptable to his client. If, however, one set of standard conditions were to become widely used, both solicitors will be familiar with them, thereby significantly shortening the time that these two reviews will take, while much typing (or word processing) will be saved, at both draft and engrossment stage, if the bulk of the document does not have to be set out in full but is dealt with by means of incorporation. Clients too, at least those who are in the property business, will also become familiar with the conditions and thus the whole process of letting business premises speeded up. The conditions would be drafted in normal English and would lend themselves to this study and familiarity.[20]

The Farrand Committee[21] said that: 'In view of [standardisation's] apparent attraction and clear potential for simplification, it may well be worthy of proper investigation by the Law Commission or some appropriate body', while the Law Commission[22] itself said: 'We think [standard terms] is an area which would repay further study'. Many will no doubt think it presumptuous for two practitioners to produce these detailed proposals without investigation or further study by an appropriate body. We would make three comments:

(a) sometimes it is helpful to put forward proposals that do not have the stamp of officialdom – if nothing else they can be produced more quickly than when a committee-structured official body is involved;

(b) 'unofficial' proposals may prove to be an answer in themselves, or may provide a starting point for a later version that may have greater status. If these conditions achieve only the latter, we would not feel that we had failed;

(c) nevertheless, we do not put these conditions forward as some kind of draft or discussion document. We believe that they immediately provide the possibility of reducing the length of documents, and the time and expense involved in drafting and negotiating commercial leases. In our view, short leases of the type set out in Forms 3–6 below are viable alternatives to the types of document with which we have been forced to become familiar over recent years and that have prompted so much concern.

1   Solicitor and former member of the Law Society's Land Law and Conveyancing Committee. We are indebted to John Stuart Colyer QC for reviewing the Conditions in draft and for his contributions.
2   'Landlord and Tenant: Reform of the Law' (1987) Law Commission No 162, para 3.6.
3   For guidance on drafting, see paras 1.1–1.5 above.
4   See para 11.1 above.
5   See for example [1987] Gazette 3 June 1626.
6   In its report (see footnote 2 above) the Law Commission wrote para 4:60 (our emphasis): 'We have already noted the dramatic rise in the number of rent review clauses in leases of business property in recent years. Although the clauses have provoked much litigation, *there is a strong case for saying that the courts and the legal profession have between them ironed out many of the problems* and can be relied upon to tackle the remainder'.
7   An example is the provisions that set out clearly when the review dates are, when the revised rent is to be determined and what happens in the meantime: see paras 6.4 and 6.52–6.55.
8   For example those assumptions or disregards that depart from reality so that the hypothetical letting (see paras 6.1, 6.2 & 6.17 above) has removed from it some factor that had a negative effect on the rent of the real letting: See paras 6.17:1 & 6.30 above).
9   See para 6.17:2 above.
10   See Chapter 14 above.

11 Thus a tenant who agreed in a lease 'to repair' would be taken to have entered into a detailed repairing obligation. This technique for shortening documents has long been in use in relation to conveyances of freehold land, where it is fully accepted (see Law of Property Act 1925, s 76).

12 Landlord and Tenant Act 1985, s 11(1) as amended by the Housing Act 1988, s 116.

13 Rent (Agriculture) Act 1976, Sch 5, para 8; Rent Act 1977, s 148; Landlord and Tenant Act 1985, s 11(6) as amended by the Housing Act 1988, s 116.

14 Housing Act 1985, s 93(1).

15 See the extract of the Law Commission's report quoted at the beginning of this Introduction.

16 See footnote 2 above, paras 3.9 and 3.10.

17 See footnote 2 above, paras 3.14 and 3.15.

18 (1979) Cmnd 7648, Annex 21.1, para 13.

19 The conditions could be bound into the lease so that all the parties' rights and liabilities will be set out in the one document, thereby achieving another of the aims set out in the extract of the Law Commission's report quoted at the beginning of this Introduction.

20 They would, for example, follow the guidelines set out in paras 11.3–11.5 above.

21 Second Report of the Conveyancing Committee (1985) para 8.11.

22 See footnote 2 above, para 3.18.

THE CONDITIONS AND HOW TO USE THEM

The Conditions

The Rosscastle Letting Conditions (see Form 1) are designed to be used in lettings of business premises in the same way as the Law Society's or the National Conditions of Sale are used in agreements for the sale of freehold and leasehold property. The aim has been to include in them the provisions that would be expected in a lease today, giving them the emphasis that a reasonable landlord would require. The worst landlord's excesses have been omitted, but the terms reflect the current market and it is suggested that they would be institutionally acceptable. They have been drafted using standard English and in a format that should be easy to follow. The Conditions are believed to be complete for a normal letting, although the draftsman can easily include additional provisions.

We decided that it would not be helpful to provide a printed form that included the Letting Conditions and on which the variables of each letting could be inserted, as is done with the conditions of sale. Instead, the Letting Conditions should be used in conjunction with (and probably bound into) a short document similar in format to a lease that sets out the parties, the property and the other key elements of that letting (see Form 2). The disadvantage with forms is that usually only limited amendments can be made (unless sheets are annexed and this is never entirely satisfactory) but with this approach the draftsman is free to add as many terms as he wishes, that may either cover additional topics not dealt with in the Conditions, or be in substitution for one or more of the Conditions. Any of the Conditions can easily be excluded (see clause 1.7 of Form 2). This flexibility is not present when a printed form has to be completed.

The Conditions are drafted essentially on the basis of a letting of the whole of a detached building but certain of the basic provisions required if the landlord retains nearby premises are included (eg Conditions 3.2:2, 3.3:2, 10.4 etc). No rights or exceptions are dealt with – we felt that these could not be standardised and that it is important for the draftsman specifically to consider in relation to each letting what rights the parties will require. The specific use to which the property must be put is dealt with in the lease, and the Conditions contain a number of general provisions (eg Conditions 3.8 and 3.9).

The Conditions provide for the landlord to insure and for the tenant to reimburse him for the premiums. If the lease specifies review dates, the Conditions dealing with rent review will be included (Conditions 7.1–7.5) and if the landlord is not the freeholder, certain general provisions relevant to an underlease will apply (Conditions 8.1–8.3). There are covenants by a guarantor (Conditions 5.1–5.2) whether originally included as a party to the lease, or who subsequently enters into covenants with the landlord following an assignment or upon the death, bankruptcy or disqualification of the original guarantor (Conditions 3.7:5 and 3.20).

A feature of the Letting Conditions is that the individual provisions have, whenever possible, been simplified by the use of an interpretation section (Conditions 2.1–2.10). Thus, for example, the granting and excepting of rights can be dealt with quite briefly because the points dealt with in Conditions 2.2:1, 2.2:3, 2.3 and 2.4 do not have to be set out, while Condition 2.2:2 deals once with an issue that is often covered throughout the document whenever the expiry or prior determination of the term is mentioned.

HOW TO USE THEM

Insert the basic provisions on a form of lease (Form 2) namely
- name and address of landlord(s)
- name and address of tenant(s)
- name and address of guarantor(s) (if any)
- brief description of the property, by reference to a plan if need be
- reference to any covenants affecting the freehold to which the lease is subject
- term for which the lease is granted
- rent, or the initial rent if there is to be rent review
- rent review dates (if any)
- decorating years
- permitted use
- details of the superior lease, where landlord not the freeholder.

Does the tenant require express rights from the landlord to enable him to use the property?

If YES, draft them. Examples are given in Forms 4, 5 and 6.

Where the tenant has been granted rights, does the landlord require (and ought he to give) covenants in relation to those rights?

If YES, draft them. Examples are given in clauses 4 and 5 of Forms 4, 5 and 6.

Should the landlord reserve rights for the benefit of nearby premises?

If YES, draft them. Examples are given under 'Exceptions' in the Forms 4, 5 and 6.

Does the property form part of a larger unit (for example an estate, or building)?

If YES consider and draft
- tenant's rights (examples are given in Forms 5 and 6)
- landlord's reservations (examples are given in Forms 5 and 6)
- service charge provisions (an example of a full service charge provisions is given in Form 6 and Form 5 shows a simpler approach)
- landlord's obligations on repair of facilities (examples are given in Forms 4 and 5).

What are the arrangements about repairs?

The Letting Conditions stipulate that the tenant is to repair (Condition 3.4) so a lease incorporating the Letting Conditions without amendment would be a full repairing lease. An example of a lease where the landlord repairs the structure and exterior and the tenant repairs the interior is given in Form 6.

What are the arrangements about insurance?

In the Letting Conditions and in the Forms 3–6, the landlord insures and recovers the cost from the tenant. If other arrangements are to apply suitable amendments will be needed – Form 7 sets out proposed amendments where insurance is by a superior landlord.

Who should determine the revised rent?

The Letting Conditions provide for an arbitrator to determine the revised rent on the rent review – Form 8 sets out proposed amendments where an expert is required.

Do any of the variations require consequential amendments?

The lease should be reviewed to check that none of the variations that have been made requires consequential amendments to the Letting Conditions. Any Condition can be excluded: see clause 1.7 of Form 2. If an alternative or additional provision is required, it can be added in the lease. There is, however, no need specifically to exclude any Conditions that self-evidently are not relevant to the letting in question: for example Conditions 3.2:2, 3.3:2 and 10.4 need not be excluded when the landlord owns no Adjoining Premises.

Is the lease acceptable to the landlord?

Finally the lease and Letting Conditions should be reviewed to check that they are 'commercially acceptable' to the landlord. Any Condition that is not acceptable can be excluded: see 1.7 in Form 2. If an alternative or additional provision is required, it can be added in the appropriate place: see 4–10 in Form 2.

Engrossment

It is suggested that a print of the Letting Conditions be bound into the engrossment thereby producing a complete document. A print could also be supplied with the draft (see footnote 1 to Form 1 below).

FORM NO 1
ROSSCASTLE LETTING CONDITIONS[1]

(1st edition)

1 DEFINITIONS

In the Letting Conditions and in the Lease the following definitions apply:[2]

1.1 'Adjoining Premises' – any nearby property in which the Landlord (or where the Landlord is a company any company that is a member of the Landlord's Group)[3] has or acquires during the Term a freehold or leasehold interest

1.2 'Bank' – any bank that is a member of the Committee of the London and Scottish Bankers and that is at any time nominated by the Landlord[4] for the purpose of making a computation under the Lease

1.3 'Building'[5] – any building or other structure that is now on the Property or that is erected on the Property during the Term

1.4 'Landlord's Group' – a group of companies of which the Landlord is or becomes a member within the meaning of the 1954 Act, s 42(1)[3]

1.5 'Lease' – the lease into which these Conditions are incorporated and references in that document and in the Letting Conditions to 'the Lease' or 'this Lease' mean that document and the Letting Conditions incorporated into it[6]

1.6 '1954 Act' – Part II of the Landlord and Tenant Act 1954 and all statutes regulations and orders included by virtue of Condition 2.2:1[7]

1.7 'Other Buildings' – any building or other structure now erected on the Adjoining Premises[8] or that is erected on the Adjoining Premises[8] during the Term

1.8 'Open Land' – any part of the Property not built upon[9]

1.9 'Plan' – the plan or plans annexed to the Lease

1.10 'Planning Acts' – Town and Country Planning Act 1971 and all statutes regulations and orders including by virtue of Condition 2.2:1[7]

1.11 'Qualified Expert' – as defined in Condition 9[10]

1.12 'Rent' – the Initial Rent[9] or the rent agreed or determined under Condition 7

1.13 'VAT' – value added tax and any tax of a similar nature substituted for it or in addition to it.[11]

2 INTERPRETATION

In the Letting Conditions and in the Lease:

2.1 the expression:

2.1:1 'conducting media' includes[12] all drains channels sewers flues conduits conducts pipes wires cables watercourses gutters culverts soakaways and other similar transmission media and installations and all fixings louvres cowls covers and other ancilliary apparatus

2.1:2 'development' has the meaning given to it by the Planning Acts[13]

2.1:3 'Landlord' includes the person for the time being entitled to the immediate possession of the Property on the expiry of the Term[14]

2.1:4 'parties' or 'party' mean the Landlord and the Tenant or either of them but (in the absence of a specific provision to the contrary in the Lease or Letting Conditions) does not include the Guarantor[15]

2.1:5 'planning control' has the meaning given to it by the Planning Acts[16]

2.1:6 'Property' includes[12] the Building all improvements and additions to the Property all fixtures on the Property (except tenant's fixtures)[17] and the conducting media[18] within the Property[19] which solely serve the Property

2.1:7 'Tenant' includes the person for the time being in whom the tenant's interest under the Lease is vested

2.2 references:

2.2:1 to a specific statute include (in the absence of any provision to the contrary in the Lease)[20] any statutory extension modification amendment or re-enactment of that statute and any regulations or orders made under it and any general reference to 'statute' or 'statutes' includes any derivative regulations or orders[21]

2.2:2 to the expiry of the Term or to the last year of the Term are (subject to Condition 10.8) to the end of the Term and the last year of the Term however the Term comes to an end whether by effluxion of time or in any other way[22]

2.2:3 to conducting media being 'in' or 'on' certain property include[12] conducting media in on under over or through that property[23]

2.2:4 to the base lending rate are to that rate or if it has been abolished to the equivalent rate that has replaced it or if none to the rate of interest most comparable with the base lending rate fixed in the absence of agreement between the parties by a Qualified Expert[24]

2.2:5 to 'losses' include[12] all liabilities incurred by the Landlord all damage and loss suffered by it all claims demands actions and proceedings made or brought against it and all costs disbursements and expenses incurred by it[25]

2.2:6 to 'damage' or 'damaged' include destruction or destroyed[26]

2.3 any right of way granted to the Tenant may (in the absence of any provision to the contrary in the Lease) also be exercised by any person expressly or by implication authorised by the Tenant (but only for proper purposes connected with the use or enjoyment of the Property)[27] and by the Landlord by any person authorised by the Landlord and by any person who is or who becomes entitled to use it[28]

2.4   if Exceptions are excepted and reserved in favour of the Landlord they may (in the absence of any provision to the contrary in the Lease) also be exercised by any person authorised by the Landlord and any person who is or who becomes entitled to exercise them[29]

2.5   any provision indicating that the Landlord's consent approval or authorisation is not to be unreasonably withheld will be construed as though it also provided that the consent approval or authorisation is not to be unreasonably delayed[30]

2.6   any consent approval or authorisation to be given by the Landlord must be in writing and signed by or on its behalf if it is to be effective under the Lease

2.7   whenever the Landlord the Tenant or the Guarantor consists of more than one person any obligation of or to that party is of or to those persons separately all together or in any combination[31]

2.8   words importing one gender include all other genders

2.9   any covenant by the Tenant not to do any act or thing include an obligation not to allow [32] that act or thing to be done by another person

2.10   the headings in the Lease and the Letting Conditions are for assistance in locating references in the text and are not to be taken into account in the construction or interpretation of the documents.[33]

3   TENANT'S COVENANTS

The Tenant covenants with the Landlord:

3.1   *Rent*

To pay the Rent without any deduction by equal quarterly payments in advance on the usual quarter days and

3.1:1   the first payment is for the period beginning with the Rent Commencement Date[34] and ending the day before the next quarter day

3.1:2   the first payment is due on the date of the Lease[35] or on the Rent Commencement Date[36] whichever is the later

3.1:3   Rent for a period of less than a year is to be apportioned on a daily basis

3.1:4   the Tenant may not exercise any claim to withhold Rent or any set-off[37] and

3.1:5   if required in writing by the Landlord the Tenant must make these payments by banker's order or credit transfer to any bank and account in the United Kingdom that the Landlord may nominate[38]

3.2   *Outgoings and VAT*

To pay and to indemnify the Landord against:

3.2:1 all rates taxes assessments impositions duties charges and outgoings[39] which now or during the Term are charged assessed or imposed upon the Property or upon the owner or occupier of it (excluding any payable by the Landlord in respect of the receipt of Rent or any other payment made by the Tenant under the Lease, except any VAT payable on the Rent or any other payment made by the Tenant under the Lease, or on any disposition or dealing with or the ownership of the reversion of the Lease) and if the Landlord loses rating relief because it has been allowed to the Tenant or any subtenant during the Term to make good that loss to the Landlord

3.2:2 the proportion properly attributable to the Property (to be fixed in the absence of agreement between the parties by a Qualified Expert)[40] of all rates taxes assessments impositions duties charges and outgoings which now or during the Term are charged assessed or imposed upon the Property and other premises or upon the owner or occupier of the Property and other premises and

3.2:3 VAT[41] chargeable on the Rent or on any payment made by the Tenant under the Lease and (except to the extent that the Landlord can reclaim it) on any payment made by the Landlord where the Tenant agrees to reimburse the Landlord

3.3 *Supplies*

3.3:1 Where the separate supply is provided to the Property to pay the supplier and to indemnify the Landlord against all charges for water electricity gas telephone and other supplies consumed on the Property and to pay all equipment rents

3.3:2 Where charges for water electricity gas telephone and any other supply are made in relation to the Property and other premises (or upon the owner or occupier of the Property and other premises) to pay the supplier and to indemnify the Landlord against the proportion of the charges properly attributable to the Property (or the owner or occupier of the Property) to be fixed from time to time in the absence of agreement between the parties by a Qualified Expert[42]

3.4 *Repairs Cleaning Decoration*

3.4:1 To repair the Property and keep it in repair[43] but the Tenant need not do so where the damage is caused by a risk against which the Landlord has insured except where the insurance money is irrecoverable through the fault of the Tenant or its subtenants[44]

3.4:2 To replace any of the Landlord's fixtures which become beyond repair during the Term

3.4:3 To clean the Property and keep it clean neat and tidy

3.4:4 To clean both sides of the windows and window frames in the Property at least once a month[45]

3.4:5 To keep the Open Land[46] adequately surfaced in good condition and free from weeds

3.4:6 Not to allow any rubbish to be on the Open Land[46]

3.4:7 To keep all landscaped areas within the Property free from weeds and properly cultivated

3.4:8   In each of the Exterior Decorating Years[47] and in the last year of the Term[48] to redecorate the exterior of the Building and in each of the Interior Decorating Years[47] and in the last year of the Term to redecorate the interior of the Building in both instances in a workmanlike way and with appropriate materials of good quality to the reasonable satisfaction of the Landlord[49]

3.4:9   To obtain the Landlord's approval (such approval not to be unreasonably withheld) of any change in the colours and patterns on each redecoration[50]

3.4:10   Where the use of conducting media boundary structures or other things is common to the Property and other premises to be responsible for and to indemnify the Landlord against all sums due from and to undertake all work that is the responsibility of the owner lessee or occupier of the Property in relation to those things

3.5   *Alterations*[51]

3.5:1   Not to erect any new building or structure on the Property nor unite the Property with any adjoining property[52]

3.5:2   Not to make any addition or alteration to the Property that affects the exterior of the Building any load bearing part of the Building or its roof or foundations[52]

3.5:3   Not to make any addition or alteration to the Property that is not prohibited by the absolute prohibitions set out in Conditions 3.5:1 and 3.5:2 unless:[52]

3.5:3.1   the consent of the Landlord has been obtained such consent not to be unreasonably withheld but in considering an application for consent the Landlord may take into account the effect that the addition or alteration may have on Adjoining Premises[53]

3.5:3.2   all necessary consents from any competent authority have been obtained

3.5:3.3   the Landlord has been supplied with drawings and where appropriate a specification in duplicate prepared by an architect or member of some other appropriate profession who must supervise the work to completion

3.5:3.4   the proper fees of the Landlord any superior landlord or mortgagee and their respective professional advisers have been paid in relation to the application for consent

3.5:3.5   such covenants as the Landlord may reasonably require about the carrying out of the addition or alteration[54] have been entered into and

3.5:3.6   in the case of substantial work and where the Landlord requires adequate security has been provided in the form of a deposit of money or a bond as assurance to the Landlord that any work allowed by the Landlord is completed

3.5:4   At the expiry of the Term to remove any addition or alteration made to the Property if requested by the Landlord to do so and to reinstate and make good any part of the Property damaged by the removal[55]

3.5:5   Not to connect with any conducting media which serve the Property unless it has obtained the approval of the competent authority and the Landlord (the Landlord's approval not to be unreasonably withheld)

3.5:6 Not to commit any waste at the Property unless it is permitted by virtue of a consent under Conditions 3.5:3 and 3.5:5[56]

3.6 *Access of Landlord and Notice to Repair*

3.6:1 To permit the Landlord and all persons authorised by the Landlord at reasonable times and on reasonable notice (except in an emergency):

3.6:1.1 to enter the Property to find out whether the provisions of the Lease have been observed[57]

3.6:1.2 to carry out work relating to any jointly used facility

3.6:1.3 to carry out work to Adjoining Premises which cannot reasonably be carried out without access to the Property

3.6:1.4 to take inventories

3.6:1.5 to exercise any right granted to or reserved to the Landlord by the Lease

3.6:1.6 to inspect in relation to rent review or any step under the 1954 Act

3.6:1.7 to view (and to open up floors and other parts of the Property where that is reasonable) the condition of the Property and

3.6:1.8 to give to the Tenant (or leave on the Property) a notice specifying any repairs maintenance or decoration that the Tenant has failed to carry out and to request the Tenant to carry them out straight away including the making good of any opening up

BUT any opening up is to be made good by or at the cost of the Landlord where it reveals no breaches of the terms of the Lease

3.6:2 Immediately to repair clean and decorate the Property as required by the notice

3.6:3 To allow the Landlord and all persons authorised by the Landlord to enter the Property to carry out the work needed to comply with the notice and to pay to the Landlord all expenses of doing so within fourteen days of a written demand if

3.6:3.1 within a month of service of the notice the Tenant has not both begun and then continued the work referred to in the notice or

3.6:3.2 the Tenant fails to complete the work within a reasonable time of service of the notice or

3.6:3.3 in the Landlord's reasonable opinion the Tenant is unlikely to complete the work within a reasonable time of the service of the notice[58]

3.7 *Alienation*

3.7:1 Except when (and to the extent) permitted under the subsequent provisions of Condition 3.7 not to:

3.7:1.1 part with possession of the Property or any part of it[60]

3.7:1.2 permit another to occupy the Property or any part of it[60]

3.7:1.3 share the occupation of the Property or any part of it[60]

3.7:1.4 hold the Property or any part of it on trust for another

3.7:2   Not to assign underlet or charge part[61] only of the Property

3.7:3   Not to assign underlet or charge the whole of the Property without the consent of the Landlord such consent not to be unreasonably withheld where the Tenant has complied with the appropriate provisions of Conditions 3.7:4–3.7:7

3.7:4[62]   To procure that any assignee enters into covenants with the Landlord to observe all the Tenant's covenants and all the other provisions of the Lease during the residue of the Term

3.7:5[62]   On an assignment to a limited company and if the Landlord reasonably[63] requires to procure that at least two directors of the company or some other persons acceptable to the Landlord (such acceptance not to be unreasonably[63] withheld) enter into covenants with the Landlord in the form of Conditions 5.1–5.2 with 'the Assignee and its successors' substituted for 'the Tenant' or in such other form as the Landlord reasonably requires[64]

3.7:6[62]   In relation to every underlease to ensure that:

3.7:6.1   it is granted without a premium at a rent approved by the Landlord (such approval not to be unreasonably withheld) and no lower than the then open market rent[65]

3.7:6.2   the rent is payable quarterly in advance on days no later than the days when rent is payable under the Lease

3.7:6.3   it contains provisions approved by the Landlord (such approval not to be unreasonably withheld):
– that provide for the upwards only review of the rent on the basis set out in Condition 7 or in such other form as the Landlord reasonably requires or approves
– that provide for the rent to be reviewed either on the Review Dates or on other dates approved by the Landlord by which the rent is reviewed no less frequently
– prohibiting the undertenant from doing or allowing any act or thing in relation to the underlet premises inconsistent with or in breach of the provisions of the Lease
– for re-entry by the underlandlord on breach of any covenant by the undertenant
– imposing an absolute prohibition against all dealings with the underlet premises other than an assignment or charge of the whole
– prohibiting any assignment or charge of the whole of the underlet premises without the consent of the Landlord under the Lease
– prohibiting the undertenant from parting with possession or permitting another to share or occupy or holding on trust for another the underlet premises or any part of them and
– imposing in relation to any permitted assignment the same obligations for consent and registration with the Landlord as are in the Lease in relation to dispositions by the Tenant

3.7:7[62]   before any permitted underletting to procure that the undertenant enters into covenants with the Landlord to the same effect as those required of an assignee

3.7:8   In relation to any permitted underlease:

3.7:8.1   to enforce the observance[57] by every undertenant of the provisions of the underlease and not at any time to waive any breach of the covenants or conditions on the part of any undertenant or assignee of any underlease nor (without the consent of the Landlord such consent not to be unreasonably withheld) to vary the terms of any permitted underlease

3.7:8.2 not to agree any reviewed rent with the undertenant without the approval of the Landlord such approval not to be unreasonably withheld

3.7:8.3 not to agree any appointment of a person as the third party determining the revised rent without the approval of the Landlord such approval not to be unreasonably withheld

3.7:8.4 to incorporate as part of its representations to that third party representations required by the Landlord and

3.7:8.5 to give the Landlord details of every rent review within 28 days of its outcome

3.7:9 Within 21 days of an assignment charge underlease or any transmission or other devolution relating to the Property to produce for registration with the Landlord's solicitor a certified copy of any relevant document and to pay the Landlord's solicitors reasonable charges for registration of at least Twenty Pounds (£20.00)[66]

3.8 *Use*[67]

3.8:1 Not to use the Property except for the Permitted Use[68]

3.8:2 Not to sleep on the Property nor use it as a residence nor keep any animal on it

3.8:3 Not to do or allow to remain upon the Property anything which may constitute a nuisance[69] or which may cause inconvenience to the Landlord or its tenants or the occupier of nearby premises or cause damage to nearby premises

3.8:4 Not to use the Property for any dangerous noisy or offensive[70] occupation nor for any illegal or immoral purposes

3.8:5 To use the Open Land only for the purposes for which it was designed or is specified on the Plan[71] and not to keep on the Open Land any caravan or temporary building[72]

3.8:6 Not to discharge into any conducting media servicing the Property:

3.8:6.1 any substance that may obstruct them or cause damage or danger or

3.8:6.2 any poisonous or radioactive matter or anything likely to pollute

3.8:7 Not to overload[73] the Property

3.8:8 Not to leave the Property continuously unoccupied for more than a month without notifying the Landlord and providing such security arrangements as the Landlord and the insurers require

3.9 *Shop*

Where the Property is a shop[74]:

3.9:1 not to play or use at the Property any apparatus that produces sound audible outside it

3.9:2 not to display any flashing lights at the Property visible outside it

3.9:3   not to install any exterior lighting exterior shade or awning at the Property

3.9:4   not to trade or to place goods on the pavement outside the Property

3.9:5   to keep the shop windows attractively dressed in a manner appropriate to the neighbourhood

3.9:6   to keep all those parts of the interior of the Property that are visible from outside attractively laid out and furnished with goods well displayed and to keep any showcases in the Property clean and attractively dressed

3.9:7   not to place or display on the exterior of the Property or on the windows[75] or inside the Property so as to be visible from outside the Property any notice sign sticker or advertisement other than:

3.9:7.1   normal price tickets attached and relating to goods sold in the display area inside the Property

3.9:7.2   the sign referred to in Condition 3.10:2 and

3.9:7.3   trade placards posters or advertisements of a temporary and not excessive nature and usual for the Permitted Use

3.10   *Aerials Signs and Advertisements*

3.10:1   Not to erect any pole mast dish or wire on the Property without the Landlord's consent such consent not to be unreasonably withheld[76]

3.10:2   If requested by the Landlord to display a sign showing the Tenant's trading name of a size and kind approved by the Landlord (such approval not to be unreasonably withheld) at a point to be specified by the Landlord

3.10:3   Not to display any other sign which is visible outside the Property[77]

3.11   *Statutory Obligations*[78]

To comply with the requirements of any statute (existing or to be passed) or of any government department local or other authority or court of competent jurisdiction whether or not the requirements are imposed upon the lessor the lessee or the occupier of the Property

3.12   *Statutory Notices*[79]

3.12:1   To produce to the Landlord a copy of any notice or proposal issued to the Tenant or served upon the Property by any government department local or other authority or court of competent jurisdiction within fourteen days of receipt

3.12:2   If required by the Landlord to produce the original document to the Landlord

3.12:3   Without delay and at the cost of the Tenant to take all steps to comply with the notice and at the request of the Landlord to make or join with the Landlord in making any reasonable representations that the Landlord requires against the notice or proposal providing they are not disadvantageous to the Tenant[80]

3.13 *Planning*

3.13:1   Not to commit any breach of planning control and to comply with the provisions of the Planning Acts[81] in relation to the Property[82]

3.13:2   Not to make any application for planning permission in relation to the Property nor to serve any notice in respect of an application without the approval of the Landlord such approval not to be unreasonably withheld[83]

3.13:3   Having obtained the Landlord's approval under Condition 3.13:2 to apply for all planning permissions and to serve all notices required for the carrying out of any operations or change of use on the Property which may constitute development[84]

3.13:4   Subject to any statutory direction to the contrary, to pay any charge that may be imposed under the Planning Acts[81] in respect of the carrying out of any development[84]

3.13:5   Even if the Landlord has given its approval under condition 3.13:2 and granted whatever other consents for the development are needed under the Lease, not to carry out any operations or change of use on the Property until:

3.13:5.1   all necessary notices under the Planning Acts have been served and copies produced to the Landlord

3.13:5.2   all necessary permissions under the Planning Acts[81] have been obtained and produced to the Landlord and

3.13:5.3   the Landlord has acknowledged that every necessary planning permission is acceptable to it (such acknowledgment not to be unreasonably withheld) although the Landlord may refuse to acknowledge its acceptance of a planning permission on the grounds that any condition contained in it or anything omitted from it or the period referred to in it would be (or would be likely to be) prejudicial to the Landlord's interest in the Property or the interest of the Landlord or (where appropriate) a company within the Landlord's Group in Adjoining Premises[53] whether during or after the expiry of the Term

3.13:6   Unless the Landlord otherwise directs, to complete before the expiry of the Term:

3.13:6.1   any works specified as having to be carried out by a date after the expiry of the Term in an agreement with the planning authority entered into as a condition to obtaining planning permission

3.13:6.2   any development[84] begun on the Property

3.13:7   In any case where a planning permission is granted subject to conditions and if the Landlord reasonably so requires, to provide security for the compliance with those conditions and not to implement the planning permission until security has been provided

3.14 *Equipment*

3.14:1   Not to install or use on the Property any equipment which causes noise or vibration detectable outside or damage to the Property

3.14:2   To keep all equipment on the Property properly maintained to renew all parts when recommended and to ensure that the equipment is properly operated

3.15   *Defective Premises*

3.15:1   To give notice immediately to the Landlord of any defect in the Property which might give rise to a liability or duty on the Landlord under the Lease the Defective Premises Act 1972 or otherwise

3.15:2   To display all notices which the Landlord may reasonably require

3.16   *Encroachments*

3.16:1   Not to stop up darken or obstruct any windows at the Property

3.16:2   To take all reasonable steps to prevent any new easement being acquired over the Property and to notify the Landlord immediately if any is attempted

3.17   *Evidence of Compliance*

If required to produce to the Landlord such evidence as the Landlord may reasonably require to satisfy itself that the provisions of the Lease have been complied with

3.18   *Indemnity*

To be responsible for and to keep the Landlord indemnified against all losses[25] resulting directly or indirectly from:

3.18:1   any negligence of the Tenant or any of its subtenants or

3.18:2   any breach by the Tenant of the provisions of the Lease

3.19   *Key Holders*

To ensure that at all times both the Landlord and the local police have written notice of the name address and home telephone number of at least two keyholders of the Property

3.20   *New Guarantor*

3.20:1   To give notice to the Landlord within fourteen days if any of the following happen to the Guarantor (or if more than one person is included in this term to any one of them) or to any person who has entered into covenants with the Landlord under Conditions 3.7:5 or 3.20:2

3.20:1.1   to an individual: death; appointment of a receiver under the Mental Health Act 1983: application for an interim order; bankruptcy petition presented; proposal made for a voluntary arrangement; deed of arrangement entered into[85]

3.20:1.2   to a company: it goes into liquidation (whether compulsory or voluntary) but not a voluntary winding up for the amalgamation or reconstruction of a solvent company; receiver manager administrative receiver or provisional liquidator appointed; petition presented for an administration order; proposal made for a voluntary arrangement or a scheme of arrangement[85]

3.20:1.3 to an individual or company: entry into an arrangement for the benefit of creditors or distress or execution levied on his or its goods

3.20:2 If required by the Landlord within 28 days of the service of a notice under Condition 3.20:1 to procure that some other person reasonably acceptable to the Landlord enters into covenants with the Landlord within 60 days of that request in the form of Conditions 5.1–5.2 (with 'the Assignee and its successors' substituted for 'the Tenant' where appropriate) or in such other form as the Landlord reasonably requires[86]

3.21 *Interest*

3.21:1 To pay interest at a yearly rate of 4% above the Bank's base lending rate from time to time on any Rent or other sum payable under this Lease that is not paid on the date on which it is due[87]

3.21:2 To pay this interest from the due date to the date of payment (both before and after any judgment) calculated on a daily basis and compounded with rests on the usual quarter days but nothing in this Condition entitles the Tenant to withhold or delay any payment or prejudices the rights of the Landlord in relation to non-payment

3.22 *Landlord's Costs*

To pay to the Landlord on an indemnity basis all costs and other expenses properly incurred by the Landlord in relation to:

3.22:1 every application made by the Tenant for consent whether it is granted refused offered subject to any qualification or withdrawn

3.22:2 the preparation and service of a notice under the Law of Property Act 1925 s 146 or incurred by or in contemplation of proceedings under ss 146 and 147 of that Act even if forfeiture is avoided otherwise than by relief granted by the court

3.22:3 the recovery of Rent or other sums due from the Tenant

3.22:4 any steps taken in connection with the preparation and service of a schedule of dilapidations during or after the expiry of the Term[88]

3.22:5 professional advice obtained by the Landlord following an application by the Tenant for a consent under the Lease

3.23 *Sale of Reversion*

To permit at reasonable times upon reasonable notice agents or prospective purchasers of any interest superior to the Lease to view the Property provided they are authorised by the Landlord or its agent[89]

3.24 *Re-letting*

To permit the Landlord or its agent at any time during the last six months of the Term (but only where the Tenant has no right to or no longer has a right to a new tenancy under the 1954 Act) to fix upon any part of the Property a notice for re-letting and during that period to permit persons with the authority of the Landlord or its agent to view the Property[69]

3.25   *Yield Up*

At the expiry of the Term:

3.25:1   to yield up the Property decorated and repaired in accordance with the terms of the Lease

3.25:2   to give up all keys of the Property to the Landlord and

3.25:3   to remove the Tenant's fixtures (if requested by the Landlord) and all signs erected by the Tenant on or near the Property and immediately to make good any damage caused by the removal.[90]

4   LANDLORD'S COVENANTS

The Landlord covenants with the Tenant:

4.1   *Quiet Enjoyment*

To permit the Tenant to hold the Property peaceably and without any interruption by the Landlord or any person claiming under or in trust for the Landlord[90]

4.2   *Exercising Rights*

In exercising all the rights involving entry to the Property to cause (and to ensure that those exercising those rights on its behalf cause) as little damage as is reasonably practicable to the Property and as little inconvenience as possible to the occupiers and immediately to make good any damage to the Property.

5   GUARANTOR'S COVENANTS

5.1   The Guarantor covenants with the Landlord named in the Lease and with all of its successors in title:[92]

5.1:1   if the Tenant does not pay the Rent or any other sum due under the Lease to pay to the Landlord on demand the Rent or other sum

5.1:2   if the Tenant is in breach of any provision of the Lease to remedy that breach on demand and to indemnify and keep indemnified the Landlord against all losses[93] suffered by the Landlord as a result (directly or indirectly) of that breach

5.1:3   in addition to the obligations set out in Conditions 5.1:1 and 5.1:2 and if the Lease is disclaimed by the Tenant's trustee in bankruptcy or liquidator:[94]

5.1:3.1   to pay to the Landlord on demand an amount equal to the Rent and other sums of a recurring nature that would have been payable under the Lease for the period beginning on the disclaimer and ending on the earlier of six months from the disclaimer, the date upon which the Property is relet or the expiry of the Term or

5.1:3.2   if requested by the Landlord within 90 days of disclaimer, to take from the Landlord a lease of the Property from the date of disclaimer for the residue of the Term at the Rent payable on disclaimer and upon the same terms as those contained in the Lease with all provisions of a periodical nature (including those relating to review of the Rent) expressed to apply on the dates that would have applied if the Lease had not been disclaimed and

5.1:3.3   to pay the costs of the Landlord properly incurred in relation to the disclaimer and where appropriate the grant of the lease to the Guarantor

5.2   The obligations of the Guarantor set out in Condition 5.1 continue to apply[95] even if:

5.2:1   the Landlord grants any time or indulgence to the Tenant or fails to enforce payment of the Rent or other sum or the performance of the terms of the Lease[96]

5.2:2   the Landlord refuses to accept the rent tendered when the Landlord was entitled (or would after the service of a notice under the Law of Property Act 1925 s 146 have been entitled) to re-enter the Property[97]

5.2:3   the terms of the Lease are varied except where the variation is prejudicial to the Guarantor[98]

5.2:4   a revised Rent has been agreed or determined under Condition 7[99]

5.2:5   the Tenant surrenders part of the Property and where this happens the liability of the Guarantor under this Lease continues for the part of the Property not surrendered after making any necessary apportionments under the Law of Property Act s 140[100] or

5.2:6   the Guarantor would have been released by any other event.

6   INSURANCE

6.1   *Landlord's Insurance Covenants*

The Landlord covenants with the Tenant:

6.1:1   To insure the Property (excluding any fixed glass insured under Condition 6.2:13) against damage by fire lightning explosion aircraft (or other aerial device) or articles dropped from them riot civil commotion malicious persons earthquake storm tempest flood bursting and overflowing of water pipes tanks and other apparatus impact by road vehicles[101] and by any other risks that the Landlord may decide although:

6.1:1.1   the obligation to insure against any particular risk is subject to insurance for that risk being ordinarily available with a reputable insurer for premises such as the Property and

6.1:1.2   this insurance will be subject to any excesses or limitations that the insurer requires

6.1:2   To effect this insurance with a reputable insurance company or with reputable underwriters[102] and through any agency that the Landlord may from time to time decide

6.1:3   That this insurance will be for the full cost of reinstatement including professional fees fees payable upon any application for planning permission or other consents that may be required for reinstatement the cost of debris removal demolition site clearance and of any works required by statute and incidental expenses[103]

6.1:4   To produce to the Tenant on request evidence of the terms of the policy and of payment of the last premium[104]

6.1:5   To procure that the interest of the Tenant is noted on the policy whenever this is permitted under the policy[105]

6.1:6   To notify the Tenant of any material change in the risks covered by the policy

6.2   *Tenant's Insurance Covenants*

The Tenant covenants with the Landlord:[106]

6.2:1   To pay as rent to the Landlord on demand and (if so demanded) in advance (but not more than 60 days in advance) of the date of renewal sums equal to:

6.2:1.1   the premiums paid or to be paid by the Landlord (inclusive of any commission[108] to be retained by the Landlord) for insuring the Property in accordance with its obligations in the Lease including any increased premiums required as a result of the Tenant's use of the Property or anything brought onto the Property

6.2:1.2   the premiums paid or to be paid by the Landlord (inclusive of any commission[108] to be retained by the Landlord) for insuring for loss of rent under the Lease for 3 years[109] or

6.2:1.3   where in the case of either of the items referred to in Conditions 6.2:1.1–6.2:1.2 the Landlord's policy includes the Property and other premises to pay the proportion of the premiums properly attributable to the Property to be fixed (in the absence of agreement between the parties) by a Qualified Expert[110]

6.2:2   To pay on demand the proportion of the sums referred to in Condition 6.2:1 for the period beginning with the Rent Commencement Date and ending on the day immediately before the next renewal date[111]

6.2:3   To comply with all the requirements and recommendations of the insurer and the fire authority

6.2:4   Not to do or omit anything that could cause the insurance effected under Condition 6.1 to become void or voidable wholly or in part or cause any additional or increased premiums to become payable unless the Tenant has previously obtained the approvals of the Landlord and the insurer the approval of the Landlord not to be unreasonably withheld

6.2:5   Where the Property is an office or a shop not to bring or store on the Property anything which is specially combustible or explosive

6.2:6   Where the Property is a factory or warehouse to bring or store on the Property anything which is specially combustible or explosive only after obtaining the approval of the insurer and the Landlord the Landlord's approval not to be unreasonably withheld

6.2:7   To keep the Property supplied with such fire fighting equipment as the insurer and the fire authority may require and to maintain it in working order and to the satisfaction of the insurer and to the reasonable satisfaction of the Landlord and at least once every six months to have any fire fighting equipment inspected by a competent person

6.2:8 Not to obstruct the access to any fire equipment or the means of escape from the Property nor to lock any fire door while the Property is occupied

6.2:9 To give notice to the Landlord immediately any event happens which might affect any insurance policy relating to the Property or any event happens against which the Landlord may have insured under the Lease

6.2:10 To inform the Landlord immediately in writing of any matter likely to affect the decision of any insurer to grant or to continue the insurance referred to in the Lease

6.2:11 If the Tenant is entitled to the benefit of any insurance on the Property to apply all money in making good the loss for which it is received[112]

6.2:12 If the Property is a shop to insure the fixed glass on the Property with a reputable insurance company or with reputable underwriters against breakage or damage for its full reinstatement cost, when required to produce to the Landlord particulars of this insurance and evidence of the payment of the premium and to reinstate any fixed glass that is broken or damaged with new glass of no less quality or thickness

6.3 *Damage or Destruction of the Property*

Conditions 6.4 and 6.5 apply whenever during the Term:

6.3:1 the Property is damaged by any of the risks against which the Landlord is obliged to insure or has insured[113] and

6.3:2 payment of the insurance money is not refused wholly or in part through the fault of the Tenant or its subtenants[113]

6.4 *Suspension of Rent*[114]

6.4:1 Whenever the situation contemplated in Condition 6.3 applies and the Property or any part of it is unfit for use the Rent (or a fair proportion of it according to the nature and extent of the damage) will not be payable until the damage is made good and the Property is (or the affected parts are) again fit for use or until three years from the damage whichever is the shorter period and the proportion and the period will be fixed (in the absence of agreement between the parties) by a Qualified Expert

6.4:2 Whenever the situation contemplated in Condition 6.3 applies for part of a quarter and the Rent for that quarter has already been paid in advance the Landlord must refund to the Tenant the proportion of the Rent (apportioned on a daily basis) attributable to the period during which Condition 6.3 applied[115]

6.5 *Reinstatement*

6.5:1 Whenever the situation contemplated in Condition 6.3 applies the Landlord must apply for and use all reasonable endeavours[116] to obtain all planning permissions building regulation consents and other consents and licences that are required to enable the Landlord to make good ('the Permissions')

6.5:2 Subject to Conditions 6.5:3–6.5:6 the Landlord must as soon as the

Permissions have been obtained (or immediately where no Permissions are required) apply all insurance money received (except sums for loss of rent) in making good[117] and the Tenant will do nothing to prevent or impede that making good

6.5:3   A 'Supervening Event' is any of the following:

6.5:3.1   failure by the Landlord to obtain the Permissions despite using all reasonable endeavours[116]

6.5:3.2   grant of any of the Permissions subject to a lawful condition with which it would be unreasonable to expect the Landlord to comply or if the Landlord is requested as a pre-condition to obtaining any of the Permissions to enter into an agreement with the planning authority[118] that would contain conditions with which it would be unreasonable to expect the Landlord to comply

6.5:3.3   some defect in the site upon which the reinstatement is to take place so that it could not be undertaken or undertaken only at a cost that would be unreasonable

6.5:3.4   inability of the Landlord to obtain access to the site to reinstate

6.5:3.5   prevention of the reinstatement by war act of God Government action strike lock-out or

6.5:3.6   any other similar circumstance that prevents reinstatement and that is beyond the control of the Landlord

6.5:4   The Landlord need not make good while prevented by a Supervening Event[119]

6.5:5   If three years from the damage it has not been made good and the Property or any part of it is still unfit for use either party may by notice served at any time within six months of the expiry of that three-year period invoke Condition 6.5:6[119]

6.5:6   Upon service of a notice in accordance with Condition 6.5:5

6.5:6.1   the Term will come to an end but without prejudice to any rights that either party may have against the other including without limitation any that the Tenant may have for breach by the Landlord of the provisions of Condition 6.5:2[119] and

6.5:6.2   all insurance money received will belong to the Landlord.[120]

7   RENT REVIEW[121]

7.1   *Application*

Conditions 7.2–7.4 apply only if reference to Review Dates or a Review Date is made in the Lease[122]

7.2   *Definitions*

In the Letting Conditions and in the Lease:

7.2:1   'Review Period' means either the period beginning with a Review Date and ending on the day before the next Review Date or the period beginning on the last or only Review Date and ending at the expiry of the Term and relevant Review Date means the Review Date at the beginning of that Review Period[123]

7.2:2 'the Assumptions'[124] are the following assumptions at the relevant Review Date:

7.2:2.1 that no work has been carried out on the Property by the Tenant its subtenants or their predecessors in title during the Term which has diminished the rental value of the Property[125]

7.2:2.2 that if the Property has been destroyed or damaged it has been fully restored[126]

7.2:2.3 that the covenants contained in the Lease on the part of the Landlord and the Tenant have been complied with[127]

7.2:2.4 that the Property[128] is available to let by a willing landlord[129] to a willing tenant[129] by one lease[130] without a premium from either party[131] and with vacant possession[132]

7.2:2.5 that the Property is equipped for immediate use by the incoming tenant[133]

7.2:2.6 that the lease by which the Property will be let ('the hypothetical lease')[124] contains the same terms as the Lease[134] (except the amount of the Initial Rent and any rent-free period allowed to the Tenant)[135] and includes the provisions for rent review[136] at the same intervals[137] as those in the Lease

7.2:2.7 that the duration of the hypothetical lease[140] is equal to the length of the Term[138] that it begins on the relevant Review Date and that the rent is payable from then[135]

7.2:2.8 that the hypothetical lease[140] provides that the tenant must decorate the Property at the same intervals as those in the Lease[139/141/142]

7.2:3 'the Disregards'[143] are the following matters at the relevant Review Date that are to be disregarded:

7.2:3.1 any effect on rent of the fact that the Tenant its subtenants or their predecessors in title have been in occupation of the Property[144]

7.2:3.2 any goodwill attached to the Property by the carrying on at the Property of the business of the Tenant its subtenants or the predecessors in title in their businesses[145]

7.2:3.3 any increase in rental value[146] of the Property attributable at the relevant Review Date to any improvement[147] to the Property carried out with the consent of the Landlord (where required)[148] by the Tenant[149] its subtenants or their predecessors in title or by any lawful occupiers during the Term[150] or during any period of occupation before the Term[151] that is either (a) not carried out in pursuance of an obligation to the Landlord[152] or (b) is carried out pursuant to Condition 3.11[153] but in making this disregard no allowance will be made for loss of use during any hypothetical period while the improvement is being carried out

7.3 *Review of Rent*

7.3:1 For each Review Period the Rent will be the greater[154] of:

7.3:1.1 the Rent payable immediately before the relevant Review Date or if payment has been suspended the Rent which would have been payable had there been no suspension or

7.3:1.2   the revised rent ascertained in accordance with this Condition

7.3:2   The revised rent for any Review Period may be agreed in writing at any time between the parties[155] or (in the absence of agreement) will be determined (but not earlier than the relevant Review Date)[156] by an arbitrator[157]

7.3:3   The revised rent will be whatever the arbitrator decides is the rent at which the Property might reasonably be expected to be let in the open market[158] at the relevant Review Date making the Assumptions and disregarding the Disregards

7.3:4   The arbitration will be conducted in accordance with the Arbitration Acts 1950 and 1979[157]

7.3:5   The arbitrator will be appointed by agreement between the parties or (in the absence of agreement) nominated by the then President of the Royal Institution of Chartered Surveyors (or his nominee)[159] on the application of either party made not earlier than six months before the relevant Review Date

7.3:6   If the arbitrator dies or declines to act the President may on the application of either party appoint another

7.3:7   The Tenant must allow the arbitrator access to the Property to do anything which the arbitrator considers necessary to carry out his function

7.3:8   If one party pays all the arbitrator's fees and expenses it may recover any part of them which the arbitrator has awarded against the other party:

7.3:8.1   in the case of the Landlord as rent in arrears

7.3:8.2   in the case of the Tenant by deduction from rent

7.3:9   When the revised rent has been fixed in accordance with this Condition memoranda will be signed by or on behalf of the parties and annexed to the Lease and its counterpart and the parties will bear their own costs of this[160]

7.4   *Arrangements Pending Revised Rent*

7.4:1   If the revised rent payable during any Review Period has not been ascertained by the relevant Review Date the then current Rent will continue to be payable on account[161] of the Rent for that Review Period

7.4:2   If the revised rent is ascertained on or before the relevant Review Date and that date is not a quarter day the Tenant must on that Review Date pay to the Landlord the difference between the Rent due for that quarter and the Rent actually paid for it

7.4:3   If the revised rent payable during any Review Period has not been ascertained by the relevant Review Date then immediately after the date it has been agreed or upon which the arbitrator's award is received by one party the Tenant must pay to the Landlord:[162]

7.4:3.1   any shortfall between the Rent which would have been paid if the revised rent had been ascertained by the Relevant Review Date and the payments made on account[162] and

7.4:3.2   interest at the Bank's base lending rate on the shortfall between the amount that would have been paid if the revised rent had been ascertained by the relevant Review Date and the payments made on account for the period beginning on the day upon which each instalment was due and ending on the day on which payment of the shortfall is made[163]

7.5 *Rent Increase Prevented*[164]

7.5:1 If at any Review Date statute restricts the Landlord's right to review rent or recover any increase the Landlord may within six months of the restriction's removal give the Tenant at least one month's written notice invoking Condition 7.5:2[164]

7.5:2 On the service of a notice under Condition 7.5:1 the Landlord can:

7.5:2.1 proceed with any review prevented or further review the rent in any review where the Landlord's right was restricted or modified and the date specified in the notice is to be treated as a Review Date but this does not vary any subsequent Review Date

7.5:2.2 recover any resulting increase in rent with effect from the earliest date permitted by law.[164]

8 UNDERLEASE

8.1 Conditions 8.1–8.3 apply whenever the Landlord is not the freeholder whether or not specific reference is made in the Lease to the superior lease and 'Superior Lease' means the lease under which the Landlord holds the Property[166]

8.2 The Tenant covenants with the Landlord:

8.2:1 To observe[167] the obligations of the lessee[168] contained in the Superior Lease and in any lease superior to it so far as they relate to the Property (but not those expressly assumed by the Landlord in the Lease) and to indemnify the Landlord against all losses[169] arising directly or indirectly from any breach[170]

8.2:2 Not do omit or allow[171] anything which might cause the Landlord to be in breach of the Superior Lease or which if done omitted or allowed by the Landlord might be a breach of the covenants on the part of the lessee or the conditions contained in the Superior Lease[172]

8.2:3 To permit the Landlord upon reasonable notice (except in emergency) to enter the Property for any purpose that is in the opinion of the Landlord necessary to enable it to comply with the covenants on the part of the lessee and the conditions contained in the Superior Lease

8.2:4 To permit any superior landlord and all persons authorised by any superior landlord to enter the Property for the purposes specified and upon the terms contained in the Superior Lease or in any lease superior to it as if the provisions in these documents dealing with the lessor's access to the Property was incorporated into this Lease

8.2:5 To pay to the Landlord on an indemnity basis all costs and other expenses properly incurred by the Landlord in enforcing the covenants on the part of the superior landlord in accordance with Condition 8.3:2[173]

8.2:6 Where the Tenant makes an application under the Lease for consent and the consent of the superior landlord is also required under the Superior Lease or any lease superior to it to pay on an indemnity basis:

8.2:6.1 all costs and other expenses properly incurred by the Landlord in relation to that application including seeking the superior landlord's consent in accordance with Condition 8.3:3 whether that application is granted refused offered subject to any qualification or withdrawn

8.2:6.2   professional advice obtained by the Landlord in relation to that application

8.2:6.3   the costs and other expenses of the superior landlords or superior landlords in relation to that application[174]

8.3   The Landlord covenants with the Tenant:

8.3:1   To pay the rent reserved by the Superior Lease and comply with the terms of it unless the Tenant is obliged to comply with them by virtue of the Lease[175]

8.3:2   On the request of the Tenant[176] to use all reasonable endeavours[177] to enforce the covenants on the part of the lessor contained in the Superior Lease

8.3:3   To use all reasonable endeavours[176/177] to obtain the consent of any superior landlord required under the Superior Lease of any lease superior to it when:

8.3:3.1   the Tenant has applied for consent under the Lease

8.3:3.2   the Landlord gives that consent or could not reasonably refuse it or gives the consent subject to consent being obtained from any superior landlord

8.3:3.3   consent is required under the Superior Lease or any lease superior to it.

9   QUALIFIED EXPERT[175]

9.1   A Qualified Expert is a person who:

9.1:1   is an associate or fellow of the Royal Institution of Chartered Surveyors or the Incorporated Society of Valuers and Auctioneers[179/180]

9.1:2   is appointed by the Landlord

9.1:3   is appointed to resolve a question of fact[180] where the Lease[181] provides for determination in this way and where the parties cannot agree

9.1:4   may be the person who is also appointed by the Landlord to collect rent[182]

9.2   In resolving any of these questions the Qualified Expert will act as an expert and not as an arbitrator and his decision will be final[183]

9.3   As soon as he is appointed the Qualified Expert must write to the parties and allow them 14 days in which to submit to him in writing their proposals on how the matter in question should be decided

9.4   The fees of the Qualified Expert for performing any of the functions given to him by the Lease will be paid by the Tenant except where the Qualified Expert directs otherwise and the Qualified Expert must order the Landlord to pay all or part of his fees when he decides a matter in the manner (or substantially in the manner) proposed by the Tenant[184]

9.5   The Tenant covenants with the Landlord to pay the fees of the Qualified Expert except where the Qualified Expert directs otherwisev

9.6 The Landlord covenants with the Tenant to pay the fees of the Qualified Expert when directed by the Qualified Expert to do so.

10 PROVISOS

10.1 *Re-entry*[185]

10.1:1 In this Condition, a 'Forfeiting Event' is any of the following:

10.1:1.1 any Rent or sum regarded as rent for the purposes of this Lease is outstanding for 21 days after becoming due whether formally demanded or not

10.1:1.2 a breach by the Tenant of any of the provisions of the Lease

10.1:1.3 in respect of an individual Tenant:[186]
– an application is made for an interim order
– a bankruptcy petition is presented
– a proposal is made for a voluntary arrangement or
– he enters into a deed of arrangement

10.1:1.4 in respect of a company Tenant:[186]
– it goes into liquidation (whether compulsory or voluntary) but not a voluntary winding up for the amalgamation or reconstruction of a solvent company
– a receiver manager administrative reciever or provisional liquidator is appointed
– a petition is presented for an administration order or
– a proposal is made for a voluntary arrangement or a scheme of arrangement or

10.1:1.5 the Tenant has any distress or execution levied on its goods at the Property

10.1:2 Whenever a Forfeiting Event exists the Landlord may enter the Property (or any part of it) at any time even if a previous right of re-entry has been waived and then the Term will end but any rights which have accrued for breach of any provision of the Lease will remain including the breach under which the re-entry is made

10.2 *Representations*

The Tenant acknowledges that it has not entered into the Lease in reliance wholly or partly on any representation made by or on behalf of the Landlord[187]

10.3 *Exclusion of Use Warranty*

Nothing in the Lease or in any consent granted by the Landlord under the Lease implies that the Property may be used for any particular purpose[188]

10.4 *Disputes with Adjoining Owners*

If any dispute arises between the Tenant and the occupier of Adjoining Premises about any right or privilege in connection with the use of the Property and of any Adjoining Premises or about any boundary structure separating the Property from the Adjoining Premises it will be decided by a Qualified Expert[189]

10.5 *Covenants Relating to Adjoining Premises*

Nothing contained in or implied by the Lease gives the Tenant the benefit of or the right to enforce (or to prevent the release or modification of) any covenant agreement or condition entered into by any tenant of any Adjoining Premises[190]

10.6 *Effect of Waiver*

Each of the Tenant's covenants will remain in full force (both at law and in equity) even if the Landlord has waived or temporarily released that covenant or waived or released (temporarily or permanently) a similar covenant in a lease of Adjoining Premises[191]

10.7 *Rights Easements etc*[192]

The Tenant will not during the Term acquire or become entitled to any easement over any Adjoining Premises and any easement exercised over any Adjoining Premises will be regarded as being by virtue of a determinable licence from the Landlord

10.8 *Extension of Term*[193]

If after the expiry of the Term there is a period of holding over extension or continuance (whether by agreement or operation of law):

10.8:1 the provisions of the Lease and the Letting Conditions (including Condition 5.1)[194] apply to that period and the expression 'Term' will be construed as applying to that period and references to the expiry of the Term or the last year of the Term will be to the end of that period however it comes to an end

10.8:2 all obligations of a periodical nature (including those contained in Conditions 3.4:8 and 3.4:9) will apply at the same intervals as those specified in the Lease

10.8:3 the Rent will only be reviewed after the expiry of the contractual term set out in the Lease if the Lease specifically provides for this and (as an illustrative example) a provision by which the Rent Review Dates are defined by anniversaries of the date upon which the Term began or of the first Review Date will not be regarded as specific under this Condition[195]

10.9 *Perpetuity Period*

The perpetuity period applicable to the Lease is 80 years beginning with the date of the Lease and whenever in the Lease either party is granted a future interest it must vest within that period and if it has not it will be void for remoteness[196]

10.10 *Compensation*[197]

Any statutory right of the Tenant to compensation from the Landlord on vacating the Property is excluded from this letting to the extent that the law allows

10.11 *Tenant's Possession*

If after the Tenant has vacated the Property on the expiry of the Term any of the Tenant's possessions remain on the Property and the Tenant fails to remove them within seven days after being requested in writing by the Landlord to do so or if after using its best endeavours the Landlord is unable to make such a request to the Tenant within 14 days from the first attempt:

10.11:1   the Landlord may as the agent of the Tenant sell the possessions and the Tenant indemnifies the Landlord against any liability incurred by it to any third party whose possessions have been sold by the Landlord in the mistaken belief (which will be presumed) that the possessions belonged to the Tenant

10.11:2   if the Landlord having made reasonable efforts is unable to locate the Tenant the Landlord is entitled to retain the proceeds of sale unless the Tenant claims them within 90 days of vacation of the Property and

10.11:3   the Tenant will be responsible for and will indemnify the Landlord against any damage caused to the Property by the possession and any losses suffered by the Landlord directly or indirectly as a result of the presence of the possessions on the Property after the Tenant has vacated the Property on the expiry of the Term

10.12   *Notices*

10.12:1   A notice[198] under the Lease must be in writing and unless the receiving party acknowledges receipt[200] is valid if (and only if)[199] it complies with the provisions of this Condition

10.12:2   The provisions are that:

10.12:2.1   the notice must be given by hand or sent by registered post or recorded delivery[201]

10.12:2.2   the notice must be served:
- where the receiving party is a company at its registered office
- where the receiving party is the Tenant at the Property
- where the receiving party is the Landlord or the Guarantor and that party is not a company at that party's address shown in the Lease or at any alternative address that is specified in a notice given by that party to the other parties

10.12:3   A notice sent by registered post or recorded delivery is to be treated as served on the third day after posting whenever and whether or not it was received[202]

10.12:4   If the receiving party is more than one person a notice to one is notice to all

10.12:5   In this Condition party includes the Guarantor.

1   Copyright in this Form is vested jointly in M J Ross and R W Castle. It may not be reproduced without their permission. Printed versions of the Form are available from M J Ross at 20 Essex Street London WC2 R 3AL. Tel: 01–836 8400, Fax: 01–240 2278. Details available on request.

2   One view would add 'unless the context otherwise requires' or 'where the context so admits' and in fact this may be implied: see *Meux v Jacobs* (1875) LR 7 HL 481 at 493; *Law Society v United Service Bureau Ltd* [1934] 1 KB 343. The better course is to use defined terms in such a way that there are no circumstances where the defined meaning does not apply. If there is a specific point, this is better dealt with where it arises in the document: see for example Conditions 2.1:4 and 2.2:1.

3   See Condition 1.4 below. Groups frequently hold properties in the names of the parent and various subsidiaries (for deliberate or accidental reasons) but the law regards ownership

strictly: see for example *Richard Roberts Holdings Ltd v Douglas Smith Stimson Partnership* (1986) 16 CSW 928. Thus but for this wording the landlord would not be regarded as owning nearby property held in the name of an associated company. This could prove relevant in for example Conditions 3.5:3.1 and 3.13:5.3.

4   It is convenient for the landlord always to be able to use his bank and the tenant's protection is that the nominated bank must be a member of the Committee.

5   This definition needs watching when the Letting Conditions are being incorporated into a lease where the demised premises form *part* of a building because this definition is not then appropriate and should be deleted by including it as one of the Excluded Conditions (see Appendix 1 Form 2 clause 1.7 below). 'Building' is used in Conditions 3.4:8 and 3.4:9 and and so these Conditions will need excluding when the definition of Building has been deleted.

6   The additional words are included so that 'in this Lease' or 'in the Lease' is all that is required in the Lease or Letting Conditions and reference does not have to be made every time to 'in the Lease and the Letting Conditions'.

7   The effect of this wording is that references in the Lease and the Letting Conditions to the Act would be to the Act as amended at the time that reference was to be made to it and not the Act as enacted at the time the Lease is granted: see paras 6.31 footnote 3 and 7.14:1 above.

8   See Condition 1.1 above.

9   This term is defined in the Lease.

10   See footnote 178 below.

11   As to VAT generally, see para 2.33 above. As to VAT in Rent Review clauses, see para 6.29 above.

12   As to the use of 'includes' compared to 'means' see para 1.5:2 footnote 6 above.

13   In view of the somewhat 'parambulatory' meaning of the term (see footnote 7 above), it is probably preferable not to refer to the specific section of the Planning Acts that currently deals with the term (s 22 of the 1971 Act).

14   The expression 'expiry of the Term' is given a special meaning by Condition 2.2:2.

15   See footnote 2 above.

16   See footnote 13 and Town and Country Planning 1971, s 87(2).

17   As to fixtures, see para 3.18 above.

18   See Condition 2.1:1 above.

19   Some leases tend to be ambiguous on this point because, where words such as 'within the Property' are omitted, it is arguable as to whether conducting media that solely serve the Property but that are outside the area defined as such (ie the area edged red on the plan) are within the demised premises and therefore, for example, the repairing covenant. It is preferable specifically to deal with this point.

20   These words are inserted as a reminder to the draftsman of the consequences of Condition 2.2:1. If he is concerned that a specific provision be given the fixed meaning at the time of the grant of the Lease, rather than any amended meaning brought about by subsequent legislation, he should so provide. See footnotes 7, 13 and 16 above.

21   Unfortunately the Interpretation Act 1978, ss 17, 23(3), do not quite go far enough to enable this clause to be dispensed with altogether particularly where a statute is modified.

22   This Condition saves numerous repetitions throughout the document of 'howsoever determined', and avoids the problem experienced by the landlord in *Dickinson v St Aubyn* [1944] KB 454, [1944] 1 All ER 379, CA.

23   See *Trailfinders Ltd v Razuki* [1988] 2 EGLR 46, [1988] 30 EG 59.

24   In view of the demise of the Bank Rate and the Minimum Lending Rate it is desirable to provide for the possibility of base rates ceasing to exist. As to construction of documents that refer to Minimum Lending Rate, see [1981] Gazette 23 September 1029. Where the Lease requires the services of an Accountant (see for example 22 Encyclopaedia of Forms and Precedents (5th edn) Forms 29–31) he would perhaps be more appropriate than the Qualified Expert to determine this matter. A further alternative would be 'a chartered accountant acting as an expert and not as an arbitrator appointed in the absence of agreement between the parties by the President (for the time being) or his nominee of the Institute of Chartered Accountants on the application of either party'.

25   Landlords are rather keen on indemnities and even those of them who support plain English (see para 1.3 above) may not be convinced that 'losses' without amplification is wide enough. Where they have suffered a loss they do not want to be involved in arguments on remoteness of damage. Nevertheless repeating this extended meaning somewhat over-complicates indemnity clauses and so it seems preferable to deal with the point once here so that the indemnities themselves can be relatively simple: see Conditions 3.18, 5.1:2, 8.2:1 and 10.11:3.

26   Probably an 'avoidance of doubt' provision but it saves repetitions without risking a loss of meaning.

27 These are vital words otherwise the tenant (no doubt for payment) could subgrant to a third party the right to use the right in question in relation, for example, to that third party's property. The landlord would not find that acceptable: he would wish to retain control and to be able to charge for granting any third party rights. See *Callard v Beeney* [1930] 1 KB 353 at 357.

28 This Condition is included so that the rights themselves can be drafted in a simple and brief way: see for example Appendix 1 Form 4 below, clause 1.3:2. If unusually a specific right of way is granted to which all or some of these words are not appropriate, then they can easily be excluded in the lease when granting that right.

29 Inserted for reasons similar to those referred to in footnote 28 above in relation to rights. For an example of simplified drafting see Appendix 1 Form 4 below, clauses 1.4:1 and 1.4:2. Again any specific exception to which these words were not appropriate can be dealt with in the Lease.

30 See para 7.5 above especially footnote 6. As to statutory obligation on the landlord relating to covenants against alienation, see para 7.6 above.

31 This wording is considered preferable to the usual 'joint and several' clause.

32 If there is a difference in meaning between permit and suffer (see *Barton v Reed* [1932] 1 Ch 362 at 375 per Luxmore J) it is suggested that 'allow' encompasses both.

33 If marginal notes rather than headings have been used the reference should be to 'marginal note'. Headings and marginal notes require the draftsman to provide a word or two to describe every clause in the document. This is not always easy and there are times when he will have to settle for something less than perfection, the only alternative being a heading or note that would be inappropriately long. It would be wrong for that title which its author might admit was not totally apposite, but was the best that he could do in a few words, to be used in construing the clause in question.

34 Note that the Rent Commencement Date could be the same date as the Lease, a date before the date of the Lease (because the tenant had been allowed into possession prior to the grant of the Lease on the basis that the liability for rent would be backdated to the date of possession) or a date after the date of the Lease (because a rent free period was being allowed).

35 This is where the Rent Commencement Date is the date of the Lease or earlier: see footnote 34.

36 This is where the Rent Commencement Date is after the date of the Lease and a rent free period is being allowed: see footnote 34 above.

37 See eg *British Anzani (Felixstowe) Ltd v International Marine Management (UK) Ltd* [1980] QB 137, [1979] 2 All ER 1063; *Lee-Parker v Izzet* [1971] 3 All ER 1099, [1971] 1 WLR 1688; 27 Halsbury's Laws (4th edn) para 232.

38 This provision has dangers for both parties. The landlord would need to instruct his bank to refuse to accept rent where there was a breach of covenant known to the landlord, otherwise the right of forfeiture would be lost (see para 12.3 above) while the tenant may feel that he requires more control over the payment of rent. Indeed the financial systems operated by many companies do not enable payments to be made in this way.

39 See para 7.27 above.

40 See para 7.27 above.

41 As to VAT generally see para 2.23 above.

42 See Condition 9 and footnote 178 below.

43 As to the meaning of repair, see para 8.1 above.

44 The landlord should consider extending this in the lease to 'or anyone at the Property expressly or by implication with the authority of the tenant or tenants'. The expression 'by implication' is intended to include a caller at the Property (such as a tradesman) where there had been no express invitation but who could not be classed as a trespasser. (This is an updated version of the time honoured term 'the Tenant and his successors in title the owners and occupiers for the time being of the Demised premises and his or their respective servants and Licensees': *Baxendale v North Lambeth Liberal and Radical Club* [1902] 2 Ch 427 at 429 per Swinfen Eady J; *Hammond v Prentice Bros Ltd* [1920] 1 Ch 201.) It is suggested, however, that the fairer course is for the landlord to ensure that the terms of the insurance policy (for which, of course, the tenant is paying) are such that the insurance money would never be irrecoverable through the fault of these third parties.

45 This Condition should be deleted where the nature of the Building is such that the tenant does not clean the outside of the windows ie where the demised premises form part of a building and the landlord is responsible for cleaning the outside of all the windows as part of the services.

46 Defined in Condition 1.8.

47 Defined in the Lease.

48   An alternative to a fixed decorating schedule is 'As often as may in the [reasonable] opinion of the Landlord [Landlord's surveyor] be necessary in order to maintain a high standard of decorative finish and attractiveness and to preserve the Building and in the last year of the Term to redecorate . . .'.

49   The tenant might consider adding a proviso to this Condition in the Lease to the effect that the obligation relating to the last year of the Term will not apply where the tenant has performed the obligation in question not less than (perhaps) 18 months prior to the expiry of the Term.

50   Landlords increasingly seem anxious to have control over *every* redecoration and not just the last one.

51   As to alterations generally, see paras 7.19–7.26 above.

52   The format of this Condition is that two absolute covenants against major work are contained in Condition 3.5:1 and 3.5:2. They are separated from the qualified covenant of Condition 3.5:3 so that the Landlord and Tenant Act 1927, s 19(2) will not apply to major work: see para 7.24:2 above. As to the drafting of Condition 3.5:2 see para 7.25:4 above. If it does not adequately describe the 'structural elements' of the building in question it should be excluded (see Appendix 1 Form 2, clause 1.7 below) and a more appropriate clause inserted in the Lease.

53   See Condition 1.1 and footnote 3 above.

54   In many leases, this covenant deals also with reinstatement but this is dealt with in Condition 3.5:4 below.

55   This clause has probably come to be inserted in leases because landlords hope that it will defeat the effect of the compensation provisions of the Landlord and Tenant Act 1927, Pt I (ss 1–17) (23 Halsbury's Statutes (4th edn) LANDLORD AND TENANT) (see para 7.24:1 above) ie because, if the improvement has been removed, it will not be an improvement to the holding at the time of quitting the premises. In fact the clause might not achieve this effect, because ibid s 9 as amended by the Landlord and Tenant Act 1954, s 49 prohibits contracting out, and it may be void under the Landlord and Tenant Act 1927, s 19(2) so far as it applies to improvements (on the grounds that it purports to fetter the court in deciding what is reasonable) for reasons that are analogous to those set out in footnote 62 below in relation to bid, s 19(1). The tenant should not, however, rely on the application of these statutory provisions and should seek to strike out the clause.

56   See para 7.21:1 above.

57   'Observe' applies to both negative and positive covenants and there is no need to state 'observe and perform': *Ayling v Wade* [1961] 2 QB 228, [1961] 2 All ER 399, CA.

58   The advantages for the landlord of this clause must be weighed against the potential liability that it creates under the Defective Premises Act 1972, s 4(4).

59   As to alienation generally see paras 7.1–7.7 above.

60   See para 7.7:4 above both generally and as to an exception for group companies.

61   Sometimes it could be vital for the tenant to be able to sublet part of the demised premises and quite reasonable on the ground of estate management to do so: see para 7.7:31 above.

62   There are conflicting views as to the validity of this and similar covenants. One is that it merely sets out a condition precedent that must be fulfilled before an assignment or underletting (for which consent cannot be unreasonably refused) and is thus unobjectionable (see *Bocardo SA v S & M Hotels Ltd* [1979] 3 All ER 737, [1980] 1 WLR 17, CA). The other is that it could be void under the Landlord and Tenant Act 1927, s 19(1) (see para 7.2 above) on the grounds that questions of reasonableness are objective ones for the court to be decided without regard to the interpretations which the parties have put on the expression (*Creery v Summersell and Flowerdew & Co Ltd* [1949] Ch 751; *Re Smith's Lease, Smith v Richards* [1931] 1 All ER 346). Thus, (so the argument goes), it must be for the court to decide if in an individual case it would be reasonable for the landlord to make its licence subject to the tenant complying with the provisions of this covenant. See also *Waite v Jennings* [1906] 2 KB 11, CA and *Balfour v Kensington Gardens Mansions Ltd* (1932) 49 TLR 29.

63   The concept of reasonableness is introduced twice in this Condition which seems appropriate.

64   Whenever a document contemplates the possibility that a second document may be entered into in the future, it is sensible for the first document to give guidance as to the terms of the second document, so as to avoid disputes then. On the other hand, it is unwise to define too precisely the terms of the second document because developments in the law and practice after the first may mean that amendments ought to be made to the second. This concern is particularly significant where its subject matter is constantly under the scrutiny of the courts. So there needs to be some flexibility in for example the form of future guarantees and the rent review provisions in any underlease.

65   See para 7.2 above. Such provisions sometimes provide that for the rent may be no lower than the rent then reserved by the lease itself although this could cause a tenant real problems if rental values have dropped in the meantime.

66 See para 7.7:5 above. Particularly where the term is a long one, a fixed fee should be avoided.

67 As to user generally see paras 7.8–7.18 above.

68 Defined in clause 1.13 of the Lease. See paras 7.8–7.18 above. Note that this is an absolute covenant: see para 7.16:1 above. This should be acceptable providing clause 1.13 of the Lease contains a wide permitted user, for example 'offices', 'shop' etc. Where it will not be acceptable to either party (see paras 7.10 and 7.11 above) will be where the permitted use is defined in clause 1.13 very narrowly, for example 'bookshop', offices 'in connection with the Lessee's business of Consulting Engineers' etc. Where the landlord wishes to control the actual trade carried on at the Property, he should specify that in clause 1.13 but add 'or any other use with the consent of the Landlord (such consent not to be unreasonably withheld) that falls within [some rather wider class]'. See for example Form No 3 below, clause 1.10, last alternative. As to the wisdom or otherwise of using the latest Use Classes Order to define that wider class, see para 7.14 above.

69 See para 7.18:1 above. 'Nuisance' is a term to be construed according to 'plain and sober and simple notions among the English people: *Walter v Selfe* (1851) 4 De G & Sm 315 at 322 per Knight-Bruce V-C. 'I have no doubt that what is a nuisance or annoyance will continue to be determined by the courts according to robust and commonsense standard': *Hampstead and Suburban Properties Ltd v Diomedous* [1969] 1 Ch 248 at 258, [1968] 3 All ER 545 at 550, per Megarry J. But a tenant can only be said to have permitted a nuisance if the landlord can show that the tenant fails to take reasonable steps to prevent the nuisance: see *Commercial General Administration Ltd v Thomsett* (1979) 250 Estates Gazette 547, CA.

70 In *Koumoudouros and Marathon Realty Co Ltd* (1978) 89 DLR (3d) 551, the lease of restaurant premises provided that they should not be used for an offensive trade or business. The tenant began to provide entertainment in the form of topless waitresses and nude dancing. The High Court of Ontario held that the word 'offensive' did not have a definite legal meaning and that it should be read in the context of the lease. Read in relation to other provisions contained in the lease, it was correct to conclude that 'offensive' did encompass the conduct complained of. Surrounding circumstances can affect whether a particular trade is offensive – see *Nussey v Provincial Bill Posting Co and Eddison* [1909] 1 Ch 734, CA and *Dunraven Securities Ltd v Holloway* (1982) 264 Estates Gazette 709, CA.

71 There is obviously an element of 'shorthand' here and this Condition is based on the assumption that the use of the Open Land is defined on the plan eg 'car park'. If it is not, then this Condition can be included as one of the Excluded Conditions (see Appendix 1 Form 2 below, clause 1.7) and the point specifically dealt with in the Lease.

72 In certain circumstances the landlord may wish to include a further covenant to the effect that the tenant will 'not being keep store stack or lay out upon the Open Land any materials equipment plant bins crates cartons boxes skips or any other recepticle for waste or any other item [which is or might become untidy unclean unsightly or in any way detrimental to the Property [or the area generally]]'.

73 It is suggested that this brief clause will usually be sufficient to deal with the point.

74 See para 7.15:2 above.

75 Retailers frequently resist this covenant to the extent that it prevents them placing stickers on the shop window. Landlords, particularly of prestige shopping centres, are often sensitive on this – a compromise is sometimes arrived at (in the lease or a side letter) by defining the extent of the window that may be obscured by stickers.

76 In this age of the satellite it is probably appropriate for this covenant to be qualified.

77 See the Town and Country Planning (Control of Advertisement) Regulations 1984. In the absence of a covenant (and subject to the above) the tenant would be entitled to exhibit advertisements on the premises including those not connected with its business: see *Clapman v Edwards* [1938] 2 All ER 507.

78 See para 7.28 above and also Condition 3.12 below.

79 See Condition 3.11 above.

80 See Condition 2.1:5 above.

81 See Condition 1.10 above.

82 Frequently in this covenant the tenant indemnifies the landlord against breach but this is unnecessary in view of the general indemnity covenant contained in Condition 3.18: any breach of Condition 3.13:1 would be a breach of the provisions of the lease and would thus be covered by Condition 3.18.

83 Landlords today generally wish to approve application for planning permissions.

84 See Condition 2.1:2 above.

85 See the Insolvency Act 1986.

86 See note 64 above.

87 It is suggested that words such as 'with a minimum of 12%' should be avoided to avoid any risk that, if interest rates drop during the term to such an extent that 12% represents significantly more than a few per cent over the basic borrowing rate, this might be held to amount to a penalty and thus be void. As to what amounts to a penalty see *Dunlop Pneumatic Tyre Co Ltd v New Garage and Motor Co Ltd* [1915] AC 79, HL; *Cellulose Acetate Silk Co Ltd v Widnes Foundry (1925) Ltd* [1933] AC 20, HL. In view of this, landlords are unwise to provide in clauses such as these for more than a few per cent over base rate.

88   The landlord should not be tempted to extend this provision to costs etc incurred by the landlord in consequence of serving a notice under the 1954 Act, s 25 because this will be void: see *Stevenson and Rush (Holdings) Ltd v Langdon* (1978) 249 Estates Gazette 743, CA.

89   The question of an estate agent's 'For Sale' or 'For Let' board being displayed at the property is often an emotive one especially for retail tenants who believe that their trade could be harmed by any suggestion (however erroneous) that they will soon be closing down or moving. Thus no right is given to display a board where a superior interest is being sold (Condition 3.23) and a reletting board is permitted only where the tenant has no right to new tenancy under the 1954 Act (Condition 3.24).

90   The question of the removal of alterations is dealt with in Condition 3.5:4.

91   See para 9.2 above.

92   There is no longer any need for the words 'without the need for express assignment': see para 5.12.

93   See Condition 2.2:5 and footnote 25 above.

94   See *Coronation Street Industrial Properties Ltd v Ingall Industries plc* (1988) 56 P & CR 348, CA; affd [1989] 1 All ER 979, [1989] 1 WLR 304, HL.

95   See para 5.7 above.

96   See para 5.7:1 above.

97   See para 5.71 footnote 3 above. The suggestion referred to there is made in Kim Lewison 'Drafting Business Leases' (2nd edn) p 197.

98   See para 5.7:2 above.

99   This is to be some extent 'avoidance of doubt' provision. It makes the point that a review of the rent is not a variation.

100   See para 5.7:2 footnote 7 above.

101   As to why it is in the tenant's interests for the range of risks to be wide: see para 10.10 above.

102   The expression 'insurance office' would probably not include a policy effected by Lloyd's Underwriters hence the specific reference.

103   See paras 10.5–10.9 above.

104   See para 10.29 above.

105   See para 10.19 above.

106   In order to comply with many of the obligations contained in this Condition, the tenant will need to have a copy of the insurance policy.

107   See para 10.25 above.

108   See para 10.26 above.

109   See paras 10.10 and 10.11 above. The landlord will need to consider if three years is adequate.

110   See Condition 9 and footnote 178 below.

111   Consideration needs to be given to this provision that assumes that the tenant's liability to contribute towards the insurance premium begins on the same day as the liability to pay rent. This need not be the case where there is a rent free period, see foonotes 34–36 above.

112   An insurance policy frequently provides that, if there is any other insurance effected by or on behalf of the insured covering the premises which are the subject of the policy, the insurers are liable only for a rateable proportion of the damage. Such provisions extend to a case where one of the policies is in the joint names of the persons interested in the premises and the other is in the name of one only of those persons: *Halifax Building Society v Keighley* [1931] 2 KB 248. Thus, at least when the insurance is in joint names, the landlord needs to ensure that the tenant will use all money received under any policy that it has effected for the purposes of reinstatement.

113   Note so far as Condition 6.3:1 is concerned, Condition 2.2:7 that would prevent a narrow interpretation of damaged while saving numerous repetitions in clauses 6.3–6.6. The landlord should perhaps consider the extension to Condition 6.3:2 referred to if footnote 44 above . . . and the tenant should resist it for the reasons set out there.

114   See paras 10.13, 10.15 and 10.23 above.

115   Some practitioners have become concerned that the Apportionment Act 1870 and the wording contained in Condition 3.1:3 may not be sufficient to put beyond doubt the position dealt with in this Condition. If this concern is justified, it makes sense to insert the specific provision. If it is not, no harm is done.

116   The extent of the duty to use best endeavours and therefore reasonable endeavours depends upon the facts in each case: see *Monkland v Jack Barclay Ltd* [1951] 2 KB 252, [1951] 1 All ER 714, CA; *Terrell v Mabie Todd & Co Ltd* [1952] 2 TLR 574; *NW Investments (Erdington) Ltd v Swani* (1970) 214 Estates Gazette 1115. In the light of *IBM United Kingdom Ltd v Rockware Glass Ltd* [1980] FSR 335, CA, it may be that there is little practical difference between a covenant to use best endeavours, a covenant to use reasonable endeavours and a covenant to take all reasonable steps. Where a 'best endeavours' covenant is given by a sublessor, there would appear to be no grounds for suggesting that the best endeavours obligation falls short of enforcement proceedings by the sublessor against the superior landlord under the terms of the superior lease. Thus such a covenant probably adds little to an express covenant to enforce the provisions of the superior lease.

117 See paras 10.13, 10.18 and 10.19–10.22 above.
118 Ie under the Town and Country Planning Act 1971, ss 33 or 52.
119 See para 10.24 above.
120 See paras 10.16 and 10.24 above. In a normal commercial lease today at a rack rent and with regular reviews it is probably appropriate for the landlord to retain the insurance moneys in the relatively unlikely event of reinstatement being prevented in order to compensate him for the loss of his investment.
121 As to rent review generally see Chapter 6 above and as to drafting principles see para 6.2.
122 It is essential for there to be no ambiguity as to whether or not parts of the Letting Conditions apply.
123 A point that can arise depending on the way in which the Review Dates are expressed in the lease is should they be construed as continuing to apply during any extension of the letting beyond the expiry of the contractual term? This point is dealt with in Condition 10.8:3.
124 As to the fundamentals of a rent review clause see paras 6.1, 6.2 and 6.17 and as to assumptions see paras 6.18–6.29 above.
125 See para 6.24 above.
126 See para 6.26 above.
127 See para 6.25 above.
128 See para 6.18:1 above.
129 See para 6.22 above.
130 See para 6.21 above.
131 See para 6.23 above.
132 See paras 6.19–6.20 above.
133 See paras 6.19:3 and 6.20:2 above.
134 See para 6.18:3 above.
135 See para 6.20:2 above.
136 See para 6.18:3(d) above. The clause should refer to reviews 'at the same intervals as those in the Lease' and not to reviews being on the 'the Review Dates' because the latter is not right bearing in mind that the term of the hypothetical lease will not be beginning on the same date as that of the actual lease.
137 See para 6.18:3 above.
138 See para 6.18:2 above.
139 See footnote 137 above.
140 Defined in Condition 7.2:2.6 above.
141 As to possible assumptions dealing with VAT, see para 6.29 above.
142 As to further possible assumptions see paras 6.27 (statutory restrictions) and 6.28 (renewal under the 1954 Act) above.
143 As to disregards generally see paras 6.30–6.40 above.
144 See para 6.32 above.
145 See para 6.33 above.
146 See para 6.40 above.
147 See paras 6.34–6.40 above. As to what is an improvement see para 6.35 above. As to how the disregard is made see para 6.37 above.
148 See para 6.36:6 above.
149 See para 6.36:2 above.
150 See para 6.31 footnote 2 above.
151 See para 6.36:1.
152 See para 6.36:3 above.
153 See para 6.36:5 above.
154 Ie an upwards only review: see paras 6.60:1 and (for a possible protection) 6.60:2 above.
155 This clause falls within the 'informal' category discussed in para 6.5 above. No notices are needed to commence or to continue the process of review.
156 The parties can agree the rent before the review date but if determination by the third party

is needed then this must wait until after the review date so that all comparables (see para 6.42 above) are available.

157 See paras 6.44–6.51 above. Where determination by an expert rather than an arbitrator is needed see Appendix 1 Form 8 below.

158 See para 6.41 above.

159 To remove any risk (however slight) of an appointment made *on behalf of* the President being invalidated.

160 See para 6.59 above.

161 See para 6.53 above.

162 See para 6.54 above.

163 See para 6.55 above.

164 See para 6.57 above.

165 As to underleases generally, see Chapter 13. As to insurance when effected by a superior landlord see Appendix 1 Form 7 below.

166 It is essential that there is no ambiguity as to whether parts of the Letting Conditions apply and a potential ambiguity would be in the case of an undisclosed headlease – ie if the lease was drafted on the basis that the landlord was the freeholder but he was in fact a tenant. This wording makes it clear that these Conditions *would* apply in these circumstances.

167 See footnote 57 above.

168 'Lessee' is used to avoid any confusion with Tenant.

169 See Condition 2.2:5 and footnote 25 above.

170 It is common to see in underleases this type of general covenant by the sublessee to observe the covenants on the part of the sublessor contained in the superior lease so far as they affect the underlet premises. No sublessee should accept such a covenant without a careful examination of the superior lease, particularly when taking an underlease of part where the need to apportion the obligations between different parts of premises demised by the superior lease could give rise to problems of interpretation. A further danger is the incorporation of a general covenant by the sublessor to observe the terms of the headlease 'so far as the Tenant is not liable . . . in this underlease . . .'. If the sublessee's covenant is similarly limited by the extent of the sublessor's obligation, the circularity of the obligations will render both ambiguous. A more satisfactory approach is to ensure that any relevant obligations on the sublessor in the superior lease are passed on in the underlease and the sublessee gives covenants to do nothing which would constitute a breach of the terms of the headlease (see condition 8.2:2). Without a covenant to observe the covenants of the superior lease, the sublessor cannot recover costs incurred as a result of the sublessee's breach of covenant. In practice most cases have arisen over covenants to repair: see *Penley v Watts* (1841) 7 M & W 601; *Pontifex v Foord* (1884) 12 QBD 152. Similarly, without a covenant for indemnity (included by virtue of Condition 3.18) a sublessor cannot recover from the sublessee costs of proceedings for relief against forfeiture: see *Clare v Dobson* [1911] 1 KB 35. Where, however, the sublessee covenants in terms to observe the covenants superior in the lease, this implies an indemnity and the sublessor is entitled to all reasonable costs: *Hornby v Cardwell* (1881) 8 QBD 329, CA. Where the covenant is to perform similar covenants to those in the superior lease, there is no implied indemnity: see *Logan v Hall* (1847) 4 CB 598; *Penley v Watts*, supra; *Walker v Hatton* (1842) 10 M & W 249. A covenant to observe the covenant in a superior lease is an express covenant to comply with the repairing covenant and not merely for indemnity: see *Ayling v Wade* [1961] 2 QB 228, [1961] 2 All ER 399, CA.

171 See footnote 32 above.

172 It is arguable that Conditions 8.2:1 and 8.2:2 are alternatives and that strictly speaking only one is needed although landlords frequently required both: see footnote 170 above.

173 See Condition 8.3:2 below and footnote 176.

174 See Condition 8.33 and footnote 176 below.

175 See footnotes 170 and 172 above.

176 Frequently 'and at its expense' or words to similar effect are inserted here but what exactly is that meant to mean – can the landlord recover his charge and disbursements or can he actually charge for the work? Conditions 8.25 and 8.26 have been inserted in the interests of certainty.

177 See footnote 116 above.

178 The Qualified Expert is an upgraded version of the landlord's surveyor and has been created so that there is an impartial professional person to hold the balance between the parties when certain disputes arise in a way similar to that adopted by the architect under a building agreement. As to his position see para 11.6 footnote 4 above. As to his role and limitations see para 11.5 above and note that the landlord should not appoint his surveyor or the managing agent to be the Qualified Expert where that person had been a party to the dispute in question: *Concorde Graphics Ltd v Andromeda Investments SA* (1982) 265 Estates Gazette 386.

179 See para 11.6 above.

180 See para 11.5 above – it is not felt that an employee of the Landlord could perform this function.

181 Note that in view of additional words in Condition 1.5 (see footnote 6 above) the words 'or the Letting Conditions' do not have to be added after 'the Lease'.

182 See footnote 178 above.

183 See paras 6.45 and 11.5 above. As to an appeal from the decision of an expert see para 6.45(c) above.

184 Clearly the Qualified Expert's position will be one of some delicacy – see *Concorde Graphics* (footnote 178 and para 11.6:4 above). This Condition may require him in certain circumstances to 'award costs' against the landlord who may a long standing client. In some ways it may be preferable for the landlord always to appoint a surveyor who would not regard him as a client even in those circumstances where the landlord would be free to invite his surveyor or the managing agent – ie where he had not previously been involved in the dispute. Nevertheless it is suggested that this format provides a fair balance. If there is no risk of the tenant having to pay the cost of independent determination, there is no incentive on him to agree the issues. He would be likely to seek independent determination every time. On the other hand, the fact that the landlord *may* have to pay the costs should encourage him to adopt a sensible attitude.

185 As to forfeiture generally see paras 12.1–12.7 above.

186 As to the various events see the Insolvency Act 1986.

187 See footnote 188 below. As to the application of the Misrepresentation Act 1967, s 3 as amended by the Unfair Contract Terms Act 1977, s 8 (29 Halsbury's Statutes (4th edn) MISREPRESENTATION AND FRAUD) see (1984) Conv (NS) 12.

188 See para 2.7 above, *Laurence v Lexcourt Holdings Ltd* [1978] 2 All ER 810, [1978] 1 WLR 1128; *Collins v Howell-Jones* (1980) 259 Estates Gazette 331, CA and the comments of Eveleigh LJ on estate agents' particulars relating to user in *Bovis Group Pension Fund Ltd v GC Flooring & Furnishing Ltd* (1984) 269 Estates Gazette 1252 at 1253, CA.

189 This provision can only work if the lease of the Adjoining Premises also contains this clause.

190 As to when tenants would be able to enforce covenants against each other see 27 Halsbury's Laws (4th edn) para 413.

191 But as to waiver of a right of forfeiture see paras 12.5–12.7 above.

192 This Condition stops short of limiting the rights to those actually granted: for example by adding: 'The operation of the Law of Property Act 1925 section 62 is excluded from this letting and the only rights granted to the Tenant are those expressly set out in the Lease'.

193 The concept dealt with here is frequently seen in the definitions clause of the lease but it is suggested that substantive points such as this should not be deal with there.

194 See para 5.7:4 above.

195 See Condition 7.2:1 and footnote 123 above.

196 See paras 4.16 and 4.17 above.

197 1954 Act, s 37: see paras 14.40–14.41 above.

198 The contents of the notice clause is likely to be vital where the lease contains for example an option or break clause.

199 Notice provisions are either mandatory (ie to be valid the notice has to be served in the way prescribed in the clause) or permissive (ie will be validly served if it complies with the clause but the clause is not exhaustive and a notice served in accordance with, for example, some relevant statutory provision will also be valid). For a discussion see *Galinski v McHugh* (1988) 57 P & CR 359, [1989] 05 EG 89, CA. Some notice provisions are carelessly drafted and it is not easy to see if the draftsman intended them to be mandatory or permissive: '(and only if)' is inserted to make it clear that this clause is mandatory.

200 This Condition states what may be thought to be the obvious but sometimes the obvious has to be stated in a mandatory clause. If receipt of the notice is acknowledged then it has been validly served, whatever method was adopted.

201 The clause deliberately does not provide for service by telex or fax. Service by telex is perhaps acceptable (at least where some form of acknowledgement is received when the message is sent) but vitally important rights should not depend upon a fax being received. Note *Ralux NV SA v Spencer Mason* [1989] CSW 8 June.

202 It is a fundamental aspect of any notice clause to provide the circumstances in which the server, provided he has complied with the requirements of clause, has for the purposes of the document served a notice, even if the recipient (claims that he) never received it.

FORM NO 2
FORM OF LEASE (FOR USE WITH THE
ROSSCASTLE LETTING CONDITIONS)[1]

[2]*THIS LEASE* dated the   19

BETWEEN:

> (1) . . . of . . . ('Landlord')[3] and

> (2) . . . of . . . ('Tenant')[4] [and]

[(3) . . . of . . . ('Guarantor')[5]   ]

WITNESSES:

1   DEFINITIONS

In this Lease and in the Letting Conditions the following definitions apply:[6]

1.1 'Property'[7]

1.2 'Rights'[8]

1.3 'Exceptions'[9]

1.4 'Encumbrances'[10]

1.5 'Term'[11] – . . . beginning on . .[12]. . . .

1.6 'Letting Conditions'[13] – the Rosscastle Letting Conditions (1st Edition) and 'Condition' means one of the Letting Conditions

[**1.7** 'Excluded Conditions'[14] – the following Conditions:]

1.8 'Initial Rent'[15]

1.9 'Rent Commencement Date'[16]

1.10 'Review Dates'[17] – . . . and 'Review Date' means one of the 'Review Dates'

1.11 'Exterior Decorating Years'[18]

1.12 'Interior Decorating Years'[18]

1.13 'Permitted Use'[19]

[**1.14** 'Superior Lease'[20] – the lease under which the Landlord holds the Property [together with other property] made on the . . . 19   between (1) . . . and (2) . . .   ];

2 THE LETTING

2.1 The Landlord lets[21] the Property to the Tenant for the Term[22]

2.2 The Landlord grants the Rights to the Tenant[8]

2.3 The Exceptions in favour of the Landlord are excepted and[9] reserved

2.4 The letting is subject to the Encumbrances[10]

3 LETTING CONDITIONS

The Letting Conditions, except for the Excluded Conditions, are part of this Lease so far as they are not varied by or inconsistent with the terms set out in this document and if this occurs the terms of this document prevail.[23]

4 DEFINITIONS AND INTERPRETATION

[Set out here in a conventional way any variations in the definitions and interpretation provisions required by the draftsman.][24]

5 TENANT'S COVENANTS

[Set out here in a conventional way any variations in the Tenant's covenants required by the draftman.][24]

6 LANDLORD'S COVENANTS

[Set out here in a conventional way any variations in the Landlord's covenants required by the draftsman.][24]

7 GUARANTOR'S COVENANTS

[Set out here in a conventional way any variations in the Guarantor's covenants required by the draftsman.][24]

8 INSURANCE

[Set out here in a conventional way any variations in the insurance provisions required by the draftsman.][24]

9 UNDERLEASE

[Set out here in a conventional way any variations in the underlease provisions required by the draftsman.][24]

10   PROVISOS

[Set out here in a conventional way any variations in the Provisos required by the draftsman.][24]
[25]

All references to Conditions are to the appropriate Condition in the Rosscastle Letting Conditions: Form No 1 above)

1   As to the use of this Form, see Appendix 1 page 370 above: 'The Letting Conditions and how to use them'. This style and format is, of course, merely the authors' suggestion and any document would be acceptable that addresses the same issues and that is drafted in connection with the Letting Conditions. Note also the comments made in the footnotes to Form No 3.

2   When the Lease will be registered at HM Land Registry (see para 15.11 above) insert the normal heading:-

HM LAND REGISTRY
LAND REGISTRATION ACTS 1925 to 1986
LEASE OF WHOLE [PART]

COUNTY and DISTRICT
or LONDON BOROUGH   :

LANDLORD'S TITLE
NUMBER   :

PROPERTY   :   [Generally insert here the description of the property contained in the Landlord's proprietorship register even in the case of a lease of part]

3   See Condition 2.1:3 so this point need not be dealt with in the Lease.
4   See Condition 2.1:7 so this point need not be dealt with in the Lease.
5   If there is no initial guarantor, then delete this reference. There is, however, no need to exclude Condition 5: see footnote 14 below and Condition 5 may be needed if a subsequent guarantor is required under Condition 3.7:5.
6   See Form No 1 footnote 2.
7   As to parcels generally, see Chapter 3 above. Note Conditions 1.3, 1.9. 2.1:6. 'All that' is legalese and should be omitted and several other words and phrases that tend to be used in the description of the parcels would also seem superfluous. In many cases, the minimum will suffice: '2 Any Street Sometown Blankshire SM1 2BB edged red [[(for identification only)] on the Plan'. If it is self-evident from the plan that it could only be for identification only, then it is suggested that these words could be omitted. Sometimes the definition might have to be expanded to clarify the extent of the demised premises, bearing in mind that the extended 'definition' of Property set out in Condition 2.1:6 is, of necessity, general and makes no reference, for example, to boundary structures. So where the ownership of these could be uncertain, add to the above description, for example, 'including the wall at the rear'. If the plan is being used to define the extent of the Property (and not merely to identify) then the description should read '. . . Blankshire SM1 2BB more particularly delineated and edged red on the Plan': see paras 3.7–3.8 above. Providing the extent of the Property is clearly defined, it matters not if this is achieved by means of words or a plan. For a description of the Property when only part of a building is being let, see Form No 6, clause 1.2.
8   Note Condition 2.3 that should shorten and simplify the description of the rights granted and the grant itself. It is suggested that clause 2 should contain the rights themselves rather than referring to them in a schedule to avoid 'leapfrogging' from one part of the document to another. Note Conditions 2.1:1 and 2.2:3 when drafting rights to use conducting media, etc. Where no rights are granted, clause 2.2 can be omitted.
9   Note Condition 2.4 and points made in footnote 8 above. These are as appropriate to the Exceptions as they are to the Rights. Note also when drafting exceptions the terms defined in Conditions 1.1 (Adjoining Premises) and 1.7 (Other Buildings). Where there are no Exceptions, Clause 2.3 can be omitted.
10   Refer here, for example, to any existing restrictions that affect the freehold title. It will generally be preferable simply to identify the restrictions rather than to set them out – for example 'restrictive covenants contained in the Third Schedule to a Conveyance made on the . . . between . . . and . . . [set out in the Charges Register to the above title]'. It is

suggested that there are two reasons for disclosing in the Lease restrictions etc, to which the freehold is subject: (a) simple fairness to the tenant and (b) removal of any possibility that the tenant could argue that he did not have notice of them and therefore is not bound. The tenant may have that notice as a matter of fact or as a matter of law: see para 2.9 above. In the case of the latter, the tenant will be bound even if he was unaware of the restriction. So if a tenant had not received actual notice (for example by the restriction being referred to in the Lease), there could be cases where he could argue that for some technical reason the statutory provisions referred to in footnotes 5 and 7 to para 2.9 above did not apply to the restriction in question and accordingly he was not bound by it.

11 See Conditions 2.2:2 and 10.8. See paras 5.18–5.21 above.

12 See paras 1.5:3 and 5.18 above.

13 See Appendix 1 Form No 1 above. It is suggested that a print of the Letting Conditions should be bound-up within the Lease so that the document is complete. As to where prints are available, see Form No 1 footnote 1 above.

14 Set out here any of the Letting Conditions that are to be excluded from the lease in question. Only those that are to be excluded for 'commercial reasons' (and that would apply to the letting if not excluded) need be excluded – ie there is no need to exclude those Conditions that are obviously not relevant to the letting. For example, if no rent review dates are specified in the lease and if the Landlord is the freeholder then Conditions 7 and 8 will not apply in the light of Conditions 7.1 and 8.1 – they do not have to be excluded. If there is no Open Land (as defined in Condition 1.8), then Conditions 3.4:5, 3.4:6 and 3.8:5 similarly will not apply, and do not have to be excluded.

15 Where there is to be no rent review, amend clause 1.8 to 'Rent' and delete clause 1.10.

16 See Appendix 1 Form No 1 above, footnotes 34–36.

17 Where there is to be no rent review, see footnote 15 above. Where there is to be one rent review, amend clause 1.10 to 'Rent Review Date'. Where there are several review dates, it is suggested that they should be set out as, for example, '24th June in the years 1990, 1995 and 2000' (assuming a 20 year term from 1985). This will avoid the problems referred to in para 1.5:4 above and Condition 10.8:3. If the landlord does require the rent to be reviewed on or after the expiry of the contractual term, then he should specifically deal with this (ie by adding the year 2005 in the above example).

18 For reasons set out in footnote 17 above, the years should be specified, but in this instance the obligation to redecorate *will* be extended into any period of holding over, etc (see Condition 10.8:2). Where the redecoration obligations are confined to the interior (for example because the demised premises form part of a larger building) amend clause 1.11 to 'Decorating Years', delete clause 1.12, include Conditions 3.4:8 and 3.4:9 as Excluded Conditions, and include in clause 5 of the lease a decorating covenant referring to the 'Decorating Years' and the interior of the Property.

19 As to use generally, see paras 7.8–7.18 above. See Form No 1, footnote 68 and Form No 3 clause 1.10. As to wisdom (or otherwise) of referring to the latest Use Classes Order, see para 7.14 above.

20 As to underleases generally see Chapter 13 and Condition 8. Note that Condition 8 will apply (for reasons explained in footnote 166 to the Letting Conditions) whenever the Landlord is not the freeholder and whether or not reference is made in the lease to the superior lease. Where the lease is an underlease, this should be stated: *Lloyds Bank Ltd v Lake* [1961] 2 All ER 30, [1961] 1 WLR 884.

21 The lease avoids using the word 'demises' preferring the more readily understood 'lets'. The two are synonymous. All that is required is words of present demise: see Hill & Redman's *Law of Landlord and Tenant* (18th edn) para A521.

22 'Yielding and paying' have also been omitted. These words are not essential – any expression showing that the parties intended that a rent will by payable will be a sufficient reservation: *Doe d Rains v Kneller* (1829) 4 C & P 3; *Attoe v Hemmings* (1614) 2 Bulst 281.

23 It is suggested that the simple 'are part of' wording is quite sufficient but 'are incorporated into and form part of this Lease' can certainly be used. It is suggested that a print of the Letting Conditions should be bound into the Lease: see Appendix 1 Form 1 footnote 1 above.

24 In drafting any additional clauses, remember the terms defined in Condition 1 and the points of interpretation in Condition 2. Note particularly Conditions 2.8–2.10. In the covenants, avoid, observe and perform – only one is needed (see *Ayling v Wade* [1961] 2 QB 228, [1961] 2 All ER 399, CA). The clause headings are there only as a reminder to the draftsman. If there is not additional clause dealing with that topic the heading is not needed.

25 No testimonium ('In Witness, etc') is required (see Coke's *Commentary on Littleton's tenure* – Co Litt – 7a). A testimonium has never been included in any Land Registry form.

FORM NO 3
LEASE OF THE WHOLE OF A BUILDING ABUTTING A
PUBLIC ROAD

The complexity of a lease depends very large upon the nature of the property being let. This form deals with the most simple of lettings – the whole of a building (office, shop or factory) that abuts a public road so that the tenant requires no rights over any adjoining land for access or conducting media. The letting incorporates all the Letting Conditions, and, because the form has been included primarily to illustrate how to use the Letting Conditions, the blanks have been completed 'to give artistic verisimilitude to an otherwise bald and unconvincing narrative'.[1] The footnotes to Form No 2 contain comments relevant to this form.

THIS LEASE dated the 2nd[2] October 1989[3]

BETWEEN:

(1) LEGALESE LIMITED of[4] 4 Hereto Street Thereby Shallshire TH1 2AB ('Landlord')

(2) BETTADRAFT LIMITED of[4] Dundrafting Redman Hill Formshire FO1 3CD ('Tenant) and

(3) MURRAY JOHN ROSS of 20 Essex Street London WC2R 3AL and RICHARD WILLIAM CASTLE of Mabor Farm Clearbrook Yelverton Devon PL20 6JD ('Guarantor')

WITNESSES:-

1   DEFINITIONS

In this Lease and in the Letting Conditions the following definitions apply:-

1.1   'Property' – Must House Short Clause Lane Precedent Parashire PR1 4EF edged red on the Plan[5]

1.2   [6]'Encumbrances' – the covenants contained in a Conveyance made on 31st March 1947 between (1) Any Vendor Limited and (2) Alice Purchaser [*or* entries numbered 1, 2 and 3 in the Charges Register of the Landlord's title to the Property (Title No PA 123456)]

1.3   'Term' – 20 years beginning on 29th September 1989[7]

1.4   'Letting Conditions' – the Rosscastle Letting Conditions (1st Edition) and 'Condition' means one of the Letting Conditions[8]

1.5   'Initial Rent' – £20,000 per year

1.6   'Rent Commencement Date' – 25th December 1989[7]

1.7 'Review Dates' – 29th September in the years 1994, 1999 and 2004 and 'Review Date' means one of the Review Dates[9]

1.8 'Exterior Decorating Years' – 1992, 1995, 1998, 2001, 2004 and 2007[9]

1.9 'Interior Decorating Years' – 1994, 1999 and 2004[9]

1.10 'Permitted Use' – offices [shop] [light industry] storage and distribution] [a bookshop or any other use with the consent of the Landlord that falls within Class A1 of the Schedule to the Town and Country Planning (Use Classes) Order 1987 (such consent not to be unreasonably withheld)][10]

2   THE LETTING

2.1   The Landlord lets the Premises to the Tenant for the Term

2.2   The letting is subject to the Encumbrances

3   LETTING CONDITIONS

The Letting Conditions are part of this Lease so far as they are not varied by or inconsistent with the terms set out in this document and if this occurs the terms of this document prevail.

On[11] *Lease*
The Common Seal of
LEGALESE LIMITED was[12] affixed
in the presence of: }

Director

Secretary

On Counterpart
The Common Seal of
BETTADRAFT LIMITED was[12]
affixed in the presence of: }

Director

Secretary

SIGNED AS A DEED[13] and DELIVERED   }
by[14] MURRAY JOHN ROSS
in the presence of: }

SIGNED AS A DEED[13] and DELIVERED
by[14] RICHARD WILLIAM CASTLE
in the presence of:

                }

(All references to Condition are to the appropriate Condition in the Rosscastle Letting Conditions: Form No 1 above)

1   W S Gilbert: 'The Mikado' Act II.
2   'Day of' adds nothing and should be deleted.
3   Most draftsmen, even those of the historical school, recognise that nothing is achieved by setting out the year in words as was once generally done.
4   Many would substitute 'whose registered office is at' for 'of' (some would add 'situate at' but this is clearly unnecessary) although it is not clear what is added by referring to the registered office in the lease. What the parties require to know when the lease is granted is the location of the other party from which property matters are managed (which may not be the registered office and may even be delegated to outside agents). At some stage during the term one party may need to know the registered office of the other when for example a notice or proceedings have to be served but a search would have to be made then – he could not rely upon the statement of the registered office contained in the lease.
5   Note particularly Form 2 footnote 7.
6   In this particular letting there are no rights or exceptions and reservations.
7   It is clear from clause 1.6 that a rent free period is being allowed. See Form No 1 footnotes 34–36 and 111.
8   In this particular letting, there are no Excluded Conditions: see Form No 2 clause 1.7 and footnote 14.
9   Note particularly Form No 2 footnote 17.
10   Note particularly Form No 1 footnote 68.
11   See Form No 2 footnote 25.
12   'Hereunto' has been deleted from the historical wording: it adds nothing.
13   See the Law of Property (Miscellaneous Provisions) Act 1989.
14   'the said' has been deleted from the historical wording; it adds nothing.

FORM NO 4
LEASE OF WAREHOUSE WITH RIGHT OF WAY

The property let by this lease is slightly more complicated than that contemplated in Form No 3. It is a warehouse and the tenant requires rights to be granted to him over a private road running across the landlord's adjoining property in order to gain access to the property, and to use conducting media under the landlord's property. The landlord covenants to maintain the road and conducting media and the tenant covenants to pay all (or a proportion) of the costs incurred by the landlord in doing so. The landlord has the right to use conducting media on the property. The footnotes to Form No 2 contain comments relevant to this form that have not been repeated here.

THIS LEASE dated the   19

BETWEEN:

      (1) . . . of . . . ('Landlord') [and]

      (2) . . . of . . . ('Tenant') [and]

[(3) . . . of . . . ('Guarantor')   ]

WITNESSES:

1   DEFINITIONS

In this Lease and in the Letting Conditions the following definitions apply:

1.1 'Property'

1.2 'Utilities'[1] – the transmission of sewage, water, gas, electricity, telecommunications and information[2]

1.3 'Rights'[3]

1.3:1 the right to pass to and from the Property along the road coloured brown on the Plan [at any time between 7 am and 6 pm on Monday to Friday each week (except public holidays)[4]] with or without vehicles of any description [*or* that are not more than 15 feet long or 20 tonnes unladen weight][5] for all purposes connected with the use of the Property but for no other purpose[6]

[7]**1.3:2** the right (subject to temporary interruption for repair alteration or replacement) to Utilities[8] to and from the Property through the conducting media that now serve the Property and that are on[9] the Adjoining Premises[10]

1.4 'Exceptions'[11]

1.4:1 the right to Utilities[8] to and from the Adjoining Premises through

411

the conducting media which are now, or may during the Term be, on the Property

1.4:2   the right at convenient times and upon reasonable notice (except in an emergency) to enter the Property[12] to maintain the conducting media on[9] the Property used (and to construct and maintain there conducting media to be used) for the provision of Utilities[8] to and from the Adjoining Premises

1.4:3   the right even if it affects the access of light and air to the Property:

1.4:3.1   to alter or raise the height of or rebuild any of the Other Buildings

1.4:3.2   to erect any new building of any height on the Adjoining Premises[13]

1.5   'Encumbrances'

1.6   'Term'

1.7   'Letting Conditions' – the Rosscastle Letting Conditions (1st Edition) and 'Condition' means one of the Letting Conditions

1.8   'Excluded Conditions' – Condition 6.3[14]

1.9   'Initial Rent'

1.10   'Rent Commencement Date'

1.11   'Review Dates' . . . and 'Review Date' means one of the Review Dates

1.12   'Exterior Decorating Years'

1.13   'Interior Decorating Years'

1.14   'Permitted Use' – any purpose that would on the date of this Lease be within Class B8 of the Schedule to the Town and Country Planning (Use Classes) Order 1987[15]

1.15   'Superior Lease' – the lease under which the Landlord holds the Premises [together with other property] made on the . . . 19 . . between (1) . . . and (2). . . .

2   THE LETTING

2.1   The Landlord lets the Property to the Tenant for the Term

2.2   The Landlord grants the Rights to the Tenant

2.3   The Exceptions in favour of the Landlord are excepted and reserved

2.4   The Letting is made subject to the Encumbrances

3 LETTING CONDITIONS

The Letting Conditions, except for the Excluded Conditions, are part of this Lease so far as they are not varied by or inconsistent with the terms set out in this document and if this occurs the terms of this document prevail.

4 THE TENANT'S COVENANTS

The Tenant covenants with the Landlord:

4.1 to refund to the Landlord [as rent][16] on demand [17][a fair proportion (to be fixed in the absence of agreement between the parties by a Qualified Expert)[18] of] any sum paid by the Landlord in or incidental to performing its obligations under clause 5

4.2 not to park any vehicles on the road coloured brown on the Plan nor on the pavements.[3]

5 THE LANDLORD'S COVENANTS

The Landlord covenants with the Tenant to repair:

5.1 the road coloured brown on the Plan until it is adopted as a highway maintainable at public expense

5.2 the conducting media on the Adjoining Premises that serve the Property.[19]

6 INSURANCE

6.1 In addition to the obligations contained in Condition 6.1:1 the landlord covenants with the Tenant also to insure the road coloured brown on the Plan and the conducting media on the Adjoining Premises that serve the Property against the risks referred to in Condition 6.1:1 on the basis that the references in the Letting Conditions to insurance effected pursuant to the Letting Conditions are to be construed as including this additional requirement[14]

6.2 In this letting, the following is substituted for Condition 6.3:
Conditions 6.4 and 6.5 apply whenever during the Term

6.3:1 the Property, the road coloured brown on the Plan or the conducting media on the Adjoining Premises that serve the Property are damaged by any of the risks against which the Landlord is obliged to insure or has insured, and

6.3:2 payment of the insurance money is not refused wholly or in part through the fault of the Tenant or its subtenants.[14]

(All references in the following footnotes to Condition are to the appropriate Condition in the Rosscastle Letting Conditions: Form No 1 above)

1   In a lease that does not contain a service charge, 'Services' would probably be a better term than 'Utilities' but it has been avoided so that the terminology in Forms 4–6 can be consistent.

2 Some of the more technical utilities may not be required in every letting.

3 As to rights of way generally, see paras 4.2–4.5 above. In particular, note that there is no right to park on a right of way: see para 4.4 above. The draftsman has wisely expressly dealt with the point in clause 4.2. As to drafting, note Condition 2.3 which means that the matters dealt with there do not have to be referred to in clauses 1.3:1 or 2.2.

4 The effect of this limitation could operate in the same way as a covenant not to occupy the Property outside normal hours (see para 7.30 above) and the same issues arise. The tenant should resist this limitation – even if it does not concern him, it might concern a potential assignee and make it more difficult for him to dispose of the lease.

5 It will be a practical point for the tenant as to whether this weight limitation is acceptable, although probably the only reason that the landlord would impose such a condition would be that the road was not constructed to take any greater weight. If this limitation would cause the tenant a problem, the only alternative would seem to be to construct a stronger road and the responsibility for the cost of this work would no doubt be 'negotiated' between the parties.

6 See Form No 1, footnote 27.

7 As to the right to use conducting media generally, see para 4.6 above.

8 See footnote 1 above.

9 See Condition 2.2:3 and *Trailfinders Ltd v Razuki* [1988] 2 EGLR 46, [1988] 30 EG 59.

10 Would the tenant also need the right to enter the Adjoining Premises in order (for example) to repair a flank wall of the Property? See para 4.7 above and Form No 5 clause 1.5:3 for a precedent.

11 As to Exceptions generally, see paras 4.10–4.17 above.

12 See para 4.12 above and *Trailfinders Ltd v Razuki* [1988] 2 EGLR 46, [1988] 30 EG 59.

13 See para 4.15 above.

14 This lease provides an example of the Excluded Conditions concept, in this instance being used to amend the Letting Conditions so that they apply to the facts of the letting in question. Assume that the landlord accepts (perhaps following a suggestion by the tenant) that the Property could be rendered unfit for use by the destruction of the access road or the conducting media on his adjoining premises. Thus he agrees to insure these, so that the suspension of rent proviso and the right to terminate if reinstatement prevented will apply if the Property is unfit for use as a result of damage to the road or the conducting media. So (a) the landlord's insuring covenant is extended (clause 6.1:1) (b) Condition 6.3 that deals with when the suspension/termination clauses operate is excluded (clause 1.8) and (c) Condition 6.3 is replaced in the lease by a clause that extends the circumstances to damage to the road or conducting media. An alternative approach would be to exclude Conditions 6.3–6.5 in their entirety and set out complete replacement clauses in the lease. This will involve more typing but less need to refer from lease to Letting Conditions.

15 Here the parties have decided that they wish the Permitted Use to be fixed and not to vary with the Use Classes Order: see para 7.14 above.

16 As to advantages and disadvantages of reserving such payments as rent, see para 11.7 above.

17 The words in square brackets will not be required where the tenant is the only person to use the road.

18 As to Qualified Expert, see Form No 1 footnote 178.

19 As to the covenant generally, see paras 11.2–11.3 above.

FORM NO 5
LEASE OF FACTORY OR WAREHOUSE ON SMALL ESTATE

The letting contemplated in this form is the whole of a building on a small estate. The tenant is granted the right to use the estate roads and the conducting media through other parts of the estate. The landlord covenants to maintain the estate roads and conducting media and to cultivate the landscaped areas forming part of the estate, and the tenant covenants to reimburse the landlord a proportion of the expenditure incurred by the landlord. The footnotes to Form No 2 contain comments relevant to this form that have not been repeated here.

THIS LEASE dated the   19

BETWEEN:

    (1) . . . of . . . ('Landlord') [and]

    (2) . . . of . . . ('Tenant') [and]

[(3) . . . of . . . ('Guarantor')   ]

WITNESSES:

1 DEFINITIONS

In this Lease and in the Letting Conditions the following definitions apply:

1.1 'Estate' – . . . and the term 'Adjoining Premises'[1] as defined in the Letting Conditions includes the Estate

1.2 'Property'

1.3 'Estate Roads' – the roads coloured brown on the Plan

1.4 'Utilities' – the transmission of sewage, water, electricity, gas, telecommunications and information

1.5 'Rights'[2]

1.5:1 the right to pass to and from the Property along the Estate Roads with or without vehicles of any description for all purposes connected with the use of the Property (but not otherwise)

1.5:2 the right (subject to temporary interruption for repair alteration or replacement) to Utilities to and from the Property through the conducting media that now serve the Property and other parts of the Estate and that are on the Adjoining Premises

1.5:3 the right at convenient times and on reasonable notice (except in an emergency) to enter the Adjoining Premises to view the condition of the

Property and to execute works to the Property that would not otherwise be practicable subject to the Tenant causing as little damage and inconvenience as possible and making good all damage caused

1.6 'Exceptions'[3]

1.6:1   the right to Utilities from and to the Adjoining Premises through the conducting media which are now, or may during the term be, on the Property

1.6:2   the right at convenient times and upon reasonable notice (except in an emergency) to enter the Property to maintain the conducting media on the Property used (and to construct and maintain there conducting media to be used) for the provision of Utilities to and from Adjoining Premises

1.6:3   the right at convenient times and on reasonable notice (except in an emergency) to enter the Property to view the condition of the Adjoining Premises and to execute works to the Adjoining Premises that would not otherwise be practicable

1.6:4   the right even if it affects the access of light and air to the Property

1.6:4.1   to alter or raise the height of or rebuild any of the Other Buildings

1.6:4.2   to put up any new building of any height on the Adjoining Property

1.7 'Encumbrances'

1.8 'Term'

1.9 'Letting Conditions' – the Rosscastle Letting Conditions (1st Edition) and 'Condition' means one of the Letting Conditions

1.10 'Excluded Conditions' – the following Conditions: 6.1, 6.2:1, 6.2:2, 6.3[4]

1.11 'Initial Rent'

1.12 'Rent Commencement Date'

1.13 'Review Dates' – . . . and 'Review Date' means one of the Review Dates

1.14 'Exterior Decorating Years'

1.15 'Interior Decorating Years'.

1.16 'Permitted Use' – any purpose[s] that fall[s] within Class[es] [B1 (except offices) *or* B2 *or* B2 *or* B8] of the Schedule to the Town and Country Planning (Use Classes) Order 1987[5]

1.17 'Tenant's Share'[6] – . . . %[7]

2   THE LETTING

2.1   The Landlord lets the Premises to the Tenant for the Term

2.2   The Landlord grants the Rights to the Tenant

2.3   The Exceptions in favour of the Landlord are excepted and reserved

2.4   The Letting is made subject to the Encumbrances.

3   LETTING CONDITIONS

The Letting Conditions, except for the Excluded Conditions, are part of this Lease so far as they are not varied by or inconsistent with the terms set out in this document and if this occurs the terms of this document prevail.

4   THE TENANT'S COVENANTS

The Tenant covenants with the Landlord:

4.1   to pay to the Landlord [as rent][8] the Tenant's Share on demand [or any other percentage that is properly attributable to the Property to be fixed in the absence of agreement between the parties by a Qualified Expert][7] of all sums incurred by the Landlord in or incidental to performing its obligations under clauses 5.1–5.3

4.2   to reimburse the Landlord [as rent] on demand for all expenditure incurred by the Landlord in or incidental to performing its obligations under clause 5

4.3   not to park any vehicles on the Estate Roads[9] or on the pavements[2]

4.4   to comply with all regulations made by the Landlord from time to time for the management of the Estate notified to the Tenant in writing [but nothing in those regulations may amend this Lease (including the Letting Conditions) and if there is any inconsistency between this Lease and the regulations, this Lease prevails].[10]

5   THE LANDLORD'S COVENANTS VARIED

The Landlord covenants with the Tenant:

5.1   to repair, maintain and keep reasonably clean the Estate Roads

5.2   to cultivate any planted or grassed parts of the Estate and to keep those parts neat and tidy

5.3[9]   to repair maintain and where necessary replace any conducting media on the Estate [(including any on the Property)][11].

6   INSURANCE

6.1   The Landlord covenants with the Tenant:–

6.1:1   to insure the Estate against damage by fire lightning explosion aircraft (or other aerial device) or articles dropped from them riot civil commotion malicious persons earthquake storm tempest flood bursting and overflowing of water pipes tanks and other apparatus impact by road vehicles and any other risks that the Landlord may decide although:–

6.1:1.1   the obligation to insure against any particular risk is subject to insurance for that risk being ordinarily available with a reputable insurer for premises such as the Estate and

6.1:1.2   this insurance will be subject to any excesses or limitations that the insurer requires

6.1:2   to effect this insurance with a reputable insurance company or with reputable underwriters and through any agency that the Landlord may from time to time decide

6.1:3   that this insurance will be for the full cost of reinstatement including professional fees fees payable upon any application for planning permission or other consents that may be required for the reinstatement the cost of debris removal demolition site clearance and of any works required by statute and incidental expenses

6.1:4   to produce to the Tenant on request evidence of the terms of the policy and of payment of the last premium

6.1:5   to procure that the interest of the Tenant is noted on the policy whenever this is permitted under the policy and

6.1:6   to notify the Tenant of any material change in the risk covered by the policy

6.2   The Tenant covenants with the Landlord to pay to the Landlord as rent on demand (and if so demanded) in advance (but not more than 60 days in advance) of the date of renewal sums equal to:–

6.2:1   the Tenant's Share [(or any other percentage that is properly attributable to the Property to be fixed in the absence of agreement between the parties by a Qualified Expert)] of the premiums paid or to be paid by the Landlord (inclusive of any commission to be retained by the Landlord) for insuring the Estate in accordance with its obligations in this Lease

6.2:2   any increased premiums required as a result of the Tenant's use of the Property or anything brought onto the Property

6.2:3   the premiums paid (or to be paid) by the Landlord (inclusive of any commission to be retained by the Landlord) for insuring for loss of rent under this Lease for 3 years or where the policy includes all the premises on the Estate to pay the Tenant's Share of the premiums [(or any other percentage that is properly attributable to the Property) to be fixed in the absence of agreement between the parties by a Qualified Expert]

6.2:4   the Tenant's Share [(or any other percentage that is properly attributable to the Property to be fixed in the absence of agreement between the parties by a Qualified Expert)] of the premiums paid or to be paid by the Landlord for insuring in such amount and on such terms as the Landlord considers appropriate against all liability of the Landlord to third parties arising out of or in connection with the Estate

6.3 The Tenant covenants with the Landlord to pay on demand the proportion of the sums referred to in Clause 6.2 for the period beginning with the Rent Commencement Date and ending on the day immediately before the next renewal date

6.4 In this letting the following is substituted for Condition 6.3:–

Conditions 6.4 and 6.5 apply whenever during the Term:–
– the Property or the Estate or the conducting media on the Estate are damaged by any of the risks against which the Landlord is obliged to insure or has insured and
– payment of the insurance money is not refused wholly or in part through the fault of the Tenant or its subtenants.

7 PROVISO

Any walls that divide the Property from structures on Adjoining Premises are party walls within the Law of Property Act 1925 s 38 and will be maintained at the equal expense of the Tenant and the other owner.[12]

(All references to Condition are to the appropriate Condition in the Rosscastle Letting Conditions: Form No 1 above)

1 The additional reference to the Adjoining Premises is 'an avoidance of doubt' provision.
2 See footnotes 4–10 of Form No 4 above.
3 See footnotes 11–13 of Form No 4 above.
4 Compare with the approach adopted in Form No 4 above explained in footnote 11. Here in Form No 5(a) the Landlord covenants to insure the Estate, not the Property. So Condition 6.1:1 has been excluded, and, in view of the references in Conditions 6.1:2 and 6.1:3 etc to 'this insurance' it seemed preferable to exclude Condition 6.1 altogether and to deal with all the points dealt with there in clause 6.1 of the lease (b) the Tenant has to reimburse not all the premium for insuring the Property but rather a proportion of the premium for insuring the Estate. The loss of rent insurance may be per unit on the Estate or that too may be dealt with on the Estate as a whole. The Landlord also requires third party public liability insurance. So Condition 6.2:1 is excluded and replaced by clause 6.2(c) Condition 6.2:2 mentions 'the sums referred to in Condition 6.2:1' and as this Condition has been excluded, Condition 6.2:2 is also excluded and replaced by clause 6.3(d) the circumstances in which the rent will be suspended and the questions of reinstatement and termination are now extended to damage to the Estate or the conducting media that could render the Property unfit for use. So Condition 3 is excluded and replaced by clause 6.4.
5 See para 7.14 and compare with Form No 4, footnote 15.
6 On the basis that all variables should be included in clause 1, it is suggested that it is preferable to set out here the percentage of the cost of insurance and services that will be the responsibility of the Tenant.
7 As to whether and why the lease should enable the percentage to be varied, see para 11.9:1. The right to vary and to refer to the Qualified Expert could have been included only once in clause 1.17, but it is just possible that it would be appropriate to vary the percentage in some instances but not in others, so it is dealt with individually.
8 As to the advantage and disadvantages of reserving such payments as rent, see para 11.7 above.
9 This lease contemplates that each tenant will be responsible for the whole of any expenditure incurred by the landlord on conducting media that solely serves only that tenant's property.

10   Any party to a document should be wary of agreeing to comply with some unknown and (at the time the lease is granted) non-existent document. The tenant's advisers need to limit the effect of this covenant by ensuring that only appropriate topics can be included in the Regulations. One way is to introduce the concept of good estates management (. . . 'made in the interest of good estate management for the Estate by the Landlord' . . .) and another is the words in square brackets.

11   The lease is, of course, a full repairing one and all conducting media within the Property form part of the Property (see Condition 2.1:6). Thus at the point where a pipe that exclusively serves the Property enters the Property, responsibility for its upkeep changes. A landlord might perhaps consider retaining responsibility for the whole length of the pipe in question providing he was reimbursed by the tenant, although consequential amendments to the repairing covenant would be needed if he chose to do this.

12   Alternatives are to include all boundary structures in one or other property, exclude them altogether and make the landlord responsible (subject to reimbursement by the tenant) or to make each tenant responsible for the decorative finishes leaving the remainder to the landlord as if part of the structure.

FORM NO 6
LEASE OF A SUITE OF OFFICES (WITH SERVICE CHARGE)

This Form relates to a suite of offices in an office building and the demised premises include only the inner finishes of the walls, floors and ceilings and the inner half of any non-structural walls that divide the premises from the remainder of the building. Thus the Tenant's repairing covenant is similarly limited. The Landlord covenants to provide services that include the repair and maintenance of those parts of the building not intended for letting such as the common parts, structure, roof and foundations. The Landlord is to be fully reimbursed by means of a service charge, the Tenant paying a fixed percentage of the cost of providing the services and any other sums incurred by the Landlord in relation to the building. The footnotes to Form No 2 contain comments relevant to this form that have not been repeated here.

THIS LEASE dated the   19

BETWEEN:

      (1) . . . of . . . ('the Landlord'), [and]

      (2) . . . of . . . ('Tenant'), [and]

[(3) . . . of . . . ('Guarantor')   ]

WITNESSES:

1 DEFINITIONS

In this Lease and in the Letting Conditions the following definitions apply:

1.1 'Building'[1] – . . . and the term 'Adjoining Premises' as defined in the Letting Conditions includes the Building[2]

1.2 'Property' – the part of the . . . floor of the Building edged red on the Plan including:[3]

1.2:1 the paint and other finishes applied to the interior of the external walls but not any other part of the external walls

1.2:2 the floor finishes but nothing below them

1.2:3 the ceiling finishes but nothing above them

1.2:4 any non-load-bearing internal walls wholly inside the Property

1.2:5 the inner half of the internal non-load-bearing walls dividing the Property from other parts of the Building

1.2:6 the doors and windows and the door and window frames

1.2:7 all additions and improvements to the Property

421

1.2:8   all fixtures in or upon the Property whether or not originally fixed to the Property except any fixture installed by the Tenant that can be removed from the Proper defacing the Property
[and]

1.2:9   the conducting media that solely serve the Property [and]

1.2:10   'the Car Park' coloured [blue] on the Plan

1.3   'Common Parts' – the pedestrian ways, forecourts [car parks] [land-scaped areas] entrance halls landings [lift-shafts] staircases passages and other areas which are from time to time during the Term provided by the Landlord for common use and enjoyment by the tenants and occupiers of the Building and all persons expressly or by implication authorised by them

1.4   'Utilities' – the transmission of [sewage] [water] electricity [gas] television telecommunications and information[4]

1.5   'Rights'[5]

1.5:1   the right to use the Common Parts for all purposes connected with the use and enjoyment of the Property

1.5:2   the right to use those toilets in the Building that are designated from time to time in writing by the Landlord[6]

1.5:3   the right (subject to temporary interruption for repair alteration or replacement) to Utilities to and from the Property through the conducting media in the Building [and on Adjoining Premises] that now serve the Property and other parts of the Building

1.5:4   the right of support and protection for the Property as now enjoyed from the Building[7]

1.6   'Exceptions'[8]

1.6:1   the right to Utilities from and to the Adjoining Premises through the conducting media which are now, or may during the Term be, on the Property

1.6:2   the right at covenient times and upon reasonable notice (except in an emergency) to enter the Property to maintain the conducting media on the Property and used (and maintain construct conducting media there to be used) for the provision of Utilities from and to Adjoining Premises

1.6:3   the right at convenient times and upon reasonable notice (except in an emergency) to enter the Property to view the condition of the Building and conducting media [and the Other Buildings] and to execute works to the Building and the conducting media [and the Other Buildings] that would not otherwise be practicable[9]

1.6:4   the right to erect scaffolding for repairing or cleaning the Building and Other Buildings[9]

1.6:5   all rights of support now or after the date of this Lease enjoyed by other parts of the Building[7] and

1.6:6   the right even if it affects the passage of light and air to the Property:

422

1.6:6.1 to alter or raise the height of the Building or to alter or raise the height of or to rebuild any of the Other Buildings

1.6:6.2 to put up any new building of any height on the Adjoining Property

1.7 'Encumbrances'

1.8 'Term'

1.9 'Letting Conditions' – the Rosscastle Letting Conditions (1st Edition) and 'Condition' means one of the Letting Conditions

1.10 'Excluded Conditions' – the following Conditions: 1.3, 2.1:6, 3.2:2, 3.4:4, 3.4:8, 3.4:9, 6.1, 6.2:1, 6.2:2, 6.3

1.11 'Initial Rent'

1.12 'Rent Commencement Date'

1.13 'Review Dates' – and 'Review Date' means one of the Review Dates

1.14 'Decorating Years'[10]

1.15 'Permitted Use' – Offices

1.16 'Tenant's Share'[11]

1.17 'Initial Provisional Service Charge'[12]

2 THE LETTING

2.1 The Landlord lets the Property to the Tenant for the Term

2.2 The Landlord grants the Rights to the Tenant

2.3 The Exceptions in favour of the Landlord are excepted and reserved

2.4 The Letting is made subject to the Encumbrances.

3 LETTING CONDITIONS

The Letting Conditions, except for the Excluded Conditions, are part of this Lease so far as they are not varied by or inconsistent with the terms set out in this document and if this occurs the terms of this document prevail.

4 THE TENANT'S COVENANTS

The Tenant covenants with the Landlord:

4.1 to clean the interior of the windows and window frames in the Property at least once a month[13]

4.2   in each of the Decorating Years and in the last year of the Term to redecorate the Property in a workmanlike way and with appropriate materials of good quality to the reasonable satisfaction of the Landlord and to obtain the Landlord's approval of any change in the colours and patterns in the last year of the Term[10]

4.3   before installing any internal demountable partitions at the Property to obtain the approval of the Landlord to the use of that type of partitioning and the installation, repositioning or removal of internal demountable partitions of a type approved by the Landlord will not be a breach of Condition 3.5

4.4   to remove any internal demountable partitions on the expiry of the Term if requested by the Landlord and to make good where the Property has been damaged by that removal

4.5   to employ for cleaning the Property a firm or company approved by the Landlord and no other firm or company[14]

4.6   not to place any thing outside the Property nor cause any obstruction of the Common Parts

4.7   to convey goods into and out of the Building and the Property only through the goods entrance and by means of the goods lift

4.8   not to interfere with the heating cooling or ventilation of the Building or to impose an additional load on any heating, cooling or ventilation plant in the Building

4.9   to operate the heating, cooling and ventilation equipment in the Property in accordance with regulations made by the Landlord from time to time

4.10   not to play or use at the Property any apparatus that produces sound audible outside and

4.11   to comply with all regulations made by the Landlord from time to time for the management of the Building but nothing in those regulations may amend this Lease and if there is any inconsistency between the terms of this Lease and the regulations, the Lease will prevail.

5   INSURANCE

5.1   The Landlord covenants with the Tenant:–

5.1:1   to insure the Building against damage by fire lightning explosion aircraft (or other aerial device) or articles dropped from them riot civil commotion malicious persons earthquake storm tempest flood bursting and overflowing of water pipes tanks and other apparatus impact by road vehicles and any other risks that the Landlord may decide although:–

5.1:1.1   the obligation to insure against any particular risk is subject to insurance for that risk being ordinarily available with a reputable insurer for premises such as the Building and

5.1:1.2   this insurance will be subject to any excesses or limitations that the insurer requires

5.1:2   to effect this insurance with a reputable insurance company or with reputable underwriters and through any agency that the Landlord may from time to time decide

5.1:3   that this insurance will be for the full cost of reinstatement including professional fees fees payable upon any application for planning permission or other consents that may be required for the reinstatement the cost of debris removal demolition site clearance and of any works required by statute and incidental expenses

5.1:4   to produce to the Tenant on request evidence of the terms of the policy and of payment of the last premium

5.1:5   to procure that the interest of the Tenant is noted on the policy whenever this is permitted under the policy and

5.1:6   to notify the Tenant of any material change in the risk covered by the policy

5.2   The Tenant covenants with the Landlord to pay to the Landlord as rent on demand (and if so demanded) in advance (but not more than 60 days in advance) of the date of renewal sums equal to:–

5.2:1   the Tenant's Share [(or any other percentage that is properly attributable to the Property to be fixed in the absence of agreement between the parties by a Qualified Expert)] of the premiums paid or to be paid by the Landlord (inclusive of any commission to be retained by the Landlord) for insuring the Building in accordance with its obligations in this Lease

5.2:2   any increased premiums required as a result of the Tenant's use of the Property or anything brought onto the Property

5.2:3   the premiums paid (or to be paid) by the Landlord (inclusive of any commission to be retained by the Landlord) for insuring for loss of rent under this Lease for 3 years or where the policy includes all the Building to pay the Tenant's Share of the premiums [(or any other percentage that is properly attributable to the Property) to be fixed in the absence of agreement between the parties by a Qualified Expert]

5.2:4   the Tenant's Share [(or any other percentage that is properly attributable to the Property to be fixed in the absence of agreement between the parties by a Qualified Expert)] of the premiums paid or to be paid by the Landlord for insuring in such amount and on such terms as the Landlord considers appropriate against all liability of the Landlord to third parties arising out of or in connection with the Building

5.3   The Tenant covenants with the Landlord to pay on demand the proportion of the sums referred to in clause 6.2 for the period beginning with the Rent Commencement Date and ending on the day immediately before the next renewal date

5.4   In this letting the following is substituted for Condition 6.3:–

Conditions 6.4 and 6.5 apply whenever during the Term:–
– the Property or the Building or the conducting media in the Building are damaged by any of the risks against which the Landlord is obliged to insure or has insured and
– payment of the insurance money is not refused wholly or in part through the fault of the Tenant or its subtenants

6   LANDLORD'S COVENANTS

6.1   *Landlord's Obligations*

The Landlord covenants with the Tenant:[16]

6.1:1   to repair and maintain the roofs and foundations of the Building, all floors and ceilings of the Building (excluding the floor and ceiling finishes) the external walls of the Building (excluding the paint and other decorative finishes applied to the internal faces of those walls) all load-bearing walls pillars and other structures of the Building (excluding the paint and other decorative finishes applied to the faces of those structures) and all other structural parts of the Building[17]

6.1:2   to repair and maintain the outer half of all internal non-load-bearing walls dividing the Property from other parts of the Building[18]

6.1:3   to repair, maintain, keep clean and decorate all parts of the Building except the Property and other areas let or available for letting, including walls, floors, ceilings, doors, door frames, windows and window frames the cleaning and decorating being to such standard as the Landlord in its discretion considers adequate[19]

6.1:4   to provide a lift service [during normal business hours][20] by the lifts now installed in the Building or by any substituted lifts as the Landlord may in its discretion decide to install

6.1:5   to supply [during normal business hours][20] hot and cold water and washing and toilet accessories in the toilets of the Building

6.1:6   to supply [during normal business hours][20] central heating and air conditioning to the Property and to the toilets, passages, halls and stairs of the Building to such temperatures as the Landlord in its discretion[19] considers adequate

6.1:7   to maintain, insure and replace when appropriate all plant which serves the Building including generators, boilers, ventilation, heating, cooling, public address and television systems and the lifts but not any plant whose maintenance is the direct responsibility of any tenant in the Building

6.1:8   to repair, maintain, clean and renew when appropriate all conducting media in or serving the Building, but not any which is the direct responsibility of any tenant in the Building

6.1:9   to maintain fire prevention and fire fighting equipment in the Building other than in the Property and other areas let or available for letting

6.1:10   to light the toilets, passages, halls, stairs, and lifts of the Building

6.1:11   to keep the garden areas of the Building neat and tidy

6.1:12   to supply and maintain bins, tools and equipment for the appearance upkeep or cleanliness of the Building and to collect and dispose of refuse from the Building and

6.1:13   to clean as frequently as it in its discretion considers necessary the outside of all windows and window frames of the Building

6.2   *Qualified Nature of Obligations*

The Landlord is not liable to the Tenant for breach of any of its obligations in Condition 6.1 where the breach was caused by something beyond the Landlord's control, except to the extent that the breach could have been prevented or shortened by the exercise of proper care by the Landlord or those undertaking the obligation on behalf of the Landlord, and provided the Landlord uses reasonable endeavours to remedy the breach.[21]

7   SERVICE CHARGE

7.1   In this Lease:

7.1:1   'Net Expenditure' means the difference between Gross Expenditure and Income

7.1:2   'Gross Expenditure'[22] means:

7.1:2.1   all the expenses incurred by the Landlord in fulfilling its obligations under this Lease (except those relating to insurance contained in clause 5)

7.1:2.2   all the fees and disbursements of any person incurred by or on behalf of the Landlord in connection with the Building any obligation under this Lease or any function referred to in this clause including (as an example):
- the managing agents retained by the Landlord to collect the rents and other sums due to the Landlord, undertake on behalf of the Landlord any of its obligations under this Lease and generally to be responsible for the management administration security maintenance and protection of the Building[23]
- any person providing reception porterage security and caretaking services at the Building[24]
- any person valuing the Building to determine the full cost of reinstatement[23]
- any professional advice sought in relation to the Building or this Lease[23]
- the Chartered Accountant referred to in clause 7.2:2.3

7.1:2.3   the cost of employing staff to undertake the Landlord's obligations under this Lease and the other functions referred to in clause 7 including insurance pension and welfare contributions the provision of uniforms and working clothes and the provision of equipment for the proper performance of their duties[25]

7.1:2.4   the [reasonable] fees of the Landlord or any company in the Landlord's Group where it rather than a third party undertakes any obligation under this Lease or other function referred to in this clause[26]

7.1:2.5   all rates assessments and outgoings which during the Term are charged assessed or imposed upon the whole Building where there is no separate charge assessment or imposition upon an individual unit or charged assessed and imposed on part of the Building other than any part of it let or available for letting

7.1:2.6   the cost of all electricity gas oil or other fuel used in performing any obligation under this Lease or other function referred to in this clause

7.1:2.7   any amount which the Landlord may be called upon to pay as a contribution towards the expense of making repairing maintaining rebuilding or cleaning anything used by the Building exclusively or by the Building and any neighbouring property including roads pavements structures or conducting media

7.1:2.8   the expense of supplying to the tenants any regulations relating to the Building

7.1:2.9   the cost of complying with making representations against or contesting the incidence of any statute byelaw regulation or notice alleged to relate to the Building (or any part of it) and for which no tenant is directly liable

7.1:2.10   the cost of abating a nuisance to any part of the Building so far as the abatement is not the direct responsibility of any tenant

7.1:2.11   the interest and fees on borrowing any money to finance its obligations under this Lease[27]

7.1:2.12   any other sum properly incurred by the Landlord in connection with the Building and[28]

7.1:2.13   any provision for expenditure in a subsequent year that the Landlord considers appropriate[29]

7.1:3   'Income' means:

7.1:3.1   any insurance money received from an insurance policy which the Landlord was obliged to take out by virtue of this Lease where the Landlord has incurred expenses in making good the insured loss itself and

7.1:3.2   any money recovered from any person (other than the service charge paid by the tenants in the Building) who was liable to contribute to the cost of compliance with the Landlord's obligations under this Lease where the Landlord has itself incurred the expense towards which the person contributed

7.1:4   'Computing Date' means 31st December or any other date that the Landlord may nominate

7.1:5   'Provisional Service Charge' means the Initial Provisional Service Charge or such other sum as may be fixed from time to time (in the absence of agreement between the parties) by a Qualified Expert as being a reasonable estimate of the Tenant's Share of the Net Expenditure for that financial year

7.2   'Payment'[30]

7.2:1   The Tenant must pay to the Landlord the Provisional Service Charge without any deduction by equal quarterly payments on the usual quarter days [(and this sum is to be treated as rent)][31] and Conditions 3.1:1–3.1:5 apply to the Provisional Service Charge as well as the Rent[30]

7.2:2 As soon as possible after every Computing Date, the Landlord must prepare and supply to the Tenant an account:

7.2:2.1 showing the Net Expenditure, the Expenditure and the Income for the period referred to in the account

7.2:2.2 containing a fair summary of the items referred to in it, and

7.2:2.3 audited by a Chartered Accountant or other person who is qualified by virtue of the Companies Act 1985, s 389(1) for appointment as auditor of a company[30]

7.2:3 This account is to be conclusive evidence of all matters of fact referred to in it[32]

7.2:4 In the case of the first Computing Date after the Rent Commencement Date, if the proportion of the Tenant's Share of the Net Expenditure shown in the account apportioned on a daily basis for the period from the Rent Commencement Date to the Computing Date:

7.2:4.1 exceeds the amount already paid as Provisional Service Charge before the first Computing Date, the Tenant must pay to the Landlord [as rent][31] the excess on demand

7.2:4.2 is less than the amount already paid as Provisional Service Charge before the first Computing Date, the Landlord will credit the excess to the Tenant against the next quarterly payment of Rent and Provisional Service Charge.[30]

7.2:5 In the case of every subsequent Computing Date, if the Tenant's Share of the Net Expenditure shown in the account for the period beginning on the day after the previous Computing Date and ending on that Computing Date:

7.2:5.1 exceeds the amount paid as Provisional Service Charge during that period, the Tenant must pay to the Landlord [as rent][31] the excess on demand

7.2:5.2 is less than the amount paid as Provisional Service Charge during that period, the Landlord will credit the excess to the Tenant against the next quarterly payment of Rent and Provisional Service Charge.

(All references to Condition are to the appropriate Condition in the Rosscastle Letting Conditions: Form No 1 above)

1 Building is being used in this lease to mean the building of which the Property forms part and not (as is the case in Condition 1.3) a building erected on the Property. So Condition 1.3 has to be excluded along with those Conditions that mention Building (Conditions 2.1:6, 3.4:8 and 3.4:9): see clause 1.10 below).

2 The latter part of this clause is very much an avoidance of doubt provision.

3 The basic concept of this lease is that only the 'inner shell' is included within the demised premises and thus the tenant is responsible for repairing/decorating only this. The landlord is responsible for all the rest of the building. Wherever a detailed description of the Property is included in the lease, the 'expanded' definition in Condition 2.1:6 must be excluded, and those parts of Condition 2.1:6 that are still required inserted in clause 1.2.

4 Specific instructions (as ever) will be needed on this clause – it may well be, for example, that no gas is available and that sewage and water is needed only in the common parts and not in the Property.

5 See Form 4 above, footnotes 3–10.

6 See para 4.9 above.

7 See para 4.8 above.

8 See Form 4 above, footnotes 11–13.

9 See para 4.13 above.

10 The concept of this letting (see footnote 3 above) is such that the tenant is responsible only for

the decoration of the interior. So there is only one set of Decorating Years while Conditions 3.4:8 and 3.4:9 are excluded and replaced by clause 4.2.

11 As to the ways of determining the Tenant's Share, see paras 11.8–11.11 above.

12 See para 11.12 above.

13 The concept of this letting (see footnote 3 above) is such that the tenant is responsible only for cleaning the interior of the windows. Thus, Condition 3.4:4 is excluded and replaced by clause 4.1.

14 Landlords are concerned with who has access to the building especially outside normal hours. Sometimes 'specified' is substituted for 'approved'. The tenant should seek 'such approval not to be unreasonably withheld'.

15 See Form 5 above, footnote 4. The approach here is identical 'Building' being substituted for Estate.

16 As to the landlord's covenant, see paras 11.14–11.16. As to the services themselves, see paras 11.17–11.20.

17 See para 11.18:3 above.

18 Where the adjoining part of the building is another let unit, the landlord will be able to recover the cost of so doing from (or to 'delegate' responsibility for doing so onto) the adjoining tenant: see 22 Encyclopaedia of Forms and Precedents (5th edn) From 30 footnote 45.

19 See para 11.19 above.

20 The tenant should watch any time limitations: see para 7.30. The lack of a lift in a tall building could make the offices on the upper floors unuseable outside normal hours at least to all but the most athletic . . . the absence of heating/air conditioning could be almost as significant.

21 See para 11.14 above.

22 Here the landlord seeks to recover the cost not only of the services that he has covenanted in clause 6 to perform but also the non-covenanted functions (see paras 11.14 and 11.17 above) that he may decide or be required to provide – in other words *all* his expenditure on the building.

23 An emotive provision so far as tenants are concerned, but probably consistent with the concept of the clear lease: see para 11.1 above.

24 Note that the landlord has not actually covenanted to provide any such services in clause 6.1.

25 See para 11.18:2 above.

26 See para 11.18 footnote 5 above.

27 See para 11.18 footnote 14 above.

28 See para 11.18:4 above.

29 As to sinking funds generally, see paras 11.21–11.29 above.

30 See paras 11.12–11.13 above.

31 See para 11.7 above.

32 See para 11.5 above.

FORM NO 7
INSURANCE BY SUPERIOR LANDLORD

The Letting Conditions are drafted on the basis that the landlord insures the property. It will be rare today for a landlord to want a tenant in occupation to insure – a more likely exception to the landlord insuring arises where the landlord has only a leasehold interest and where his lease provides for the insurance to be effected by the superior landlord. In these circumstances, all the Conditions dealing with insurance should be excluded – by stating in the Lease that Conditions 6.1–6.5 are Excluded Conditions – and a clause such as the following inserted in the Lease.

---

4   INSURANCE

4.1   The Landlord covenants with the Tenant:

4.1:1   to pay promptly to the superior landlord all sums relating to insurance required under the Superior Lease ('Insurance Payments')

4.1:2   to request from the superior landlord as often as is permitted under the Superior Lease [whenever reasonably requested by the Tenant] evidence of the terms of the policy under which the Property is insured and of payment of the last premium and to pass on to the Tenant the evidence obtained from the superior landlord

4.1:3   to pass on to the Tenant copies of all communications about the insurance of the Property received from the insurers or the superior landlord or any person on their behalf; and

4.1:4   to take all reasonable steps to procure that the interest of the Tenant is noted on the policy

4.2   The Tenant covenants with the Landlord:

4.2:1   to pay as rent to the Landlord on demand sums equal to:

4.2:1.1   all the Insurance Payments made by the Landlord to the superior landlord

4.2:1.2   the premiums paid or to be paid by the Landlord (inclusive of any commission to be retained by the Landlord) for insuring for loss of rent under this Lease for [3] years or

4.2:1.3   where in the case of either of the items referred to in clause 4.2:1.1–4.2:1.2 the Insurance Payments or the policies in question include the Property and other premises, to pay the proportion of the Insurance Payments or the premiums properly attributable to the Property to be fixed (in the absence of agreement between the parties) by a Qualified Expert

4.2:2   to pay on demand the proportion of the sums referred to in Condition 4.2:1 for the period beginning with the Rent Commencement Date and ending on the day immediately before the next renewal date

4.2:3   not to do or omit anything that could cause any insurance on the Property to become void or voidable wholly or in part nor anything by which additional or increased insurance premiums may become payable

4.2:4   to keep the Property supplied with such fire fighting equipment as the insurer and the fire authority may require and to maintain it in working order and to the satisfaction of the insurer and the superior landlord and to the reasonable satisfaction of the Landlord and at least once every six months to have any fire fighting equipment inspected by a competent person

4.2:5   to comply with the requirements and recommendations of the insurer and the fire authority

4.2:6   not to obstruct the access any fire equipment or the means of escape from the Property nor to lock any fire door while the Property is occupied

4.2:7   to give notice to the Landlord immediately any event happens which might affect any insurance policy relating to the Property or when any event happens against which the Landlord or a superior landlord may have insured under the Lease

4.2:8   to inform the Landlord immediately in writing of any matter likely to affect the decision of any insurer to grant or to continue insurance of the Property

4.2:9   if the Tenant is entitled to the benefit of any insurance on the Property, to apply all money in making good the loss for which it is received and

4.2:10   [to insure any] [if the Property is a shop, to insure the] fixed glass on the Property with a reputable insurance company or with reputable underwriters against breakage or damage for its full reinstatement cost, when required to produce to the Landlord particulars of the insurance and evidence of the payment of the premium, and to reinstate any fixed glass that is broken or damaged with new glass of no less quality or thickness

4.3   The Rent under the Lease will be suspended for as long as the rent reserved by the Superior Lease is suspended, and if the payment of any other recurring item is suspended under the Superior Lease, it will be similarly suspended under the Lease.

FORM NO 8
REVIEWED RENT DETERMINED BY AN EXPERT RATHER THAN AN ARBITRATOR

The Letting Conditions are drafted on the basis that the revised rent will be determined on the rent reviews by an arbitrator. If an expert is required, the Lease should indicate that Conditions 7.3 and 7.4 are Excluded Conditions and the following should be inserted in the Lease.

---

4 RENT REVIEW

4.1 For each Review Period, the Rent will be the greater of:

4.1:1 the Rent payable immediately before the relevant Review Date, or, if payment of the Rent has been suspended, the Rent which would have been payable had there been no suspension, or

4.1:2 the revised rent ascertained in accordance with this clause

4.2 The revised rent for any Review Period may be agreed in writing at any time between the parties or (in the absence of agreement) will be determined but not earlier than the relevant Review Date by an expert

4.3 The revised rent will be whatever the expert decides is the rent at which the Property might reasonably be expected to be let in the open market at the relevant Review Date making the Assumptions and disregarding the Disregards

4.4 The fees and expenses of the expert including the cost of his appointment will be borne equally by the parties who will otherwise each bear their own costs

4.5 The expert is to be appointed by agreement between the parties, or (in the absence of agreement) nominated by the then President of the Royal Institution of Chartered Surveyors (or his nominee) on the application of either party made not earlier than six months before the relevant Review Date

4.6 If the expert dies or declines to act the President may on the application of either party appoint another

4.7 The Tenant must allow the expert access to the Property to do anything which the expert considers necessary to carry out his function

4.8 The expert will allow each party to make representations to him [and to make written counter-representations] but will not be in any way fettered by the representations [and counter-representations] and will rely on his own judgement

4.9 When the Rent has been fixed in accordance with this clause, memoranda will be signed by or on behalf of the parties and annexed to the Lease and its counterpart and the parties will bear their own costs of this

4.10   If the revised rent payable during any Review Period has not been ascertained by the relevant Review Date, the then current Rent will continue to be payable on account of the Rent for that Review Period

4.11   If the revised rent is ascertained on or before the relevant Review Date and that date is not a quarter day, the Tenant must on that Review Date pay to the Landlord the difference between the Rent due for that quarter and the Rent actually paid for it

4.12   If the revised rent payable during any Review Period has not been ascertained by the relevant Review Date, then immediately after the date it has been agreed or upon which the expert's decision is made, the Tenant must pay to the Landlord:

4.12:1   any shortfall between the Rent which would have been paid if the revised rent had been ascertained by the relevant Review Date and the payment made on account, and

4.12:2   interest at the Bank's base lending rate on the shortfall between the amount that would have been paid if the revised rent had been ascertained by the relevant Review Date and the payments made on account for the period beginning on the day upon which each instalment was due and ending on the day on which payment of the shortfall is made.

ADDITIONAL CLAUSES

Clause

A   LATENT DEFECTS: CLAUSE FOR INCLUSION IN LEASE OF THE WHOLE OF A NEW BUILDING

This clause takes up the suggestion set out in para 8.15:2 above. There is nothing absolute about the headings to the proposed form of lease (see Form No 2 above) and where a number of provisions are to be included, all relating to the same topic, it seems sensible to group them together under a descriptive heading (in the way in which, for example, the insurance provisions are set out in the Letting Conditions). No Letting Conditions have to be excluded because clause 4.1 indicates that the Letting Conditions are subject to this clause. The latent defect is defined (see para 8.7 above) and there is optional wording that would exclude from the definition anything that the Tenant ought to have discovered prior to the Lease.

---

4   Latent defects

4.1   The Tenant's obligations relating to the repair of the Property contained in the Letting Conditions are subject to the provisions of this clause

4.2   'Defect' means any defect in the Property attributable to design, workmanship or materials, supervision of construction or installation, or preparation of the site [but excludes any defect which would have been apparent to a competent professional either on inspection immediately before the grant of this Lease or from any plans or documents copies of which were
of this Lease or from any plans or documents copies of which were made available to the Tenant before the date of this Lease]

4.3   The Tenant need not remedy and the Landlord must remedy at its own expense:

4.3:1   any Defect notified to the Landlord by the Tenant within the first [six] years of the Term

4.3:2   any disrepair revealed at any time in the Term caused directly or indirectly by a Defect that has been notified in accordance with clause 4.3:1

435

B   LATENT DEFECTS: CLAUSE FOR INCLUDING IN A LEASE OF PART OF A NEW BUILDING

This clause aims to do for a lease of part of a building what clause A does for a whole building. It is assumed that a service charge is payable and so the clause excludes from the service charge any expenditure incurred by the landlord in relation to latent defects, and requires the landlord to remedy them at his own expense.

4   Latent defects

4.1   (Clause 4.1 of A)

4.2   (Clause 4.2 of A with 'Building' substituted for 'Property')

4.3   The Tenant need not remedy, and the Landlord cannot directly or indirectly recover from the Tenant the cost relating to the remedy of but the Landlord must remedy at its own expense:–

4.3:1   any Defect revealed within the first [six] years of the Term

4.3:2   any disrepair revealed at any time in the Term caused directly or indirectly by a Defect notified within the first [six] years of the Term

C   ALIENATION: CLAUSE PERMITTING OCCUPATION BY A GROUP COMPANY

See para 7.7:4 above. No Letting Conditions have to be excluded.

Condition 3.7:1 is amended so that the Tenant may [having given notice to the Landlord] permit a company that is a member of the same Group as the Tenant (within the meaning of s 42 of the 1954 Act) to occupy the Property or share with the Tenant the occupation of the Property but only for so long as both companies remain members of that group and only in a way that does not transfer or create a legal estate.

D   ALIENATION: UNDERLETTING ONLY PERMITTED IF 1954 ACT EXCLUDED

Landlords sometimes wish to make this addition to the list of provisions set out in Condition 3.7:6.3.

The Tenant covenants with the Landlord not to underlet [the whole or] any part of the Property without producing to the Landlord an Order of the Court authorising the agreement between the parties to the underlease to exclude the operation of the 1954 Act ss 24 to 28 in relation to that underlease.

E   TENANT'S COVENANT: COMPENSATION FOR MAJOR WORK

Tenants are often concerned by the prospect of being required to undertake major work towards the end of the term under the repairing covenant

(Condition 3.4:1), or the covenants to comply with statute (Conditions 3.11 and 3.12). This worry is sometimes met by providing that any such work is looked upon as if it were an improvement for which the tenant was entitled to compensation under the Landlord and Tenant Act 1927.

Where any provision of this Lease obliges the Tenant [in the last [5] years of the Term] to carry out any work costing more than [75]% of the annual rent at the beginning of the work then when the Tenant quits the Property the Landlord will pay him compensation based on an assessment of the work as if it was an improvement for which the Landlord had to pay compensation to an outgoing tenant under the Landlord and Tenant Act 1927 and the compensation will be agreed between the parties or determined by an arbitrator appointed in the absence of agreement between the parties by the then President of the Royal Institution of Chartered Surveyors or his nominee on the application of either party.

F   REINSTATEMENT: LANDLORD NOT OBLIGED TO REINSTATE EXACTLY AS BEFORE

It is difficult to recreate a building that has been destroyed and this is all the more so in the case of old buildings. Few buildings are in fact destroyed or significantly damaged, and no doubt when this does arise the parties can usually agree upon the various issues. If, however, the building was particularly unusual, a clause along the following lines may well reassure the landlord. Note that Condition 2.2:7 provides that 'damaged' includes destroyed.

If the Property is substantially damaged the Landlord may reinstate with any modifications called for by the Permissions, adopted to reflect contemporary building practice or that the Landlord may reasonably require but the Landlord must provide the Tenant with accommodation not less convenient or spacious and ancillary facilities no less appropriate than those which existed immediately before the damage.

G   TERMINATION OF LEASE: TENANT'S OPTION TO BREAK CLAUSE

See paras 12.8 and 12.9 above. It is suggested that the two dates referred to in this clause should be set out rather than relying upon expressions like 'on the expiry of the third year of the Term' or 'not less than 3 months notice'. This approach should avoid the difficulties referred to in paras 1.5:3 and 1.5:4 above and it also better communicates these important points to the parties or their successors. As to whether or not the clause should be subject to the tenant complying with the provisions of the lease, see para 12.9. As to why 'observes' is sufficient and there is not need to add 'and performs' see *Ayling v Wade* [1961] 2 QB 228, [1961] 2 All ER 399, CA.

At any time before [Date 1] the Tenant may serve a notice to terminate the Term on [Date 2 – 6 months later] and if it does so [and if the Tenant [reasonably] observes the provisions of this Lease up to [Date 2]] the Term will end at 12 noon on [Date 2] (rent being paid for all that day) but the termination will not affect any claim that the Landlord may have for breaches by the Tenant of the provisions of this Lease.

H   TERMINATION OF LEASE: TENANT'S OPTION WHERE PROPERTY UNFIT FOR OCCUPATION FOR ANY REASON NOT INVOLVING TENANT'S DEFAULT

The Letting Conditions give either party the right to terminate if the Property is not fit for use 3 years after the damage. There can be very few tenants who would not prefer the flexibility of being able to terminate the lease immediately and to seek alternative accommodation at once rather than having to wait for the landlord to reinstate. The tenant will probably need alternative accommodation in the meantime and, especially where reinstatement could be problematical, they will not know for some time if their occupation of the Property will merely be suspended or will be terminated. That being so, a tenant in a strong negotiating position might well advance a provision giving him the right to terminate immediately.

If through no fault of the Tenant or its subtenants the Property becomes unfit for use the Tenant may give the Landlord [3] months notice to terminate this Lease and on the expiry of the notice the Term will end but this will not affect any claim that either party may have for breaches by the other of the provisions of this Lease.

I   ARBITRATION

See paras 12.10–12.12 above. As to 'under out of or in connection with' see *Fillite (Runcorn) Ltd v Aqua-Lift (a firm)* (1989) Times, 28 February, CA. It is inappropriate for matters concerning forfeiture to be referred to (and potentially delayed by) arbitration and the second exception makes it clear that, where the lease provides for determination of questions of fact to be made by (for example) the Landlord's surveyor or the Qualified Expert, it is not open to a party to refer the question to arbitration. The risk is probably slight but there does seem some merit in permitting the nomination to be made by somebody on behalf of the President, to eliminate the possibility of an aggrieved party seeking the removal of an arbitrator who was not personally appointed by the President. It will be noted that there is no mention of the Arbitration Act 1950 and 1979. A reference can certainly be included but it is suggested that this is unnecessary. The Acts apply to an 'arbitration agreement' and this is defined (1950 Act, s 32) as a 'written agreement to submit present or future differences to arbitration, whether an arbitrator is named therein or not'. As the clause below is clearly such an agreement the Arbitration Acts apply without specific reference.

Any dispute that arises under out of or in connection with this Lease (except where it relates to forfeiture or where the means of resolving the dispute in question is specifically set out in this Lease) will be determined by an arbitrator appointed by the parties or in the absence of agreement nominated on the application of either party at any time by the then President of the [Law Society] [Royal Institution of Chartered Surveyors] or a person appointed to make nominations on behalf of and in the name of the President.

Appendix 2

Checklist for tenant's solicitor

It is unlikely that anyone, however well versed in a subject, would be able to recall at any given moment, and without any prompting, every point that should be considered when reviewing a complex and lengthy legal document. It is equally unlikely that anyone could list *all* the items that would be relevant to *every* lease, and certainly no such claim is made here. The aim of this checklist is to ensure that no significant point is overlooked by the tenant's solicitor, when instructed in a 'normal' commercial letting. Each item has been kept as brief as possible, with a reference to the paragraph number etc, that deals with the topic in question. Practitioners may find it helpful to produce their own lists based on this format, so that they will be able to work through a list in relation to a specific matter, perhaps marking each point with a tick as they deal with it, or a cross as they decide that it is not relevant to that particular case.

A   PRELIMINARY

1	Is the draft complete?	1.13
2	Do the major terms comply with instruction?	1.13
3	Acknowledge receipt	1.13
4	Copy to Client/Surveyor	1.13
5	Will a site inspection be necessary?	2.17
6	Agents' particulars/photographs	2.18
7	Deny authorised to sign	1.9
8	Has survey been undertaken? If so obtain copy	2.16
9	Did survey extend to plant and equipment? If not advise client that it should where these will be significant	2.16
10	Landlord's consent needed, applied for	2.3
11	Preliminary comments on client on Lease	1.17
12	Is lease being renewed under the 1954 Act? If so remember what court would order if negotiations break down	14.42–14.62

B   SEARCHES ENQUIRIES ETC

1	Local search	2.12
2	Mining search, if needed	2.13
3	Commons search, map index search, if needed	2.12/fn1
4	Preliminary enquiries	2.14
5	Additional Enquiries:	

5.1	Is tenant's proposed use permitted under	
5.1:1	– Planning Acts	2.5–2.6
5.1:2	– Freehold Title	2.8–2.10
5.1:3	– Headlease	2.8
5.2	Will consent of mortgagees be required?	15.4
5.3	Copies of all documents mentioned in the draft (headlease, insurance policy, regulations etc)	2.15
5.4	Title deduced?	2.9–2.10
5.5	Inventory of landlord's fixtures	3.19
6	Planning enquires re surrounding area?	2.12

C   TAXATION

1	Has the client received advice?	2.22
2	General Taxes	2.22
3	Value Added Development Land Tax implications	2.23–2.26
4	Capital Allowances	3.20
5	Length of Term and Stamp Duty	5.20

D   AGREEMENT FOR LEASE

1	Needed?	2.19
2	Needed urgently?	2.20
3	Registration	2.21
4	Stamping	2.21
5	Recite in the Lease	5.17

E   THE PARTIES

1	Is landlord as expected? If unknown, search	2.11, 5.3
2	Will landlord give significant covenants in Lease (ie services, maintenance of structure etc)? If so, and if landlord unknown, search	5.3
3	Is tenant correctly described?	5.4
4	Does the client wish the lease to be taken by the company named in the draft?	5.4

F   GUARANTOR/ORIGINAL TENANT

1	Had a guarantor for tenant been previously agreed?	5.5
2	Amend to apply only when lease vested in tenant	5.10:1
3	If not:	
3.1	served with copies of notices etc	5.10:2
3.2	informed if late in paying rent	5.10:3
3.3	rent review	5.10:5
3.4	assign on default	5.10:6
4	Deed between guarantor and tenant	5.10:7
5	Protect original tenant after assignment	5.5, 5.14–5.16

G RECITALS

1	Needed?	5.17

H THE DEMISED PREMISES

1	Do the words and plan define with absolute certainty?	3.1–3.9
2	Where lease is of part of a building, are the boundaries precisely defined?	3.11–3.17
3	Is ownership of boundary walls fences etc dealt with?	3.2
4	If plan inadequate:	
4.1	– is better plan essential?	3.7
4.2	– could premises be defined in words?	3.9
4.3	– should boundary be pegged out?	3.10
5	Is plan correctly referred to ('for identification only' etc)?	3.7–3.8
6	Fixtures – is drafting appropriate?	3.18–3.19
7	Upper limit defined?	3.5
8	Any airspace sub-soil problems?	3.4–3.6

I RIGHTS

1	Does tenant have all that he requires to use premises?	4.1–4.9
2.1	Right of way – does it extend to highway?	4.2–4.3
2.2	Right of way – does it include vehicles?	4.3
3	Parking – will extra rights be required?	4.4
4	With whom is the right of way shared?	4.5
5	Are rights required for services through conducting media etc on adjoining property?	4.6
6	Will access to neighbouring land/air space to repair be needed?	4.7
7	Is support/protection required?	4.8
8	Are rights needed to toilets?	4.9
9	Is the upkeep of those items, through or over which the rights will be enjoyed, properly dealt with by means of	
	– landlord's covenants	11.2–11.3
	– service charge	11.4–11.20

J EXCEPTIONS AND RESERVATIONS

1	Any access should only be on reasonable notice etc, reasonable times during day, on prior appointment etc	4.12
2	Landlord to make good on exercising rights	4.14
3	Are other exceptions and reservations necessary reasonable?	4.14
4	Is exclusion of right of light reasonable?	4.15

K   DATES AND PERIODS

1	Any doubt when term commences – use 'from and including' or 'commencing on'?	1.5:3
2	Clear when rent begins to be payable?	5.19
3	Are all other dates and periods certain?	1.5:4
4	Rent payable in advance or arrears?	5.22

L   RENT REVIEW

1	Has other than open market rent been agreed (Index, turnover etc)? If so, is client aware of dangers?	6.61–6.65
2	Send copy of clause to client's surveyor	6.17:3
3	Informal type of clause? If not, do clients really want formalistic clause?	6.5
4	If notices etc, is time of the essence?	6.6–6.14
5	Could landlord delay indefinitely then activate?	6.15–6.16
6	Could landlord's rent prevail on tenant's default? If so, object	6.13–6.14
7	Could tenant activate?	6.44
8	Upwards only? Accepted?	6.60:1
9	Tenant to terminate after review?	6.60:2
10	Review Dates clear and as previously agreed?	1.5:4 and 6.4
11	Complete initial period?	6.4:2
12	Term-end review date?	6.4:3
13	Hypothetical letting properly dealt with	6.2/fn1
14	Any unusual assumptions/disregards? Appropriate?	6.17:1
15	Does nature of property etc require special assumptions/disregards?	6.18:1(d)
16	Assumptions:	
16.1	no work diminished rental value	6.24
16.2	Premises restored	6.26
16.3	covenants complied with: landlord/tenant	6.25
16.4	willing landlord/willing tenant	6.22
16.5	one lease	6.21
16.6	premium	6.23
16.7	vacant possession	6.19–6.20
16.8	equipped for immediate use	6.20:2
16.9	other terms of letting (including user, alteration covenants etc)	6.18:3
16.10	including rent review provisions	6.18:3
16.11	length of hypothetical term	6.18:2
16.12	statutory consents etc	6.27
16.13	renewal under 1954 Act	6.28
16.14	VAT	6.29
17	Disregards	
17.1	false	6.30
17.2	occupation: Tenant/subtenants/predecessors	6.32
17.3	goodwill: Tenant/subtenants/predecessors	6.33
18	Disregard improvements:	6.34–6.40

442

M ALIENATION

N USE

O ALTERATIONS

2	Are terms ('Structure' 'structural repairs' etc) clear?	7.25:3/4
3	If certain alterations are permitted/or permitted with consent while all others prohibited, can permitted class clearly be identified?	7.24, 7.25:5/7
4	Onerous procedural requirements?	7.25:6
5	Resist obligation to reinstate at end of term	7.25:9
6	Relationship with other clauses etc especially planning	7.21

P OTHER COVENANTS

1	Does landlord covenant to maintain shared items?	7.29, 11.2–11.3
2	Normal hours: avoid excessive limitation	7.30
3	Interest: payable at once?	7.31
4	Landlords legal fees	7.32
5	Whenever practical ensure qualified covenants	7.33

Q REPAIRING COVENANT

1	Ensure relevant terms (where used) adequately defined:	
1.1	– 'the demised premises'	8.4
1.2	– 'interior'	8.5
1.3	– 'structure', 'structural repair'	8.6
1.4	– 'inherent defect'	8.7
2	Resist covenant that goes beyond repair	8.10
3	Exclude liability where repair prevented	8.11 f/n 4
4	Exclude liability for damage etc by an insured risk	8.11 f/n 4
5	Is full repairing lease of part of a building practical?	8.9
6	In a short letting, is the covenant appropriate?	8.11 f/n 3
7	Do the landlord's and tenant's covenants together deal with everything?	8.8
8	Will rights of access to adjoining property etc be required to comply with covenant?	4.7
9	Old Buildings	8.12
10	Generally	8.12–8.13
10.1	schedule of condition	8.13:2
10.2	proviso of fair wear and tear	8.13:3
11	New Buildings	8.14
11	Generally	
11.1	relieve tenant of liability for inherent defects and impose upon landlord	8.15
11.2	if unsuccessful, propose that this operates for a limited term	8.15:2
11.3	if dealing with agreement for lease, propose 'prevention is better than cure' provision	8.15:3
11.4	duty of Care Agreement	8.15:3
11.5	landlord to pursue remedies	8.15:4
11.6	exclude service charge	8.16

444

R LANDLORD'S COVENANTS

1	Quiet enjoyment	9.2
2	Restriction on letting adjoining premises for competing trade	9.4
3	Maintain items that tenants agree to contribute towards	11.3

S INSURANCE

1	Copy of policy provided?	10.28
2	Landlord's covenant to insure adequate?	10.1, 10.18
3	Practical to insure in joint names?	10.18
4	Tenant's interest noted	10.19
5	Landlord obliged to insure against cost of reinstatement?	10.4–10.9
6	Landlord obliged to produce to tenant evidence of insurance, change of terms etc?	10.29
7	Deal with subrogation?	10.18
8	Commission dealt with?	10.26
9	If landlord insures with other premises, is method of apportioning premium fair?	10.25
10	Are insured risks adequate?	10.10
11	Landlord obliged to reinstate?	10.19, 10.22
12	Landlord to make-up shortfall?	10.20
13	Suspension of rent included?	10.14, 10.15, 10.23
14	Suspension of rent limitations (others payments suspended, only insured risk, limited time, tenant default excluded proportion and time determination): worth trying to amend?	10.23
15	Termination if reinstatement prevented?	10.24
16	Ownership of insurance moneys if rebuilding prevented?	10.16

T SERVICE CHARGE

1	Only professionally qualified 'Accountant' and 'Surveyor'	11.6
2	Are determinations and certifications acceptable?	11.5
3	Is the basis upon which tenant's share determined reasonable?	11.8–11.11
4	Are the arrangements for payment on account reasonable?	11.12
5	Landlord to pay service charge for unlet parts	11.13
6	Cesser of rent proviso to extend to service charge	10.23
7	Are exclusions from landlord's covenant to perform services reasonable?	11.14–11.16
8	The Services	11.17–11.20

8.1	– resist reasonable standard being replaced by the landlord's standard and absolute discretion	11.19
8.2	– resist extension beyond services (or at least advise client) especially re structure etc	11.18:3
8.3	– the 'mopping up' provision	11.18:4
8.4	– staff	11.18:2
9	Consultation/traders association	11.20
10.1	Sinking Fund – general	11.21
10.2	– taxation	11.22
11	Ensure client *fully* understands concept of clear lease	11.1

U   PROVISOS

1	Limitations on forfeiture for bankruptcy/liquidation	12.4
2	Break clause	12.8–12.9
3	Resist (unless specifically agreed, exclusion of security of tenure provisions 1954 Act)	14.18
4	Resist exclusion of compensation under 1954 Act	14.41
5	Arbitration	12.10–12.12

V   UNDERLEASES

1	Acquire copy of superior lease(s)	2.15
2	Consider alienation provisions of superior lease(s): is underletting the subject of absolute or qualified covenant? Advise client	7.1:2, 7.3–7.6
3	Consent applied for? (Change of use needed too? Absolute/qualified/advise client)	2.3
4	Relationship of key covenants in superior lease(s): repair, alterations etc	13.2, 13.9
5	Tenant's covenant to 'perform' under superior lease(s) appropriate?	13.4, Rosscastle: 13.2, 13.9, 8.2:1, 8.2:2
6	Covenant by landlord to 'perform' under superior lease	13.4, Rosscastle: 8.3:1, 8.3:2
7	Covenant by landlord to seek consent from superior landlord when requested by tenant	Rosscastle: 8.3:3
8	Service charge properly dealt with in underlease	13.10
9	Is insurance by superior landlord properly dealt with in underlease?	Appendix 1 Form 7
10	Are any break options in superior lease(s) properly dealt with in underlease?	13.12–13.14

W   PRE-COMPLETION

X   AFTER COMPLETION

Appendix 3

Landlord and Tenant Act 1954, ss 23–46, 55, 64 and 69

Tenancies to which Part II applies

23. Tenancies to which Part II applies

(1) Subject to the provisions of this Act, this Part of this Act applies to any tenancy where the property comprised in the tenancy is or includes premises which are occupied by the tenant and are so occupied for the purposes of a business carried on by him or for those and other purposes.

(2) In this Part of this Act the expression 'business' includes a trade, profession or employment and includes any activity carried on by a body of persons, whether corporate or unincorporate.

(3) In the following provisions of this Part of this Act the expression 'the holding', in relation to a tenancy to which this Part of this Act applies, means the property comprised in the tenancy, there being excluded any part thereof which is occupied neither by the tenant nor by a person employed by the tenant and so employed for the purposes of a business by reason of which the tenancy is one to which this Part of this Act applies.

(4) Where the tenant is carrying on a business, in all or any part of the property comprised in a tenancy, in breach of a prohibition (however expressed) of use for business purposes which subsists under the terms of the tenancy and extends to the whole of that property, this Part of this Act shall not apply to the tenancy unless the immediate landlord or his predecessor in title has consented to the breach or the immediate landlord has acquiesced therein.

In this subsection the reference to a prohibition of use for business purposes does not include a prohibition of use for the purposes of a specified business, or of use for purposes of any but a specified business, but save as aforesaid includes a prohibition of use for the purposes of some one or more only of the classes of business specified in the definition of that expression in subsection (2) of this section.

Continuation and renewal of tenancies

24. Continuation of tenancies to which Part II applies and grant of new tenancies

(1) A tenancy to which this Part of this Act applies shall not come to an end

unless terminated in accordance with the provisions of this Part of this Act; and, subject to the provisions of section twenty-nine of this Act, the tenant under such a tenancy may apply to the court for a new tenancy–

(a) if the landlord has given notice under [s 25 of this Act] to terminate the tenancy, or

(b) if the tenant has made a request for a new tenancy in accordance with section twenty-six of this Act.

(2) The last foregoing subsection shall not prevent the coming to an end of a tenancy by notice to quit given by the tenant, by surrender or forfeiture, or by the forfeiture of a superior tenancy [unless–

(a) in the case of a notice to quit, the notice was given before the tenant had been in occupation in right of the tenancy for one month; or

(b) in the case of an instrument of surrender, the instrument was executed before, or was executed in pursuance of an agreement made before, the tenant had been in occupation in right of the tenancy for one month.]

(3) Notwithstanding anything in subsection (1) of this section,–

(a) where a tenancy to which this Part of this Act applies ceases to be such a tenancy, it shall not come to an end by reason only of the cesser, but if it was granted for a term of years certain and has been continued by subsection (1) of this section then (without prejudice to the termination thereof in accordance with any terms of the tenancy) it may be terminated by not less than three nor more than six months' notice in writing given by the landlord to the tenant;

(b) where, at a time when a tenancy is not one to which this Part of this Act applies, the landlord gives notice to quit, the operation of the notice shall not be affected by reason that the tenancy becomes one to which this Part of this Act applies after the giving of the notice.

NOTES
Sub-ss (1), (2): amended by the Law of Property Act 1969, ss 3(2), 4(1).

24A. Rent while tenancy continues by virtue of s 24

[(1) The landlord of a tenancy to which this Part of this Act applies may,–

(a) if he has given notice under s 25 of this Act to terminate the tenancy; or

(b) if the tenant has made a request for a new tenancy in accordance with s 26 of this Act;

apply to the court to determine a rent which it would be reasonable for the tenant to pay while the tenancy continues by virtue of section 24 of this Act, and the court may determine a rent accordingly.

(2) A rent determined in proceedings under this section shall be deemed to be the rent payable under the tenancy from the date on which the proceedings were commenced or the date specified in the landlord's notice or the tenant's request, whichever is the later.

(3) In determining a rent under this section the court shall have regard to the rent payable under the terms of the tenancy, but otherwise subsections (1) and (2) of s 34 of this Act shall apply to the determination as they would apply to the determination of a rent under that section if a new tenancy from year to year of the whole of the property comprised in the tenancy were granted to the tenant by order of the court.]

NOTES
Commencement: 1 January 1970.
Added by the Law of Property Act 1969, s 3(1).

25. Termination of tenancy by the landlord

(1) The landlord may terminate a tenancy to which this Part of this Act applies by a notice given to the tenant in the prescribed form specifying the date at which the tenancy is to come to an end (hereinafter referred to as 'the date of termination'):

Provided that this subsection has effect subject to the provisions of Part IV of this Act as to the interim continuation of tenancies pending the disposal of applications to the court.

(2) Subject to the provisions of the next following subsection, a notice under this section shall not have effect unless it is given not more than twelve nor less than six months before the date of termination specified therein.

(3) In the case of a tenancy which apart from this Act could have been brought to an end by notice to quit given by the landlord–

(a) the date of termination specified in a notice under this section shall not be earlier than the earliest date on which apart from this Part of this Act the tenancy could have been brought to an end by notice to quit given by the landlord on the date of the giving of the notice under this section; and

(b) where apart from this Part of this Act more than six months' notice to quit would have been required to bring the tenancy to an end, the last foregoing subsection shall have effect with the substitution for twelve months of a period six months longer than the length of notice to quit which would have been required as aforesaid.

(4) In the case of any other tenancy, a notice under this section shall not specify a date of termination earlier than the date on which apart from this Part of this Act the tenancy would have come to an end by effluxion of time.

(5) A notice under this section shall not have effect unless it requires the tenant, within two months after the giving of the notice, to notify the landlord in writing whether or not, at the date of termination, the tenant will be willing to give up possession of the property comprised in the tenancy.

(6) A notice under this section shall not have effect unless it states whether the landlord would oppose an application to the court under this Part of this Act for the grant of a new tenancy and, if so, also states on which of the grounds mentioned in section thirty of this Act he would do so.

26. Tenant's request for a new tenancy

(1) A tenant's request for a new tenancy may be made where the tenancy under which he holds for the time being (hereinafter referred to as 'the current tenancy') is a tenancy granted for a term of years certain exceeding one year, whether or not continued by section twenty-four of this Act, or granted for a term of years certain and therafter from year to year.

(2) A tenant's request for a new tenancy shall be for a tenancy beginning with such date, not more than twelve nor less than six months after the making of the request, as may be specified therein:

Provided that the said date shall not be earlier than the date on which apart from this Act the current tenancy would come to an end by effluxion of time or could be brought to an end by notice to quit given by the tenant.

(3) A tenant's request for a new tenancy shall not have effect unless it is made by notice in the prescribed form given to the landlord and sets out the tenant's proposals as to the property to be comprised in the new tenancy (being either the whole or part of the property comprised in the current

tenancy), as to the rent to be payable under the new tenancy and as to the other terms of the new tenancy.

(4) A tenant's request for a new tenancy shall not be made if the landlord has already given notice under the last foregoing section to terminate the current tenancy, or if the tenant has already given notice to quit or notice under the next following section; and no such notice shall be given by the landlord or the tenant after the making by the tenant of a request for a new tenancy.

(5) Where the tenant makes a request for a new tenancy in accordance with the foregoing provisions of this section, the current tenancy shall, subject to the provisions of subsection (2) of section thirty-six of this Act and the provisions of Part IV of this Act as to the interim continuation of tenancies, terminate immediately before the date specified in the request for the beginning of the new tenancy.

(6) Within two months of the making of a tenant's request for a new tenancy the landlord may give notice to the tenant that he will oppose an application to the court for the grant of a new tenancy, and any such notice shall state on which of the grounds mentioned in section thirty of this Act the landlord will oppose the application.

27. Termination by tenant of tenancy for fixed term

(1) Where the tenant under a tenancy to which this Part of this Act applies, being a tenancy granted for a term of years certain, gives to the immediate landlord, not later than three months before the date on which apart from this Act the tenancy would come to an end by effluxion of time, a notice in writing that the tenant does not desire the tenancy to be continued, section twenty-four of this Act shall not have effect in relation to the tenancy [unless the notice is given before the tenant has been in occupation in right of the tenancy for one month].

(2) A tenancy granted for a term of years certain which is continuing by virtue of section twenty-four of this Act may be brought to an end on any quarter day by not less than three months' notice in writing given by the tenant to the immediate landlord, whether the notice is given . . . after the date on which apart from this Act the tenancy would have come to an end [or before that date, but not before the tenant has been in occupation in right of the tenancy for one month].

NOTES
Amended by the Law of Property Act 1969, s 4(2).

28. Renewal of tenancies by agreement

Where the landlord and tenant agree for the grant to the tenant of a future tenancy of the holding, or of the holding with other land, on terms and from a date specified in the agreement, the current tenancy shall continue until that date but no longer, and shall not be a tenancy to which this Part of this Act applies.

Application to court for new tenancies

29. Order by court for grant of a new tenancy

(1) Subject to the provisions of this Act, on an application under subsection (1) of section twenty-four of this Act for a new tenancy the court shall make an

order for the grant of a tenancy comprising such property, at such rent and on such other terms, as are hereinafter provided.

(2) Where such an application is made in consequence of a notice given by the landlord under section twenty-five of this Act, it shall not be entertained unless the tenant has duly notified the landlord that he will not be willing at the date of termination to give up possession of the property comprised in the tenancy.

(3) No application under subsection (1) of section twenty-four of this Act shall be entertained unless it is made not less than two nor more than four months after the giving of the landlord's notice under section twenty-five of this Act or, as the case may be, after the making of the tenant's request for a new tenancy.

30. Opposition by landlord to application for a new tenancy

(1) The grounds on which a landlord may oppose an application under subsection (1) of section twenty-four of this Act are such of the following grounds as may be stated in the landlord's notice under section twenty-five of this Act or, as the case may be, under subsection (6) of section twenty-six thereof, that is to say:–

(a) where under the current tenancy the tenant has any obligations as respects the repair and maintenance of the holding, that the tenant ought not to be granted a new tenancy in view of the state of repair of the holding, being a state resulting from the tenant's failure to comply with the said obligations;

(b) that the tenant ought not to be granted a new tenancy in view of his persistent delay in paying rent which has become due;

(c) that the tenant ought not to be granted a new tenancy in view of other substantial breaches by him of his obligations under the current tenancy, or for any other reason connected with the tenant's use or management of the holding;

(d) that the landlord has offered and is willing to provide or secure the provision of alternative accommodation for the tenant, that the terms on which the alternative accommodation is available are reasonable having regard to the terms of the current tenancy and to all other relevant circumstances, and that the accommodation and the time at which it will be available are suitable for the tenant's requirements (including the requirement to preserve goodwill) having regard to the nature and class of his business and to the situation and extent of, and facilities afforded by, the holding;

(e) where the current tenancy was created by the sub-letting of part only of the property comprised in a superior tenancy and the landlord is the owner of an interest in reversion expectant on the termination of that superior tenancy, that the aggregate of the rents reasonably obtainable on separate lettings of the holding and the remainder of that property would be substantially less than the rent reasonably obtainable on a letting of that property as a whole, that on the termination of the current tenancy the landlord requires possession of the holding for the purpose of letting or otherwise disposing of the said property as a whole, and that in view thereof the tenant ought not to be granted a new tenancy;

(f) that on the termination of the current tenancy the landlord intends to demolish or reconstruct the premises comprised in the holding or a substantial part of those premises or to carry out substantial work of construction on the holding or part thereof and that he could not reasonably do so without obtaining possession of the holding;

(g) subject as hereinafter provided, that on the termination of the current tenancy the landlord intends to occupy the holding for the purposes, or partly for the purposes, of a business to be carried on by him therein, or as his residence.

(2) The landlord shall not be entitled to oppose an application on the ground specified in paragraph (g) of the last foregoing subsection if the interest of the landlord, or an interest which has merged in that interest and but for the merger would be the interest of the landlord, was purchased or created after the beginning of the period of five years which ends with the termination of the current tenancy, and at all times since the purchase or creation thereof the holding has been comprised in a tenancy or successive tenancies of the description specified in subsection (1) of section twenty-three of this Act.

[(3) Where the landlord has a controlling interest in a company any business to be carried on by the company shall be treated for the purposes of subsection (1)(g) of this section as a business to be carried on by him.

For the purposes of this subsection, a person has a controlling interest in a company if and only if either–

(a) he is a member of it and able, without the consent of any other person, to appoint or remove the holders of at least a majority of the directorships; or

(b) he holds more than one-half of its equity share capital, there being disregarded any shares held by him in a fiduciary capacity or as a nominee for another person;

and in this subsection 'company' and 'share' have the meanings assigned to them by s 455(1) of the Companies Act 1948 and 'equity share capital' the meaning assigned to it by section 154(5) of that Act.]

NOTES
Commencement: Before 1 January 1970 (sub-ss (1), (2)); 1 January 1970 (sub-s (3)).
Sub-s (3): added by the Law of Property Act 1969, s 6.

31. Dismissal of application for new tenancy where landlord successfully opposes

(1) If the landlord opposes an application under subsection (1) of section twenty-four of this Act on grounds on which he is entitled to oppose it in accordance with the last foregoing section and establishes any of those grounds to the satisfaction of the court, the court shall not make an order for the grant of a new tenancy.

(2) Where in a case not falling within the last foregoing subsection the landlord opposes an application under the said subsection (1) on one or more of the grounds specified in paragraphs (d), (e) and (f) of subsection (1) of the last foregoing section but establishes none of those grounds to the satisfaction of the court, then if the court would have been satisfied of any of those grounds if the date of termination specified in the landlord's notice or, as the case may be, the date specified in the tenant's request for a new tenancy as the date from which the new tenancy is to begin, had been such later date as the court may determine, being a date not more than one year later than the date so specified,–

(a) the court shall make a declaration to that effect, stating of which of the said grounds the court would have been satisfied as aforesaid and specifying

the date determined by the court as aforesaid, but shall not make an order
for the grant of a new tenancy;

(b) if, within fourteen days after the making of the declaration, the tenant so
requires the court shall make an order substituting the said date for the
date specified in the said landlord's notice or tenant's request, and
thereupon that notice or request shall have effect accordingly.

31A. Grant of new tenancy in some cases where section 30(1)(f) applies

[(1) Where the landlord opposes an application under section 24(1) of this
Act on the ground specified in paragraph (f) of section 30(1) of this Act the
court shall not hold that the landlord could not reasonably carry out the
demolition, reconstruction or work of construction intended without obtaining
possession of the holding if–

(a) the tenant agrees to the inclusion in the terms of the new tenancy of terms
giving the landlord access and other facilities for carrying out the work
intended and, given that access and those facilities, the landlord could
reasonably carry out the work without obtaining possession of the holding
and without interfering to a substantial extent or for a substantial time
with the use of the holding for the purposes of the business carried on by
the tenant; or

(b) the tenant is willing to accept a tenancy of an economically separable part of
the holding and either paragraph (a) of this section is satisfied with respect
to that part or possession of the remainder of the holding would be
reasonably sufficient to enable the landlord to carry out the intended work.

(2) For the purposes of subsection (1)(b) of this section a part of a holding
shall be deemed to be an economically separable part if, and only if, the
aggregate of the rents which, after the completion of the intended work, would
be reasonably obtainable on separate lettings of that part and the remainder of
the premises affected by or resulting from the work would not be substantially
less than the rent which would then be reasonably obtainable on a letting of
those premises as a whole.]

NOTES

Commencement: 1 January 1970.

Added by the Law of Property Act 1969, s 7(1).

32. Property to be comprised in new tenancy

(1) [Subject to the following provisions of this section], an order under section
twenty-nine of this Act for the grant of a new tenancy shall be an order for the
grant of a new tenancy of the holding; and in the absence of agreement between
the landlord and the tenant as to the property which constitutes the holding
the court shall in the order designate that property by reference to the
circumstances existing at the date of the order.

[(1A) Where the court, by virtue of paragraph (b) of section 31A(1) of this
Act, makes an order under section 29 of this Act for the grant of a new tenancy
in a case where the tenant is willing to accept a tenancy of part of the holding,
the order shall be an order for the grant of a new tenancy of that part only.]

(2) The foregoing provisions of this section shall not apply in a case where
the property comprised in the current tenancy includes other property besides
the holding and the landlord requires any new tenancy ordered to be granted

under section twenty-nine of this Act to be a tenancy of the whole of the property comprised in the current tenancy; but in any such case–

(a) any order under the said section twenty-nine for the grant of a new tenancy shall be an order for the grant of a new tenancy of the whole of the property comprised in the current tenancy, and

(b) references in the following provisions of this Part of this Act to the holding shall be construed as references to the whole of that property.

(3) Where the current tenancy includes rights enjoyed by the tenant in connection with the holding, those rights shall be included in a tenancy ordered to be granted under section twenty-nine of this Act [except as otherwise agreed between the landlord and the tenant or, in default of such agreement, determined by the court].

NOTES

Commencement: Before 1 January 1970 (sub-ss (1), (2), (3)); 1 January 1970 (sub-s (1A)).
Amended by the Law of Property Act 1969, ss 7(2), 8.

33. Duration of new tenancy

Where on an application under this Part of this Act the court makes an order for the grant of a new tenancy, the new tenancy shall be such tenancy as may be agreed between the landlord and the tenant, or, in default of such an agreement, shall be such a tenancy as may be determined by the court to be reasonable in all the circumstances, being, if it is a tenancy for a term of years certain, a tenancy for a term not exceeding fourteen years, and shall begin on the coming to an end of the current tenancy.

34. Rent under new tenancy

[(1)] The rent payable under a tenancy granted by order of the court under this Part of this Act shall be such as may be agreed between the landlord and the tenant or as, in default of such agreement, may be determined by the court to be that at which, having regard to the terms of the tenancy (other than those relating to rent), the holding might reasonably be expected to be let in the open market by a willing lessor, there being disregarded–

(a) any effect on rent of the fact that the tenant has or his predecessors in title have been in occupation of the holding,

(b) any goodwill attached to the holding by reason of the carrying on thereat of the business of the tenant (whether by him or by a predecessor of his in that business),

[(c) any effect on rent of an improvement to which this paragraph applies],

(d) in the case of a holding comprising licensed premises, any addition to its value attributable to the licence, if it appears to the court that having regard to the terms of the current tenancy and any other relevant circumstances the benefit of the licence belongs to the tenant.

[(2) Paragraph (c) of the foregoing subsection applies to any improvement carried out by a person who at the time it was carried out was the tenant, but only if it was carried out otherwise than in pursuance of an obligation to his immediate landlord, and either it was carried out during the current tenancy or the following conditions are satisfied, that is to say,–

(a) that it was completed not more than twenty-one years before the application for the new tenancy was made; and

(b) that the holding or any part of it affected by the improvement has at all

455

times since the completion of the improvement been comprised in
tenancies of the description specified in s 23(1) of this Act; and
(c) that at the termination of each of those tenancies the tenant did not quit.]

[(3) Where the rent is determined by the court the court may, if it thinks fit,
further determine that the terms of the tenancy shall include such provision for
varying the rent as may be specified in the determination.]

NOTES

Commencement: Before 1 January 1970 (sub-s (1)); 1 January 1970 (remainder).
Amended by the Law of Property Act 1969, ss 1(1), 2.

35. Other terms of new tenancy

The terms of a tenancy granted by order of the court under this Part of this Act
(other than terms as to the duration thereof and as to the rent payable
thereunder) shall be such as may be agreed between the landlord and the
tenant or as, in default of such agreement, may be determined by the court;
and in determining those terms the court shall have regard to the terms of the
current tenancy and to all relevant circumstances.

36. Carrying out of order for new tenancy

(1) Where under this Part of this Act the court makes an order for the grant of
a new tenancy, then, unless the order is revoked under the next following
subsection or the landlord and the tenant agree not to act upon the order, the
landlord shall be bound to execute or make in favour of the tenant, and the
tenant shall be bound to accept, a lease or agreement for a tenancy of the
holding embodying the terms agreed between the landlord and the tenant or
determined by the court in accordance with the foregoing provisions of this
Part of this Act; and where the landlord executes or makes such a lease or
agreement the tenant shall be bound, if so required by the landlord, to execute
a counterpart or duplicate thereof.

(2) If the tenant, within fourteen days after the making of an order under
this Part of this Act for the grant of a new tenancy, applies to the court for the
revocation of the order the court shall revoke the order; and where the order is
so revoked, then, if it is so agreed between the landlord and the tenant or
determined by the court, the current tenancy shall continue, beyond the date
at which it would have come to an end apart from this subsection, for such
period as may be so agreed or determined to be necessary to afford to the
landlord a reasonable opportunity for reletting or otherwise disposing of the
premises which would have been comprised in the new tenancy; and while the
current tenancy continues by virtue of this subsection it shall not be a tenancy
to which this Part of this Act applies.

(3) Where an order is revoked under the last foregoing subsection any
provision thereof as to payment of costs shall not cease to have effect by reason
only of the revocation; but the court may, if it thinks fit, revoke or vary any
such provision or, where no costs have been awarded in the proceedings for the
revoked order, award such costs.

(4) A lease executed or agreement made under this section, in a case where
the interest of the lessor is subject to a mortgage, shall be deemed to be one
authorised by section ninety-nine of the Law of Property Act 1925 (which
confers certain powers of leasing on mortgagors in possession), and subsection
(13) of that section (which allows those powers to be restricted or excluded by
agreement) shall not have effect in relation to such a lease or agreement.

37. Compensation where order for new tenancy precluded on certain grounds

(1) Where on the making of an application under section twenty-four of this Act the court is precluded (whether by subsection (1) or subsection (2) of section thirty-one of this Act) from making an order for the grant of a new tenancy by reason of any of the grounds specified in paragraphs (e), (f) and (g) of subsection (1) of section thirty of this Act and not of any grounds specified in any other paragraph of that subsection [or where no other ground is specified in the landlord's notice under section 25 of this Act or, as the case may be, under section 26(6) thereof, than those specified in the said paragraphs (e), (f) and (g) and either no application under the said section 24 is made or such an application is withdrawn], then, subject to the provisions of this Act, the tenant shall be entitled on quitting the holding to recover from the landlord by way of compensation an amount determined in accordance with the following provisions of this section.

(2) The said amount shall be as follows, that is to say,–

(a) where the conditions specified in the next following subsection are satisfied it shall be [the product of the appropriate multiplier and] twice the rateable value of the holding,

(b) in any other case it shall be [the product of the appropriate multiplier and] the rateable value of the holding.

(3) The said conditions are–

(a) that, during the whole of the fourteen years immediately preceding the termination of the current tenancy, premises being or comprised in the holding have been occupied for the purposes of a business carried on by the occupier or for those and other purposes;

(b) that, if during those fourteen years there was a change in the occupier of the premises, the person who was the occupier immediately after the change was the successor to the business carried on by the person who was the occupier immediately before the change.

(4) Where the court is precluded from making an order for the grant of a new tenancy under this Part of this Act in the circumstances mentioned in subsection (1) of this section, the court shall on the application of the tenant certify that fact.

(5) For the purposes of subsection (2) of this section the rateable value of the holding shall be determined as follows:–

(a) where in the valuation list in force at the date on which the landlord's notice under section twenty-five or, as the case may be, subsection (6) of section twenty-six of this Act is given a value is then shown as the annual value (as hereinafter defined) of the holding, the rateable value of the holding shall be taken to be that value;

(b) where no such value is so shown with respect to the holding but such a value or such values is or are so shown with respect to premises comprised in or comprising the holding or part of it, the rateable value of the holding shall be taken to be such value as is found by a proper apportionment or aggregation of the value or values so shown;

(c) where the rateable value of the holding cannot be ascertained in accordance with the foregoing paragraphs of this subsection, it shall be taken to be the value which, apart from any exemption from assessment to rates, would on a proper assessment be the value to be entered in the said valuation list as the annual value of the holding;

and any dispute arising, whether in proceedings before the court or otherwise, as to the determination for those purposes of the rateable value of the holding shall be referred to the Commissioners of Inland Revenue for decision by a valuation officer.

An appeal shall lie to the Lands Tribunal from any decision of a valuation officer under this subsection, but subject thereto any such decision shall be final.

(6) The Commissioners of Inland Revenue may by statutory instrument make rules prescribing the procedure in connection with references under this section.

(7) In this section–

the reference to the termination of the current tenancy is a reference to the date of termination specified in the landlord's notice under section twenty-five of this Act or, as the case may be, the date specified in the tenant's request for a new tenancy as the date from which the new tenancy is to begin;

the expression 'annual value' means rateable value except that where the rateable value differs from the net annual value the said expression means net annual value;

the expression 'valuation officer' means any officer of the Commissioners of Inland Revenue for the time being authorised by a certificate of the Commissioners to act in relation to a valuation list.

[(8) In subsection (2) of this section 'the appropriate multiplier' means such multiplier as the Secretary of State may by order made by statutory instrument prescribe.

(9) A statutory instrument containing an order under subsection (8) of this section shall be subject to annulment in pursuance of a resolution of either House of Parliament.]

NOTES
    Commencement: Before 1 January 1970 (sub-ss (1)–(7)); 25 March 1981 (remainder).
    Sub-s (1): amended by the Law of Property Act 1969, s 11.
    Sub-s (2): amended by the Local Government, Planning and Land Act 1980, s 193, Sch 33.
    Sub-ss (8), (9): added by the Local Government, Planning and Land Act 1980, s 193, Sch 33.

38. Restriction on agreements excluding provisions of Part II

(1) Any agreement relating to a tenancy to which this Part of this Act applies (whether contained in the instrument creating the tenancy or not) shall be void [(except as provided by subsection (4) of this section)] in so far as it purports to preclude the tenant from making an application or request under this Part of this Act or provides for the termination or the surrender of the tenancy in the event of his making such an application or request or for the imposition of any penalty or disability on the tenant in that event.

(2) Where–
(a) during the whole of the five years immediately preceding the date on which the tenant under a tenancy to which this Part of this Act applies is to quit the holding, premises being or comprised in the holding have been occupied for the purposes of a business carried on by the occupier or for those and other purposes, and
(b) if during those five years there was a change in the occupier of the premises, the person who was the occupier immediately after the change was the successor to the business carried on by the person who was the occupier immediately before the change,

any agreement (whether contained in the instrument creating the tenancy or not and whether made before or after the termination of that tenancy) which purports to exclude or reduce compensation under the last foregoing section shall to that extent be void, so however that this subsection shall not affect any agreement as to the amount of any such compensation which is made after the right to compensation has accrued.

(3) In a case not falling within the last foregoing subsection the right to compensation conferred by the last foregoing section may be excluded or modified by agreement.

[(4) The court may–

(a) on the joint application of the persons who will be the landlord and the tenant in relation to a tenancy to be granted for a term of years certain which will be a tenancy to which this Part of this Act applies, authorise an agreement excluding in relation to that tenancy the provisions of ss 24 to 28 of this Act; and

(b) on the joint application of the persons who are the landlord and the tenant in relation to a tenancy to which this Part of this Act applies, authorise an agreement for the surrender of the tenancy on such date or in such circumstances as may be specified in the agreement and on such terms (if any) as may be so specified;

if the agreement is contained in or endorsed on the instrument creating the tenancy or such other instrument as the court may specify; and an agreement contained in or endorsed on an instrument in pursuance of an authorisation given under the subsection shall be valid notwithstanding anything in the preceding provisions of this section.]

NOTES

Commencement: Before 1 January 1970 (sub-ss (1)–(3)); 1 January 1970 (sub-s (4)).
Amended by the Law of Property Act 1969, s 5.

General and supplementary provisions

39. Saving for compulsory acquisitions

(1) . . .

(2) If the amount of the compensation which would have been payable under section thirty-seven of this Act if the tenancy had come to an end in circumstances giving rise to compensation under that section and the date at which the acquiring authority obtained possession had been the termination of the current tenancy exceeds the amount of [the compensation payable under s 121 of the Lands Clauses Consolidation Act 1845 or s 20 of the Compulsory Purchase Act 1965 in the case of a tenancy to which this Part of this Act applies], that compensation shall be increased by the amount of the excess.

(3) Nothing in section twenty-four of this Act shall affect the operation of the said section one hundred and twenty-one.

NOTES
Amended by the Land Compensation Act 1973, ss 47, 86, Sch 3.

40. Duty of tenants and landlords of business premises to give information to each other

(1) Where any person having an interest in any business premises, being an interest in reversion expectant (whether immediately or not) on a tenancy of

those premises, serves on the tenant a notice in the prescribed form requiring him to do so, it shall be the duty of the tenant to notify that person in writing within one month of the service of the notice–

(a) whether he occupies the premises or any part thereof wholly or partly for the purposes of a business carried on by him, and

(b) whether his tenancy has effect subject to any sub-tenancy on which his tenancy is immediately expectant and, if so, what premises are comprised in the sub-tenancy, for what term it has effect (or, if it is terminable by notice, by what notice it can be terminated), what is the rent payable thereunder, who is the sub-tenant, and (to the best of his knowledge and belief) whether the sub-tenant is in occupation of the premises or of part of the premises comprised in the sub-tenancy and, if not, what is the sub-tenant's address.

(2) Where the tenant of any business premises, being a tenant under such a tenancy as is mentioned in subsection (1) of section twenty-six of this Act, serves on any of the persons mentioned in the next following subsection a notice in the prescribed form requiring him to do so, it shall be the duty of that person to notify the tenant in writing within one month after the service of the notice–

(a) whether he is the owner of the fee simple in respect of those premises or any part thereof or the mortgagee in possession of such an owner and, if not,

(b) (to the best of his knowledge and belief) the name and address of the person who is his or, as the case may be, his mortgagor's immediate landlord in respect of those premises or of the part in respect of which he or his mortgagor is not the owner in fee simple, for what term his or his mortgagor's tenancy thereof has effect and what is the earliest date (if any) at which that tenancy is terminable by notice to quit given by the landlord.

(3) The persons referred to in the last foregoing subsection are, in relation to the tenant of any business premises,–

(a) any person having an interest in the premises, being an interest in reversion expectant (whether immediately or not) on the tenant's, and

(b) any person being a mortgagee in possession in respect of such an interest in reversion as is mentioned in paragraph (a) of this subsection:

and the information which any such person as is mentioned in paragraph (a) of this subsection is required to give under the last foregoing subsection shall include information whether there is a mortgagee in possession of his interest in the premises and, if so, what is the name and address of the mortgagee.

(4) The foregoing provisions of this section shall not apply to a notice served by or on the tenant more than two years before the date on which apart from this Act his tenancy would come to an end by effluxion of time or could be brought to an end by notice to quit given by the landlord.

(5) In this section–

the expression 'business premises' means premises used wholly or partly for the purposes of a business;

the expression 'mortgagee in possession' includes a receiver appointed by the mortgagee or by the court who is in receipt of the rents and profits, and the expression 'his mortgagor' shall be construed accordingly;

the expression 'sub-tenant' includes a person retaining possession of any premises by virtue of [the Rent Act 1977] after the coming to an end of a sub-tenancy, and the expression 'sub-tenancy' includes a right so to retain possession.

NOTES

Sub-s (5): amended by the Rent Act 1977, s 155, Sch 23, para 17.

41. Trusts

(1) Where a tenancy is held on trust, occupation by all or any of the beneficiaries under the trust, and the carrying on of a business by all or any of the beneficiaries, shall be treated for the purposes of section twenty-three of this Act as equivalent to occupation or the carrying on of a business by the tenant; and in relation to a tenancy to which this Part of this Act applies by virtue of the foregoing provisions of this subsection–

(a) references (however expressed) in this Part of this Act and in the Ninth Schedule to this Act to the business of, or to carrying on of business, use, occupation or enjoyment by, the tenant shall be construed as including references to the business of, or to carrying on of business, use, occupation or enjoyment by, the beneficiaries or beneficiary;

(b) the reference in paragraph (d) of [subsection (1) of] section thirty-four of this Act to the tenant shall be construed as including the beneficiaries or beneficiary; and

(c) a change in the persons of the trustees shall not be treated as a change in the person of the tenant.

(2) Where the landlord's interest is held on trust the references in paragraph (g) of subsection (1) of section thirty of this Act to the landlord shall be construed as including references to the beneficiaries under the trust or any of them; but, except in the case of a trust arising under a will or on the intestacy of any person, the reference in subsection (2) of that section to the creation of the interest therein mentioned shall be construed as including the creation of the trust.

NOTE
Amended by the Law of Property Act 1969, s 1(2).

41A. Partnerships

[(1) The following provisions of this section shall apply where–

(a) a tenancy is held jointly by two or more persons (in this section referred to as the joint tenants); and

(b) the property comprised in the tenancy is or includes premises occupied for the purposes of a business; and

(c) the business (or some other business) was at some time during the existence of the tenancy carried on in partnership by all the persons who were then the joint tenants or by those and other persons and the joint tenants' interest in the premises was then partnership property; and

(d) the business is carried on (whether alone or in partnership with other persons) by one or some only of the joint tenants and no part of the property comprised in the tenancy is occupied, in right of the tenancy, for the purposes of a business carried on (whether alone or in partnership with other persons) by the other or others.

(2) In the following provisions of this section those of the joint tenants who for the time being carry on the business are referred to as the business tenants and the others as the other joint tenants.

(3) Any notice given by the business tenants which, had it been given by all the joint tenants, would have been–

(a) a tenant's request for a new tenancy made in accordance with s 26 of this Act; or

(b) a notice under subsection (1) or subsection (2) of s 27 of this Act;

shall be treated as such if it states that it is given by virtue of this section and sets out the facts by virtue of which the persons giving it are the business tenants; and references in those sections and in s 24A of this Act to the tenant shall be construed accordingly.

(4) A notice given by the landlord to the business tenants which, had it been given to all the joint tenants, would have been a notice under section 25 of this Act shall be treated as such a notice, and references in that section to the tenant shall be construed accordingly.

(5) An application under s 24(1) of this Act for a new tenancy may, instead of being made by all the joint tenants, be made by the business tenants alone; and where it is so made–

(a) this Part of this Act shall have effect, in relation to it, as if the references therein to the tenant included references to the business tenants alone; and

(b) the business tenants shall be liable, to the exclusion of the other joint tenants, for the payment of rent and the discharge of any other obligation under the current tenancy for any rental period beginning after the date specified in the landlord's notice under s 25 of this Act or, as the case may be, beginning on or after the date specified in their request for a new tenancy.

(6) Where the court makes an order under s 29(1) of this Act for the grant of a new tenancy on an application made by the business tenants it may order the grant to be made to them or to them jointly with the persons carrying on the business in partnership with them, and may order the grant to be made subject to the satisfaction, within a time specified by the order, of such conditions as to guarantors, sureties or otherwise as appear to the court equitable, having regard to the omission of the other joint tenants from the persons who will be the tenant under the new tenancy.

(7) The business tenants shall be entitled to recover any amount payable by way of compensation under s 37 or s 59 of this Act.]

NOTES
Commencement: 1 January 1970.
Added by the Law of Property Act 1969, s 9.

42. Groups of companies

(1) For the purposes of this section two bodies corporate shall be taken to be members of a group if and only if one is a subsidiary of the other or both are subsidiaries of a third body corporate.

In this subsection 'subsidiary' has the same meaning as is assigned to it for the purposes of the Companies Act 1948, by section one hundred and fifty-four of that Act.

(2) Where a tenancy is held by a member of a group, occupation by another member of the group, and the carrying on of a business by another member of the group, shall be treated for the purposes of section twenty-three of this Act as equivalent to occupation or the carrying on of a business by the member of the group holding the tenancy; and in relation to a tenancy to which this Part of this Act applies by virtue of the foregoing provisions of this subsection–

(a) references (however expressed) in this Part of this Act and in the Ninth Schedule to this Act to the business of or to use occupation or enjoyment by the tenant shall be construed as including references to the business of or to use occupation or enjoyment by the said other member;

(b) the reference in paragraph (d) of [subsection (1) of] section thirty-four of this Act to the tenant shall be construed as including the said other member; and

(c) an assignment of the tenancy from one member of the group to another shall not be treated as a change in the person of the tenant.

[(3) Where the landlord's interest is held by a member of a group–

(a) the reference in paragraph (g) of subsection (1) of s 30 of this Act to intended occupation by the landlord for the purposes of a business to be carried on by him shall be construed as including intended occupation by any member of the group for the purposes of a business to be carried on by that member; and

(b) the reference in subsection (2) of that section to the purchase or creation of any interest shall be construed as a reference to a purchase from or creation by a person other than a member of the group.]

NOTES

Commencement: Before 1 January 1970 (sub-ss (1), (2)); 1 January 1970 (sub-s (3)).
Amended by the Law of Property Act 1969, ss 1(2), 10.

43. Tenancies excluded from Part II

(1) This Part of this Act does not apply–

(a) to a tenancy of an agricultural holding [or a tenancy which would be a tenancy of an agricultural holding if the proviso to subsection (1) of section two of the Agricultural Holdings Act 1948, did not have effect or, in a case where the appoval of the Minister of Agriculture, Fisheries and Food was given as mentioned in the said subsection (1), if that approval had not been given];

(b) to a tenancy created by a mining lease;

(c) . . .

[(d) to a tenancy of premises licensed for the sale of intoxicating liquor for consumption on the premises, other than–

(i) premises which are structurally adapted to be used, and are bona fide used, for a business which comprises one or both of the following, namely, the reception of guests and travellers desiring to sleep on the premises and the carrying on of a restaurant, being a business a substantial proportion of which consists of transactions other than the sale of intoxicating liquor;

(ii) premises adapted to be used, and bona fide used, only for one or more of the following purposes, namely, for judicial or public administrative purposes, or as a theatre or place of public or private entertainment, or as public gardens or picture galleries, or for exhibitions, or for any similar purpose to which the holding of the licence is merely ancillary;

(iii) premises adapted to be used, and bona fide used, as refreshment rooms at a railway station.]

(2) This part of this Act does not apply to a tenancy granted by reason that the tenant was the holder of an office, appointment or employment from the grantor thereof and continuing only so long as the tenant holds the office, appointment or employment, or terminable by the grantor on the tenant's ceasing to hold it, or coming to an end at a time fixed by reference to the time at which the tenant ceases to hold it:

Provided that this subsection shall not have effect in relation to a tenancy granted after the commencement of this Act unless the tenancy was granted by an instrument in writing which expressed the purpose for which the tenancy was granted.

(3) This Part of this Act does not apply to a tenancy granted for a term certain not exceeding [six months] unless–

(a) the tenancy contains provisions for renewing the term or for extending it beyond [six months] from its beginning; or

(b) the tenant has been in occupation for a period which, together with any period during which any predecessor in the carrying on of the business carried on by the tenant was in occupation, exceeds [twelve months].

NOTES
Sub-s (1): para (a) amended by the Agriculture Act 1958, s 8(1), Sch 1, Part I, para 29; para (c) repealed by the Housing Act 1980, s 152, Sch 26; para (d) substituted by the Finance Act 1959, s 2(6), Sch 2, para 5.
Sub-s (3): amended by the Law of Property Act 1969, s 12.

43A. Jurisdiction of county court to make declaration

[Where the rateable value of the holding is such that the jurisdiction conferred on the court by any other provision of this Part of this Act is, by virtue of s 63 of this Act, exercisable by the county court, the county court shall have jurisdiction (but without prejudice to the jurisdiction of the High Court) to make any declaration as to any matter arising under this Part of this Act, whether or not any other relief is sought in the proceedings.]

NOTES
Commencement: 1 January 1970.
Added by the Law of Property Act 1969, s 13.

44. Meaning of 'the landlord' in Part II, and provisions as to mesne landlords, etc

(1) Subject to the next following subsection, in this Part of this Act the expression 'the landlord', in relation to a tenancy (in this section referred to as 'the relevant tenancy'), means the person (whether or not he is the immediate landlord) who is the owner of that interest in the property comprised in the relevant tenancy which for the time being fulfils the following conditions, that is to say–

(a) that it is an interest in reversion expectant (whether immediately or not) on the termination of the relevant tenancy, and

[(b) that it is either the fee simple or a tenancy which will not come to an end within fourteen months by effluxion of time and, if it is such a tenancy, that no notice has been given by virtue of which it will come to an end within fourteen months or any further time by which it may be continued under section 36(2) or section 64 of this Act.]

and is not itself in reversion expectant (whether immediately or not) on an interest which fulfils those conditions.

(2) References in this Part of this Act to a notice to quit given by the landlord are references to a notice to quit given by the immediate landlord.

(3) The provisions of the Sixth Schedule to this Act shall have effect for the application of this Part of this Act to cases where the immediate landlord of the tenant is not the owner of the fee simple in respect of the holding.

NOTES
Sub-s (1): amended by the Law of Property Act 1969, s 14(1).

46. Interpretation of Part II

In this Part of this Act:–

'business' has the meaning assigned to it by subsection (2) of section twenty-three of this Act;

'current tenancy' has the meaning assigned to it by subsection (1) of section twenty-six of this Act;

'date of termination' has the meaning assigned to it by subsection (1) of section twenty-five of this Act;

subject to the provisions of section thirty-two of this Act, 'the holding' has the meaning assigned to it by subsection (3) of section twenty-three of this Act;

'mining lease' has the same meaning as in the Landlord and Tenant Act 1927.

55. Compensation for possession obtained by misrepresentation

(1) Where under Part I of this Act an order is made for possession of the property comprised in a tenancy, or under Part II of this Act the court refuses an order for the grant of a new tenancy, and it is subsequently made to appear to the court that the order was obtained, or the court induced to refuse the grant, by misrepresentation or the concealment of material facts, the court may order the landlord to pay to the tenant such sum as appears sufficient as compensation for damage or loss sustained by the tenant as the result of the order or refusal.

(2) In this section the expression 'the landlord' means the person applying for possession or opposing an application for the grant of a new tenancy, and the expression 'the tenant' means the person against whom the order for possession was made or to whom the grant of a new tenancy was refused.

64. Interim continuation of tenancies pending determination by court

(1) In any case where–
(a) a notice to terminate a tenancy has been given under Part I or Part II of this Act or a request for a new tenancy has been made under Part II thereof, and
(b) an application to the court has been made under the said Part I or the said Part II, as the case may be, and
(c) apart from this section the effect of the notice or request would be to terminate the tenancy before the expiration of the period of three months beginning with the date on which the application is finally disposed of,
the effect of the notice or request shall be to terminate the tenancy at the expiration of the said period of three months and not at any other time.

(2) The reference in paragraph (c) of subsection (1) of this section to the date on which an application is finally disposed of shall be construed as a reference to the earliest date by which the proceedings on the application (including any proceedings on or in consequence of an appeal) have been determined and any time for appealing or further appealing has expired, except that if the application is withdrawn or any appeal is abandoned the reference shall be construed as a reference to the date of the withdrawal or abandonment.

69. Interpretation

(1) In this Act the following expressions have the meanings hereby assigned to them respectively, that is to say:–

'agricultural holding' has the same meaning as in the Agricultural Holdings Act 1948;

'development corporation' has the same meaning as in the New Towns Act 1946;

'local authority' has the same meaning as in the Town and Country Planning Act 1947;

'mortgage' includes a charge or lien and 'mortgagor' and 'mortgagee' shall be construed accordingly;

'notice to quit' means a notice to terminate a tenancy (whether a periodical tenancy or a tenancy for a term of years certain) given in accordance with the provisions (whether express or implied) of that tenancy;

'repairs' includes any work of maintenance, decoration or restoration, and references to repairing, to keeping or yielding up in repair and to state of repair shall be construed accordingly;

'statutory undertakers' has the same meaning as in the Town and Country Planning Act 1947, except that it includes the National Coal Board;

'tenancy' means a tenancy created either immediately or derivatively out of the freehold, whether by a lease or underlease, by an agreement for a lease or underlease or by a tenancy agreement or in pursuance of any enactment (including this Act), but does not include a mortgage term or any interest arising in favour of a mortgagor by his attorning tenant to his mortgagee, and references to the granting of a tenancy and to demised property shall be construed accordingly;

'terms', in relation to a tenancy, includes conditions.

(2) References in this Act to an agreement between the landlord and the tenant (except in section seventeen and subsections (1) and (2) of section thirty-eight thereof) shall be construed as references to an agreement in writing between them.

(3) References in this Act to an action for any relief shall be construed as including references to a claim for that relief by way of counterclaim in any proceedings.

NOTES

New Towns Act 1946: see now New Towns Act 1965, s 2.

Town and Country Planning Act 1947: see now Town and Country Planning Act 1971.

NOTES PREPARED ON BEHALF OF THE STANDING COMMITTEE OF THE LAW SOCIETY ON LAND LAW AND CONVEYANCING[1]

Renewing business tenancies[2]

The strict time-limits imposed by statute on the exercise of the tenant's right to renew a business tenancy continue to cause difficulty and hardship, because the right is lost if by misunderstanding or oversight on the part of the tenant or his adviser, a counter-notice is not given, or an application to the court is not made, in time.

Efforts have been made to amend the law so as to relax the strict time-limits but these have been unsuccessful (see [1981] *Gazette*, 11 February, 142).

In the majority of cases where the tenant does apply to the court within the given period, the application turns out to be unnecessary because the new lease is later granted by agreement. These difficulties can be avoided. Appropriate action on the part of the parties to a lease can extend the period, to give adequate time to negotiate a new lease, and to avoid the need to commence proceedings.

When a landlord gives a tenant notice to terminate a business tenancy, under s 25 of the Landlord and Tenant Act 1954, the Act requires the tenant to take two steps if he wants to claim a new lease. First, within two months after the notice is given, he must notify the landlord in writing that he is not willing to give up possession of the property (ss 25(5) and 29(2)). Secondly, not less than two months nor more than four months after the landlord's notice is given, he must make an application to the court (s 29(3)). The court has no power to extend these time limits (*Kammins Ballrooms Co Ltd v Zenith Investments (Torquay) Ltd* [1971] AC 850).

The limits can, nevertheless, be altered. In deciding that the court did not have jurisdiction to extend the time-limits, four out of five members of the House of Lords held that the parties could themselves do so by agreement. Accordingly, it is open to solicitors acting for landlords and tenants to agree between them to extend the time-limits. This will often enable tenants to avoid the trouble and expense of commencing proceedings. Not only will the clients' costs be reduced, but the courts will be relieved of a lot of unnecessary paperwork and the risks of negligence actions from missed time-limits will be eliminated.

It is suggested that the following guide-lines should be observed:

(1) solicitors should obtain the prior written authority of their clients to agree a waiver of the statutory time-limits;

(2) the agreement between the parties' solicitors should be in writing, and may conveniently be reached in correspondence;

(3) agreement to waive the time-limit for proceedings should be reached before the four-month period expires, so that an application to court can still be made if there is no agreement; and

(4) an agreed extension should be indefinite, to avoid merely exchanging the trap of one time-limit for a different one, although the landlord should reserve the right to impose a new limit on reasonable notice.

A possible form of agreement to extend the time-limit for taking proceedings is:

"[The landlord] agrees that the time allowed to [the tenant] for taking proceedings under s 24(1) of the Landlord and Tenant Act 1954 for the grant of a new tenancy of [the premises] shall be extended until such time as [the landlord] serves written notice on (the tenant] to impose a new expiry date on the period allowed for taking those proceedings. That new expiry date shall not be earlier than (a) the expiration of the period of four months referred to in s 29(3) nor (b) three weeks after service of the notice imposing it.'

This allows the landlord to reimpose the time-limit at any time after the original four months, while giving the tenant three weeks in which to commence proceedings after receiving the landlord's new notice.

1 Reproduced with the permission of the Law Society.
2 Published [1981] Gazette 29 July 853, by Mr T M Aldridge. See para 14.11 above.

Business tenancy applications – need to register a pending action[1]

Once again, the wide scope of the meaning of a pending action relating to land has been shown, because in *Selim Ltd v Bickenhall Engineering Ltd* [1981] 1 WLR 1318, Megarry VC ruled that a summons to the court for leave (under the Leasehold Property (Repairs) Act 1938) to commence forfeiture proceedings was a pending action and had properly been protected by registration of a caution. In *Whittingham v Whittingham* [1979] Fam 9, a mortgagee was held not to be bound by a wife's application for a property adjustment order in her divorce petition as it had not been registered. Thus proceedings to acquire an interest in land and to terminate such an interest are now held both to fall within the statutory definition.

Applications to the court for new tenancies under Pt II of the Landlord and Tenant Act 1954 seem undeniably to be pending actions relating to land; at present it appears that few are protected by registration, but attention is drawn to the dangers of omitting this step. In the absence of registration, a purchaser of the reversion would only be bound if he had express notice of the application, and the tenant might well have difficulty in proving that state of affairs. The simple precaution of registration at the Land Charges Department or relevant district land registry is both easier and safer.

Similar considerations apply to various applications under Pt I of the Landlord and Tenant Act 1954, the Leasehold Reform Acts and other statutes, as well as to ordinary actions for forfeiture and possession.

1 Published [1982] Gazette 13 January 30, by Professor J E Adams. See paras 8.36 and 14.14 above.

Index